# on the Market!

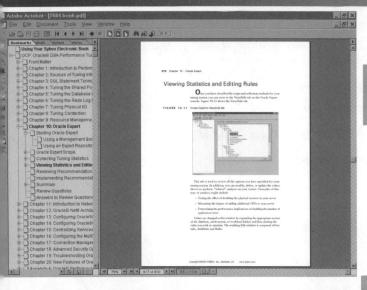

## Search the DBA Study Guide ebook in PDF

- Access the entire *Oracle8i DBA Study Guide*, complete with figures and tables, in electronic format.

- Use the Adobe Acrobat Reader (included on the CD-ROM)t o view the electronic book.

- Search chapters to find information on any topic in seconds.

## Oracle8i Evaluation Version

- Preview Oracle8i in this downloadable evaluation version.

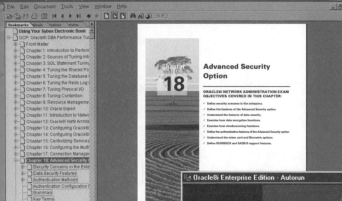

D1727448

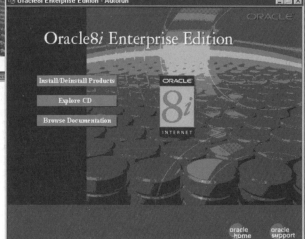

**Actual comments about Joe Johnson taken from student evaluation forms while teaching at Greenbrier & Russel's Oracle Approved Education Centers:**

*"Joe was a great teacher. He made it clear which things would have the most impact. Sometimes you are overwhelmed and you don't know what settings to look at, but he gave us a good idea where to start."*

*"I found the instructor's ability to explain things he learned from his experience as a DBA especially helpful."*

*"Fantastic instructor. Even the 'dry' topics were interesting."*

*"Joe is an excellent instructor—explains things well and in a straight forward way."*

*"Joe was excellent at presenting material in a simple way, so even the inexperienced (like myself) were able to understand."*

*"Excellent instructor—knows how to teach and explain. Best I've had for Oracle."*

*"Joe's presentation was natural, knowledgeable, and highly effective."*

*"Joe Johnson is the best technical instructor I've ever had."*

**Actual comments about Matthew Weishan taken from student evaluation forms while teaching at Greenbrier & Russel's Oracle Approved Education Centers:**

*"Best instructor I have ever had for a technical class."*

*"Matt was able to clarify many of the nagging technical questions I had about Oracle Database Administration."*

*"I have attended two of Matt's classes, and both of them have helped me pass my OCP exams. One for Intro to Oracle and the other for Database Administration."*

*"Very knowledgeable of the Oracle subject matter."*

*"Excellent instructor. He had an answer to everyone's questions."*

*"Related real-world business issues into the classroom. Explained the topics extremely well."*

*"Very well done. Matt was an effective and competent instructor. I would definitely take another class with Matt."*

*"Give him a raise!"*

# OCP: Oracle8i DBA Performance Tuning and Network Administration Study Guide

# OCP: Oracle8i™ DBA Performance Tuning and Network Administration Study Guide

Joseph C. Johnson

Matthew Weishan

San Francisco • Paris • Düsseldorf • Soest • London

SYBEX

Associate Publisher: Richard Mills
Contracts and Licensing Manager: Kristine O'Callaghan
Acquisitions & Developmental Editor: Kim Goodfriend
Editor: Malka Geffen
Production Editor: Jennifer Campbell
Technical Editors: Ganesh Raghavan, Ashok Hanumanth
Book Designer: Bill Gibson
Graphic Illustrator: Tony Jonick
Electronic Publishing Specialist: Susie Hendrickson
Proofreaders: Andrea Fox, Camera Obscura, Laurie O'Connell, Nancy Riddiough, Nathan Whiteside
Indexer: Nancy Guenther
CD Coordinator: Kara Eve Schwartz
CD Technician: Keith McNeil
Cover Designer: Archer Design
Cover Illustrator/Photographer: Photo Researchers

Library of Congress Card Number: 00-106114

ISBN: 0-7821-2684-7

Manufactured in the United States of America

10 9 8 7 6 5 4

# Software License Agreement: Terms and Conditions

*This book is dedicated to my wife Brenda and daughter Emily, without whose support, patience, and understanding, this project would have never been completed.*
—Joe Johnson

*This book is dedicated to the four most wonderful people in my life: my wife Karen, and my three daughters Rachel, Laura, and Alyssa.*
—Matt Weishan

# Acknowledgments

I would like to acknowledge the many people who helped shape the professional experiences that lead to my writing of this book. This includes Rich Vertrees for talking me into applying for my first DBA position in 1994. Also to Tony Gastel, Leslie Girardin, and Audrey Smith for putting in many long hours with me in the early days at Highland Community College.

This also includes my friends and mentors at Oracle Education: Terry Wojtkunski, Bruce Ernst, and Jason Schiedemeyer. Included, too, are my Oracle colleagues at Greenbrier & Russel, Inc.: Sandy Carlsson, Christopher Guillaume, Jesus Quinoines, Tammie Guillaume, Mary Lee, Rodney Woodard, John Bradford, Jim Whittle, Betty MacEwen, Bob Bryla, and Terry Anderson.

I also wish to acknowledge the clients who have offered me many challenging Oracle experiences over the years, including: Jim Schwarz and Reginald Bron at Marquette University, Barb Cooley at The Falk Corporation, Gary Coyne, Pete Bognar, and Steve Hahn at Johnson Controls, Inc., Bill Ebner and Mike Talbot at B.C. Ziegler and Company, and Dave Hill, Doug VanHorn, and Keith Brockman at University of Wisconsin System Administration.

I must also thank my parents, Bob and Chris, for teaching me that hard work and a good sense of humor would take me far in life. Thanks for giving me the tools that have enabled me to become the person I am today.

Finally I wish to thank Matt Weishan for being such a great co-author to work with, and the team from Sybex, Inc.: Kim Goodfriend, Malka Geffen, and Jennifer Campbell, who helped make the whole process go smoothly.

—Joe Johnson


I would like to thank my parents for always being there when I needed them and teaching me that anything is possible if you set your mind to it. I would like to thank Jim Maldonado, who I learned so much from when I was first starting in this business. He served as a mentor to this somewhat green computer programmer and showed me what it takes to be successful in this field. There have been countless others who have influenced me over the years, but I would especially like to thank Roney Pate, Christopher Barwick, Virginia Duris, and my colleagues in education at Greenbrier & Russel, Inc. for their support in this and other endeavors during my career. Finally, I would like to thank Joe Johnson for believing in me and working with me on this very challenging and rewarding project.

—Matt Weishan

# Contents at a Glance

# Contents

# Introduction

There is high demand and competition for professionals in the Information Technology (IT) industry, and the Oracle Certified Professional (OCP) certification is the hottest credential in the database realm. You have made the right decision to pursue certification. Being an OCP will give you a distinct advantage in this highly competitive market.

Many readers may already be familiar with Oracle Corporation and its products and services. For those who aren't familiar with the company, Oracle Corporation, founded in 1977, is the world's leading database company and second largest independent software company with revenues of more than $9.7 billion, serving over 145 countries. Oracle's CEO, Lawrence J. Ellison, saw the future of information technology in Internet computing, and the Oracle8i database was created to meet the needs of this technological evolution.

This book is intended to help you continue on your exciting new path towards obtaining the Oracle8i certified database administrator certification. The book will give you the necessary knowledge of the Oracle Server architecture and the hands-on skills you need to pass Exams 1Z0-024 and 1Z0-026. Although the OCP exams for Database Administration can be taken in any order, it is generally recommended that the Oracle8i OCP certification exam for Performance and Tuning and the Oracle8i OCP certification exam for Network Administration be the final exams taken in the series.

# Why Become an Oracle Certified Professional?

The number one reason to become an Oracle Certified Professional is to gain more visibility and greater access to the industry's most challenging opportunities. The OCP program is Oracle's commitment to provide top-quality resources for technical professionals who want to become Oracle specialists in specific job roles. The certification tests are scenario-based, which is the most effective way to access your hands-on expertise and critical problem-solving skills.

Certification is proof of your knowledge and shows that you have the skills required to support Oracle's core products according to the standards established by Oracle. The OCP program can help a company identify proven performers who have demonstrated their skills to support the company's investment in Oracle technology. It demonstrates that you have a solid understanding of your job role and the Oracle products used in that role.

So, whether you are beginning a career, changing careers, securing your present position, or seeking to refine and promote your position, this book is for you!

# Oracle Certifications

**O**racle has several certification tracks designed to meet different skill levels. Each track consists of several tests that can be taken in any order. The following tracks are available:

- Oracle Database Administrator

- Oracle Application Developer

- Oracle Database Operator

- Oracle Java Developer

- Oracle Financial Applications Consultant

## Oracle Database Administrator (DBA)

The role of Database Administrator (DBA) has become a key to success in today's highly complex database systems. The best DBAs work behind the scenes, but are in the spotlight when critical issues arise. They plan, create, and maintain databases to ensure that the databases meet the data management needs of the business. DBAs also monitor the databases for performance issues and work to prevent unscheduled downtime. Being an effective DBA requires broad understanding of the architecture of Oracle database and expertise in solving system-related problems. The Oracle8i certified administrator track consists of the following five tests:

- 1Z0-001: Introduction to Oracle—SQL and PL/SQL

- 1Z0-023: Oracle8i—Architecture and Administration

- 1Z0-024: Oracle8i—Performance and Tuning

- 1Z0-025: Oracle8i—Backup and Recovery

- 1Z0-026: Oracle8i—Network Administration

## Oracle Application Developer

This track tests your skills in client-server and Web-based application development using Oracle application development tools such as Developer/2000, SQL, PL/SQL, and SQL*Plus. The following five tests comprise this track:

- 1Z0-001: Introduction to Oracle—SQL and PL/SQL
- 1Z0-101: Develop PL/SQL Program Units
- 1Z0-121: Developer/2000 Build Forms I
- 1Z0-122: Developer/2000 Build Forms II
- 1Z0-123: Developer/2000 Build Reports

## Oracle Database Operator (DBO)

A Database Operator (DBO) performs simple operational tasks on Oracle databases in a support role to the DBA. DBOs need an introductory knowledge of the commands and utilities associated with managing a database. DBOs also install and set up databases, create users, and perform routine backups. You need take the following test to be certified as a Database Operator:

- 1Z0-401: Database Operator

## Oracle Java Developer

This certification track is part of the Certification Initiative for Enterprise Development, a multi-vendor collaboration with Sun Microsystems, IBM, Novell, and the Sun-Netscape Alliance to establish standards for knowledge and skill levels for enterprise developers in the Java technology. The Initiative recognizes three levels of certification requiring five tests. At each skill level, a certificate is awarded to candidates who successfully pass the required exams in that level.

- **Level 1: Sun Certified Programmer**
    - 1Z0-501: Sun Certified Programmer for the Java 2 Platform
- **Level 2: Certified Solution Developer**
    - 1Z1-502: Oracle JDeveloper: Develop Database Applications with Java (Oracle JDeveloper, Release 2)

        *or*

        1Z1-512: Oracle JDeveloper: Develop Database Applications with Java (Oracle JDeveloper, Release 3)

- 1Z0-503: Object Oriented Analysis and Design with UML
- **Level 3: Certified Enterprise Developer**
    - 1Z0-504: Enterprise Connectivity with J2EE
    - 1Z0-505: Enterprise Development on the Oracle Internet Platform

## Oracle Financial Applications Consultant

This certification tests your expertise in Oracle Financial applications. These exams are designed to test your knowledge of the business processes incorporated into the Oracle Financial applications software. The following three tests comprise this track, and the third exam offers a specialization in either Procurement or Order Fulfillment:

- 1Z0-210: Financial Management R11
- 1Z0-220: Applied Technology R11
- 1Z0-230: Procurement R11

*or*

- 1Z0-240: Order Fulfillment

## More Information

The most current information about Oracle certification can be found at `http://education.oracle.com`. Follow the Certification Home Page link and choose the track you are interested in. Read the Candidate Guide for the test objectives and test contents, and keep in mind that they can change at any time without notice.

# OCP: Database Administrator Track

The Oracle8i Database Administrator certification consists of five tests, and Sybex offers several study guides to help you achieve the OCP Database Administrator Certification. There are three books in this series:

- *OCP: Oracle8i™ DBA SQL and PL/SQL Study Guide*
- *OCP: Oracle8i™ DBA Architecture & Administration and Backup & Recovery Study Guide*

- *OCP: Oracle8i™ DBA Performance Tuning and Network Administration Study Guide*

Additionally, these three books are offered in a boxed set:

- *OCP: Oracle8i™ DBA Certification Kit*

The following table shows the number of questions and required passing percentage for each of the five OCP DBA exams.

| Exam# | Title | Total Questions | Questions Correct | Passing % | Sybex Study Guide |
|---|---|---|---|---|---|
| 1Z0-001 | Introduction to Oracle—SQL & PL/SQL | 57 | 39 | 68% | *OCP: Oracle8i™ DBA SQL and PL/SQL Study Guide* |
| 1Z0-023 | Oracle8i: Architecture and Administration | 65 | 38 | 58% | *OCP: Oracle8i™ DBA Architecture & Administration and Backup & Recovery Study Guide* |
| 1Z0-024 | Oracle8i: Performance and Tuning | 57 | 38 | 67% | *OCP: Oracle8i™ DBA Performance Tuning and Network Administration Study Guide* |
| 1Z0-025 | Oracle8i: Backup and Recovery | 60 | 34 | 57% | *OCP: Oracle8i™ DBA Architecture & Administration and Backup & Recovery Study Guide* |
| 1Z0-026 | Oracle8i: Network Administration | 59 | 41 | 71% | *OCP: Oracle8i™ DBA Performance Tuning and Network Administration Study Guide* |

## Skills Required for DBA Certification

- Understanding RDBMS concepts

- Writing queries and manipulating data

- Creating and managing users and database objects

- Knowledge of PL/SQL programming and constructs

- Strong knowledge of Oracle Server architecture—Database and Instance

- Complete understanding of physical and logical database storage concepts

- Managing data—storage, loading and reorganization

- Managing roles, privileges, password and resources

- Understanding of backup and recovery options

- Archiving redo log files and hot backups

- Using Recovery Manager (RMAN) to perform backup and recovery operations

- Creating and managing Standby database

- Identifying and tuning database and SQL performance

- Interpreting data dictionary views and database parameters

- Configuring Net8 on the server side and client side

- Using multi-threaded server, connection manager and Oracle Names

- Understanding of graphical and character mode backup, recovery and administration utilities

## Tips for Taking OCP Exams

- Each OCP test contains about 60–80 questions to be completed in about 90 minutes. Answer the questions you know first, so that you do not run out of time.

- Many questions on the exam have answer choices that at first glance look identical. Read the questions carefully. Don't just jump to conclusions. Make sure that you are clear about exactly what each question asks.

- Many of the test questions are scenario-based. Some of the scenarios contain non-essential information and exhibits. You need to be able to identify what's important and what's not.

- Do not leave any questions unanswered. There is no negative scoring. You can mark a difficult question or a question you are unsure about and come back to it later.

- When answering questions that you are not sure about, use a process of elimination to get rid of the obviously incorrect answers first. Doing this greatly improves your odds if you need to make an educated guess.

# What Does This Book Cover?

This book covers everything you need to know to pass the OCP: Oracle8i Performance and Tuning and OCP: Oracle8i Network Administration exams. The first part of the book covers the most critical areas of database performance tuning and how to follow and implement Oracle's recommended tuning methodology. The second part covers the topics of network administration including configuring the necessary client and server components of an Oracle network and helps you develop an understanding of the Oracle 8i Net8 architecture.

### Part One: OCP: Oracle8i Performance Tuning

Chapter 1 starts with an overview of the Oracle Tuning Methodology and how it is used to perform effective database tuning.

Chapter 2 discusses the sources of information related to database performance tuning. This includes data dictionary views, trace files, and log files.

Chapter 3 introduces you to SQL statement tuning and application design. Methods of gathering and analyzing SQL statement processing are discussed.

Chapter 4 covers how to monitor and tune the Shared Pool. Techniques for improving Shared Pool performance, including package pinning and reserved areas, are discussed.

Chapter 5 is dedicated to techniques for monitoring and tuning the Database Buffer Cache. The use of multiple buffer pools to enhance Database Buffer Cache performance is also explored.

Chapter 6 discusses the Redo Log Buffer and how to tune its performance. Tuning considerations related to minimizing redo generation and the I/O activities of LGWR are covered in detail.

Chapter 7 covers all aspects of tuning database operations related to physical I/O. Segment, extent, and block I/O are all addressed.

Chapter 8 introduces tuning database contention. This includes a discussion of latches and locking.

Chapter 9 discusses the Oracle Resource Management utilities and how they can be used to manage database performance.

Chapter 10 explores the Oracle Enterprise Manager graphical tuning aid called Oracle Expert.

### Part Two: OCP Oracle8i Network Administration

Chapter 11 introduces the basic network architecture. You will learn about the areas to consider when designing and implementing an Oracle network. You will also be introduced to the standard features of Oracle8i Net8 and the some of the optional configuration features of Net8.

Chapter 12 discusses the architecture of Net8 and how clients establish connections with an Oracle Server. You will also be introduced to the Net8 stack and the responsibilities of each of the layers of the Net8 stack.

Chapter 13 deals with server-side configuration. You will learn how to configure and manage the main network components and network configuration of the server.

Chapter 14 covers client side configuration. You will learn about the main network components and configuration of clients in an Oracle environment. You will learn about the various ways that clients can locate Oracle Servers and how to configure the most critical client-side files.

Chapter 15 covers the Oracle Names Server. You will learn about how a Names Server operates, the benefits of Names Servers and how to configure and manage Names Servers.

Chapter 16 discusses the Mulithreaded Server option. You will gain knowledge of what Multithreaded Server is, when it is appropriate to configure Multithreaded Server and how to configure and tune the Mulththreaded Server.

Chapter 17 covers the Connection Manager middle-tier component of Net8. You will learn the various benefits that Connection Manager offers and how to configure Connection Manager.

Chapter 18 deals with the Oracle Advanced Security option. You will discover and examine each of the features of the Advanced Security option.

Chapter 19 discusses how to troubleshoot connection problems in an Oracle network. You will learn about what kinds of connection problems can occur and how to diagnose and troubleshoot these problems. You will also learn what tools are available to assist you if connection problems should occur.

Chapter 20, a bonus chapter on the CD, deals with the new features of Oracle8i Net8. You will learn what the features are, the benefits they provide, and how to configure them.

Each chapter ends with review questions that are specifically designed to help you retain the knowledge presented. To really nail down your skills, read each question carefully and answer the questions.

# Where Do You Take the Exam?

**Y**ou may take the exams at any of the more than 800 Sylvan Prometric Authorized Testing Centers around the world. For the location of a testing center near you, call 1-800-891-3926. Outside of the United States and Canada, contact your local Sylvan Prometric Registration Center. The tests can be taken in any order.

To register for an Oracle Certified Professional exam:

- Determine the number of the exam you want to take.

- Register with the nearest Sylvan Prometric Registration Center. At this point, you will be asked to pay in advance for the exam. At the time of this writing, the exams are $125 each and must be taken within one year of payment. You can schedule exams up to six weeks in advance or as soon as one working day prior to the day you wish to take it. If something comes up and you need to cancel or reschedule your exam appointment, contact Sylvan Prometric at least 24 hours in advance.

- When you schedule the exam, you'll get instructions regarding all appointment and cancellation procedures, the ID requirements, and information about the testing-center location.

You can also register for the test online at http://www.2test.com/register /frameset.htm. If you live outside the US, register online at http:// www.2test.com/register/testcenterlocator/ERN_intl_IT&FAA.htm.

# How to Use This Book

This book can provide a solid foundation for the serious effort of preparing for the Oracle Certified Professional Performance and Tuning, and Net8 Administration exams. To best benefit from this book, use the following study method:

1. Take the Assessment Tests immediately following this introduction. (The answers are at the end of each test.) Carefully read over the explanations for any questions you get wrong, and note which chapters the material comes from. This information should help you plan your study strategy.

2. Study each chapter carefully, making sure that you fully understand the information and the test objectives listed at the beginning of each chapter. Pay extra close attention to any chapter where you missed questions in the Assessment Tests.

3. Closely examine the sample queries that are used throughout the book. You may find it helpful to type in the samples and compare the results shown in the book to those on your system. Once you're comfortable with the content in the chapter, answer the review questions related to that chapter. (The answers appear at the end of the chapter, after the review questions.)

When typing in examples from the book, do not type the line numbers that appear in the sample output; the Oracle query tools automatically number lines for you.

4. Note the questions that confuse you, and study those sections of the book again.

5. Take the Practice Exams in this book. You'll find them in Appendix A and Appendix B. The answers appear at the end of the exams.

6. Before taking the exam, try your hand at the bonus exams that are included on the CD that comes with this book. The questions in these exams appear only on the CD. This will give you a complete overview of what you can expect to see on the real thing.

7.  Remember to use the products on the CD that is included with this book. The electronic flashcards and the EdgeTest exam preparation software have all been specifically picked to help you study for and pass your exams. Oracle also offers sample exams on their certification Web site: `http://education.oracle.com/certification/sts.html`.

8.  The electronic flashcards can be used on your Windows computer or on your Palm device.

To learn all the material covered in this book, you'll have to apply yourself regularly and with discipline. Try to set aside the same time period every day to study, and select a comfortable and quiet place to do so. If you work hard, you will be surprised at how quickly you learn this material. All the best!

# What's on the CD?

**W**e worked hard to provide some really great tools to help you with your certification process. All of the following tools should be loaded on your workstation when studying for the test.

## The EdgeTest for Oracle Certified DBA Preparation Software

Provided by EdgeTek Learning Systems, this test preparation software prepares you to successfully pass the OCP Performance and Tuning and Net8 Administration exams. In this test engine, you will find all of the questions from the book, plus additional Practice Exams that appear exclusively on the CD. You can take the Assessment Tests, test yourself by chapter, take the Practice Exams that appear in the book or on the CD, or take an exam randomly generated from any of the questions.

## Electronic Flashcards for PC and Palm Devices

After you read the book, read the review questions at the end of each chapter and study the practice exams included in the book and on the CD. But wait, there's more! Test yourself with the Flashcards included on the CD. If you can get through these difficult questions, and understand the answers, you'll know you're ready for the OCP: Oracle8i Performance and Tuning and Net8 Administration exams.

The flashcards include 150 questions specifically written to hit you hard and make sure you are ready for the exam. Between the review questions, practice exam, and flash cards, you'll be more than prepared for the exam.

### *OCP: Oracle8i™ DBA Performance Tuning and Network Administration Study Guide* Ebook

Sybex is now offering the Oracle Certification books on CD, so you can read them on your PC or laptop. It is in Adobe Acrobat format. Acrobat Reader 4 is also included on the CD.

This will be extremely helpful to readers who fly and don't want to carry a book, as well as to readers who find it more comfortable reading from their computer.

# How to Contact the Authors

You can reach Matthew Weishan via e-mail at mweishan@yahoo.com. You may contact Joe Johnson via e-mail at jjohnson@gr.com.

# About the Authors

Joe Johnson is an Oracle Certified Professional with over six years of experience managing production databases. He is currently working as a Senior Database Administrator for Greenbrier & Russel, Inc. in Milwaukee, Wisconsin. Formerly Joe worked as an Oracle instructor at Greenbrier & Russel's Oracle Approved Education Centers (OAEC) where he received the OAEC Instructor of the Year Award from Oracle Education in 1998.

Matthew Weishan is an Oracle Certified Professional and Certified Technical Trainer with more than seven years experience with Oracle databases. He is currently Content Services Architect for Kedestra. Located in Brookfield, Wisconsin, the company is developing Internet-based collaboration services and content syndication for the commercial real estate industry. Formerly, he was a Senior Instructor specializing in the Oracle Database Administration Curriculum for Greenbrier & Russel, Inc. in Madison, Wisconsin. He has over 16 years of experience in the Information Technology industry and has worked in various capacities, including Senior System Analyst, Lead Consultant, and Lead Database Administrator for several large corporations, including Fortune 500 companies.

# Assessment Test

1. Which of the following are advantages of Names Servers over other net service name resolution options? (Choose all that apply.)

   **A.** Centralizes service names

   **B.** Allows for easier administration

   **C.** No setup required on the client

   **D.** Can store service names in a database

2. It is important to establish tuning benchmarks for all of the following reasons *except*:

   **A.** Without benchmarks it is hard to track your tuning progress.

   **B.** Benchmarks help you determine when to stop tuning one area and move on to another.

   **C.** Benchmarks are always the best measure of tuning success.

   **D.** Benchmarks are quantitative statistical measures of tuning effectiveness.

3. Which of the following contain tuning information for the Shared Pool (choose two)?

   **A.** V$LIBRARYCACHE

   **B.** V$DICTIONARYCACHE

   **C.** V$ROWCACHE

   **D.** V$SHARED_POOL_SIZE

4. Which of the other OEM GUI tools can Oracle Expert use as a source of SQL performance statistics when generating tuning recommendations?

   **A.** Tablespace Manager

   **B.** Storage Manager

   **C.** Oracle Trace

   **D.** Instance Manager

5. Which of these are roles of Net8 in the Oracle Network architecture? Choose all that apply.

   A. Handles communications between the client and server

   B. Handles server-to-server communications

   C. Used to establish an initial connection to an Oracle Server

   D. Acts as a messenger, which passes requests between clients and servers

   E. All of the above

6. Which of the following are advantages of Multithreaded Server (choose all that apply)?

   A. Fewer server processes

   B. Manages more connections with the same or less memory

   C. Better client response time

   D. All of the above

7. Which of the following methods of activating user tracing can be done by the DBA to another connected user?

   A. `ALTER SESSION SET SQL_TRACE=TRUE;`

   B. Use the `DBMS_SYSTEM.SET_SQL_TRACE_IN_SESSION` package.

   C. Use the `DBMS_UTILITY.SET_SQL_TRACE_IN_SESSION` package.

   D. Any of the above can be used to activate tracing.

8. Which of the following forms of SQL statement tuning output reports information about how much CPU time a statement consumed?

   A. TKPROF

   B. AUTOTRACE

   C. Explain Plan

   D. All of the above contain CPU usage information.

**9.** Which of the following shows the `init.ora` entry to create a Keep Pool that is 20MB in size and managed by 20 LRU latches? (Assume a database block size of 2K.)

**A.** BUFFER_POOL_KEEP = (BUFFERS:200, LRU_LATCHES:20)

**B.** BUFFER_POOL_KEEP = (BUFFERS:10240, LRU_LATCHES:20)

**C.** BUFFER_POOL_KEEP = (BUFFERS:200, LRU_LATCHES:200)

**D.** BUFFER_POOL_KEEP = (BUFFERS:2048, LRU_LATCHES:50)

**10.** Lock contention can occur when which of the following happens? (Choose all that apply.)

**A.** Application developers use a non-Oracle development tool

**B.** Application developers code unnecessarily high lock levels

**C.** Application developers use an old version of SQL*Net

**D.** Application developers use an old version of Net8

**11.** Which of the following is not a consideration when deciding whether to use multiple Database Writers?

**A.** The number of CPUs in the server

**B.** The number of tables in the database

**C.** The number of physical devices use to store the datafiles

**D.** Whether or not I/O slaves are being used

**12.** Which of the following must be up-to-date in the database in order for the cost-based optimizer to make good access path choices?

**A.** Database security

**B.** Database snapshots

**C.** Database statistics

**D.** Database views

**13.** The Shared Pool performs all of the following functions except:

    **A.** Caches frequently issued SQL statements

    **B.** Caches data dictionary data

    **C.** Caches transaction recovery information

    **D.** Caches shared session information when using the MTS option

**14.** Which of the following are advantages of the hostnaming method? (Choose all that apply.)

    **A.** Does not require any client configuration

    **B.** Reduces administrative work

    **C.** Takes advantage of Connection Manager

    **D.** All of the above

**15.** All of the following `init.ora` parameters affect the amount of server memory an Oracle instance consumes *except*:

    **A.** ARCHIVE_LOG_DEST

    **B.** SHARED_POOL_SIZE

    **C.** LOG_BUFFER

    **D.** DB_BLOCK_BUFFERS

**16.** Which of the following is *true* about dispatchers?

    **A.** They listen for client connection requests.

    **B.** They take the place of dedicated servers.

    **C.** They place client requests on a response queue.

    **D.** All of the above

**17.** Which of the following is not a method for improving the Shared Pool hit ratio?

    **A.** Increase the value for the SHARED_POOL parameter in the `init.ora`.

    **B.** Increase the value for the SHARED_POOL_SIZE parameter in the `init.ora`.

    **C.** Increase the value for the SHARED_POOL_BYTES parameter in the `init.ora`.

    **D.** Increase the value for the SIZE_SHARED_POOL parameter in the `init.ora`.

**18.** What happens when a database that is in archive log mode fills the disk drive specified by the `init.ora` parameter LOG_ARCHIVE_DEST with archived redo logs?

    **A.** The database will hang until space is made available in that location.

    **B.** The database will crash and cause possible data corruption.

    **C.** The Archiver background process will write messages to the alert log, but processing will continue.

    **D.** The archive logs that are more than three days old will be purged.

**19.** For which statistic in V$LATCH do you query when examining the instance for latch contention?

    **A.** Database Buffer Cache LRU latch

    **B.** Cache Buffers LRU latch

    **C.** Cache Buffers LRU chain

    **D.** Cache Buffers contention

**20.** Which of the following is *not* a common method of improving datafile I/O?

    **A.** Separate tables and indexes into different tablespaces.

    **B.** Make sure that only data dictionary information is stored in the SYSTEM tablespace.

    **C.** Store each table and index in its own tablespace.

    **D.** Striping datafiles and segments across multiple devices.

**21.** Which of the following statements is true of both materialized views and stored outlines?

   **A.** Both store a predefined execution plan.

   **B.** Both store statistics like MAX and MIN in a pre-summarized form.

   **C.** Both allow you to skip using the actual underlying table and instead use the view or stored plan.

   **D.** Both are designed to speed up the performance of user queries.

**22.** When a deadlock situation occurs, which session will be rolled back in order to resolve the deadlock?

   **A.** The session that causes the deadlock

   **B.** The session that detects the deadlock

   **C.** The session that has done the least amount of work

   **D.** The session that logged in last

**23.** What type of lock is taken out when the LOCK TABLE ... IN EXCLUSIVE MODE command is issued? (Choose all that apply.)

   **A.** Exclusive

   **B.** Shared

   **C.** Explicit

   **D.** Implicit

**24.** Which best describes a domain?

   **A.** A collection of related Oracle services

   **B.** A connect descriptor

   **C.** A Net service name

   **D.** An Oracle Server

**25.** What is the primary configuration file of the localnaming option?

    **A.** `sqlnet.ora`

    **B.** `tnsnames.ora`

    **C.** `listener.ora`

    **D.** `names.ora`

**26.** What are the two types of load balancing?

    **A.** Connection load balancing

    **B.** Server load balancing

    **C.** Client load balancing

    **D.** Network load balancing

**27.** How many default resource consumer groups are created at database creation?

    **A.** One

    **B.** Two

    **C.** Three

    **D.** Four

**28.** What is the maximum number of active pending areas at one time?

    **A.** One

    **B.** Two

    **C.** Three

    **D.** Four

**29.** Which of the following commands would be used to dynamically change the active resource plan for the instance?

    **A.** `ALTER DATABASE SET RESOURCE_MANAGER_PLAN...`

    **B.** `ALTER SYSTEM SET RESOURCE_MANAGER_PLAN...`

    **C.** `ALTER DATABASE SET RESOURCE_PLAN...`

    **D.** `ALTER SYSTEM SET RESOURCE_PLAN ...`

**30.** Which of the following types of information cannot be found in the alert log?

    **A.** Instance startups and shutdowns

    **B.** Redo log switches

    **C.** Creation of database users

    **D.** Tablespace creation

**31.** When assigning a user to a resource consumer group, which procedure in the RDBMS_RESOURCE_MANAGER_PRIVS package is used?

    **A.** ASSIGN_RSRC_CONSUMER_GROUP

    **B.** ASSIGN_RSG_TO_USER

    **C.** GRANT_SWITCH_CONSUMER_GROUP

    **D.** GRANT_RSRC_CONSUMER_GROUP

**32.** Which of the following resource consumer groups cannot be defined as the user's initial RCG?

    **A.** A resource consumer group that the user did not create

    **B.** A resource consumer group that was granted via a role

    **C.** A resource consumer group that has only CPU allocations defined in its plan directives

    **D.** A resource consumer group that uses more than four levels to define degree-of-parallelism allocations

**33.** Which of the following methods of connecting to Oracle Expert will not cause a repository to be built in the target database? Choose two.

    **A.** The database is using the Parallel Server option.

    **B.** The database already has an Oracle Expert repository.

    **C.** The connection is made through an Oracle Management Server.

    **D.** The default Oracle Expert schema uses the SYSTEM tablespace to store its objects.

**34.** Which of the following best describes connection pooling?

    **A.** It allows clients to share connections.

    **B.** It allows dispatchers to handle multiple clients.

    **C.** It allows clients to use dedicated connections.

    **D.** It is considered a "middleware" piece of software.

**35.** What of the following areas should be monitored when establishing benchmarks?

    **A.** Response time

    **B.** CPU utilization statistics

    **C.** Physical I/O and memory consumption

    **D.** All of the above should be monitored.

**36.** What is the default sample frequency on the Collect tab of the Oracle Expert main window?

    **A.** Every 12 minutes

    **B.** 12 times per hour

    **C.** Five times per hour

    **D.** Every 15 minutes

**37.** How do the UNRECOVERABLE and NOLOGGING options differ?

    **A.** The NOLOGGING option is only in effect at table creation, while the UNRECOVERABLE option is a table attribute.

    **B.** The NOLOGGING option can only be used on new tables, while the UNRECOVERABLE option can be added to existing tables.

    **C.** The UNRECOVERABLE option is only in effect at table creation, while the NOLOGGING option is a table attribute.

    **D.** The NOLOGGING does not log DML of any kind, while the UNRECOVERABLE option only skips logging direct loads using SQL*Loader.

**38.** Performing what operation on a suggestion on the Recommendations tab allows you to decline a suggested recommendation?

    **A.** Double click and select `Decline` from the pop-up menu

    **B.** Single click and select `Decline` from the pop-up menu

    **C.** Right-click and select `Decline` from the pop-up menu

    **D.** Drag and select `Decline` from the pop-up menu

**39.** What are the two Names Server configurations?

    **A.** Using an `sdns.ora` file to store service names

    **B.** Using a `tnsnames.ora` file to store service names

    **C.** Using a database to store service names

    **D.** Using a `sqlnet.ora` file to store service names

**40.** What is the function of the client cache option?

    **A.** Allows clients to store connect descriptor information from recent Names Server contacts

    **B.** Allows clients to store retrieved data from an Oracle Server

    **C.** Allows clients to keep track of information about Names Servers

    **D.** All of the above

**41.** What does it mean when a listener autoregisters with a Names Server?

    **A.** A listener listens for Names Server connections.

    **B.** A listener provides information to a Names Server about services that the listener is listening for.

    **C.** A listener gets information from the Names Server about what services the Names Server knows about.

    **D.** None of the above

**42.** Which best describes multi-protocol interchange?

    **A.** Allows clients and servers using different protocols to communicate

    **B.** Sets up rules to allow or disallow connections to Oracle Servers

    **C.** Funnels client connections into a single outgoing connection to the Oracle Server

    **D.** None of the above

**43.** Which of the following is not a level at which the optimizer mode can be set?

    **A.** Instance level

    **B.** Session level

    **C.** Statement level

    **D.** Any of the above levels can be used to set the optimizer mode.

**44.** Which best describes client access control?

    **A.** Allows clients and servers using different protocols to communicate

    **B.** Sets up rules to allow or disallow connections to Oracle Servers

    **C.** Funnels client connections into a single outgoing connection to the Oracle Server

    **D.** None of the above

**45.** Changing the values on which tab of the Oracle Expert main window allows you to perform a "what-if" analysis?

    **A.** Scope

    **B.** Collect

    **C.** View/Edit

    **D.** Recommendations

**46.** What is in the `cman_profile` section of the `cman.ora` file?

    **A.** Sets up the listening location of the Connection Manager

    **B.** Allows you to configure optional Connection Manager parameters

    **C.** Configures Connection Manager rules

    **D.** None of the above

**47.** The main difference between logging and tracing is:

    **A.** Tracing cannot be disabled.

    **B.** Logging cannot be disabled.

    **C.** Logging records only significant events.

    **D.** Tracing records only significant events.

**48.** If you were concerned about the number of clients connecting to a listener and the burden on the listener, what could you configure? (Choose the best answer.)

    **A.** Listener load balancing

    **B.** Client load balancing

    **C.** Connection load balancing

    **D.** All of the above

**49.** What utility is used to format trace files?

    **A.** Oracle Trace

    **B.** Oracle Trace Assistant

    **C.** Oracle Net8 Trace

    **D.** Oracle Trace Utility

**50.** Which of the following statements about the differences between the V$SESSTAT and V$SYSSTAT views is incorrect? (Choose two.)

    **A.** V$SESSTAT shows per session statistics, V$SYSSTAT shows instance wide statistics.

    **B.** V$SESSTAT includes the user name, V$SYSSTAT does not.

    **C.** V$SESSTAT shows statistics for connected sessions, V$SYSSTAT shows cumulative statistics for all sessions that have connected since instance startup.

    **D.** The statistics in V$SESSTAT and V$SYSSTAT are most accurate right after instance startup.

**51.** What utility can be used to check if a client can see an Oracle Listener?

    **A.** `netstat`

    **B.** `namesctl`

    **C.** `tnsping`

    **D.** `lsnrctl`

    **E.** None of the above

**52.** What information does the adapter utility provide on UNIX-based systems?

    **A.** A summary of all listeners on the server

    **B.** A list of supported protocols

    **C.** A list of linked protocol adapters

    **D.** Information regarding installed network protocols

**53.** Which of the following is *true* about shared servers?

    **A.** They talk to dispatchers.

    **B.** They execute client requests.

    **C.** They talk directly to the listener.

    **D.** They talk directly to a client process.

**54.** Assume that V$SYSSTAT shows the following statistics: consistent gets 230444, physical reads 19288, db block gets 341789. What is the Database Buffer Cache hit ratio?

    **A.** 3.37 percent

    **B.** .0337 percent

    **C.** 96.63 percent

    **D.** .9963 percent

**55.** Which of the following is *false* about instance failover?

    **A.** (Failover = ON)

    **B.** It involves multiple instances.

    **C.** It involves a single instance.

    **D.** It can be used with a dedicated server.

**56.** In Oracle8i, what has replaced the Oracle SID definition passed to the listener?

   **A.** A listener name

   **B.** Service naming

   **C.** A network location

   **D.** An Oracle Names Server location

**57.** Which of these is *not* a layer of the Net8 Stack?

   **A.** Two-Task Common

   **B.** Transparent Network Substrate

   **C.** Oracle Call Interface

   **D.** Application

   **E.** All of the above are part of the Net8 Stack.

**58.** Which of the following runs as a separate OS process on each server that hosts an Oracle instance? This process monitors the actions you have requested and reports any occurrences of these events back to the Oracle Enterprise Manager Console.

   **A.** Net8 Listener

   **B.** Oracle Intelligent Agent

   **C.** Server Manager

   **D.** SQL*Worksheet

**59.** Put these steps of connecting to a client in proper order.

   **A.** The client attempts to resolve the location of the Oracle Server.

   **B.** The client enters connection information.

   **C.** If the request fails, an error message is sent back to the client about why the connection was failed.

   **D.** The server receives the connection request and determines if it is valid.

   **E.** If the location is resolved, the client contacts the Oracle Server.

   **F.** If the server accepts the request, it sends a response back to the client and the connection is established.

**60.** Which of these is *not* a way to resolve a net service name?

   **A.** Localnaming

   **B.** Hostnaming

   **C.** Oracle Name Server

   **D.** Internal Naming

**61.** What are the two ways a client can terminate a session?

   **A.** Normal termination

   **B.** Immediate termination

   **C.** Abnormal termination

   **D.** Aborted termination

**62.** What does OSI stand for?

   **A.** Oracle Standard Implementation

   **B.** Oracle System Information

   **C.** Open Standard Interconnection

   **D.** Open Systems Interconnection

**63.** Why do bind variables help improve Library Cache hit ratios?

   **A.** They are easier for programmer to use than real values.

   **B.** They are not limited to storing just VARCHAR data like non-bind variables.

   **C.** If two statements differ by only the value in the bind variable, a cache hit will occur.

   **D.** None of the above are correct because bind variables actually hinder the Library Cache hit ratio.

**64.** Which best describes the function of the Net8 Assistant?

   **A.** A graphical tool to configure critical Oracle network files

   **B.** A tool to configure the Oracle protocols

   **C.** A graphical tool used to monitor Oracle connections

   **D.** A tool to troubleshoot Oracle connection problems

**65.** What configuration file controls the listener?

   **A.** tnsnames.ora

   **B.** listener.ora

   **C.** sqlnet.ora

   **D.** names.ora

**66.** What Shared Pool component is responsible for caching SQL and PL/SQL statements?

   **A.** Data Dictionary Cache

   **B.** Library Cache

   **C.** User Global Area

   **D.** Large Pool

**67.** Which optional parameter allows you to register listeners with Oracle Names Servers? (Choose two.)

   **A.** ORACLE_SERVICE

   **B.** INSTANCE_NAME

   **C.** ORACLE_NAME

   **D.** SERVICE_NAME

**68.** Which command line utility is used to start and stop the listener?

   **A.** listener

   **B.** lsnrctl

   **C.** listen

   **D.** listen_ctl

**69.** Which of the following statements is true about RADIUS?

   **A.** The RADIUS server and the Oracle server can be on the same machine.

   **B.** The RADIUS server and the Oracle server must be on different machines.

   **C.** The RADIUS server and the authentication server must be on different machines.

   **D.** None of the above is true.

**70.** While B-Tree Indexes, Reverse Key Indexes, and Index Organized Tables, are all designed for different situations, they share which of the following attributes?

   **A.** These objects can only be used by users with DBA privileges.

   **B.** These objects all use a B-Tree structure to store their data.

   **C.** These objects all store their data as bit maps.

   **D.** These objects cannot be used by the cost-based optimizer.

**71.** What role does the `init.ora` play in database performance tuning?

   **A.** Determines the size of Oracle's Memory structures

   **B.** Stores the locations of the datafiles

   **C.** Stores transaction recovery information

   **D.** All of the above are correct.

**72.** Which method of security scrambles messages during transmission?

   **A.** Checksumming

   **B.** Encryption

   **C.** Distributed Computing Environment

   **D.** Token Cards option

**73.** Which parameter is used in operating system authentication and defaults to OPS$?

   **A.** `SQLNET.AUTHENTICATION_SERVICES`

   **B.** `REMOTE_AUTHENT_CLIENT`

   **C.** `OS_AUTHENT_PREFIX`

   **D.** `SQLNET.OS_AUTHENT_CLIENT`

**74.** Buffer Cache cache misses do not always result in a disk I/O because of the presence of:

   **A.** Hardware controller caches

   **B.** The System Global Area

   **C.** The Redo Log Buffer

   **D.** The Dirty List

**75.** Improving the Database Buffer Cache hit ratio by bypassing the Buffer Cache using Parallel DML should only be considered when:

   **A.** CPU utilization is low.

   **B.** There are several CPUs.

   **C.** Both of the above

   **D.** None of the above

**76.** What are some of the issues of network complexity that the database administrator should consider? Choose all that apply.

   **A.** How much time will it take to configure a client

   **B.** What type of work clients will be performing

   **C.** What type of protocols being used

   **D.** The size and number of transactions that will be done

   **E.** All of the above

**77.** What are the three primary network configurations?

   **A.** N-tier architecture

   **B.** Single-tier architecture

   **C.** Multi-tier architecture

   **D.** Two-tier architecture

**78.** What statistic in V$SYSSTAT indicates that migrated or chained rows may exist in the database?

   **A.** `table chain count`

   **B.** `table fetch for continued row`

   **C.** `chain_cnt`

   **D.** `continued row fetch`

**79.** Which of the following is not a component of an Oracle Database?

   **A.** System Global Area

   **B.** Control files

   **C.** Datafiles

   **D.** Redo logs

**80.** Why does deleting and reinserting migrated rows fix the migration problem?

   **A.** Rows only migrate when inserted.

   **B.** Rows only migrate when deleted.

   **C.** Rows only migrate when updated.

   **D.** Deleting and reinserting rows does not fix the problem of row migration.

**81.** Checkpoint activity is closely related to the performance of the Redo Log Buffer because:

   **A.** The contents of the Redo Log Buffer are copied to the archive destination at a database checkpoint.

   **B.** The contents of the Redo Log Buffer are flushed to the online Redo Log at a database checkpoint.

   **C.** The contents of the Redo Log Buffer are flushed to the Datafiles at a database checkpoint.

   **D.** The contents of the online Redo Log are copied into the Redo Log Buffer at a database checkpoint.

**82.** What features do the Oracle Gateway products provide? Choose all that apply.

   **A.** They allow organizations to bridge communications between desperate databases.

   **B.** They allow clients and servers to communicate across multiple protocols.

   **C.** They restrict access to databases by certain clients.

   **D.** They allow for seamless integration of existing systems.

**83.** Which two dynamic performance views can be used to examine Redo Log Buffer performance on a per-user basis?

**A.** V$SYSTEM and V$SGA

**B.** V$SYSSTAT and V$SESSION

**C.** V$SESSION_WAIT and V$SESSION

**D.** V$SESSION and V$LOGBUFFER

**84.** How does Multithreaded Server differ from dedicated server (choose all that apply)?

**A.** Clients use dispatchers instead of dedicated connections.

**B.** The System Global Area contains request and response queues.

**C.** Shared server processes execute client requests.

**D.** All of the above

**85.** What is a cache replication used for?

**A.** To keep track of client connections

**B.** To synchronize client and server connections

**C.** To keep Names Servers in a region synchronized with net service information

**D.** None of the above

**86.** Which best describes connection concentration?

**A.** Allows clients and servers using different protocols to communicate

**B.** Sets up rules to allow or disallow connections to Oracle Servers

**C.** Funnels client connections into a single outgoing connection to the Oracle Server

**D.** None of the above

87. Which of the following is not a hardware resource that must be considered when tuning the Oracle Server?

    A. Memory utilization

    B. Power consumption

    C. CPU utilization

    D. I/O activity

88. What statistic do you query for in V$SYSTEM_EVENT when examining the instance for Free List contention?

    A. free list

    B. buffer busy wait

    C. segment header

    D. None of the above

89. What is a disadvantage of the hostnaming option?

    A. Cannot use bequeath connections

    B. Cannot use multithreaded server connections

    C. Cannot use client load balancing

    D. All of the above

90. Which of the following is not a step in using the UTLBSTAT.SQL and UTLESTAT.SQL scripts?

    A. Run the UTLESTAT.SQL script at the beginning of the reporting period.

    B. Let at least ten minutes pass between running each script.

    C. Examine the resulting REPORT.TXT file for information.

    D. Copies of some V$ views are made and then used to calculate performance statistics.

**91.** What does IIOP stand for?

**A.** Internet Interactive Objects Protocol

**B.** Internet Instance Objects Protocol

**C.** Internet Inter-Orb Protocol

**D.** Internet Inter-Objects Protocol

**E.** None of the above

**92.** Select the `init.ora` entry that will result in an error at instance startup:

**A.** BUFFER_POOL_KEEP = (BUFFERS:200, LRU_LATCHES:20)

**B.** BUFFER_POOL_KEEP = (BUFFERS:10240, LRU_LATCHES:20)

**C.** BUFFER_POOL_RECYCLE = (BUFFERS:150, LRU_LATCHES:2)

**D.** BUFFER_POOL_RECYCLE = (BUFFERS:2048, LRU_LATCHES:50)

**93.** Which of the following might indicate that the Redo Log Buffer is too small? (Choose two.)

**A.** The ratio of `redo buffer allocation retries` to `redo entries` in V$SYSSTAT is less than 1 percent.

**B.** The ratio of `redo buffer allocation retries` to `redo entries` in V$SYSSTAT is more than 1 percent.

**C.** The value for `redo log space requests` in V$SYSSTAT is steadily decreasing.

**D.** The value for `redo log space requests` in V$SYSSTAT is steadily increasing.

# Answers to Assessment Test

1. **A, B, D.** The Names Server allows for centralized administration of service names in the enterprise. This allows for easier administration and ensures more accurate service name information. See Chapter 15 for more information.

2. **C.** Without tuning benchmarks it is very difficult to determine what effects your tuning efforts are having on the system. Rather than just subjectively noticing that "the system runs faster," you need to be able to measure exactly which areas are running faster and by how much. Without initial benchmark statistics, it is also difficult to know when to stop tuning in one area and move to another. For example, if the throughput of a particular query has been reduced from 2 minutes to 15 seconds, further attention to tuning of this statement may not be warranted if other possible tuning bottlenecks have also been identified. See Chapter 1 for more information.

3. **A, C.** The V$LIBRARYCACHE view can be used to monitor the hit ratio of the Library Cache. The V$ROWCACHE view can be used to monitor the performance of the Data Dictionary Cache. Both of these areas are also included in the output of REPORT.TXT. See Chapter 4 for more information.

4. **C.** Trace information that has been gathered by the Oracle Trace GUI tool can be used directly by Oracle Expert in generating tuning recommendations. See Chapter 10 for more information.

5. **E.** Net8 is responsible for handling client-to-server and server-to-server communications in an Oracle environment. It manages the flow of information in the Oracle Network infrastructure. Net8 is used to establish the initial connection to the Oracle Server and then acts as the messenger, which passes requests from the client back to the server or between two Oracle Servers. See Chapter 11 for more information.

**6.** A, B.  Multithreaded Server allows Oracle servers to manage a greater number of connections utilizing the same amount or less memory and process resources. If an Oracle server is constrained by these resources, Multithreaded Server can be an alternative configuration that can provide relief. See Chapter 16 for more information.

**7.** B.  A connected user's session can be traced by the DBA by using the DBMS_SYSTEM.SET_SQL_TRACE_IN_SESSION PL/SQL package, or by setting the init.ora parameter SQL_TRACE=TRUE. See Chapter 2 for more information.

**8.** A.  The output of the TKPROF command contains information on the resources (including CPU) that a given SQL statement is consuming during the Parse, Execute, and Fetch phases of statement processing. The EXPLAIN PLAN FOR command allows you to see how Oracle is executing a statement from the standpoint of table access methods, index usage, and joins. The AUTOTRACE facility also allows you to see some resource usage and Explain Plan output, but does so automatically, with each statement executed. See Chapter 3 for more information.

**9.** B.  If each database block is 2K, then 10,240 buffers are required to create a 20MB pool: 2048 bytes per buffer * 10,240 buffers = 20,971,520 bytes = 20MB. See Chapter 5 for more information.

**10.** B.  Application developers who code long-running transactions that do not commit frequently can also contribute to lock contention. See Chapter 8 for more information.

**11.** B.  Servers with only one CPU do not generally benefit from multiple Database Writer processes. You should also limit the number of Database Writers to about two per physical device. If I/O slaves are used then multiple Database Writers cannot be used. See Chapter 7 for more information.

**12.** C.  When using the cost-based optimizer mode, the optimizer needs current statistics in order to be able to make the appropriate choices from all the possible execution plans. Without these statistics the optimizer will likely make poor choices about index usage, causing many queries to needlessly perform full table scans when retrieving their data. See Chapter 3 for more information.

**13.** C.   The Shared Pool caches the SQL statements and data dictionary information issued by the application accessing the instance. The Shared Pool caches this information so that users can share one another's parsed statements and data dictionary information, thus reducing the amount of overhead associated with each statement. See Chapter 4 for more information.

**14.** A, B.   The hostnaming method is used in simple Oracle networks that have few Oracle servers. The advantage of this method is that it does not require any configuration files to be present on the clients. This reduces the amount of administrative work that you have to do for client connections. See Chapter 14 for more information.

**15.** A.   The location of the archived Redo logs does not impact the amount of server memory needed by the Oracle instance. See Chapter 6 for more information.

**16.** B.   Dispatchers, discussed in Chapter 16, take the place of the dedicated server processes. The dispatchers are responsible for responding to client requests by placing the requests on a request queue in the SGA and retrieving completed requests placed on a response queue and passing them back to the client. See Chapter 16 for more information.

**17.** B.   The Shared Pool hit ratios can be improved by increasing the size of the shared pool, reserving space in the shared pool for large PL/SQL objects, pinning frequently used PL/SQL objects in memory, and re-writing applications using strict coding standards and bind variables. See Chapter 4 for more information.

**18.** A.   Unless secondary locations for archive logs are specified in the `init.ora` using the `LOG_ARCHIVE_DUPLEX_DEST` or `LOG_ARCHIVE_DEST_n` parameters, the database will stop processing DML transactions until space is made available in the archive log destination. See Chapter 7 for more information.

**19.** C.   The hit ratio for the `cache buffers LRU chain` latch should be in excess of 99 percent on well-tuned systems. See Chapter 8 for more information.

**20.** C. While tables and indexes should be separated from one another's tablespaces to improve I/O, placing every table and index in its own tablespace creates a difficult to manage environment. See Chapter 7 for more information.

**21.** D. While both materialized views and stored outlines are designed to speed up query processing, each does so in a different manner. Stored outlines improve query performance by storing a predefined execution plan for the optimizer to follow. This way the optimizer does not have to take time to evaluate possible execution plans. Instead, it will always pick the plan that you have determined is the best plan. Materialized views improve query performance by physically storing the results of summary queries in a view. This minimizes I/O by allowing the query to access the materialized view for its data instead of having to read the data from the underlying tables and perform the summary calculations dynamically. See Chapter 3 for more information.

**22.** B. The session that detects that deadlock situation is rolled back in order to resolve the deadlock situation. See Chapter 8 for more information.

**23.** A. Explicitly locking a table using the LOCK TABLE command will take out an exclusive lock, prohibiting all other users from performing any DML on rows in the table. See Chapter 8 for more information.

**24.** A. A domain is nothing more than a collection of related Oracle services. The domain groups may be defined along some boundary. Examples would be logical boundaries, such as grouping like applications services together, or physical boundaries, such as by geographic locations. See Chapter 14 for more information.

**25.** B. The main characteristic of the localnaming method is that it uses the tnsnames.ora file to resolve service names. In fact, this method is sometimes called the tnsnames.ora method. This file contains information about the service names and connect descriptors for each service name that a client can contact. See Chapter 14 for more information.

26. **A, C.** Connection load balancing evenly distributes a set of connections across a set of dispatchers in a multithreaded server environment. Client load balancing randomly selects from a list of listener locations for a net service name to evenly distribute connections across multiple listeners. This balancing prevents any one listener to become strained by servicing too many connection requests simultaneously. See Chapter 14 for more information.

27. **D.** Four resource consumer groups, SYS_GROUP, LOW_GROUP, DEFAULT_CONSUMER_GROUP, and OTHER_GROUPS, are created at database creation. See Chapter 9 for more information.

28. **A.** Only one pending area can be active at a time. See Chapter 9 for more information.

29. **B.** ALTER SYSTEM SET RESOURCE_MANAGER_PLAN=*ResourcePlanName* can be used to dynamically change the current resource plan that is active in the instance. See Chapter 9 for more information.

30. **C.** Examples of information contained in the alert log includes instance startups and shutdowns, redo log switches, tablespace and datafile creation, block corruption errors, and segment space allocation errors. See Chapter 2 for more information.

31. **C.** The GRANT_SWITCH_CONSUMER_GROUP procedure not only grants the resource consumer group to the user, but also allows them to make this RCG active by using the SWITCH_CURRENT_CONSUMER_GROUP procedure in the DBMS_SESSION PL/SQL package. See Chapter 9 for more information.

32. **B.** Resource consumer groups that have been assigned to a user through a role may not be defined as the user's initial RCG. The resource consumer group must be granted to the user directly. See Chapter 9 for more information.

33. **B, C.** If a connection is made without the Oracle Management Server and no prior repository exists, then the Repository Manager window will pop up and ask you whether you want to build a repository. See Chapter 10 for more information.

**34.** A.  Connection pooling allows clients to share connections. Clients will wait for a connection to become idle. They then can take over an existing connection to get their request processed. This allows for an even greater number of connections being supported. See Chapter 16 for more information.

**35.** D.  All areas of the application and database should be monitored when establishing performance benchmarks. These areas include throughput and response times of SQL statements, statistical data on CPU and memory consumption, and information regarding physical I/O. See Chapter 1 for more information.

**36.** B.  Other valid sample frequencies are one sample per hour, four samples per hour, and six samples per hour. See Chapter 10 for more information.

**37.** C.  All subsequent direct path activities on a `NOLOGGING` table will avoid generating any redo information. Only the initial inserts skip generating redo entries when creating an `UNRECOVERABLE` table using the `CREATE TABLE AS SELECT`... syntax. See Chapter 6 for more information.

**38.** C.  Right-clicking a suggested tuning change brings up a pop-up menu from which you can select the Decline option. See Chapter 10 for more information.

**39.** A, C.  A Names Server can be configured to use an operating system file called a Checkpoint file to store information, or it can be configured to store information in a region database. For small installations, the check-point file may be sufficient, but Oracle recommends using a database for larger installations. See Chapter 15 for more information.

**40.** A.  The client cache option allows you to store connect descriptor infor-mation collected from recent contacts with Names Servers on the client. This can save trips to the Names Server because the client will attempt to use the cached connect descriptor information before making a Names Server request. See Chapter 15 for more information.

**41.** C.   Listeners can automatically register their service names with the Names Server if you set the `use_plug_and_play` parameter in the `listener.ora` file. This enables you to automatically update Names Servers if changes are made to the listener. See Chapter 15 for more information.

**42.** A.   Multi-protocol interchange allows clients and Oracle Servers that are using different network protocols to communicate with one another. Connection Manager acts as an interpreter, compensating for the differences in the network protocols. See Chapter 17 for more information.

**43.** D.   The optimizer mode can be set at the instance level using `OPTIMIZER_MODE` in the `init.ora`, the session level using the `ALTER SESSION` command, or the statement level using hints. A statement level hint always supercedes all other settings. If no hints exist, then the session-level setting will take precedence. If the optimizer mode has not been set that the session level, then the instance-level setting takes effect. See Chapter 3 for more information.

**44.** B.   Client access control is a feature of Connection Manager that makes Connection Manager function similar to a firewall. Connections can be accepted or rejected on the basis of the client location, the destination server and the Oracle service the client is attempting to connect to. This gives the DBA flexibility in configuring access control to the Oracle environment. The `cman_rules` section of the `cman.ora` file is where rules are specified. See Chapter 17 for more information.

**45.** C.   By changing values on the View/Edit tab and then regenerating tuning recommendations, you can test how possible changes to server hardware resources, etc., might impact the database's performance. See Chapter 10 for more information.

**46.** B.   The `cman_profile` section of the `cman.ora` file contains optional configuration parameters such as the maximum number of concurrent connections Connection Manager can manage, logging and tracing parameters, and timeout parameters. See Chapter 17 for more information.

**47.** C.  Logging records significant events, such as starting and stopping the listener, along with certain kinds of network errors. Tracing records all events that occur even when an error does not happen. The trace file provides a great deal of information that logs do not. See Chapter 19 for more information.

**48.** B.  Client load balancing could be configured to distribute connection requests across multiple listeners. See Chapter 20 for more information.

**49.** B.  The Oracle Trace Assistant utility is used to format trace files. It is a command-line utility with optional parameters. The utility takes a trace file and produces a more readable report from the information in trace files. See Chapter 19 for more information.

**50.** B and D.  The V$SESSTAT view shows statistics for all sessions that are connected to the instance. The V$SYSSTAT view does not contain any session-specific statistics, only summary statistics for the entire instance. Since the contents of the V$ views are cleared at instance shutdown, no V$ view contains useful statistics right after instance startup. See Chapter 2 for more information.

**51.** C.  The tnsping utility can be used to check if a client can contact a listener. The command format is tnsping <*databasename*> <*number of tries*>. For example, tnsping DBA 3 would attempt to contact the DBA database three times. This utility also provides information on how long it takes to contact the listener. See Chapter 19 for more information.

**52.** C.  The adapter utility provides a list of all of the protocol adapters that are linked into the Oracle environment. It is useful to run this utility if there is a question of whether or not the right protocol adapters are installed. See Chapter 19 for more information.

**53.** B.  The shared server processes are responsible for executing the client requests. They retrieve the requests from a request queue and place the completed request in the appropriate dispatcher response queue. See Chapter 16 for more information.

**54.** C. The hit ratio is .9663 or 96.63 percent calculated as 1 – ( 19288 / (230444+341789)). See Chapter 5 for more information.

**55.** C.   Instance failover involves more than a single instance. See Chapter 20 for more information.

**56.** B.   Service naming has replaced the Oracle SID definition. See Chapter 20 for more information.

**57.** E.   All of these are part of the Net8 Stack. The stack consists of: Application, OCI, Two-Task Common, TNS, Oracle Protocol Adapters, and Network Protocol. See Chapter 12 for more information.

**58.** B.   The Oracle Intelligent Agent reports database event information back to the OEM Console and performs Fixit Jobs as required.  See Chapter 2 for more information.

**59.** B, A, E, D, F, C.   In Chapter 12, the steps were outlined as follows:

1. The client enters connection information. (B)

2. The client attempts to resolve the location of the Oracle Server. (A)

3. If the location is resolved, the client contacts the Oracle Server. (E)

4. The server receives the connection request and determines if it is valid. (D)

5. If the server accepts the request, it sends a response back to the client and the connection is established. (F)

6. If the request fails, an error message is sent back to the client about why the connection was failed. (C )

See Chapter 12 for more information.

**60.** D.   Localnaming, Hostnaming, Oracle Names Server, External Naming Service. See Chapter 12 for more information.

**61.** A, C.   Normal termination and Abnormal termination. See Chapter 12 for more information.

**62.** D.   OSI Stands for Open Systems Interconnection. This is a layered approach to network communications and is the foundation of the Net8 layer technology. See Chapter 12 for more information.

**63.** C.   Bind variables help improve the Library Cache hit ratio by improving the likelihood that two SQL statements will hash to the same value. This occurs because the bind variable is used when hashing the SQL statement instead of the actual value stored in the variable. See Chapter 4 for more information.

**64.** A.   The Net8 Assistant is a graphical tool that provides a way to configure most of the critical network files for the Oracle Server. See the section in Chapter 13 on starting and using the Net8 Assistant for further details.

**65.** B.   The `listener.ora` file contains the configuration information for the listener. The file contains information about the listening locations, the service names that the listener is listening for, and a section for optional listener parameters such as logging and tracing parameters. There should  only be one `listener.ora` file on a machine. If multiple listeners are used, each listener should have its own entry in the `listener.ora` file. See Chapter 13 for more information on the `listener.ora` file.

**66.** B.   The components of the Shared Pool are the Library Cache and the Data Dictionary Cache. The Library Cache is where parsed copies of the issued SQL statements are stored. The Data Dictionary Cache is where data dictionary information used by the cached statements is stored. See Chapter 4 for more information.

**67.** B, D.   The `INSTANCE_NAME` and `SERVICE_NAME` parameters must be configured in the `init.ora` file to enable the Oracle Server to use the Autoregistration facility. Autoregistration alleviates the need to manually configure services with a listener. The section on Autoregistration in Chapter 13 contains further information about its configuration.

**68.** B.   The `lsnrctl` command line utility is used to start and stop the listener. You can also use this utility to get information about the status of the listener and make modifications to the `listener.ora` file. For further information, see the section on the `lsnrctl` command line utility in Chapter 13.

**69.** **A.** The RADIUS server and the Oracle Server can be on the same machine. See Chapter 18 for more information.

**70.** **B.** B-Tree indexes store the data from the indexed column, plus the row ID of the location of the column's data in the associated table, in a B-Tree structure. Reverse Key Indexes reverse the data in the indexed column before building the B-Tree structured index. Index Organized Tables are much like B-Tree indexes except that they store the entire row data for the indexed column, not just a row ID that points to the row data in an associated table. See Chapter 3 for more information.

**71.** **A.** The `init.ora` has many parameters that affect database performance. Among other things, these parameters control memory usage, sort resources, tracing, and I/O resources. Understanding which `init.ora` parameters are important for tuning and determining at what level to set these parameters is a topic discussed throughout this book. See Chapter 1 for more information.

**72.** **B.** Encryption is used to scramble messages during transmission. See Chapter 18 for more information.

**73.** **C.** The `OS_AUTHENT_PREFIX` defaults to OPS$. This parameter should be set to NULL when using the Advanced Security option. See Chapter 18 for more information.

**74.** **A.** Some modern caching controllers contain upwards of 500MB of memory, which is used to cache O/S blocks that would otherwise result in a physical I/O request. Because reading from these caches is thousands of times faster than reading from disk, a Database Buffer Cache cache miss that only results in a cache I/O instead of a disk I/O is not as significant a performance issue. See Chapter 5 for more information.

**75.** **C.** Parallel DML improves the Database Buffer Cache hit ratio by using a separate memory area for performing DML statements. This feature places extra demand on the CPUs so excess CPU capacity is important. See Chapter 5 for more information.

**76.** B, C, D.   The DBA needs to consider such items as the number of clients the network will need to support, the type of work the clients will be doing, the locations of the clients in the network, and the size of transactions that will be done in the network. See the section in Chapter 11 on Network considerations for details.

**77.** A, B, D.   The three primary network configurations are single-tier, two-tier, and n-tier architecture. Single-tier was the predominant architecture for the many years when the mainframe dominated the corporate environment. Two-tier architecture came into vogue with the introduction of the PC and has been a dominant architecture ever since. With the inception of the Internet, more organizations are turning towards n-tier architecture as a means to leverage many computers and enhance flexibility and performance of their applications. See the discussion in Chapter 11 on network architecture.

**78.** B.   The `table fetch for continued` row statistic indicates how often more than one block had to be read in order to retrieve a single row. See Chapter 7 for more information.

**79.** A.   An Oracle instance consists of the memory structures that Oracle uses to manage user interaction with the database. This includes the SGA and all Oracle background processes (SMON, PMON, DBW0, LGWR, and CKPT). An Oracle database consists of all the physical files that make up the database: control files, datafiles, and redo logs. See Chapter 1 for more information.

**80.** C.   When a row is updated to be larger than the available free space in the block where the row is stored, it migrates to a new block. By deleting and reinserting the migrated rows, the rows will automatically be assigned to a block that can hold the entire row without migration. See Chapter 7 for more information.

**81.** B.   At a database checkpoint event both Database Writer (DBW0) and Log Writer (LGWR) empty the contents of their respective SGA caches to disk. DBW0 writes committed data buffers to the Datafiles and LGWR writes the contents of the Redo Log Buffer to the online Redo Log. See Chapter 6 for more information.

**82.** A, D. The Oracle Gateway products allow organizations to bridge the communication gaps between desperate databases and the Oracle environment. There are two gateway products: the Procedural Gateway and the Transparent Gateway. Both allow organizations seamless integration of Oracle with their existing databases. Oracle supports over 30 database types that allow for a wide degree of integration. See the section on the gateway products in Chapter 11 for more information.

**83.** C. The V$SESSION dynamic performance view contains information on currently connected users. By joining this view to V$SESSION_WAIT, which contains information about the waits that these users are experiencing, you can identify which users are waiting to access the Redo Log Buffer by querying for the statistic log buffer space. See Chapter 6 for more information.

**84.** D. Multithreaded Server used a shared model. Clients share processes called dispatchers that handle their requests. Clients also share processes called shared servers that execute their requests. The sharing is done through modifications to the SGA. See Chapter 16 for more information.

**85.** C. Cache Replication is used when you configure the checkpoint file configuration. Cache replication ensures that all Names Servers are kept synchronized with current net service names information. Each Names Server passes net service name and connect descriptor information to other Name Servers in a region. See Chapter 15 for more information.

**86.** C. Connection concentration allows Connection Manager to funnel incoming client connections into a single outgoing connection to the Oracle Server. This reduces the number of concurrent processes the Oracle Server machine must manage, thus reducing the resource load on the machine. See Chapter 17 for more information.

**87.** B.  Every database tuning effort will impact three areas: memory, CPU, and I/O. Increasing the performance of one area generally has a negative impact on another area. For example, improving I/O by increasing the size of the memory structures so they can cache more data blocks will increase the demands on memory and CPU. See Chapter 1 for more information.

**88.** B.  Occurrences of the `buffer busy wait` statistic in V$SYSTEM_EVENT indicate that the instance may be experiencing Free List contention. See Chapter 8 for more information.

**89.** C.  The disadvantage is that certain functionality such as client load balancing and failover is not available when you use the hostnaming method. See Chapter 14 for more information.

**90.** A.  The `UTLBSTAT.SQL` script copies the structure and content of several of the V$ views at the beginning of the reporting period. At the end of the reporting period the `UTLESTAT.SQL` script captures the structure and contents of the same tables, and then calculates differences in the statistics between the two points in time. These calculated differences are produced in the `REPORT.TXT` output. See Chapter 2 for more information.

**91.** C.  The Internet Inter-Orb Protocol is supported by Net8 to allow for support of Enterprise JavaBeans and CORBA. See Chapter 20 for more information.

**92.** A.  Each LRU latch must control at least 50 buffers. If you want 200 buffers in the Keep Pool, you can only use a maximum of four latches to manage them. If you want to use 20 LRU latches to manage the Keep Pool, you must have at least 1,000 buffers assigned to them. See Chapter 5 for more information.

**93.** B, D.  The ratio of redo entries to redo allocation retries should be less than 1 percent, and space requests should be steady or decreasing over time on a well-tuned system. See Chapter 6 for more information.

# Introduction to Performance Tuning

## ORACLE8i PERFORMANCE AND TUNING EXAM OBJECTIVES COVERED IN THIS CHAPTER:

✓ List the roles associated with the database tuning process.

✓ Define the steps associated with the tuning process.

✓ Identify tuning goals.

Exam objectives are subject to change at any time without prior notice and at Oracle's sole discretion. Please visit Oracle's Training and Certification Web site (http://education .oracle.com/certification/index.html) for the most current exam objectives listing.

**W**hy is the system so slow?" The ability to answer this question definitively and authoritatively is one of the most important skills for an Oracle DBA to possess. Acquiring this skill requires a thorough understanding of the Oracle Server architecture, as well as knowledge of how Oracle processes SQL statements and how Oracle interacts with host operating systems and server hardware. Consequently, tuning an Oracle database can be a daunting task. Oracle8i is *so* tunable and *so* feature-rich that it's often difficult to know where to begin your tuning effort. Because of this, the application of a proven tuning methodology is the key to a successful tuning exercise.

# The Oracle Tuning Methodology

**O**racle recommends a top-down approach to tuning that emphasizes examining the highest performance payoff areas first, and leaving areas with less impact on performance for later inspection. Oracle outlines its recommended tuning methodology in Chapter 2: Performance Tuning Methods of the *Oracle8i Tuning, Release 8.1.5* documentation (Part Number A67775-01).

The full library of Oracle documentation is available online at Oracle's free Technet Web site: http://technet.oracle.com. This site also features trial software downloads and user forums.

The prioritized list of tuning areas is as follows:

Step 1: Tuning the Business Rules

Step 2: Tuning the Data Design

Step 3: Tuning the Application Design

Step 4: Tuning the Logical Structure of the Database

Step 5: Tuning Database Operations

Step 6: Tuning the Access Paths

Step 7: Tuning Memory Allocation

Step 8: Tuning I/O and Physical Structure

Step 9: Tuning Resource Contention

Step 10: Tuning the Underlying Platform(s)

Understand that tuning any one of these areas can effect several of the others. For example, improvements to access paths (Step 6) may necessitate changes in the areas of memory utilization (Step 7) and I/O (Step 8). Because of this, Oracle Server performance tuning tends to be an ongoing, iterative process. However, for the purposes of our initial discussion, we will break down this methodology into two broad categories: application tuning and database tuning.

## Application Tuning

The first three steps of the Oracle tuning methodology focus on issues related to tuning the application design. Steps four through six focus on issues related to application implementation. These application-related steps must be completed before any database tuning issues are ever examined. This is an excellent strategy, since nearly 90 percent of all tuning issues are application-related. Interestingly, as packaged applications become more prevalent, this aspect of tuning becomes increasingly difficult because many of these factors are under the control of the application provider.

The Oracle8i Performance and Tuning exam does not draw heavily on concepts from the first three steps, since these topics tend to be more appropriate for application designers and developers. However, the exam does address some of the topics in steps four through six. These topics will be addressed in Chapter 3: SQL Statement Tuning and Application Design, but only to the extent that these apply to database tuning.

## Database Tuning

Once any application issues are addressed, steps seven through ten of the Oracle methodology focus on performance tuning issues that are directly related to Oracle Server tuning. These areas include tuning the memory structures, disk I/O activity, and resource contention in the database. Performance problems in these areas are identified using Oracle supplied scripts, queries against the data dictionary, and GUI tools such as Oracle Enterprise Manager, Oracle Expert, and Oracle Trace.

The Oracle8i Performance and Tuning exam concentrates heavily on these three areas. In general, the exam requires that you understand how each of these architecture mechanisms work, which measures are available to gauge the performance of these mechanisms, how to interpret the results of these measurements, and what changes are appropriate to improve the performance of these mechanisms. Additionally, topics such as the special tuning considerations for Decision Support Systems (DSS) and Online Transaction Processing Systems (OLTP) as well as the features of Oracle's Multithreaded Server (MTS) option are also incorporated into the exam. All of these topics are addressed in the performance tuning section of this book with the exception of the Multithreaded Server feature. MTS tuning is discussed in Chapter 16 of Part II, which is  the Net8 section of the book. Be sure to review this tuning-related information even if you are not yet preparing for the Oracle8i Network Administration exam.

# Goal-Oriented Tuning

**B**efore undertaking a tuning effort using the Oracle methodology, it is important to set specific tuning goals and then measure your progress toward those goals throughout the tuning process. This is not unlike the process a physician uses when treating a patient, where the physician records standard "performance" measures (i.e. blood pressure, temperature, respiration, heart rate, etc.) and then uses these measures throughout the course of treatment to track the progress of the patient's condition.

# Establishing a Benchmark

You should measure exactly how the system is currently performing before beginning any tuning effort. Using this benchmark, it is then possible to formulate an idea of how you would like the system to perform after the initial tuning effort is complete. As in medicine, it is important to take a holistic view of the system when gathering this benchmark performance data. No single area should be examined in seclusion. Some of the items that should be included in your initial measurements are:

- The performance of client machines used to access the system

- The performance of the network used to access the system

- The performance of the server hardware used to host the system

- The performance of the operating system used to manage the system hardware

- The performance of the Oracle database used as the repository for the application data

Ideally, all of these areas would be monitored simultaneously, for a meaningful duration of time, while the system is under a normal workload. This monitoring will likely require the expertise of many people including system designers, application developers, system and network administrators, and power users. Outputs from monitoring consist primarily of statistics and timings.

## Statistics

Important benchmark statistics can be gathered in all of the design, application, and developer areas listed above. These statistics might include:

- Client PC CPU and memory utilization

- Network traffic efficiency

- Server CPU and memory utilization

- Server disk I/O and controller activity

- Oracle instance memory utilization

- Oracle database I/O activity

These statistics can be gathered using vendor-supplied utilities, third-party tuning tools, or empirical observations. Oracle Server statistics are typically gathered by running Oracle-supplied scripts, monitoring activity through the use of a GUI tool, or by examining database trace and log files. The resulting statistics are frequently expressed in terms of ratios and percentages. Other statistics are expressed in terms of throughput. *Throughput* is the amount of processing that a computer or system can perform in a given amount of time. An example of throughput might be "How many customer deposits can we post to the appropriate accounts in four hours under regular workloads?"

### Timings

Timings related to performance tuning are usually related to response times. *Response time* is the amount of time it takes for a single user's request to return the desired result while using an application. An example of response time might be "How long does it take for the system to return a listing of all the customers who have purchased products that require service contracts?"

## Setting Performance Goals

Once you have established a good baseline against which you'll measure your tuning activities, you need to establish measurable tuning goals. These goals should be specific and stated in a measurable way that allows you to use your existing data for comparison. Consider the following goals:

- "I'd like to pin the five most frequently used PL/SQL packages in memory so that the users can access them faster."

- "I'd like to reduce the time it takes to enter a customer's checking account deposit, post the funds to their account, and issue a receipt to 10 seconds or less."

These are both good examples of measurable tuning goals. They are much more useful tuning goals than something generic like "I'd like the system to run faster."

### Benefits

This explicit statement of goals is important for several reasons. First, it limits the tuning effort to a narrow scope. Changing too many factors at once has foiled many well-intentioned tuning campaigns. By limiting your tuning activities to one or two target areas, the effect of each change can be more easily measured and its effectiveness evaluated.

Second, explicit goals allow you to stop that part of the tuning process once the goals are achieved. While overall tuning is an ongoing and iterative process, it is possible to "tune a system to death" by endlessly tweaking obscure components that produce little or no real performance benefit. Setting tuning targets helps to prevent this problem by allowing you to move to new tuning areas once you have achieved your specific goals.

# General Tuning Concepts

**Y**ou now have an understanding of Oracle's tuning methodology and can appreciate the roles that goal setting and performance measurement play in this model. Additional performance tuning concepts will be introduced in this section and will form the framework of our subsequent discussions.

## Understanding Tradeoffs

There is an old saying that states, "Oracle is not really a software company at all; it's merely a front for a consortium of CPU, disk, and memory manufacturers." It probably seems that way to many purchasing managers after approving yet another purchase order for Oracle-related hardware.

However, this saying does demonstrate that, even with the application of a proven tuning methodology that utilizes extensive benchmarks, most tuning efforts involve some degree of compromise. This occurs because every Oracle Server is constrained by the availability of three key resources: CPU, disk (I/O), and memory.

### CPU

Tuning Oracle's memory and I/O activity will provide little benefit if the server's processor is already overburdened. However, even in high-end, multi-CPU servers, consideration should be given to the impact that changing memory or device configurations will have on CPU utilization. Oracle is also a very "CPU-aware" product. This means that several Oracle Server configuration parameters change dynamically when CPUs are added or removed from the server.

### Disk (I/O)

The more Oracle Server activity that occurs in memory, the lower the physical I/O will be. However, placing too many demands on the available memory by oversizing Oracle's memory structures can cause undesirable additional I/O in the form of operating system paging and swapping. Modern disk-caching hardware and software also complicate database I/O tuning, since I/O activity on these systems may result in reads from the disk controller's cache and not directly from disk.

### Memory

The availability of memory for Oracle's memory structures is key to good performance. Managing that memory is important so that it is used to maximum benefit without wasting any that could be better used by other server processes. Oracle offers several memory tuning options that help you make the most efficient use of the available memory.

## Two Tuning Rules of Thumb

Several different performance tuning topics and concepts will be discussed in subsequent chapters. Many of these topics involve new Oracle Server configuration parameters or the calculation of ratios and interpretation of data dictionary queries. When you focus on all these details, it's easy to lose sight of the big tuning picture. Try to keep these two simple performance tuning tenets in mind while reading this book:

- Add more.

- Make it bigger.

At the end of a lengthy tuning analysis, either or both of these suggestions will frequently be the solution to your tuning problem.

### Add More

Oracle's performance tuning methodology helps identify which resources are causing bottlenecks because they are being demanded more frequently than they can be supplied. The easiest way to fix a performance problem of this type is to add more of that resource to the system.

### Make It Bigger

Oracle's performance tuning methodology also helps ascertain which resources are experiencing performance difficulties not because there are too few of that particular resource, but because the resource is too small to service the requests made against it. The easiest way to fix a performance problem of this type is to make each of those resources larger.

The dreaded ORA-01555 "Snapshot Too Old" error, where a database's rollback segments are too small and/or too few to service the database transactions properly, is a classic example of this concept. This error is discussed in further detail in Chapter 7 of this book.

# Review of the Oracle Architecture

To succeed as an Oracle DBA, you need to completely understand Oracle's underlying architecture and its mechanisms. Understanding the relationship between Oracle's memory structures, background processes, and I/O activities is critical before any tuning of these areas can be undertaken. The Oracle architecture model is reviewed here briefly.

## Logical versus Physical Structures

The Oracle Server architecture can be broken into two main categories: logical (or memory) structures and physical (or file) structures. Memory structures are tuned first in the Oracle tuning methodology. Only after logical tuning goals are met is physical tuning of the database examined. The Oracle Server memory structures are collectively known as the Oracle *instance*. Oracle's physical memory structures are collectively known as the Oracle *database*.

### The Oracle Instance

An Oracle Server instance is made up of Oracle's main memory structure, called the *System Global Area (SGA),* and the Oracle background processes. The SGA, at a minimum, is made up of three components: the Shared Pool, the Database Buffer Cache, and the Redo Log Buffer. Other components of the SGA, like the Large Pool, may also exist on your system depending on what optional features you chose to use. The Oracle background processes are, at a minimum: *System Monitor (SMON), Process Monitor (PMON), Database Writer (DBW0), Log Writer (LGWR),* and the *Checkpoint Process (CKPT).* Several other Oracle background processes may also be running on your system, depending on which optional features you have decided to implement. Figure 1.1 summarizes the responsibilities of each of these mechanisms. Each of these areas will be discussed in greater detail with regard to performance tuning later in the book.

**FIGURE 1.1** System Global Area Components

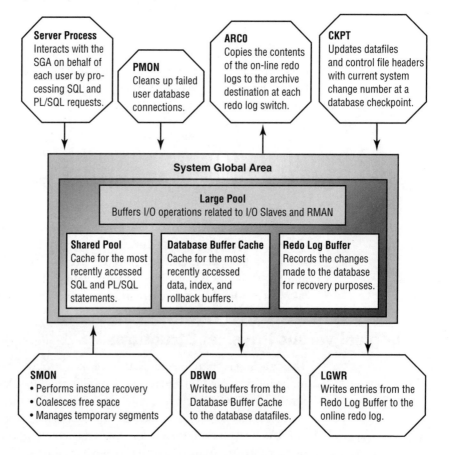

## The Oracle Database

An Oracle database is made up of *control files, datafiles,* and *redo logs.* Additional physical files that are associated with the Oracle database are the *init.ora, trace* and *alert log* files, *password file,* and any *archived redo log* files. Table 1.1 summarizes the role that each of these files plays in the database architecture. Each of these areas will be discussed in greater detail with regard to performance tuning later in the book.

**TABLE 1.1**   Oracle Physical Files

| File Name | Information Contained in File |
| --- | --- |
| control file | Locations of other physical files, database name, database block size, database character set, and recovery information |
| datafile | Data blocks from all database segments including tables and indexes |
| redo log | A record of all changes made to the database, used for recovery |
| init.ora | A listing of configuration parameters for the instance and database |
| archived log file | Copy of the contents of previous online Redo logs, used for recovery |
| password file | Users who have been granted the SYSDBA and SYSOPER privilege |
| alert log file | Information messages and error messages generated by database activity |
| trace files | Information messages and error messages generated by users or background processes |

The init.ora file is of great importance to Oracle Server performance tuning. Many tuning modifications are implemented by making changes to the parameters in the init.ora. The default location for the init.ora is $ORACLE_HOME/dbs on UNIX systems, and %ORACLE_HOME%\database on Windows NT systems. On UNIX systems the init.ora is generally a symbolic link to a file stored in $ORACLE_BASE/admin/*SID*/pfile, where *SID* is the name of the instance associated with that init.ora. Some init.ora parameters can be changed dynamically while the database is open, but others require that the instance be shut down and restarted before they take effect.

There are about 200 different documented init.ora parameters in Oracle8i. Thankfully, you do not need to know every one of them to succeed at performance tuning. The init.ora parameters related to performance tuning are discussed throughout the book. One init.ora parameter that is important to remember for database performance tuning is TIMED_STATISTICS. Whenever you undertake a tuning effort, you should set this parameter to TRUE and then shut down and restart the instance, or use the ALTER SYSTEM SET TIMED_ STATISTICS=TRUE command to dynamically activate this feature. This parameter causes Oracle to gather timing information for actions taken against the database. The additional overhead inflicted on the system by these timings far outweigh the useful information they provide.

There are also many performance tuning modifications that can be made to the database without changing the init.ora. These modifications are made by issuing SQL commands against the Oracle Server, which are most often used to make structural changes to the database. Examples of these changes include modifying tablespaces, rollback segments, datafiles, and redo logs. These commands are issued from the appropriate Oracle management tools like SQL*Plus, SQL*Plus Worksheet, or one of the Oracle Enterprise Manager tools.

# Summary

**A**dopting a proven tuning methodology is the key to Oracle Server performance tuning. Since thorough tuning efforts require an analysis of the entire system, application designers, developers, and DBAs should all participate in the process. Oracle's recommended methodology stresses tuning Oracle Server issues only after application issues are addressed. Among Oracle Server issues, memory and I/O tuning are given attention before resource contention and OS tuning. Taking into consideration all the tradeoffs involved, tuning must take place within a framework of accurate benchmarks and measurable goals in order for the tuning effort to succeed.

## Key Terms

Before you take the exam, make sure you're familiar with the following terms:

throughput

response time

System Global Area (SGA)

System Monitor (SMON)

Process Monitor (PMON)

Database Writer (DBW0)

Log Writer (LGWR)

Checkpoint Process (CKPT)

control file

datafile

redo log

`init.ora`

trace file

alert log file

password file

archive log file

# Review Questions

1. Which of the following is the first step in Oracle's recommended tuning methodology?

   **A.** Tune the database

   **B.** Tune the network

   **C.** Tune the application

   **D.** All of the above are equally important.

2. The first tuning step in Oracle's methodology that is generally under the DBA's direct control is:

   **A.** Tune resource contention

   **B.** Tune the logical structure

   **C.** Tune the operating system

   **D.** Tune memory allocation

3. Moving a datafile to a new disk drive in order to improve performance is an example of which step in the Oracle tuning methodology?

   **A.** Tune I/O and physical structure

   **B.** Tune the access paths

   **C.** Tune resource contention

   **D.** None of the above

4. Increasing the size of the System Global Area in order to improve performance is an example of which step in the Oracle tuning methodology?

   **A.** Tune the Underlying Platform

   **B.** Tune Database Operations

   **C.** Tune Memory Allocation

   **D.** Tune the Data Design

**5.** Which of the following steps would be performed last when using Oracle's Tuning Methodology?

   **A.** Tune Memory Allocation

   **B.** Tune the Application Design

   **C.** Tune Resource Contention

   **D.** Tune I/O and Physical Structure

**6.** It is important to set tuning goals because:

   **A.** Goals allow you to focus your tuning efforts.

   **B.** Goals help identify system bottlenecks.

   **C.** Goals can be written be monitored via SQL scripts.

   **D.** None of the above are correct.

**7.** Benchmarks should be taken:

   **A.** For the database only

   **B.** For the network only

   **C.** For the client PCs only

   **D.** All of the above

**8.** Which of the following are not an example of a pre-tuning benchmark?

   **A.** Statistics

   **B.** Timings

   **C.** Both of these are good pre-tuning benchmarks.

   **D.** Neither of these is a good pre-tuning benchmark.

**9.** Which of the following is the best way to gather pre-tuning benchmarks on a system that utilizes PC clients that access the database over a network?

    **A.** Gather statistics and timings from the PC clients, network, and database, but not simultaneously.

    **B.** Gather the statistics and timings at a time when the system is not being utilized so as not to interfere with regular processing.

    **C.** Gather the statistics and timings for only a short period of time, preferably less than two minutes.

    **D.** Gather the statistics and timings for a useful period of time, during regular processing, on the PC clients, network, and database.

**10.** Response time is a measure of:

    **A.** The time it takes for a single user to receive a result set back when working from within the application

    **B.** How much processing the system can do during a given amount of time

    **C.** How fast a user's PC can refresh the screen with new data

    **D.** How long it takes for Oracle to find data without using an index

**11.** Throughput is a measure of:

    **A.** The time it takes for a single user to receive a result set back when working from within the application

    **B.** How much processing the system can do during a given amount of time

    **C.** How fast a user's PC can refresh the screen with new data

    **D.** How long it takes for Oracle to find data without using an index

**12.** Which of the following is not a way in which database performance statistics and timings are gathered?

   **A.** Using Oracle-supplied scripts

   **B.** Using Oracle's GUI tools

   **C.** Examining Oracle log and trace files

   **D.** All of these are good sources of database performance statistics.

**13.** The hardware resource that is most impacted by performance tuning changes is:

   **A.** The server CPU

   **B.** The server memory

   **C.** The server I/O system

   **D.** All of the above are affected by tuning changes.

**14.** Which of the following components of the Oracle architecture are not found in the System Global Area (choose two)?

   **A.** Redo log

   **B.** Shared Pool

   **C.** Control file

   **D.** Database Buffer Cache

**15.** An Oracle instance is made up of:

   **A.** SGA and the `init.ora`

   **B.** SGA and the background processes

   **C.** SGA, datafiles, control files, and redo logs

   **D.** SGA, alert log, and trace files

**16.** An Oracle database is made up of:

**A.** Datafiles, redo logs, and trace files

**B.** Datafiles, control files, and `init.ora`

**C.** Datafiles, redo logs, and control files

**D.** Redo logs, archived redo logs, and password file

**17.** Which of the following Oracle background processes writes blocks from the Database Buffer Cache to the datafiles?

**A.** LGWR

**B.** DBW0

**C.** CKPT

**D.** SMON

**18.** Which of the following Oracle background processes detects failed user processes and rolls back their transactions?

**A.** PMON

**B.** DBW0

**C.** SMON

**D.** CKPT

**19.** Which of the following components of System Global Area caches recently accessed data, index, and rollback blocks?

**A.** Shared Pool

**B.** Database Buffer Cache

**C.** Large Pool

**D.** Redo Log Buffer

**20.** Which of the following components of the System Global Area records changes made to the database for recovery purposes?

**A.** Shared Pool

**B.** Database Buffer Cache

**C.** Large Pool

**D.** Redo Log Buffer

# Answers to Review Questions

1. C. Tuning the application's functionality and design is done before any database tuning in Oracle's methodology.

2. D. Tuning memory allocation is the biggest tuning payoff area that is under the DBA's direct control.

3. A. Relocating the database's physical files, whether they are datafiles, control files, or redo logs, are all forms of I/O tuning.

4. C. The System Global Area is Oracle's main memory structure. Changing its size will impact the amount of server memory allocated to the Oracle instance on the server.

5. C. Oracle's recommended tuning methodology emphasizes tuning the application first and the Oracle Server second. Memory allocation, I/O, and contention are all examples of Oracle Server tuning.

6. A. Tuning goals allow you to focus on areas of greatest importance first and then move on to lesser objectives after the goals are met.

7. D. All aspects of the system should have benchmarks established before testing the tuning process. This allows you to confirm that your tuning changes are having a positive effect and are not just coincidental to some other change.

8. C. Before any tuning changes are implemented, a good baseline measurement should be taken so that the effects of the tuning changes can be properly evaluated. System statistics and timings are both good examples of such benchmark statistics.

9. D. Accurate measures of pre-tuning performance must include all aspects of the system and should be taken over a long enough duration to provide meaningful results. These measurements should also be taken during a period of normal, or even heavy, processing so that the system will be under stress at the time.

10. A. Response time is an example of a measure that helps determine whether end-users are benefiting from the tuning process.

11. B. Throughput is an example of a measure that helps determine whether batch processing and overall processing is benefiting from the tuning process.

12. D. All of these areas can provide useful statistics and timings. Each of these areas will be discussed in much greater detail later in the book.

13. D. CPU, memory, and I/O are all affected by tuning changes. For example, changes made to reduce I/O generally increase the demands on memory and CPU.

14. A and C. Redo logs and control files are components of the physical database, not the System Global Area.

15. B. The System Global Area and its associated PMON, SMON, DBW0, LGWR, and CKPT background processes make up the Oracle instance.

16. C. An Oracle database consists of the control files, redo logs, and datafiles. The trace files, archived redo logs, password file, and init.ora are not considered part of the database.

17. B. Database Writer (DBW0) is responsible for writing blocks from the Database Buffer Cache to the database datafiles.

18. A. Process Monitor (PMON) cleans up failed user connections by rolling back their transactions and releasing any locks they held.

19. B. The Database Buffer Cache holds the data, index, and rollback blocks that users are accessing via the application. Database Writer (DBW0) writes these blocks to the database datafiles.

20. D. The Redo Log Buffer holds a record of changes made to the database so that they can be redone in the event of a device failure. Log Writer (LGWR) writes these changes to the online redo log file.

# Chapter

# 2

# Sources of Tuning Information

## ORACLE8i PERFORMANCE TUNING EXAM OBJECTIVES COVERED IN THIS CHAPTER:

- ✓ Describe the location and usefulness of the alert log file.
- ✓ Describe the location and usefulness of the background and user process trace files.
- ✓ Collect statistics using dynamic performance views, REPORT.TXT, Oracle wait events and Oracle Enterprise Manager tools.

Exam objectives are subject to change at any time without prior notice and at Oracle's sole discretion. Please visit Oracle's Training and Certification Web site (http:/ /education.oracle.com/certification/ index.html) for the most current exam objectives listing.

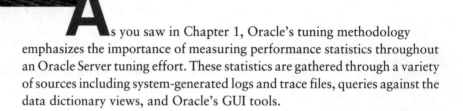

As you saw in Chapter 1, Oracle's tuning methodology emphasizes the importance of measuring performance statistics throughout an Oracle Server tuning effort. These statistics are gathered through a variety of sources including system-generated logs and trace files, queries against the data dictionary views, and Oracle's GUI tools.

# The Alert Log

The Oracle *alert log* records informational and error messages for a variety of activities that have occurred against the database during its operation. These activities are recorded in chronological order from the oldest to most recent. A sample alert log from a UNIX Oracle8i Server is shown here.

```
Starting ORACLE instance (normal)
LICENSE_MAX_SESSION = 0
LICENSE_SESSIONS_WARNING = 0
LICENSE_MAX_USERS = 0
Starting up ORACLE RDBMS Version: 8.1.5.0.0.
System parameters with non-default values:
  processes               = 200
  shared_pool_size        = 12000000
  control_files           = /u02/oradata/PROD/
control101.ctl
  db_block_buffers        = 20000
  log_archive_start       = TRUE
```

```
    log_archive_dest              = /u01/oradata/PROD/arch
    log_archive_format            = PROD_%s.arc
    log_buffer                    = 163840
    db_file_multiblock_read_count= 32
    sort_area_size                = 655360
    db_name                       = PROD
    background_dump_dest          = /u01/oracle/admin/PROD/bdump
    user_dump_dest                = /u01/oracle/admin/PROD/udump
    core_dump_dest                = /u01/oracle/admin/PROD/cdump
PMON started with pid=2
DBW0 started with pid=3
LGWR started with pid=4
CKPT started with pid=5
SMON started with pid=6
Mon Aug 21 15:56:14 2000
RECO started with pid=7
Mon Aug 21 15:56:14 2000
alter database  mount
Mon Aug 21 15:56:22 2000
Successful mount of redo thread 1, with mount id
2939412134.
Mon Aug 21 15:56:22 2000
Database mounted in Exclusive Mode.
Completed: alter database  mount
Mon Aug 21 15:56:22 2000
alter database open
Picked Lamport Server scheme to generate SCNs
Mon Aug 21 15:56:22 2000
Thread 1 opened at log sequence 54
  Current log# 3 seq# 54 mem# 0: /u01/oradata/PROD/
log3a.dbf
  Current log# 3 seq# 54 mem# 1: /u01/oradata/PROD/
log3b.dbf
Successful open of redo thread 1.
Mon Aug 21 16:45:47 2000
ORA-1652: unable to extend temp segment by 102400 in
tablespace ORADBA
```

```
Tue Aug 22 09:53:20 2000
ALTER DATABASE
    DATAFILE '/u04/oradata/PROD/index02.dbf' RESIZE 500M
Tue Aug 22 09:53:21 2000
Completed: ALTER DATABASE
    DATAFILE '/u04/oradata/PROD
Tue Aug 22 10:00:17 2000
alter database backup controlfile to trace
Tue Aug 22 10:00:17 2000
Completed: alter database backup controlfile to trace
Shutting down instance (normal)
License high water mark = 6
Tue Aug 22 10:13:02 2000
ALTER DATABASE CLOSE NORMAL
```

The Alert log is found in the directory specified by the `init.ora` parameter `BACKGROUND_DUMP_DEST`. On systems that follow the *Optimal Flexible Architecture (OFA)* model recommended by Oracle, this directory will be `$ORACLE_BASE/admin/SID/bdump` on UNIX systems and `%ORACLE_BASE%\admin\SID\bdump` on Windows NT systems, where *SID* represents the name of the Oracle instance that will be creating the alert log.

The Optimal Flexible Architecture model is discussed in detail in Chapter 1: Overview of *Oracle8i Migration, Release 8.1.5* (Part Number A67774-01).

The name of the alert log also varies by operating system. On UNIX systems, it is of the form `alert_SID.log`. On Windows NT systems, it is of the form `SIDalrt.log`. In both cases, *SID* represents the name of the Oracle instance the alert log belongs to.

The alert log will frequently give you a quick indication of whether gross tuning problems exist in the database. Tables that are unable to acquire additional storage, sorts that are failing, and problems with rollback segments all show up as messages in the alert log. Because of this, you should examine your alert log daily to see if any of these obvious tuning problems exist. The alert log also contains information related to backup and recovery issues, including datafile and redo log corruption. In particular, the alert log should be examined regularly for ORA-0600 errors. These ambiguous internal errors are largely undocumented. However, they can be indicators of data corruption or other structural database problems. Resolution of these errors should be undertaken with the assistance of Oracle Worldwide Support at `http://support.oracle.com`.

## Alert Log Tuning Information

A sampling of alert log entries that are related to performance tuning issues are shown in Table 2.1. This is not a complete list, and not all of these messages will appear in every alert log.

**NOTE**  Explanations of Oracle errors that are identified by ORA- codes can be found in the *Oracle8i Error Messages, Release 8.1.5* (Part Number A67785-01).

**TABLE 2.1**  Common Alert Log Messages Related To Performance Tuning

| Alert Log Message | Message Description |
| --- | --- |
| Unable to Extend Temp Segment by *n* in Tablespace *x* | Identified by the error code ORA-01652, this error occurs when a user's Server Process cannot find enough contiguous free space in their temporary tablespace to perform the required sort operation. Tuning of sort activity is discussed in Chapter 7: Tuning Physical I/O. |
| Unable to Extend Table *x* by *n* in Tablespace *x* | Identified by the error code ORA-01653, this error occurs when a table segment is attempting to acquire an additional extent, but cannot do so because there is not enough contiguous free space in the tablespace. Extent management is discussed in Chapter 7: Tuning Physical I/O. |
| Unable to Extend Rollback Segment *x* by String in Tablespace *x* | Identified by the error code ORA-01650, this error occurs when a rollback segment needs to grow, but is unable to because there is insufficient contiguous free space in the tablespace where the rollback segment resides. Rollback segment tuning is discussed in Chapter 7: Tuning Physical I/O. |

**TABLE 2.1** Common Alert Log Messages Related To Performance Tuning *(continued)*

| Alert Log Message | Message Description |
|---|---|
| Max # Extents *n* Reached in Table *x* | Identified by the error code ORA-01631, this error occurs when a table segment needs to grow, but is unable to because it would exceed its maximum allowed number of extents. Segment extent tuning is discussed in Chapter 7: Tuning Physical I/O. |
| Checkpoint Not Complete | This message occurs when a database checkpoint event started, but did not complete before the next checkpoint event began. Tuning of this mechanism is discussed in Chapter 6: Tuning the Redo Log Buffer. |
| Thread *n* Advanced to Log Sequence *n* | This message indicates that a log switch between online redo logs has occurred. The message will also include information about which redo log file was being written to at the time. These messages are generated during the normal course of log switching and do not necessarily indicate a performance problem unless they happen excessively. Redo log tuning is discussed in Chapter 7: Tuning Physical I/O. |

## Managing the Alert Log

The alert log is constantly appended to while the database is in operation. If left unmanaged, it can grow very large. While the information in the alert log is an excellent tuning aid, a large alert log containing information dating back several months or years is difficult to work with. You can manage the alert log's size by regularly renaming, trimming, or deleting it. You may want to perform this maintenance following your nightly or weekly database backups. Oracle automatically creates a new alert log if the prior one was renamed or deleted.

# Background, Event, and User Trace Files

Oracle trace files are text files that contain session information for the process that created them. Trace files can be generated by the Oracle background processes, through the use of `init.ora` trace events, or by user Server Processes. All of these trace files contain useful information for performance tuning and system troubleshooting.

## Background Trace Files

*Background process trace files* are found in the directory specified by the init.ora parameter BACKGROUND_DUMP_DEST. On systems that follow the OFA model, this directory will be $ORACLE_BASE/admin/*SID*/bdump on UNIX systems and %ORACLE_HOME%\admin\\*SID*\bdump on Windows NT systems, where *SID* is the name of the Oracle instance that generated the file. Background process trace files incorporate the name of the background process that generated them in the trace file name. Examples of UNIX and Windows NT background trace file names are shown in Table 2.2.

**TABLE 2.2**  Sample Background Process Trace File Names

| Process Name | UNIX System | Windows NT System |
|---|---|---|
| Process Monitor (PMON) | pmon_nnnn.trc | sidPMON.trc |
| System Monitor (SMON) | smon_nnnn.trc | sidSMON.trc |
| Database Writer (DBW0) | dbw0_nnnn.trc | sidDBW0.trc |
| Log Writer (LGWR) | lgwr_nnnn.trc | sidLGWR.trc |
| Checkpoint Process (CKPT) | ckpt_nnnn.trc | sidCKPT.trc |
| Archive Process (ARC0) | arc0_nnnn.trc | sidARC0.trc |

## Event Tracing

The Oracle8i Server also has special options that you can configure to enable the collection of detailed tracing information for particular database events. A *database event* is a specific action or activity that occurs in the database. You may occasionally be asked to activate tracing for some of these events by Oracle Worldwide Support (OWS) as part of a troubleshooting or tuning effort.

Tracing of these events is usually done at the instance level by adding new lines to the `init.ora`. If several trace events are being added to the `init.ora`, they should be grouped together and commented appropriately. The `init.ora` entries will look like this:

```
EVENT="10046 trace name context forever, level 12"
```

The double quotes are part of the actual syntax of this parameter. Notice that each event entry is made up of two components:

- The event to be traced, designated by a number (10046 in the example above)

- The level to which tracing will be performed, designated by a number (12 in the example above)

The numeric values for both the events and their associated levels are not widely documented. In most cases, OWS will provide you with these values when the need for using trace events arises. Setting them to the proper values is important for the event tracing to work properly.

## User Trace Files

*User trace files* are found in the directory specified by the `init.ora` parameter USER_DUMP_DEST. On systems that follow the OFA model, this directory will be `$ORACLE_BASE/admin/`*SID*`/udump` on UNIX systems and `%ORACLE_HOME%\admin\`*SID*`\udump` on Windows NT systems, where *SID* is the name of the Oracle instance that generated the file. User process trace files incorporate the OS process identifier in the trace file name. On UNIX systems, they also incorporate the name of the instance that the user was connected to when they were generated. Examples of UNIX and Windows NT background trace file names are shown here:

- UNIX System: `ora_prod_4327.trc`

- Windows NT System: `ora00117.trc`

A query can be performed against the V$PROCESS and V$SESSION dynamic performance views in order to identify which user generated a particular trace file. The following code demonstrates how to match a user trace file to the user session that generated it.

```
SQL> SELECT s.username, p.spid
  2  FROM v$session s, v$process p
  3  WHERE s.paddr = p.addr
  4  AND p.background is null;
```

| USERNAME | SPID |
| --- | --- |
| SCOTT | 4292 |
| DBSNMP | 4377 |
| SYSTEM | 4372 |
| JOE | 4437 |
| BRENDA | 4368 |
| EMILY | 4469 |

Using the output from this SQL query, it can be seen that a trace file with the name ora_prod_4292.trc or ora04292.trc would belong to Scott's session. Note that tracings from sessions that are connected via Multithreaded Server, Transaction Managers that use the XA X/Open Interface, or the Oracle Call Interface may generate more than one trace file per user session.

## Activating User Tracing

Oracle occasionally creates a user trace file when processing errors occur in a user's Server Process. The code listing below shows a portion of the output from a user trace file that was generated on a Windows NT Oracle8i Server when a deadlock error occurred. Deadlock errors are discussed in more detail in Chapter 8: Tuning Contention.

```
Dump file c:\app\oracle\admin\PROD\udump\ORA00190.TRC
Tue Aug 15 09:48:21 2000
ORACLE V8.1.5.0.0 - Production vsnsta=0
vsnsql=d vsnxtr=3
Windows NT V4.0, OS V5.101, CPU type 586
Oracle8i Enterprise Edition Release 8.1.5.0.0 - Production
With the Partitioning and Java options
```

```
PL/SQL Release 8.1.5.0.0 - Production
Windows NT V4.0, OS V5.101, CPU type 586
Instance name: prod

Redo thread mounted by this instance: 1

Oracle process number: 9

Windows thread id: 190, image: ORACLE.EXE


*** 2000.08.15.09.48.21.799
*** SESSION ID:(7.25) 2000.08.15.09.48.21.719
ksqded1:  deadlock detected via did
DEADLOCK DETECTED
Current SQL statement for this session:
update apps.customer set name = 'Acme' where name = 'XYZ'
The following deadlock is not an ORACLE error. It is a
deadlock due to user error in the design of an application
or from issuing incorrect ad-hoc SQL. The following
information may aid in determining the deadlock:
Deadlock graph:
```

While events such as deadlocks automatically generate trace files, full scale tracing of user sessions does not occur unless the user or DBA requests it. Full user tracing can be activated at either the instance level or session level using any of the following methods.

### Instance-Level Tracing

By setting the `init.ora` parameter SQL_TRACE=TRUE, all processes against the instance will create their own trace files. This particular method of tracing should be used with care since it creates a great deal of overhead against the system. The default value for this parameter is FALSE.

### User-Level Self Tracing

A user can turn SQL tracing on or off in their own session using the following SQL commands:

```
ALTER SESSION SET SQL_TRACE=TRUE;
```

To start the tracing process, and

```
ALTER SESSION SET SQL_TRACE=FALSE;
```

to end the tracing process.

### User-Level DBA Tracing

Most applications do not provide the user with a mechanism for issuing SQL commands from within the application. Therefore, the ALTER SESSION SQL commands shown in the previous section cannot be used to initiate tracing in these types of environments. In this situation you can initiate tracing against the user's session using the Oracle-supplied PL/SQL package called DBMS_SYSTEM. This PL/SQL package contains a procedure called SET_SQL_TRACE_IN_SESSION that allows you to activate tracing in another user's session by supplying the user's system identifier (sid) and serial number (serial#) values for that user from the V$SESSION view. The following example demonstrates how first to identify, and then activate tracing in a session for the user Scott.

1. Identify the sid and serial# for Scott's session by querying V$SESSION:

```
SQL> select username, sid, serial#
  2  from v$session
  3  where username is not null;
```

| USERNAME | SID | SERIAL# |
| --- | --- | --- |
| SYSTEM | 6 | 2301 |
| SCOTT | 10 | 2642 |

2. Activate tracing in Scott's session by using the DBMS_SYSTEM PL/SQL package and the values for sid and serial#:

```
SQL> execute sys.dbms_system.set_sql_trace_in_
session(10,2642,TRUE);


PL/SQL procedure successfully completed.
```

3. Scott's session is now generating a trace file listing to the directory specified in USER_DUMP_DEST in the init.ora. Once the activity you wish to trace is complete, you can disable the tracing on Scott's session using the DBMS_SYSTEM package again.

```
SQL> execute sys.dbms_system.set_sql_trace_in_
session(10,2642,FALSE);


PL/SQL procedure successfully completed.
```

Tracing is now stopped in Scott's session.

### Interpreting User Trace File Output

Once the user trace file is generated using any of the above methods, it can be used to aid many aspects of performance tuning. Details of how to interpret the contents of user trace files using the TKPROF utility are covered in Chapter 3: SQL Statement Tuning and Application Design.

## Managing Trace Files

Once tracing is activated in a user's session, every action the user takes against the instance is included in the trace file output. If tracing is left on for an extended period of time, the files generated may be very large. In fact, a trace file could grow large enough to fill the entire disk location specified in the USER_DUMP_DEST init.ora parameter.

The init.ora parameter MAX_DUMP_FILE_SIZE allows you to limit the size to which a user trace file can grow. This value can be expressed in either OS blocks or bytes. Table 2.3 shows the various ways in which this parameter can be specified.

**TABLE 2.3**  Specifying the Value for MAX_DUMP_FILE_SIZE

| Parameter Specification | Resulting Maximum Size of User Trace |
| --- | --- |
| MAX_DUMP_FILE_SIZE=10000 | 10000 OS blocks |
| MAX_DUMP_FILE_SIZE=500K | 500,000 bytes |
| MAX_DUMP_FILE_SIZE=10M | 10 megabytes |
| MAX_DUMP_FILE_SIZE=unlimited | No limit on file size |

Like the Alert log file, background, event, and user trace files should also be renamed, trimmed, or deleted occasionally so it is easier to find the most recent trace file data when needed.

# Performance Tuning Views

There are two broad categories of performance tuning views: the V$ *dynamic performance views* and the DBA *data dictionary views*. The data contained in these two families of views are beneficial for both performance tuning benchmarking and subsequent performance monitoring. Before examining the contents of these views in detail, let's look at a brief summary of how these two types of views differ:

- The names of the V$ views are generally singular whereas the DBA views usually have plural names. For example V$DATAFILE vs. DBA_DATA_FILES.

- Many of the V$ views are available when the database in a nomounted or mounted state. DBA views are only available when the database is open.

- The data contained in the V$ views is generally lowercase. The data contained in the DBA views is usually uppercase. This is important to remember when specifying WHERE clauses in your queries against these views.

- The V$ views contain dynamic performance data which is lost each time the instance is shutdown. Because of this, these views always contain statistics that have been gathered since the instance was started. From a performance tuning perspective, *when* you examine the data in these views can be as important as *how* you examine the data in these views. The data contained in the DBA views is more static and is not cleared at instance shutdown. Because of the dynamic nature of the V$ views, you will find that they are the more commonly used data dictionary views for performance tuning.

## V$ Views Commonly Used in Performance Tuning

There are over 175 V$ dynamic performance views in an Oracle8i database. These views are based on dynamic tables collectively know as the X$ tables. These virtual tables exist only in memory and are largely undocumented, having cryptic names like X$KSMSP and X$KWQSI. Most performance tuning information can be obtained from the V$ tables themselves.

Table 2.4 contains a partial listing of the V$ views that are more frequently used in performance tuning.

**TABLE 2.4** Sample of Dynamic Performance Views

| View name | View Description |
| --- | --- |
| V$SGASTAT | Shows information about the size of the System Global Area's components. |
| V$EVENT_NAME | Shows database events that may require waits when requested by the system or by an individual session. There are approximately 200 possible wait events. |
| V$SYSTEM_EVENT | Shows events for which waits have occurred for all sessions accessing the system. |
| V$SESSION_EVENT | Shows events for which waits have occurred, individually identified by session. |
| V$SESSION_WAIT | Shows events for which waits are presently occurring, individually identified by session. |
| V$STATNAME | Matches the name to the statistics listed only by number in V$SESSTAT and V$SYSSAT. |
| V$SYSSTAT | Shows overall system statistics for all sessions, both currently and previously connected. |
| V$SESSTAT | Shows statistics on a per-session basis for currently connected sessions. |
| V$SESSION | Shows current connection information on a per-session basis. |
| V$WAITSTAT | Shows statistics related to block contention. |

In general, queries that incorporate V$SYSSTAT will show statistics for the entire instance since the time it was started. By joining this view to the other relevant views, you get the overall picture of performance in the database. Alternatively, queries that incorporate V$SESSTAT will show statistics for a particular session. These queries are better suited for examining the performance of an individual operation or process.

A complete description of all the V$ views can be found in Chapter 3: Dynamic Performance (V$) Views of *Oracle8i Reference, Release 8.1.5* (Part Number A67790-01).

## DBA Views Commonly Used in Performance Tuning

There are approximately 150 DBA data dictionary views in an Oracle8i database. The tables underlying these views are the physical tables that make up the Oracle data dictionary. Like the X$ virtual tables, these tables are also generally undocumented and have only mildly meaningful names like OBJ$ and FILE$. However, in most cases, the DBA views themselves will provide the information you need to begin performance tuning. Table 2.5 contains a partial listing of some of the DBA views that are used when you undertake performance tuning on a database.

**TABLE 2.5** Sample of Static Dictionary Views

| View Name | View Description |
| --- | --- |
| DBA_TABLES | Table storage, row, and block information |
| DBA_INDEXES | Index storage, row, and block information |
| INDEX_STATS | Index depth and dispersion information |
| DBA_DATA_FILES | Datafile location, naming, and size information |
| DBA_SEGMENTS | General information about any space consuming segment in the database |
| DBA_HISTOGRAMS | Histogram definition information |

A complete description of all the DBA views can be found in Chapter 2: Static Data Dictionary Views of *Oracle8i Reference, Release 8.1.5* (Part Number A67790-01).

## Sample Queries on Views

In order to demonstrate the usefulness of these views for performance tuning, a brief example of each type will be presented here. Each subsequent chapter also contains examples of relevant queries on the V$ and DBA views for the topic addressed in that section.

### Sample *V$* View Query

When querying the V$ views, it is not uncommon to join two or more of these views together in order to get all the information you require. For example, querying V$SESSTAT will give you detailed statistics about events within a particular user's session, but will not tell you the name of each statistic. To get the meaning of each statistic, you will have to join V$SESSTAT to V$STATNAME. An example of this type of query is shown in the following code listing. This query would show all the session statistics for a user called Scott.

```
select s.username, n.name, t.value
from v$session s, v$statname n, v$sesstat t
where s.sid=t.sid
and t.statistic#=n.statistic#
and s.username = 'SCOTT';
```

Keep in mind that joining any view to V$SYSSTAT will give you system-wide performance information while joining any view to V$SESSTAT will give you performance information for an individual user.

### Sample *DBA* View Query

Queries against the DBA views are also useful for performance tuning. For example, you may wish to know which tables have rows in them that are either chained or migrated. The query shown below would provide that information for a user named Scott whose schema has been recently analyzed.

```
select table_name, chain_cnt
from dba_tables
where owner = 'SCOTT'
and chain_cnt !=0;
```

Chaining, migration, and the process of analyzing tables are discussed in more detail in Chapter 3: SQL Statement Tuning and Application Design and Chapter 7: Tuning Physical I/O.

# Oracle-Supplied Tuning Scripts

There are several scripts supplied with the Oracle Server that you can use to help you identify possible database performance problems. These scripts are located in `$ORACLE_HOME/rdbms/admin` on UNIX systems and `%ORACLE_HOME%\rdbms\admin` on Windows NT systems. Some commonly used Oracle-supplied tuning scripts include:

- `UTLBSTAT.SQL/UTLESTAT.SQL` (Discussed in the following section)
- `UTLLOCKT.SQL` (Chapter 8: Tuning Contention)
- `CATBLOCK.SQL` (Chapter 8: Tuning Contention)
- `CATPARR.SQL` (Chapter 5: Tuning the Database Buffer Cache)
- `DBMSPOOL.SQL` (Chapter 4: Tuning the Shared Pool)
- `UTLCHAIN.SQL` (Chapter 7: Tuning Physical I/O)
- `UTLXPLAN.SQL` (Chapter 3: SQL Statement Tuning and Application Design)

Some of these scripts are run only once, to build tables or views that are useful for performance tuning. Other scripts are run every time you perform a tuning exercise. All of these scripts are discussed in detail in later chapters. However, because the output from the `UTLBSTAT.SQL` and `UTLESTAT.SQL` scripts encompass all aspects of database performance, an introductory discussion of them is included here.

## UTLBSTAT.SQL and UTLESTAT.SQL

The Oracle-supplied `UTLBSTAT.SQL` and `UTLESTAT.SQL` scripts are probably the two most useful tools at your disposal for Oracle Server performance tuning. The purpose of these scripts is to capture and summarize into a single report virtually all database and instance performance activity for a specific period of time. Since the process of running the `UTLBSTAT.SQL` and `UTLESTAT.SQL` scripts and the content of the resulting output is the same on all platforms and operating systems, it is an important tool for you to understand.

The *B* in UTLBSTAT.SQL stands for *beginning*. The *E* in UTLESTAT.SQL stands for *end*. As these names would imply, the UTLBSTAT.SQL script is run at the beginning of the tuning measurement period and UTLESTAT.SQL is run at the end of the tuning measurement period.

## Running the *UTLBSTAT.SQL* Script

Before running the UTLBSTAT.SQL script, it is important that the instance has been up long enough to allow the V$ dynamic performance views to be populated with meaningful statistics. Usually this means that you will want to wait and run the UTLBSTAT.SQL script after the database has been open for at least thirty minutes of normal user activity.

When the UTLBSTAT.SQL script is executed, it will do the following:

- First, it will drop any of the tables that the UTLBSTAT.SQL script is about to create—if they already exist. These tables may exist if a previous execution of UTLBSTAT.SQL was not followed by the execution of UTLESTAT.SQL. Because the tables may not exist, it is normal to see ORA-00942 "Table or View Does Not Exist" errors during the execution of UTLBSTAT.SQL.

- Next, the UTLBSTAT.SQL script creates a series of temporary tables that are copies of the contents of some of the V$ views as they exist at that moment in time. For example, UTLBSTAT.SQL will create a table called stats$begin_event that is a copy of the v$system_event view.

The UTLBSTAT.SQL script is executed using the following command in either SQL*Plus or Server Manager:

- UNIX: SQL> @$ORACLE_HOME/rdbms/admin/utlbstat.sql

- Windows NT: @%ORACLE_HOME%\rdbms\admin\utlbstat.sql

Because the script performs a CONNECT INTERNAL during its processing, you may be prompted for a password if your system uses a password file.

## Running the *UTLESTAT.SQL* Script

A meaningful amount of time should be allowed to pass between the time that UTLBSTAT.SQL is run and the time UTLESTAT.SQL is run. Generally this duration should be at least fifteen minutes, but could be several hours or even days.

If the instance is shutdown between the time you run UTLBSTAT.SQL and UTLESTAT.SQL, your results will not be useable. This occurs because all the statistics in the V$ views that are used by these two scripts are cleared at instance shutdown and then repopulated at instance startup.

When the UTLESTAT.SQL script is executed, it will do the following:

- First, it will drop any of the tables that the UTLESTAT.SQL script is about to create—if they already exist. These tables may exist if a previous execution of UTLESTAT.SQL failed. Because the tables may not exist, it is normal to see ORA-00942 "Table or View Does Not Exist" errors during the execution of UTLESTAT.SQL.

- Next, the UTLESTAT.SQL script creates a series of temporary tables that are copies of the contents of the same V$ views that UTLBSTAT.SQL copied. This time, however, the tables have names like stats$end_event and will contain statistics as they exist at that moment in time.

- Then, it calculates metrics between the statistics in the stats$begin tables, which were created by UTLBSTAT.SQL at the beginning of the tuning period, and the stats$end tables created by UTLESTAT.SQL at the end of the tuning period.

- Finally, it generates a text file, REPORT.TXT, which contains the results of these calculations. This text file contains all the information needed for most database tuning activities.

The UTLESTAT.SQL script is executed using the following command in either SQL*Plus or Server Manager:

- UNIX: SQL> @$ORACLE_HOME/rdbms/admin/utlestat.sql

- Windows NT: SQL> @%ORACLE_ HOME%\rdbms\admin\utlestat.sql

Because the script performs a CONNECT INTERNAL during its processing, you may be prompted for a password if your system uses a password file. The resulting REPORT.TXT file will be written to the operating system in the users current directory.

## Interpreting the Contents of *REPORT.TXT*

Once generated by the UTLBSTAT.SQL and UTLESTAT.SQL, the resulting REPORT.TXT file will contain all the tuning statistics for the period between the time UTLBSTAT.SQL was executed and the time when UTLESTAT.SQL was executed. REPORT.TXT is a simple text file that can be viewed with any editor. Upon initial examination, deciphering the contents of a REPORT.TXT file may seem like a daunting task. However, with practice and experience, you will quickly be able to spot problem areas in a lengthy REPORT.TXT file with a minimum of effort. References to relevant portions of the REPORT.TXT file will be made throughout the remainder of this book.

A section from a sample REPORT.TXT file generated on an Oracle8i UNIX system is shown in Figure 2.1.

**FIGURE 2.1** Sample section of REPORT.TXT file

```
SQL>
SQL> set charwidth 12
SQL> set numwidth 10
SQL> Rem Select Library cache statistics.  The pin hit rate should be high.
SQL> select namespace library,
  2        gets,
  3        round(decode(gethits,0,1,gethits)/decode(gets,0,1,gets),3)
  4          gethitratio,
  5        pins,
  6        round(decode(pinhits,0,1,pinhits)/decode(pins,0,1,pins),3)
  7          pinhitratio,
  8        reloads, invalidations
  9    from stats$lib;

LIBRARY             GETS GETHITRATIO     PINS PINHITRATIO   RELOADS INVALIDATIONS
---------------- ---------- ----------- ---------- ----------- ---------- -------------
BODY                  37        .865        38        .789          3             0
CLUSTER              386        .995       594        .993          0             0
INDEX                  4         .75         5          .6          0             0
OBJECT                 0           1         0           1          0             0
PIPE                   0           1         0           1          0             0
SQL AREA           16317        .969     99239        .988        161            79
TABLE/PROCEDURE     1700        .857     60291        .989        118             0
TRIGGER               71        .887        71        .577         11             0
8 rows selected.

SQL>
SQL> set charwidth 27;
SQL> set numwidth 12;
```

**NOTE** Oracle8i version 8.1.6 includes a new set of performance tuning scripts called Statspack. These scripts are similar to UTLBSTAT.SQL and UTLESTAT.SQL in that they are designed to monitor the statistical performance of an Oracle instance. The new Statspack scripts contain many new statistics that more accurately measure the performance of the new features in Oracle8i and display this information more clearly than do UTLBSTAT.SQL and UTLESTAT.SQL. See http://www.oracle.com/oramag/oracle/00-Mar/o20tun.html for more details on Statspack.

# Graphical Performance Tuning Tools

Oracle provides several *Graphical User Interface (GUI)* database management tools that can be used to aid a tuning effort. These GUI tools are divided into three product categories:

- Oracle Enterprise Manager/Oracle DBA Management Pack
- Oracle Diagnostics Pack
- Oracle Tuning Pack

The Oracle Enterprise Manager is bundled with Oracle DBA Management Pack. These two tools are included with the basic Oracle Server software. The Diagnostics and Tuning Packs are extra-cost options that require a separate license with Oracle.

## Oracle Enterprise Manager/DBA Management Pack

*Oracle Enterprise Manager (OEM)* and DBA Management Pack make up the core of Oracle's GUI database management tools. The OEM tool is used to monitor and manage databases using the tools within the DBA Management Pack toolkit. The DBA Management Pack is made up of the DBA Studio and SQL*Plus Worksheet. The components of the DBA Management Pack and their uses are shown in Table 2.6.

**TABLE 2.6** Components of the DBA Management Pack

| Component | Purpose |
| --- | --- |
| Instance Manager | Starting, stopping, and managing Oracle instances |
| Schema Manager | Creating and managing Oracle database objects. |
| Security Manager | Creating and managing Oracle users, privileges, and roles |

**TABLE 2.6** Components of the DBA Management Pack *(continued)*

| Component | Purpose |
| --- | --- |
| Storage Manager | Creating and managing tablespaces and datafiles |
| SQL*Plus Worksheet | GUI environment for issuing command line SQL statements |

OEM, with its centralized management console, is a very useful tool for performance tuning since it allows you to monitor database activity that impacts performance in real time. Figure 2.2 shows what a configured OEM Console looks like.

**FIGURE 2.2** Oracle Enterprise Manager Console

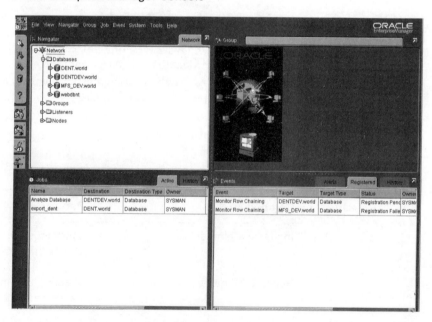

The OEM Console seamlessly integrates components of the DBA Management, Tuning, and Diagnostic Packs into one centralized GUI environment from which you can administer all your databases. OEM's management tools also allow you to schedule jobs against databases and monitor databases in real time for a variety of events. These jobs and events are monitored and performed by the OEM Intelligent Agent.

## The OEM Intelligent Agent

The OEM Console performs its event monitoring and job scheduling with the help of an autonomous process which runs on each server (or node) that the OEM tool is monitoring. This process is called the *Oracle Intelligent Agent*. There is only one agent on each server node that OEM is monitoring regardless of how many databases exist on that node. The Intelligent Agent and the databases it monitors represent the third tier in Oracle's three-tier OEM architecture. The middle tier of the OEM architecture is the Oracle Management Server (OMS), which acts as the repository for the OEM configuration. The OMS is accessible from a variety of clients including UNIX workstations and Web browsers. These clients represent the first tier of the OEM architecture. An overview of the OEM three-tier architecture model is shown in Figure 2.3.

**FIGURE 2.3** The three-tier OEM architecture model

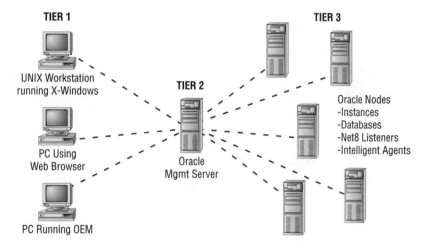

The Intelligent Agent process on each node connects to the databases on that node as the user DBSNMP. Once connected, the Intelligent Agent performs actions, on behalf of the Oracle Management Server, that have been configured using the OEM clients. The Agent then reports the results of those actions back to Oracle Management Server where they are then displayed in the Event and Job panes at the bottom of the OEM Console. In this way, the OEM Intelligent Agent is able to monitor a database for specific database events and take specific actions when some events occur.

## Event Monitoring

OEM includes a sophisticated event management system. These events can be very useful tools for performance tuning. For example, you can use OEM events and the Intelligent Agent to notify you via e-mail or paging whenever a table containing chained rows is detected in the database (row chaining is discussed in Chapter 7: Tuning Physical I/O). Oracle supplies a number of predefined events in the OEM console so that you can immediately start monitoring for common events that are of interest to you. These events include monitoring whether the database is up or down, whether the Net8 Listener is up or down, and whether the server node that the database resides on is up or down. When extra-cost options like the Tuning or Diagnostic Packs are added, they provide additional built-in event monitoring for excessive extent growth and low tablespace storage availability, as well memory utilization statistics and contention for certain database resources. You can also create your own custom events for the Intelligent Agent to monitor by using the TCL command language.

Additional information on using TCL scripting to create custom OEM events can be found in Chapter 5: Job and Event Scripts of *Oracle Intelligent Agent Users Guide, Release 8.1.5* (Part Number A67825-01).

### Fixit Jobs

Event monitoring can be configured so that whenever the Intelligent Agent detects that a particular event has occurred, a specified task, known as a *Fixit Job*, is performed in response to that event. Therefore, problems that would normally require manual intervention can be fixed immediately according to your predefined specifications.

## Oracle Diagnostics Pack

The *Oracle Diagnostics Pack* is made up of several tools designed to help you identify, diagnose, and repair problem areas in your databases. Table 2.7 shows the components of the Diagnostics Pack.

**TABLE 2.7**  Components of the Diagnostics Pack

| Component | Purpose |
| --- | --- |
| Capacity Planner | Estimates future system requirements based on current workloads |

**TABLE 2.7** Components of the Diagnostics Pack *(continued)*

| Component | Purpose |
|---|---|
| Performance Manager | Presents real-time performance information in a graphical format |
| TopSessions | Monitors user session activities including resource consumption and locking |
| Trace Data Viewer | Graphical tool for viewing trace file output |
| Trace Manager | Collects trace event data for specified application operations |

Performance Manager, Top Sessions, and Trace Manager are particularly useful for performance tuning.

## Performance Manager

*Performance Manager* is a GUI performance monitoring tool that allows you to observe database performance indicators in your databases in real time. The indicators Performance Manager tracks are the same ones that we will discuss throughout this book. However, rather than issuing queries or inspecting REPORT.TXT files for this information, it is presented visually in the form of charts and graphs. Figure 2.4 shows a sample of Performance Manager's graphical output.

**FIGURE 2.4** Performance Manager output

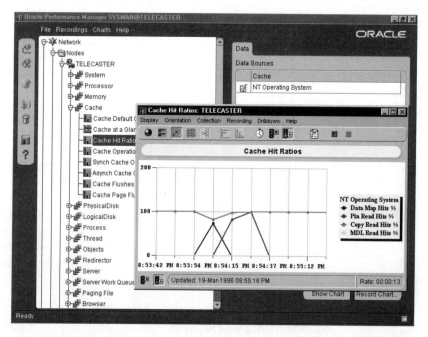

One unique feature of Performance Manager is that the performance data can be recorded for several hours and then graphically "played back" at an accelerated rate in order to help you identify spikes in activity that may be negatively impacting your system.

## TopSessions

*TopSessions* is a graphical tool for identifying in real time which users are consuming the most server resources. Resources that can be monitored include CPU, memory, file I/O, and transactions. Figure 2.5 shows a sample TopSessions screen that indicates which users are consuming the most CPU.

**FIGURE 2.5** TopSessions CPU usage by user

| USERNAME | SID | OSUSER | PARSE TIME CPU | COMMAND | STATUS | MACHINE | PROGRAM |
|----------|-----|--------|----------------|---------|--------|---------|---------|
| BACKGROUN... | 5 | oracle | 253 | UNKNOWN | ACTIVE | stratocaster | oracle@stratocaster (SMON) |
| SYSTEM | 8 | bbjj | 226 | UNKNOWN | ACTIVE | EXPLORER | VMS.EXE |
| JOE | 11 | oracle | 214 | SELECT | INACTIVE | stratocaster | sqlplus@stratocaster (TNS V... |
| SCOTT | 14 | bbjj | 143 | SELECT | ACTIVE | EXPLORER | PLUS80W.EXE |
| BACKGROUN... | 6 | oracle | 79 | UNKNOWN | ACTIVE | stratocaster | oracle@stratocaster (RECO) |
| DBSNMP | 7 | oracle | 66 | UNKNOWN | INACTIVE | stratocaster | ? @stratocaster (TNS V1-... |
| DBSNMP | 10 | oracle | 25 | UNKNOWN | INACTIVE | stratocaster | ? @stratocaster (TNS V1-... |
| | 9 | | 0 | UNKNOWN | ACTIVE | | |
| BACKGROUN... | 4 | oracle | 0 | UNKNOWN | ACTIVE | stratocaster | oracle@stratocaster (CKPT) |
| BACKGROUN... | 3 | oracle | 0 | UNKNOWN | ACTIVE | stratocaster | oracle@stratocaster (LGWR) |

TopSessions is also useful for identifying locking issues, which may cause excessive waits for other database users. Locking is discussed in detail in Chapter 8: Tuning Contention.

## Trace Manager

Many Oracle servers are accessed by applications that are not Oracle-centric in nature. These applications only use the Oracle database as a repository for the application's data. All the application logic and processing happens outside the database. Gathering and analyzing performance data from these types of applications can be difficult. Oracle's *Trace Manager* GUI tool allows you to collect performance data for specific events within these types of applications. This is accomplished through the use of an Application Program Interface (API). An API designed specifically for this purpose has been incorporated in the Oracle Server since Oracle 7.3. The types of data that can be collected via this API generally relate to resource usage, execution times, and application specific data. Additionally, you can also use Trace Manager to gather performance information related to regular database events.

See Chapter 15: Using Oracle Trace in *Oracle8i Tuning, Release 8.1.5* (Part Number A67775-1) for more details on configuring, scheduling, and administering the Oracle Trace Manager GUI utility.

## Oracle Tuning Pack

The Oracle Tuning Pack is designed specifically to assist you with database performance tuning issues. Table 2.8 shows the components of the Tuning Pack.

**TABLE 2.8**    Components of the Tuning Pack

| Component | Purpose |
| --- | --- |
| Oracle Expert | Wizard-based database tuning tool based on the Oracle Tuning Methodology |
| SQL Analyze | Analyzes and rewrites SQL statements to improve their performance |
| Tablespace Manager | Reports on and manages the space utilization within tablespaces |

Oracle Expert and Tablespace Manager are particularly useful for database-level performance tuning.

### Tablespace Manager

*Tablespace Manager* allows you to examine and tune the content of Oracle tablespaces. Using this tool, you can determine which tablespace and datafiles a segment's extents are stored in, how big those extents are, and which block IDs the extents are using. Figure 2.6 shows the Tablespace Manager output for the System tablespace on a Windows NT system.

**FIGURE 2.6** Tablespace Manager output

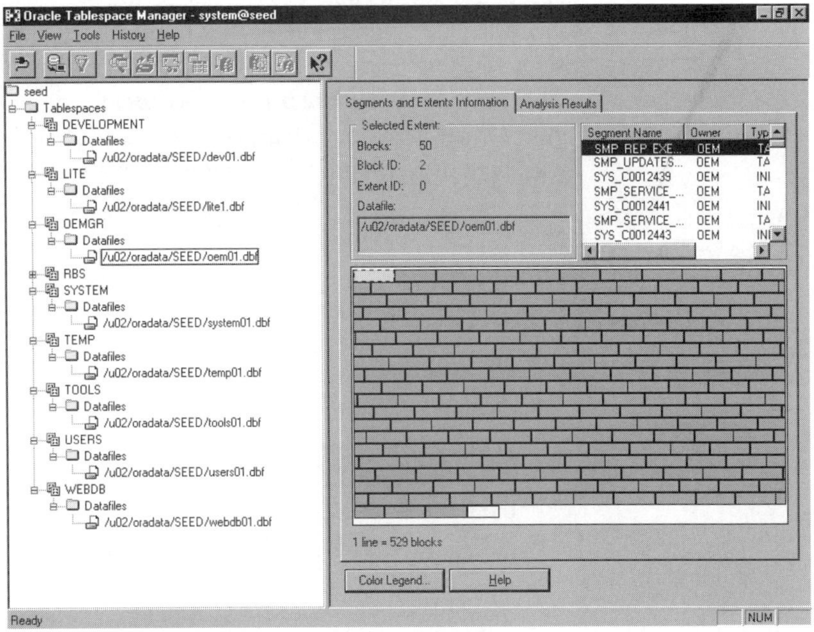

You can also use Tablespace Manager to analyze tables and indexes, coalesce tablespace free space, and reorganize segments. Many of these topics will be addressed in Chapter 7: Tuning Physical I/O.

### Oracle Expert

*Oracle Expert* is a GUI tool that gathers and analyzes performance tuning data according to your specifications. Once the data is gathered, Oracle Expert then uses its built-in inference engine to formulate tuning recommendations. These recommendations can include a summary report, SQL scripts, and new init.ora parameters. Oracle Expert is discussed in detail in Chapter 10: Oracle Expert.

# Summary

**H**aving accurate and complete information is critical both before and during the tuning process. This information can be gathered from several locations. The alert log contains a variety of instance-wide event information, while the background and user trace files can be used to more narrowly identify what is happening in the database. Oracle's dynamic V$ and DBA data dictionary views also allow you to gather important statistics and information that are needed for database tuning.

Oracle supplies the UTLBSTAT.SQL and UTLESTAT.SQL scripts so that you can capture statistics for a determinate period of time and then analyze those statistics using the resulting REPORT.TXT. The Oracle Enterprise Manager Console also provides useful tuning information through its event monitoring via the Intelligent Agent. Several useful performance tuning add-on packs are also available for the Oracle Enterprise Manager. These include the Diagnostic and Tuning Packs, both of which provide additional performance tuning capabilities.

## Key Terms

Before you take the exam, make sure you're familiar with the following terms:

alert log

Optimal Flexible Architecture

BACKGROUND_DUMP_DEST

USER_DUMP_DEST

MAX_DUMP_FILE_SIZE

trace file

Oracle Enterprise Manager (OEM)

Fixit Job

TopSessions

Tablespace Manager

database event

UTLBSTAT.SQL

UTLESTAT.SQL

dynamic performance view

data dictionary view

Graphical User Interface (GUI)

Intelligent Agent

Performance Manager

Trace Manager

Oracle Expert

# Review Questions

1. The alert log contains information on all but which of the following:

   **A.** Instance startup and shutdown

   **B.** Creation of new database users

   **C.** Redo log switches

   **D.** All of the above are in the alert log.

2. Which of the following is an appropriate way to manage the size of the alert log?

   **A.** Delete it following a good backup.

   **B.** Trim it by deleting the oldest entries first.

   **C.** Rename it following a good database backup.

   **D.** Any of the above are appropriate methods.

3. On a UNIX system, the trace file for the SMON background process would have a name like which of the following?

   **A.** 1234_trc.smon

   **B.** 1234_smon.trc

   **C.** smon_1234.trc

   **D.** trc_smon.1234

4. Which of the following views can be used to determine which user generated a particular user trace file? (Choose all that apply.)

   **A.** V$SYSTEM

   **B.** V$SESSION

   **C.** V$USER

   **D.** V$PROCESS

5. Which of the following `init.ora` parameters activates tracing at the instance level?

   **A.** TRACE_ON

   **B.** TRACE_SQL

   **C.** SQL_FILE

   **D.** SQL_TRACE

6. Users can activate tracing of their own session using which of the following commands?

   **A.** ALTER USER SET SQL_TRACE=TRUE;

   **B.** ALTER USER ACTIVATE SQL_TRACE;

   **C.** ALTER SESSION SET SQL_TRACE=TRUE;

   **D.** ALTER SESSION SET TRACE ON;

7. Which of the following Oracle-supplied PL/SQL packages can be used to activate tracing in another user's session?

   **A.** DBMS_SYSTEM

   **B.** DBMS_SESSION

   **C.** DBMS_TRACE

   **D.** DBMS_UTILITY

8. What utility is used to format trace file output?

   **A.** EXP

   **B.** TKPROF

   **C.** SQLLDR

   **D.** ORAPWD

**9.** Setting MAX_DUMP_FILE_SIZE=30000 would allow a user's trace file to grow to a maximum of:

**A.** 30,000 OS blocks

**B.** 30,000 Oracle blocks

**C.** 30,000 bytes

**D.** 30 megabytes

**10.** Which of the following statements about the V$ dynamic performance views are true? (Choose all that apply.)

**A.** Their contents are cleared at instance shutdown.

**B.** The V$ views are not useful for performance tuning, only auditing.

**C.** The V$ views are only available when the database is open.

**D.** Many of the V$ views used in performance tuning contain data that is stored in lowercase.

**11.** Which of the following views contains information about overall system statistics, both previously and currently connected?

**A.** V$SGASTAT

**B.** V$STATNAME

**C.** V$SESSTAT

**D.** V$SYSTAT

**12.** Which DBA view would show storage, row, and block information for an individual table?

**A.** DBA_TABLES

**B.** DBA_OBJECTS

**C.** DBA_TABLE_SIZE

**D.** DBA_TAB_PRIVS

13. What database event would cause the statistics generated by
    UTLBSTAT.SQL and UTLSTAT.SQL to be invalid?

    **A.** The addition of a datafile

    **B.** An instance shutdown and restart

    **C.** A user connection that is idle for the whole period

    **D.** An export of the SYSTEM schema

14. The name of the file that is generated by UTLBSTAT.SQL and
    UTLESTAT.SQL is called:

    **A.** REPORT.TXT

    **B.** REPORT.LOG

    **C.** REPORT.LST

    **D.** REPORT.SQL

15. On UNIX systems, the UTLBSTAT.SQL script is located in:

    **A.** $ORACLE_HOME/rdbms/admin

    **B.** $ORACLE_HOME/network/admin

    **C.** $ORACLE_HOME/sqlplus/admin

    **D.** $ORACLE_HOME/orainst/admin

16. The autonomous process that runs on each Oracle server to manage
    jobs and monitor events on that node is called:

    **A.** Net8 Listener

    **B.** Enterprise Manager Console

    **C.** Intelligent Agent

    **D.** Data Gatherer

**17.** A job that is scheduled to run when a particular event occurs is called a:

    **A.** Agent Job

    **B.** RMAN Job

    **C.** OEM Job

    **D.** Fixit Job

**18.** The OEM GUI tool that records and reports database performance statistics graphically in real time is called:

    **A.** TopSessions

    **B.** Performance Manager

    **C.** Trace Manager

    **D.** Tablespace Manager

**19.** The Oracle Tuning Pack is made of all of the following products except:

    **A.** Oracle Expert

    **B.** SQL Analyze

    **C.** Trace Manager

    **D.** Tablespace Manager

**20.** The GUI tool that gathers performance data, analyzes that data, and then makes appropriate tuning recommendations is called:

    **A.** SQL Analyze

    **B.** Oracle Expert

    **C.** Trace Expert

    **D.** SQL Expert

# Answers to Review Questions

1. B. The alert log does not contain any user information.

2. D. The alert log can be deleted, renamed, or trimmed in order to keep it from growing to an unmanageable size.

3. C. All background processes on UNIX systems generate trace files that incorporate a process ID as well as the process name in the trace file name.

4. B and D. Joining the V$SESSION and V$PROCESS views allows you to associate a username with a process ID. This process ID is included in the user's trace file name.

5. D. Setting the init.ora parameter SQL_TRACE = TRUE will activate tracing for every session that connects to the instance.

6. C. ALTER SESSION SET SQL_TRACE=TRUE is used to activate tracing in a user's own session. ALTER SESSION SET SQL_TRACE=FALSE stops tracing a users session.

7. A. The SET_SQL_TRACE_IN_SESSION procedure in DBMS_SYSTEM is used to activate tracing in another user's session using the user's sid and serial# from V$SESSION.

8. B. The TKPROF utility can be used to format user trace files. This utility is discussed in more detail in Chapter 3: SQL Statement Tuning and Application Design.

9. A. If the value following the MAX_DUMP_FILE parameter is not denoted by either K or M, then it represents the maximum size of the trace file in OS blocks.

**10.** A and D.  The V$ views contain very useful information for database tuning. The V$ views are available when the database is nomounted, mounted, and open. The data in the V$ views is lowercase for the most part, but you should wait to examine this data until after the instance has been up for a time because the content of the V$ views is cleared at instance shutdown and then repopulated at the next startup.

**11.** D.  V$SYSTAT shows overall system statistics for all sessions both current and historical, since instance startup.

**12.** A.  Once analyzed, a table's storage utilization, blocks usage, and row length information can be found in DBA_TABLES.

**13.** B.  Shutting down the instance between the time UTLBSTAT.SQL and UTLESTAT.SQL are run clears the statistics in the V$ views that form the basis of their output.

**14.** A.  The UTLESTAT.SQL script generates the REPORT.TXT file by performing calculations on the stat$begin tables created by UTLBSTAT.SQL and the stats$end tables created by UTLESTAT.SQL.

**15.** A.  Nearly all the Oracle-supplied tuning scripts, including UTLBSTAT.SQL, are located in $ORACLE_HOME/rdbms/admin.

**16.** C.  The Oracle Intelligent Agent runs on each node that contains an Oracle database. The agent monitors the databases on that node on behalf of the Oracle Enterprise Manager Console.

**17.** D.  Fixit Jobs are associated with database events. When the database event occurs, the Fixit Job will run in response to the event—generally to remedy the problem reported by that event.

**18.** B.  The OEM Performance Manager GUI tool displays database performance data in a graphical format.

**19.** C.  Trace Manager is a component of the Diagnostics Pack, not the Tuning Pack.

**20.** B.  The Oracle Expert tool analyzes database statistics according to your specifications before making tuning recommendations. Oracle Expert is discussed in detail in Chapter 10: Oracle Expert.

# SQL Statement Tuning and Application Design

---

## ORACLE8i PERFORMANCE TUNING EXAM OBJECTIVES COVERED IN THIS CHAPTER:

✓ Identify the role of the DBA in application tuning.

✓ Use optimizer modes to enhance SQL statement performance.

✓ Manage stored outlines to store execution plans as a series of hints.

✓ Use the available data access methods to tune the physical design of the database.

✓ Monitor and tune indexes.

✓ Identify the demands of online transaction processing (OLTP) systems.

✓ Identify the demands of decision support systems (DSS).

✓ Reconfigure systems on a temporary basis for particular needs.

Exam objectives are subject to change at any time without prior notice and at Oracle's sole discretion. Please visit Oracle's Training and Certification Web site ( http://education.oracle.com/certification/index.html ) for the most current exam objectives listing.

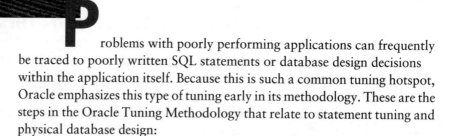

**P**roblems with poorly performing applications can frequently be traced to poorly written SQL statements or database design decisions within the application itself. Because this is such a common tuning hotspot, Oracle emphasizes this type of tuning early in its methodology. These are the steps in the Oracle Tuning Methodology that relate to statement tuning and physical database design:

Step 4: Tuning the Logical Structure of the Database

Step 5: Tuning Database Operations

Step 6: Tuning Access Paths

Appropriate tuning changes in these three areas depend heavily on the type of system that is being evaluated. Online transactional systems have different SQL and design considerations than do Decision Support Systems. No matter the type of system, you must accurately measure the performance of the current SQL and understand the tuning options available to you before you can begin evaluating these three areas for possible improvement.

# Measuring SQL Performance

**T**uning in any of the areas mentioned in these three steps requires that you take accurate and timely measurements of specific SQL activity occurring within the application. Once these measurements are taken, you can attempt to improve their performance using a variety of techniques. A complete discussion of SQL statement tuning techniques is beyond the scope of this book and the Performance Tuning OCP exam. However, as a DBA, it is important for you to understand the three most commonly used tools for measuring the performance of SQL statements: the TKPROF utility, Explain Plans, and AUTOTRACE.

# The *TKPROF* Utility

The Trace Kernel Profile, or *TKPROF*, utility is used to format user trace files that were generated using one of the user session tracing techniques discussed in Chapter 2. User trace files contain all the SQL statements that the user issued while tracing was active, information about how long each statement took to execute, and the number of resources the statement consumed. Because the contents of a raw, unformatted trace file is difficult to interpret, the TKPROF utility is used to convert the trace file into a form you can more easily understand.

## Formatting a User Trace File Using *TKPROF*

The TKPROF utility is a stand-alone utility that is executed directly from the OS prompt. The following shows a simple TKPROF formatting example taken from a UNIX system:

```
$ tkprof ora_12558.trc trace.txt
```

This example would format a user trace file called `ora_12558.trc` and store the formatted version in a file called `trace.txt`. As this example shows, the first two parameters to follow the TKPROF command are the name of the trace file and the output file, respectively. The TKPROF utility has several additional command line arguments that can also be used when formatting the trace file depending on what information is desired. These options are specified on the command line immediately after the required trace file name and output file name parameters. A listing of these options is shown in Table 3.1:

**TABLE 3.1**  TKPROF Command Line Options

| Option | Definition and Usage |
|---|---|
| EXPLAIN | Generates an Explain Plan for each statement in the trace file by using the PLAN_TABLE in the schema specified by this command. This option must include a valid Oracle username and password. |
| TABLE | Using the schema specified by the EXPLAIN option, the execution plan is stored in the specified table rather than default table, PLAN_TABLE. |

**TABLE 3.1** TKPROF Command Line Options *(continued)*

| Option | Definition and Usage |
|---|---|
| SYS | Indicates whether the formatted file should include recursive SQL statements (i.e. statements implicitly issued against the data dictionary in support of the primary SQL statements). |
| SORT | Determines the order in which the statements in the formatted trace file will be sorted. The 22 sort options are listed in Tables 3.2, 3.3, and 3.4. |
| RECORD | Specifies the filename into which the SQL statements in the trace file should be written. Allows you to isolate the SQL statements without any accompanying resource usage information. |
| PRINT | Limits the number of SQL statements included in the resulting formatted trace file to the specified value |
| INSERT | Creates an SQL script that, when executed, will create a table called TKPROF_TABLE and then populate this table with the raw statistics contained in this trace file |
| AGGRE-GATE | Determines whether the statistics from multiple issuers of the same SQL statement will be counted together or independently |

Several examples demonstrating the use of TKPROF with some of these options are shown below.

The following demonstrates the use of the TKPROF with SYS and EXPLAIN parameters:

```
$ tkprof ora_1234.trc trace.txt sys=no explain=joe/sidney
```
This use of the TKPROF would:

- Format the trace file ora_1234.trc and store the results in an output file called trace.txt.

- Cause any recursive SQL in the original trace file to be omitted from the formatted trace file, trace.txt.

- Include in the formatted trace file, `trace.txt`, Explain Plans of each SQL statement issued. The `PLAN_TABLE` in the user Joe's schema would be used to generate the Explain Plans.

The following demonstrates the use of TKPROF with RECORD and PRINT parameters:

```
C:\> tkprof ora_1234.trc trace.txt print=10 record=sql.txt
```

This use of the TKPROF utility would:

- Format the trace file `ora_1234.trc` and store the first 10 SQL statements in an output file called `trace.txt`.

- Create a file called `sql.txt` that would contain the first ten SQL statements in the original trace file.

The following demonstrates the use of TKPROF with INSERT and SORT parameters:

```
$ tkprof ora_1234.trc trace.txt insert=trace.sql
sort=(fchrow)
```

This use of the TKPROF utility would:

- Format the trace file `ora_1234.trc` and store the results, sorted by the number of rows returned by each statement, in an output file called `trace.txt`. A discussion of other TKPROF sorting options appears in the next section.

- Create a second file called `trace.sql` that contains the SQL commands needed to create a table called `TKPROF_TABLE` and then populate it with the statistics for the SQL statements in the trace file.

Without a sort parameter like FCHROW, the TKPROF utility would list the SQL statements in the formatted output file in the order in which they were executed. When this default sort order is not desired, TKPROF has several additional sorting parameters. The formatted output will be sorted in descending order, according to the option you specify. Multiple sort parameters can also be used simultaneously. In these cases the sorted output will be sorted in the order specified, but is based on the sum of the values for the sorted option.

### *TKPROF* Sorting Parameters

Each parameter is related to one of the three phases of SQL statement processing: Parse, Execute, or Fetch. *Parsing* refers to the process of getting an SQL statement ready to execute. This process includes checking the statement for syntactic correctness and determining the user's privileges on objects referenced in the statement. TKPROF sort options related to the parse phase of SQL statement processing are shown in Table 3.2.

**TABLE 3.2**   Sort Options for the Parse Phase of Statement Processing

| Option | Sort Order |
| --- | --- |
| PRSCNT | Number of times the statement was parsed |
| PRSCPU | Amount of CPU time spent parsing the statement |
| PRSELA | Elapsed time spent parsing the statement |
| PRSDSK | Number of disk reads that occurred while the statement was being parsed |
| PRSMIS | Number of rollback blocks read from the SGA while the statement was being parsed |
| PRSCU | Number of data blocks read from the SGA while the statement was being parsed |

The second step in SQL statement processing, *Execute*, occurs when the SQL statement performs the action specified in the statement. Examples of execution might be selecting, inserting, updating, or deleting data from a segment, or creating a user, tablespace, or datafile. Table 3.3 shows the TKPROF sort options related to the execute phase of SQL statement processing.

**TABLE 3.3**   Sort Options for the Execute Phase of Statement Processing

| Option | Sort Order |
| --- | --- |
| EXECNT | Number of times the statement was executed |
| EXECPU | Amount of CPU time spent executing the statement |
| EXEELA | Elapsed time spent executing the statement |

**TABLE 3.3** Sort Options for the Execute Phase of Statement Processing *(continued)*

| Option | Sort Order |
| --- | --- |
| EXEDSK | Number of disk reads that occurred while the statement was being executed |
| EXEQRY | Number of rollback blocks read from the SGA while the statement was executing |
| EXECU | Number of data blocks read from the SGA while the statement was executing |

If the SQL statement that was issued is a SELECT statement, it will also perform the last step in SQL statement processing—a Fetch operation. The *Fetch* phase occurs when the result set returned by the SQL statement is sent back to the user. TKPROF sort options related to the fetch phase of SQL statement processing are shown in Table 3.4.

**TABLE 3.4** Sort Options for the Fetch Phase of Statement Processing

| Option | Sort Order |
| --- | --- |
| FCHCNT | Number of row fetches that occurred |
| FCHCPU | Amount of CPU time spent fetching rows |
| FCHELA | Elapsed time spent fetching rows |
| FCHDSK | Number of disk reads that occurred while the rows were being fetched |
| FCHQRY | Number of rollback blocks read from the SGA while the rows where being fetched |
| FCHCU | Number of data blocks read from the SGA while the rows were being fetched |
| FCHROW | Number of rows fetched by the statement |

## Interpreting a Trace File Formatted Using *TKPROF*

Once a user trace file has been formatted using the TKPROF utility, the contents of the resulting file can be used as an excellent measure of SQL performance. A sample trace file formatted with TKPROF is shown in Figure 3.1.

**FIGURE 3.1**   Sample output from TKPROF formatted trace file

```
select u.name,o.name
from
obj$ o,user$ u,trigger$ t where t.baseobject=:1 and t.obj#=o.obj# and
  o.owner#=u.user# order by o.obj#

call     count       cpu    elapsed      disk      query    current       rows
------- ------  --------  ---------  --------  ---------  ---------  ---------
Parse        1      0.01       0.01         0          0          0          0
Execute      1      0.01       0.01         0          0          0          0
Fetch        1      0.00       0.00         0          1          0          0
------- ------  --------  ---------  --------  ---------  ---------  ---------
total        3      0.02       0.02         0          1          0          0

. . .

INSERT INTO employee (employee_id, last_name, first_name)
VALUES (295,'Joe','Johnson')

call     count       cpu    elapsed      disk      query    current       rows
------- ------  --------  ---------  --------  ---------  ---------  ---------
Parse        1      0.08       0.12         0          0          0          0
Execute      1      0.04       0.20         5          3         11          1
Fetch        0      0.00       0.00         0          0          0          0
------- ------  --------  ---------  --------  ---------  ---------  ---------
total        2      0.12       0.32         5          3         11          1

. .

SELECT last_name, title, department_id
FROM employee

call     count       cpu    elapsed      disk      query    current       rows
------- ------  --------  ---------  --------  ---------  ---------  ---------
Parse        1      0.01       0.01         0          0          0          0
Execute      5      0.08       0.09         0          0          0          0
Fetch      250      0.09       0.10        54        202         64        245
------- ------  --------  ---------  --------  ---------  ---------  ---------
total        4      0.18       0.20        54        202         64        245
```

The CPU and Elapsed timings shown in the example above will only be non-zero if the init.ora parameter TIMED_STATISTICS=TRUE.

When you examine the above trace file, you will notice the following elements:

- The first listing is for a recursive statement that was issued against the data dictionary to support the INSERT statement that follows. Since this level of detail is rarely useful, the SYS=NO option can be used during formatting to eliminate these types of entries from the output file.

- The third statement, a SELECT statement, contains information for the Parse, Execute, and Fetch phases. Table 3.5 shows the descriptions of each of the columns in the formatted TKPROF output file:

**TABLE 3.5**   TKPROF Output Descriptions

| Statistic Name | Statistic Description |
| --- | --- |
| Count | The number of times the Parse, Execute, or Fetch phase occurred |
| CPU | Total number of seconds the CPU spent processing all the Parse, Execute, or Fetch calls in the statement |
| Elapsed | Total number of seconds spent processing the all the Parse, Execute, or Fetch calls in the statement |
| Disk | Total number of data blocks read from disk during the Parse, Execute, and Fetch calls in the statement |
| Query | Total number of rollback blocks (blocks in consistent mode) read from the SGA during the Parse, Execute, and Fetch calls in the statement |
| Current | Total number of data blocks (blocks in current mode) read from the SGA during the Parse, Execute, and Fetch calls in the statement |
| Rows | The number of rows effected by the Execute phase for INSERT, UPDATE, and DELETE statements, or Fetch phase for SELECT statements |

Using these statistics, you can see that the third statement was parsed once, executed five times, and performed 250 fetches. This processing consumed a total of .18 seconds of CPU time, and .20 seconds elapsed while the statement was processed. The statement required that 54 data blocks be read from disk and 266 from the SGA, and returned 245 rows. The TKPROF utility will also display these statistics in summary form at the end of the output file. These statistics will provide overall totals for both recursive and non-recursive statements.

### Identifying Statements That May Require Tuning

Using the formatted output from TKPROF, it is relatively easy to zero in on SQL statements that may require further tuning. In general you would look for statements that:

- Consume excess CPU resources

- Take a long time to Parse, Execute, or Fetch

- Read too many data blocks from disk and too few from the SGA

- Access many data blocks but return only a few rows

Once you have identified these statements you can use the Explain Plan facility to further determine why these statements are performing poorly.

## The Explain Plan Facility

Oracle's *Explain Plan* facility is used to determine how a particular SQL statement is processing. With this information, it is possible to improve the statement's performance by rewriting the SQL code to eliminate unwanted behavior. While a complete discussion of interpreting Explain Plan output is beyond the scope of this text and the Oracle8i Performance Tuning OCP exam, you should have a basic understanding of this important tool as well.

### Generating Explain Plans Using *TKPROF*

As you saw in the previous section, the EXPLAIN parameter can be used to generate Explain Plans for SQL statements when formatting a user trace file with the TKPROF utility. Figure 3.2 shows what this Explain Plan output would look like.

**FIGURE 3.2** Explain Plan output generated by TKPROF

```
select w.id, w.city, w.state, w.zip_code, r.name, e.last_name
from s_warehouse w, s_region r, s_emp e
where e.id = w.manager_id
and r.id = w.region_id

call      count       cpu   elapsed      disk     query   current      rows
-------  -------  -------  -------   -------   -------   -------   -------
Parse         1      0.13      0.09         0         0         0         0
Execute       1      0.00      0.00         0         0         0         0
Fetch         2      0.01      0.04         7        24         4         5
-------  -------  -------  -------   -------   -------   -------   -------
total         4      0.14      0.13         7        24         4         5

Misses in library cache during parse: 1
Optimizer goal: CHOOSE
Parsing user id: 60  (SCOTT)

Rows     Row Source Operation
-------  ---------------------------------------------------
    5    NESTED LOOPS
    6     NESTED LOOPS
    6      TABLE ACCESS FULL S_WAREHOUSE
   10      TABLE ACCESS BY INDEX ROWID S_EMP
   10       INDEX UNIQUE SCAN (object id 15747)
    5     TABLE ACCESS BY INDEX ROWID S_REGION
   10      INDEX UNIQUE SCAN (object id 15754)


Rows     Execution Plan
-------  ---------------------------------------------------
    0    SELECT STATEMENT   GOAL: CHOOSE
    5     NESTED LOOPS
    6      NESTED LOOPS
    6       TABLE ACCESS (FULL) OF 'S_WAREHOUSE'
   10       TABLE ACCESS (BY INDEX ROWID) OF 'S_EMP'
   10        INDEX (UNIQUE SCAN) OF 'S_EMP_ID_PK' (UNIQUE)
    5      TABLE ACCESS (BY INDEX ROWID) OF 'S_REGION'
   10       INDEX (UNIQUE SCAN) OF 'S_REGION_ID_PK' (UNIQUE)
```

However, formatting a large trace file using the EXPLAIN parameter can take a prohibitively long time. In these cases, you will probably want to examine the formatted trace file for poorly performing SQL statements and then generate Explain Plans for only those statements that use the techniques discussed in the next section.

## Generating Explain Plans Using *EXPLAIN PLAN FOR*

Once a poorly performing SQL statement has been identified, you can use the EXPLAIN PLAN FOR command to generate an Explain Plan for this statement. The steps to generate an Explain Plan using this technique are:

- Create a PLAN_TABLE table using the utlxplan.sql script found in $ORACLE_HOME/rdbms/admin on UNIX systems or %ORACLE_HOME%\rdbms\admin\ on Windows NT systems. This step only needs to be performed once:

  SQL> @$ORACLE_HOME/rdbms/admin/utlxplan.sql
  Table created.

- Populate the PLAN_TABLE with the SQL statement's execution plan using the EXPLAIN PLAN FOR command:

```
SQL> EXPLAIN PLAN FOR
  2 SELECT dist.distributor_id,
  3         dist.city,
  4         dist.state,
  5         dist.zip_code,
  6         district.name,
  7         emp.last_name
  8 FROM    distributor dist, district, employee emp
  9 WHERE   emp.employee_id = dist.manager_id
 10 AND     district.district_id = dist.district_id;
```

Explained.

- The EXPLAIN PLAN FOR command will populate the PLAN_TABLE with the execution plan for the query. The query itself does not execute. Only its execution plan is generated.

Be sure to either truncate the PLAN_TABLE or use the SET STATEMENT_ID= syntax between executions of the EXPLAIN PLAN FOR command. Otherwise, the execution plans of several tables will be stored in the PLAN_TABLE at the same time, making interpretation difficult.

- You now can query the PLAN_TABLE in order to see how the explained statement would be executed:

```
SQL> SELECT LPAD(' ',4*(LEVEL-2))||
  2                  operation||' '||
  3                  options||' '||
  4                  object_name "Execution Plan"
  5 FROM plan_table
  6 START WITH id = 0
  7 CONNECT BY PRIOR id = parent_id;
```

- The output from this query on the PLAN_TABLE looks like the following sample:

```
Execution Plan
----------------------------------------------
SELECT STATEMENT
NESTED LOOPS
    NESTED LOOPS
        TABLE ACCESS FULL DISTRIBUTOR
        TABLE ACCESS BY INDEX ROWID EMPLOYEE
            INDEX UNIQUE SCAN EMPLOYEE_ID_PK
    TABLE ACCESS BY INDEX ROWID DISTRICT
        INDEX UNIQUE SCAN DISTRICT_ID_PK
```

Whether generated by TKPROF or EXPLAIN PLAN FOR, you will need to examine the output from the PLAN_TABLE to identify if any of the individual operations in the SQL processing can benefit from tuning.

## Interpreting Explain Plan Output

In general, Explain Plan output is interpreted by starting at the innermost operation in the Explain Plan. This operation is always executed first, unless it is an index access. In this case the table operation directly above the index access would begin the execution plan. From this starting point, you examine the Explain Plan's remaining operations, working your way up and out toward the leftmost operations in the plan.

If two operations appear at the same level and are both the innermost operations, the operation on top is executed first.

Gaining proficiency at reading Explain Plans takes practice. In order to introduce you to this process, the output from the previous example is interpreted here:

- The innermost operation of this plan is INDEX UNIQUE SCAN EMPLOYEE_ID_PK.

- Because this step involves an index and not a table, the operation directly above this step, TABLE ACCESS BY INDEX ROWID EMPLOYEE, is instead considered as the possible start to this execution plan. You do this because the index lookup and the table access are essentially one step, not two.

- However, at the same level as the access of EMPLOYEE, is the operation TABLE ACCESS FULL DISTRIBUTOR. Since these two operations appear at the same level, the operation on top, TABLE ACCESS FULL DISTRIBUTOR, is where the execution plan begins. Note that while the operation INDEX UNIQUE SCAN DISTRICT_ID_PK is also on the same level as the access of EMPLOYEE and DISTRIBUTOR, this index access is ignored at this time because it involves a table that is on another, more outer level.

A TABLE ACCESS FULL operation in an Explain Plan indicates that a Full Table Scan (FTS) occurred. These operations cause every row in a table to be accessed. This can be a costly operation depending on the number of rows in a table and the proportion of those rows returned by the query. The appropriate use of indexing helps minimize performance problems associated with FTS. Indexing is discussed later in this chapter.

- Working your way out and up, the next operation you encounter is NESTED LOOPS. In this operation, the DISTRIBUTION table is joined to the EMPLOYEE table via the EMPLOYEE_ID_PK index. A NESTED LOOPS join occurs whenever Oracle takes the resulting rows from the first operation (the FTS of DISTRIBUTOR) and then compares the results of that operation to each row in the second operation (access of EMPLOYEE via an index).

To better understand what has occurred up to this point in the execution plan, look at the example below, which has numbered each operation in the Explain Plan in the order it occurs:

```
Order    Execution Plan
-------------------------------------------------------

         SELECT STATEMENT
         NESTED LOOPS
4            NESTED LOOPS
1                TABLE ACCESS FULL DISTRIBUTOR
3                TABLE ACCESS BY INDEX ROWID EMPLOYEE
2                    INDEX UNIQUE SCAN EMPLOYEE_ID_PK
             TABLE ACCESS BY INDEX ROWID DISTRICT
                 INDEX UNIQUE SCAN DISTRICT_ID_PK
```

Now consider the interpretation:

- Since the NESTED LOOPS join and TABLE ACCESS BY INDEX ROWID DISTRICT both appear at this level, we consider them next. These operations imply that the results of the first operation, a NESTED LOOPS join of DISTRIBUTOR and EMPLOYEE, is itself joined to DISTRICT via the DISTRICT_ID_PK index using a second NESTED LOOPS join found on the next level.

- The only operation left is to return the rows to the user. This step is not expressed in the Explain Plan, but is implied by the SELECT STATEMENT keyword that appears at the beginning of the Explain Plan output.

To conclude the previous example, the final stages of the Explain Plan are numbered in the order in which they occur:

```
Order    Execution Plan
-----------------------------------------------------
8        SELECT STATEMENT
7        NESTED LOOPS
4           NESTED LOOPS
1              TABLE ACCESS FULL DISTRIBUTOR
3              TABLE ACCESS BY INDEX ROWID EMPLOYEE
2                 INDEX UNIQUE SCAN EMPLOYEE_ID_PK
6           TABLE ACCESS BY INDEX ROWID DISTRICT
5              INDEX UNIQUE SCAN DISTRICT_ID_PK
```

# The *AUTOTRACE* Utility

The Oracle *Autotrace* utility combines elements of both the TKPROF utility and the EXPLAIN PLAN FOR facility. Unlike TKPROF, AUTOTRACE does not require you to format a trace file to get resource usage information. This information is automatically included in the AUTOTRACE output along with the execution plan of the SQL statement that was issued. No separate query on the PLAN_TABLE is required. However, unlike the EXPLAIN PLAN FOR facility, AUTOTRACE actually executes the statement being examined before generating an execution plan.

## Preparing to Use *AUTOTRACE*

Before using the AUTOTRACE utility, you must first perform several initial setup operations. These operations are performed only once.

First, each user who wishes to use the AUTOTRACE utility will need a PLAN_ TABLE table in their schema. This table can be created using the utlxplan.sql script found in $ORACLE_HOME/rdbms/admin on UNIX systems or %ORACLE_ HOME%\rdbms\admin on Windows NT systems. Unlike EXPLAIN PLAN FOR, AUTOTRACE will automatically clean out the contents of the PLAN_TABLE between executions.

Second, you will then need to create a database role called PLUSTRACE by running an Oracle-supplied script called plustrce.sql while logged on as the user SYS. This script is located in $ORACLE_HOME/sqlplus/admin on UNIX systems or %ORACLE_HOME%\sqlplus\admin on Windows NT systems.

Finally, you will have to grant the new PLUSTRACE role to every user who will be using the AUTOTRACE utility.

## Using *AUTOTRACE*

The AUTOTRACE utility is only available from within a SQL*Plus session. AUTOTRACE can be activated in a SQL*Plus session by issuing the SET AUTOTRACE ON command. The following example demonstrates the output of the AUTOTRACE utility:

```
SQL> set autotrace on
SQL> SELECT dist.distributor_id "ID",
   2 dist.city,
   3 dist.state,
   4 dist.zip_code,
   5 district.name,
   6 emp.last_name
   7 FROM    distributor dist,
   8         district,
   9         employee emp
  10 WHERE   emp.employee_id
  11           = dist.manager_id
  12 AND    district.district_id
  13           = dist.district_id;


ID CITY    STATE ZIP_CODE   NAME          LAST_NAME
--- ------- ----- ---------- ------------ -------------
101 Maidson  WI     53704     Northern        Bryla
110 Freeport IL     61032     Midwest         Gastel
```

```
205 Phoenix     AZ      85024     Southwest    Girardin
355 El Cajon    CA      92020       Western    Anderson
451 Boston      MA      02152       Eastern       Terry
```

Execution Plan
```
----------------------------------------------------------
0   SELECT STATEMENT Optimizer=CHOOSE
 0   NESTED LOOPS
2 1     NESTED LOOPS
3 2       TABLE ACCESS (FULL) OF 'S_WAREHOUSE'
4 2       TABLE ACCESS (BY INDEX ROWID) OF 'S_EMP'
5 4         INDEX (UNIQUE SCAN) OF 'S_EMP_ID_PK' (UNIQUE)
6 1     TABLE ACCESS (BY INDEX ROWID) OF 'S_REGION'
7 6       INDEX (UNIQUE SCAN) OF 'S_REGION_ID_PK' (UNIQUE)
```

Statistics
```
---------------------------------------------------
     0 recursive calls
     4 db block gets
    24 consistent gets
     0 physical reads
     0 redo size
  1717 bytes sent via SQL*Net to client
   786 bytes received via SQL*Net from client
     4 SQL*Net roundtrips to/from client
     1 sorts (memory)
     0 sorts (disk)
     5 rows processed
```

The statistics listed at the end of the AUTOTRACE output will be explained in more detail in Chapter 7: Tuning Physical I/O.

In addition to ON, the SET AUTOTRACE command also has the four additional options shown in Table 3.6.

**TABLE 3.6** Options for AUTOTRACE Utility

| Option | Description |
|---|---|
| ON EXPLAIN | Displays query results and execution plan, but no statistics |
| TRACEONLY | Displays the execution plan and the statistics, but no query results* |
| TRACEONLY STATISTICS | Displays the statistics only, no execution plan or query results* |
| OFF | Turns off the AUTOTRACE utility |

*The query is still executed even though the query results are not shown.

# Understanding the Oracle Optimizer

**A**s you learned in the previous section, several tools exist that will allow you to see a particular SQL statement's execution plan. A single SQL statement often has many different possible execution plans, all of which return the same result, but only one of which is optimal. It is the job of the Oracle optimizer to choose the best execution plan.

There are essentially two optimizer modes in Oracle: Rule and Cost. As you will see in the following sections, these two optimizer modes differ in terms of how they select the optimal execution plan from among the many possible execution plans for a given statement.

## Rule-Based Optimization

The *rule-based optimizer* (RBO) uses a set of predefined "rules of thumb" to decide how to best execute a query. These guidelines include rules like "if a table column referenced in a WHERE clause has an index on it, always use the index when accessing the corresponding table data." However, these rules are not flexible enough to consider factors like table size, the number of rows in the table, or the cardinality of the data in the indexed columns. *Cardinality* refers to the variation in the data within a column. Columns that contain many different values are said to have high cardinality. Columns that contain very few different values are said to have low cardinality. At times this inability to consider cardinality leads the RBO to follow inefficient SQL execution plans. For instance, in the example from the previous section, the RBO would use the index to access the table even if the table only contained a few rows. This requires the SQL statement to perform two I/Os (one on the index and one on the table) when the entire table could just have easily been accessed with only one I/O.

In early versions of Oracle, such as Version 6 and older, application developers frequently used their knowledge of these rules to directly influence the behavior of the RBO. However, because of its superior efficiency, Oracle now recommends that the cost-based optimizer (CBO) be used in favor of the RBO in all new development environments. Switching an older system from using the RBO to using cost-based optimization can also be considered after careful testing. This does not work in all cases, however. Since some older systems may have been coded to specifically exploit features of the RBO, they may actually perform worse when converted to the CBO. In fact, Oracle's own suite of enterprise resource planning applications (i.e. Oracle Financials, Oracle Human Resources, etc.) all used the older RBO mode in versions prior to 11i.

Only the CBO is capable of considering newer Oracle features like Stored Execution Plans and Index-organized Tables when generating execution plans.

## Cost-Based Optimization

Unlike the rule-based optimizer that has only its predefined guidelines to follow when executing a query, the *cost-based optimizer* (CBO) considers many different execution plans and then selects the one with the lowest execution cost. The costs considered are primarily related to CPU and I/O. In order to determine the relative cost of each execution plan, the CBO relies heavily on the presence of statistics about the tables and indexes in the database. These statistics are stored in the data dictionary and include:

- The size of each table or index
- The number of rows each table or index contains
- The number of database blocks used by each table or index
- The length of each table row
- The cardinality of the column data in indexed columns

By default, these statistics are not present in the database. The statistics are gathered and stored in the database when the tables and indexes are analyzed.

Table and index statistics need to be kept current in order for the CBO to perform effectively. Out-of-date statistics that no longer reflect the actual underlying table data may cause the CBO to select less than optimal execution plans.

## Analyzing Individual Tables and Indexes

You can use the following command to analyze an individual table or index in order to gather its statistics:

```
SQL> ANALYZE TABLE employee COMPUTE STATISTICS;
Table analyzed.
```

This command gathers the statistics for the EMPLOYEE table by examining every row in the table. It will also gather statistics on all the indexes associated with the EMPLOYEE table. If EMPLOYEE is a very large table, this method could be time consuming and resource intensive. Larger tables can be analyzed using this command:

```
SQL> ANALYZE INDEX distributor_id_pk ESTIMATE STATISTICS;
Table analyzed.
```

Using ESTIMATE in place of COMPUTE causes Oracle to estimate the tables statistics using a sample of the table or index data instead of using the entire table. The default sample size is 1,064 rows. In most cases, the ESTIMATE parameter provides statistics that are nearly as accurate as those collected using the COMPUTE option. You can specify your own sample size in terms of rows or a percentage of the overall table using the following commands:

```
SQL> ANALYZE TABLE distributors ESTIMATE STATISTICS
  2   SAMPLE 500 ROWS;
Table analyzed.

SQL> ANALYZE INDEX distributor_id_pk ESTIMATE STATISTICS
  2   SAMPLE 35 PERCENT;
Table analyzed.
```

If you specify a value for SAMPLE that exceeds 50 percent of the rows in the table, Oracle will generate the statistics using a COMPUTE instead of ESTIMATE.

If you desire an even more focused analysis of the data in the tables and indexes, you can include the FOR clause with the ANALYZE TABLE command:

```
SQL> ANALYZE TABLE distributors ESTIMATE STATISTICS
  2  FOR COLUMNS district_id SIZE 200;
Table analyzed.
```

This command would limit the analysis of the table to the just the DISTRICT_ID column instead of the default behavior of examining all columns. The SIZE parameter specifies how many slices to divide the column's values into before examining the cardinality of data within each slice. The more slices that are taken, the more accurate a picture the CBO will have regarding the distribution of the data within the column. The default value for SIZE is 75. The acceptable range of values is 1 through 254. Without this information, the CBO assumes that the data is normally distributed when, in fact, it may not be. Additional options for the FOR clause of the ANALYZE command appear in Table 3.7.

**TABLE 3.7**  Options of the FOR Clause of the ANALYZE Command

| Option | Description |
| --- | --- |
| FOR TABLE | Gathers only table statistics, without column statistics |
| FOR ALL COLUMNS | Gathers columns statistics only, on all columns |
| FOR ALL INDEXED COLUMNS | Gathers columns statistics on only columns that are indexed |
| FOR ALL LOCAL INDEXES | Gathers column statistics on all local indexes of a partitioned table |

The ANALYZE command also has a DELETE option that can be used to remove statistics if needed:

```
SQL> ANALYZE TABLE employee DELETE STATISTICS;
```

## Analyzing by Schema

In order for the CBO to perform best, all the tables and indexes involved in a SQL statement should be analyzed. Oracle provides two PL/SQL packages, DBMS_UTILITY and DBMS_STATS, which can be used to analyze every table

## The Importance of Histograms

When a table is analyzed, Oracle stores the lowest and highest data values in each column as part of the table's statistics. The Oracle optimizer assumes that the data between these two data values is normally distributed. In other words, the optimizer assumes that most of the data in the column falls between these high and low values, and less of the data in the column will be found at either of the two extremes. If this assumption is not true, the optimizer may make very poor choices about how to execute SQL statements that involve that column.

On one occasion, we experienced a query that was running against a large table whose indexed columns did not have normally distributed data. A particular query on this table was taking over 17 hours to parse, execute, and fetch its rows. After we realized that, instead of being normally distributed between a low and high value, the data had spikes of high and low values throughout, we analyzed the table using the following options:

```
SQL> ANALYZE TABLE finaid COMPUTE STATISTICS FOR COLUMNS award
SIZE 100;
```

This command created a histogram that divided the data in the AWARD column of the FINAID table into 100 separate slices. The histogram then determined the high and low value for each of the slices and stored those as part of the table and index statistics. These statistics gave the optimizer a much more accurate view of the data and the usefulness of the associated indexes.

As a result, the same query that had taken 17 hours to complete now ran in only three minutes. This clearly demonstrates the importance of using histograms when the column data being accessed is not normally distributed. Histogram information is can be found in the DBA_HISTOGRAMS data dictionary view.

and index in a user's schema without having to individually specify each segment by name.

### DBMS_UTILITY

The DBMS_UTILITY package accepts several arguments that are similar to those you saw for the ANALYZE command in the previous section. An example using several of these arguments is shown here:

```
SQL> EXECUTE DBMS_UTILITY.ANALYZE_
SCHEMA('SCOTT','ESTIMATE',0,40,'FOR
      ALL INDEXED COLUMNS SIZE 40');
PL/SQL procedure successfully completed.
```

Each of the arguments used in this example is described in Table 3.8.

**TABLE 3.8**   Arguments for DBMS_UTILITY.ANALYZE_SCHEMA

| Argument Used In Example | Description |
| --- | --- |
| SCOTT | The schema to be analyzed. |
| ESTIMATE | The type of analysis to be done. If COMPUTE is used, the next two arguments have no effect. |
| 0 | The number of rows to use in the estimate. If the estimate will be specified as a percentage of rows, enter a zero here. |
| 40 | The percentage of the total rows to be used in the estimate. If the previous argument is non-zero, then this argument has no effect. |
| FOR ALL INDEXED COLUMNS SIZE 40 | Additional options as shown in Table 3.7. |

The DBMS_UTILITY package can also be used to analyze the entire database. A database level analysis can use the same arguments that were discussed in Table 3.8, with the exception of the schema argument. The following is an example of a complete database analysis using the same sample size as the previous example:

```
SQL> EXECUTE SYS.DBMS_UTILITY.ANALYZE_
DATABASE('ESTIMATE',0,40,'FOR ALL INDEXED COLUMNS SIZE
40');
PL/SQL procedure successfully completed.
```

Because the recursive data dictionary queries rely heavily on specific access paths to run efficiently, you should never analyze the segments in the SYS schema. Using the ANALYZE DATABASE command will cause statistics to be gathered for the SYS schema. You should use the DBMS_UTILITY.ANALYZE_
SCHEMA('SYS','DELETE'); command to remove them.

### DBMS_STATS

The DBMS_STATS package offers several additional analyzing options that are not available in the DBMS_UTILITY package. Some of these options include:

- The ability to back up old statistics before new statistics are gathered. This very useful feature allows you to restore some or all of the original statistics if the CBO performs poorly after updated statistics have been gathered.

- The ability to take a random sample of *blocks*, not just rows, when estimating statistics.

- The ability to gather table statistics much faster by performing the analysis in parallel.

- The ability to automatically gather statistics on highly volatile tables and bypass gathering statistics on static tables.

The following example shows how the DBMS_STATS packages would be used to gather statistics on the EMPLOYEE table in Joe's schema:

```
SQL> EXECUTE DBMS_STATS.GATHER_TABLE_STATS
('JOE','EMPLOYEE');
```

Like the DBMS_UTILITY package, the DBMS_STATS package can also be used to analyze indexes, an entire schema, or the whole database using the procedures shown in Table 3.9.

**TABLE 3.9** Procedures within the DBMS_STATS Package

| Procedure Name | Description |
| --- | --- |
| GATHER_INDEX_STATS | Used to gather statistics on a specified index |
| GATHER_SCHEMA_STATS | Used to gather statistics on a specified schema |
| GATHER_DATABASE_STATS | Used to gather statistics on an entire database |

For complete details of the many options available in the DBMS_STATS package, see Chapter 49: DBMS_STATS of *Oracle8i Supplied Packages Reference, Release 8.1.5* (Part Number A68001-01).

## Viewing Table and Index Statistics

Once statistics have been gathered using one of the previously defined methods, you can examine them by querying several data dictionary views. Except for tables that are using the dynamic monitoring feature of the DBMS_STATS package, these views will only contain the statistics as they existed at the time they were gathered.

Statistics for analyzed tables can be found in the DBA_TABLES data dictionary view. Figure 3.3 shows a query that demonstrates the difference between the statistics in DBA_TABLES for an unanalyzed and analyzed EMPLOYEE table.

**FIGURE 3.3**    Analyzed vs. Unanalyzed Table

```
SQL*Plus: Release 8.0.5.0.0 - Production on Thu Mar 9 21:3:22 2000

(c) Copyright 1998 Oracle Corporation.  All rights reserved.


Connected to:
Oracle8i Enterprise Edition Release 8.1.5.0.2 - Production
With the Partitioning and Java options
PL/SQL Release 8.1.5.0.0 - Production

SQL> SELECT num_rows, blocks, empty_blocks, avg_space, chain_cnt
  2          avg_row_len, avg_space_freelist_blocks, num_freelist_blocks
  3  FROM dba_tables
  4  WHERE table_name = 'EMPLOYEE';

 NUM_ROWS     BLOCKS EMPTY_BLOCKS AVG_SPACE AVG_ROW_LEN AVG_SPACE_FREELIST_BLOCKS NUM_FREELIST_BLO
--------- ---------- ------------ --------- ----------- ------------------------- ----------------


SQL> ANALYZE TABLE joe.employee COMPUTE STATISTICS;

Table analyzed.

SQL> SELECT num_rows, blocks, empty_blocks, avg_space, chain_cnt
  2          avg_row_len, avg_space_freelist_blocks, num_freelist_blocks
  3  FROM dba_tables
  4  WHERE table_name = 'EMPLOYEE';

 NUM_ROWS     BLOCKS EMPTY_BLOCKS AVG_SPACE AVG_ROW_LEN AVG_SPACE_FREELIST_BLOCKS NUM_FREELIST_BLO
--------- ---------- ------------ --------- ----------- ------------------------- ----------------
    15815        605           19       242           0                         0

SQL>
```

A description of the contents of each of the columns that stores statistics in the DBA_TABLES data dictionary view is included in Table 3.10.

**TABLE 3.10** Description of DBA_TABLES Statistic Columns

| Column Name | Description |
| --- | --- |
| NUM_ROWS | Number of rows in the table |
| BLOCKS | Number of blocks below the High Water Mark |
| EMPTY_BLOCKS | Number of blocks above the High Water Mark |
| AVG_SPACE | Average available free space in the table |
| CHAIN_CNT | Number of chained or migrated rows |
| AVG_ROW_LENGTH | Average length, in bytes, taken up by row data and row overhead |
| AVG_SPACE_FREELIST_ BLOCKS | Average free space, in bytes, of the blocks on the table's Freelist |
| NUM_FREELIST_BLOCKS | Number of blocks on the table's Freelist |
| SAMPLE_SIZE | Size of the sample used to last analyze the table |
| LAST_ANALYZED | Date the table was last analyzed |

Index statistics are found in the DBA_INDEXES data dictionary view. Figure 3.4 shows a query that demonstrates the difference between the statistics in DBA_INDEXES for an unanalyzed and analyzed EMPLOYEE_ID_PK index.

**FIGURE  3.4**    Analyzed vs. Unanalyzed Index

```
With the Partitioning and Java options
PL/SQL Release 8.1.5.0.0 - Production

SQL> SELECT blevel, leaf_blocks, distinct_keys, avg_leaf_blocks_per_key,
  2        avg_data_blocks_per_key, clustering_factor, num_rows,
  3        sample_size, last_analyzed
  4  FROM dba_indexes
  5  WHERE index_name = 'EMPLOYEE_ID_PK';

   BLEVEL LEAF_BLOCKS DISTINCT_KEYS AVG_LEAF_BLOCKS_PER_KEY AVG_DATA_BLOCKS_PER_KEY
--------- ----------- ------------- ----------------------- -----------------------

CLUSTERING_FACTOR  NUM_ROWS SAMPLE_SIZE LAST_ANAL
----------------- --------- ----------- ---------



SQL> ANALYZE INDEX joe.employee_id_pk COMPUTE STATISTICS;

Index analyzed.

SQL> SELECT blevel, leaf_blocks, distinct_keys, avg_leaf_blocks_per_key,
  2        avg_data_blocks_per_key, clustering_factor, num_rows,
  3        sample_size, last_analyzed
  4  FROM dba_indexes
  5  WHERE index_name = 'EMPLOYEE_ID_PK';

   BLEVEL LEAF_BLOCKS DISTINCT_KEYS AVG_LEAF_BLOCKS_PER_KEY AVG_DATA_BLOCKS_PER_KEY
--------- ----------- ------------- ----------------------- -----------------------

CLUSTERING_FACTOR  NUM_ROWS SAMPLE_SIZE LAST_ANAL
----------------- --------- ----------- ---------
        1         148         15815                       1                       1
                  605         15815             0 09-MAR-00

SQL> |
```

A description of the contents of each of the columns that stores statistics in the DBA_INDEXES data dictionary view is included in Table 3.11.

**TABLE  3.11**    Description of DBA_INDEXES Statistic Columns

| Column Name | Description |
| --- | --- |
| BLEVEL | Number of levels between the index's root block and its leaf blocks |
| LEAF_BLOCKS | Number of leaf blocks in the index |
| DISTINCT KEYS | Number of distinct values in the indexed column – a measure of the column's cardinality. |
| AVG_LEAF_BLOCKS_ PER_KEY | Average number of leaf blocks used for each distinct key value in the index |
| AVG_DATA_BLOCKS_ PER_KEY | Average number of data blocks for each distinct key value in the index |

**TABLE 3.11** Description of DBA_INDEXES Statistic Columns *(continued)*

| Column Name | Description |
| --- | --- |
| CLUSTERING_FACTOR | A measure of how ordered the data is in the index's underlying table |
| NUM_ROWS | Number of rows contained in the index |
| SAMPLE_SIZE | Size of the sample used to last analyze the index |
| LAST_ANALYZED | Date the index was last analyzed |

Even greater granularity of the contents of tables and their indexed columns can be found in the DBA_TAB_COL_STATISTICS data dictionary view. A description of the contents of each of the columns that stores statistics in the DBA_TAB_COL_STATISTICS data dictionary view is included in Table 3.12.

**TABLE 3.12** Description of DBA_TAB_COL_STATISTICS Columns

| Column Name | Description |
| --- | --- |
| TABLE_NAME | Name of the table |
| COLUMN_NAME | Name of the table column |
| NUM_DISTINCT | Number of distinct values in the column—a measure of cardinality |
| LOW_VALUE | Lowest value in the column |
| HIGH_VALUE | Highest value in the column |
| DENSITY | A measure of how dense the column data is |
| NUM_NULLS | Number of values in the column that are NULL |
| NUM_BUCKETS | Number of "slices" the data was divided into when it was last analyzed |
| SAMPLE_SIZE | Size of the sample used to last analyze the table |

**TABLE 3.12**  Description of DBA_TAB_COL_STATISTICS Columns *(continued)*

| Column Name | Description |
|---|---|
| LAST_ANALYZED | Date the table was last analyzed |
| GLOBAL_STATS | Indicates whether statistics were generated using partition data |
| USER_STATS | Indicates whether the statistics were entered by the user |
| AVG_COL_LENGTH | Average length, in bytes, of the column |

Note that the DBA_TAB_COL_STATISTICS data dictionary view lacks an owner column to distinguish between tables from two schemas that have the same name. Use the USER_TAB_COL_STATISTICS data dictionary view to see each table's column statistics.

## Copying Statistics between Databases

One of the common drawbacks of development environments is that they do not accurately reflect the volume of data that will be used in the final production systems. This can lead to unexpectedly poor performance when applications are moved from development to production. To minimize this problem, Oracle8i allows you to copy your optimizer statistics from your production system to a smaller development system. Even though the data volumes on the development system may be smaller, the optimizer behaves the same way it will when presented with the data volume of the production system. This is extremely useful for developers because they can now see the execution plans that will be used in the production environment once the application is migrated.

This statistics migration process is accomplished by exporting the statistics from the production system and then importing them into the development system. The following steps show you how to use the DBMS_STATS package to perform the export and import operations:

1. In the production database, create the STATS table in the TOOLS tablespace. This table will be used to hold the production schema statistics.

```
SQL> EXECUTE DBMS_STATS.CREATE_STAT_TABLE
  2  ('JOE','STATS','TOOLS');
```

2. Capture the current statistics for Joe's schema and store them in the newly created STATS table.

```
SQL> EXECUTE DBMS_STATS.EXPORT_SCHEMA_STATS
('JOE','STATS');
```

3. Use the Oracle Export utility from the OS command line to export the contents of the STATS table from the production database.

```
$ exp joe/sidney@PROD file=stats.dmp tables=(STATS)
log=stats.log
```

4. Move the export dump file from the production server to the Development server using FTP.

```
$ ftp devl
Connected to DEVL
220 DEVL FTP server (Tue Sep 21 16:48:12 EDT 1999)
ready.
Name (DEVL:jjohnson): johnson
331 Password required for johnson.
Password:
230 User johnson logged in.
Remote system type is UNIX.
Using binary mode to transfer files.
ftp> put stats.dmp
200 PORT command successful.
150 Opening BINARY mode data connection for stats.dmp
226 Transfer complete.
ftp> bye
```

5. In the Development database, create the STATS table in the TOOLS tablespace. This table will hold the exported contents of the STATS table from the production database.

```
SQL> EXECUTE DBMS_STATS.CREATE_STAT_TABLE
  2  ('JOE','STATS','TOOLS');
```

6. Use the Oracle Import utility form the OS command line to import the STATS dump file created on the production server into the STATS table on the Development server.

```
$ imp joe/sidney@DEVL file=stats.dmp log=stats.log full=y
```

7. Move the statistics in the STATS table into the Development database's data dictionary.

```
SQL> EXECUTE DBMS_STATS.IMPORT_SCHEMA_STATS
('JOE','STATS');
```

# Setting the Optimizer Mode

**N**ow that you know how the rule-based and cost-based optimizers differ and understand the importance of timely statistics to proper CBO operation, you're ready for this section's discussion on how to configure your database to run in the optimizer mode of your choosing. The optimizer mode can be set at the following three levels:

- Instance level
- Session level
- Statement level

The following sections discuss each of these methods of setting the optimizer mode.

## Optimizer Mode: Instance Level

The optimizer mode is set at the instance level through the use of the `OPTIMIZER_MODE init.ora` parameter. Once set, this parameter will determine the default optimizer mode used by all sessions operating against the instance. The `OPTIMIZER_MODE` parameter can be set to one of the following four values:

- RULE
- CHOOSE
- FIRST_ROWS
- ALL_ROWS

### *RULE* Mode

Setting `OPTIMIZER_MODE=RULE` in the `init.ora` places the instance into rule-based optimization mode. The presence or absence of statistics has no effect on the optimizer while operating in this mode (unless hints are used).

### *CHOOSE* Mode

Setting `OPTIMIZER_MODE=CHOOSE` in the `init.ora` places the instance into either rule-based optimization mode or cost-based optimization mode. If `OPTIMIZER_MODE=CHOOSE` and statistics exist for any one of the tables involved in a query, then the instance will use cost-based optimization when executing that query. Any missing statistics will be estimated "on the fly" by the optimizer. If `OPTIMIZER_MODE=CHOOSE` and no statistics exist on any tables or indexes in the query, then the instance will use rule-based optimization when executing the query. CHOOSE is the default setting for OPTIMIZER_MODE in the init.ora.

### FIRST_ROWS Mode

Setting OPTIMIZER_MODE=FIRST_ROWS in the init.ora also places the instance into either rule-based or cost-based optimization mode based on the presence or absence of table and indexes statistics. In this mode, if statistics exist, then the instance will use a variation of CBO designed to return the first rows fetched by a query as quickly as possible. This mode is designed to improve the overall response time of queries.

### ALL_ROWS Mode

Setting OPTIMIZER_MODE=ALL_ROWS in the init.ora also places the instance into either rule-based or cost-based optimization mode based on the presence or absence of table and indexes statistics. In this mode, if statistics exist, then the instance will use a variation of CBO designed to return all the rows fetched by a query as quickly as possible. This mode is used to improve the overall throughput of queries. ALL_ROWS is the default CBO mode.

## Optimizer Mode: Session Level

Once the init.ora optimizer mode is set at the instance level, all users connecting to the instance will utilize that optimization mode as the default for processing their queries. However, it is possible for a user to change the optimizer mode for their session using only the ALTER SESSION command. The following example shows the current session being changed to cost-based optimization mode:

```
SQL> ALTER SESSION SET OPTIMIZER_MODE=CHOOSE;
```

The possible values for the optimizer mode at the session level are the same as those at the instance level: RULE, CHOOSE, FIRST_ROWS, and ALL_ROWS. This optimizer mode is retained by the session until the user either resets it using the ALTER SESSION command again or logs out.

## Optimizer Mode: Statement Level

The optimizer can also be influenced at the statement level through the use of hints. *Hints* are specific instructions that make the optimizer perform in a particular way. Hints are embedded within the actual SQL statements itself by surrounding the hint with the symbols /*+ and */. An example of a hint that would make the specified SQL statement run in rule-based optimization mode is shown here:

```
SQL> SELECT /*+ RULE */ dist.distributor_id,
  2  dist.city,
  3  dist.state,
  4  dist.zip_code,
  5  district.name,
  6  emp.last_name
  7  FROM   distributor dist, district, employee emp
  8  WHERE  emp.employee_id = dist.manager_id
  9  AND district.district_id = dist.district_id;
```

Make sure you have the + immediately after the /* when specifying a hint. If you have a space or any other characters than /*+ preceding the hint, Oracle will treat the hint specification as a comment and ignore it.

The four instance- and session-level optimizer modes you have already seen (RULE, CHOOSE, FIRST_ROWS, and ALL_ROWS) can also be specified as hints. There are also several other more specialized hints. There are nearly 40 different optimizer hints available in Oracle8i. It is beyond the scope of this text and the Oracle8i Performance Tuning OCP exam to discuss them all in detail. However, some more commonly used hints are described in Table 3.13.

**TABLE 3.13**  Commonly Used Optimizer Hints

| Hint Name | Example | Description |
| --- | --- | --- |
| FULL | /*+ FULL SALES */ | Forces optimizer to use a full table scan when accessing the SALES table |
| INDEX | /*+ INDEX SALES_ ID_PK */ | Forces the optimizer to use the index SALES_ID_PK when accessing the SALES table the index is built on |
| REWRITE | /*+ REWRITE */ | Forces the optimizer to dynamically rewrite the query in order to make use of a materialized view if one is available |
| PARALLEL | /*+ PARALLEL */ | Causes the specified operation to execute in parallel |

All hints, with the exception of RULE, cause the CBO to be used when the query is executed.

A complete list of all the Oracle hints can be found in Chapter 7: Optimizer Modes, Plan Stability, and Hints of *Oracle8i Tuning, Release 8.1.5* (Part Number A67775-01).

### Optimizer Precedence Rules

Since the optimizer mode can be set at the instance, session, or statement level in the form of a hint, it is important to understand which setting will take precedence when a statement is actually executed:

- Statement level hints override session and instance level optimizer modes.

- Session level optimizer settings override instance level optimizer settings.

- Instance level settings take effect if no session level optimizer settings or hints are specified.

- The default instance optimizer mode is CHOOSE. If statistics exist on any table or index involved in a query, then CBO is used. If no statistics exist, then RBO is used.

# Improving Application Performance

**G**athering and analyzing application information in the form of trace files and execution plans is the first step to understanding how your application is performing. Knowing how the application is affected by the behavior of the Oracle optimizer is important as well. Drawing on this information, the next section will examine the options available to you for improving the performance of an application. These techniques fall into two broad categories: improving execution paths by storing optimal plans and using materialized views, and minimizing I/O by using indexes and clusters.

# Improving Execution Paths

Depending on the complexity of the query, the size of the tables, and the number of alternatives considered by the Oracle optimizer, the mere formulation of an execution plan can contribute to degraded query performance. Oracle8i introduces two new concepts, plan stability and materialized views, to help minimize the performance impact that execution plan determination has on a query's execution.

## Plan Stability

Changes that you make to the database may inadvertently affect execution plans. For example, changes made to init.ora parameters to improve one aspect of database tuning may cause the Oracle optimizer to behave differently than it did before—possibly to the detriment of previously well-tuned SQL processing. Oracle8i allows you to address this problem by giving specified execution plans "stability." Plan stability is accomplished by storing the preferred execution plan for a given SQL statement in the data dictionary.

### Stored Outlines

Oracle8i maintains these predefined execution plans in the data dictionary in the form of *stored outlines*. These stored outlines represent the execution plan the optimizer will use whenever the SQL statement associated with the stored outline is executed. This stored execution plan remains constant even if new statistics are gathered or optimizer-related changes are made to the init.ora. A stored outline is essentially a collection of hints that will reproduce the execution plan that the optimizer used when it originally executed a statement.

Through a process known as *plan equivalence,* a SQL statement must *exactly* match the original statement used to generate an outline in order for the stored outline to be used. Even an identical statement with the addition of a hint or comment will not be considered equivalent for stored outline usage.

### Using Stored Outlines

Several configuration steps must be performed before using the shared out-lines feature. These steps are listed here in the order they should be performed:

1. Determine which statements you would like to store execution plans for. It is likely that these statements will involve tables and indexes whose data is relatively static. Queries that utilize tables

and indexes of highly volatile data will probably benefit from the normal, dynamic nature of the CBO. If you wish to generate stored outlines for every statement, simply set the init.ora parameter CREATE_STORED_OUTLINES=TRUE. This option should be used sparingly since it is unlikely that stored outlines are appropriate for every SQL statement. If this option is used, steps 2–4 do not apply.

2. Ascertain whether the statements you have identified can be lumped into two or more broad categories of statements. Doing so will help you determine whether a statement is eligible for stored outline execution. Examples of categories might include "Queries that access the EMPLOYEE table" or "Queries that do a lookup on the ADDRESS column of the DISTRIBUTOR table." At outline creation, if you do not specify which category a stored outline should belong to, it will be stored in a category called DEFAULT.

3. Alter the OUTLN schema. This schema stores all the stored outlines for the database.

   - For security purposes, change the OUTLN schema's password. The default password (OUTLN) is well documented.

   - Alter the OUTLN schema's default and temporary tablespaces to something other than the SYSTEM tablespace.

   - Move the two tables that the OUTLN schema uses to store outlines (OL$ and OL$HINTS) out of the SYSTEM tablespace and into OUTLN's new default tablespace. The Export and Import utility can be used for this operation.

4. To create the stored outlines for the statements you identified, use the following commands:

```
SQL> CREATE OR REPLACE OUTLINE employee_mgr_last_name
  2  FOR CATEGORY employee_queries ON
  3  SELECT lastname
  4  FROM employee
  5  WHERE job_title = 'MGR';
```

where EMPLOYEE_MGR_LAST_NAME is the name of the new stored outline and EMPLOYEE_QUERIES is the name of the category to which it is assigned. Alternatively, you can activate outlines for a particular category in your session and then issue each of the commands you wish to create outlines for:

```
SQL> ALTER SESSION SET CREATE_STORED_OUTLINES =
employee_queries;
SQL> SELECT lastname
  2  FROM employee
  3  WHERE job_title = 'MGR';
SQL> ALTER SESSION SET CREATE_STORED_OUTLINES = false;
```

where EMPLOYEE_QUERIES is the name of the category that this stored outline will be assigned. The name of the stored outline will be system generated.

**5.** Next, activate the stored outlines feature using one of the following methods:

- Set the init.ora parameter USE_STORED_OUTLINES=TRUE and restart the instance.

- Place the instance into stored outlines mode dynamically using:

```
SQL> ALTER SYSTEM SET USE_STORED_OUTLINES = true;
```

The above command will activate stored outlines in all categories. To activate categories selectively use:

```
SQL> ALTER SYSTEM SET USE_STORED_OUTLINES =
employee_queries;
```

- Turn on the stored outline feature at the session level by using:

```
SQL> ALTER SESSION SET USE_STORED_OUTLINES = true;
```

The above command will activate stored outlines in all categories. To activate categories selectively use:

```
SQL> ALTER SESSION SET USE_STORED_OUTLINES =
employee_queries;
```

### Managing Stored Outlines

Stored outline requirements change over time. Outlines may need to be dropped, renamed, or moved from one category to another. These types of maintenance operations are performed using the Oracle-supplied package OUTLN_PKG and the ALTER OUTLINE and DROP OUTLINE commands.

**USING OUTLN_PKG**

The OUTLN_PKG package contains three procedures. The names and descriptions of these procedures are shown in Table 3.14.

**TABLE 3.14** Procedures in the OUTLN_PKG

| Procedure Name | Description |
| --- | --- |
| DROP_UNUSED | Drops outlines in current schema that have not been used since they were created |
| DROP_BY_CAT | Drops the specified category and all outlines contained in it |
| UPDATE_BY_ CAT | Creates the new category name specified and moves all the outlines in the old category specified into the new category |

The following examples demonstrate the use of each of these procedures:

```
SQL> EXECUTE OUTLN_PKG.DROP_UNUSED;
PL/SQL procedure successfully completed.

SQL> EXECUTE OUTLN_PKG.DROP_UNUSED ('EMPLOYEE_QUERIES');
PL/SQL procedure successfully completed.

SQL> EXECUTE OUTLN_PKG.UPDATE_BY_CAT ('DEFAULT','DSS_QUERIES');
PL/SQL procedure successfully completed.
```

**USING ALTER AND DROP OUTLINE**

The ALTER OUTLINE and DROP OUTLINE commands can also be used to manage stored outlines. Table 3.15 shows the available options for the ALTER OUTLINE command.

**TABLE 3.15** Options for ALTER OUTLINE

| Command | Description |
|---|---|
| REBUILD | Generates a new execution plan for the specified stored outline using current statistics |
| RENAME TO | Changes the name of the stored outline to the new name specified |
| CHANGE CATEGORY TO | Changes the category to which the stored outline belongs |

The following examples demonstrate the use of each of these options:

```
SQL> ALTER OUTLINE employee_mgr_last_name REBUILD;
Outline altered.

SQL> ALTER OUTLINE employee_mgr_last_name RENAME TO
employee_lname;
Outline altered.

SQL> ALTER OUTLINE employee_lname CHANGE CATEGORY TO emp_
queries;
Outline altered.
```

If an outline is no longer needed, you can use the DROP OUTLIN command to delete it from the system. An example of this syntax is shown here:

```
SQL> DROP OUTLINE employee_lname;
Outline dropped.
```

If the stored outline that is dropped is the last outline in its category, the category will also be dropped. Oracle does not maintain categories that do not contain stored outlines.

### Viewing Stored Outline Data

The data dictionary views DBA_OUTLINE_HINTS and DBA_OUTLINES contain information about all the stored outlines in the database. A description of the contents of each of these views is contained in Table 3.16 and Table 3.17.

**TABLE 3.16** Contents of the DBA_OUTLINE_HINTS View

| Column Name | Description |
| --- | --- |
| NAME | The name of the stored outline |
| OWNER | The schema name of the stored outline's owner |
| CATEGORY | The category the stored outline is associated with |
| USED | Indicates whether the outline has ever been used (values are USED/UNUSED) |
| TIMESTAMP | Date and time the stored outline was created |
| VERSION | Oracle RDBMS version that created the stored outline |
| SQL_TEXT | The actual text of the original SQL query associated with the stored outline |

**TABLE 3.17** Contents of the DBA_OUTLINES View

| Column Name | Description |
| --- | --- |
| NAME | The name of the stored outline |
| OWNER | The schema name of the stored outline's owner |

**TABLE 3.17** Contents of the DBA_OUTLINES View *(continued)*

| Column Name | Description |
| --- | --- |
| NODE | The identifier indicating to which SQL statement the hint belongs |
| JOIN_POS | The position of the table in the SQL query's original join order |
| HINT | The actual text of the hint used in the original SQL query associated with the stored outline |

## Materialized Views

Stored outlines help speed up queries by telling the optimizer how to tackle the query execution associated with a particular SQL statement. *Materialized views* are also designed to speed up queries by storing data from queries in a pre-joined, pre-summarized format. Materialized views are intended primarily for use in data warehouses and Decision Support Systems where large volumes of data are accessed and summarized using queries. As with a stored outline, the optimizer recognizes when the use of a materialized view is appropriate and dynamically adjusts the query to make use of the associated view. However, unlike a stored outline, a query does not have to match exactly the SQL statement used to create the materialized view. Instead, the optimizer can dynamically rewrite a query that is close to the original definition so that the materialized view can be used in place of the actual tables.

### Using Materialized Views

Several configuration steps must be performed before using the materialized view feature. These steps are listed here in the order they should be performed:

1. Determine the statements for which you would like create materialized views. It is likely that these statements will involve large fact tables that are joined to one another and include summary functions like COUNT, MAX, MIN, or SUM.

2. Decide whether or not you wish to keep the data in the view in sync with the underlying base tables. If you do not want to keep the data in sync, you will specify the NEVER option during the creation of the view. If you do want the data to be kept in sync, you will specify the FORCE option during the creation of the view. FORCE is the default sync mode.

3. If you use the FORCE option during view creation, the sync or refresh of the data will occur in one of the following ways:

   - Complete: The materialized view is truncated and then completely repopulated with data from the base tables in the query.

   - Fast: The materialized view is only populated with data from the base tables that has changed since the last re-sync. The refresh is performed using the view's log data or by ROWID.

   Oracle will try to use the fast refresh first, and then the complete refresh if the fast refresh is not available.

4. Next, ascertain how often you would like your chosen refresh process to occur. There are two possible refresh modes:

   - On Commit: The materialized view data will be refreshed with every committed transaction on the base tables.

   - By Time: By using the START WITH and NEXT options during view creation, the materialized view data can be refreshed at specified times on specified dates. These refresh times and dates are submitted as jobs to the Oracle job queue.

5. Set the init.ora parameters related to materialized views. A list of these parameters and their descriptions is in Table 3.18.

**TABLE 3.18** Materialized View init.ora Parameters

| Parameter | Description |
| --- | --- |
| JOB_QUE_PROCESSES | The number of background job queue processes to start |
| JOB_QUE_INTERVAL | How often the job queue background processes wake up and check for pending jobs (in seconds) |
| QUERY_REWRITE_ENABLED | Allows optimizer to dynamically rewrite queries to take advantage of materialized views when set to TRUE |

**TABLE 3.18**   Materialized View `init.ora` Parameters *(continued)*

| Parameter | Description |
|---|---|
| QUERY_REWRITE_ INTEGRITY | Determines the degree to which the data consistency is to be adhered to when accessing materialized views. Options are: ENFORCED: Query rewrites only occur when Oracle can guarantee data currency (default); TRUSTED: Query rewrites can occur when declared relationships exist, but without complete data currency; STALE_TOLERATED: Query rewrites can occur even when the view's data and the underlying table data are not current. |
| OPTIMIZER_MODE | Must be set to one of the cost-based optimizer modes |

The QUERY_REWRITE_ENABLED parameter can also be set at the session level using the ALTER SESSION command. The system privilege GLOBAL QUERY REWRITE and/or QUERY REWRITE must be granted to users who wish to alter their session in this manner.

Users only need privileges on the base tables underlying the materialized view in order to use it, not on the view itself.

### Creating Materialized Views

Once you have identified the SQL statements for which you would like to create materialized views, you are ready to build the materialized views. The sample code below shows how a materialized view would be built on the DISTRICT, DISTRIBUTOR, and EMPLOYEE tables:

```
SQL> CREATE MATERIALIZED VIEW EMP_BY_DISTRICT
  2  TABLESPACE MVIEW_DATA
  3  PARALLEL (DEGREE 2)
  4  REFRESH FAST
  5  ENABLE QUERY REWRITE
  6  AS
```

```
 7  SELECT d.id, COUNT(e.last_name)
 8  FROM distributor dist, district d, employee e
 9  WHERE e.id = dist.manager_id
10  AND d.id = dist.district_id
11  GROUP BY d.id;
Materialized view created.
```

For the complete syntax for the CREATE MATERIALIZED VIEW command see Chapter 7: SQL Statements of *Oracle8i SQL Reference, Release 8.1.5* (Part Number A67779-01).

## Managing Materialized Views

Once your materialized views are created you will need to know how to refresh, disable, and drop them.

### Refreshing Materialized Views

Materialized views can be set up to refresh manually or automatically. Manual refreshes are performed with the DBMS_MVIEW package. Automatic refreshes are accomplished by creating the materialized view with the COMMIT option or by scheduling the refresh using the DBMS_MVIEW package.

#### MANUAL REFRESHES

Refreshes can be generated manually using the DBMS_MVIEW package and one of its three procedures: REFRESH, REFRESH_DEPENDENT, REFRESH_ALL_MVIEWS. Each of these procedures is described in Table 3.19.

**TABLE 3.19** Procedures for Manual Refresh of Materialized Views

| Procedure Name | Description |
| --- | --- |
| REFRESH | Refreshes the specified materialized view |
| REFRESH_DEPENDENT | Refreshes all materialized views that utilize this table |
| REFRESH_ALL_MVIEWS | Refreshes all materialized views in the schema that have not been refreshed since the last bulk load of data to the base tables |

The following examples demonstrate the use of each of these procedures:

```
SQL> EXECUTE DBMS_MVIEW.REFRESH ('EMP_BY_DISTRICT');
PL/SQL procedure successfully completed.


SQL> EXECUTE DBMS_MVIEW.REFRESH_DEPENDENT ('EMPLOYEE');
PL/SQL procedure successfully completed.


SQL> EXECUTE DBMS_MVIEW.REFRESH_ALL_MVIEWS;
PL/SQL procedure successfully completed.
```

### AUTOMATIC REFRESHES

A materialized view that was created with the REFRESH FAST ON COMMIT or REFRESH COMPLETE ON COMMIT option will be refreshed automatically after each commit. This can cause significant overhead if the base tables involved in the query are frequently updated. You could also create the views with the REFRESH FAST ON DEMAND or REFRESH COMPLETE ON DEMAND option and then demand their refresh using the Oracle-supplied PL/SQL packages DBMS_MVIEW and DBMS_JOB. The submission of a refresh job for a materialized view called EMP_BY_DISTRICT that executes every Sunday at 2:00 am can be done using the PL/SQL procedure shown below:

```
CREATE OR REPLACE PROCEDURE refresh_emp_by_district
IS
v_job_num NUMBER;
BEGIN
DBMS_JOB.SUBMIT(
   v_job_num,
   'DBMS_MVIEW.REFRESH (''EMP_BY_DISTRICT'');',
   SYSDATE,
   'NEXT_DAY(TRUNC(SYSDATE),''SUNDAY'') + 2/24'
                );
END;
/
```

## Disabling Materialized Views

Materialized views can be disabled at the instance, session, or statement level by using one of the following four methods:

- Set the init.ora parameter QUERY_WRITE _ENABLED and restart the instance.

- Dynamically set the value of QUERY_WRITE _ENABLED using the ALTER SYSTEM command.

- Set QUERY_REWRITE_ENABLED=FALSE at the session level using the ALTER SESSION command.

- At the statement level, use the NOREWRITE hint in a query.

### Dropping Materialized Views

The following example demonstrates the syntax for dropping a materialized view:

```
SQL> DROP MATERIALIZED VIEW emp_by_district;
Materialized view dropped.
```

Dropping a materialized view does not affect any of the data in the base tables that the view was built on.

# Minimizing I/O Using Indexes and Clusters

Stored outlines and materialized views aid query performance by reducing the options that the optimizer must consider when developing an execution plan. This section deals with the other half of the query execution equation—the speed with which the data is actually retrieved once the plan is executed. One of the most effective methods for reducing the time it takes for the Oracle Server to find and return rows is achieved through the use of indexes and clusters.

## Indexes

The appropriate use of indexing is probably the single most effective tuning tool in the DBA's arsenal. This is true because indexes cut down greatly on unnecessary I/O, which contributes greatly to the response time of a query. The four index types available in Oracle8i are:

- B-Tree index

- Bitmap index

- Reverse Key Index (RKI)

- Index Organized Table (IOT)

### B-Tree Indexes

Balanced tree, or *B-Tree*, indexes are the most common type of index found in modern relational databases. B-Tree indexes sort the column data of the table columns they are built on in ascending order. In addition to the sorted column data, the B-Tree index also stores a row ID indicating where the rest of that row's data is stored in the indexed table. The index then stores these values in a tree-structured format.

For example, suppose your application had a table called EMPLOYEE that contained the following data:

```
SQL> SELECT *
  2  FROM employee;
```

| EMP_ID | LAST_NAME | FIRST_NAME | TITLE | DEPT_ID | G |
|--------|-----------|------------|-------|---------|---|
| 100 | Baker | Brenda | Dir Web Development | 601 | F |
| 101 | Douglass | Laura | Dir of Research | 301 | F |
| 102 | Schwarz | Jim | Dir of IS | 401 | M |
| 110 | Block | Robin | Corporate Counsel | 501 | F |
| 106 | Bron | Reginald | Dir of Marketing | 601 | M |
| 108 | Weishan | Matt | Technical Writer | 601 | M |
| 107 | Gastel | Tony | Oracle DBA | 401 | M |

By examining trace files and Explain Plans, you have determined that an B-Tree index on the LAST_NAME column of the table will likely help performance of querying against the EMPLOYEE table:

```
SQL> CREATE INDEX employee_last_name_idx
  2  ON employee (last_name)
  3  STORAGE (INITIAL 250K NEXT 250K PCTINCREASE 0)
  4  TABLESPACE APPL_IDX;
```

```
Index created.
```

The resulting index would store the values for the LAST_NAME column, along with the row IDs for those values, in a B-Tree structure as shown in Figure 3.5.

**FIGURE  3.5**  Index contents and structure for B-Tree Index on LAST_NAME column of EMPLOYEE

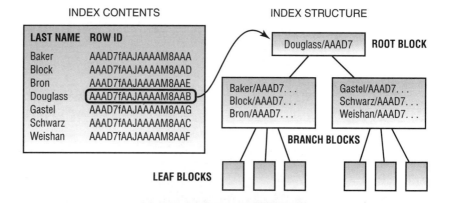

By first searching the index, which is arranged in the multi-leveled tree structure, and then accessing the required table data by row ID, costly full table scan operation is avoided and query performance is enhanced. B-Tree indexes are very useful when executing queries that will return only a small number of the overall rows found in a table. As a rule of thumb, Oracle recommends considering a B-Tree indexing strategy whenever queries frequently return less than 5 percent of the total rows in the table. The best candidates for B-Tree indexes are those columns having high cardinality in their data. These columns should also be frequently used in SQL statement WHERE clauses.

By design, B-Tree indexes are always balanced. This is true because the Oracle Server continually splits full index blocks as new values are added to the table that the index is built on. However, as insert and delete activity occurs on a table, its associated indexes can develop many levels. This tends to degrade the efficiency of the B-Tree index because it takes the Oracle Server longer to work its way from the root, or starting block, down to the level that actually contains the index entry for the data in question. You can determine how "deep" an index is by analyzing the index and then performing the following query on DBA_INDEXES:

```
SQL> SELECT index_name, blevel
  2   FROM dba_indexes
  3   WHERE blevel >= 4;
```

The above query will display all the indexes that have four or more levels between their root block and their deepest leaf blocks. These indexes are good candidates for rebuild. Rebuilding these indexes will reduce the number of levels and improve the performance of the index. You can use the following command to rebuild an index that fits this situation:

```
SQL> ALTER INDEX emp_last_namd_idx REBUILD;
```

Another indication that an index may benefit from a rebuild is evident when the deleted entries in the index represent more than 20 percent of the overall entries. When this is the case, the index is using more space than it needs to store index entries and therefore increasing the number of blocks that must be accessed to retrieve an entry. The following SQL commands show how to identify indexes with this problem:

```
SQL> ANALYZE INDEX employee_last_name_idx VALIDATE
STRUCTURE;
```

The VALIDATE STRUCTURE option for the ANALYZE command populates the data dictionary view INDEX_STATS with values. You can then query this view to see if any space is being wasted in the index:

```
SQL> SELECT (DEL_LF_ROWS_LEN/LF_ROWS_LEN) * 100
  2   "Wasted Space"
  3   FROM index_stats
  4   WHERE index_name = 'EMPLOYEE_LAST_NAME_IDX';

     Wasted Space
     -----------
             34
```

Using this calculation, Oracle recommends rebuilding any index whose wasted space exceeds 20 percent.

For more information on the ALTER INDEX ... REBUILD and the ALTER INDEX ... VALIDATE STRUCTURE commands see Chapter 16: Managing Indexes of *Oracle8i Administrator's Guide, Release 8.1.5* (Part Number A67772-01).

### Bitmap Indexes

B-Tree indexes work best on columns whose data has high cardinality. For columns with low cardinality, a *Bitmap* index may be a more effective indexing option. Unlike B-Tree indexes, Bitmap indexes create a binary mapping of the rows in the table and store that map in the index blocks. This means the resulting index will require significantly less space to store the index data and retrieves the rows of an equality match on the indexed column more quickly than an equivalent B-Tree index.

For example, if you decide from your examination of trace files and Explain Plans that an index should be built on the GENDER column of the EMPLOYEE table, a Bitmap index would be a good choice because the column's data has low cardinality. This is true because only two possible values, M or F, are allowed for this column:

```
SQL> SELECT *
  2   FROM employee;
```

```
EMP_ID LAST_NAME   FIRST_NAME TITLE                DEPT_ID G
------ ----------  ---------- -------------------- ------- -
100 Baker          Brenda     Dir Web Development   601 F
101 Douglass       Laura      Dir of Research       301 F
102 Jim            Schwarz    Dir of IS             401 M
110 Block          Robin      Corporate Counsel     501 F
106 Bron           Reginald   Dir of Marketing      601 M
108 Weishan        Matt       Technical Writer      601 M
107 Gastel         Tony       Oracle DBA            401 M
```

```
SQL> CREATE BITMAP INDEX employee_gender_idx
  2    ON employee (gender)
  3    STORAGE (INITIAL 50K NEXT 50K PCTINCREASE 0)
  4    TABLESPACE APPL_IDX;
```

The Bitmap index would then store the two possible values and the binary mapping for each value as it relates to the column data. The bitmap index stores a 1 if the value is true for that row, and a 0 if it is not. Figure 3.6 shows the manner in which a Bitmap index would store the data from the GENDER column.

**FIGURE 3.6**  Bitmap Index for GENDER column

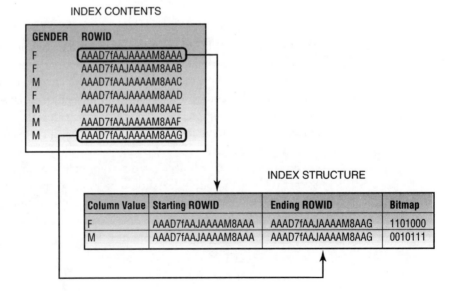

Subsequent queries on EMPLOYEE that include an equality match on GENDER in the WHERE clause can now locate all row IDs of the rows that satisfy the query with only one I/O.

Bitmap indexes should not be used on tables that have high INSERT, UPDATE, or DELETE activity. These DML operations are costly in terms of performance because they require that the entire bitmap for all possible values be rebuilt dynamically. However, each bitmap is only updated once per DML activity, even when several rows are changed.

Consideration should be given to the SORT_AREA_SIZE, CREATE_BITMAP_AREA_SIZE, and BITMAP_MERGE_AREA_SIZE init.ora parameters whenever bitmap indexes are used. Increasing the size of each of these parameters generally enhances the speed with which bitmap indexes can be created and manipulated. These three parameters are described in Table 3.20.

**TABLE 3.20** Important init.ora Parameters Related to Bitmap Indexes

| Parameter | Description |
| --- | --- |
| SORT_AREA_SIZE | Size in bytes of the buffer where sorted bitmap column and row ID information is stored until batch commit |
| CREATE_BITMAP_AREA_ SIZE | Amount of memory, in bytes, assigned to bitmap creation |
| BITMAP_MERGE_AREA_ SIZE | Amount of memory allocated for bitmap merges following an index range scan |

### Reverse Key Indexes

The *Reverse Key Index (RKI)* is a special type of B-Tree index. The RKI is useful when an index is built on a column that contains sequential numbers. If a traditional B-Tree index is built on a column containing this type of data, the index tends to develop many levels. Since having more than four levels of depth in a B-Tree can degrade performance, an RKI is well suited to this situation.

Reverse Key indexes solve this problem by simply reversing the data in the indexed column, and then indexing on the new reversed data, which is generally more evenly distributed across a range of values than the original sequential data was. If you have determined that an index is needed on the EMP_ID column of the EMPLOYEE table, a Reverse Key index would be appropriate since the data is sequential:

```
SQL> SELECT *
  2  FROM employee;


EMP_ID LAST_NAME  FIRST_NAME TITLE                DEPT_ID G
------ ---------- ---------- -------------------- ------- -
   100 Baker      Brenda     Dir Web Development      601 F
   101 Douglass   Laura      Dir of Research         301 F
   102 Jim        Schwarz    Dir of IS               401 M
   110 Block      Robin      Corporate Counsel       501 F
   106 Bron       Reginald   Dir of Marketing        601 M
   108 Weishan    Matt       Technical Writer        601 M
   107 Gastel     Tony       Oracle DBA              401 M


SQL> CREATE INDEX employee_emp_id_idx
  2  ON employee (emp_id)
  3  REVERSE
  4  STORAGE (INITIAL 250K NEXT 250K PCTINCREASE 0)
  5  TABLESPACE APPL_IDX;

Index created.
```

Figure 3.7 shows an example of how an RKI on the EMP_ID column of the EMPLOYEE table would look internally.

**FIGURE 3.7** Reverse Key index on EMPLOYEE_ID

ORIGINAL & REVERSED KEYS

| ORIGINAL ID | REVERSED ID | ROWID |
|---|---|---|
| 100 | 001 | AAAD7fAAJAAAAM8AAA |
| 101 | 101 | AAAD7fAAJAAAAM8AAB |
| 102 | 201 | AAAD7fAAJAAAAM8AAC |
| 110 | 011 | AAAD7fAAJAAAAM8AAD |
| 106 | 601 | AAAD7fAAJAAAAM8AAE |
| 108 | 801 | AAAD7fAAJAAAAM8AAF |
| 107 | 701 | AAAD7fAAJAAAAM8AAG |

RESULTING INDEX CONTENTS

| ORIGINAL ID | REVERSED ID | ROWID |
|---|---|---|
| 100 | 001 | AAAD7fAAJAAAAM8AAA |
| | 011 | AAAD7fAAJAAAAM8AAD |
| 101 | 101 | AAAD7fAAJAAAAM8AAB |
| | 201 | AAAD7fAAJAAAAM8AAC |
| 106 | 601 | AAAD7fAAJAAAAM8AAE |
| 107 | 701 | AAAD7fAAJAAAAM8AAG |
| 108 | 801 | AAAD7fAAJAAAAM8AAF |

The fact that an index is reverse-keyed is transparent to the application developer and the user. No special syntax is required to use it in your queries.

Because of the reversed values stored in the index, queries that perform range scans on columns (i.e. using BETWEEN, >, <, etc.) that are Reverse Key indexed will experience full table scans

### Index Organized Tables

You will recall that the performance gain offered by the use of B-Tree indexes resulted from the fact that the index entry points directly to the row ID of the row data in the underlying table. *Index Organized Tables (IOT)* take this idea one step further. Instead of storing a row ID pointer to where the rest of the row data is stored, the row data is actually stored in its entirety in the index itself. Therefore, the extra I/O caused by reading the index and then the table is eliminated, because the data in an IOT has the additional benefit of being stored in a B-Tree structure. If you frequently access the data in a table using its primary key, an IOT will return the rows more quickly than a traditional table.

Suppose you have decided to create a new application table called EMPLOYEE_HISTORY that will store employee information by EMP_ID. Since you expect to access this table by EMP_ID, an IOT might be a good choice for creating this table:

```
SQL> CREATE TABLE employee_history
  2   (employee_id number primary key,
  3    last_name varchar2(20),
  4    first_name varchar2(20),
  5    title varchar2(30),
  6    hire_date date,
  7    departure_date date)
  8   ORGANIZATION INDEX TABLESPACE appl_idx
  9   PCTTHRESHOLD 25
 10   INCLUDING first_name
 11   OVERFLOW TABLESPACE appl_of;

Table created.
```

The important parts of the CREATE TABLE syntax that are related to IOT creation are summarized in Table 3.21.

**TABLE 3.21** Syntax for Index IOT Creation

| Clause | Description |
| --- | --- |
| ORGANIZATION INDEX | Specifies that this table is an IOT table |
| PCTTHRESHOLD | Specifies what percentage of the entire data block to hold open in order to store the row data associated with a primary key value |

**TABLE 3.21**    Syntax for Index IOT Creation *(continued)*

| Clause | Description |
|---|---|
| INCLUDING | Specifies at which column to break a row into two pieces when a row's length exceeds the size set aside in PCTTHRESHOLD |
| OVERFLOW TABLESPACE | Specifies the tablespace where the second half of the row data will be stored when the row's length exceeds the size set aside in PCTTHRESHOLD |

After populating this table with data, the contents might look something like those shown in Figure 3.8.

**FIGURE 3.8**    Contents of the EMPLOYEE_HISTORY table

```
SQL> SELECT *
  2  FROM employee_history;

EMPLOYEE_ID LAST_NAM FIRST_NA TITLE                                            HIRE_DATE DEPART
----------- -------- -------- ------------------------------------------------ --------- ------
        100 Baker    Brenda   Dir of Web Dev                                   07-FEB-98
        101 Douglass Laura    Dir of Research                                  10-JAN-97 11-JUN
        102 Schwarz  Jim      Dir of IS                                        13-MAR-98
        106 Bron     Reginald Dir of Marketing                                 29-NOV-96
        107 Gastel   Tony     Oracle DBA                                       11-JUL-97
        108 Weishan  Matt     Technical Writer                                 23-NOV-99 15-MAY
        110 Block    Robin    Corporate Counsel                                03-JUN-96
        112 Macomber Bart     Head Honcho Big Cheese Boss Guy and Supreme Leader 07-FEB-98
```

Figure 3.9 shows how the data for this table would be physically stored between the IOT Segment and the IOT Overflow Segment.

**FIGURE 3.9**    Physical storage of the EMPLOYEE_HISTORY data

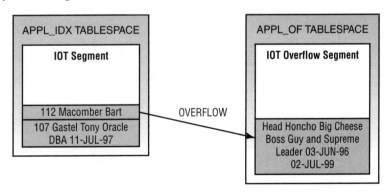

Notice in Figure 3.9 that the entire row of data associated with employee 107, Gastel, fits into one of the blocks allocated to the EMPLOYEE_HISTORY IOT. However, employee 112, Macomber, has a title that is too long to fit into the space reserved by PCTTHRESHOLD. Therefore, the row for Macomber is cut off at the INCLUDING column (FIRST_NAME), and the remaining row data is instead stored in a block belonging to the overflow segment in another tablespace. Finding the name of this overflow segment is discussed in the following section.

## Index Data Dictionary Views

The data dictionary views DBA_INDEXES, DBA_SEGMENTS, and DBA_TABLES all contain information about one or more of the index types you have seen so far. Sample queries showing index information on the indexes we have just discussed are shown in Figure 3.10.

**FIGURE 3.10**   Sample query showing index types

```
SQL> SELECT index_name,
  2         index_type,
  3         table_name
  4  FROM   dba_indexes
  5  WHERE  table_name in
  6         ('EMPLOYEE','EMPLOYEE_HISTORY');

INDEX_NAME                      INDEX_TYPE              TABLE_NAME
------------------------------  ----------------------  ------------------
EMPLOYEE_LAST_NAME_IDX          NORMAL                  EMPLOYEE
EMPLOYEE_GENDER_IDX             BITMAP                  EMPLOYEE
EMPLOYEE_EMPLOYEE_ID_IDX        NORMAL/REV              EMPLOYEE
SYS_IOT_TOP_16102               IOT - TOP               EMPLOYEE_HISTORY
```

Note that the type of index is indicated in the INDEX_TYPE column: NORMAL for regular B-Tree, BITMAP for Bitmap, NORMAL/REV for Reverse Key, and IOT-TOP for the index segment of an Index Organized Table. The only information lacking in this query is specifics on the overflow segment for the IOT. This information is available from DBA_SEGMENTS, as shown below.

```
SQL> SELECT segment_name,
  2    segment_type,
  3    tablespace_name
  4  FROM dba_segments
  5  WHERE segment_name LIKE '%IOT%';


SEGMENT_NAME          SEGMENT_TYPE  TABLESPACE_NAME
--------------------  ------------  ----------------
SYS_IOT_OVER_16102    TABLE         APPL_OF
SYS_IOT_TOP_16102     INDEX         APPL_IDX
```

This query shows the two components of the IOT EMPLOYEE_HISTORY: the index itself, SYS_IOT_TOP_16102, and the overflow segment SYS_IOT_OVER_16102. The numeric portion of the names was system generated at the creation of the IOT. In order to more clearly see the relationship between an IOT and its associated overflow segment we can query DBA_TABLES, as shown below.

```
SQL> SELECT table_name,
  2  iot_name,
  3  iot_type,
  4  tablespace_name
  5  FROM dba_tables
  6  WHERE table_name = 'EMPLOYEE_HISTORY'
  7  OR iot_name = 'EMPLOYEE_HISTORY';


TABLE_NAME          IOT_NAME          IOT_TYPE     TABLESPACE
------------------  ----------------  ------------ ----------
EMPLOYEE_HISTORY                      IOT
SYS_IOT_OVER_16102  EMPLOYEE_HISTORY  IOT_OVERFLOW APPL_OF
```

Note that the table SYS_IOT_OVER_16102 has the entry EMPLOYEE_HISTORY as its associated table. Further, observe that the entry for TABLESPACE_NAME for the EMPLOYEE_HISTORY table is NULL since the actual segment that stores the data is an index, not a table.

## Index and Hash Clusters

Indexes improve the performance of queries because they eliminate full table scans by directing Oracle to the precise location on the requested rows. This reduces the total number of data blocks that must be read in order to satisfy a query. A second mechanism for improving performance by minimizing I/O can be effected through the use of clusters. A *cluster* is a group of one or more tables whose data is stored together in the same data blocks. In this way, queries that utilize these tables via a table join don't have to read two sets of data blocks to get their results; they only have to read one. There are two types of clusters available in Oracle8i: the Index cluster and the Hash cluster.

### Index Clusters

*Index clusters* are used to store the data from one or more tables in the same physical Oracle blocks. The usefulness of clusters is limited to very specific situations. In general, clustered tables should:

- Always be queried together and only infrequently on their own

- Have little or no DML activity performed on them after the initial load

- Have roughly equal numbers of child records for each parent key

If you have tables that meet these criteria, you may want to consider creating an Index cluster to store the data for these tables. Clustered tables behave just like unclustered tables, but their storage space is taken not from a tablespace, but from a cluster, which itself is a segment stored in a tablespace. The cluster is accessed via an index that contains entries that point to the specific key values on which the tables are joined (i.e. clustered).

Suppose you have two tables, TEACHER and STUDENT, that contain the following data:

```
SQL> SELECT *
  2  FROM teacher;
```

| TEACHER_ID | LAST_NAME | FIRST_NAME | ROOM_NUMBER |
| ---------- | --------- | ---------- | ----------- |
| 100 | Viola | Bangasser | 222 |
| 101 | Jeanne | Massingil | 223 |
| 102 | Jennings | Steve | 224 |
| 103 | Dortch | Neil | 225 |

```
SQL> SELECT *
  2  FROM student;
```

| STUDENT_ID | LAST_NAME | FIRST_NAME | TEACHER_ID |
| ---------- | --------- | ---------- | ---------- |
| 345891001 | Anderson | Jerry | 100 |
| 345097651 | Smith | Audrey | 100 |
| 348990122 | Johnson | Emily | 100 |
| 365778012 | Anderson | Ian | 100 |
| 368791033 | St. Ubbins | David | 100 |
| . | | | |
| . | | | |
| . | | | |
| 368211431 | Smalls | Derek | 103 |

You have noticed that the application rarely retrieves teacher information without the accompanying student information. If the number of students per teacher is uniform, you may decide to cluster the data from these two tables into the same physical blocks to improve query performance. The following example shows the SQL statements required to create a cluster called TEACHER_STUDENT, an index on the cluster called TEACHER_STUDENT_IDX, and tables TEACHER and STUDENT in the cluster:

```
SQL> CREATE CLUSTER teacher_student
  2  (teacher_id number)
  3  SIZE 1000
  4  STORAGE (initial 500K next 500K pctincrease 0);
  5  TABLESPACE apps_clst;

Cluster created.
```

The above command creates a cluster called TEACHER_STUDENT and specifies that the column TEACHER_ID will be the cluster key or column around which the two table's data will be clustered. This column was chosen because it will be the column that the TEACHER and STUDENT tables will have in common. The parameter SIZE specifies how many cluster keys we expect to have per Oracle block. If we have a 2048-byte (2K) Oracle block size, then this parameter indicates that we expect to get about two (2048/1000 = 2.048) cluster keys per block. In other words, you expect to store the data for two teachers and all of their students in each Oracle block. Choosing the proper value for SIZE is difficult if all the cluster key values (teachers) don't have the same number of clustered records (students). However, setting this value properly is critical to gaining optimal cluster performance:

```
SQL> CREATE INDEX TEACHER_STUDENT_IDX
  2  ON CLUSTER teacher_student
  3  TABLESPACE apps_idx;

Index created.
```

Notice that the indexed column is not specified when creating an index on a cluster segment. The index is automatically created on the cluster key column, TEACHER_ID.

Now that the cluster structure exists, you can create the TEACHER and STUDENT tables in the cluster:

```
SQL> CREATE TABLE TEACHER
  2  (teacher_id number,
  3   last_name varchar2(20),
  4   first_name varchar2(20),
```

```
    5   room_number number)
    6  CLUSTER teacher_student
    7  (teacher_id);
```

Table created.

```
SQL> CREATE TABLE student
    2  (student_id number,
    3   last_name varchar2(20),
    4   first_name varchar2(20),
    5   teacher_id number)
    6  CLUSTER teacher_student
    7  (teacher_id);
```

Table created.

Note that no tablespace specification is given when creating the tables in the cluster. This is not because we want to use the default tablespace for the user, but because the cluster itself is the storage area for each table's data. In this way, any data inserted into the TEACHER or STUDENT table will be stored in the same physical blocks—the blocks of the cluster segment they are contained in. Figure 3.11 shows the relationship between two clustered tables, the cluster itself, the cluster index, and the tablespaces they are both stored in.

**FIGURE 3.11**   Index cluster and table relationship

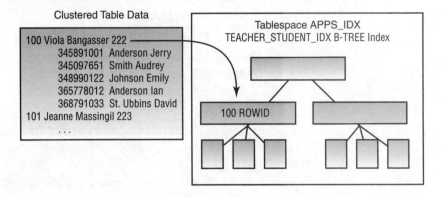

### Hash Clusters

*Hash clusters* are used in place of a traditional index to quickly find rows stored in a table. Rather than examine an index and then retrieve the rows from a table, a Hash cluster's data is stored so queries against the cluster can use a hashing algorithm to determine directly where a row is stored with no intervening index required.

Comparing the differences between a Hash cluster and non-Hash cluster table, assume you issue the following query on the EMPLOYEE table:

```
SQL> SELECT *
2  FROM employee
3  WHERE emp_id = 100;
```

If the EMPLOYEE table were created as a non-Hash cluster table, a query like this would result in the following operations:

- Find the EMP_ID in the index on the EMP_ID column.

- Use the row ID value stored in the index to locate the row in the table.

- Read the row from the table, and return the information to the user.

This requires at least two I/Os to retrieve the row information, one (or more) on the index and one on the table. If, however, this table was created using a Hash cluster, then the query would involve these operations instead:

- The value in the WHERE clause (100) is passed through the same hashing algorithm that is used when inserting rows. This process occurs in memory and requires no I/O. The resulting value produced by the algorithm points directly to the location of the row in the table.

- The row is read, and the information is returned to the user.

In this case, only one I/O was required to retrieve the row, instead of the two or more with the traditional table/B-Tree index combination.

Careful testing should be performed before implementing Index clusters and Hash clusters. Trying to apply them when the table data is not appropriate for their usage, or specifying their storage parameters incorrectly at cluster creation, can actually hinder performance instead of improve it.

# OLTP vs. DSS Tuning Requirements

**S**o far, you have examined the indexing techniques available to you for improving query execution. Now it is time to consider how the appropriateness of those options differs when considering the two primary types of database systems in use today: Online Transaction Processing Systems and Decision Support Systems.

## Transactional Tuning Considerations

*Online Transaction Processing Systems* (OLTP) tend to be accessed by large numbers of users doing short DML transactions. Order taking, inventory management, and scheduling systems are all examples of OLTP systems. Users of OLTP systems are primarily concerned with throughput: the total time it takes place and order, remove an item from inventory, or schedule an appointment.

OLTP systems need enough B-Tree indexes to meet performance goals but not so many as to slow down the performance of INSERT, UPDATE, and DELETE activity. The table and index statistics should be gathered regularly if the CBO is used because data volumes tend to change quickly in OLTP systems.

## Decision Support Tuning Considerations

*Decision Support Systems* (DSS) and data warehouses represent the other end of the tuning spectrum. These systems tend to have very little if any INSERT, UPDATE, and DELETE activity, except when data is mass loaded or purged at the end of the week, month, quarter, or year. Users of these systems are concerned with response time, which is the time it takes to get the results from their queries.

DSS makes heavy use of full table scans so the appropriate use of indexes and Hash clusters are important. Index Organized Tables can also be important tuning options for large DSS systems. Bitmap indexes may be considered where the column data has low cardinality but is frequently used as the basis for queries. Thought should also be given to selecting the appropriate optimizer mode and gathering new statistics whenever data is loaded or purged. The use of histograms may also help improve DSS response time. Finally, consideration should be given to database block size, init.ora parameters related to sorting, and the possible use of the Oracle Parallel Query option.

## Hybrid Systems: OLTP and DSS

Some systems are a combination of both OLTP and DSS. These *hybrid* systems can present a significant challenge because the tuning options that help one type of system frequently hinder the other. However, through the careful use of indexing and resource management, some level of coexistence can usually be achieved. As the demands on each of these systems grows, you will probably ultimately have to split the two types of systems into two separate environments in order to meet the needs of both user communities.

# Summary

Understanding how to use TKPROF, Explain Plans, and AUTOTRACE to analyze application SQL processing is important for every DBA. These tools allow you to understand not only how the application SQL is being executed, but also what resource costs are associated with those executions.

One major determinant of database performance is the extent to which the Oracle optimizer makes good SQL execution choices. These choices are influenced by the optimizer mode and the presence or absence of database statistics. These statistics can be gathered at the segment, schema, or database level. The statistics can also be moved between databases so that testing of optimizer behavior can be done with realistic data.

A variety of methods are available to improve application performance. These methods include: stored outlines, materialized views, B-Tree indexes, Bitmap indexes, Reverse Key indexes, Index Organized Tables, Index clusters, and Hash clusters. The appropriateness of these options varies with the type of system managed. OLTP systems have different indexing strategies than DSS environments.

## Key Terms

Before you take the exam, make sure you're familiar with the following terms:

TKPROF

parse

execute

fetch

AUTOTRACE

rule-based optimizer

cost-based optimizer

hints

materialized view

B-Tree

Bitmap

Reverse Key Index (RKI)

Index Organized Table (IOT)

cluster

Hash cluster

Online Transaction Processing

Decision Support System

# Review Questions

1. Which of the following utilities allows you to see how much CPU time a SQL statement spent parsing, executing, and fetching?

   **A.** AUTOTRACE

   **B.** Explain Plan

   **C.** TKPROF

   **D.** Materialize view

2. Which of the following types of SQL statements has a Fetch phase?

   **A.** Select

   **B.** Insert

   **C.** Update

   **D.** Delete

3. TKPROF output can be sorted by all of the following except:

   **A.** Parse elapsed time

   **B.** Network elapsed time

   **C.** Fetch elapsed time

   **D.** Execution elapsed time

4. In order for the TKPROF output to include timing information, which init.ora parameter must be set to TRUE?

   **A.** TIMINGS

   **B.** TIME_QUERY

   **C.** STATISTICS

   **D.** TIMED_STATISTICS

5. Some execution plans show all blocks from a table being accessed in order to satisfy a query. This type of table access is called a:

   **A.** Full table scan

   **B.** Nested loop

   **C.** Range scan

   **D.** None of the above

6. Which of the following methods of SQL execution plan analysis actually executes the statement before displaying the statement's execution plan?

   **A.** TKPROF

   **B.** AUTOTRACE

   **C.** EXPLAIN PLAN FOR

   **D.** DBMS_STATS

7. Which of the following roles needs to be granted to a user before they can use the AUTOTRACE command?

   **A.** RESOURCE

   **B.** PLUSTRACE

   **C.** CONNECT

   **D.** CREATE SESSION

8. Which of the following is *not* a valid value for the init.ora parameter OPTIMIZER_MODE?

   **A.** COST

   **B.** RULE

   **C.** CHOOSE

   **D.** All of the above are valid values.

9. If the `init.ora` optimizer mode is set to CHOOSE, but no statistics have been gathered for the application's tables and indexes, which optimizer mode will Oracle use?

   **A.** Cost

   **B.** Rule

   **C.** Hint

   **D.** None of the above

10. Which of the following Oracle-supplied packages can be used to analyze all the objects in a particular schema?

    **A.** DBMS_PACKAGE

    **B.** DBMS_STATS

    **C.** DBMS_SYSTEM

    **D.** DBMS_ANALYZE

11. Following an ANALYZE command, which of the following data dictionary views will contain statistics on the number of rows in a table?

    **A.** DBA_ROWS

    **B.** DBA_TABLE_ROWS

    **C.** DBA_TABLES

    **D.** DBA_STATISTICS

12. Histograms are useful because they allow the optimizer to have a better idea of how the data in an indexed column is:

    **A.** Sorted

    **B.** Named

    **C.** Entered

    **D.** Distributed

13. The optimizer mode can be set at which of the following levels?

    **A.** Instance

    **B.** Session

    **C.** Statement

    **D.** All of the above

14. The ability to store predefined execution plans so that the optimizer knows in advance which execution plan is best is called:

    **A.** Stored outlines

    **B.** Materialized views

    **C.** Hash cluster

    **D.** Index Organized Table

15. If you do not specify which category a stored outline belongs to, which category will it be assigned to?

    **A.** SYSTEM

    **B.** TEMP

    **C.** USERS

    **D.** DEFAULT

16. If a materialized view is refreshed each time a commit occurs in one of the tables that the view is based on, then this view was created with which option?

    **A.** REFRESH SYNC

    **B.** REFRESH FAST

    **C.** REFRESH COMPLETE

    **D.** REFRESH TOTAL

17. Which `init.ora` parameter must be set to TRUE if materialized views are to be used?

    **A.** FAST_REFRESH

    **B.** QUERY_REWRITE

    **C.** QUERY_REWITE_ENABLED

    **D.** MATERIALIZED_VIEWS

18. Which of the following types of indexes stores the indexed column's values and associated row IDs as a binary string?

    **A.** B-Tree index

    **B.** Reverse Key index

    **C.** Bitmap index

    **D.** Bitwise index

19. Which of the following factors would not make a column a good candidate for a B-Tree index?

    **A.** The data in the column has low cardinality.

    **B.** The column is frequently used in SQL statement WHERE clauses.

    **C.** Most queries on the table return only a small portion of all rows.

    **D.** None of the above.

20. Index Organized Tables store row data that exceeds the index's PCTTHRESHOLD in what type of segment?

    **A.** Chain Segment

    **B.** Excess Segment

    **C.** Overflow Segment

    **D.** Index segment

# Answers to Review Questions

1. C. After formatting a user trace file using TKPROF, the formatted trace file will contain timings for both CPU and elapsed time for the Parse, Execute, and Fetch phases of a query (assuming the init.ora parameter TIMED_STATISTICS = TRUE).

2. A. Only Select statements perform a fetch operation.

3. B. A number of TKPROF sort options exist for the parse, execute, and fetch phases. TKPROF does not include any network timings.

4. D. If the init.ora parameter TIMED_STATISTICS is not set to TRUE, then all timings in a formatted TKPROF file will be 0.

5. A. Full table scans cause Oracle to read every row of a table. When full table scans are performed on a table, but very few of the total rows in the table are returned by the query, an appropriate indexing strategy should be investigated.

6. B. AUTOTRACE always executes the SQL being examined, even if the TRACEONLY option is used.

7. B. The PLUSTRACE role must be granted to users who wish to use the AUTOTRACE command. This role is created by running the plustrce.sql script while connected as the user SYS.

8. A. The valid optimizer modes for the init.ora are RULE, CHOOSE, FIRST_ROWS, and ALL_ROWS.

9. B. Even if the optimizer mode is set to CHOOSE in the init.ora, the rule-based optimization will be used if statistics do not exist.

10. B. The DBMS_STATS package can be used to analyze all the objects in a given schema, index, or the entire database.

**11.** C. The DBA_TABLES data dictionary view also contains statistics about the number of blocks the table uses, and the average length of each table row.

**12.** D. Histograms offer a better view of how data is distributed by dividing the column data into pieces before analyzing the data within each piece.

**13.** D. The optimizer mode can be set at the instance level using the init.ora parameter OPTIMIZER_MODE, at the session level using the ALTER SESSION command, or at the statement level using hints.

**14.** A. Stored outlines use the execution plan that was generated at their creation for any subsequent SQL statements that match the original SQL statement exactly.

**15.** D. Unless a category is assigned, stored outlines will be stored in the DEFAULT category. Stored outlines can be moved to another category using the OUTLN_PKG.UPDATE_BY_CAT package.

**16.** C. The REFRESH COMPLETE option causes a materialize view to be refreshed with each commit on the underlying tables. The REFRESH FAST option only updates the view with the data that has been added since the last refresh.

**17.** C. Materialized views can also be enabled at the statement level by using the /*+ REWRITE */ hint.

**18.** C. Bitmap indexes store their indexed column values as a binary string of 1s and 0s.

**19.** A. Columns with high cardinality are best suited for B-Tree indexing. Columns with low cardinality are better suited for Bitmap indexes.

**20.** C. Oracle will store any row whose length exceeds the value of PCTTHRESHOLD in an overflow segment. The first part of the row, up to the column specified in the INCLUDING clause is stored in the index. The remainder of the row is stored in the overflow segment.

# Tuning the Shared Pool

## ORACLE8i PERFORMANCE TUNING EXAM OBJECTIVES COVERED IN THIS CHAPTER:

✓ Tune the Library Cache and the Data Dictionary Cache.

✓ Measure the Shared Pool hit ratio.

✓ Size the Shared Pool appropriately.

✓ Pin objects in the Shared Pool.

✓ Tune the Shared Pool reserved space.

✓ Describe the User Global Area (UGA) and session memory considerations.

✓ Configure the large pool.

Exam objectives are subject to change at any time without prior notice and at Oracle's sole discretion. Please visit Oracle's Training and Certification Web site (http://education .oracle.com/certification/index.html) for the most current exam objectives listing.

he previous chapter showed how to identify and remedy performance bottlenecks in an application's SQL code. This is a very important part of database tuning, as rewriting poorly performing SQL can make a huge difference in how well an Oracle-based application performs. However, what if your application is a purchased, third-party application, an application that does not lend itself to modifications of the delivered code? In these cases, you have options when it comes to tuning:

- Complain to the vendor and hope they do something about the poor performance.

- Add your own indexes to the delivered product in the hopes that they will improve performance.

- Tune Oracle's shared memory structure, the SGA, and try to improve application performance by minimizing the overhead associated with SQL statement processing and the accessing of the application's data and index blocks.

The last option falls into the category addressed by the next step in the Oracle tuning methodology:

Step 7:Tuning Memory Allocation

The next three chapters will address the issue of tuning Oracle's memory allocation. This chapter deals with tuning the Shared Pool; Chapter 5 discusses tuning the Database Buffer Cache, and Chapter 6 covers tuning the Redo Log Buffer.

# Understanding the Shared Pool

T he *Shared Pool* is the portion of the SGA that caches the SQL and PL/ SQL statements that have been recently issued by application users. The Shared Pool is managed by a *Least Recently Used (LRU)* algorithm. Once the Shared Pool is full, this algorithm makes room for subsequent SQL statements by aging out the statements which have been least recently accessed. In this manner, the Oracle server keeps the "popular" SQL and PL/SQL statements in the Shared Pool while the less commonly used statements are phased out. By caching these frequently used statements in memory, an application user who issues the same SQL or PL/SQL statement as that of a previous user benefits from the fact that the statement is already in memory, ready to be executed. This is very useful for the subsequent application user as that user can skip some of the overhead that was incurred when the statement was originally issued.

## The Benefits of Statement Caching

When an application user issues an SQL or PL/SQL statement against an Oracle instance, several operations take place before the statement is actually executed. For example, let's examine what happens when the following SQL statement is issued:

```
SQL> SELECT last_name, first_name
  2  FROM customers
  3  WHERE customer_id = 2201;
```

First, Oracle converts the characters in the statement to their ASCII equivalent numeric codes. Next, this string of ASCII characters is passed through a hashing algorithm, which in turn produces a single hashed value. The user's Server Process then checks to see if that hashed value already exists in the Shared Pool. If it does, the user's Server Process uses the cached version of the statement to execute the statement. If the hashed value does not exist in the Shared Pool, the user's Server Process goes about the process of parsing the statement, then executes it. This extra step of parsing adds overhead to each SQL operation because the parse step must:

- Check the statement for syntactic correctness

- Perform object resolution where the names and structures of the referenced objects are checked against the data dictionary

- Gather statistics regarding the objects referenced in the query by examining the data dictionary

- Prepare and select an execution plan from among the available plans, including the determination of whether Stored Outlines or Materialized views are relevant

- Determine the security for the objects referenced in the query by examining the data dictionary

- Generate a compiled version of the statement (called *P-Code*)

The parse operation is expensive because of this extra preparation. Parsing can be avoided by making sure that most statements find a parsed version of themselves already in the Shared Pool. Finding a matching SQL statement in the Shared Pool is referred to as a *cache hit*. Not finding a matching statement and having to perform the parse operation is considered a *cache miss*. In order for a cache hit to occur, the two SQL statements must match *exactly*; the ASCII equivalents of the two statements must be identical for them to hash to the same value in the Shared Pool. Therefore, even a minor difference between two statements, like lowercase versus uppercase, will cause a cache miss to occur. Maximizing cache hits and minimizing cache misses is the goal of all Shared Pool tuning.

However, before you can begin to tune the Shared Pool, you must first understand what functions each of the components of the Shared Pool performs.

# Components of the Shared Pool

The Shared Pool is made up of three components: the Library Cache, the Data Dictionary Cache, and the User Global Area. Each of these components plays a role in the performance of SQL and PL/SQL statements.

## Library Cache

The Shared Pool's *Library Cache* is the location where Oracle caches the SQL and PL/SQL statements that have been recently issued by application users. PL/SQL statements can be in the form of procedures, functions, packages, triggers, anonymous PL/SQL blocks, or JAVA classes. Once cached, these cached statements have several components:

- The actual text of the statement itself

- The hashed value associated with the statement

- The P-code for the statement

- Any statistics associated with the statement
- The execution plan for the statement

Many of these components for the statement issued earlier can be viewed in the V$SQLAREA dynamic performance view as shown in the following query:

```
SQL> SELECT sql_text, hash_value, optimizer_mode
  2  FROM v$sqlarea
  3  WHERE users_executing !=0


SQL_TEXT                        HASH_VALUE OPTIMIZER_MODE
------------------------------- ---------- --------------
SELECT last_name, first_name 1.603E+09  CHOOSE
FROM customer
WHERE customer_id = '2201'
```

This view can also be used to see which statements application users are actually issuing against the instance at that moment in time, how many times a statement has been issued, and how many disk and buffer reads and sorts a statement did. The V$SQLAREA view contains only the first eighty characters of the SQL or PL/SQL statements that are being issued. The complete text of these SQL or PL/SQL statements can be found in the SQL_TEXT column of the data dictionary view V$SQLTEXT.

 Since they are dynamic performance views, the V$SQLAREA and V$SQLTEXT views will only show information for statements that are actually executing at the moment you query them.

If you are only looking for more general information about the types of SQL statements application users are issuing, you can use the V$SESSION view. This view contains a COMMAND column, which can be used to identify generically the type of statement a user is issuing. There are 100 possible values for COMMAND; each represents a different type of SQL command. Table 4.1 shows a sample of some of the values that you may want to use when querying the COMMAND column in this view.

**TABLE 4.1** Values for COMMAND in V$SESSION

| Command | Description |
| --- | --- |
| 2 | Insert |
| 3 | Select |

**TABLE 4.1** Values for COMMAND in V$SESSION *(continued)*

| Command | Description |
| --- | --- |
| 6 | Update |
| 7 | Delete |
| 26 | Lock table |
| 44 | Commit |
| 45 | Rollback |
| 47 | PL/SQL Execute |

For example, you could use the following query on the V$SESSION view to see which users are currently issuing UPDATE commands:

```
SQL> SELECT username
  2  FROM v$session
  3  WHERE command = 6;


USERNAME
--------
ZOE
MAX
ROBIN
JIM
```

Detailed information and the dynamic performance views V$SQLAREA, V$SQLTEXT, and V$SESSION can be found in Chapter 3: Dynamic Performance (V$) Views of *Oracle8i Reference, Release 8.1.5* (Part Number A67790-01).

## Data Dictionary Cache

Whenever an SQL or PL/SQL statement is issued, the data dictionary must also be examined to make sure that the tables referenced in the statement exist, that the column names and data types are correct, and that the application user issuing the statement has sufficient privileges on the segments involved. Like the statement itself, this information is also cached in memory in the Shared Pool's *Data Dictionary Cache*. This memory area is also managed using an LRU mechanism.

By using the Data Dictionary Cache, the Oracle Server caches the data dictionary information in a separate memory area than it does the associated SQL statements. This is useful for two reasons:

- The LRU mechanisms for the Library Cache and Data Dictionary Cache work independently. This tends to keep data dictionary information in memory longer.

- Subsequent application users who issue similar, but not identical statements as previous users benefit from the fact that the data dictionary information associated with the tables in their statement may be in memory—even if the actual statement is not.

### User Global Area

The User Global Area (UGA) is only present in the Shared Pool if Oracle's Multithreaded Server (MTS) option is being used. In the MTS architecture, the *User Global Area* is used to cache application user session information. This information must be in a shared location because the MTS architecture uses several different shared server processes to process SQL and PL/SQL activity against the instance. Since the shared server process that starts a transaction may not be the one that also finishes it, access to this session information must be stored in the UGA. In a non-MTS or dedicated server situation, this session information is maintained in the application user's private *Process Global Area* or PGA.

See "Tuning Multithreaded Server" in Chapter 16 of this book for more details on MTS.

# Measuring the Performance of the Shared Pool

The primary indicator of the performance of the Shared Pool is the cache-hit ratio. High cache-hit ratios indicate that your application users are frequently finding the SQL and PL/SQL statements they are issuing already in memory. Hit ratios can be calculated for both the Library Cache and the Data Dictionary Cache.

# Library Cache

The performance of the Library Cache is measured by calculating its hit ratio. This hit ratio information can be found in two places: the V$LIBRARYCACHE dynamic performance view and the REPORT.TXT file generated by running UTLBSTAT.SQL and UTLESTAT.SQL.

## Using *V$LIBRARYCACHE*

A Library Cache miss can occur at either the parse or execute phases of SQL statement processing. The cache hit ratio related to the parse phase is shown in the GETHITRATIO column of V$LIBRARYCACHE. The cache hit ratio related to the execution phase is shown in the PINHITRATIO column of V$LIBRARYCACHE. The RELOADS and INVALIDATIONS columns of V$LIBRARYCACHE are also useful for Library Cache tuning. A sample query on V$LIBRARYCACHE showing these columns is included here in Figure 4.1.

**FIGURE 4.1** Sample query on V$LIBRARYCACHE

```
SQL> SELECT namespace, gethitratio, pinhitratio, reloads, invalidations
  2  FROM v$librarycache
  3  WHERE namespace in ('SQL AREA',
  4                      'TABLE/PROCEDURE',
  5                      'BODY',
  6                      'TRIGGER');

NAMESPACE        GETHITRATIO PINHITRATIO  RELOADS INVALIDATIONS
---------------- ----------- -----------  ------- -------------
SQL AREA         .915877437  .937549722       10             2
TABLE/PROCEDURE  .799093656  .807164634        0             0
BODY             .7          .625              0             0
TRIGGER          1           1                 0             0
```

The NAMESPACE column in the above figure shows the source of the cached code. Table 4.2 shows the definition of each namespace type.

**TABLE 4.2** Code Source by Namespace Type

| Namespace | Code Source |
| --- | --- |
| SQL AREA | SQL statement |
| TABLE/PROCEDURE | PL/SQL stored procedure or function |
| BODY | PL/SQL package body |
| TRIGGER | PL/SQL trigger |

The other values for NAMESPACE found in V$LIBRARYCACHE refer to information used to determine dependencies between cached objects and statements. These values are of little value to you in terms of database tuning.

### GETHITRATIO

In V$LIBRARYCAHE, Oracle uses the term *get* to refer to a type of lock, called a *Parse Lock*, that is taken out on an object during the parse phase for the statement that references that object. Each time a statement is parsed, the value for GETS in the V$LIBRARYCACHE view is incremented by 1. The column GETHIT stores the number of times that the SQL and PL/SQL statements issued by the application found a parsed copy of themselves already in memory. When this occurs, there is no parsing of the statement required. The user's Server Process just executes the copy already in memory instead. The ratio of parsed statements (GETS) to those that did not require parsing (GETHITS) is calculated in the GETHITRATIO column of V$LIBRARYCACHE. In the sample output in Figure 4.1, our application users are finding the SQL statements they are issuing already in the Library Cache (i.e. GETHITRATIO) 91 percent of the time. The higher this number is, the better the application is performing.

Acording to Oracle, well-tuned OLTP systems can expect to have Library Cache GETHITRATIOs of 95 percent or higher. DSS and data warehouse applications often have lower hit ratios because of the ad hoc nature of the queries against them.

### PINHITRATIO

PINS, like GETS, are also related to locking. However, while GETS are associated with locks that occur at parse time, PINS are related to locks that occur at execution time. These locks are the short-term locks used when accessing an object. Therefore, each library cache GET also requires an associated PIN, in either Shared or Exclusive mode, before accessing the statement's referenced objects. Each time a statement is executed, the value for PINS is incremented by 1. The PINHITRATIO column in V$LIBRARYCACHE indicates how frequently executed statements found the associated parsed SQL already in the Library Cache. In the sample output in Figure 4.1, this is occurring 93.7 percent (i.e. PINHITRATIO) of the time.

Oracle recommends that well-tuned OLTP systems strive for a Library Cache `PINHITRATIO` that exceeds 90 percent. DSS and data warehouse applications will generally be lower.

### RELOADS

The RELOADS column shows the number of times that an executed statement had to be re-parsed because the Library Cache had aged out or invalidated the parsed version of the statement. Reload activity can be monitored by comparing the number of statements that have been executed (PINS) to the number of those statements that required a reload (RELOADS):

```
SQL> SELECT SUM(reloads)/SUM(pins) "Reload Ratio"
  2  FROM v$librarycache;


Reload Ratio
------------
  .001506251
```

In this example our Reload Ratio is .0015, or 0.15 percent. This means that we are not re-parsing statements that were previously loaded in the Library Cache very often.

Oracle considers well-tuned systems to be those with Reload Ratios of less than 1 percent.

### INVALIDATIONS

Invalidations occur when a cached SQL statement is marked as invalid and therefore forced to parse even though it was already in the Library Cache. Cached statements are marked as invalid whenever the objects they reference are modified in some way. For example, re-compiling a view that was used by previously cached SQL statements will cause those cached statements to be marked as invalid. Therefore, any subsequent statements that use this view will need to be parsed even though an exact copy of that statement may already be cached. High values for INVALIDATIONS mean additional overhead for the application. Therefore, performing activities that might cause invalidations should be weighed against the expected benefit of those activities.

## Using *REPORT.TXT* Output

The REPORT.TXT file generated by running UTLBSTAT.SQL and UTLESTAT.SQL also contains a section that shows GETHITRATIO, PINHITRATIO, RELOADS, and INVALIDATIONS information for the library cache. Figure 4.2 shows the relevant section of a REPORT.TXT file.

**FIGURE 4.2** REPORT.TXT output showing Library Cache statistics

```
SQL>
SQL> set charwidth 12
SQL> set numwidth 10
SQL> Rem Select Library cache statistics.  The pin hit rate should be high.
SQL> select namespace library,
  2      gets,
  3         round(decode(gethits,0,1,gethits)/decode(gets,0,1,gets),3)
  4           gethitratio,
  5      pins,
  6         round(decode(pinhits,0,1,pinhits)/decode(pins,0,1,pins),3)
  7           pinhitratio,
  8         reloads, invalidations
  9    from stats$lib;

LIBRARY               GETS GETHITRATIO    PINS PINHITRATIO   RELOADS INVALIDATIONS
---------------- ---------- ----------- ---------- ----------- ---------- -------------
BODY                    37       .865       38       .789         3         0
CLUSTER                386       .995      594       .993         0         0
INDEX                    4        .75        5        .6          0         0
OBJECT                   0          1        0          1         0         0
PIPE                     0          1        0          1         0         0
SQL AREA             16317       .969    99239       .988       161        79
TABLE/PROCEDURE       1700       .857    60291       .989       118         0
TRIGGER                 71       .887       71       .577        11         0
8 rows selected.

SQL>
SQL> set charwidth 27;
SQL> set numwidth 12;
SQL> Rem The total is the total value of the statistic between the time
```

# Data Dictionary Cache

Like the Library Cache, the measure of the effectiveness of the Data Dictionary Cache is expressed in terms of a hit ratio. This Dictionary Cache hit ratio shows how frequently the application finds the data dictionary information it needs in memory, instead of having to read it from disk. This hit-ratio information is contained in a dynamic performance view called V$ROWCACHE. The output from REPORT.TXT also contains statistics related to the Data Dictionary Cache hit ratio.

## Using *V$ROWCACHE*

The V$ROWCACHE view contains two columns, GETS and GETMISSES, that are used to calculate the Data Dictionary Cache hit ratio. The statistics in this view are not generally examined individually, but in aggregate using the query shown here:

```
SQL> SELECT 1 - (SUM(getmisses)/SUM(gets))
```

```
     2   "Data Dictionary Hit Ratio"
     3   FROM v$rowcache;

Data Dictionary Hit Ratio
-------------------------
                .969700203
```

The result of this query shows that your application is finding the data dictionary information it needs, already in memory, 96.9 percent of the time.

Oracle recommends that consideration be given to tuning the Shared Pool if the Data Dictionary hit ratio is less than 85 percent.

Data Dictionary information is also contained in the REPORT.TXT output produced by UTLBSTAT.SQL and UTLESTAT.SQL. Since the statistics are shown individually for each of the data dictionary elements that are cached, you will need to add the GET_REQS and GET_MISS columns yourself before calculating the hit ratio. Figure 4.3 shows the relevant section of a REPORT.TXT file.

**FIGURE 4.3**   REPORT.TXT output showing Data Dictionary Cache statistics

```
SQL> set numwidth 8;
SQL> Rem get_miss and scan_miss should be very low compared to the requests.
SQL> Rem cur_usage is the number of entries in the cache that are being used.
SQL> select * from stats$dc
  2    where get_reqs != 0 or scan_reqs != 0 or mod_reqs != 0;

NAME                   GET_REQS GET_MISS SCAN_REQS SCAN_MISS MOD_REQS    COUNT CUR_USAGE
--------------------   -------- -------- --------- --------- --------  -------- ---------
dc_tablespaces            85242        2         0         0        0       10         5
dc_free_extents            3765     1273      1260         0     3744       25         5
dc_segments                1979      172         0         0     1328       74        73
dc_rollback_segments        127        0         0         0        0       16         8
dc_used_extents            1282     1266         0         0     1282      852       850
dc_tablespace_quotas       1253        2         0         0     1253        3         2
dc_files                      1        1         0         0        0       14         1
dc_users                   3306       22         0         0        0       16        11
dc_user_grants             2941       21         0         0        0       11         9
dc_objects                 1280      278         0         0       82      188       179
dc_synonyms                  13        1         0         0        0       12        11
dc_usernames                337        1         0         0        0       21        11
dc_object_ids               933      185         0         0       25      122       121
dc_constraints               17        6         0         0       17       11        10
dc_sequences               1926        0         0         0     1895       10         9
dc_profiles                  10        0         0         0        0        4         1
dc_histogram_defs             0        0        20         0        0       10         9

17 rows selected.

SQL>
SQL>
```

## Monitoring Shared Pool Using OEM

Both the Library Cache and Data Dictionary Cache hit ratios can be monitored using the Performance Manager component of OEM Diagnostics Pack. Figure 4.4 shows a sample Performance Manager graphic for the Library Cache, and Figure 4.5 shows similar output for the Data Dictionary Cache.

**FIGURE 4.4** Performance Manager Library Cache statistics

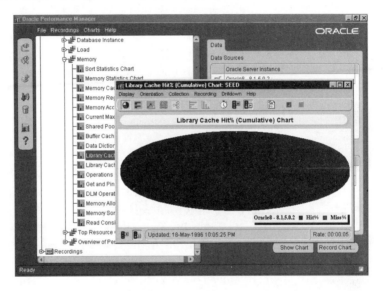

**FIGURE 4.5** Performance Manager Data Dictionary Cache statistics

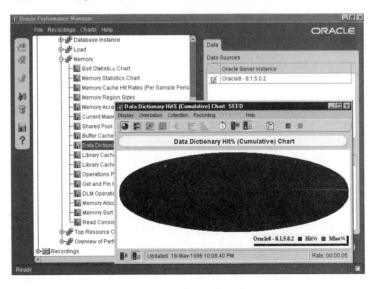

# Improving Shared Pool Performance

**N**ow that you know about the components of the Shared Pool and can measure the performance of each, you can examine methods for improving Shared Pool performance. The objective of all these methods is to increase Shared Pool performance by improving Library Cache and Data Dictionary Cache hit ratios. These techniques fall into five categories:

- Make it bigger
- Make room for large PL/SQL statements
- Keep important PL/SQL code in memory
- Encourage code reuse
- Create a Large Pool

## Make It Bigger

The simplest way to improve the performance of the Library and Data Dictionary Caches is to increase the size of the Shared Pool. Because the Oracle Server dynamically manages the relative sizes of the Library and Data Dictionary Caches from amongst the total space available to the Shared Pool, making the Shared Pool larger lessens the likelihood that cached information will be moved out of either cache by the LRU mechanism. This has the effect of improving both the Library Cache and Data Dictionary Cache hit ratios.

It is rare to see a situation where the Library Cache's hit ratios are good, but the Data Dictionary Cache's are bad, or vice versa. The hit ratios for both of these caches tend to move together as a result of this dynamic allocation of space between the two caches.

The size of the Shared Pool is determined by the init.ora parameter SHARED_POOL_SIZE. This parameter is specified in bytes and by default is set to 64MB on 64-bit operating systems and 16MB on 32-bit operating systems. If you are using Oracle's Java capabilities, it is important to make sure the Shared Pool is at least 50MB in size. Over 4,000 Java classes are loaded at instance startup, and they require at least this much Shared Pool space to function properly. By default, Oracle8i configures a third pool of size 10MB specified by the init.ora parameter JAVA_POOL_SIZE. This pool is used to cache Java state and runtime execution information.

See Chapter 4: JServer Environment Details in *Oracle8i Java Developers Guide, Release 8.1.5* (Part Number A64682-01) for more information on sizing the Java Pool.

## Make Room for Large PL/SQL Statements

If an application makes a call to a large PL/SQL package or trigger, several other cached SQL statements may be moved out of memory by the LRU mechanism when this large package is loaded into the Library Cache. This has the effect of reducing the Library Cache hit ratio if these statements are subsequently re-read into memory later. To avoid this problem, Oracle gives you the ability to set aside a portion of the Library Cache for use by large PL/SQL packages. This area of the Shared Pool is called the *Shared Pool Reserved Area*.

The init.ora parameter SHARED_POOL_RESERVED_SIZE can be used to set aside a portion of the Shared Pool for exclusive use by large PL/SQL packages and triggers. The value of SHARED_POOL_RESERVED_SIZE is specified in bytes and can be set to any value up to 50 percent of the value specified by SHARED_POOL_SIZE. By default, SHARED_POOL_RESERVE_SIZE will be 5 percent of the size of the Shared Pool.

One way to determine the optimal size of your reserve pool is to monitor a dynamic performance view called V$DB_OBJECT_CACHE. This view shows the names and sizes of the objects (in bytes) that are cached in the Library Cache. The following query can be used to see the names and sizes of the PL/SQL packages that are currently cached in memory:

```
SQL> SELECT owner, name, sharable_mem
  2  FROM v$db_object_cache
  3  WHERE type IN ('PACKAGE','PACKAGE BODY')
  4  ORDER BY SHARABLE_MEM DESC;

OWNER  NAME                    SHARABLE_MEM
------ --------------------    ------------
SYS    STANDARD                      218260
SYS    DBMS_SPACE_ADMIN               19312
SYS    DBMS_STANDARD                  15809
```

| | | |
|---|---|---|
| SYS | DBMS_OUTPUT | 14171 |
| SYS | DBMS_APPLICATION_INFO | 12629 |
| SYS | DBMS_OUTPUT | 6231 |
| SYS | DBMS_SPACE_ADMIN | 5324 |
| SYS | DBMS_APPLICATION_INFO | 2865 |

The dynamic performance view V$SHARED_POOL_RESERVE can be used to monitor the use of the Shared Pool Reserved Area and help determine if it is properly sized. Indications that you have over-allocated memory for the reserved area include:

- The statistics in the REQUEST_MISS column are consistently zero or static.

- The statistics in the FREE_MEMORY column are more than 50 percent of the total size allocated to the reserved area.

Non-zero or steadily increasing values for the statistic REQUEST_FAILURES indicate that the reserved area is too small.

Oracle recommends that you aim to have REQUEST_MISSES and REQUEST_FAILURES near zero in V$SHARED_POOL_RESERVED when using the Shared Pool Reserved Area.

## Keep Important PL/SQL Code in Memory

Applications that make heavy use of PL/SQL packages and triggers or Oracle sequences can improve their Shared Pool hit ratios by permanently caching these frequently used PL/SQL objects in memory until the instance is shutdown. This process is known as *pinning* and is accomplished by using the Oracle-supplied PL/SQL package DBMS_SHARED_POOL. Pinned packages are stored in the space set aside for this purpose by the init.ora parameter SHARED_POOL_RESERVED_SIZE.

### Building *DBMS_SHARED_POOL*

The DBMS_SHARED_POOL package is not built by the CATPROC.SQL script that is run at database creation. Instead, it must be built by running the DBMSPOOL.SQL script located in $ORACLE_HOME/rdbms/admin on UNIX systems and %ORACLE_HOME%\rdbms\admin on Windows NT systems while logged in as the user SYS:

```
SQL> @$ORACLE_HOME/rdbms/admin/dbmspool.sql
```

## Using *DBMS_SHARED_POOL*

The DBMS_SHARED_POOL PL/SQL package contains two procedures, KEEP and UNKEEP, which are used to pin or unpin (respectively) a package, trigger, or sequence in memory. The following example demonstrates how to pin an application PL/SQL package called APPROVE_PO:

```
SQL> EXECUTE DBMS_SHARED_POOL.KEEP ('APPROVE_PO');
```

## Identifying Pinned Objects

You can identify the objects that have been pinned using DBMS_SHARED_POOL by issuing the following query:

```
SQL> SELECT owner, name, type
  2  FROM v$db_object_cache
  3  WHERE kept = 'YES';
```

| OWNER | NAME | TYPE |
| --- | --- | --- |
| APPS | APPROVE_PO | PACKAGE |
| APPS | APPLY_TAX | TRIGGER |
| APPS | ASSIGN_ORG | PROCEDURE |

## What to Pin

Determining which objects should be pinned requires a thorough knowledge of the application and its components. One way to gather information on which objects are being frequently accessed in your database is to activate Oracle's auditing feature on the objects that you are considering pinning. If you audit the PL/SQL packages, triggers, and sequences in the application for a period of normal processing, you can go back and see which of those objects were heavily accessed during that time and then consider pinning those items. Some vendors will also recommend pinning strategies for their products.

## When to Pin

To get the maximum benefit from pinning, the objects to be pinned should be loaded into memory right after instance startup. This is usually accomplished through the use of a SQL script that is executed immediately after the instance is started. While some application vendors supply scripts for pinning their frequently used packages, many do not. In these cases, you will have to write a script yourself, consisting of an EXECUTE DBMS_SHARED_POOL.KEEP command for each package you wish to pin.

Anonymous blocks of PL/SQL code cannot be easily pinned using the `DBMS_SHARED_POOL` package as shown in the previous section. Applications with low Library Cache hit ratios, which also make heavy use of anonymous blocks, may benefit from rewriting those blocks as stored procedures so they can in turn be pinned.

Even the command `ALTER SYSTEM FLUSH SHARED_POOL` does not flush pinned objects. However, pinned objects will be removed from memory at the next instance shutdown.

## Encourage Code Reuse

Another way to improve the hit ratio for the Shared Pool is to use the code that is already cached there whenever possible. A new statement is only considered to be equivalent to a cached statement when the two statements have the same hash value. To increase the likelihood that this will occur, it is important for application developers to use coding standards that specify the appropriate use of case, spacing, and lines in the application code. Use of generic code should also be considered where possible.

Another method to improve code reuse is through the use of bind variables. *Bind variables* allow an application developer to use generic variables in their code rather than specific values. For example, suppose two users, User A and User B, both issue similar SQL statements. User A Looks For Customer 2204:

```
SQL> SELECT last_name, first_name
     FROM app.customer
     WHERE customer_id = '2204';
```

User B Looks For Customer 2301:

```
SQL> SELECT last_name, first_name
     FROM app.customer
     WHERE customer_id = '2301';
```

As you have seen earlier in this chapter, these two statements will not hash to the same value and will therefore cause a Library Cache cache miss. However, if these two statements had been issued using bind variables, User A looking for Customer 2204 using a bind variable would look like this:

```
:customer_id = 2204

SQL> SELECT last_name, first_name
     FROM app.customer
```

```
         WHERE customer_id = :customer_id;
```
User B looking for Customer 2301 using a bind variable would look like this:
```
:customer_id = 2301
```

```
SQL> SELECT last_name, first_name
     FROM app.customer
     WHERE customer_id = :customer_id;
```
In this case, the two statements will hash to the same value and result in a Library Cache cache hit because the bind variable itself, not the value stored in it, is used to generate the hash value.

The use of bind variables also has a tuning downside. Since bind variables are only containers for values, not actual values, they tend to confuse the cost-based optimizer, which is forced to make a blind guess at how the value in the container might affect the optimal execution plan.

## Create a Large Pool

Increasing the size of the Shared Pool, setting up a reserved area, and pinning PL/SQL packages are all effective methods of improving the performance of the Shared Pool. However, even with all these options in place, the performance of the Shared Pool can still be negatively impacted by heavily SQL-intensive operations like those that occur when using the multiple I/O server processes, Oracle's Recovery Manager (RMAN) utility, or MTS.

Oracle provides the ability to create a special area in the SGA, called the *Large Pool*, which can be used to process these types of requests. To create a Large Pool, set the init.ora parameter LARGE_POOL_SIZE to the desired size in bytes. By default, this parameter is zero (i.e., no Large Pool exists) unless the PARALLEL_AUTOMATIC_TUNING parameter is set to TRUE, in which case the size of the Large Pool is set automatically. When configuring the Large Pool manually, the minimum non-zero value allowed for LARGE_POOL_SIZE is 600K. Once configured, the Oracle Server will use the Large Pool to allocate memory to I/O server processes, RMAN, and MTS connections. By doing this, the memory allocated to the Shared Pool will not be consumed by these processes, but instead will be available to application users. You can use the POOL column in the dynamic performance view V$SGASTAT to track which objects are using the Large Pool:

```
SQL> SELECT name, bytes
     2  FROM v$sgastat
```

```
3  WHERE pool = 'large pool';
```

| NAME                        | BYTES   |
| --------------------------- | ------- |
| PX msg pool                 | 2347781 |
| free memory                 | 612030  |

---

### How Big Should I Make the Shared Pool on My New Server?

When setting up a new server where no previous statistics are available, you are forced to take educated guesses at the sizing of SGA components like the Shared Pool. While Oracle provides some suggested values (small, medium, and large) for the various SGA components in its sample init.ora, these are rarely useful since "small, medium, and large" are only relative terms.

**Initial SGA Size Calculation**

Instead of using the Oracle sample values, we use the following rule of thumb when setting the SGA size for a new system:

- Server Physical Memory x .55 = Total Amount of Memory to Allocate to All SGAs (TSGA)

- TSGA/Number of Oracle Instances on the Server = Total SGA Size Per Instance (TSGAI)

Using this TSGAI value, you can then calculate the SGA sizing for each individual instance:

- TSGAI x .45 = Total Memory Allocated to the Shared Pool

- TSGAI x .45 = Total Memory Allocated to the Database Buffer Cache (Chapter 5)

- TSGAI x .10 = Total Memory Allocated to the Redo Log Buffer (Chapter 6)

In most cases, reserving 10 percent of the SGA space for the Redo Log Buffer will be overkill. However, memory can always be taken away from this area and given to the Shared Pool, Database Buffer Cache, and Large Pool once tuning statistics become available.

> **Considerations**
>
> This calculation is intended to make the best use of the available memory while still leaving adequate memory for the operating system, Oracle background processes, user Server Processes, and any other non-Oracle processes that run on the server. The amount of memory required by the operating system varies widely between Windows NT systems (which generally need more) and UNIX-based systems (which generally need less), so you may want to adjust your calculations accordingly. This rule of thumb works pretty well on servers whose overall memory is less than 1GB. On servers with more than 1GB of memory, you should adjust the initial 55 percent reduction used in the TSGA calculation to a larger value (i.e. 60–75 percent).

The value for `free memory` shown in this view can be used to help tune the size of the Large Pool. If `V$SGASTAT` shows high or increasing values for `free memory`, you have probably over-allocated space to the Large Pool. If you have low or decreasing values for `free memory`, you may need to consider increasing the Large Pool size.

# Summary

The Shared Pool plays an important role in the processing of SQL statements issued against the instance by the application. It acts as the cache where previously issued statements are stored so subsequent requests for the same command can avoid parsing the command.

The Shared Pool caches its information in two areas: the Library Cache and the Data Dictionary Cache. The Library Cache is used to cache SQL statements, PL/SQL procedures, functions, and triggers, and sequences while the Data Dictionary Cache stores information about the objects in the database used by the cached SQL statements. Shared Pool performance is measured in terms of the hit ratios of these two caches.

The cache-hit ratio for the Shared Pool can be improved by increasing the size of the Shared Pool, setting up a Shared Pool Reserved Area, pinning frequently used PL/SQL code and sequences in memory, and by rewriting application SQL code to encourage the re-use of parsed statements.

## Key Terms

Before you take the exam, make sure you're familiar with the following terms:

Shared Pool

Least Recently Used (LRU)

cache hit

cache miss

Library Cache

Data Dictionary Cache

Process Global Area

User Global Area

parse lock

Shared Pool Reserve Area

bind variables

# Review Questions

1. Tuning the Shared Pool is included in which step in the Oracle tuning methodology?

    **A.** Tuning the data design

    **B.** Tuning database operations

    **C.** Tuning memory allocation

    **D.** Tuning I/O and physical structure

2. The contents of the Shared Pool are managed using what type of algorithm?

    **A.** Least Recently Needed

    **B.** Least Recently Used

    **C.** Least Recently Accessed

    **D.** Least Recently Parsed

3. The process of preparing a statement for execution is called:

    **A.** Caching

    **B.** Hashing

    **C.** Parsing

    **D.** None of the above

4. Finding a statement already cached in the Library Cache is referred to as a:

    **A.** Cache hit

    **B.** Cache miss

    **C.** Cache match

    **D.** Cache parse

5. To determine if a new statement is a match for an existing statement already in the Shared Pool, Oracle compares each statement's:

   **A.** Result set

   **B.** Security

   **C.** Execution plan

   **D.** Hashed value

6. In order for two statements to result in a cache hit, which of the following must be true?

   **A.** The statements must use the same case—either upper, lower, or mixed.

   **B.** The statements must be issued against the same table.

   **C.** The statements must be on the same number of lines.

   **D.** All of the above must be true.

7. Which of the following dynamic data dictionary views contains the entire SQL statement issued by a user?

   **A.** V$LIBRARYCACHE

   **B.** V$SQLTEXT

   **C.** V$SQLAREA

   **D.** V$ROWCACHE

8. The User Global Area, or UGA, is associated with which Oracle option?

   **A.** Parallel Server

   **B.** Symmetric Replication

   **C.** Hot Standby Database

   **D.** Multithreaded Server

9. Which dynamic data dictionary view contains information about the Library Cache hit ratio?

    **A.** V$ROWCACHE

    **B.** V$LIBRARYCACHE

    **C.** V$DICTIONARYCACHE

    **D.** All of the above

10. According to Oracle, what value for GETHITRATIO in V$LIBRARYCACHE should you strive for on an OLTP system?

    **A.** Less than 10 percent

    **B.** Between 60 and 80 percent

    **C.** Higher than 95 percent

    **D.** Between 10 and 20 percent

11. Changes in values for which of the following columns in V$LIBRARYCACHE indicates that a previously parsed statement was aged out of the cache, having to be subsequently re-parsed?

    **A.** INVALIDATIONS

    **B.** RELOADS

    **C.** PINHITRATIO

    **D.** GETHITRATIO

12. According to Oracle, what Reload Ratio would a well-tuned system have?

    **A.** 90 percent or higher

    **B.** 10 percent or higher

    **C.** Less than 1 percent

    **D.** More than 1 percent

**13.** If a sequence is altered to increment by a new value, each of the cached SQL statements that referenced this sequence will be:

**A.** Pinned in the Library Cache.

**B.** Marked as invalid in the Library Cache.

**C.** Hashed to a new value in the Library Cache.

**D.** This change to the sequence will have no effect on the Library Cache.

**14.** The output from REPORT.TXT does not show information on which of the following areas of the Library Cache?

**A.** GETHITRATIO

**B.** RELOADS

**C.** INVALIDATIONS

**D.** All of the above are included in the REPORT.TXT output.

**15.** Which of the following dynamic performance views has information on the hit ratio for the Data Dictionary Cache?

**A.** V$LIBRARYCACHE

**B.** V$DICTIONARYCACHE

**C.** V$ROWCACHE

**D.** V$SQLAREA

**16.** According to Oracle, what should the Data Dictionary hit ratio be for a well-tuned OLTP system?

**A.** More than 85 percent

**B.** Less than 85 percent

**C.** Between 50 and 60 percent

**D.** None of the above

**17.** Which of the following GUI tools can be used to monitor the Library and Data Dictionary Cache hit ratios?

   **A.** Oracle Trace Manager

   **B.** Oracle Tablespace Manager

   **C.** Oracle Memory Manager

   **D.** Oracle Performance Manager

**18.** Which of the following is not an accepted method of improving the hit ratio for the Shared Pool?

   **A.** Decrease the SHARED_POOL_SIZE init.ora parameter

   **B.** Increase the SHARED_POOL_RESERVED_SIZE init.ora parameter

   **C.** Pin PL/SQL packages in the Shared Pool

   **D.** Rewrite application code to make more use of bind variables

**19.** Which of the following Oracle-supplied PL/SQL packages is used to pin PL/SQL packages into the Shared Pool?

   **A.** DBMS_UTILITY

   **B.** DBMS_SYSTEM

   **C.** DBMS_SHARED_POOL

   **D.** DBMS_KEEP

**20.** Which dynamic performance view can be used to monitor the effectiveness of the Shared Pool Reserved Area?

   **A.** V$LIBRARYCACHE

   **B.** V$ROWCACHE

   **C.** V$DB_OBJECT_CACHE

   **D.** V$SHARED_POOL_RESERVE

# Answers to Review Questions

**1.** C.   The Shared Pool is one of the three memory structures found in the SGA.

**2.** B.   The LRU mechanism for managing the Shared Pool assures that the most recently used statements will remain in memory, while older statements are moved out.

**3.** C.   The parse process involves checking the statement for syntactic correctness, object resolution (i.e., table names, column names, and data types), and determination of an execution plan.

**4.** A.   Cache hits occur whenever an application finds a parsed version of a statement already cached in memory.

**5.** D.   Once reduced to its ASCII equivalent, each Oracle statement is then passed through a hashing algorithm. This hash value is compared to the hashed values associated with the statements that are cached in the Library Cache to determine if a parse needs to take place.

**6.** D.   Two statements must match exactly in order to be considered a cache hit.

**7.** B.   V$SQLAREA only contains the first 80 characters of the SQL statement issued.

**8.** D.   The MTS option requires that some user session information be stored in the User Global Area in the Shared Pool.

**9.** B.   The GETHITRATIO and PINHITRATIO columns of V$LIBRARYCACHE show the hit ratios for the Library Cache.

**10.** C.   A well-tuned OLTP system should have a GETHITRATIO for the Library Cache in excess of 95 percent.

**11.** B.  A non-zero value for RELOADS column of V$LIBRARYCACHE indicates that statements are being re-parsed shortly after they are flushed from the Library Cache.

**12.** C.  A Reload Ratio of less than 1 percent is considered appropriate for most systems.

**13.** B.  If an object that is referenced by a cached SQL statement is altered or dropped, all cached statements that refer to this object will be marked as invalid and will require a re-parse at the next execution of the statement.

**14.** D.  The first section of a REPORT.TXT file contains Library Cache information for the GETHITRATIO, PINHITRATIO, RELOADS, and INVALIDATIONS.

**15.** C.  The V$ROWCACHE view contains two columns, GETMISSES and GETS, that can be used to calculate the hit ratio for the Data Dictionary Cache.

**16.** A.  A well-tuned OLTP system will have a hit ratio of 85 percent or higher.

**17.** D.  The Performance Manager GUI found in the OEM Diagnostics Pack can graphically display the hit ratios for the Library Cache and Data Dictionary Cache.

**18.** A.  Increasing, not decreasing, the size of the Shared Pool will improve the Shared Pool hit ratios.

**19.** C.  The KEEP and UNKEEP procedures of the DBMS_SHARED_POOL package can be used to pin and unpin PL/SQL packages in the Shared Pool.

**20.** D.  The statistics for FREE_MEMORY, REQUEST_MISS, and REQUEST_FAILURES found in the V$SHARED_POOL_RESERVE view can all be used to determine if the Shared Pool Reserve Area is sized appropriately.

# Tuning the Database Buffer Cache

## ORACLE8i PERFORMANCE TUNING EXAM OBJECTIVES COVERED IN THIS CHAPTER:

- ✓ Describe how the Database Buffer Cache is managed.
- ✓ Calculate and tune the Database Buffer Cache hit ratio.
- ✓ Tune the Buffer Cache hit ratio by adding or removing buffers.
- ✓ Create and size multiple Buffer Pools.
- ✓ Monitor Database Buffer Cache usage.
- ✓ Make appropriate use of table caching.

Exam objectives are subject to change at any time without prior notice and at Oracle's sole discretion. Please visit Oracle's Training and Certification Web site (http://education.oracle.com/certification/index.html) for the most current exam objectives listing.

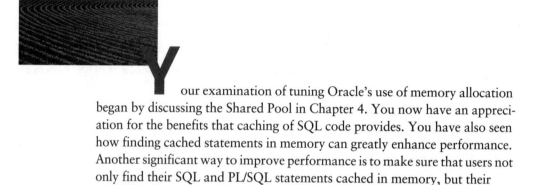

Your examination of tuning Oracle's use of memory allocation began by discussing the Shared Pool in Chapter 4. You now have an appreciation for the benefits that caching of SQL code provides. You have also seen how finding cached statements in memory can greatly enhance performance. Another significant way to improve performance is to make sure that users not only find their SQL and PL/SQL statements cached in memory, but their requested data as well. This is the role of the Database Buffer Cache.

Knowing how the Database Buffer Cache's mechanisms work, how to monitor its performance, and how to tune it when needed all fall into Step 7 of the Oracle Tuning Methodology: Tuning Memory Allocation.

# Understanding the Database Buffer Cache

The *Database Buffer Cache*, or Buffer Cache, is the portion of the SGA that caches the data blocks of the segments the application users have been most recently accessing in the database. Each buffer in the Buffer Cache corresponds in size to, and holds the contents of, one database block. These blocks may belong to:

- Tables

- Indexes

- Clusters

- Large Object (LOB) segments

- LOB indexes

- Rollback segments

- Temporary segments

Tuning of rollback and temporary segments are discussed in Chapter 7: Tuning Physical I/O.

The Database Buffer Cache is managed by a combination of processes including an LRU List, a Dirty List, user Server Processes, and Database Writer (DBW0).

## The LRU List

Like the Shared Pool, the Database Buffer Cache is also managed by *a Least Recently Used* (LRU) algorithm. Once the Buffer Cache's buffers are full of copies of data blocks, the LRU algorithm makes room for subsequent requests for new data blocks to be copied into the SGA by aging out the blocks that have been least recently accessed. This allows the Oracle Server to keep the most recently requested data buffers in the Buffer Cache while the less commonly used data buffers are flushed. By caching the data buffers in this manner, an application user who needs the same data buffers as a previous user, benefits from the fact that the buffers are already in memory and therefore do not need to be read from disk by the user's Server Process. This is beneficial because reads from memory are thousands of times faster than reads from disk. Similar to the Shared Pool, a Database Buffer Cache cache hit occurs when a user finds that a data buffer they need is already in memory. Having to read that data from disk into a buffer is considered a cache miss.

You can think of the LRU list that manages the buffers in the Database Buffer Cache as being similar to a conveyor belt. Figure 5.1 illustrates this concept.

**FIGURE 5.1** How the LRU List Manages the Buffer Cache

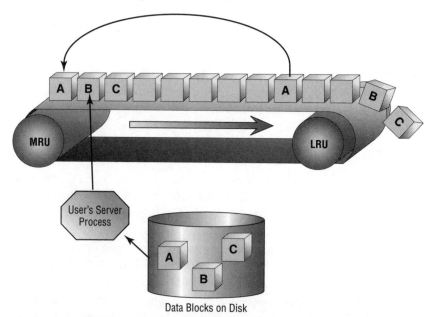

Data Blocks on Disk

When a request is made for data, the user's Server Process places the newly read blocks (A, B, C) from disk into buffers at the beginning (Most Recently Used) of the LRU List. These buffers stay on the LRU List but move toward the least recently used end as additional data blocks are read into memory. If a buffer (A) is accessed during the time it is on the LRU List, the buffer is moved back to the beginning of the LRU List (i.e., back to the MRU end). If buffers are not accessed again before they reach the end of the LRU List, the buffers (B and C) are marked as free and overwritten by another block being read from disk.

The behavior of the LRU List is slightly different when a table is accessed during a full table scan (FTS). During an FTS, the table buffers are placed immediately at the least recently used end of the LRU List. While this has the effect of immediately causing these blocks to be flushed from the cache, it also prevents an FTS on a large table from pushing all other buffers out of the cache.

## The Dirty List

There are three types of buffers found in the Database Buffer Cache. These types are shown in Table 5.1.

**T A B L E   5 . 1**   Possible Statuses for Database Buffer Cache Buffers

| Status | Description |
|--------|-------------|
| Free | Buffer is not currently in use. |
| Pinned | Buffer is currently in use by a Server Process. |
| Dirty | Buffer is not in use, but contains committed data that has not yet been written to disk by Database Writer. |

Initially, the copies of the database blocks that are stored in free buffers contain the same data as the blocks on disk. In other words, the blocks and their copies in the buffers are in sync. Dirty buffers are those buffers whose copy in the Buffer Cache does not match the version of the block on disk. These blocks and their copies in the buffers are not in sync. The Oracle Server can freely overwrite the contents of a free buffer when a new block needs to be placed in memory. Dirty buffers cannot be overwritten by new blocks being read from disk until after the contents of the dirty buffers have been written to disk.

The mechanism for managing these dirty buffers is called the *Dirty List*. This list keeps track of all the blocks that have been modified by application users through the use of INSERT, DELETE, or UPDATE statements, but have not yet been written to disk. Dirty buffers are written to disk by the Oracle background process Database Writer (DBW0).

## User Server Process

When a user's Server Process does not find the data it needs already in the Buffer Cache, it must read the data from disk. It is the user's Server Process that performs this copying of the requested data blocks into the Database

Buffer Cache. Before it can be read from disk, however, a free buffer must be found to hold the copy of the data block in memory. When searching for a free buffer to hold the block that is to be read, the Server Process makes use of both the LRU List and the Dirty List:

- While searching the LRU List for a free block, the Server Process moves any dirty blocks it finds on the LRU List to the Dirty List.

- As the Dirty List has buffers added to it, it grows longer and longer. When it hits a predetermined threshold length, DBW0 writes the dirty buffers to disk.

- DBW0 can also write dirty buffers to disk even if the Dirty List has not reached its threshold length. This occurs when a user's Server Process has examined too many buffers without successfully finding a free buffer. In this case, DBW0 will write dirty buffers directly from the LRU List (as opposed to moving them to the Dirty List first, as above) to disk.

When a user's Server Process needs a buffer and finds that buffer in memory, the buffer may contain uncommitted data or data that has changed since the time the user's transaction began. Since the Oracle Server never allows a user to see uncommitted data or committed data that was changed after their transaction began, the Server Process uses a buffer that contains the before-image of the data to provide a read-consistent view of the database. This before-image is stored in a rollback segment whose blocks are also cached in the Buffer Cache.

## Database Writer

Not only can a user's Server Process cause DBW0 to write dirty buffers to disk, there are several other database events that can cause Database Writer to write the dirty buffers to disk. The complete list of events that can cause DBW0 to write to disk is summarized in Table 5.2.

**TABLE 5.2**   Events that Cause Database Writer to Write to Disk

| Event | How DBW0 Writes |
| --- | --- |
| When Dirty List reaches its threshold length | DBW0 writes dirty buffers from Dirty List. |
| When LRU List is searched too long without finding a free buffer | DBW0 writes dirty buffers directly from the LRU List. |
| When three seconds pass | DBW0 moves dirty buffers from the LRU List to the Dirty List. If the threshold length is exceeded, a write to disk occurs. |
| At Checkpoint | DBW0 moves all dirty buffers from the LRU List to the Dirty List and then writes them to disk. |
| At Tablespace Hot Backup | DBW0 moves the dirty buffers for that tablespace from the LRU List to the Dirty List and then writes them to disk. |
| At Tablespace Offline Temporary | DBW0 moves the dirty buffers for that tablespace from the LRU List to the Dirty List and then writes them to disk. |
| At Drop Segment | Dropping a table or index causes DBW0 to first write the dirty blocks for that segment to disk. |

# Measuring the Performance of the Database Buffer Cache

The primary indicator of the performance of the Database Buffer Cache is the cache hit ratio. High cache hit ratios indicate that your application users are frequently finding the data buffers they need already in memory. The hit ratio information for the Database Buffer Cache can be found in several places: the V$SYSSTAT, V$SESS_IO, and V$SESSION dynamic performance views, the output from UTLBSTAT.SQL and UTLESTAT.SQL (REPORT.TXT), and the OEM Performance Manager GUI tool. Additionally, there are also non-hit ratio measures of Database Buffer Cache effectiveness.

## Using *V$SYSSTAT*

Cache misses occur when a user's Server Process does not find the data buffer it needs in memory, causing a read from disk to occur. The V$SYSSTAT dynamic performance view keeps track of three statistics that are used to calculate the Buffer Cache hit ratio:

**Physical Reads**   The number of data blocks read from disk into the Buffer Cache since instance startup (i.e. tables, indexes, and rollback segments).

**DB Block Gets**   The total number of requests for data that were satisfied by using buffers that were already cached in the Database Buffer Cache.

**Consistent Gets**   The total number of requests for data that were satisfied by using rollback segment buffers (for read consistency) that were already cached in the Database Buffer Cache.

Using these statistics we can compare the number of times a block had to be read from disk (Physical Reads) to the total number of blocks that were accessed (DB Block Gets and Consistent Gets), as shown in the following query:

```
SQL> SELECT 1 -
  2 (physical.value / (blockgets.value+consistent.value))
  3  "Buffer Cache Hit Ratio"
  4  FROM v$sysstat physical,
  5  v$sysstat blockgets,
  6  v$sysstat consistent
```

```
7  WHERE physical.name = 'physical reads'
8  AND blockgets.name = 'db block gets'
9  AND consistent.name = 'consistent gets';

Buffer Cache Hit Ratio
----------------------
            .889616116
```

According to Oracle, a well-tuned OLTP system should have Database Buffer Cache hit ratios of 90 percent or higher.

This query returns the hit ratio for the Database Buffer Cache for the entire instance. The following section discusses how to view the Database Buffer Cache hit ratio for an individual session.

## Using *V$SESS_IO* and *V$SESSION*

Occasionally, you may want to view the Database Buffer Cache hit ratio from the perspective of an individual user. This is useful when overall database performance is acceptable, but one user seems to be experiencing performance issues. When joined, the V$SESS_IO and V$SESSION views contain the statistics required to calculated a per-session Database Buffer Cache hit ratio, as the following query displays:

```
SQL> SELECT username, osuser,
  2      1 -
  3      (io.physical_reads/
  4      (io.block_gets+io.consistent_gets))
  5      "Hit Ratio"
  6  FROM v$sess_io io, v$session sess
  7  WHERE io.sid = sess.sid
  8  AND (io.block_gets + io.consistent_gets) ! = 0
  9  AND username IS NOT NULL;

USERNAME                OSUSER      Hit Ratio
```

```
-------------------- -------- ----------
DBSNMP              oracle   .693430657
SYS                 oracle   .935706068
APPS                OraUser  .872109221
```

Complete descriptions of the contents of the V$SYSSTAT, V$SESS_IO, V$SESSION, and V$SYSTEM_EVENT views can be found in Chapter 3: Dynamic Performance (V$) Views in *Oracle8i Reference, Release 8.1.5* (Part Number A67790-01).

## Using *REPORT.TXT* Output

The REPORT.TXT file generated by running UTLBSTAT.SQL and UTLESTAT.SQL also contains a section that shows the statistics needed to calculate the Database Buffer Cache hit ratio. The relevant sections of a sample REPORT.TXT are shown in Figure 5.2.

**FIGURE 5.2** REPORT.TXT Output Showing Data Dictionary Cache Statistics

```
SQL> Rem The total is the total value of the statistic between the time
SQL> Rem bstat was run and the time estat was run.  Note that the estat
SQL> Rem script logs on as "internal" so the per_logon statistics will
SQL> Rem always be based on at least one logon.
SQL> select n1.name "Statistic",
  2         n1.change "Total",
  3         round(n1.change/trans.change,2) "Per Transaction",
  4         round(n1.change/logs.change,2)  "Per Logon",
  5         round(n1.change/(to_number(to_char(end_time,   'J'))*60*60*24 -
  6                    to_number(to_char(start_time, 'J'))*60*60*24 +
  7                    to_number(to_char(end_time,   'SSSSS')) -
  8                    to_number(to_char(start_time, 'SSSSS')))
  9            , 2) "Per Second"
 10   from stats$stats n1, stats$stats trans, stats$stats logs, stats$dates
 11   where trans.name='user commits'
 12     and  logs.name='logons cumulative'
 13     and  n1.change != 0
 14   order by n1.name;

Statistic                        Total  Per Transaction   Per Logon  Per Second
-------------------------------- ------ ----------------  ---------- ------------
<snip>
consistent gets                 2509227        13563.39   156826.69      929.69
<snip>
db block gets                    590521         3192.01    36907.56      218.79
<snip>
physical reads                  1544643         8349.42    96540.19       572.3
```

## Monitoring Buffer Cache Using OEM

The Database Buffer Cache hit ratios can be monitored using the Performance Manager component of OEM Diagnostics Pack. Figure 5.3 shows a sample Performance Manager graphic for the Database Buffer Cache hit ratio.

**FIGURE 5.3** Performance Manager Database Buffer Cache statistics

## Non-Hit Ratio Performance Measures

There are also several non-hit ratio measures of Database Buffer Cache performance. These statistics are related to the number of buffers that a user's server process has to examine before finding a free buffer in the Database Buffer Cache. There are three statistics that measure this activity:

**Free Buffer Inspected**   Number of buffers inspected before finding a free one

**Free Buffer Waits**   Number of waits during Free Buffer Inspected activity

**Buffer Busy Waits**   Number of waits for a free buffer to become available

High or steadily increasing values for any of these statistics indicate that user Server Processes are spending too much time searching for free buffers in the Database Buffer Cache. The following query on V$SYSSTAT can be used to monitor these statistics:

```
SQL> SELECT name, value
  2  FROM v$sysstat
  3  WHERE name IN ('free buffer inspected',
  4                 'free buffer waits',
  5                 'buffer busy waits');


NAME                                VALUE
------------------------------- ----------
free buffer inspected                2578
buffer busy waits                    1267
```

These statistics are also included in the output from REPORT.TXT.

# Improving Buffer Cache Performance

**N**ow that you know how the Database Buffer Cache management mechanisms work and how to monitor their performance, you can examine methods for improving the performance. The objective of these methods is to increase Database Buffer Cache performance by improving its hit ratio. These techniques fall into five categories:

- Make it bigger
- Use multiple buffer pools
- Cache tables in memory
- Bypass Buffer Cache
- Use indexes appropriately

## Make It Bigger

The easiest way to improve the performance of the Database Buffer Cache is to increase its size. The larger the Database Buffer Cache, the less likely cached buffers are to be moved out of the cache by the LRU List. The longer buffers are stored in the Database Buffer Cache, the higher the hit ratio will be.

The size of the Database Buffer Cache is determined by the init.ora parameters DB_BLOCK_SIZE and DB_BLOCK_BUFFERS. Database block size is specified in bytes by the DB_BLOCK_SIZE parameter. This value is set at database creation and can only be changed by recreating the database. The default value for DB_BLOCK_SIZE varies by platform. On most UNIX systems, it is between 2K and 8K. Windows NT systems have a default block size of 2K. No matter the default, most systems can use 2K, 4K, 8K, 16K, 32K, or 64K block sizes. The number of database buffers to create in the SGA is specified by number by the DB_BLOCK_BUFFERS parameter. The product of these two values, DB_BLOCK_SIZE and the number of DB_BLOCK_BUFFERS, determines the size of the Database Buffer Cache.

In general, it is an acceptable tuning practice to keep making the Database Buffer Cache larger by increasing the value for DB_BLOCK_BUFFERS until no further improvement in the Database Buffer Cache hit ratio occurs or until the available memory is exhausted. Note that increases to the Database Buffer Cache are not a direct relationship. Doubling the value for DB_BLOCK_BUFFERS will not necessarily double the Buffer Cache hit ratio.

Not all I/Os are physical. With the advent of modern caching disk controllers, it is common for database servers to do the majority of cache miss reads from the controller cache, not directly from disk. The best way to determine the overall effectiveness of your Database Buffer Cache is to monitor not only the Buffer Cache hit ratio, but also how many "physical reads" are being done from disk as opposed to the disk controller's cache.

Not only will increasing the Buffer Cache improve its hit ratio, it should also lower the number of waits reported by the free buffer inspected, buffer busy waits, and free buffer waits system statistics. These statistics are a good secondary measure of the effectiveness of your changes to the Database Buffer Cache.

# Use Multiple Buffer Pools

By default, all database segments compete for use of the same Database Buffer Cache buffers. This can lead to a situation where some infrequently accessed tables that are only of interest to a few application users can push more frequently used data buffers out of memory. To avoid this, Oracle provides you with the ability to divide the Database Buffer Cache into as many as three separate areas called *buffer pools*. Segments are then explicitly assigned to use the appropriate buffer pool as determined by the DBA.

## Buffer Pool Types

Before you create any buffer pools, you must determine which types of pools you wish to use. Each buffer pool is used to cache a different type of segment:

**Keep Pool**   Used to cache segments that you rarely, if ever, want to leave the Database Buffer Cache.

**Recycle Pool**   Used to cache segments that you rarely, if ever, want to retain in the Database Buffer Cache.

**Default Pool**   Used to cache segments that are not designated for either the Keep or Recycle Pools.

Unless you specify otherwise in the `init.ora`, only the Default Pool is created at instance startup.

## Determining Which Segments to Cache

Next, you must determine which segments to cache and in which pools to cache them. This requires a thorough knowledge of the application, its segments, and how they are accessed. As with deciding which PL/SQL packages to pin in the Shared Pool, database auditing can be useful to determine which segments should be cached. Another way to determine which segments should be assigned to each buffer pool is by querying the V$BH and DBA_ SEGMENTS views. The V$BH view is actually intended for use when tuning Oracle Servers with the Oracle Parallel Server (OPS) option selected. However, it can also be useful for tuning non-OPS systems because it displays how many cached buffers from each cached segment are currently in the Database Buffer Cache. By querying the V$BH and DBA_SEGMENTS views using the common column OBJECT_ID, you can also see which segments are currently cached in the Buffer Cache along with the segment's owner, name, and type:

```
SQL> SELECT obj.owner,
  2          obj.object_name,
  3          obj.object_type,
  4          COUNT(DISTINCT bh.block#) "Num. Buffers"
  5   FROM   dba_objects obj, v$bh bh
  6   WHERE  obj.object_id = bh.objd
  7   AND    owner != 'SYS'
  8   GROUP BY obj.owner,
  9            obj.object_name,
 10            obj.object_type
 11 ORDER BY 4;

OWNER  OBJECT_NAME    OBJECT_TYPE Num. Buffers
------ -------------- ----------- ------------
APPS   EMPLOYEE       TABLE                 12
APPS   EMPLOYEE_PK_ID INDEX                 10
APPS   REGION         TABLE                  8
```

Segments owned by the user SYS are excluded from this query because they are most likely data dictionary segments that are nearly always kept on the LRU List during normal processing. Another way to find similar information is by querying the V$CACHE and DBA_USERS views like this:

```
SQL> SELECT username "Owner",
  2          name "Seg. Name",
  3          kind "Seg. Type",
  4          COUNT(DISTINCT block#) "Num. Buffers"
  5   FROM v$cache, dba_users
  6   WHERE v$cache.owner#=dba_users.user_id
  7   GROUP BY name, username, kind
  8   HAVING COUNT(DISTINCT block#) > 10
  9   ORDER BY 3 DESC;
Owner Seg. Name          Seg. Type  Num. Buffers
-------------------- ---------- ------------
APPS   EMPLOYEE           TABLE                12
APPS   EMPLOYEE_PK_IDX    INDEX                10
APPS   REGION             TABLE                 8
```

Before using the V$CACHE view, you must create it by running the Oracle-supplied script CATPARR.SQL while logged in as the user SYS. This script can be found in $ORACLE_HOME/rdbms/admin on UNIX systems and %ORACLE_HOME%\rdbms\admin on Windows NT systems. The V$CACHE dynamic performance view, like V$BH, is actually intended for use in OPS tuning.

For the purposes of our example, assume you have determined that the application segments shown in Table 5.3 should be specifically cached in the pools shown.

**TABLE 5.3**   Example Segments and Their Assigned  Buffer Pools

| Segment Name | Segment Type | Buffer Pool |
|---|---|---|
| EMPLOYEE | Table | Keep Pool |
| REGION | Table | Keep Pool |
| DIVISION | Table | Recycle Pool |
| EMPLOYEE_FIRST_NAME_IDX | Index | Keep Pool |
| EMPLOYEE_ID_PK | Index | Keep Pool |
| SALES_HISTORY | Table | Recycle Pool |

Any other application segments not specifically allocated to the Keep or Recycle Pools will use the Default Pool.

## Determining the Size of Each Pool

After determining which segments you wish to cache, you need to determine how large each pool should be. Making this determination is easy if the segments to be cached have been analyzed. The BLOCKS column of the DBA_TABLES and DBA_INDEXES data dictionary views can be used to determine how many Database Buffer Cache buffers would be needed to cache an entire segment or portion of that segment. For the purposes of our example, assume you have decided to create three buffer pools with the following sizes:

- Keep Pool: 150MB

- Recycle Pool: 50MB

- Default Pool: 300MB

Figure 5.4 shows what these three buffer pools would conceptually look like in the SGA once they are created.

**FIGURE 5.4** Keep, Default, and Recycle Buffer Pools

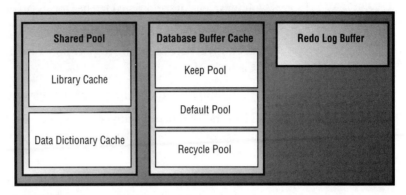

## Creating the Buffer Pools

Next, the buffer pools must be created with the selected sizes by setting the appropriate init.ora parameters. These parameters are detailed in Table 5.4.

**TABLE 5.4** init.ora Parameters Used to Configure Buffer Pools

| Parameter | Description |
| --- | --- |
| DB_BLOCK_BUFFERS | The total number of database buffers to create in the Database Buffer Cache for the entire instance |
| DB_BLOCK_LRU_LATCHES | The total number of latches to create for accessing the Database Buffer Cache for the entire instance |
| BUFFER_POOL_KEEP | The number of the DB_BLOCK_BUFFERS and DB_BLOCK_LRU_LATCHES that are allocated to the Keep Pool |
| BUFFER_POOL_RECYCLE | The number of DB_BLOCK_BUFFERS and DB_BLOCK_LRU_LATCHES that are allocated to the Recycle Pool |

*Latches* are used to protect access to all of Oracle's shared memory structures, including the Database Buffer Cache. Since only the Default Pool exists by default, the Oracle Server has only one latch configured for accessing the Default Pool. As you configure additional Buffer Cache pools using the above parameters, you must allocate additional latches for the management of each pool. When assigning values to these parameters you must follow these rules:

- Each LRU Latch must be responsible for managing at least 50 Buffer Cache buffers.

- Each buffer pool must be assigned at least one LRU Latch.

- The total number of buffers assigned to the Keep and Recycle Pools are taken from the total number of buffers specified by the DB_BLOCK_ BUFFERS parameter.

- The total number of latches assigned to the Keep and Recycle Pools are taken from the total number of latches specified by the DB_BLOCK_ LRU_LATCHES parameter. At least one latch must be left for use by the Default Pool.

Using our desired values of 150MB for the Keep Pool, 50MB for the Recycle Pool, and 300MB for the Default Pool, we might configure our init.ora like this:

```
# DB Block size is 8K
DB_BLOCK_SIZE = 8192
# 8K/buffer * 64000 buffers = 500MB, the
# desired total size of
# the Database Buffer Cache
DB_BLOCK_BUFFERS = 64000
# Create 30 LRU latches to manage the
# entire Database
# Buffer Cache
DB_BLOCK_LRU_LATCHES = 30
# Use 19,200 of the 64,000 buffers (150MB)
# for the Keep Pool.
# Manage the 19,200 buffers in the Keep Pool
# using 10 of the 30 total LRU Latches
BUFFER_POOL_KEEP=(BUFFERS: 19200, LRU_LATCHES: 10)
# Use 6,400 of the remaining 44,800 buffers (50MB)
```

```
# for the Recycle Pool
# Manage the 6,400 buffers in the Recycle Pool
# using 5 of the 20 remaining LRU Latches
BUFFER_POOL_RECYCLE=(BUFFERS: 6400, LRU_LATCHES: 5)
# The remaining buffers (38,400) and LRU # Latches (15)
are used to manage the Default Pool
```

**WARNING**

Incorrectly specifying the Buffer pool init.ora parameters in any way results in a ORA-00378 "Buffer Pools Cannot Be Created as Specified" error.

While the number of buffers for each pool has to be specified according to the size you desire each pool to be, the number of latches assigned to manage those buffers will vary according to your application requirements. In general, the more latches you have managing a buffer pool, the less likely there is to be contention for those latches when access to the buffer pool is requested. The default value for DB_BLOCK_LRU_LATCHES is 1 or half the number of CPUs in the server, whichever is larger. The maximum value for DB_BLOCK_LRU_LATCHES is twice the number of CPUs. The Default Pool will use whatever buffer and latches are not assigned to the Keep Pool or the Recycle Pool to manage its buffer storage.

**NOTE**

The issue of latch contention is covered in detail in Chapter 8: Tuning Contention.

## Assigning Segments to Pools

Now that the appropriate buffer pools are created, you must use the ALTER command to assign each segment to its specified buffer pool. The following is an example:

```
SQL> ALTER TABLE apps.employee
  2   STORAGE (BUFFER_POOL KEEP);

SQL> ALTER TABLE apps.region
  2   STORAGE (BUFFER_POOL KEEP);

SQL> ALTER TABLE apps.divison
```

```
 2   STORAGE (BUFFER_POOL RECYCLE);

SQL> ALTER INDEX apps.employee_first_name_idx
 2   STORAGE (BUFFER_POOL KEEP);

SQL> ALTER INDEX apps.employee_id_pk
 2   STORAGE (BUFFER_POOL KEEP);

SQL> ALTER TABLE apps.sales_history
STORAGE (BUFFER_POOL RECYCLE);
```

You can view which segments have been assigned non-default buffer pools by using the following query on DBA_SEGMENTS:

```
SQL> SELECT owner, segment_type,
 2   segment_name, buffer_pool
 3   FROM dba_segments
 4  WHERE buffer_pool != 'DEFAULT';
```

| OWNER | SEGMENT_TYPE | SEGMENT_NAME | BUFFER_ |
|-------|--------------|-------------------------|---------|
| APPS | TABLE | EMPLOYEE | KEEP |
| APPS | TABLE | REGION | KEEP |
| APPS | TABLE | DIVISION | RECYCLE |
| APPS | INDEX | EMPLOYEE_FIRST_NAME_IDX | KEEP |
| APPS | INDEX | EMPLOYEE_ID_PK | KEEP |
| APPS | TABLE | SALES_HISTORY | KEEP |

Any segment buffers that were cached prior to the ALTER command will remain in their current pool. The buffers will not be moved to the newly specified buffer pool until the next time they are re-read from disk.

## Monitoring the Performance of Multiple Buffer Pools

After making the appropriate changes to the init.ora and specifying which segments to cache in which buffer pools, the instance must be shut down and restarted for the changes you have made to take effect. After restarting, you can monitor the performance of the buffer pools using the V$BUFFER_POOL and V$BUFFER_POOL_STATISTICS dynamic performance views.

### Using *V$BUFFER_POOL*

The V$BUFFER_POOL dynamic performance view contains information about the configuration of the multiple buffer pools themselves. You can query this view to examine the size and number of latches assigned to each buffer pool:

```
SQL> SELECT name, set_count "Latches", buffers
  2  FROM v$buffer_pool
  3  WHERE id !=0;
```

| NAME | Latches | BUFFERS |
| --- | --- | --- |
| KEEP | 10 | 19200 |
| RECYCLE | 5 | 6400 |
| DEFAULT | 15 | 38400 |

The results of this query clearly shows that the buffers and latches that are not assigned to the Keep or Recycle Pools are assigned to the Default Pool.

### Using *V$BUFFER_POOL_STATISTICS*

The V$BUFFER_POOL_STATISTICS dynamic performance view contains many of the same statistics that we saw in V$SYSSTAT. Before using this view, you must create it by running the Oracle-supplied script CATPERF.SQL while logged in as the user SYS. This script can be found in $ORACLE_HOME/rdbms/admin on UNIX systems and %ORACLE_HOME%\rdbms\admin on Windows NT systems. Once built, you can use V$BUFFER_POOL_STATISTICS to calculate hit ratios for each of the individual buffer pools with a query very similar the one used to calculate the overall Database Buffer Cache hit ratio below:

```
SQL> SELECT name "Buffer Pool",
  2  1 -
  3  (physical_reads / (db_block_gets + consistent_gets))
  4  "Buffer Pool Hit Ratio"
  5  FROM sys.v$buffer_pool_statistics
  6  ORDER BY name;
```

| Buffer Pool | Buffer Pool Hit Ratio |
| ------------------- | --------------------- |
| DEFAULT | .713179916 |
| KEEP | .9721 |
| RECYCLE | .238907 |

As you might expect, if you have tuned the multiple buffer pools properly, the hit ratio should be very high for the Keep Pool and low for the Recycle Pool. The hit ratio for the Default Pool should be somewhere in between these two values, but typically should be in the range of 70-80 percent.

## Cache Tables in Memory

No matter how many buffer pools you decide to use, each one is still managed by an LRU List. Normally, blocks that are accessed by application users are placed at the most recently used end of the LRU List. However, as was noted earlier in this chapter, tables that are accessed via a full table scan (FTS) place their blocks immediately at the least recently used end of the LRU List.

This behavior can present an interesting tuning dilemma. If the cost-based optimizer sees that a frequently used table (like a validation or lookup table) is small, it is likely to be accessed with a FTS. But, this FTS places the tables buffers at the least recently used end of the LRU List where they are quickly removed from the Buffer Cache, only to be reread into memory when they are needed again by a subsequent application user.

One way to manage this problem, particularly with small tables, is to make use of cached tables. Tables designated as being *cache tables* do not have their buffers placed at the least recently used end of the LRU List when they are accessed via an FTS. Instead, these buffers are placed at the most recently used end of the LRU List just as if they had not been full table scanned. This has the effect of keeping these buffers in memory longer while still accessing in the most efficient manner. Cache tables can be implemented in three ways: at table creation, by altering the table after creation, or by using a hint.

### Caching at Table Creation

You can make a table a cache table by including the keyword CACHE when the table is created, as follows:

```
SQL> CREATE TABLE phone_list
  2  ( employee_id   number,
  3  phone_number   varchar2(11),
```

```
4   extension     varchar2(4))
5   TABLESPACE appl_tab
6   STORAGE (INITIAL 50K NEXT 50K PCTINCREASE 0)
7   CACHE;
```

By default, all tables are created as NOCACHE tables unless the CACHE option is specified.

## Using *ALTER TABLE* to Create Cache Table

You can change an existing table into a cache table using the keyword CACHE with the ALTER TABLE command:

```
SQL> ALTER TABLE employee CACHE;
```

The NOCACHE option is used to change a table back to its regular FTS behavior.

## Using Hints to Cache

You can also dynamically CACHE or NOCACHE tables using the appropriate hint:

```
SQL> SELECT /*+ CACHE */ last_name, first_name
  2  FROM employee;
```

The hint will only affect this query; all other accesses of the EMPLOYEE table would still use the table's default cache mode.

## Displaying Cache Table Information

You can use the CACHE column in the DBA_TABLES view to determine which tables are cached, as shown here:

```
SQL> SELECT owner, table_name
  2  FROM dba_tables
  3  WHERE LTRIM(cache) = 'Y';


OWNER          TABLE_NAME
------------   ------------------
APPS           EMPLOYEE
APPS           PHONE_LIST
```

## Bypass Buffer Cache

Another technique for improving the performance of the Database Buffer Cache is to bypass the Buffer Cache completely for certain types of buffer requests. By bypassing the Buffer Cache, buffers that are already stored there are not moved down or off the LRU List during processing. The two types of transactions that can be configured to bypass the Database Buffer Cache are:

- Sort Direct Writes (Covered in Chapter 7: Tuning Physical I/O)

- Parallel DML

Parallel Data Manipulation Language (DML) involves doing bulk inserts, updates, and deletes in parallel by starting multiple processes to perform the action. Several `init.ora` parameters must be set properly before parallel execution can be used effectively. A complete discussion of these configuration procedures is beyond the scope of this text and the Oracle8i Performance Tuning OCP exam. However, parallel execution should only be considered when your server has multiple underutilized CPUs, suitable I/O subsystems, and adequate memory to support the parallel execution.

See Chapter 26: Tuning Parallel Execution and Chapter 27: Parallel Execution Tuning Tips in *Oracle8i Tuning, Release 8.1.5* (Part Number A67775-01) for more information on configuring and using parallel DML.

## Use Indexes Appropriately

The biggest impact you can make on the performance of the Database Buffer Cache from an application SQL code perspective is to ensure that unnecessary full table scans are avoided through the appropriate use of indexes. The fewer full table scans that occur, the higher the Database Buffer Cache hit ratio will be. One simple way to try and encourage the use of indexes is to build indexes on the foreign key columns of tables that reference a primary key column in another table. This will not only help to improve the effectiveness of multi-table joins, but it will also minimize Buffer Cache intensive FTS sort-and-merge joins between the two tables.

# Summary

**T**he role of the SGA's Database Buffer Cache is to cache the most frequently used segments so application users can avoid physical disk I/O when accessing data. The size of the Database Buffer Cache is specified by the `init.ora` parameters `DB_BLOCK_BUFFERS` and `DB_BLOCK_SIZE`. Each Buffer Cache buffer holds the data from one segment block. The activity of the Database Buffer Cache is managed by an LRU algorithm, a Dirty List, and Database Writer (DBW0).

The performance of the Database Buffer Cache is measured by a hit ratio that compares the total number of reads performed in the instance to the number of reads that were done from disk. A Buffer Cache hit ratio of 90 percent or better is expected for well-tuned OLTP systems. The hit ratio can be calculated by querying `V$SYSSTAT`, `V$SESSIO`, `V$SESSION`, and the output from `REPORT.TXT`. Graphical representations of the hit ratio can be viewed using the Oracle Enterprise Manager Performance Manager tool.

The options for improving the hit ratio of the Database Buffer Cache include: making the Buffer Cache larger, using multiple buffer pools, caching tables in the Buffer Cache, bypassing the Buffer cache for I/O intensive operations, and using the indexes to minimize full table scans appropriately.

## Key Terms

Before you take the exam, make sure you're familiar with the following terms:

Dirty List

latch

Keep Pool

Recycle Pool

Default Pool

# Review Questions

1. Which of the following mechanisms does the Database Buffer Cache use to manage its memory?

   **A.** LRU List

   **B.** Dirty List

   **C.** DBW0

   **D.** All of the above play a role in managing the Database Buffer Cache.

2. Which of the following is *not* cached in the Database Buffer Cache?

   **A.** Tables

   **B.** Redo logs

   **C.** Indexes

   **D.** Rollback segments

3. Which of the following processes copy the segment blocks from disk into the Database Buffer Cache buffers?

   **A.** DBW0

   **B.** LGWR

   **C.** Server Process

   **D.** PMON

4. Unless a full table scan occurs, at which end of the LRU list does a user's Server Process place its buffers in the Database Buffer Cache?

   **A.** MRU

   **B.** LRU

   **C.** Middle

   **D.** None of the above

**5.** Each time a buffer of the Database Buffer Cache LRU List is accessed, it is moved to the:

   **A.** MRU

   **B.** LRU

   **C.** Middle

   **D.** None of the above

**6.** A buffer whose copy in the Database Buffer Cache does not match the copy of the segment block on disk is called a:

   **A.** Pinned buffer

   **B.** Free buffer

   **C.** Dirty buffer

   **D.** Rollback buffer

**7.** Which mechanism does a user's Server Process use when locating a free buffer in the Database Buffer Cache?

   **A.** LRU List

   **B.** Dirty List

   **C.** DBW0

   **D.** All of the above

**8.** At which of the following times does DBW0 write dirty buffers to disk?

   **A.** When the Dirty List reaches a threshold length

   **B.** When a user's Server Process searches the LRU List too long without finding a free buffer

   **C.** At a checkpoint

   **D.** All of the above

9. The primary measure of the performance of the Database Buffer Cache is:

    **A.** Average LRU List length

    **B.** Maximum Dirty List miss ratio

    **C.** Database Buffer Cache hit ratio

    **D.** All of the above

10. Which of the following dynamic performance views is used to calculate the Database Buffer Cache hit ratio?

    **A.** V$BUFFERCACHE

    **B.** V$SYSTEMSTATS

    **C.** V$SYSSTAT

    **D.** V$SGASTAT

11. According to Oracle, a well-tuned Database Buffer Cache in an OLTP system should have a hit ratio of:

    **A.** 10 percent or less

    **B.** 50 percent

    **C.** 60-80 percent

    **D.** 90 percent or higher

12. Which of the following statistics in V$SYSSTAT refers to the number of physical reads that have occurred since instance startup?

    **A.** physical reads

    **B.** preads

    **C.** disk reads

    **D.** phyread

**13.** Using the statistics from V$SYSSTAT, which of the following formulas can be used to calculate a Database Buffer Cache hit ratio?

**A.** 1 − ((rollback gets + buffer gets)/ physical reads )

**B.** 1 − (db block gets / (physical reads + consistent gets))

**C.** 1 − (physical reads / (consistent gets + db block gets))

**D.** 1 − (consistent gets / ( physical reads + db block gets))

**14.** Which of the following is a source of information about hit ratios related to the Database Buffer Cache?

**A.** V$SYSSTAT

**B.** V$SESS_IO

**C.** V$SESSION

**D.** All of the above contain Database Buffer Cache hit ratio information.

**15.** Which of the following does not show Database Buffer Cache hit ratio information?

**A.** V$SYSSTAT

**B.** V$SGASTAT

**C.** REPORT.TXT

**D.** OEM Performance Manager

16. Increasing the size of the Database Buffer Cache improves performance because:

    **A.** Server Processes are more likely to find free buffers when needed.

    **B.** Buffers are less likely to be moved out of the cache prematurely by the LRU mechanism.

    **C.** Both of the above are correct.

    **D.** Neither of the above is correct.

17. Which of the following buffer pools can be used to cache segments you have determined to be frequently accessed?

    **A.** Kept

    **B.** Keep

    **C.** Cache

    **D.** Pin

18. Which of the following views can be used to determine which segments might make good candidates for the Keep Pool?

    **A.** V$BH

    **B.** DBA_OBJECTS

    **C.** V$CACHE

    **D.** Any of the above

19. At a maximum, how many buffers must each Database Buffer Cache LRU latch manage?

    **A.** 100

    **B.** 50

    **C.** 500

    **D.** There is no maximum.

**20.** Tables whose buffers are placed at the most recently used end of the LRU List, even when full table scanned, are called:

**A.** Pinned Tables

**B.** Cache Tables

**C.** Kept Tables

**D.** None of the above

# Answers to Review Questions

1. A. The LRU list is used to keep frequently accessed buffers in memory. The Dirty List keeps track of buffers whose copy in memory has changed. Database Writer (DBW0) writes dirty buffers to disk.

2. B. Table, index, cluster, LOB indexes, LOB segments, rollback segments, and temporary segments can all be cached in the Database Buffer Cache.

3. C. Each user's Server Process copies the requested blocks into the Database Buffer Cache.

4. A. Segment blocks are copied into buffers that are placed at the most recently used end of the LRU List.

5. A. Once accessed, any cached buffers are moved from their current location on the LRU List to the beginning, or most recently used end, of the LRU List.

6. C. Dirty buffers store data that has been changed by the application user but has not yet been written to disk by DBW0.

7. D. As the Server Process searches the LRU List for free buffers, dirty buffers are moved to the Dirty List where they are written to disk by DBW0 when the Dirty List reaches its threshold length.

8. D. In addition to these times, DBW0 also writes dirty buffers to disk when tablespaces that store blocks for those segments are placed in hot backup or offline mode and when segments are dropped.

9. C. The Database Buffer Cache hit ratio finds the percentage of buffer requests that were able to be satisfied using the existing cached buffers.

10. C. The V$SYSSTAT dynamic performance view contains statistics on the total number of buffers read and the number of those that were read from disk.

**11.** D. Hit ratios may be lower for non-OLTP systems.

**12.** A. The value for the `physical reads` statistic in V$SYSSTAT is the number of physical I/Os that have occurred since instance startup.

**13.** C. Comparing physical reads to the total number of buffers read produces the Database Buffer Cache hit ratio.

**14.** D. V$SYSSTAT contains statistics for calculating an overall Database Buffer Cache hit ratio. V$SESS_IO, and V$SESSION contain statistics for calculating session-specific Database Buffer Cache hit ratios.

**15.** B. The dynamic performance view V$SGASTAT does not contain Database Buffer Cache hit ratio information.

**16.** C. Increasing the size of the Database Buffer Cache makes more free buffers available and cuts down on unwanted LRU flushing of buffers.

**17.** B. You can assign frequently accessed application segments in the Keep buffer pool by using the STORAGE (BUFFER_POOL KEEP) parameter with the ALTER command.

**18.** D. The V$BH and V$CACHE dynamic performance views as well as the DBA_SEGMENTS and DBA_USERS data dictionary views can be used to determine which segments currently have their buffers in memory.

**19.** D. Each LRU latch in the Database Buffer Cache must manage at least 50 buffers, but there is no strict maximum number of buffers a latch can manage.

**20.** B. Tables that have been created or altered using the CACHE keyword, or accessed using the CACHE hint, will have their buffers placed at the most recently used end of the LRU list during a full table scan.

# Tuning the Redo Log Buffer

---

## ORACLE8i PERFORMANCE TUNING EXAM OBJECTIVES OFFERED IN THIS CHAPTER:

- ✓ Determine if processes are waiting for space in the Redo Log Buffer.
- ✓ Size the Redo Log Buffer appropriately.
- ✓ Reduce redo operations.

Exam objectives are subject to change at any time without prior notice and at Oracle's sole discretion. Please visit Oracle's Training & Certification Web site (http://education.oracle.com/certification/index.html) for the most current exam objectives listing.

In this chapter, you will see how the role of the last component of the SGA, the Redo Log Buffer, complements the functionality of the two SGA structures you have already explored in Chapter 4: Tuning the Shared Pool and Chapter 5: Database Buffer Cache. This chapter will discuss the role of the Redo Log Buffer, its mechanisms, how to monitor its performance, and how to tune it when needed. This is the final chapter dealing with Step 7 in the Oracle Tuning Methodology: Tuning Memory Allocation.

# Understanding the Redo Log Buffer

The *Redo Log Buffer*, is the portion of the SGA that records the information needed to redo an application user's transactions in the event of media failure or user error. These transactions may be DML statements like INSERT, UPDATE, or DELETE, or DDL statements like CREATE, ALTER, or DROP. It is the job of each application user's Server Process to copy redo information into the Redo Log Buffer.

Unlike the Shared Pool and Database Buffer Cache, the Redo Log Buffer is not managed by an LRU mechanism. Instead of the conveyor belt concept of the LRU List, the Redo Log Buffer's management mechanism can be thought of as funnel, where transaction redo information enters at the top of the funnel and is then occasionally emptied out the bottom of the funnel. It is the Oracle background process *Log Writer* (LGWR) which empties the contents of the Redo Log Buffer. These contents are written by LGWR to the online redo log on disk. To keep up with the volume of incoming Redo Log

Buffer entries, LGWR is prompted to empty the entire contents of the Redo Log Buffer whenever any of the following events occur:

- An application user issues a `COMMIT` command.

- Every three seconds.

- Redo Log Buffer is one-third full.

- A Database Checkpoint occurs.

Because LGWR is triggered to write by any and all of these events, LGWR generally does a pretty good job of keeping up with managing the contents of the Redo Log Buffer. In fact, only the last two triggering events are somewhat under the DBA's control.

The DBA can control the size of the Redo Log Buffer and therefore can control how quickly it fills to one-third its total size. Sizing the Redo Log Buffer is discussed in the next section.

A *Database Checkpoint* event represents the moment in time when the database is in a consistent state. When the checkpoint event occurs:

- All buffers in the Database Buffer Cache that contain committed transactions are written to disk.

- All the contents of the Redo Log Buffer are written to the online redo log.

- Database control files and datafile headers are updated to indicate that the checkpoint event has occurred.

Checkpoints are important because, following instance failure, only those transactions that occurred after the last checkpoint have to be recovered during instance recovery. Database checkpoints occur in the database whenever:

- The instance is shutdown using any method except `ABORT`.

- When the online redo log switches from the current log to the next redo log in the sequence.

- When the DBA issues the `ALTER SYSTEM CHECKPOINT` command.

- When the value specified by the `init.ora` parameter `LOG_CHECKPOINT_INTERVAL` is exceeded.

- When the value specified by the `init.ora` parameter `LOG_CHECKPOINT_TIMEOUT` is exceeded.

The `init.ora` parameter `LOG_CHECKPOINT_INTERVAL` specifies the number of bytes that can be written to the online redo log before a database checkpoint occurs. The number of bytes for this parameter is specified in terms of operating system blocks. For example, if your OS block size is 512 bytes and you would like a checkpoint to occur every time 1MB of redo have been generated, you would set LOG_CKECKPOINT_INTERVAL=2048 (1048576 bytes between check-points ÷ 512 bytes per OS block = 2048 OS blocks between checkpoints).

The init.ora parameter LOG_CHECKPOINT_TIMEOUT indicates how many seconds should be allowed to pass between database checkpoints. Therefore, setting LOG_CHECKPOINT_TIMEOUT=1800 would cause a checkpoint to occur every 30 minutes.

To reduce the time it takes to perform instance recovery, Oracle recommends that a database checkpoint occurs every 20 to 30 minutes. This can be achieved either through proper redo log sizing or the use of the LOG_CHECKPOINT_INTERVAL and LOG_CHECKPOINT_TIMEOUT init.ora parameters.

Completing the redo mechanism is *Archiver* (ARC0), the Oracle background process which copies the contents of inactive logs to a secondary location if the database is operating in archive log mode. Figure 6.1 demonstrates the concept of the Redo Log Buffer mechanism.

**FIGURE 6.1** Conceptual Redo Log Buffer Mechanism

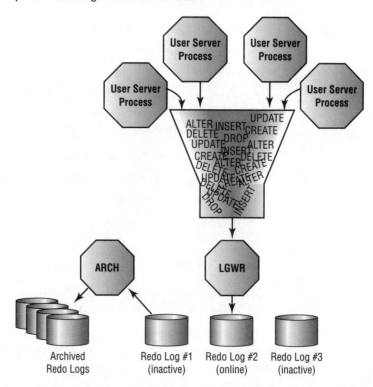

# Measuring the Performance of the Redo Log Buffer

**O**ne way the performance of the Redo Log Buffer can be measured is in terms of the number and length of waits that user Server Processes experience when trying to place entries in the Redo Log Buffer. These waits can be viewed in the V$SYSSTAT and V$SESSION_WAIT dynamic performance views. These same statistics can also be found in REPORT.TXT and by using the OEM Performance Manager tool. Checkpoint and archiving activity relating to the redo logs and the Redo Log Buffer are also important performance indicators. These areas can be monitored using V$SYSTEM_EVENT, REPORT.TXT, and the contents of alert log.

## Using *V$SYSSTAT*

The database statistics recorded in V$SYSSTAT that are relevant to tuning the Redo Log Buffer are redo buffer allocation retries, redo entries, and redo log space requests.

The statistic redo entries reports the number of entries that have been placed in to the Redo Log Buffer by the user Server Processes since instance startup. The statistic redo buffer allocation retries refers to the number of times user Server Processes had to wait and then retry placing their entries in the Redo Log Buffer because LGWR had not yet written the current entries to the online redo log. Using these two statistics, it is possible to calculate a Redo Log Buffer Retry Ratio using the following query on V$SYSSTAT:

```
SQL> SELECT retries.value/entries.value "Redo Log Buffer
Retry Ratio"
  2  FROM v$sysstat retries, v$sysstat entries
  3  WHERE retries.name = 'redo buffer allocation retries'
  4  AND entries.name = 'redo entries';

Redo Log Buffer Retry Ratio
---------------------------
                    .000345
```

Ideally you would like the user Server Processes to never have to wait for access to the Redo Log Buffer. High or increasing values for this ratio indicates that the Redo Log Buffer may need tuning.

Oracle recommends that this Redo Log Buffer Retry Ratio should be less than 1 percent.

The statistic `redo log space requests` in V$SYSSTAT measures how often LGWR is waiting for a redo log switch to occur when moving from the current online redo log to the next:

```
SQL> SELECT name, value
  2    FROM v$sysstat
  3    WHERE name = 'redo log space requests';


name                          value
-----------------------       -----
redo log space requests        34
```

During a redo log switch, LGWR cannot empty the contents of the Redo Log Buffer. This may cause user Server Processes to experience a wait when trying to access the Redo Log Buffer. This wait generates a retry request as explained in the previous section. Therefore, high or increasing values for `redo log space requests` indicates that your redo logs may be too small and thus contributing to the Redo Log Buffer Retry Ratio. This can also indicate a problem with I/O contention. Tuning physical I/O is discussed in the next chapter.

See Appendix C: Statistic Descriptions in *Oracle8i Reference, Release 8.1.5* (Part Number A67790-01) for definitions of all the statistics found in V$SYSSTAT.

## Using *V$SESSION_WAIT*

Unlike V$SYSSTAT, which shows statistics for the entire instance, V$SESSION_WAIT shows how long, and for which events, individual user sessions have waited. The `log buffer space` statistic indicates how long the user session had to wait to place an entry in the Redo Log Buffer because LGWR had not yet finished writing the contents of the Redo Log Buffer to the online redo log.

You can use the following query on both V$SESSION_WAIT and V$SESSION to monitor this activity on a per-user basis:

```
SQL> SELECT username, wait_time, seconds_in_wait
2    FROM v$session_wait, v$session
3    WHERE v$session_wait.sid = v$session.sid
4    AND event LIKE 'log buffer space';

USERNAME SECONDS_IN_WAIT               STATE
-------- --------------- -----------------
     JOE              20           WAITING
    MATT             213 WAITED SHORT TIME
```

Table 6.1 shows the possible values for STATE in V$SESSION_WAIT and the descriptions for each of these states.

**TABLE 6.1**  Column Values and Descriptions for STATE in V$SESSION_WAIT

| Value | Description |
|-------|-------------|
| WAITING | The session is waiting at that moment. |
| WAITED UNKNOWN TIME | Duration of the last wait is undetermined.* |
| WAITED SHORT TIME | The last wait lasted less than 1/100th of a second. |
| WAITED KNOWN TIME | The value in the WAIT_TIME column is the actual wait time. |

*On operating systems that do not support a fast timing mechanism, this value may always be displayed until the init.ora parameter TIMED_STATISTICS is set to TRUE.

High or increasing values for waits related to log buffer space may indicate that the Redo Log Buffer needs to be tuned.

See Appendix A: Oracle Wait Events in *Oracle8i Reference, Release 8.1.5* (Part Number A67790-01) for definitions of all the statistics found in V$SESSION_WAIT and V$SYSTEM_EVENT.

## Using *REPORT.TXT* Output

The REPORT.TXT file generated by running UTLBSTAT.SQL and UTLESTAT.SQL also contains a section that shows the same statistics related to Redo Log Buffer performance that are found in V$SYSSTAT. The relevant sections of a sample REPORT.TXT are shown in Figure 6.2.

**FIGURE 6.2** REPORT.TXT output showing Redo Log Buffer statistics

```
SQL> Rem The total is the total value of the statistic between the time
SQL> Rem bstat was run and the time estat was run.  Note that the estat
SQL> Rem script logs on as "internal" so the per_logon statistics will
SQL> Rem always be based on at least one logon.
SQL> select n1.name "Statistic",
  2         n1.change "Total",
  3         round(n1.change/trans.change,2) "Per Transaction",
  4         round(n1.change/ logs.change,2)  "Per Logon",
  5         round(n1.change/(to_number(to_char(end_time,   'J'))*60*60*24 -
  6                  to_number(to_char(start_time, 'J'))*60*60*24 +
  7                  to_number(to_char(end_time,  'SSSSS')) -
  8                  to_number(to_char(start_time, 'SSSSS')))
  9            , 2) "Per Second"
 10   from stats$stats n1, stats$stats trans, stats$stats logs, stats$dates
 11   where trans.name='user commits'
 12    and  logs.name='logons cumulative'
 13    and  n1.change != 0
 14   order by n1.name;

Statistic                         Total   Per Transaction    Per Logon   Per Second
-------------------------------- -------- ----------------- ----------- ------------
redo buffer allocation retries        139              .75        8.69          .05
redo entries                       265916          1437.38    16619.75        98.52
redo log space requests                33  |            .18        2.06          .01
```

Information about the performance of checkpoints can also be found in the REPORT.TXT file as shown in Figure 6.3.

**FIGURE 6.3** REPORT.TXT output showing Checkpoint statistics

```
8 rows selected.

SQL>
SQL> set charwidth 27;
SQL> set numwidth 12;
SQL> Rem The total is the total value of the statistic between the time
SQL> Rem bstat was run and the time estat was run.  Note that the estat
SQL> Rem script logs on as "internal" so the per_logon statistics will
SQL> Rem always be based on at least one logon.
SQL> select n1.name "Statistic",
  2         n1.change "Total",
  3         round(n1.change/trans.change,2) "Per Transaction",
  4         round(n1.change/ logs.change,2)  "Per Logon",
  5         round(n1.change/(to_number(to_char(end_time,   'J'))*60*60*24 -
  6                  to_number(to_char(start_time, 'J'))*60*60*24 +
  7                  to_number(to_char(end_time,  'SSSSS')) -
  8                  to_number(to_char(start_time, 'SSSSS')))
  9            , 2) "Per Second"
 10   from stats$stats n1, stats$stats trans, stats$stats logs, stats$dates
 11   where trans.name='user commits'
 12    and  logs.name='logons cumulative'
 13    and  n1.change != 0
 14   order by n1.name;

Statistic                        Total Per Transaction   Per Logon   Per Second
-------------------------------- ----- --------------- ----------- ------------
background checkpoints completed     23            .12        1.44          .01
background checkpoints started       23            .12        1.44          .01
|
```

Generally, the value for background checkpoints started, should be equal to or at least not significantly different from, the number of background checkpoints completed. If these statistics differ by more than 1, then checkpoints have been started that were never completed.

## Monitoring Redo Log Buffer Using OEM

The performance of the Redo Log Buffer can also be monitored using the Performance Manager component of OEM Diagnostics Pack. Figure 6.4 shows a sample Performance Manager graphic for the statistics related to the Redo Log Buffer.

**FIGURE 6.4**   Performance Manager Redo Log Buffer statistics

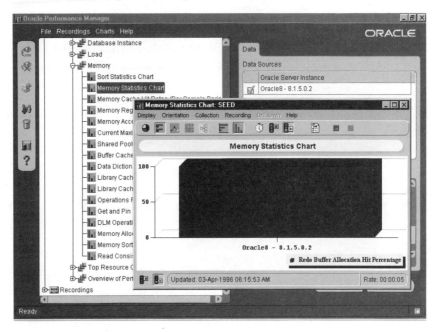

## Using *V$SYSTEM_EVENT*

Occasionally, checkpoint events are started, but do not complete successfully because a second checkpoint request occurs very soon after the first. You can detect checkpoints that are started but not completed by querying

for the statistic `log file switch (checkpoint incomplete)` in
V$SYSTEM_EVENT. This dynamic performance view reports the number of
waits that have occurred since instance startup for a variety of events:

```
SQL> SELECT event, total_waits, average_wait
2    FROM V$SYSTEM_EVENT
3    WHERE event like 'log file switch%';
EVENT                       TOTAL_WAITS AVERAGE_WAIT
----------------------      ----------- ------------
log file switch                       5         18.8
(checkpoint incomplete)
```

Table 6.2 describes the contents of the V$SYSTEM_EVENT columns used in
this query.

**TABLE 6.2**   Descriptions of Selected Columns In V$SYSTEM_EVENT

| Column Name | Description |
| --- | --- |
| EVENT | The name of the event associated with the wait |
| TOTAL_WAITS | The total number of times a wait occurred for this event |
| TIME_WAITED | The total time, in 100th of second, spent waiting for this event |
| AVERAGE_WAIT | The average time, in 100th of second, spent waiting for this event |

The statistic `log file switch (archiving needed)` indicates how often
the writing of the contents of the Redo Log Buffer to the online redo log by
LGWR was interrupted by a wait for the ARC0 Oracle background process to
copy the contents of a redo log to the archive destination.

## Using the Alert Log

The alert log also contains important information regarding checkpoint
activity. When found in the alert log, the following messages indicate that the
redo logs are switching too fast and not allowing enough time for a checkpoint that has been started to complete normally:

```
Thread 1 advanced to log sequence 293
Current log# 1 seq# 293 mem# 0: /u03/oradata/PROD/
log1a.dbf
```

```
Current log# 1 seq# 293 mem# 1: /u04/oradata/PROD/
log1b.dbf
Thread 1 cannot allocate new log, sequence 294
Checkpoint not complete
```

# Improving Redo Log Buffer Performance

**N**ow that you know how the Redo Log Buffer mechanism works and how to monitor its performance, you can examine methods for improving its performance. The objective of Redo Log Buffer tuning is to make sure that user Server Processes have access to, and can place entries in, the Redo Log Buffer without experiencing a wait. These techniques fall into four categories:

- Make it bigger
- Improve efficiency of checkpoints
- Speed up archiving
- Reduce redo generation

## Make It Bigger

The easiest way to improve the performance of the Redo Log Buffer is to increase its size. The larger the Redo Log Buffer is, the less likely user Server Processes are to experience a wait when trying to place redo entries into the buffer.

The size of the Redo Log Buffer is specified in bytes using the init.ora parameter LOG_BUFFER. The default value for LOG_BUFFER varies by platform. However, Oracle's own documentation gives some conflicting information on this point. According to some Oracle documentation, the default size is 500K or 128K × the number of CPUs, whichever is larger. Other documentation says the default size for the Redo Log Buffer is four times the maximum Oracle block size for your platform. Check your system-specific documentation for your default value.

If you make the size of the Redo Log Buffer too small by setting LOG_BUFFER to a very low value, the Oracle Server will override your settings and increase the Redo Log Buffer to its default size.

As with the Shared Pool and the Database Buffer Cache, it is an acceptable tuning practice to continue increasing the size of the Redo Log Buffer until the Redo Log Buffer Retry Ratio shows no further improvement or the value for the statistic log buffer space in V$SESSION_WAIT ceases to diminish.

## Improve Efficiency of Checkpoints

As this chapter has shown, the checkpoint event is an I/O intensive event in the database. Once a checkpoint is started, you would like it to complete successfully. If it does not, the checkpoint event ends up causing unnecessary I/O by prompting DBW0 and LGWR to empty the Database Buffer Cache and Redo Log Buffer, but provides no recovery benefits.

If V$SYSTEM_EVENT, REPORT.TXT, or the alert log show evidence of checkpoints not completing, try increasing the size of the redo log members so they fill and switch less quickly.

You can also use the LOG_CHECK_POINT_TIMEOUT and LOG_CHECKPOINT_ INTERVAL init.ora parameters described in the previous section to explicitly manage checkpoint activity. The default value for LOG_CHECKPOINT_TIMEOUT is 900 seconds for Oracle8i and 1800 for Oracle8i Enterprise Edition. The acceptable range of values for LOG_CHECKPOINT_TIMEOUT is 0 (ignore the parameter) to unlimited. The default value for LOG_CHECKPOINT_INTERVAL is operating system dependent. The acceptable range of values for this parameter is 1 to unlimited.

## Speed Up Archiving

Another potential bottleneck for the performance of the Redo Log Buffer is the frequency and efficiency with which the archive background process, ARC0, copies the contents of the redo log files to the archive destination when the database is operating in archive log mode. If LGWR needs to write to a redo log that is currently being archived by ARC0, LGWR will wait until ARC0 finishes copying the redo log's contents to the archive destination. To reduce the likelihood of this occurrence, LGWR will automatically start additional archive background processes (ARC1, ARC2, etc.) when demands on the system warrant them. The number of Archiver processes can also be set using the init.ora parameter LOG_ARCHIVE_MAX_PROCESSES. This parameter can be set to any value between 1 and 10.

You can also reduce the likelihood that the ARC0 process will create a Redo Log Buffer bottle neck by specifying a device with fast I/O capabilities as the location of for your archive redo log files.

# Reduce Redo Generation

Another way to improve the performance of the Redo Log Buffer is to reduce the demands placed upon it by reducing the amount of redo information generated by certain DML statements. This technique is implemented using one of the following methods:

- UNRECOVERABLE keyword
- NOLOGGING keyword

## *UNRECOVERABLE* Keyword

The UNRECOVERABLE keyword is used when creating a table using the CREATE TABLE AS SELECT... SQL command:

```
SQL> CREATE TABLE employee_history
  2  AS
  3  SELECT *
  4  FROM employee
  5  UNRECOVERABLE;
```

Tables created in this manner do not generate any redo information for the inserts generated by the CREATE statement's sub-query. However, any subsequent DML on the table will generate entries in the Redo Log Buffer. By default, all tables created using the CREATE TABLE AS SELECT... syntax are recoverable.

The UNRECOVERABLE/RECOVERABLE keyword cannot be used when creating partitioned tables, index-organized tables, or tables containing Large Objects (LOBS). For this reason, it has been largely replaced by the NOLOGGING option since Oracle version 8.0.x.

## *NOLOGGING* Keyword

Like UNRECOVERABLE, the NOLOGGING option also allows you to specify which tables should skip generating redo entries when certain types of DML are performed on them. However, unlike UNRECOVERABLE, NOLOGGING is an attribute of the table that stays in effect until you disable it.

The NOLOGGING keyword can be specified during table creation:

```
SQL> CREATE TABLE employee_history
2    (employee_id number,
3    last_name varchar2(30)
4    first_name varchar2(30)
5    hired_date date,
6    start_date date,
7    end_date date)
8    TABLESPACE appl_tab
9    STORAGE (INITIAL 500k NEXT 500k PCTINCREASE 0)
10   NOLOGGING;
```

The NOLOGGING option can also be specified in the ALTER TABLE command:

```
SQL> ALTER TABLE employee_history NOLOGGING;
SQL> ALTER TABLE employee_history LOGGING;
```

All tables are LOGGING tables unless the NOLOGGING option is specified at either table creation or by using the ALTER TABLE command.

In both cases, redo entry generation will be suppressed for all subsequent DML on the EMPLOYEE_HISTORY table if that DML is of the following types:

- Direct Path loads using SQL*Loader

- Direct load inserts using the /*+ DIRECT */ hint

Any subsequent DML on a NOLOGGING table that does not fall into one of these two categories will still generate regular redo entries in the Redo Log Buffer. You can determine which tables have the NOLOGGING attribute set by querying DBA_TABLES:

```
SQL> SELECT owner, table_name
  2  FROM dba_tables
  3  WHERE logging = 'NO';

OWNER         TABLE_NAME
------        ----------------
SYS              ATEMPTAB$
SYSTEM     DEF$_TEMP$LOB
APPS     EMPLOYEE_HISTORY
```

In addition to the CREATE TABLE and ALTER TABLE commands shown above, the following DDL commands can also be used with the NOLOGGING option:

- CREATE TABLE AS SELECT…
- CREATE INDEX…
- ALTER INDEX… REBUILD

Specifying the NOLOGGING attribute on a table means that any data that was loaded using the direct path methods will be lost if media recovery is required before the new data that was added has been included in a scheduled cold or hot database backup.

# Summary

This chapter has shown you the important role that the Redo Log Buffer plays in maintaining Oracle's high degree of transaction recoverability. The significance of the database checkpoint event was also described. At times, however, this component of the SGA can be a performance bottleneck.

You can identify whether the Redo Log Buffer is experiencing any performance problems by querying the V$SYSSTAT, V$SESSION_EVENT, and V$SYSTEM_EVENT dynamic performance views. The REPORT.TXT file, OEM Performance Manager, and alert log also give you important tuning information about the Redo Log Buffer and database checkpoints.

Techniques for improving the performance of the Redo Log Buffer include increasing its size, improving the efficiency of checkpoints, improving the performance of the Archiver Oracle background process, and reducing redo entries by using the UNRECOVERABLE and NOLOGGING options.

## Key Terms

Before you take the exam, make sure you're familiar with the following terms:

Redo Log Buffer

Database Checkpoint

Log Writer

Archiver

# Review Questions

1. Which of the following processes helps manage the contents of the Redo Log Buffer?

   **A.** LRU List

   **B.** Dirty List

   **C.** LGWR

   **D.** All of the above play a role in managing the Redo Log Buffer.

2. Which of the following command types do not place entries in the Redo Log Buffer?

   **A.** INSERT

   **B.** SELECT

   **C.** UPDATE

   **D.** DROP TABLE

3. Which process places the transaction redo information into the Redo Log Buffer?

   **A.** LGWR

   **B.** ARC0

   **C.** DBW0

   **D.** None of the above is correct.

4. Which of the following actions cause LWGR to empty the contents of the Redo Log Buffer to the online redo log? (Choose two.)

   **A.** Occurrence of a database Checkpoint event.

   **B.** ARC0 copies a redo log to the archive destination.

   **C.** Any user issues a COMMIT.

   **D.** DBW0 writes to a datafile.

5. Which of the following `init.ora` parameters would cause a database checkpoint to occur every 20 minutes?

   **A.** LOG_CHECKPOINT_INTERVAL = 1200

   **B.** LOG_CHECKPOINT_TIMEOUT = 20

   **C.** LOG_CHECKPOINT_TIME_OUT = 1200

   **D.** LOG_CHECKPOINT_TIMEOUT = 1200

6. Which of the following `init.ora` parameters would cause a checkpoint event to occur every time 5K of data has been written from the Redo Log Buffer to the online redo log? Assume a 512-byte OS block size.

   **A.** LOG_CHECKPOINT_BYTES=10

   **B.** LOG_CHECKPOINT_INTERVAL=10

   **C.** LOG_CHECKPOINT_INTERVAL=5000

   **D.** LOG_CHECKPOINT_INTERVAL=512

7. All of the following will cause a database checkpoint *except*:

   **A.** DBA performs a SHUTDOWN TRANSACTIONAL.

   **B.** An application user issues a COMMIT.

   **C.** Redo log switches.

   **D.** Any of the above can cause a database checkpoint event to occur.

8. Which dynamic performance view can be used to calculate the Redo Log Buffer Retry Ratio?

   **A.** V$SYSSTAT

   **B.** V$SESSION

   **C.** V$SYSTEM_EVENT

   **D.** V$SGASTAT

9. Which statistic in the V$SESSION_WAIT dynamic performance view can be used to determine which users are currently experiencing waits for access to the Redo Log Buffer?

   A. buffer wait

   B. redo log buffer wait

   C. log buffer space

   D. log buffer wait

10. Which statistics in the output from a REPORT.TXT file can be used to identify excessive checkpoint activity?

    A. check point start/ checkpoint stop

    B. database checkpoints started/ database checkpoint ended

    C. background checkpoints started/ background checkpoints completed

    D. background checkpoint start time/ background checkpoint end time

11. Excessive checkpoint activity that results in checkpoints being started that are not completed can be found in (choose two):

    A. V$SYSTEM_EVENT

    B. V$SESSION

    C. Alert log

    D. V$LIBRARYCACHE

12. According to Oracle, in a well-tuned database user Server Processes will find space in the Redo Log Buffer without waiting around:

    A. 1 percent of the time

    B. 99 percent of the time

    C. 55 percent of the time

    D. 80 percent of the time

**13.** Which of the following methods can be used to improve the performance of the Redo Log Buffer?

    **A.** Increase the value for the LOG_BUFFER init.ora parameter.

    **B.** Reduce the amount of redo generated by using the NOLOGGING option.

    **C.** Avoid unnecessary checkpoints.

    **D.** All of the above are effective methods of improving the performance of the Redo Log Buffer.

**14.** Creating a table with the NOLOGGING option will cause no redo entries to be placed in the Redo Log Buffer except when the following types of DML are performed on the table:

    **A.** Direct path SQL*Loader loads

    **B.** Regular DML

    **C.** Inserts done with the /*+ DIRECT */ hint

    **D.** Inserts done as a result of a CREATE TABLE AS SELECT ... subquery.

**15.** How do the NOLOGGING and UNRECOVERABLE options differ?

    **A.** The NOLOGGING option can only be used on small tables, while UNRECOVERABLE can be used on any table.

    **B.** Only users with DBA privileges can access NOLOGGING tables, while any user can access an UNRECOVERABLE table.

    **C.** The UNRECOVERABLE option can only be specified at table creation, while NOLOGGING can be added to a table at any time.

    **D.** The UNRECOVERABLE option only works when users issue the SET TRANSACTION UNRECOVERABLE command, while NOLOGGING works without any additional commands.

**16.** The size of the Redo Log Buffer is specified by which of the following `init.ora` parameters?

**A.** LOG_BUFFER_SIZE

**B.** REDO_LOG_BUFFER

**C.** REDO_LOG_BUFFER

**D.** LOG_BUFFER

**17.** Which of the following `init.ora` parameters would create a Redo Log Buffer that is 1MB in size?

**A.** LOG_BUFFER=1048576

**B.** LOG_BUFFER=1M

**C.** LOG_BUFFER=1

**D.** LOG_BUFFER=1024

**18.** LGWR starts to write the contents of the Redo Log Buffer to disk when it reaches:

**A.** two-thirds full

**B.** one-third full

**C.** one-half full

**D.** 100 percent full

**19.** Tuning the Redo Log Buffer falls into which step in the Oracle Tuning Methodology?

**A.** Step 4: Tuning the Logical Structure of the Database

**B.** Step 8: Tuning I/O and Physical Structure

**C.** Step 7: Tuning Memory Allocation

**D.** Step 5: Tuning Database Operations

**20.** Which of the following SGA components will typically make up the smallest portion of the total SGA size?

**A.** Shared Pool

**B.** Database Buffer Cache

**C.** Redo Log Buffer

**D.** All of them are equally sized.

# Answers to Review Questions

1. C. The LGWR background process writes the contents of the Redo Log Buffer to the online redo log to ensure that user Server Processes can find room for their entries in the buffer.

2. B. Only DML and DDL statements require entries in the Redo Log Buffer.

3. D. The user's Server Process places the redo entries associated with the user's transaction into the Redo Log Buffer.

4. A and C. LGWR also writes every three seconds and whenever the Redo Log Buffer is one-third full.

5. D. The value for LOG_CHECKPOINT_TIMEOUT is expressed in seconds. Twenty minutes = 1200 seconds.

6. B. The value for LOG_CHECKPOINT_INTERVAL is expressed in OS blocks. Ten OS blocks = $512 \times 10 = 5120 = 5K$.

7. B. A user COMMIT causes LGWR to empty the contents of the Redo Log Buffer to the online redo log, but does not cause a database checkpoint.

8. A. The V$SYSSTAT dynamic performance view contains the redo entries and redo buffer allocation retries statistics that can be used to calculate how often user Server Processes are waiting to place entries in the Redo Log Buffer.

9. C. The statistic log buffer space indicates which users are currently waiting, or have recently waited, for access to the Redo Log Buffer.

10. C. If the number of background checkpoints started and number of background checkpoints completed differ by more than 1, checkpoints are not always completing before the next one begins.

**11.** A, C. The V$SYSTEM_EVENT dynamic performance view will contain the statistic log file switch (checkpoint incomplete) when excessive checkpoints are a problem. The alert log will also contain checkpoint not complete messages.

**12.** B. The ratio of Redo Log Buffer entries to Redo Log Buffer retries should be less than 1 percent.

**13.** D. Another option for improving the performance of the Redo Log Buffer is to improve the speed of redo log archiving.

**14.** B. Regular application DML is still recorded in the Redo Log Buffer even if a table is a NOLOGGING table.

**15.** C. You can use the ALTER TABLE command to add or remove the NOLOGGING attribute from a table.

**16.** D. The size of the Redo Log Buffer is specified in bytes using the LOG_BUFFER parameter in the init.ora.

**17.** A. The value for LOG_BUFFER cannot be specified using *M* for megabyte or *K* for kilobyte.

**18.** B. The LGWR background process writes the contents of the Redo Log Buffer to the online redo log when the buffer is one-third full. This helps ensure that space will always be available for subsequent transactions.

**19.** C. Since the Redo Log Buffer is a portion of the SGA, tuning its performance is associated with tuning memory allocation.

**20.** C. Because it is constantly being emptied by LGWR, the Redo Log Buffer is generally much smaller that the other components of the SGA.

# Chapter 7

# Tuning Physical I/O

## ORACLE8i PERFORMANCE TUNING EXAM OBJECTIVES COVERED IN THIS CHAPTER:

- ✓ Diagnose inappropriate use of SYSTEM, RBS, TEMP, DATA, and INDEX tablespaces.
- ✓ Use locally managed tablespaces to avoid space management issues.
- ✓ Detect I/O problems.
- ✓ Ensure that files are distributed to minimize I/O contention and use appropriate type of devices.
- ✓ Use striping where appropriate.
- ✓ Tune Checkpoints.
- ✓ Tune DBWn process I/O.
- ✓ Determine an appropriate block size.
- ✓ Optimize space usage within blocks.
- ✓ Detect and resolve row migration.
- ✓ Identify the SQL operations that require sorting.
- ✓ Ensure that sorting is done in memory where possible.
- ✓ Reduce the number of I/Os required to perform sort runs.
- ✓ Allocate temporary space accordingly.
- ✓ Use the dynamic performance views to check rollback segment performance.
- ✓ Reconfigure and monitor rollback segments.
- ✓ Define the number and sizes of rollback segments.
- ✓ Appropriately allocate rollback segments to transactions.

Exam objectives are subject to change at any time without prior notice and at Oracle's sole discretion. Please visit Oracle's Training & Certification Web site (http://education.oracle.com/certification/index.html) for the most current exam objectives listing.

**N**early every action that occurs in the database will result in some type of logical or physical I/O. By properly tuning the components of the System Global Area, you can minimize the physical I/Os caused by user transaction. However, no degree of memory tuning will completely eliminate physical I/O activity. Therefore, the next step in the tuning methodology, Step 8: Tuning I/O and Physical Structure, addresses this important area of database tuning.

This chapter discusses the mechanisms related to physical I/O and recommends ways to measure and tune the physical I/O of datafiles, data blocks, and sorting to improve performance. Many activities in the database will cause physical I/O to occur. These activities include:

- Database Writer (DBW0) writing data buffers from the Database Buffer Cache to the database's datafiles

- DBW0 writing data to rollback segment blocks to maintain read consistency

- User Server Processes reading data blocks to copy their contents into the Database Buffer Cache

- Log Writer (LGWR) writing transaction recovery information from the Redo Log Buffer to the online redo log

- Archiver (ARC0) reading the contents of redo logs and writing those contents to the archive destination

- Application user activity temporarily writing large sort requests to disk

- Rollback segment usage

Any of these actions can cause performance difficulties if they occur excessively or are done inefficiently. Therefore, the goals when tuning physical I/O are generally to:

- Minimize physical I/O whenever possible by properly sizing the SGA

- Perform any remaining physical I/O as fast as possible when it is required

Minimizing I/O by properly sizing the SGA was the topic of Chapters 4, 5, and 6. The remainder of this chapter examines how to monitor and tune physical I/O to perform the I/O as quickly as possible when it is required. In order to get a good understanding of how the database is currently performing in terms of physical I/O, several measures must be taken on a number of different database components. The following sections will discuss how to measure and tune the performance of the following database structures as they relate to physical I/O:

- Datafiles

- DBW0

- Individual data blocks

- Redo logs and LGWR

- Checkpoints and CKPT

- Database archiving and ARCH0

- Sort activity and temporary segments

These measures will be taken using queries on V$ and DBA views, examining the contents of REPORT.TXT, and using the OEM Performance and Diagnostic Pack utilities.

# Tuning Datafile I/O Performance

The database's datafiles are made up of individual database blocks. These blocks store the data for each segment. These blocks are read into the Database Buffer Cache by each user's Server Process, and are written by the DBW0 Oracle background process.

# Measuring Datafile I/O

Measuring the physical I/O performance of the datafiles in the database can be done using the V$FILESTAT and V$DATAFILE dynamic performance views, the OEM Performance Manager GUI tool, and the output from REPORT.TXT.

## Using *V$FILESTAT* and *V$DATAFILE*

The V$FILESTAT and V$DATAFILE dynamic performance views can be used to monitor the performance of the read and write activity against the individual datafiles and tablespaces in the database. Figure 7.1 shows a query on these two views.

**FIGURE 7.1** Performance query on V$FILESTAT and V$DATAFILE

```
SQL> SELECT name, phyrds, phywrts,
  2         avgiotim, miniotim,
  3         maxiowtm, maxiortm
  4  FROM v$filestat, v$datafile
  5  WHERE v$filestat.file#=v$datafile.file#;

NAME                                  PHYRDS    PHYWRTS   AVGIOTIM   MINIOTIM   MAXIOWTM   MAXIORTM
----------------------------------    --------  --------  ---------  ---------  ---------  ---------
/u02/oradata/SEED/system01.dbf        455014    156       0          0          6          20
/u02/oradata/SEED/temp01.dbf          269       421       0          0          2          1
/u02/oradata/SEED/appl_data01.dbf     1174      641       0          0          1          1
/u02/oradata/SEED/oem01.dbf           4         2         0          0          1          1
/u02/oradata/SEED/rbs01.dbf           38        601       0          0          4          5
/u02/oradata/SEED/tools01.dbf         7         13        0          0          1          1
/u02/oradata/SEED/users01.dbf         4         2         0          0          1          1
/u02/oradata/SEED/webdb01.dbf         4         2         1          1          1          1
/u02/oradata/SEED/appl_idx01.dbf      4         2         0          0          2          2

9 rows selected.

SQL> |
```

In order to interpret what you see in this output, you need to understand what each of these column values represents. Table 7.1 describes the contents of the V$FILESTAT columns shown in the query in Figure 7.1.

**TABLE 7.1** Descriptions of V$FILESTAT Columns Used in Query*

| Column Name | Description |
| --- | --- |
| PHYRDS | Number of physical reads done on that datafile |
| PHYWRTS | Number of physical writes done to that datafile |
| AVGIOTIM | Average time, in 100th of a second, spent performing I/O on that datafile |

**TABLE 7.1** Descriptions of V$FILESTAT Columns Used in Query *(continued)*\*

| Column Name | Description |
| --- | --- |
| MINIOTIM | Minimum time, in 100th of a second, spent performing I/O on that datafile |
| MAXIOWTM | Maximum time, in 100th of a second, spent writing to that datafile |
| MAXIORTM | Maximum time, in 100th of a second, spent reading from that datafile |

\* The init.ora parameter TIMED_STATISTICS must be set to TRUE in order for these timings to be generated.

Using the output in Figure 7.1, you can see that the physical writes are fairly evenly disbursed among three datafiles: appl_data01.dbf, rbs01.dbf, and temp01.dbf, which are the datafiles for the application tables, rollback segments, and temporary segments respectively. The majority of physical reads are occurring on the datafile that makes up the SYSTEM tablespace, which often occurs because the data dictionary tables that Oracle uses to perform recursive SQL are located in the SYSTEM tablespace. However, excessive write activity to the SYSTEM tablespace may indicate that non-data dictionary segments are stored there.

For a complete listing of all columns in the V$FILESTAT and V$DATAFILE views, see Chapter 3: Dynamic Performance (V$) Views in *Oracle8i Reference, Release 8.1.5* (Part Number A67790-01).

## Using *REPORT.TXT*

The REPORT.TXT file generated by UTLBSTAT.SQL and UTLESTAT.SQL also contains file I/O information at both the tablespace level and datafile level. Figure 7.2 shows the REPORT.TXT output that displays tablespace I/O statistics. Figure 7.3 shows the section of REPORT.TXT that contains tablespace and datafile I/O statistics.

**FIGURE 7.2** Sample REPORT.TXT showing tablespace I/O statistics

```
SQL>
SQL> set charwidth 80;
SQL> set numwidth 10;
SQL> Rem Sum IO operations over tablespaces.
SQL> select
  2     table_space||'
  3      table_space,
  4     sum(phys_reads) reads,  sum(phys_blks_rd) blks_read,
  5     sum(phys_rd_time) read_time,  sum(phys_writes) writes,
  6     sum(phys_blks_wr) blks_wrt,  sum(phys_wrt_tim) write_time,
  7     sum(megabytes_size) megabytes
  8   from stats$files
  9   group by table_space
 10   order by table_space;

TABLE_SPACE       READS    BLKS_READ  READ_TIME     WRITES   BLKS_WRT WRITE_TIME  MEGABYTES
--------------- ---------- ---------- ---------- ---------- ---------- ---------- ----------
APPL_DATA          298338    1382905          0      20969      20969          0        367
APPL_IDX               17         17          0         17         17          0         10
OEMGR                  17         17          0         17         17          0         21
RBS                132519     132519          0      18190      18190          0         21
SYSTEM              24886      31221          0       4821       4821          0        157
TEMP                  543        906          0        911        911          0         52
TOOLS                  40         40          0         84         84          0         26
USERS                  17         17          0         17         17          0          1
WEBDB                  17         17          0         17         17          0        105

9 rows selected.

SQL>
```

**FIGURE 7.3** Sample REPORT.TXT showing tablespace and datafile I/O statistics

```
SQL> set charwidth 48;
SQL> set numwidth 10;
SQL> Rem I/O should be spread evenly accross drives. A big difference between
SQL> Rem phys_reads and phys_blks_rd implies table scans are going on.
SQL> select table_space, file_name,
  2        phys_reads reads, phys_blks_rd blks_read, phys_rd_time read_time,
  3        phys_writes writes, phys_blks_wr blks_wrt, phys_wrt_tim write_time,
  4        megabytes_size megabytes
  5   from stats$files order by table_space, file_name;

TABLE_SPACE FILE_NAME                              READS  BLKS_READ  READ_TIME     WRITES   BLKS
----------- ----------------------------------- ---------- ---------- ---------- ---------- -----
APPL_DATA   /u02/oradata/SEED/appl_data01.dbf      298338    1382905          0      20969      2
APPL_IDX    /u02/oradata/SEED/appl_idx01.dbf           17         17          0         17
OEMGR       /u02/oradata/SEED/oem01.dbf                17         17          0         17
RBS         /u02/oradata/SEED/rbs01.dbf            132519     132519          0      18190      1
SYSTEM      /u02/oradata/SEED/system01.dbf          24886      31221          0       4821
TEMP        /u02/oradata/SEED/temp01.dbf              543        906          0        911
TOOLS       /u02/oradata/SEED/tools01.dbf              40         40          0         84
USERS       /u02/oradata/SEED/users01.dbf              17         17          0         17
WEBDB       /u02/oradata/SEED/webdb01.dbf              17         17          0         17
|
9 rows selected.

SQL>
SQL>
SQL> set charwidth 25
SQL> Rem The times that bstat and estat were run.
```

In Figure 7.2, you can see that the majority of the read and write activity I/O took place on the APPL_DATA, RBS, and SYSTEM tablespaces. You can also see that in some cases, multiple blocks were read and written with a single I/O. For example, the APPL_DATA tablespace had 298,338 physical reads performed against it, reading 1,382,905 blocks. This is approximately four to five database blocks read for every physical read on that tablespace. Tuning this type of multiblock read is discussed in the datafile and tablespace tuning section later in this chapter.

## Using Performance Manager

The Performance Manager GUI tool can also report physical I/O tuning information at the tablespace and datafile level. Figure 7.4 shows the OEM Performance Manager screen that shows datafile I/O in terms of reads and writes per second.

**FIGURE 7.4** OEM Performance Manager Datafile I/O

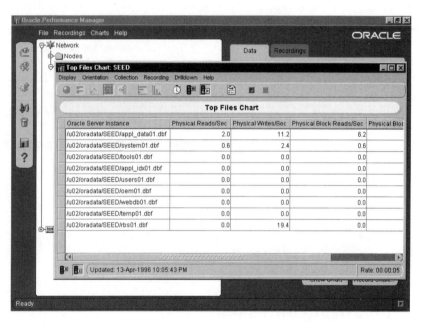

Figure 7.5 shows another screen from OEM Performance Manager, which provides an overall summary of the I/O occurring in the database in terms of write activity per second and read activity per second.

**FIGURE 7.5** OEM Performance Manager Overall I/O

There is no standard rule as to which datafiles should be receiving the most or least I/O. In general, however, you should strive to balance the I/O requests across several datafiles.

# Improving Datafile I/O

All database segments are stored in tablespaces. These tablespaces are made up of physical OS files called datafiles. The datafiles store the actual data blocks that make up each segment's extents. Tuning tablespaces and datafiles generally involves making sure that the I/O against these structures is balanced and fast.

## Balancing Datafile I/O

The simplest way to balance the I/O between the segments in the database is to allocate the storage for those segments to the appropriate tablespaces. At a minimum, this would entail separating the major components of the database into their own tablespaces and making sure that database users do not have the SYSTEM tablespace assigned as their default tablespace. Very excessive I/O on the SYSTEM tablespace datafiles can indicate that non-data dictionary segments may be stored in the SYSTEM tablespace.

Table 7.2 shows a minimum tablespace configuration that could be used to achieve these goals.

**TABLE 7.2**  Suggested Minimum Tablespace Names and Uses

| Tablespace Name | Description |
| --- | --- |
| SYSTEM | Objects owned by the user SYS (i.e., the data dictionary) |
| TOOLS | Default tablespace for the user SYSTEM |
| USERS | Default tablespace for all other database users |
| TEMP | Location for temporary segments used for sorting |
| RBS | Location for rollback segments |
| APPL_DATA | Location for application tables, default tablespace for the application schema |
| APPL_IDX | Location for the application indexes |

Applications that make use of stored PL/SQL procedures, functions, triggers, and packages will still store their PL/SQL source code in the data dictionary in the SYSTEM tablespace.

The separation of temporary segment and rollback segment tablespaces from the SYSTEM tablespace is important for both tuning and management purposes. Table 7.2 also shows a common technique for balancing tablespace I/O: separating application tables from their associated indexes. This technique helps improve performance on busy OLTP systems when tables and their associated indexes are having their blocks read while the blocks are also having rows inserted into them.

This concept can be taken a step further by segregating segments by functional area (i.e., separating Accounting tables and indexes from Inventory tables and indexes) or size (i.e., separating large tables and indexes from small tables and indexes).

## Performing Datafile I/O Quickly

After balancing the I/O requests by separating tables and indexes into their own tablespaces, you can try to perform the I/Os against these structures as quickly as possible. Performing datafile I/O quickly is achieved in four ways: by placing high I/O datafiles on separate disk drives and controllers, striping tablespaces, using locally managed tablespaces, and tuning the DB_FILE_ MULTIBLOCK_READ_COUNT init.ora parameter.

### Segregating Datafiles by Drive and Controller

Improving I/O performance by separating table segments from their associated indexes was explained in the previous section. By additionally ensuring that two different devices are used to store these datafiles and that these devices are attached to two separate disk controllers, I/O performance can be improved even more.

### Datafile Striping

The idea of separating datafiles onto distinct devices can be extended even further through a technique called *striping*. When a datafile is striped, it is stored across several devices, not just one. This increases I/O performance because multiple sets of disk drive heads are brought into use when a read or write of the datafile is required. The easiest way to stripe a datafile is to store the datafile on a *RAID* device. A RAID, or Redundant Array of Independent Disks, consists of several physical disks that can be managed and accessed as if they were one or more physical devices. Therefore, placing a datafile on a RAID device implicitly causes the file to be striped across all the devices in the RAID. This technique does not require any special action on the part of the DBA.

Datafiles can also be manually striped across devices in the absence of a RAID array. Manual striping is accomplished by creating a tablespace made up of several datafiles, where each datafile is placed on a separate physical device. Next, a segment is created so that its extents are stored in each of the datafiles associated with the tablespace, effectively striping the segment across the available devices. The following steps show how a SQL statement could be used to accomplish this for a table called EMP.

1. First, create the EMP table's initial extent:

```
SQL> CREATE TABLE emp
  2  (emp_id number,
  3  last_name varchar2(20),
  4  first_name varchar2(30),
  5  dept_id number)
  6  STORAGE (INITIAL 4M NEXT 4M PCTINCREASE 0)
  7  TABLESPACE appl_data;


Table created.
```

2. Next, add two additional datafiles, each located on separate devices from the other datafiles, to the tablespace where the EMP table is stored:

```
SQL> ALTER TABLESPACE appl_data
  2  add datafile '/u02/oradata/PROD/appl_data02.dbf'
  3  size 5M;


Tablespace altered.


SQL> ALTER TABLESPACE appl_data
  2  add datafile '/u03/oradata/PROD/appl_data03.dbf'
  3  size 5M;


Tablespace altered.
```

3. Finally, manually allocate two new extents for the EMP table using the datafiles that were created:

```
SQL> ALTER TABLE emp
  2  ALLOCATE EXTENT
  3  (DATAFILE
  4   '/u02/oradata/PROD/appl_data02.dbf'
  5  SIZE 4M);

Table altered.

SQL> ALTER TABLE emp
  2  ALLOCATE EXTENT
  3  (DATAFILE
  4   '/u03/oradata/PROD/appl_data03.dbf'
  5   SIZE 4M);

Table altered.
```

Figure 7.6 compares these two methods of striping a datafile.

**FIGURE 7.6** Comparison of RAID-based and manual datafile striping

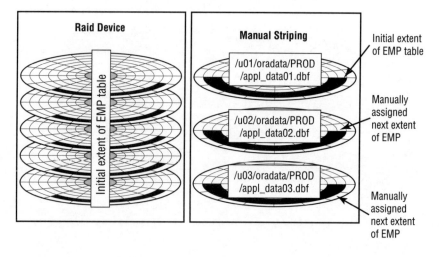

Manual striping tends to be a time consuming activity that may not yield benefits in proportion to the time spent managing it.

### Locally Managed Tablespaces

Datafile I/O can also be reduced through the use of *Locally Managed Tablespaces (LMT)*. A Locally Managed Tablespace uses a bitmap stored in the header of each of the tablespace's datafiles instead of the data dictionary to manage the allocation of space within the tablespace. This allows LMTs to allocate and de-allocate space from the tablespace more quickly, without having to access the data dictionary in the SYSTEM tablespace. Segments stored in LMTs also have the added advantage of being able to have thousands of extents without incurring any performance degradation.

See Chapter 3: Tablespaces and Datafiles in *Oracle8i Concepts, Release 8.1.5* (Part Number A67781-01) for more details on the creation and management of locally managed tablespaces.

### *DB_FILE_MULTIBLOCK_READ_COUNT init.ora* Parameter

This init.ora parameter determines the maximum number of database blocks that are read by a user's Server Process whenever a full table scan (FTS) read operation is performed. The default value for this parameter is 8. The maximum value for this parameter varies by OS. Setting this parameter to a value greater than 8 benefits performance most when the database blocks are being accessed via full table scans. By increasing this parameter, more blocks are accessed with each I/O, thereby cutting down on the total I/Os required.

Before setting this parameter, you can use the following query on V$SYSSTAT to determine how often your application is performing full table scans:

```
SQL> SELECT name, value
  2  FROM v$sysstat
  3  WHERE name = 'table scans (long tables)';


NAME                                  VALUE
-----------------------------   ----------
table scans (long tables)               948
```

High values for this statistic indicate that your application is performing frequent full table scans and may benefit from an increase in the DB_FILE_MULTIBLOCK_ READ_COUNT parameter.

The behavior of the Cost-based Optimizer is also affected by this parameter. If fewer I/Os are required to access all the rows of a table via a full table scan, then the CBO may now choose to access that table using a FTS instead a previously used index.

Another view useful for monitoring FTS operations is V$SESSION_LONGOPS. This view shows activity associated with selected long-running operations like snapshot refreshes, recovery operations, and parallel query jobs. You can also register your application's long-running tasks with this view using the DBMS_ APPLICATION_INFO.SET_SESSION_LONGOPS procedure.

See Chapter 3: DBMS_APPLICATION_INFO in *Oracle8i Supplied Packages Reference, Release 8.1.5* (Part Number A68001-01) for more details on registering application jobs with the V$SESSION_LONGOPS view.

### Raw vs. Cooked: How Do You Like Your Disks?

When a new disk is added to a UNIX-based Oracle Server, the UNIX System Administrator has two choices for managing the I/O activities against disks:

- Create a UNIX file system on the disk

- Leave the device in its raw format without a UNIX file system on it

Disk partitions that contain file systems are referred to as "cooked" or *synchronous* devices. Disk partitions that do not contain file systems are referred to as "raw" or *asynchronous* devices. Which of these two device types to use on Oracle Servers has frequently been a source of hot debate among database administrators. The argument stems from the fact that, since they do not contain a file system, raw devices do not incur the additional overhead of OS intermediation when a read or write request is made to these devices. This makes the I/O activity against the device very fast, thus improving database performance. However, the management of raw devices is generally more difficult than those with file systems. For example, UNIX commands to list the contents of a device (1s) or copy files from one device to another (cp) cannot be used on raw devices. Historically, this meant the DBA was forced to give up ease of management to gain higher performance.

With the advent of caching controllers, faster disk drives, and improved logical volume managers, the performance gap between raw and cooked devices on modern systems has narrowed considerably. Today, the choice of using raw or cooked devices is largely one of personal preference, not one driven by performance requirements.

# Tuning DBW0 Performance

**D**atabase Writer (DBW0) is responsible for writing database buffers from the Database Buffer Cache to the database datafiles. As you saw in Chapter 5: Tuning the Database Buffer Cache, DBW0 performs this write activity at database checkpoints and when user Server Processes are searching for free buffers in the Database Buffer Cache.

## Measuring DBW0 I/O

The V$SYSTEM_EVENT and V$SYSSTAT dynamic performance views and the REPORT.TXT file can be used to determine whether DBW0 is experiencing any difficulty in meeting its obligations to fulfill write requests.

## Using *V$SYSTEM_EVENT*

The system events `buffer busy wait` and `db file parallel write` are both possible indicators of I/O performance problems related to DBW0. The event called `buffer busy wait` indicates that waits are being experienced for buffers in the Database Buffer Cache. Some of these waits may be due to inefficient writing of dirty buffers by DBW0. The event called `db file parallel write` indicates DBW0 may be experiencing waits when writing many blocks in parallel. These waits may be due to a slow device on which the datafiles reside, or the fact that DBW0 cannot keep up with the write requests it is being asked to perform. The following query shows how to determine what the values for these events are in your database:

```
SQL> SELECT event, total_waits, average_wait
  2  FROM v$system_event
  3  WHERE event IN ('buffer busy wait',
  4                  'db file parallel write');

EVENT                      TOTAL_WAITS AVERAGE_WAIT
-------------------------- ----------- ------------
db file parallel write             239   .034454825

1 row selected.
```

This query shows that waits for DBW0 to perform parallel writes have occurred 239 times since instance startup. However, since the AVERAGE_WAIT column value is expressed in 100th of a second, these waits are not yet significant in this particular case. Note that the lack of output for the `buffer busy wait` statistic indicates that this event has not occurred since instance startup.

The event `write complete waits` can also be used to monitor DBW0 I/O activity. Occurances of this event indicate that user sessions have been experiencing waits for buffers to be written from the Database Buffer Cache by DBW0.

High or steadily increasing values for `buffer busy wait`, `db file parallel write`, or `write complete waits` may indicate that DBW0 is not performing its write activities efficiently.

## Using *V$SYSSTAT*

The statistics `redo log space requests`, `DBWR buffers scanned`, and `DBWR lru scans` found in the V$SYSSTAT view are also useful for measuring the performance of DBW0. The statistic `redo log space request` indicates that a wait occurred for a redo log to become available following a log switch. Since a database checkpoint occurs at a log switch, both DBW0 and LGWR have to complete their write activity from the Database Buffer Cache and Redo Log Buffer respectively before LGWR can start writing to the next redo log. If DBW0 is not writing the contents of the Database Buffer Cache fast enough, `redo log space requests` may result. The following query on V$SYSSTAT shows example output for this statistic:

```
SQL> SELECT name, value
  2  FROM v$sysstat
  3  WHERE name = 'redo log space requests';

NAME                            VALUE
----------------------- ----------
redo log space requests             5
```

High or steadily increasing values for redo log space requests in V$SYSSTAT may indicate that DBW0 is not performing its write activities efficiently.

The `DBWR buffers scanned` and `DBWR lru scans` statistics can be used to monitor the effectiveness of DBW0. The statistic `DBWR buffers scanned` indicates the total number of buffers in the Database Buffer Cache that were examined in order to find dirty buffers to write. Since DBW0 performs this action, DBW0 may perform writes ineffectively if it is busy examining the LRU List for dirty buffers when it is signaled to write. Dividing `DBWR buffers scanned` by the value for `DBWR lru scans` will yield the average number of buffers examined with each LRU scan. The following query on V$SYSSTAT shows this calculation:

```
SQL> SELECT scanned.value/scans.value
  2         "Avg. Num. Buffers Scanned"
  3  FROM v$sysstat scanned, v$sysstat scans
  4  WHERE scanned.name = 'DBWR buffers scanned'
  5  AND scans.name = 'DBWR lru scans';
```

```
Avg. Num. Buffers Scanned
-------------------------
             20.2711864
```

Using this query, high or steadily increasing values for the Average Number of Buffers Scanned may indicate that DBW0 is not performing its write activities efficiently.

## Using *REPORT.TXT*

All of the events and statistics mentioned so far in this section can also be found in the output file REPORT.TXT. Figures 7.7, and 7.8 show the sections of REPORT.TXT that contain the information regarding the events from the V$SYSTEM_EVENT view and statistics from the V$SYSSTAT view.

**FIGURE 7.7** Sample REPORT.TXT showing V$SYSTEM_EVENT events

```
SQL> Rem System wide wait events for background processes (PMON, SMON, etc)
SQL> select  n1.event "Event Name",
  2          n1.event_count "Count",
  3          n1.time_waited "Total Time",
  4          round(n1.time_waited/n1.event_count, 2) "Avg Time"
  5    from stats$bck_event n1
  6    where n1.event_count > 0
  7    order by n1.time_waited desc;

Event Name                               Count    Total Time    Avg Time
------------------------------------ ------------- ------------- -------------
buffer busy waits                          904             0             0
...
db file parallel write                    3007             0             0
...
```

**FIGURE 7.8**  Sample REPORT.TXT showing V$SYSSTAT statistics

```
SQL> set numwidth 12;
SQL> Rem The total is the total value of the statistic between the time
SQL> Rem bstat was run and the time estat was run.  Note that the estat
SQL> Rem script logs on as "internal" so the per_logon statistics will
SQL> Rem always be based on at least one logon.
SQL> select n1.name "Statistic",
  2         n1.change "Total",
  3         round(n1.change/trans.change,2)  "Per Transaction",
  4         round(n1.change/logs.change,2)   "Per Logon",
  5         round(n1.change/(to_number(to_char(end_time,   'J'))*60*60*24 -
  6                     to_number(to_char(start_time, 'J'))*60*60*24 +
  7                     to_number(to_char(end_time,   'SSSSS')) -
  8                     to_number(to_char(start_time, 'SSSSS')))
  9                , 2) "Per Second"
 10    from stats$stats n1, stats$stats trans, stats$stats logs, stats$dates
 11    where trans.name='user commits'
 12      and  logs.name='logons cumulative'
 13      and  n1.change != 0
 14    order by n1.name;

Statistic                      Total Per Transaction   Per Logon   Per Second
--------------------------- ---------- --------------- ------------ ------------
DBWR buffers scanned            44918           242.8      2807.38        16.64
...
DBWR lru scans                   2818           15.23       176.13         1.04
...
redo log space requests            33             .18         2.06          .01
...
```

# Improving DBW0 I/O

Two init.ora parameters can be used to tune the performance of
DBW0's activities:

- DBWR_IO_SLAVES
- DB_WRITER_PROCESSES

## DBWR_IO_SLAVES

This init.ora parameter specifies the number of Database Writer slave processes to start at instance startup. Database Writer slave processes are similar
to the actual DBW0 process itself, except they can only perform write operations, not move buffers from the LRU List to the Dirty List in the Database
Buffer Cache as DBW0 does. The purpose of these slaves is to simulate asynchronous I/O on systems that only support synchronous I/O (see the next
sidebar). Archiver (ARC0), Log Writer (LGWR) and Recovery Manager
(RMAN) can also use similar I/O slaves to perform their read and write
activities. The default value for this parameter is 0. The maximum value for
this parameter is OS-dependent. However, setting DBWR_IO_SLAVES to any
non-zero value will automatically start four I/O slaves for ARC0, LGWR,

and RMAN. The naming convention for the DBW0 slaves for an instance called PROD are shown here:

- First DBW0 I/O slave: `ora_i101_PROD`

- Second DBW0 I/O slave: `ora_i102_PROD`

- *n*th DBW0 I/O slave: `ora_i10n_PROD`

---

## How I/O Slaves Simulate Asynchronous I/O

As mentioned in the previous sidebar, devices can be configured as either raw or cooked. From the perspective of the DBW0, each read or write request to a cooked device is punctuated by a wait for the OS to signal that the operation is complete. Since each write request is blocked from continuing because of the wait for the OS's signal, this type of I/O is also referred to as "blocking I/O." A request to write five database blocks to a datafile on a cooked device might look like the pattern shown in the following graphic.

| Write request occurs | Write request is processed | Write request occurs | Write request is processed | Write request occurs | Write request is processed | Write request occurs | Write request is processed |
|---|---|---|---|---|---|---|---|

Unlike the blocking I/O shown here, Database Writer does not have to wait for the write request to be processed before the next write request is serviced when using raw devices. Therefore, raw devices are generally faster at performing I/O operations than cooked devices because there is no wait for OS to signal the completion of the I/O on asynchronous devices. Multiple DBW0 slaves allow the DBA to simulate asynchronous (raw) I/O on synchronous (cooked) I/O devices by interleaving read/write requests with read/write processing. The following graphic illustrates this process.

| | Write request | Write request is processed | Write Request | Write request is processed | Write Request | Write request is processed | |
|---|---|---|---|---|---|---|---|
| **DBW0** → | Write request | Write request is processed | Write Request | Write request is processed | Write Request | Write request is processed | |
| **DBW0 Slave** → | | Write request | Write request is processed | Write Request | Write request is processed | Write Request | Write request is processed |

### DB_WRITER_PROCESSES

While DBW0 slaves can help improve I/O performance, they are not able to perform all the functions of DBW0 (like managing the Dirty and LRU Lists in the Database Buffer Cache). If DBW0 needs assistance performing these tasks as well, you can start additional, full-fledged, Database Writer processes using the DB_WRITER_PROCESSES parameter in the init.ora. The default value for this parameter is 1. The maximum value for this parameter is 10. Note that DBWR I/O slaves and multiple DBWR processes cannot be used simultaneously. If you specify a non-zero value for DBWR_IO_SLAVES, then the value for DBWR_WRITER_PROCESSES has no effect. When adjusting the DBWR_WRITER_PROCESSES parameter, you should also adjust the DB_BLOCK_LRU_LATCHES parameter so that each DBWR process is allocated the same number of latches.

Having more than one DBWR process is not useful on servers with only one CPU.

# Tuning Segment Block I/O

**S**egments like tables and indexes store their data in Oracle blocks. The Oracle block size is determined at database creation and represents the smallest unit of I/O that is possible in an Oracle database. While the default block size is 2K or 4K on most operating systems, Oracle blocks can be 2K, 4K, 8K, 16K, 32K, or 64K. All segments in the database will have the same block size.

You can determine your current database block size by using the SHOW PARAMETER DB_BLOCK_SIZE command in SQL*Plus, Server Manager, or SQL*Plus Worksheet.

## Understanding Block I/O

When a segment is created, it is allocated a chunk of contiguous blocks, called an *extent*, from within a datafile that is associated with the tablespace that the segment is stored in. A user's Server Process copies these blocks into buffers in the Database Buffer Cache during normal database processing. The first block of this initial extent, called the header block, contains a road map to the locations of all the other blocks in the extent. Figure 7.9 shows the relationship between the following table, called EMPLOYEE, its initial extent of 250KB, the tablespace called APPL_DATA, and its associated data-files, `appl_data01.dbf` and `appl_data02.dbf`:

```
SQL> CREATE TABLE employee
  2  ( emp_id    number,
  3    last_name    varchar2(20),
  4    first_name   varchar2(20),
  5    start_date   date)
  6  PCTFREE 20 PCTUSED 30
  7  INITTRANS 5
  8  STORAGE (initial 250K
  9           next 250K
 10           pctincrease 0
 11           freelists 1)
 12  TABLESPACE appl_data;

Table created.
```

**FIGURE 7.9**  Relationship between the EMPLOYEE table, initial extent, tablespace, and datafiles

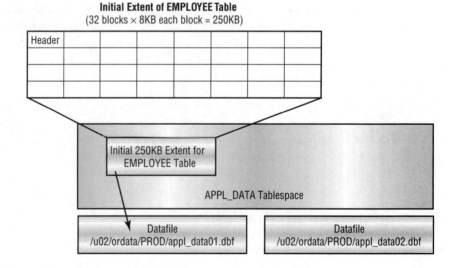

If you were to zero in on one block from the 32 blocks allocated to the initial 250KB extent of the EMPLOYEE table, you will see that it has the structure shown in Figure 7.10.

**FIGURE 7.10**    Structure of an individual EMPLOYEE table block

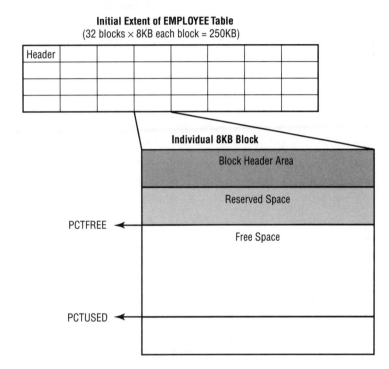

Each block is divided into three sections:

- Block header area

- Reserved space

- Free space

## Block Header Space

Every segment block uses some of its allocated space to store header information about the contents of that block. This header information includes the transaction slots specified by the INITRANS parameter at table creation, a directory of the rows that are contained within the block, and other general header information needed to manage the contents of the block. This block header information generally consumes between 50 to 200 bytes of the block's total size.

## Reserved Space

The parameter PCTFREE tells Oracle how much space to set aside in each block to store row updates. This value is specified as a percentage of the overall size of the block. For example, if you create a table with a PCTFREE setting of 20, then 20 percent of the block's storage will be set aside to hold updated row information. Once a block is filled with data to the level of PCTFREE, the block will no longer accept new inserts, leaving the remaining space to store updates to the existing rows already stored in the block.

The process of removing a block from the list of available blocks is performed by the table's *Free List*. You can think of a Free List as a clipboard that contains a listing of the block IDs that belong to a particular segment. Whenever a user's Server Process wants to insert a new row into a segment, the Server Process consults the Free List to find the block ID of a block that is available to accept the insert. If the subsequent insert should cause the block to fill to above the cutoff determined by PCTFREE, then the block is taken off the Free List, and no other inserts will be made to that block.

A block stays off of the Free List until enough data is deleted so that the block's available space falls below that specified by PCTUSED. When this occurs, the block will go back to the top of the Free List where it can be used again to store new inserts. The default values for PCTFREE and PCTUSED are 10 percent and 40 percent respectively. PCTFREE and PCTUSED can be set at segment creation or changed after creation using the ALTER command. However, the ALTER command does not change the PCTFREE and PCTUSED for blocks that currently contain data. Only new blocks or blocks that are returned to the Free List will have the new setting for PCTFREE and PCTUSED.

Segments from which you expect little or no update can have their PCTFREE value set to a very low (even zero) value. This has the benefit of packing the blocks as fully as possible, causing fewer blocks to be read when accessing a segment's data.

There is no PCTUSED value associated with index blocks. Index blocks go back on the Free List only when they are completely empty.

## Free Space

The remaining space in the segment block, after allowances for the block header and the PCTFREE reserved space, is free space that is used to store the row data for the segment. The number of rows that will fit into each block is dependent upon the size of the block and the average row length of the data stored in that segment.

# Improving Segment Block I/O

In terms of performance tuning block I/O, there are several key areas that must be considered:

- The cost associated with dynamic extent allocation
- The performance impact of extent sizing
- The performance impact of block sizing
- How row chaining and migration affect performance
- The role of the High Water Mark during full table scans

## Dynamic Extent Allocation

When all the available extents assigned to a segment are full, the next insert operation will cause the segment to acquire a new extent. On rapidly growing tables, this dynamic allocation of segment extents incurs undesirable I/O overhead. This I/O stems from the queries that Oracle must perform against the data dictionary in the SYSTEM tablespace and the actual acquisition of the extent space in the appropriate datafile. In order to avoid this dynamic allocation, you must first identify tables that are close to needing an additional extent, and then proactively assign them additional extents. The following SQL commands show how this could be done for a table called SALES:

```
SQL> SELECT owner, table_name,
  2         1-(empty_blocks/(empty_blocks+blocks))
  3         "% Blocks Used"
  4  FROM dba_tables
  5  WHERE owner != 'SYS'
  6  AND 1 - (empty_blocks/(empty_blocks+blocks)) > .95
  7  ORDER BY 1;

OWNER           TABLE_NAME              % Blocks Used
-------------   --------------------    -------------
APPL            SALES                               1
APPL            EMPLOYEE                     .96654275
APPL            DEPARTMENT                   .96899225

SQL> ALTER TABLE appl.sales
  2  ALLOCATE EXTENT;
```

For optimal performance, Oracle states that the maximum number of extents for a segment should not exceed 1,000 (or 2,000 if the segment is stored in a locally managed tablespace).

## Extent Sizing and Performance

Closely related to the dynamic allocation of extents is the size of each extent. Larger extent sizes offer slightly better performance than smaller extents because they are less likely to dynamically extend and can also have all their locations identified from a single block (called the *extent map*) stored in the header of the segment's first extent.

## Block Size and Performance

Since extents are made up of contiguous blocks, database block size is closely related to I/O performance. The appropriate block size for your system will depend on your application, OS specifications, and available hardware. Generally, OLTP systems use smaller block sizes because:

- Small blocks provide better performance for the random-access nature of the OLTP systems.

- Small blocks reduce block contention, since each block contains fewer rows.

- Small blocks are better for storing the small rows that are common in OLTP systems.

However, small block sizes do add to Database Buffer Cache overhead because more blocks must generally be accessed, since each block stores fewer rows.

Conversely, DSS systems use larger block sizes because:

- Large blocks pack more data and index entries into each block.

- Large blocks favor the sequential I/O common in most DSS systems.

However, larger block sizes also increase the likelihood of block contention and require larger Database Buffer Cache sizes to accommodate all the buffers required to achieve acceptable Database Buffer Cache hit ratios.

Block size also impacts two important block-related tuning issues: row chaining and row migration.

### Row Chaining

When a row that is inserted into a table exceeds the size of the database block, the row will spill over into two or more blocks. Whenever a row spans multiple blocks in this manner, it is referred to as a *chained row*. Row chaining is bad for performance because multiple blocks must be read to return a single row. The only way to fix a chained row is to decrease the size of the insert or increase the Oracle block size.

### Row Migration

*Row migration* occurs when a previously inserted row is updated. If the update to the row causes the row to grow larger than the space available in the block specified by PCTFREE, Oracle moves (or migrates) the row to a new block. When migration occurs, a pointer is left at the original location, which points to the row's new location in the new block. Row migration is bad for performance because Oracle must perform at least two I/Os (one on the original block, and one on the block referenced by the row pointer) in order to return a single row. Row migration can be minimized by setting PCTFREE to an appropriate value so updated rows find sufficient space in the same block to store the new data.

Since row migration only occurs during an update, it can be corrected by merely deleting and then reinserting the migrated rows. The following steps show how row migration can be identified and remedied in a table called SALES.

### Identifying Chained and/or Row Migration

The following ANALYZE TABLE command is used to identify whether chained or migrated rows exist in a table:

```
SQL> ANALYZE TABLE sales COMPUTE STATISTICS;

Table analyzed.

SQL> SELECT table_name, chain_cnt
  2  FROM dba_tables
  3  WHERE table_name = 'SALES';

TABLE_NAME                     CHAIN_CNT
------------------------------ ----------
SALES                                  5
```

The ANALYZE command populates the CHAIN_CNT column of DBA_TABLES, which is otherwise null. The resulting CHAIN_CNT of 5 indicates that the SALES table has five rows that are chained and/or migrated. Unfortunately, this view does not distinguish between rows that are migrated and rows that are chained.

Next, the Oracle-supplied script UTLCHAIN.SQL is used to build a table called CHAINED_ROWS. This table is then used to identify the chained and/or migrated rows by using the ANALYZE command with the LIST CHAINED ROWS parameter. The UTLCHAIN.SQL script, shown below, is located in $ORACLE_HOME/rdbms/admin on UNIX systems and %ORACLE_HOME%\rdbms\admin on Windows NT systems.

```
SQL> @$ORACLE_HOME/rdbms/admin/utlchain.sql
Table created.
SQL> ANALYZE TABLE sales LIST CHAINED ROWS;
Table analyzed.
```

Now the CHAINED_ROWS table can be queried to identify which rows are migrated and/or chained in the SALES table by using the HEAD_ROWID column of the CHAINED_ROWS table and the ROWID pseudo column of the SALES table:

```
SQL> SELECT owner_name, table_name, head_rowid
  2  FROM chained_rows
  3  WHERE table_name = 'SALES';


OWNER_NAME TABLE_NAME HEAD_ROWID
---------- ---------- ------------------

APPL       SALES      AAAEHvAAGAAABnUAAD
APPL       SALES      AAAEHvAAGAAABnUAAE
APPL       SALES      AAAEHvAAGAAABnUAAF
APPL       SALES      AAAEHvAAGAAABnUAAG
APPL       SALES      AAAEHvAAGAAABnUAAH
```

Next, you need to copy the chained rows to a temporary table so that you can subsequently delete them from the SALES table, and then reinsert them into the SALES table:

```
SQL> CREATE TABLE temp
  2  AS SELECT *
  3     FROM sales
  4     WHERE rowid IN (SELECT head_rowid
  5                     FROM chained_rows);
```

```
Table created.

SQL> DELETE FROM sales
  2  WHERE rowid IN (SELECT head_rowid
  3                         FROM chained_rows);

5 rows deleted.

SQL> INSERT INTO sales
  2  SELECT * FROM temp;

5 rows created.
```

Finally, you can reanalyze the SALES table with the COMPUTE STATISTICS option. Any non-zero value remaining in the CHAIN_CNT column of DBA_TABLES indicates that those rows are chained, not migrated, since deleting and reinserting those rows did not fix the row:

```
SQL> ANALYZE TABLE sales COMPUTE STATISTICS;

Table analyzed.

SQL> SELECT table_name, chain_cnt
  2  FROM dba_tables
  3  WHERE table_name = 'SALES';

TABLE_NAME                     CHAIN_CNT
------------------------------ ----------
SALES                                  1
```

In this example, one row was actually chained and not migrated, so it was not fixed by deleting and reinserting the rows.

A second method for identifying the existence of row chaining and migration in the database is by querying V$SYSSTAT for occurances of the statistic table fetch continued row:

```
SQL> SELECT name, value
  2  FROM v$sysstat
```

```
 3  WHERE name = 'table fetch continued row';


NAME                                   VALUE

----------------------------   ----------

table fetch continued row                450
```

This statistic is also found in the REPORT.TXT output as shown in Figure 7.11.

**FIGURE 7.11**   Sample REPORT.TXT showing chained/migrated row statistic

```
SQL> set charwidth 27;
SQL> set numwidth 12;
SQL> Rem The total is the total value of the statistic between the time
SQL> Rem bstat was run and the time estat was run.  Note that the estat
SQL> Rem script logs on as "internal" so the per_logon statistics will
SQL> Rem always be based on at least one logon.
SQL> select n1.name "Statistic",
  2          n1.change "Total",
  3          round(n1.change/trans.change,2) "Per Transaction",
  4          round(n1.change/logs.change,2)  "Per Logon",
  5          round(n1.change/(to_number(to_char(end_time,   'J'))*60*60*24 -
  6                          to_number(to_char(start_time, 'J'))*60*60*24 +
  7                          to_number(to_char(end_time,   'SSSSS')) -
  8                          to_number(to_char(start_time, 'SSSSS')))
  9                , 2) "Per Second"
 10     from stats$stats n1, stats$stats trans, stats$stats logs, stats$dates
 11     where trans.name='user commits'
 12       and  logs.name='logons cumulative'
 13       and  n1.change != 0
 14     order by n1.name;

Statistic                         Total Per Transaction   Per Logon   Per Second
------------------------------  ------------ ----------------  ------------  ------------
...
table fetch continued row            58              .31        3.63            .02
...
```

## High Water Mark and Performance

Another important consideration when tuning database I/O related to individual database blocks is the concept of *High Water Mark*. As a segment uses the database blocks allocated to its extents, the Oracle Server keeps track of the highest block ID that has ever been used to store segment data. This block ID is called the High Water Mark (HWM). Figure 7.12 illustrates this mechanism.

**FIGURE 7.12** High Water Mark mechanism

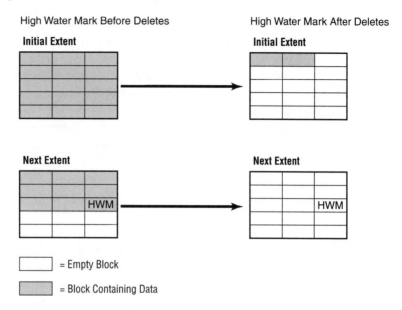

The HWM is significant because a user's Server Process reads all the segment blocks up to the HWM when performing a full table scan against a segment. Since the HWM does not move when rows are deleted from a segment, many empty blocks may end up being scanned during a FTS even though they no longer contain data. Additionally, if the segment is static (no additional rows are expected to be added to the segment), the space above the HWM will be wasted.

After using the ANALYZE command, the EMPTY_BLOCKS column in DBA_TABLES shows the number of blocks that a table has above its High Water Mark. The BLOCKS column in DBA_TABLES shows the number of blocks below the HWM; these blocks may, or may not, contain data.

# Tuning Redo Log and LGWR I/O

**S**ince LGWR and the redo logs play a central role in database recovery, they must be tuned—not only to ensure optimal performance, but also optimal recovery.

### Measuring Redo Log and LGWR I/O

Measuring the performance of the database redo logs is difficult because Oracle does not provide any data dictionary views that directly show I/O activity against the redo logs. One way to gather I/O information about the redo logs is to use the V$LOGFILE view to determine the locations of the redo log files and then use an OS utility to monitor I/O on those devices. The UNIX utilities sar and iostat are both useful for monitoring disk I/O on the devices where redo logs are located. Performance Monitor can be used for similar monitoring on Windows NT systems. However, LGWR is rarely the source of any significant performance problems.

### Improving Redo Log and LGWR I/O

By using the techniques described in Chapter 6 to tune the Redo Log Buffer, you can assure that the I/O activities of LGWR and the redo logs is performing properly. If the Redo Log Buffer is too small, the actions of LGWR and the redo logging mechanism can cause I/O performance bottlenecks.

One of the easiest ways to ensure that the redo logs will not cause any I/O performance issues is to separate them from datafiles onto their own devices. This generally helps the performance of both the database datafiles and redo logs since the I/O activity of the former is typically random and the I/O activity of the latter is sequential.

# Tuning Checkpoints and CKPT I/O

**C**losely related to the tuning of LGWR and the redo logs is tuning of database Checkpoints and the CKPT background process. As mentioned in Chapter 6, the database checkpoint is an I/O intensive event where both DBW0 and LGWR write portions of the contents of their respective SGA caches to disk. Perform database checkpoints frequently enough to ensure quick instance recovery, but not so much as to cause unnecessary I/O.

### Measuring Checkpoint and CKPT I/O

As shown in Chapter 6, checkpoints can be monitored using the background checkpoints started and background checkpoints completed statistics in V$SYSSTAT and REPORT.TXT.

## Improving Checkpoint and CKPT I/O

Chapter 6 also discussed the usage of the init.ora parameters LOG_
CHECKPOINT_TIMEOUT and LOG_CHECKPOINT_INTERVAL to tune the frequency
with which checkpoints occur in the database. Two additional parameters:
FAST_START_IO_TARGET and DB_BLOCK_MAX_DIRTY_TARGET can also be used
to tune database checkpoint activity.

### FAST_START_IO_TARGET

This init.ora parameter is used to limit the number of I/Os that would be
required to perform instance recovery if the database were to fail at that moment.
The default value for this parameter is equal to the number of buffers specified by
DB_BLOCK_BUFFERS. Valid values are zero (i.e. disable the parameter) or anything
between 1000 and the value specified by DB_BLOCK_BUFFERS.

### DB_BLOCK_MAX_DIRTY_TARGET

Like FAST_START_IO_TARGET, this init.ora parameter is also used to specify the maximum number of dirty buffers that are allowed to collect in the
Database Buffer Cache before DBW0 writes them to disk. However, because
it does not impose a hard limit on the number of I/Os for recovery, this
parameter is less precise than FAST_START_IO_TARGET. The default value
for this parameter is equal to the number of buffers specified by DB_BLOCK_
BUFFERS. Valid values are zero (i.e. disable the parameter) or anything
between 1000 and the value specified by DB_BLOCK_BUFFERS.

The FAST_START_IO_TARGET parameter is only available on the Oracle8i
Enterprise Edition.

# Tuning Archiving and ARC0 I/O

The process of *archiving* refers to the copying of the redo log files'
contents to a secondary destination so that the archived logs can be used
for database recovery in the event of media failure or user error. While
this mechanism is an important part of the backup and recovery aspect
of administering a database, it can also be a significant source of I/O
performance problems.

## Measuring Archiving and ARC0 I/O

The two most common performance problems related to the archiving process are:

- The archive destination fills with archived logs, causing database processing to halt until additional space is made available.

- The ARC0 background process does not keep up with the redo log switching activity, causing a wait to occur when the redo logs wrap before ARC0 has completed archiving the contents of the log.

These events can be monitored using the V$ARCHIVE_DEST, V$ARCHIVED_LOG, V$ARCHIVED_PROCESSES, and V$SYSSTAT dynamic data dictionary views.

### Filling the Archive Location

The location of the archived redo log files is specified using the init.ora parameter LOG_ARCHIVE_DEST or LOG_ARCHIVE_DEST_$n$ where $n$ is a value between 1 and 5, which allows you to specify up to five archive destinations for extra assurance of recoverability.

The init.ora parameter LOG_ARCHIVE_DEST_$n$ is only available in the Oracle8i Enterprise Edition. ARCHIVE_LOG_DEST must be used to specify the archive location in the Oracle8i Standard Edition.

When the archive destination becomes full, database processing halts, and an error message is written to the database Alert log. Figure 7.13 shows an example of what this error message looks like.

**FIGURE 7.13**   Alert log error message when archive destination is full

```
Tue Apr 18 22:05:09 2000
Thread 1 advanced to log sequence 301
  Current log# 1 seq# 301 mem# 0: /u03/oradata/SEED/log1a.dbf
  Current log# 1 seq# 301 mem# 1: /u04/oradata/SEED/log1b.dbf
Tue Apr 18 22:05:09 2000
ARC0: Beginning to archive log# 2 seq# 300
ARC0: Error creating archivelog file '/u05/oradata/SEED/SEED_300.arc'
ARC0: Archiving not possible: error count exceeded
ARC0: Failed to archive log# 2 seq# 300
ARCH: Archival stopped, error occurred. Will continue retrying
Tue Apr 18 22:05:09 2000
ORACLE Instance SEED - Archival Error
ARCH: Connecting to console port...
Tue Apr 18 22:05:09 2000
ORA-16014: log 2 sequence# 300 not archived, no available destinations
ORA-00312: online log 2 thread 1: '/u03/oradata/SEED/log2a.dbf'
ORA-00312: online log 2 thread 1: '/u04/oradata/SEED/log2b.dbf'
ARCH: Connecting to console port...
ARCH:
 ORA-16014: log 2 sequence# 300 not archived, no available destinations
ORA-00312: online log 2 thread 1: '/u03/oradata/SEED/log2a.dbf'
ORA-00312: online log 2 thread 1: '/u04/oradata/SEED/log2b.dbf'
Tue Apr 18 22:05:22 2000
LGWR: prodding the archiver
Tue Apr 18 22:05:22 2000
ARC0: received prod
```

When this error occurs, the database will remain halted until space is made available in the archive location. You can also temporarily change the archive location using the following command:

```
SQL> ALTER SYSTEM ARCHIVE LOG ALL TO
  2  '/u04/oradata/PROD';
```

Once space is made available in the archive destination, archiving will resume, and a message will be written to the alert log to indicate that archiving has resumed.

## ARC0 Processes Causing Waits at Log Switch

If the redo logs are switching too frequently, LGWR may wrap around and try to write to a redo log that has not yet been archived by ARC0. Since a database in archive log mode cannot reuse a redo log until it has been archived, LGWR will hang for a moment until the redo log has been archived and becomes available. To prevent this, LGWR automatically starts new archive processes (i.e. ARC1, ARC2, etc.) any time it detects that the current number of Archiver processes are not keeping up with the switching of the redo logs. The DBA can also start additional Archiver processes at instance startup by setting the init.ora parameter LOG_ARCHIVE_MAX_PROCESSES to a value between 2 and 10 (1 is the default).

You can actively monitor the need for additional Archiver processes by querying the V$ARCHIVE_PROCESSES dynamic performance view. This view shows the status of each Archiver process and whether it is currently busy or idle.

If any of the statistics listed in Table 7.3 are present in V$SYSTEM_EVENT or V$SESSION_EVENT, this indicates that actions of LGWR may be held up by the actions of ARC0.

**TABLE 7.3** Wait Events in V$SYSSTAT That Can Indicate ARC0 I/O Bottlenecks

| Statistic | Description |
| --- | --- |
| log file switch (archiving needed) | How often LGWR is experiencing a wait because the redo log it wants to switch to has not finished archiving yet. |
| log file switch completion | How long it takes for a redo log switch to complete. High or steadily increasing values for this statistic may indicate a problem with ARC0. |
| log buffer space | How often user Server Processes are experiencing waits when trying to place redo entries in the Redo Log Buffer. These waits may be due to LGWR being held up by ARC0 from writing to the online redo log. |
| log parallel write | How long it takes LGWR I/Os to complete. High or steadily increasing values for this statistic may also indicate that the activities of LGWR are being interrupted by ARC0. |

These statistics can also be found in the REPORT.TXT output file.

## Improving Archiving and ARC0 I/O

If you have identified the archiving mechanisms or ARC0 itself as a performance bottleneck, you can improve the performance of these processes by adding more redo logs, increasing the size of the existing redo logs, actively managing the archive destinations, and creating additional ARC0 processes to assist with the archiving process.

## Add More

Every Oracle database must have at least two redo log groups. However, by adding additional redo log groups to your database, you decrease the likelihood that LGWR will wrap around through all the redo logs and back to the one that may still be archiving. There is no magic number of redo log groups that is correct for all situations, but between five and 20 logs is generally adequate on most OLTP systems.

In addition to having an adequate number of redo log groups, each group should have at least two members. Having multiple redo log members in each group minimizes possible data loss due to the corruption or loss of an online redo log.

## Make It Bigger

In addition to adjusting the quantity of redo logs, increasing their size can also cut down on the frequency of log switches and the archiving overhead that comes with them. For the purposes of checkpointing and recoverability, Oracle recommends that a log switch take place approximately every 20 to 30 minutes. However, as we have seen, checkpoint frequency can be tuned using the LOG_CHECKPOINT_TIMEOUT, LOG_CHECKPOINT_INTERVAL, FAST_IO_TARGET, and DB_BLOCK_MAX_DIRTY_TARGET parameters in the init.ora. Therefore, it is possible to increase the size of your redo logs without negatively affecting checkpoint frequency.

## Tune Archive Destinations

There are several init.ora parameters that you can use to lessen the likelihood of a database stoppage due to a filled archive location. These parameters allow you to specify multiple, concurrent archive destinations so that database transaction processing can continue even if one of the other locations fills with archive logs.

### LOG_ARCHIVE_DUPLEX_DESTINATION

This parameter is used in conjunction with the LOG_ARCHIVE_DEST parameter discussed in the previous section. By setting this parameter, ARC0 is instructed to write archived redo logs to both locations. When used in conjunction with LOG_ARCHIVE_MIN_SUCCEED_DEST shown in the next section, ARC0 can continue to archive redo log files even if one of the two locations is full.

### LOG_ARCHIVE_DEST_n

This parameter is used in conjunction with the LOG_ARCHIVE_DEST parameter, which was discussed in the previous section. By setting the LOG_ARCHIVE_DEST_*n* parameter, ARC0 is instructed to write archived redo logs to multiple locations. These locations can be local or remote and can be specified as either required or optional when used in conjunction with LOG_ARCHIVE_MIN_SUCCEED_DEST and LOG_ARCHIVE_DEST_STATE_*n*. As shown in the next sections, ARC0 can continue to archive redo log files even if one of the locations is full.

### LOG_ARCHIVE_MIN_SUCCEED_DEST

When used with LOG_ARCHIVE_DUPLEX_DEST and LOG_ARCHIVE_DEST_*n*, this parameter specifies the number of locations to which ARC0 must be able to successfully write archive log files before an error is raised. The default value is 1. Valid values are 1 or 2 when used with LOG_ARCHIVE_DUPLEX_DEST, or between 1 and 5 when used with LOG_ARCHIVE_DEST_*n*.

### LOG_ARCHIVE_DEST_STATE_n

This init.ora parameter is used in conjunction with LOG_ARCHIVE_DEST_*n*. A LOG_ARCHIVE_DEST_STATE_*n* is specified for each corresponding LOG_ARCHIVE_DEST_*n* parameter. The valid values for this parameter are ENABLE or DEFER. The following sample from an init.ora shows how these parameters might be specified on a UNIX system running Oracle8i Enterprise Edition.:

```
log_archive_dest_1       = /u01/oradata/PROD
log_archive_dest_2       = /u02/oradata/PROD
log_archive_dest_3       = /u03/oradata/PROD
log_archive_dest_state_1 = enable
log_archive_dest_state_2 = defer
log_archive_dest_state_3 = enable
```

Using these parameters, ARC0 would copy the contents of the redo logs to two locations: /u01/oradata/PROD and /u03/oradata/PROD. Although the location /u02/oradata/PROD is configured as an archive location, it would not be used until its status is changed from DEFER to ENABLE. Changing a location's status from DEFER to ENABLE can be accomplished by either editing the init.ora, or by issuing the ALTER SYSTEM SET LOG_ARCHIVE_DEST_STATE_n = ENABLE command.

The dynamic data dictionary views V$ARCHIVE_DEST and V$ARCHIVED_LOG can be used to monitor the location and status of the archive activity in each archive destination.

### Create Additional ARC0 Processes

While Oracle states that multiple Archiver processes are rarely needed, you may want to experiment with starting additional Archiver processes if ARC0 appears to be causing a performance bottleneck. Additional Archiver processes are started by using the LOG_ARCHIVE_MAX_PROCESSES parameter in the init.ora. The number of Archiver processes to start is somewhat dependent upon the number of archive destinations you have specified and the speed of the storage devices that are behind those locations. The default value for this parameter is 1. The valid values for this parameter are from 1 to 10. These archive processes will start immediately at instance startup.

The dynamic data dictionary view V$ARCHIVE_PROCESSES can be used to monitor the number and activity of multiple Archiver processes.

# Tuning Sort I/O

**S**orting occurs whenever data must be placed in a specified order. When a sort occurs in an Oracle instance, it can take place in one of two locations: in memory or on disk. Sorts in memory are the least expensive in terms of performance. Sorts to disk are the most expensive because of the extra overhead of the disk I/Os. In general, the primary tuning goal with regard to sorting is to minimize sort activity, but when it must be done, perform it in memory whenever possible.

Many changes were made to the area of tuning sort I/O in Oracle8i. Five init.ora parameters that were used in Oracle 7.3 and Oracle8 were made obsolete in Oracle8i. In many ways, this has made the process of tuning sorts easier in Oracle8i.

## Understanding Sort Activity

The types of SQL statements that can cause database sorts to occur include the following:

- ORDER BY
- GROUP BY

- SELECT DISTINCT
- UNION
- INTERSECT
- MINUS
- ANALYZE
- CREATE INDEX
- Joins between tables on columns that are not indexed

The amount of memory set aside for each user's Server Process to perform these sort operations is specified by the init.ora parameters SORT_AREA_SIZE and SORT_AREA_RETAINED_SIZE.

### SORT_AREA_SIZE

The default value for SORT_AREA_SIZE is OS-dependent. The minimum size for this parameter is equivalent to six Oracle blocks. The maximum size is OS-dependent. SORT_AREA_SIZE specifies how much memory each user's Server Process should set aside to perform in-memory sort operations. If a sort operation is smaller than this size, the sort will be performed in memory. If the sort operation is larger than this size, the sort is broken up into chunks. Each chunk is then sorted individually, with the intermediate sorted chunks being written to the user's temporary tablespace. Once all the chunks have been sorted, the final, sorted result is created when the separate sorted chunks are merged together and returned to the user.

The SORT_AREA_SIZE parameter can be set using the init.ora, or by issuing the ALTER SYSTEM SET SORT_AREA_SIZE=*n* DEFERRED command, or by using the ALTER SESSION SET SORT_AREA_SIZE=*n* command.

When using the Multithreaded Server option, each user's sort area is taken from the UGA, not the server's main memory.

### SORT_AREA_RETAINED_SIZE

By default, the value for SORT_AREA_RETAINED_SIZE is equal to the size of SORT_AREA_SIZE. The minimum size for this parameter is the equivalent of two Oracle blocks. The maximum size is limited to the value of SORT_AREA_SIZE. Once a sort operation is complete, the user's Server Process reduces the memory set aside for sorting by SORT_AREA_SIZE to the value specified by SORT_AREA_RETAINED_SIZE.

The SORT_AREA_RETAINED_SIZE parameter can be set using the init.ora, by using the ALTER SYSTEM SET SORT_AREA_RETAINED_SIZE=*n* DEFERRED command, or by using the ALTER SESSION SET SORT_AREA_RETAINED_SIZE=*n* command.

> Depending on the degree of parallelism specified, sorts performed using the Oracle Parallel Query option can require several times the amount of memory specified by SORT_AREA_SIZE.

## Measuring Sort I/O

Sort activity can be monitored using the V$SYSSTAT and V$SORT_SEGMENT dynamic data dictionary views, using the output from REPORT.TXT, and by using OEM's Performance Manager GUI tool. The V$SORT_SEGMENT and V$SORT_USAGE views are also useful for monitoring sort activity and are discussed in the "Improving Sort I/O" section of this chapter.

### Using *V$SYSSTAT*

The V$SYSSTAT dynamic performance view has two statistics, sorts (memory) and sorts (disk), that can be used to monitor sort user activity. Using these two statistics, the following sample query shows how you can calculate an in-memory sort ratio:

```
SQL> SELECT mem.value/(disk.value + mem.value)
  2          "In-memory Sort Ratio"
  3  FROM v$sysstat mem, v$sysstat disk
  4  WHERE mem.name = 'sorts (memory)'
  5  AND disk.name = 'sorts (disk)';

In-memory Sort Ratio
--------------------
             .99233
```

> Oracle's recommended tuning goal with regard to sorting is to have at least 95 percent of all sorts happen in memory.

## Using *REPORT.TXT*

Figure 7.14 shows the information from REPORT.TXT that indicates the number of sorts that were performed in memory and to disk.

**FIGURE 7.14** REPORT.TXT sort statistics

```
SQL> Rem The total is the total value of the statistic between the time
SQL> Rem bstat was run and the time estat was run. Note that the estat
SQL> Rem script logs on as "internal" so the per_logon statistics will
SQL> Rem always be based on at least one logon.
SQL> select n1.name "Statistic",
  2            n1.change "Total",
  3            round(n1.change/trans.change,2) "Per Transaction",
  4            round(n1.change/logs.change,2)  "Per Logon",
  5            round(n1.change/(to_number(to_char(end_time,   'J'))*60*60*24 -
  6                             to_number(to_char(start_time, 'J'))*60*60*24 +
  7                             to_number(to_char(end_time,   'SSSSS')) -
  8                             to_number(to_char(start_time, 'SSSSS')))
  9                        , 2) "Per Second"
 10     from stats$stats n1, stats$stats trans, stats$stats logs, stats$dates
 11     where trans.name='user commits'
 12      and  logs.name='logons cumulative'
 13      and  n1.change != 0
 14     order by n1.name;

Statistic                     Total Per Transaction    Per Logon   Per Second
---------------------- ------------ ---------------- ------------ -----------
sorts (disk)                      6              .03          .38           0
sorts (memory)                  857             4.63        53.56         .32
sorts (rows)                  54223            293.1      3388.94       20.09
```

## Using Performance Manager

Oracle Enterprise Manager's Performance Manager GUI tool can also report sorting information. Figure 7.15 shows the OEM Performance Manager screen that displays cumulative sort activity for the instance.

**FIGURE 7.15** OEM Performance Manager sort statistics

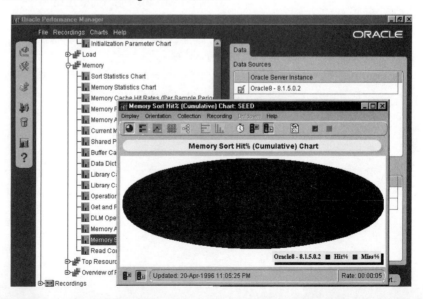

# Improving Sort I/O

Sort activity can cause excessive I/O when performed to disk instead of memory, so you should try to tune sort activity so that its impact is minimized. There are several possible methods of improving sort performance, including: avoiding SQL statements that cause sorts, increasing the init.ora parameters related to sorting, using temporary tablespaces, and improving the reads related to sort I/O.

## Avoid Sorts

One way to improve sort performance is to minimize the number of sorts being performed by application code and ad-hoc queries. Examples of this technique include:

- Using the UNION ALL operator in place of UNION

- Ensuring that columns used in table joins are properly indexed

- Building indexes on columns used in ORDER BY and GROUP BY clauses

- Creating indexes using the NOSORT option where appropriate

- Using the COMPUTE option when analyzing tables and indexes

See *Oracle8i SQL Reference, Release 8.1.5* (Part Number A67779-01) for a complete explanation of each of these commands.

## Make It Bigger

Another technique for improving I/O related to sorting is to minimize the number of sorts that are done to disk by increasing the value of SORT_AREA_ SIZE in the init.ora. Care must be taken when increasing this parameter, however. The value specified by SORT_AREA_SIZE is assigned on a *per user* basis. Therefore, if SORT_AREA_SIZE is set to 1MB, and 20 users connect to the database, each user's Server Process will consume 1MB of server memory, 20MB total, whether they are actively sorting or not. Make sure you consider the effect these increased memory demands will have on the performance of the server before assigning large sort areas at the instance level.

Oracle states that the default value for SORT_AREA_SIZE is adequate for most OLTP systems. Oracle also advises that a SORT_AREA_SIZE of 1MB is generally optimal for systems that use the Oracle Parallel Query option.

## Creating Temporary Tablespaces

When a user's Server Process writes a sort chunk to disk, it writes the data to the user's temporary tablespace. This tablespace, although it is referred to as the user's *temporary* tablespace, can have the tablespace attribute of being either permanent or temporary. Table 7.4 compares temporary and permanent tablespaces.

**TABLE 7.4** Comparison of Temporary and Permanent Tablespaces

| Tablespace Type | Description |
| --- | --- |
| Permanent | Can contain permanent segments like tables and indexes, as well as multiple temporary sort segments that are owned by each individual user's Server Process |
| Temporary | Can contain only a single temporary segment that is shared by all users performing sorts to disk |

You can use the following query on the DBA_TABLESPACES data dictionary view to determine whether a tablespace is permanent or temporary:

```
SQL> SELECT tablespace_name, contents
  2  FROM dba_tablespaces;


TABLESPACE_NAME                   CONTENTS
------------------------------    ---------
SYSTEM                            PERMANENT
TEMP                              TEMPORARY
APPL_DATA                         PERMANENT
OEMGR                             PERMANENT
RBS                               PERMANENT
TOOLS                             PERMANENT
USERS                             PERMANENT
WEBDB                             PERMANENT
APPL_IDX                          PERMANENT
```

If a user's temporary tablespace is a permanent tablespace, each user who performs a sort must build, and then drop, a sort segment within the tablespace. This dynamic management of individual sort segments is expensive both in terms of I/O and recursive data dictionary calls.

Unlike a sort segment stored in a permanent tablespace, the sort segment in the temporary tablespace is not dropped when the user's sort completes. Instead, the first sort operation following instance startup creates a sort segment that remains in the temporary tablespace for reuse by subsequent users who also perform sorts to disk. This sort segment will remain in the temporary tablespace until instance shutdown. You can monitor the size and usage of the sort segment using the V$SORT_SEGMENT and V$SORT_USAGE dynamic performance views.

### Using *V$SORT_SEGMENT*

The V$SORT_SEGMENT view allows you to monitor the size and growth of the sort segment that resides in the temporary tablespace. The sort segment will grow dynamically as users place demands on it. The following query shows three of the more useful columns in this view:

```
SQL> SELECT tablespace_name,
  2          current_users,
  3          max_sort_blocks
  4  FROM v$sort_segment;


TABLESPACE_NAME CURRENT_USERS MAX_SORT_BLOCKS
--------------- ------------- ---------------
TEMP                       11             300
```

This query output shows that 11 users are currently using to the sort segment stored in the TEMP tablespace. In addition, the largest single sort by an individual user was the equivalent of 300 Oracle blocks in size. This last statistic in particular, MAX_SORT_BLOCKS, can be useful when trying to determine what the optimal setting for SORT_AREA_SIZE and SORT_AREA_RETAINED_SIZE should be. By setting these init.ora parameters to at least MAX_SORT_BLOCKS * DB_BLOCK_SIZE, you can accommodate more sorts in memory and reduce I/O.

### USING *V$SORT_USAGE*

While V$SORT_SEGMENT shows overall sort operations well, it does not allow you to see which individual users are causing large sorts to disk. However, the V$SORT_USAGE view does include a USER column which can be used to monitor sort activity by user as shown by the following query:

```
SQL> SELECT user, tablespace,
  2          blocks
  3  FROM v$sort_usage
  4  ORDER BY blocks;
```

| USER | TABLESPACE | BLOCKS |
| --- | --- | --- |
| APPS | TEMP | 200 |
| JOE | TEMP | 110 |
| BRENDA | TEMP | 20 |

The TABLESPACE column tells you in which tablespace the sorts are being performed. The BLOCKS column indicates size of the sort activity in Oracle blocks. Monitoring this value can also be useful when setting the init.ora parameters SORT_AREA_SIZE and SORT_AREA_RETAINED_SIZE.

The V$SORT_USAGE view only contains entries when at least one sort is in progress. If you query this view while no users are connected, or when no sort activity is being performed, no rows will be returned.

---

### Sorting: The Whole Story

Knowing which user is performing the most sorting in your database is useful information. However, it is generally even more useful to know exactly what SQL operations they are performing to cause the sorts. With this information, you may be able to identify a SQL statement that could have its sorting eliminated by creating a new index or rewriting some application code.

The following query on V$SESSION, V$SQLAREA, and V$SORT_USAGE shows how the SQL being issued by users with high sort activity can be identified:

```
SQL> SELECT sess.username,
  2          sql.sql_text,
  3          sort.blocks
```

```
    4   FROM v$session sess,
    5        v$sqltext sql,
    6        v$sort_usage sort
    7   WHERE sess.serial# = sort.session_num
    8   AND    sort.sqladdr = sql.address
    9   AND    sort.sqlhash = sql.hash_value
   10   AND    sort.blocks > 200;
USERNAME SQL_TEXT                                       BLOCKS
-------- ---------------------------------- ----------
APPS     SELECT customer_id, customer_name       210
         FROM customer
         ORDER BY city, state
```

### Tuning Sorts with *SORT_MULTIBLOCK_READ_COUNT*

When a user's Server Process finishes sorting the individual chunks of a large, multi-chunk sort, it then has to merge the sort segments on disk into the final sorted result. This merging process requires that one or more read operations from disk occur. In order to make the I/Os associated with these reads as efficient as possible, the init.ora parameter SORT_MULTIBLOCK_READ_COUNT should be tuned. This parameter tells the user Server Process how many database blocks to read from the sort segment with each I/O. Increasing this value causes Oracle to perform fewer I/Os when performing the sort/merge operation.

The default value for this parameter is 2. The minimum allowed value is 1 and the maximum is OS-dependent.

In order to improve the overall throughput of sort activity, care should be taken so that the value of SORT_AREA_SIZE, is equal to, or a multiple of, the default INITIAL and NEXT extent storage values for the temporary tablespace. The value for SORT_ MULTIBLOCK_READ_COUNT should also be set to a value that will allow multiple sort/ merge fetches to completely fill the sort area specified by SORT_AREA_SIZE.

# Tuning Rollback Segment I/O

**R**ollback segments play a critical role in every database DML transaction. When a user starts a DML transaction, the before-image of the changed data is written to a rollback segment. This before-image data stored in the rollback segment is used for three important purposes:

- It can be used to restore the original state of the data if the user performing the DML command issues a ROLLBACK command.

- It provides a read-consistent view of the changed data to other users who access the same data prior to the DML user issuing a COMMIT command.

- It is used during instance recovery to undo uncommitted transactions that were in progress just prior to an instance failure.

Unless you ask for a specific rollback segment using the SET TRANSACTION USE ROLLBACK SEGMENT command, the Oracle Server assigns transactions to rollback segments in such a way as to try and have each rollback segment manage about the same number of transactions. The total number of transactions a rollback segment can handle is dependent on the Oracle block size of your database. Within each rollback segment, Oracle uses the extents in a circular fashion until the rollback segment is full. Once the rollback segment is full, no new transactions will be assigned to it until some of the rollback segment space is released when a user issues a COMMIT or ROLLBACK command.

A single rollback segment can store the before-images for several different transactions. However, a transaction writes its before-image information to only one rollback segment. Additionally, once a transaction is assigned to a rollback segment, the transaction never switches to a different rollback segment, even if the original rollback segment was not the most appropriate choice. If the before-image of a transaction that starts in one extent of a rollback segment grows to fill that extent, the transaction will wrap into the adjacent extent and continue writing before-image information to that extent. If the adjacent extent already contains before-image information for some other active transaction, Oracle will not overwrite that information, but will instead add a new extent to the rollback segment in order to store the transaction's growing before-image. As you will see, the frequency with which transactions cause wrapping and extending of rollback segments will be key to the tuning of their performance.

Rollback segment tuning can be one of the most elusive aspects of database administration. Even when rollback activity has reached a steady state and no problems are apparent, one large transaction can cause a rollback segment error to occur. This can lead to frustrating rollback segment tuning problems that never completely go away. The goals of rollback-segment tuning usually involve the following:

- Making sure that database users always find a rollback segment to store their transaction before-images without experiencing a wait

- Making sure that database users always get the read-consistent view they need to complete their transactions

- Making sure that the database rollback segments do not cause unnecessary I/O

Every database contains at least one rollback segment, which is the system rollback segment. Once other rollback segments are created in the database, this segment is used only for data dictionary read consistency and transaction control.

# Measuring Rollback Segment I/O

In general, there are four areas that you should monitor when trying to tune the performance of rollback segments:

- Contention for the header of the rollback segments

- Contention for the rollback segment extents

- Wrapping of transactions from one extent to another within rollback segments

- Dynamic extent allocation by the rollback segments

Because rollback segments can be used to "undo" a user's DML and restore the original data using the before-image, many of the statistics in these views use the term *undo* rather than *rollback segment* in their names.

## Rollback Segment Header Contention

The Oracle Server uses a transaction table stored in the header block of each rollback segment to track the transactions that use the segment to store their before-images. This header block is generally cached in the Database Buffer Cache so that all users can access it when trying to store their transaction before-images. On a busy OLTP system, users may experience a wait for access to these rollback segment header blocks, thereby causing their transaction performance to decline.

You can measure the frequency with which these waits are occurring using the V$SYSTEM_EVENT, V$WAITSTAT, and V$ROLLSTAT dynamic performance views as well as the output from REPORT.TXT.

### Using *V$SYSTEM_EVENT*

The V$SYSTEM_EVENT view tracks performance related information on rollbacks segments via the undo segment tx slot statistic. The following query shows how to display this information:

```
SQL> SELECT event, total_waits,
  2         time_waited, average_wait
  3  FROM v$system_event
  4  WHERE event like '%undo%';


EVENT                 TOTAL_WAITS TIME_WAITED AVERAGE_WAIT
--------------------- ----------- ----------- ------------
undo segment tx slot        28070          18   .000641254
```

Ideally, the value of the AVERAGE_WAIT statistic should be consistently at or near zero.

### Using *V$WAITSTAT*

The V$WAITSTAT view contains information on block contention statistics. Included in these statistics are counts for the number of times application users have experienced a wait for access to the header block of rollback segments. The following query shows how this information appears in the V$WAITSTAT view:

```
SQL> SELECT class, count
  2  FROM v$waitstat
  3  WHERE class IN ('undo header',
  4                  'system undo header')


CLASS                  COUNT
------------------- ----------
system undo header         0
undo header               12
```

The statistic for system header undo relates to the system rollback segment. The undo header statistic is for the non-system rollback segments.

Ideally, the counts for these waits should be consistently at or near zero.

### Using *V$ROLLSTAT*

The V$ROLLSTAT view contains detailed information regarding the behavior of the rollback segments in the database. In particular, the columns USN, GETS and WAITS are particularly useful for measuring contention for the rollback segment header. Table 7.5 shows the descriptions of each of these columns

**TABLE 7.5** V$ROLLSTAT Columns Used to Measure Header Contention

| Column | Description |
| --- | --- |
| USN | Undo Segment Number, the internal system-generated number assigned to the rollback segment |
| GETS | Number of times a user's Server Process needed to access the rollback segment header and did so successfully |
| WAITS | Number of times a user Server Process needed to access the rollback segment header and experienced a wait |

Using these columns, you can construct a query that will return the get ratio for each rollback segment header in your database:

```
SQL> SELECT n.name, s.usn,
  2          DECODE (s.waits,0,1
  3                     ,1-(s.waits/s.gets))
  4          "RBS Header Get Ratio"
  5    FROM v$rollstat s, v$rollname n
  6    WHERE s.usn = n.usn
  7    ORDER BY usn;
NAME                      USN  RBS Header Get Ratio
--------------- ---------- ---------------------
SYSTEM                      0                     1
```

| | | |
|-----------|---|--------|
| RBS01 | 1 | .97 |
| RBS02 | 2 | 1 |
| RBS03 | 3 | 1 |
| RBS04 | 4 | .8425 |
| RBS05 | 5 | 1 |
| RBSBIG | 6 | 1 |

Oracle recommends that a well-tuned OLTP system have a rollback segment header get ratio of 95 percent or higher for all rollback segments.

### Using *REPORT.TXT*

Rollback segment header contention statistics are also written to the REPORT.TXT file. Figures 7.16 and 7.17 show the sections from REPORT.TXT, which contain the information of rollback segment header contention.

**FIGURE 7.16** REPORT.TXT showing V$WAITSTAT wait statistics

```
SQL>
SQL> Rem Buffer busy wait statistics.  If the value for 'buffer busy wait' in
SQL> Rem the wait event statistics is high, then this table will identify
SQL> Rem which class of blocks is having high contention.  If there are high
SQL> Rem 'undo header' waits then add more rollback segments.  If there are
SQL> Rem high 'segment header' waits then adding freelists might help.  Check
SQL> Rem v$session_wait to get the addresses of the actual blocks having
SQL> Rem contention.
SQL> select * from stats$waitstat
  2    where count != 0
  3    order by count desc;

CLASS                      COUNT                TIME
-------------------- -------------------- --------------------
data block                   636                   0
undo header                  221                   0
segment header                46                   0
undo block                     1                   0

4 rows selected.
```

**FIGURE 7.17** REPORT.TXT showing V$ROLLSTAT statistics

```
SQL>
SQL> set numwidth 19;
SQL> Rem Waits_for_trans_tbl high implies you should add rollback segments.
SQL> select * from stats$roll;

UNDO_SEGMENT TRANS_TBL_GETS TRANS_TBL_WAITS UNDO_BYTES_WRITTEN SEGMENT_SIZE_BYTES XACTS SHRINKS WRAPS
------------ -------------- --------------- ------------------ ------------------ ----- ------- -----
           0             10               0                  0             407552     0       0     0
           1          18008              62            7545280            4093952     0       0    33
           2          11919              82            9431392            4093952     0       0    42
           3          18104              71            7123280            4093952     0       0    31
           4          31412              15            6437242            4093952     0       0    12
           5          22080              10            3945280            4093952     0       0    23
           6          12019               0           29431392           69099520     0       0     0

3 rows selected.
```

## Rollback Segment Extent Contention

Even when there are no waits occurring for access to the rollback segment header blocks, there may still be waits occurring for access to the blocks within the individual extents of each rollback segment. Statistics for these waits can also be found in the V$WAITSTAT and V$SYSTEM_EVENT dynamic performance views and the output from REPORT.TXT.

### Using *V$WAITSTAT*

In addition to showing information on waits for rollback segment header blocks, the V$WAITSTAT view also contains statistics on waits for access to rollback segment extent blocks. The following query shows how to determine whether these waits are occurring in the database:

```
SQL> SELECT class, count
  2  FROM v$waitstat
  3  WHERE class IN ('undo block',
  4                  'system undo block')

CLASS                   COUNT
------------------ ----------
system undo block           0
undo block                 22
```

The output from this query shows that your application users experienced 22 waits for access to rollback segment blocks since instance startup. You can determine what percentage of the total number of requests that is by querying V$SYSSTAT for the consistent gets statistic and then calculating a ratio:

```
SQL> SELECT value
  2  FROM v$sysstat
  3  WHERE name = 'consistent gets';

     VALUE
----------
   7804633
```

The consistent gets statistic refers to the number of times rollback segment extent blocks were accessed in the Database Buffer Cache. By using the values from these two queries, you can calculate a wait ratio for access to rollback segment extent blocks: 22 waits ÷ 7,804,633 attempts to access a rollback segment block = .000003 or .0003 percent wait ratio.

If the wait ratio for rollback segment extent blocks exceeds 1 percent, Oracle recommends that you consider tuning your rollback segments.

### Using *REPORT.TXT*

The section of REPORT.TXT shown in Figure 7.16 also shows the wait information for rollback segment extent blocks. In this example, there were 221 waits for access to a rollback segment header between the time UTLBSTAT.SQL and UTLESTAT.SQL were run.

## Rollback Segment Transaction Wrapping

When a transaction's before-image exceeds the size of the extent to which it has been allocated, the transaction will wrap into the next extent if it is available. This dynamic wrapping incurs a small I/O cost and should be avoided if possible. You can examine the V$ROLLSTAT dynamic performance view and the output from REPORT.TXT to determine whether transaction wrapping is occurring in your rollback segments.

### Using *V$ROLLSTAT*

You can query the WRAPS column of V$ROLLSTAT to see how often transactions have wrapped from one extent to another since instance startup:

```
SQL> SELECT n.name, s.usn, s.wraps
  2  FROM v$rollname n, v$rollstat s
  3  WHERE n.usn = s.usn;
```

| NAME   | USN | WRAPS |
| ------ | --- | ----- |
| SYSTEM | 0   | 0     |
| RBS01  | 1   | 10    |
| RBS02  | 2   | 0     |
| RBS03  | 3   | 22    |
| RBS04  | 4   | 35    |
| RBS05  | 5   | 8     |
| RBSBIG | 6   | 0     |

Frequent wrapping indicates that the extent sizes of each rollback segment may be too small.

### Using *REPORT.TXT*

The extent wrapping statistics are also available in the output from REPORT.TXT as shown in Figure 7.17.

## Dynamic Extent Allocation of Rollback Segments

When a transaction's before-image exceeds the size of the extent to which it has been allocated, but cannot wrap to the next extent because there are still active transactions in that extent, the rollback segment will add a new extent and wrap into that one instead. This dynamic extent allocation incurs an I/O cost that should be avoided if possible. You can examine the V$ROLLSTAT and V$SYSTEM_EVENT dynamic performance views and the output from REPORT.TXT to determine whether dynamic extent allocation is occurring in your rollback segments.

### V$SYSTEM_EVENT

The statistic undo segment extension in the V$SYSTEM_EVENT dynamic performance view records how long user Server Processes had to wait for rollback segments to add extents to handle transaction processing:

```
SQL> SELECT event, total_waits,
  2         time_waited, average_wait
  3  FROM v$system_event
  4  WHERE event like '%undo%';

EVENT                   TOTAL_WAIT TIME_WAITED AVERAGE_WAIT
----------------------- ---------- ----------- ------------
undo segment extension       28070          18   .000641254
```

High or steadily increasing values for these wait statistics indicate that you either have too few rollback segments, too small rollback segments, or both.

### Using *V$ROLLSTAT*

The V$ROLLSTAT view contains a column called EXTENDS. This column indicates how often the rollback segment was forced to add extents to support database transaction activity:

```
SQL> SELECT n.name, s.usn, s.extends
  2  FROM v$rollname n, v$rollstat s
  3  WHERE n.usn = s.usn;
```

| NAME | USN | EXTENDS |
|------|-----|---------|
| SYSTEM | 0 | 0 |
| RBS01 | 1 | 55 |
| RBS02 | 2 | 2 |
| RBS03 | 3 | 12 |
| RBS04 | 4 | 16 |
| RBS05 | 5 | 8 |
| RBSBIG | 6 | 52 |

If your rollback segments are frequently adding extents to support the transaction activity in your database, then the rollback segments are probably too small.

### Using *REPORT.TXT*

As shown in Figure 7.17, information on rollback segment extending is also contained in the output from REPORT.TXT.

## Improving Rollback Segment I/O

After measuring the performance of your rollback segments, you may decide to tune them for improved performance. When you tune rollback segments, consider these four tuning categories:

- Add more.
- Make them bigger.
- Explicitly manage rollback segments for large transactions.
- Minimize the need for rollback space.

The tricky question becomes *how much* bigger to make the rollback segments and *how many* more rollback segments to create. While an exact determination of these two issues can be elusive, several useful guidelines are mentioned in the following sections.

## Add More

The easiest way to minimize contention for both rollback segment headers and rollback segment extent blocks is to make more of those two resources available. To add these resources, you have to add more rollback segments to the database.

Oracle recommends one rollback segment for every four concurrent transactions, for up to a maximum of 20 rollback segments.

## Make It Bigger

Not only do you need to have enough rollback segments available in the database, but you must also make sure that they are large enough to handle the before-images that will be placed in them. The optimal size of rollback segments varies with the type of system (i.e. OLTP vs. DSS) and the types of transactions being performed in the database. Table 7.6 compares the relative costs of each type of DML command.

**TABLE 7.6**    Comparison of Rollback Cost for DML Operations

| Command | Entry Stored In Rollback Segment | Relative Rollback Segment Cost |
|---------|----------------------------------|-------------------------------|
| INSERT | The ROWID of the inserted row | Low |
| UPDATE | The column data for the changed columns | Medium |
| DELETE | The entire deleted row | High |

If the table the DML is being performed on also has an associated index or indexes, the demands on the rollback segment will be even greater since the index before-images must also be maintained.

To more accurately determine how much rollback space your users need, you can monitor how much they are currently using via the V$TRANSACTION, V$SESSION, and V$ROLLSTAT dynamic performance views.

### Using *V$TRANSACTION* and *V$SESSION*

By joining the V$SESSION and V$TRANSACTION views you can see how much space each session is using in the database rollback segments:

```
SQL> SELECT s.osuser, s.username, t.used_ublk
  2  FROM v$session s, v$transaction t
  3  WHERE s.taddr = t.addr;
```

| OSUSER | USERNAME | USED_UBLK |
| --- | --- | --- |
| rbron | SYSTEM | 2 |
| rbron | APPS | 280 |
| jschwarz | APPS | 16 |
| jjohnson | APPS | 12 |
| tgastel | APPS | 8 |

This output shows the amount of rollback activity currently being generated by each user at the moment the query was issued.

### Using *V$ROLLSTAT*

If you have a large transaction that seems to be having trouble with rollback segments, you may have difficulty using the above query on V$SESSION and V$TRANSACTION to track its rollback segment usage. In these cases, it is usually easier to use the V$ROLLSTAT view to determine how much rollback segment space the transaction needs. The procedure to do so is outlined here:

**1.** Take all but one rollback segment offline:

```
SQL> ALTER ROLLBACK SEGMENT rbs01 OFFLINE;
SQL> ALTER ROLLBACK SEGMENT rbs02 OFFLINE;
SQL> ALTER ROLLBACK SEGMENT rbs03 OFFLINE;
SQL> ALTER ROLLBACK SEGMENT rbs04 OFFLINE;
SQL> ALTER ROLLBACK SEGMENT rbs05 OFFLINE;
```

**2.** Query the V$ROLLSTAT and V$ROLLNAME views to determine how many bytes of before-image data have been written to the rollback segment so far. This statistic is contained in the WRITES column of V$ROLLSTAT:

```
SQL> SELECT n.name, s.usn, s.writes
  2  FROM v$rollname n, v$rollstat s
  3  WHERE n.usn = s.usn
  4  AND name != 'SYSTEM';
```

| NAME  | USN | WRITES |
| ----- | --- | ------ |
| RBS06 | 6   | 4498   |

**3.** Next, run the transaction that is experiencing rollback segment problems:

```
SQL> DELETE FROM sales_history
  2  WHERE sale_date < '01-JAN-95';
```

**4.** Now, rerun the query on V$ROLLSTAT and V$ROLLNAME views to see how many bytes have been written to the rollback segment now:

```
SQL> SELECT n.name, s.usn, s.writes
  2  FROM v$rollname n, v$rollstat s
  3  WHERE n.usn = s.usn
  4  AND name != 'SYSTEM';
```

| NAME  | USN | WRITES  |
| ----- | --- | ------- |
| RBS06 | 6   | 6198468 |

Since the WRITES column records the number of bytes that have been written to each rollback segment, the difference between the value for WRITES in Step 2 and the value for WRITES in Step 4 will indicate the size of the transaction's rollback requirements. In this example: 6,198,468 – 4,498 = 6,193,970 bytes. This means that the overall size of your rollback segments will need to be at least 6MB if they are to be expected to handle this transaction. However, this method can be wasteful of disk space if each rollback segment is sized for your largest transaction. The next section, "Explicitly Managing Rollback Segments," discusses how to alleviate this problem.

### More and Bigger: The Special Case of "Snapshot Too Old"

The bane of many a DBA is the unpredictable occurrence of the ORA-01555 "Snapshot Too Old" (rollback segment too small) error. These errors can be hard to resolve because they don't always occur in a consistent manner. The following scenario illustrates how a "Snapshot Too Old" error might occur and why they are hard to tune away.

- 11:30 am: Malka updates a customer's unpaid balance, thereby writing the before-image of the data to the database's rollback segment. She is then interrupted by a phone call, leaving her changes temporarily uncommitted.

- 11:32 am: Jennifer starts a job that generates a report showing all unpaid balances on customer accounts, including the customer that Malka is in the process of updating. For read consistency, the Oracle Server notes the time (using the System Change Number or SCN) that Jennifer's query starts in order to show Jennifer the data, as it exists at that moment in time, throughout her query.

- 11:33 am: Malka finishes her phone call and commits her changes to the customer's unpaid balance. This releases the rollback segment entry that previously stored the before-image of her transaction. However, the Oracle Server does note on the Interested Transaction List that Jennifer's process is "interested" in Malka's before-image, since Jennifer's transaction needs the data for read consistency.

- 11:48 am: In order to maintain read consistency, Jennifer's long-running report needs to show the data for the customer that Malka changed, as it existed at 11:32 am. Since Malka committed her changes, this data no longer exists in the table, only in the rollback segment. If no other user has happened to use the rollback segment blocks where Malka stored her before-image, Jennifer's Server Process will simply read the blocks and continue. If another user has overwritten the blocks that used to contain Malka's before-image, Jennifer's query will fail with a ORA-01555 "Snapshot Too Old" (rollback segment too small) error because read consistency for Jennifer could not be maintained.

The best protection against the "Snapshot Too Old" error is two-fold. First, try to avoid executing long-running queries while short transactions are occurring on the tables underlying those queries. Second, increase the size and number of rollback segments to decrease the likelihood that a released rollback segment entry, which is needed by another session, will be overwritten before they are able to use it.

When we create rollback segments on new systems, we use standard sizing values of INITIAL 512K, NEXT 512K, and a MINEXTENTS of 20. This formula will result in a 10MB rollback segment. These values tend to prevent most rollback segment problems, but should be monitored nonetheless to determine whether they are too big or too small.

## Explicitly Managing Rollback Segments

Very large transactions, like those associated with batch processing runs, frequently require large rollback segments that are not necessarily appropriate for regular OLTP transactions. In these cases, it is best to create one or two large rollback segments and dedicate them to this purpose. However, since the Oracle Server normally assigns transactions to rollback segments automatically, you will need to add a few extra steps to your batch processing in order to utilize this technique:

1. Create a new, large rollback segment for storing the before-images of large batch jobs:

```
SQL> CREATE PRIVATE ROLLBACK SEGMENT rbsbatch
  2   STORAGE (INITIAL 10M NEXT 10M)
  3   TABLESPACE rbs;
```

Right after creation, the new rollback segment will be in an offline state. Leave the rollback segment offline until it is time to do the batch processing.

2. Just before starting the batch processing jobs, put the rollback segment online:

```
SQL> ALTER ROLLBACK SEGMENT rbsbatch ONLINE;
```

3. Next, assign the batch job to this rollback segment using the SQL command SET TRANSACTION or the DBMS_TRANSACTION stored procedure:

```
SQL> SET TRANSACTION USE ROLLBACK SEGMENT rbsbatch;
```

*or*

```
SQL> EXECUTE DBMS_TRANSACTION.USE_ROLLBACK_
SEGMENT('rbsbatch');
```

4. Now, start the batch processing job:

    SQL> EXECUTE posting_job;

5. Next, immediately take the large rollback segment offline:

    SQL> ALTER ROLLBACK SEGMENT rbsbatch OFFLINE;

    The rollback segment will not actually go offline until the batch trans-action is complete. However, because it has been marked to go offline in the data dictionary, no other transactions will be assigned to it.

Any commit that occurs within the batch job will cause the large rollback seg-ment to go offline and become unavailable. Therefore, you must bring the rollback segment back online and re-issue the SET TRANSACTION or DBMS_ TRANSACTION command after each commit to keep the batch job from using some other rollback segment.

## Minimizing Rollback Segment Activity

Another way to minimize performance problems related to rollback seg-ments is to try and minimize the number and size of entries that are written to the rollback segments. This goal can be accomplished by performing fre-quent commits to minimize large rollback entries, using the COMMIT=Y and BUFFER options when performing database imports, forgoing the use of the CONSISTENT option when using the database EXPORT utility, and setting an appropriate COMMIT value when using the SQL*Loader utility.

See *Oracle8i Utilities, Release 8.1.5* (Part Number A67792-01) for more information on the options for the EXPORT, IMPORT, and SQL*Loader utilities.

# Summary

**O**racle background processes and user transaction activity both cause I/O to occur during normal operation. While proper tuning of the SGA can greatly minimize unnecessary I/O, you should still monitor and tune the I/O specific operations in the database. Effective I/O tuning includes managing datafile I/O, read and write activities of the DBW0, LGWR, and ARC0 background processes, block-level I/O, sort activities, and rollback segments.

Datafile and tablespace I/O is generally tuned by separating application data from data dictionary objects, segregating application tables and indexes, and locating datafiles on several different physical devices via striping and the use of locally managed tablespaces.

DBW0 performance is tuned by monitoring its performance and starting Database Writer I/O slaves or additional Database Writer processes as needed.

Block-level I/O is dependent on several factors including block size, extent size, and update frequency. Common I/O problems related to Oracle blocks include row migration and row chaining.

The LGWR background process generally is not a significant source of I/O performance problems, but I/O slaves can be created to help LGWR perform its operations if needed.

The activities of the CKPT background process can be tuned to help assure checkpoints occur frequently enough to guarantee quick recovery, but not so often as to add unnecessary I/O. Checkpoint frequency can be specified in terms of maximum desired recovery times and in terms of transaction volume.

The process of archiving redo log entries to the archive destination can cause a significant performance problem if the archive device fills. Multiple archive destinations can be specified, and concurrent Archiver processes can be started to help prevent this problem.

I/O occurs any time a user's Server Process performs a sort that is larger than the value specified by SORT_AREA_SIZE in the init.ora. The use of true temporary tablespaces helps improve the performance of disk sorts.

Rollback segments represent a special challenge to database tuning. Because every user must be able to get a read-consistent view of the database and be able to write before-image data for their transactions, rollback segments have a tendency to grow dynamically and be the source of heavy I/O. Minimizing wrapping and dynamic extension of rollback segments are two key I/O tuning goals.

## Key Terms

Before you take the exam, make sure you're familiar with the following terms:

Redo Log Buffer

striping

asynchronous

Free List

row chaining

High Water Mark

Archiving

extent

synchronous

extent map

row migration

Log Writer

RAID

Locally Managed Tablespace

# Review Questions

1. Which of the following dynamic performance views contain information related to tuning I/O? (Choose all that apply.)

   **A.** V$SYSSTAT

   **B.** V$LIBRARYCACHE

   **C.** V$SYSTEM_EVENT

   **D.** V$FILESTAT

2. Which of the following is not a possible source for I/O related performance issues?

   **A.** Datafiles

   **B.** Oracle blocks

   **C.** Control files

   **D.** Redo logs

3. The values for MINIOTIM and AVGIOTIM in V$FILESTAT are expressed in:

   **A.** Minutes

   **B.** Seconds

   **C.** 100th of a second

   **D.** 1000th of a second

4. Suppose you have determined that the EMP table and its index on LAST_NAME are frequently being used in application processing. What would be one way to try and improve the I/O of this operation?

   **A.** Make sure the table and its index are in the same tablespace.

   **B.** Make sure the table and its index are on the same physical device.

   **C.** Ask users to commit their work more often.

   **D.** Separate the table and its index onto separate datafiles and physical devices.

5. Separating an application's accounting tables from its manufacturing tables is an example of:

   A. Segregating segments by size

   B. Segregating segments by functional area

   C. Segregating segments by growth potential

   D. None of the above is correct.

6. Which of the following is *not* an example of a datafile striping technique?

   A. Placing a single datafile on a RAID device

   B. Creating a tablespace with several datafiles, and placing the datafiles on one device

   C. Creating a tablespace with several datafiles, and placing each datafile on a separate device

   D. Creating a tablespace with several datafiles, and placing the datafiles on a RAID device

7. Locally managed tablespaces offer a performance advantage because:

   A. Their storage management is performed in memory.

   B. Their extents are larger than those of a regular tablespace.

   C. They do not use the data dictionary to manage their storage allocations.

   D. They can be of the type temporary or permanent.

8. Which of the following describes the advantage of asynchronous over synchronous I/O?

   A. They do not rely on the OS layer to perform their write operations.

   B. They can use disks larger than 1GB.

   C. They can be backed up to tape.

   D. They generally require more skill to create and manage.

9. How do the actions of a Database Writer I/O slave and the DBW0 background process differ?

   **A.** I/O slaves are only used during recovery.

   **B.** DBW0 only performs write activities, while the I/O slaves also manages the Database Buffer Cache LRU List.

   **C.** I/O slaves can only read from datafiles, not write to them.

   **D.** I/O slaves only performs write activities, while DBW0 also manages the Database Buffer Cache LRU List.

10. What statistic in V$SYSTAT indicates that DBW0 may not be writing the contents of the Database Buffer Cache to disk fast enough?

    **A.** redo log space requests

    **B.** buffer busy wait

    **C.** db file parallel write

    **D.** busy buffer wait

11. Which two init.ora parameters are used to tune the performance of Database Writer?

    **A.** DB_BLOCK_WRITERS

    **B.** DBWR_IO_SLAVES

    **C.** DB_WRITER_PROCESSES

    **D.** DB_WRITERS

12. What happens to a database block once it has been filled to PCTFREE?

    **A.** The rows in the block are migrated to a new block.

    **B.** Any new rows will be chained to another block.

    **C.** The block goes onto the Used List.

    **D.** The block comes off the Free List.

13. A row is updated so that it fills all the available space in the block where the row resides. Any subsequent updates to rows in that block will cause:

    **A.** Row chaining

    **B.** Row migration

    **C.** Row compression

    **D.** Row corruption

14. Which of the following is identified using the ANALYZE TABLE ... LIST CHAINED ROWS command? Select all that apply.

    **A.** Row migration

    **B.** Row chaining

    **C.** Row corruption

    **D.** Row length

15. During a full table scan, the user's Server Process reads all the table's blocks up to the:

    **A.** Last extent

    **B.** PCTFREE value

    **C.** High Water Mark

    **D.** User's tablespace quota

16. Which of the following init.ora parameters is used to tune CKPT frequency?

    **A.** FAST_MAX_DIRTY_TARGET

    **B.** FAST_START_IO_TARGET

    **C.** FAST_IO_START_TARGET

    **D.** DB_BLOCK_MAX_START_TARGET

**17.** The primary determinant of whether a sort will happen in memory or to disk is:

**A.** The amount of memory in the user's PC

**B.** The amount of memory in the server

**C.** The amount of server memory reserved for sorting by the SORT_AREA_SIZE init.ora parameter

**D.** The number of tables involved in the query causing the sort

**18.** Following a sort, the Oracle Server shrinks the sort area assigned to each user's PGA to the value specified by:

**A.** SORT_AREA_SIZE

**B.** SORT_AREA_RETAINED_SIZE

**C.** SORT_AREA_MIN_SIZE

**D.** SORT_AREA_MAX_SIZE

**19.** When a rollback segment continues writing its before-image from one extent to the next adjacent extent in a rollback segment, this is referred to as:

**A.** Wrapping

**B.** Extending

**C.** Snapshot Too Old

**D.** None of the above

**20.** Which of the following might be possible solutions for resolving an ORA-01555 "Snapshot Too Old" error? Select all that apply.

**A.** Add more rollback segments.

**B.** Make the existing rollback segments larger.

**C.** Avoid running long queries against tables that are frequently updated.

**D.** All of the above are possible solutions.

# Answers to Review Questions

1. A, C, D. The V$LIBRARYCACHE view contains information about the Shared Pool, not I/O.

2. C. Very little I/O occurs against the database control files. They are only briefly updated at a checkpoint event by the CKPT background process.

3. C. The columns MAXIOWTM and MAXIORTM in V$FILESTAT are also expressed in 100th of a second.

4. D. Separating the table from its indexes will help improve the performance of OLTP transactions that access both segments during processing.

5. B. Separating segments by functional area helps to balance the I/O between application components that are used by different user groups.

6. B. Effective datafile striping requires that the datafile or datafiles for a tablespace be placed on multiple devices, either via a RAID or manual placement on physical disks.

7. C. Instead of the data dictionary, locally managed tablespaces use a bitmap in the file header of each datafile to store space allocation information.

8. A. Asynchronous, or raw, devices are written to directly by Oracle without waiting for a signal from the OS as is required by synchronous, or cooked, devices.

9. D. I/O slaves are only designed to assist Database Writer with its write activities. They do not move blocks from the LRU List to the Dirty List.

10. A. If DBW0 is not writing the contents of the Database Buffer Cache to disk fast enough at a database checkpoint, LGWR will not be able to empty the contents of the Redo Log Buffer, causing a redo log space request to occur.

11. B, C. DBWR_IO_SLAVES is used to start I/O slaves. DB_WRITER_ PROCESSES is used to start additional Database Writer processes.

**12.** D. Blocks that have been filled to their PCTFREE value are removed from the Free List and can no longer accept new inserts. The blocks go back on the Free List once the block's storage drops below PCTUSED.

**13.** B. Rows that are located in a block whose PCTFREE space is completely consumed are migrated to another block when they are updated.

**14.** A, B. The LIST CHAINED ROWS phrase identifies chained and/or migrated rows by populating the CHAIN_CNT column in DBA_TABLES with a numeric value.

**15.** C. All table blocks up to the High Water Mark are read during full table scans, whether or not those blocks contain data.

**16.** B. The FAST_START_IO_TARGET parameter allows you to specify the maximum number of I/Os allowed for instance recovery. DB_BLOCK_MAX_DIRTY_TARGET is used in a similar manner to specify the maximum number of dirt buffers that are allowed to collect in the Database Buffer Cache.

**17.** C. The SORT_AREA_SIZE parameter allows you to specify how much memory to dedicate to sorting in each user's PGA. If the sort is larger than this value, the sort will be done to disk in several chunks.

**18.** B. Following a sort, the amount of sort space allocated to a user's PGA is decreased to the value specified by SORT_AREA_RETAINED_SIZE. These two values are equal by default.

**19.** A. A wrap occurs whenever a user's before-image fills the extent they were assigned to and then moves to store the remaining before-image in the adjacent extent. If the adjacent extent is in use, the rollback segment will add an additional extent.

**20.** D. The ORA-01555 error is associated with long-running queries that cannot find the read consistent view of the database that they require. This error can be remedied by making sure that before-images are maintained as long as possible after they are released by creating larger, and more numerous rollback segments.

# Tuning Contention

## ORACLE8i PERFORMANCE TUNING EXAM OBJECTIVES COVERED IN THIS CHAPTER:

✓ Define the different latch types in Oracle8i.

✓ Know how to diagnose and tune LRU latch contention.

✓ Describe how to avoid Free List contention.

✓ Define types and modes of locking.

✓ List possible causes of lock contention.

✓ Describe how to use Oracle utilities to detect lock contention.

✓ Understand how to resolve lock contention.

✓ Identify how to prevent locking problems.

✓ Understand the causes and indicators of deadlock problems.

Exam objectives are subject to change at any time without prior notice and at Oracle's sole discretion. Please visit Oracle's Training and Certification Web site (http://education .oracle.com/certification/index.html) for the most current exam objectives listing.

This chapter deals with Step 9 in the Oracle Tuning Methodology, Tuning Resource Contention. Since this is the second to last step in the tuning methodology (Step 10: Tuning the Underlying Platform(s), is last) you might think that this topic is the least important. In some cases, this is probably true. For example, the topic of latch contention tuning is a relatively low payoff tuning area when compared with the SGA and physical I/O tuning that has been discussed in previous chapters. On the other hand, lock contention can have a huge performance impact if application users are frequently experiencing a complete halt in their processing due to restrictive locking. In this case, you might consider contention to be one of the most important tuning areas.

For the purposes of this discussion, we will break the topic of contention into three areas: latch contention, Free List contention, and lock contention.

# Latch Contention

Latches are used to protect access to Oracle's memory structures. A *latch* is a specialized type of lock that is used to serialize access to a particular memory structure or mechanism. Each latch protects a different structure or mechanism as indicated by the name of the latch. Only one process at a time may access a latch; processes are allowed to access a latch only when the latch is not already in use by another process. In this manner, Oracle makes sure that no two processes are accessing the same data structure simultaneously.

If a process needs a latch that is busy when the process requests it, the process will experience a wait. This wait behavior varies with the type of latch being accessed:

- If the latch is a *Willing-to-Wait* latch, the process requesting the latch will wait for a short period and then request the latch again, perhaps waiting several more times, until it succeeds.

- If the latch is an *Immediate* latch, the process immediately tries to obtain the latch again, without waiting, until it succeeds.

The V$LATCH dynamic performance view is used to monitor the activity of both Willing-to-Wait and Immediate latches. Table 8.1 shows some of the columns found in V$LATCH that are important for monitoring latch contention.

**TABLE 8.1**  Columns in V$LATCH Used to Monitor Latch Contention

| Column Name | Description |
| --- | --- |
| NAME | The name of the latch |
| GETS | The number of times a Willing-to-Wait latch was acquired without waiting |
| MISSES | The number of times a Willing-to-Wait latch was not acquired and a wait resulted |
| SLEEPS | The number of times a process had to wait before obtaining a Willing-to-Wait latch |
| IMMEDIATE_GETS | The number of times an Immediate latch was acquired without waiting |
| IMMEDIATE_MISSES | The number of times an Immediate latch was not acquired and a retry resulted |

In terms of performance tuning, we would like to minimize the number of times processes find either type of latch unavailable at the time they request them. This is generally achieved by increasing the number of latches available to the instance.

While there at least 142 Willing-to-Wait and Immediate latches in an Oracle8i database (depending on which options you have decided to install), only a few are of interest to the DBA from a tuning perspective. In terms of the content of the OCP Performance Tuning exam, only one—the Cache Buffers LRU Chain latch—is included in the exam objectives.

## The Cache Buffers LRU Chain Latch

The Cache Buffers LRU Chain latch is accessed by user Server Processes when they are searching for free blocks in the Database Buffer Cache using the LRU List. The total number of these latches is determined by the init.ora parameter DB_BLOCK_LRU_LATCHES.

To monitor whether latch contention is occurring for the Database Buffer Cache LRU List latch, you can use V$LATCH and REPORT.TXT.

### Using *V$LATCH*

The following query on V$LATCH calculates the hit ratio on the Database Buffer Cache LRU List latch:

```
SQL> SELECT 1- (sleeps/gets)
  2          "LRU Latch Hit Ratio"
  3  FROM v$latch
  4  WHERE name = 'cache buffers lru chain';

LRU Latch Hit Ratio
-------------------
          .999996896
```

Database Buffer Cache LRU List hit ratios lower than 99 percent indicate that contention is occurring for the LRU list in the Database Buffer Cache.

### Using *REPORT.TXT*

Figure 8.1, the output from REPORT.TXT, shows the gets and waits for the Database Buffer Cache LRU latch.

**FIGURE  8.1**    Sample REPORT.TXT showing Database Buffer Cache LRU latch statistics

```
SQL> set charwidth 18;
SQL> set numwidth 11;
SQL> Rem Latch statistics. Latch contention will show up as a large value for
SQL> Rem the 'latch free' event in the wait events above.
SQL> Rem Sleeps should be low.     The hit_ratio should be high.
SQL> select name latch_name, gets, misses,
  2    round((gets-misses)/decode(gets,0,1,gets),3)
  3      hit_ratio,
  4    sleeps,
  5    round(sleeps/decode(misses,0,1,misses),3) "SLEEPS/MISS"
  6    from stats$latches
  7    where gets != 0
  8    order by name;

LATCH_NAME                          GETS    MISSES  HIT_RATIO    SLEEPS SLEEPS/MISS
-----------------------------  -----------  ------- ----------- ------- -----------
cache buffers lru chain         3077566         273          1       327       1.198
```

The fourth column in the REPORT.TXT output, HIT_RATIO, shows how often processes that requested the Database Buffer Cache LRU latch were able to obtain it without waiting. Ideally, you would like this hit ratio to be 99 percent or higher. In our example, the cache buffers lru chain hit ratio is 100 percent (after rounding).

In general, the time spent waiting for a latch to become available is very short (1/100th of a second or less). This is why tuning latch contention has a low priority in the Oracle Tuning Methodology.

## Tuning Latch Contention

If contention for the Database Buffer Cache LRU latch exists on your system, consider increasing the DB_BLOCK_LRU_LATCHES parameter in the init.ora file. Oracle's recommended guidelines for setting this parameter is to set DB_BLOCK_LRU_LATCHES equal to:

- 6 × the number of CPUs in your server

- DB_BLOCK_BUFFERS ÷ 50

Be careful not to set the DB_BLOCK_LRU_LATCHES parameter too high. Remember from Chapter 5: Tuning the Database Buffer Cache, that each LRU latch in the Database Buffer Cache must control at least 50 buffers; otherwise an error is returned when the instance is started.

# Free List Contention

In Chapter 7: Tuning Physical I/O, we discussed how Oracle segments use blocks to store their data. That chapter also discussed how each segment keeps a Free List that contains a listing of which of the segment's blocks are able to accept new rows. You should recall that blocks on the Free List have not yet been filled to the PCTFREE value specified for the table.

If your application has many users performing frequent inserts, the application user's Server Processes may experience waits when trying to access the Free List for a frequently inserted table. These waits are called *Free List contention*. The tuning goal with regard to Free Lists is to minimize this type of contention by making sure that all processes can access a segment's Free List without experiencing a wait.

## Detecting Free List Contention

Free List contention can be detected by querying V$WAITSTAT, V$SYSTEM_EVENT, and V$SESSION_WAIT dynamic performance views, and the DBA_SEGMENTS data dictionary view. Free List statistics are also available in the Performance Manager GUI Tool.

### Using *V$SYSTEM_EVENT*

The V$SYSTEM_EVENT view shows statistics regarding wait events that have occurred in the database since instance startup. Occurrences of the buffer busy wait event indicate that Free List contention may exist in the database. The following query can be used to determine if buffer busy waits are occurring in your instance:

```
SQL> SELECT event, total_waits
  2  FROM v$system_event
```

```
   3  WHERE event = 'buffer busy waits';
EVENT                 TOTAL_WAITS
------------------    -----------
buffer busy waits            1033
```

Finding the `buffer busy wait` in your V$SYSTEM_EVENT view does not in and of itself indicate a problem with Free List contention. The V$WAITSTAT view should also be examined.

## Using *V$WAITSTAT*

The V$WAITSTAT view contains statistics about the number of waits that have occurred for individual segment blocks. The following query returns the number of Free List waits that have occurred since instance startup:

```
SQL> SELECT class, count
  2  FROM v$waitstat
  3  WHERE class IN ('free list',
  4                  'segment header');

CLASS                 COUNT
------------------    ----------
segment header           12
free list                 4
```

Non-zero counts for either of these statistics indicate that contention for Free Lists is occurring. If you determine that Free List contention is present, next you must determine which segments are experiencing the contention. This can be achieved using a query on V$SESSION_WAIT and DBA_SEGMENTS as discussed in the next section.

## Using *V$SESSION_WAIT* and *DBA_SEGMENTS*

The V$SESSION_WAIT view can be joined to the DBA_SEGMENTS view to determine which segments are experiencing Free List contention. The following query shows how you can join these two tables using the P1, P2, HEADER_FILE, and HEADER_BLOCK columns:

```
SQL> SELECT s.segment_name, s.segment_type, s.freelists
  2  FROM dba_segments s, v$session_wait w
  3  WHERE w.p1 = s.header_file
  4  AND    w.p2 = s.header_block
  5  AND    w.event = 'buffer busy waits';
```

```
SEGMENT_NAME          SEGMENT_TYPE FREELISTS
------------------    ------------ ---------
EMPLOYEE              TABLE                1
```

### Using Performance Manager

The Performance Manager GUI tool also can monitor Free List contention. Figure 8.2 shows the Performance Manager screen that displays the Free List hit ratio for all segments in the database.

**FIGURE 8.2**  Performance Manager Free List statistics

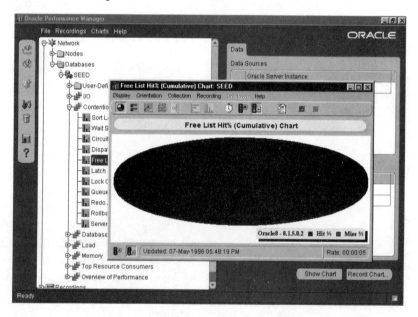

## Tuning Free List Contention

The number of Free Lists assigned to a segment is determined at segment creation and cannot be changed dynamically. Therefore, once you identify the segment that is experiencing Free List contention, you must drop and re-create it using the FREELISTS option in order to add more Free Lists. By default, all segments are assigned one Free List.

Generally, Free List contention is only a serious problem in Oracle Parallel Server environments. This is true because many users and multiple instances access one database in that configuration.

# Lock Contention

**A**s you have seen, Oracle uses latches to protect access to memory structures. Latches are held for only short periods of time, and waits for busy latches are also very brief.

Oracle's locking mechanisms are similar to the latching mechanisms, but *locks* are used to protect access to data, not memory structures. Locks are also less restrictive than latches. In some cases, several users can share a lock on a segment. This is not possible with latches, which are never shared between processes.

Additionally, unlike latches, lock requests can be queued up in the order they are requested and then applied accordingly. This queuing mechanism is referred to as an *enqueue*. The enqueue keeps track of users who are waiting for locks, which lock mode they need, and in what order they asked for their locks.

*Lock contention* can occur any time two users try to lock the same resource at the same time. Lock contention usually arises when you have many users performing DML on a relatively small number of tables. When this situation causes two users to try modifying the same row in the same table, lock contention results.

In general, locks are used to preserve *data consistency*. This means that the data a user is changing stays consistent within their session, even if other users are also changing it. Oracle's automatic locking processes lock data at the lowest possible level so as not to needlessly restrict access to application data. Since this type of locking model allows many users to access data at the same time, application users achieve a high degree of *data concurrency*.

Once taken out, a lock is maintained until the locking user issues either a COMMIT or a ROLLBACK command. Because of this, locks that are too long in duration or too restrictive in nature can adversely affect performance for other application users who need to access the locked data. In most cases, this locking is done at the row level. Using Oracle's default locking mechanism, multiple users can do the following:

- Change different rows in the same table with no locking issues

- Change the same row in the same table with enqueues determining who will have access to the row and when, and with System Change Numbers (SCN) deciding whose change will be the final one

Figure 8.3 demonstrates these two locking situations (two users updating different rows and the same row) when two users are updating and querying data in a table called DEPT.

**FIGURE 8.3** Example of Oracle's locking mechanism

As illustrated in this figure, when Joe issues his UPDATE statement, he locks the row associated with DEPT_ID 20. When Matt issues his UPDATE command, he locks the row associated with the Sales department. Since Joe and Matt are each locking a different row, neither is affected by the other's lock. When Joe queries the DEPT table looking for the Sales department data, Matt's lock will not prevent Joe from seeing the Sales data. However, since Matt has not yet committed his changes, Joe will use the before-image data in Matt's rollback segment entry to build a read consistent view of the Sales data. Finally, when Matt tries to change the Accounting department's name by updating the row whose DEPT_ID is 20, Matt will experience a wait, stuck behind Joe's lock on the same row. Matt's session will continue to wait until Joe issues either a COMMIT or a ROLLBACK.

# Lock Types and Modes

Oracle uses two lock types to perform its locking operations: a *DML* or *data lock* and a *DDL* or *dictionary lock*. When performing these locking functions, Oracle also uses two different locking modes to achieve its goals of data concurrency and data consistency. The first lock mode, exclusive, is the most restrictive. An *exclusive lock* locks a resource until the transaction that took out the lock is complete. No other user can modify the resource while it is locked in exclusive mode. The second lock mode, shared, is the least restrictive. A *share lock* locks the resource, but allows other users to also obtain additional share locks on the same resource.

## DML Locks

DML or data locks are denoted by TM and are used to lock tables when users are performing INSERT, UPDATE, and DELETE commands. Data locks can either be at the table level or row level. Every user who performs DML on a table actually gets two locks on the table: a share lock at the table level and an exclusive lock at the row level. These two locks are *implicit*, meaning that Oracle performs the locking actions for the user. *Explicit locks* can also be taken out when performing DML commands. An explicit lock requires that you manually request a specified lock type. Table 8.2 compares modes used for DML locks.

**TABLE 8.2** Comparison of the Oracle DML Lock Modes

| Kind of Lock | Lock Mode (Lock Symbol) | Command | Description |
|---|---|---|---|
| Implicit | Row Exclusive (RX) | INSERT, UPDATE, DELETE | Other users can still perform DML of any other row in the table. |
| Implicit | Table Row Share (RS) | SELECT ... FOR UPDATE | Other users can still perform DML on the rows in the table that were not returned by the SELECT statement. |
| Implicit | Share (S) | UPDATE and DELETE on parent tables with Foreign Key relationships to child tables | Users can still perform DML on any other row in either the parent or child table as long as an index exists on the child table's Foreign Key column. |
| Implicit | Share Row Exclusive (SRX) | DELETE on Parent tables with Foreign Key relationships to Child tables | Users can still perform DML on any other row in either the parent or child table as long as an index exists on the child table's Foreign Key column. |
| Explicit | Exclusive (X) | LOCK TABLE ... IN EXCLUSIVE MODE | Other users can only query the table until the locking transaction is either committed or rolled back. |

* Oracle will take out a more restrictive lock on the child table whenever appropriate indexes on the Foreign Key columns of a child table are not present.

## DDL Locks

DDL or dictionary locks are denoted by TX and are used to lock tables when users are creating, altering, or dropping tables. This type of lock is always at the table level and is designed to prevent two users from modifying a table's structure simultaneously. Table 8.3 shows a comparison of the different modes used for DDL locks.

**TABLE 8.3**    Comparison of the Oracle DDL Lock Modes

| Lock Type | Lock Mode | Command | Description |
|---|---|---|---|
| Implicit | Exclusive (X) | CREATE, DROP, ALTER | Prevents other users from issuing DML or SELECT statements against the referenced table until after the CREATE, DROP, or ALTER operation is complete |
| Implicit | Shared (S) | CREATE PROCEDURE, AUDIT | Prevents other users from altering or dropping the referenced table until after the CREATE PROCEDURE or AUDIT operation is complete |
| Implicit | Breakable Parse | - | Used by statements cached in the Shared Pool; never prevents any other types of DML, DDL, or SELECT by any user |

# Monitoring Lock Contention

When left to its default mechanisms, Oracle generally does a very effective job of managing locking. When it does occur, lock contention can be identified using the V$LOCK and V$LOCKED_OBJECT dynamic performance views as well as the TopSessions GUI tool.

## Using *V$LOCK*

The V$LOCK dynamic performance view contains data regarding the locks that are being held in the database at the time a query is issued against the

view. As shown below, this view can be joined to DBA_OBJECTS and
V$SESSION to also see who is holding the lock and on which objects:

```
SQL> SELECT s.username,
  2            DECODE(l.type,'TM','TABLE LOCK',
  3                          'TX','ROW LOCK',
  4                          NULL) "LOCK LEVEL",
  5         o.owner, o.object_name, o.object_type
  6  FROM v$session s, v$lock l, dba_objects o
  7  WHERE s.sid = l.sid
  8  AND o.object_id = l.id1
  9  AND s.username IS NOT NULL;
```

| USERNAME | LOCK LEVEL | OWNER | OBJECT_NAM | OBJECT_TYPE |
|----------|------------|-------|------------|-------------|
| JOE | TABLE LOCK | JOE | EMP | TABLE |
| SCOTT | TABLE LOCK | JOE | EMP | TABLE |

This example shows that the users Scott and Joe are both locking the
EMP table owned by Joe. If Joe had called to complain that his application session appeared to not be responding, this query might help you
determine whether Joe's transaction is stuck waiting for Scott to commit or roll back his transaction. However, this query does not explicitly
indicate which user is blocking another user.

## Using *V$LOCKED_OBJECT*

The V$LOCKED_OBJECT view also lists all the locks currently held by every
user on the system. However, it also includes blocking information showing
who is performing the locking transaction that is causing other application
users to experience a wait. The following query can be used to determine
who is locking which objects and the user who holds the blocking lock:

```
SQL> SELECT LPAD(' ',DECODE(l.xidusn,0,3,0))
  2         ||l.oracle_username "User Name",
  3         o.owner, o.object_name, o.object_type
  4         FROM v$locked_object l, dba_objects o
  5  WHERE l.object_id = o.object_id
  6  ORDER by o.object_id, 1 desc;
```

| User Name | OWNER | OBJECT_NAM | OBJECT_TYPE |
| --- | --- | --- | --- |
| SCOTT | JOE | EMP | TABLE |
| BRENDA | JOE | EMP | TABLE |
| JOE | JOE | EMP | TABLE |
| ROBIN | APPS | PAYROLL | TABLE |
| REGI | APPS | PAYROLL | TABLE |

The query output shows that Scott, Joe, and Brenda are all locking rows in Joe's EMP table while Robin and Regi are locking rows in the application PAYROLL table. Furthermore, the leftmost username indicates the user who holds the lock that is preventing the other users from continuing their work. In the first example, this means that Scott's transaction on Joe's EMP table is blocking Brenda and Joe's transactions. Likewise, Robin's transaction on the PAYROLL table is blocking Regi's transaction on that same table. Techniques for resolving these types of blocking transactions are covered in the next section.

## Using the TopSessions GUI Tool

The Oracle TopSessions GUI tool is also useful for monitoring lock contention. Locking information is displayed in TopSessions by double-clicking the session you wish to examine. This opens the TopSessions Details window. By selecting the Locks tab on this window, TopSessions displays the lock information related to the user you selected. Figure 8.4 shows the Locks tab of the TopSessions Details window for the user Joe's session.

**FIGURE  8.4**    The Locks tab of the TopSessions Details window

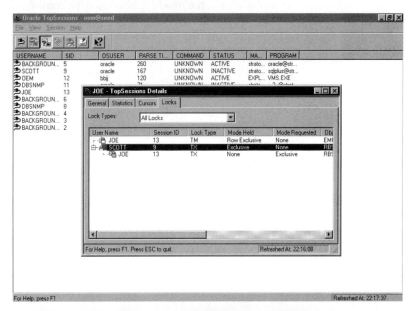

This figure shows that Joe is requesting a lock on a rollback segment but is waiting behind Scott's transaction, which must commit or roll back, before Joe can obtain the lock.

## Resolving Lock Contention

As mentioned earlier, lock contention occurs when two users try to lock the same resource in exclusive mode at the same time. When using Oracle's default locking mechanisms, lock contention is usually only a problem when your application has many users performing DML on a relatively small number of tables. Since Oracle's enqueue mechanism assigns locks in the order in which they were requested, a user who wishes to lock a row that is already locked by another user may experience a delay for an indeterminate length of time while waiting for the other user to commit or roll back their transaction. Once the users involved in the lock contention are identified using the techniques shown in the previous section, there are only two ways to resolve the contention:

- Contact the blocking user and ask them to commit or roll back their changes.

- Kill the blocking session using an SQL command, OEM's Instance Manager, or the TopSessions GUI tool.

### Using SQL

When lock contention occurs, you can use the ALTER SYSTEM KILL SESSION command to kill the blocking session. This command disconnects the blocking user's session and rollbacks any uncommitted transactions they had open. Before you can kill a blocking user's session, however, you must identify the SID and SERIAL# for their session using V$SESSION. The following example shows how to determine Scott's SID and SERIAL # if he were the blocking user causing lock contention:

```
SQL> SELECT sid, serial#
  2  FROM v$session
  3  WHERE username = 'SCOTT';

       SID    SERIAL#
---------- ----------
        12       8881
```

If all users connect to the application using the same Oracle username, try adding the V$SESSION columns OSUSER, MACHINE, or PROGRAM to your query to help identify which user's session you should kill.

Once you have identified the SID and SERIAL# for the session to be killed, you can issue the ALTER SYSTEM command to actually kill the session:

```
SQL> ALTER SYSTEM KILL SESSION '12,8881';
```

The user whose session was killed does not get an immediate indication that this has occurred unless they are accessing the database at that moment. If they are idle when their session is killed, they will not receive the ORA-00028 "Your Session Has Been Killed" error message until they initiate activity against the database.

## Using Instance Manager

OEM's Instance Manager tool can also be used to kill sessions causing lock contention. Sessions are killed in Instance Manager by:

- Expanding the Sessions branch in the left-hand side of the Instance Manager Window

- Clicking once on the username of the session you wish to kill

- Selecting Sessions ➤ Disconnect ➤ Immediate from the Instance Manager menu

Figure 8.5 shows the Instance Manager screen after Scott's session has been killed using the technique described above.

**FIGURE 8.5** Instance Manager's killed session screen

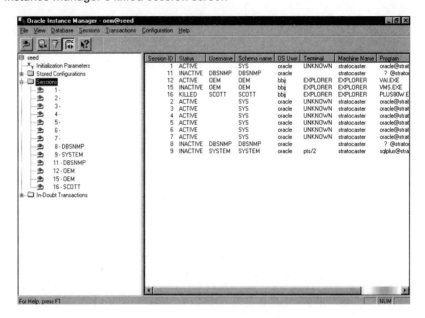

## Using TopSessions

Like Instance Manager, TopSessions can also be used to kill a session that is blocking another user's ability to obtain a lock. Session are killed in TopSessions by:

- Clicking once on the username of the session you wish to kill

- Selecting Sessions ➤ Kill from the TopSessions menu

Figure 8.6 shows the TopSessions confirmation window that pops up when a kill of Scott's session has been initiated using the technique described above.

**FIGURE 8.6**   TopSessions' kill session screen

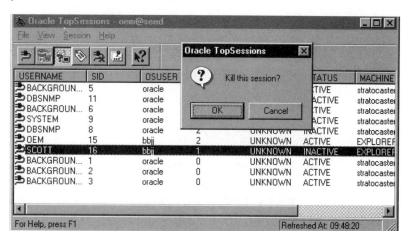

---

### A Deadly Embrace: The Special Case of Deadlocks

A *deadlock* (or sometimes referred to as a "deadly embrace") occurs when-ever two or more users are waiting for locks on data that are already locked by the one of the two or more users. Sound confusing? A simple example will help clarify the definition:

**1.** Malka updates the EMP table by changing the last name of employee 20 to Jones:

```
SQL> UPDATE emp
  2   SET last_name = 'Jones'
  3   WHERE id = 20;
1 row updated.
```

**2.** Next, Jennifer updates the EMP table, changing the salary of employee 25 to $50,000:

```
SQL> UPDATE emp
  2   SET salary = 50000
  3   WHERE id = 25;
1 row updated.
```

**3.** Malka also updates employee 25, changing the last name to Smith. At this point, Malka is stuck waiting behind Jennifer's lock on the same row, so Malka's session hangs:

```
SQL> UPDATE emp
```

```
 2   SET last_name = 'Smith'
 3   WHERE id = 25;
```

**4.** Now, Jennifer starts to update employee 20 (the row Malka locked in the first step) and tries to change their salary to $60,000:

```
SQL> UPDATE emp
 2   SET salary = 60000
 3   WHERE id = 20;
```

This leaves Jennifer stuck waiting behind Malka's lock on the same row. Both users are waiting for the other user to release their lock, but neither user can issue a COMMIT or ROLLBACK to release their locks because their sessions are hung up. This is a deadlock situation.

If there was no resolution to this situation, these two users would wait indefinitely for each other to release their locks. Luckily, Oracle automatically resolves deadlocks for you by simply rolling back one of the blocking transactions, thus releasing one of the locks involved in the deadlock. The transaction that gets rolled back will belong to the session that detects the deadlock situation. In our example, this would be Malka's session, and she would see the following error:

```
ORA-00060: deadlock detected while waiting for resource
```

Malka's session will also generate a trace file in the directory specified as the USER_DUMP_DEST in the init.ora. This trace file will indicate when, and on which table, the deadlock event occurred. A portion of Malka's trace file is shown here:

```
*** 2000.05.13.10.07.14.777
*** SESSION ID:(16.43) 2000.05.13.10.07.14.750
ksqded1:  deadlock detected via did
DEADLOCK DETECTED
Current SQL statement for this session:
UPDATE emp
SET last_name = 'Smith'
WHERE id = 25
The following deadlock is not an ORACLE error. It is a
deadlock due to user error in the design of an application
or from issuing incorrect ad-hoc SQL. The following
information may aid in determining the deadlock:
Deadlock graph:...
```

# Tuning Lock Contention

When lock contention causes performance-related problems, it is generally due to one of three factors:

- Application developers have coded excessively high lock levels.

- Application developers code long-running transactions without frequent commits.

- Application users start transactions and leave them uncommitted for extended periods.

Users waiting to obtain locks that are currently held by another user will perceive the resulting wait for those locks to be a performance issue. Therefore, finding and minimizing the effects of these locking-related issues can help improve performance.

## Excessive Lock Levels

Many commercial business applications are designed so that the customer can use the products with the database software of their choosing. Therefore, these products are not designed to take advantage of the unique features of any particular database vendor. Since not all relational databases share Oracle's propensity for row-level locking, developers who write these commercial packages sometimes explicitly code locks into the application that are higher than Oracle's default locking mechanisms in an effort to make the application more portable across databases. If these explicit locks cause locking contention to occur, there is very little a DBA can do to correct it, because the application code may either be unavailable or too costly to modify.

## Infrequent Commits

Commercial business application code that incorporates long-running transactions that do not commit at regular intervals can also cause locking-related performance issues. While some of these long transactions are necessary to perform the required processing, others may be the result of poor coding or application design. Locking issues of this type will occasionally cause the "Snapshot Too Old" error discussed in Chapter 7. As with explicit locks, these types of lock-related tuning problems are difficult to correct unless the application code itself is changed.

### Open User Transactions

Some users of an application will start a transaction and then leave the transaction open for a long period of time as they attend to other duties or tasks that interrupt their work. If the task they are performing in the application is locking many rows, other users may wait a long time for the locks to be released.

One way the DBA can prevent this problem is to disconnect users who are idle for a specified period of time through the use of Oracle's Profile feature. By creating a profile that is allowed a specified period of inactivity before disconnecting, and then assigning each user to this profile, the DBA can ensure that users who start transactions will have those transactions rolled back if they are idle for too long.

See Chapter 23, *Managing Users and Resources*, of *Oracle8i Administrator's Guide* (Part Number A67772-01) for details on how to set up Oracle's Profile feature.

# Summary

This chapter discussed the tuning-related aspects of contention for latches, Free Lists, and locking. Latches are used to protect access to memory structures. Although there are many types of latches, the Database Buffer Cache LRU latch (i.e., `cache buffers LRU chain latch`) is one of the most useful in terms of contention tuning. The number of LRU latches for the Database Buffer Cache is tuned using the `init.ora` parameter `DB_BLOCK_LRU_LATCHES`. `V$LATCH`, and the output from `REPORT.TXT` can be used to identify latch contention.

Free List contention can also be a performance tuning consideration on systems that perform frequent insert activity. The number of Free Lists for a table can only be changed by dropping and re-creating the table. The dynamic performance views `V$SYSTEM_EVENT`, `V$SESSION_WAIT`, and `V$WAITSTAT` as well as the Performance Manager GUI tool can be used to determine if Free List contention is occurring in your database.

Locking issues can also be a source of performance tuning problems. While Oracle's default locking mechanisms are primarily at the row level, performance issues can still occur when applications code excessively high lock levels, long transactions, or when users leave transactions uncommitted for extended periods. The Oracle Server automatically resolves deadlocks whenever they occur. You can use the V$LOCK and V$LOCKED_OBJECT dynamic performance views and the TopSessions GUI tool to monitor lock contention in the database.

When lock contention becomes severe, you can use the ALTER SYSTEM command as well as the Instance Manager and TopSessions GUI tools to kill the sessions that are holding the restrictive locks.

## Key Terms

Before you take the exam, make sure you're familiar with the following terms:

latch

Willing-to-Wait

Immediate

Free List contention

lock contention

enqueue

data consistency

data concurrency

data lock

dictionary lock

deadlock

# Review Questions

1. Which of the following latch types does not wait before attempting to re-obtain a busy latch?

   **A.** Immediate

   **B.** Instant

   **C.** Willing-to-Wait

   **D.** Unwilling-to-Wait

2. Which of the following latch types waits before attempting to re-obtain a busy latch?

   **A.** Immediate

   **B.** Instant

   **C.** Willing-to-Wait

   **D.** Unwilling-to-Wait

3. Which of the following mechanisms is used to protect access to memory structures?

   **A.** Enqueue

   **B.** Lock

   **C.** Latch

   **D.** `init.ora`

4. The number of times a user Server Process has successfully obtained a Willing-to-Wait latch without waiting is recorded in which column in V$LATCH?

   **A.** `MISSES`

   **B.** `GETS`

   **C.** `SLEEPS`

   **D.** `IMMEDIATE_GETS`

**5.** The number of times a user Server Process has successfully obtained an Immediate latch without waiting is recorded in which column in V$LATCH?

   **A.** MISSES

   **B.** GETS

   **C.** SLEEPS

   **D.** IMMEDIATE_GETS

**6.** Which latch is used by Server Processes when looking for room to copy blocks in the Database Buffer Cache?

   **A.** LRU latch

   **B.** Buffer Cache latch

   **C.** Cache Buffers LRU Chain latch

   **D.** Chain LRU latch

**7.** The number of latches assigned to the Database Buffer Cache LRU List is determined by setting which init.ora parameter?

   **A.** CACHE_BUFFERS_CHAIN

   **B.** DBBC_LRU_LATCH

   **C.** DB_BLOCK_LRU_LATCHES

   **D.** DB_BLOCK_BUFFERS

**8.** The desired hit ratio for the Database Buffer Cache LRU List is:

   **A.** 99 percent

   **B.** 85 percent

   **C.** 1 percent

   **D.** 5 percent

9. Segment blocks go on and off the Free List according to what values associated with the table?

   A. INITIAL/NEXT

   B. PCTFREE/PCTUSED

   C. TABLESPACE/DATAFILE

   D. MINEXTENTS/MAXEXTENTS

10. Free List contention can be detected using which of the following dynamic performance views? (Choose all that apply.)

   A. V$SYSTEM_EVENT

   B. V$SESSION

   C. V$SESSION_WAIT

   D. V$WAITSTAT

11. Resolving Free List contention is difficult because:

   A. Free List contention only occurs on large tables.

   B. The number of Free Lists is specified only at segment creation.

   C. The size of the Free List is dependent on the OS block size.

   D. Free List contention is only a problem when you have a small number of users.

12. The process of making sure that a user sees a consistent view of the database throughout their transaction is referred to as:

   A. Data concurrency

   B. Data constancy

   C. Data consistency

   D. Data contention

**13.** By default, most Oracle exclusive locks related to DML are at what level?

   **A.** Table level

   **B.** Column level

   **C.** Block level

   **D.** Row level

**14.** When the SELECT FOR UPDATE command is used, what type of lock is taken out of the selected rows?

   **A.** Table lock

   **B.** Row exclusive

   **C.** Table row share

   **D.** Exclusive

**15.** Which of the following lock types is the most restrictive?

   **A.** Exclusive

   **B.** Unique

   **C.** Exclusion

   **D.** None of the above is restrictive

**16.** Which lock type is taken out when creating, dropping, or altering a table?

   **A.** Restrictive

   **B.** Exclusive

   **C.** Explicit

   **D.** Shared

**17.** Which of the following GUI tools can be used to monitor lock contention? (Choose all that apply.)

   **A.** Instance Manager

   **B.** Performance Manager

   **C.** TopSessions

   **D.** Lock Manager

**18.** Which of the following is a method of resolving lock contention in an emergency? (Choose all that apply.)

   **A.** Kill the session using the `ALTER SYSTEM KILL SESSION` command.

   **B.** Kill the session using TopSessions.

   **C.** Kill the session using Schema Manager.

   **D.** Kill the session using Instance Manager.

**19.** If you wanted to kill the session for a user Jim, and the contents of `V$SESSION` showed his `SID` and `SERIAL#` to be 20 and 2369, what command would you issue to kill the session?

   **A.** `ALTER SYSTEM KILL SESSION (20,2369);`

   **B.** `ALTER SESSION KILL SYSTEM '20,2369';`

   **C.** `ALTER SYSTEM KILL SESSION '20','2369';`

   **D.** `ALTER SYSTEM KILL SESSION '20,2369';`

**20.** When an Oracle deadlock occurs, where is the deadlock information recorded after it is resolved?

   **A.** Alert log

   **B.** `V$DEADLOCK`

   **C.** User trace file

   **D.** TopSessions

# Answers to Review Questions

1. A. Immediate latches try to obtain the requested busy latch without waiting.

2. C. Willing-to-Wait latches sleep before trying to obtain a previously requested latch that was busy.

3. C. Latches are used to protect access to memory structures like the LRU lists and the Redo Log Buffer.

4. B. The GETS column of V$LATCH shows the number of times that a Willing-to-Wait latch was obtained without waiting.

5. D. The IMMEDIATE_GETS column of V$LATCH shows how often Immediate latches were obtained without waiting.

6. C. User Server Processes search the LRU list using the Cache Buffers LRU Chain latch when placing copies of blocks into the Database Buffer Cache.

7. C. The DB_BLOCK_LRU_LATCHES parameter in the init.ora file determines how many latches are assigned to the Database Buffer Cache's LRU List. The value for the parameter must be at least DB_BLOCK_BUFFERS/50.

8. A. A hit ratio of at least 99 percent is desired for the Database Buffer Cache LRU List.

9. B. Segment blocks are taken off the Free List when they are filled to PCTFREE and placed back on the Free List when they are emptied to PCTUSED.

10. A, C, D. The V$SYSTEM_EVENT view contains statistics on the buffer busy wait event. V$WAITSTAT contains statistics about waits for Free List blocks. V$SESSION_WAIT can be joined to DBA_SEGMENTS to determine which segments are experiencing Free List contention.

**11.** B. A table experiencing Free List contention must be exported, dropped, and re-created with a higher value for FREELISTS before importing the table data.

**12.** C. Oracle uses rollback segments and SCNs to ensure that users always see a read consistent view of the database.

**13.** D. While Oracle does take out a share lock at the table level, an exclusive lock on the data being changed is only taken out at the row level.

**14.** C. The SELECT FOR UPDATE command takes out a table row share lock, preventing other users from performing DML on the selected rows.

**15.** A. An exclusive lock is the most restrictive type, allowing other users to perform only SELECT statements until the lock is released.

**16.** B. Performing DDL on a table requires that an exclusive lock be taken out of that table.

**17.** C. You can observe the locks that are held in any current session by clicking the session in the TopSessions tool. Lock Manager also displays locking information by session.

**18.** A, B, D. Using SID and SERIAL# for the blocking session, you can use the ALTER SYSTEM command to disconnect the specified user. The TopSessions and Instance Manager GUI tools can also be used to disconnect a user holding an excessive lock.

**19.** D. The values for SID and SERIAL# must be enclosed in single quotes and separated by commas when killing a session with the ALTER SYSTEM command.

**20.** C. The user whose session detects the deadlock and has their transaction rolled back will generate a trace file in the USER_DUMP_DEST location specified in the init.ora.

# Resource Management

## ORACLE8i PERFORMANCE TUNING EXAM OBJECTIVES COVERED IN THIS CHAPTER:

✓ Describe the features of Database Resource Manager.

✓ Limit the use of resources using Database Resource Manager.

Exam objectives are subject to change at any time without prior notice and at Oracle's sole discretion. Please visit Oracle's Training and Certification Web site (http://education .oracle.com/certification/index.html) for the most current exam objectives listing.

As you have seen in the preceding chapters, Oracle utilizes many hardware resources while application users are accessing an instance. In cases where these resources are scarce, the DBA must allocate the resources so that the needs of the users are met most effectively. In Oracle versions prior to Oracle8i, DBAs could only manage user resource consumption through the use of profiles. However, profiles did not offer enough granularity to be considered a complete resource management solution.

Oracle8i introduces a new method of allocating and managing the resources needed by application users. Utilizing the new Resource Manager feature, a DBA can now create resource groups and assign them specific resource limits. These resource groups can in turn be assigned to application users who inherit the resource limits assigned to that group. A new set of data dictionary tables are also available to monitor the resources and users assigned to each group.

> **NOTE** Oracle Resource Manager is only available in the Oracle8i Enterprise Edition.

At the time of this writing, detailed documentation on Resource Manager was scant. Within all the volumes that make up the Oracle8i Documentation Library, less than 75 pages are dedicated to the topic of implementing and managing the Resource Manager feature. As this powerful feature matures, expect to see more complete details in the documentation on how it can best be implemented. However, this chapter does explain the basic functionality of Resource Manager within the scope of the objectives specified for the Performance and Tuning OCP exam.

For more details on using Resource Manager see Chapter 11: Using the Database Resource Manager in *Oracle8i Administrator's Guide, Release 8.1.5* (Part Number A67772-01) and Chapter 39: DBMS_RESOURCE_MANAGER in *Oracle8i Supplied Packages Reference, Release 8.1.5* (Part Number A68001-01).

# Resource Manager Overview

The Oracle8i Resource Manager uses three components to achieve the goal of effective resource management: *resource consumer groups, resource plans,* and *resource plan directives*. Table 9.1 shows the descriptions of each of these Resource Manager components.

**TABLE 9.1**    Descriptions of Resource Manager Components

| Component | Description |
| --- | --- |
| Resource consumer group | A group of users who have similar needs for database resources |
| Resource plan | A collection of resource plan directives that are used to implement resource management |
| Resource plan directive | Specifies how many CPU and parallel query resources are allocated to each resource consumer group |

Only two resources can currently be controlled through the use of Resource Manager:

- The amount of CPU allocated to each user who is a member of the resource consumer group

- The degree of parallelism allowed for parallel queries performed by a user who is a member of the resource consumer group

The CPU resources are allocated using the *emphasis method*, which allows you to assign varying weights for the resources at several levels. These weights are expressed in terms of a percentage between zero and 100. The resources associated with a parallel query (i.e., maximum degree of parallelism) are assigned using the *absolute method*. This means that maximum degree of parallelism is an absolute, specified value.

When allocating CPU and degree-of-parallelism priority to database users, Resource Manager allows you to define up to eight different levels of priority to which users can be assigned. For example, suppose we wanted to create a resource consumer group called POWER_USERS for your most sophisticated application users. Within this group, you may want to further specify the CPU and parallelism requirements by dividing the POWER_USERS resource consumer group between the FUNCTIONAL and TECHNICAL resource plans. These two resource plans could then be assigned CPU and parallelism priority on up to eight levels of granularity. Figure 9.1 conceptually shows how this resource allocation can be broken down.

**FIGURE 9.1** Relationship of resource consumer group, resource plan, and plan directive

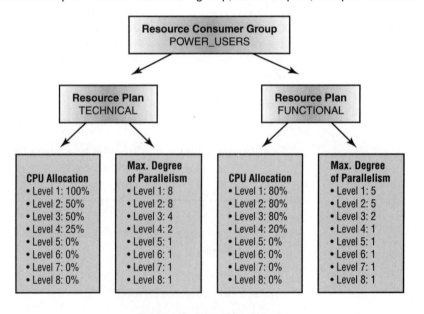

**Resource Plan Directives**

Notice that the TECHNICAL resource plan is allocated 100 percent of CPU at the first level, 50 percent at the second and third levels, 25 percent at the fourth level, and zero percent at the remaining levels. This means that users in the TECHNICAL resource plan will be able to use 100 percent of the CPU resources they need. If they do not use all the CPU resources, then users assigned to this resource consumer group will use the remaining CPU resources in this manner:

- 50 percent of any remaining CPU resources after Level 1 needs are serviced

- 50 percent of any remaining CPU resources after Level 2 needs are serviced

- 25 percent of any remaining CPU resources after Level 3 needs are serviced

Resource Manager allocates priority for the degree of parallelism associated with parallel queries in a similar manner. For example, the FUNCTIONAL resource plan can utilize up to five parallel query processes when performing parallel query operations. If any parallel query resources are left over, then the remaining parallel query resources will be allocated in this manner:

- Up to five additional query processes can be started if any resources remain after Level 1 needs are serviced.

- Up to two additional query processes can be started if any resources remain after Level 2 needs are serviced.

- One additional query process can be started for each of the remaining levels if any resources remain from the previous level.

Resource Manager can only manage the resources (i.e., CPU) that are allocated to the instance by the server's operating system. If other OS resource management tools are already managing the allocation of resources to Oracle at the OS level, then Resource Manager's effectiveness may be limited.

# Configuring Resource Management

In order to use the resource management features of Oracle8i, you must first perform a few simple configuration operations. These operations include granting resource management privileges to the proper users, creating the resource management objects, assigning those resources to individual users, and setting the overall resource objectives for the instance.

## Granting Resource Manager Privileges

By default, users with DBA privileges can also create and manage resource consumer groups. If a non-DBA user is going to be allowed to manage resource groups, plans, and directives, they must be granted the ADMINISTER_RESOURCE_MANAGER privilege. Unlike traditional system privileges, which can be granted with the GRANT ... TO ... command, the ADMINISTER_RESOURCE_MANAGER privilege must be granted using an Oracle-supplied PL/SQL package called DBMS_RESOURCE_MANAGER_ PRIVS. This package requires three arguments: GRANTEE_NAME, PRIVILEGE_NAME, and ADMIN_OPTION. GRANTEE_NAME is the name of the Oracle user being granted the privilege. PRIVILEGE_NAME is the name of the privilege being granted (i.e. DBMS_RESOURCE_MANAGER_ PRIVS). ADMIN_OPTION indicates whether the user receiving the privilege can pass that privilege along to other users. Figure 9.2 shows how this package could be used to grant the ADMINISTER_RESOURCE_ MANAGER privilege to the user Regi with the ADMIN option.

**FIGURE 9.2** Granting Resource Manager privilege

```
SQL> EXECUTE dbms_resource_manager_privs.grant_system_privilege (grantee_name => 'REGI', privilege_name => 'ADM
INISTER_RESOURCE_MANAGER', admin_option => TRUE);

PL/SQL procedure successfully completed.
```

 The => in the above Figure is part of the actual syntax for executing the DBMS_ RESOURCE_MANAGER_PRIVS package. You must also type all the parameters on one line, as shown in Figure 9.2, in order for the package to execute successfully.

If you need to revoke the privilege to administer Resource Manager, you will use the REVOKE_SYSTEM_PRIVILEGE procedure in the DBMS_RESOURCE_ MANAGER_PRIVS package. This procedure accepts two arguments: REVOKEE_ NAME and PRIVILEGE_NAME. Figure 9.3 shows how the Resource Manager privilege could be revoked from the user Regi.

**FIGURE 9.3** Revoking Resource Manager privilege

```
SQL> EXECUTE dbms_resource_manager_privs.revoke_system_privilege (revokee_name => 'REGI', privilege_name => 'AD
MINISTER_RESOURCE_MANAGER');

PL/SQL procedure successfully completed.
```

# Creating the Resource Manager Objects

Once the proper privileges have been assigned to the users who will be administering the Resource Manager, you must then build the database objects needed by Resource Manager. Setting up Resource Manager requires the following steps:

- Creation of a pending area
- Creation of one or more resource consumer groups
- Creation of one or more resource plans
- Creation of one or more resource plan directives
- Validation of the resource consumer groups, plans, and directives
- Saving of the resource consumer groups, plans, and directives to the database

## Creating the Pending Area

Whenever a new resource consumer group, plan, or directive is created, they are temporarily stored in the pending area until they are validated and written to the database. The purpose of the pending area is to give the DBA an opportunity to confirm that the definition of each consumer group, plan, and directive is correct before implementing it. The pending area is created using the DBMS_RESOURCE_MANAGER package and the CREATE_PENDING_AREA procedure:

```
SQL> EXECUTE dbms_resource_manager.create_pending_area;
```

 The database can only have one pending area at a time.

## Creating Resource Consumer Groups

A *resource consumer group (RCG)* is used to define a group of application users who have similar resource requirements. RCGs are similar to Oracle roles, except RCGs are used to manage resources, whereas roles are used to manage database object and system privileges. By default, every application user belongs to at least one RCG, which is called the DEFAULT_CONSUMER_GROUP. In addition to the DEFAULT_CONSUMER_GROUP, several other RCGs are constructed at database creation. The names and descriptions of these RCGs are shown in Table 9.2.

**TABLE 9.2** Default Resource Consumer Groups

| Resource Group Name | Description |
|---|---|
| SYS_GROUP | This group has the highest priority for resource access. The users SYS and SYSTEM are assigned to this RCG by default. |
| LOW_GROUP | This group receives the lowest priority for database resources. Every user has access to this RCG. |
| DEFAULT_CONSUMER_GROUP | Every user who is not explicitly assigned to another RCG is assigned to this RCG by default. |
| OTHER_GROUPS | The group that all users belong to when they are not members of the specific resource plan that is currently active in the instance. |

If you want to create your own RCG, you will use the DBMS_RESOURCE_MANAGER package and the CREATE_CONSUMER_GROUP procedure. Figure 9.4 shows this package being used to create a RCG called POWER_USERS.

**FIGURE 9.4** Creating a new resource consumer group

```
SQL> EXECUTE dbms_resource_manager.create_consumer_group ( consumer_group => 'POWER_USERS', comment => 'Users who will always receive preference for resources');

PL/SQL procedure successfully completed.
```

At this point, the new POWER_USERS resource consumer group is stored in the pending area, which you created in the previous section. The new RCG will not be written to the database and will not be made available until it is committed. Committing new RCGs to the database is covered later in this chapter.

## Creating Resource Plans

*Resource plans* are used to organize plan directives. A group of plan directives can be assigned to a resource plan, which can in turn be assigned to one or more resource groups. Only one resource plan can be active in the instance at a time. Determining which resource plan is active in the instance is discussed in the "Setting Instance Resource Objectives" section later in this chapter.

Suppose you wanted to create two resource plans within the POWER_USERS resource consumer group, one for the functional users and one for the technical users. Figure 9.5 shows how these two resource plans could be created.

**FIGURE 9.5** Creating new resource plans

```
SQL> EXECUTE dbms_resource_manager.create_plan ( plan => 'FUNCTIONAL', comment => 'Functional power users');
PL/SQL procedure successfully completed.
SQL> EXECUTE dbms_resource_manager.create_plan ( plan => 'TECHNICAL', comment => 'Technical power users');
PL/SQL procedure successfully completed.
```

A default resource plan, called SYSTEM_PLAN, is created at database creation.

As with the creation of a new resource consumer group, the new FUNCTIONAL and TECHNICAL resource plans are stored in the pending area until they are committed. Committing new resource plans to the database is also covered in later in this chapter.

## Creating Plan Directives

A *plan directive* is used to link a resource consumer group to a resource plan. The plan directive is where the appropriate allocation of the two resources controlled by Resource Manager (CPU and degree of parallelism) is specified. Figure 9.6 shows the assignment of CPU and parallelism resources to the FUNCTIONAL and TECHNICAL resource groups in the POWER_USERS resource consumer group.

**FIGURE 9.6** Creating a new plan directive

```
SQL> EXECUTE dbms_resource_manager.create_plan_directive ( plan => 'FUNCTIONAL', group_or_subplan => 'POWER_USE
RS', comment => 'Plan directive for functional power users', cpu_p1 => 80, parallel_degree_limit_p1 => 5);
PL/SQL procedure successfully completed.
SQL> EXECUTE dbms_resource_manager.create_plan_directive ( plan => 'TECHNICAL', group_or_subplan => 'POWER_USER
S', comment => 'Plan directive for functional power users', cpu_p1 => 100, parallel_degree_limit_p1 => 8);
PL/SQL procedure successfully completed.
```

The CPU_P1 argument shown in Figure 9.6 is used to specify what percentage of the overall CPU the resource consumer group/resource plan combination is allowed to use. You can also define up to eight levels of resource allocation for parallel query using `parallel_degree_limit_p1`, `parallel_degree_limit_p2`, etc., through `parallel_degree_limit_p8`. Each plan directive must also include a reference to the default resource consumer group OTHER_GROUPS. This is the resource consumer group that is active for a user when the user is not included in the resource plan that is active at the instance level. Figure 9.7 shows the assignment of FUNCTIONAL and TECHNICAL resource plans to the OTHER_GROUPS resource consumer group.

**FIGURE 9.7** Allocating a plan directive to OTHER_GROUPS

```
SQL> EXECUTE dbms_resource_manager.create_plan_directive ( plan => 'FUNCTIONAL', group_or_subplan => 'OTHER_GRO
UPS', comment => 'OTHER_GROUP default', cpu_p2 => 50, parallel_degree_limit_p1 => 1);

PL/SQL procedure successfully completed.

SQL>
SQL> EXECUTE dbms_resource_manager.create_plan_directive ( plan => 'TECHNICAL', group_or_subplan => 'OTHER_GROU
PS', comment => 'OTHER_GROUP default', cpu_p2 => 50, parallel_degree_limit_p1 => 1);

PL/SQL procedure successfully completed.
```

## Validating Consumer Resource Group, Plans, and Directives

Once a resource consumer group has been defined and assigned a resource plan and directive, the entire package must be validated before being written to the database. Verification of these Resource Manager components is performed using the VALIDATE_PENDING_AREA procedure of the DBMS_RESOURCE_MANAGER package as shown here:

```
SQL> EXECUTE dbms_resource_manager.validate_pending_area
();
```

If you forget to include a reference to the OTHER_GROUPS default resource consumer group when defining the FUNCTIONAL and TECHNICAL plan directives, you will see the error shown in Figure 9.8 when validation is performed.

**FIGURE 9.8** Error returned when OTHER_GROUPS is omitted from the plan directive

```
SQL> execute dbms_resource_manager.validate_pending_area;
BEGIN dbms_resource_manager.validate_pending_area; END;

*
ERROR at line 1:
ORA-00604: error occurred at recursive SQL level
ORA-01001: invalid cursor
ORA-29382: validation of pending area failed
ORA-29377: consumer group OTHER_GROUPS is not part of top-plan TECHNICAL
ORA-29377: consumer group OTHER_GROUPS is not part of top-plan FUNCTIONAL
ORA-06512: at "SYS.DBMS_RMIN", line 249
ORA-06512: at "SYS.DBMS_RESOURCE_MANAGER", line 254
ORA-06512: at line 1
```

### Saving Resource Consumer Groups, Plans, and Directives

Once the pending resource consumer groups, plans, and directives have been validated, they must be committed to the database before they can be assigned to database users. This commit is performed using the SUBMIT_PENDING_AREA procedure in the DBMS_RESOURCE_MANAGER package as shown here:

```
SQL> EXECUTE dbms_resource_manager.submit_pending_area;
```

# Assigning Resources to Users

Once you have created resource consumer groups, assigned them resource plans, and associated resource directives with those plans, it is time to assign the resource consumer groups to application users. You can assign a resource consumer group to a database user by either granting the RCG directly to an individual user, or by granting the RCG to a database role. Figure 9.9 shows how the GRANT_SWITCH_CONSUMER_GROUP procedure in the DBMS_RESOURCE_MANAGER_PRIVS package is used to assign the POWER_USERS RCG to a user named Betty, without the ability to pass the privileges along to other users (i.e. lacking GRANT OPTION).

**FIGURE 9.9** Assigning a resource consumer group to a user

```
SQL> EXECUTE dbms_resource_manager_privs.grant_switch_consumer_group ( grantee_name => 'BETTY', consumer_group
=> 'POWER_USERS', grant_option => FALSE);

PL/SQL procedure successfully completed.
```

Since a user can be a member of several RCGs at one time, it is usually preferred to specify a default RCG that will be active for the user when they initially connect to the database. A user's default RCG is assigned using the SET_INITIAL_CONSUMER_GROUP procedure of the DBMS_RESOURCE_MANAGER package. Figure 9.10 shows how Betty would be assigned the default RCG of POWER_USERS. If a user is not assigned a default consumer group, their initial RCG will be the public group DEFAULT_CONSUMER_GROUP.

**FIGURE 9.10** Assigning a user a default resource consumer group

```
SQL> EXECUTE dbms_resource_manager.set_initial_consumer_group ( user => 'BETTY', consumer_group => 'POWER_USERS
');

PL/SQL procedure successfully completed.
```

While RCGs can be assigned via roles, a resource consumer group that was granted through a role cannot be specified as a user's default RCG.

The active RCG for a user can also be changed dynamically with the application by using the DBMS_SESSION package and the SWITCH_CURRENT_CONSUMER_GROUP procedure. This is a useful feature that allows an application to activate and deactivate various RCGs for users as they navigate through an application and perform activities that have varying levels of resource requirements. Figure 9.11 shows sample PL/SQL code that could be embedded in an application to use DBMS_SESSION to change a users current RCG to POWER_USERS when performing a resource-intensive calculation.

**FIGURE 9.11** Using DBMS_SESSION to change the active resource consumer group

```
SQL> CREATE OR REPLACE PROCEDURE calc_tax
  2
  3  IS
  4
  5  v_original_rcg varchar2(30);
  6  v_previous_rcg varchar2(30);
  7
  8  CURSOR c_sales IS
  9  SELECT sales_amount
 10  FROM sales;
 11
 12  v_tax number;
 13
 14  BEGIN
 15
 16  -- set the user's RCG to POWER_USERS before calculating the tax
 17  -- the current RCG will be stored in the v_initial_rcg variable
 18
 19  DBMS_SESSION.SWITCH_CURRENT_CONSUMER_GROUP ( new_consumer_group => 'POWER_USERS', old_consumer_group => v_
original_rcg, initial_group_on_error => FALSE);
 20
 21  FOR r_sales IN c_sales LOOP
 22  v_tax := r_sales.sales_amount * .065;
 23  dbms_output.put_line (v_tax);
 24  END LOOP;
 25
 26  -- switch back to the original RCG
 27
 28  DBMS_SESSION.SWITCH_CURRENT_CONSUMER_GROUP ( new_consumer_group => v_original_rcg, old_consumer_group => v
_previous_rcg, initial_group_on_error => TRUE);
 29
 30  END;
 31  /

Procedure created.
```

# Setting Instance Resource Objectives

Any of the defined resource plans can be activated for the instance. However, only one resource plan can be active at a time. The active resource plan for the instance can be defined using the RESOURCE_MANAGER_PLAN parameter in the init.ora, or by dynamically issuing the ALTER SYSTEM SET RESOURCE_MANAGER_PLAN command. If this parameter is not set, then the features of Resource Manager are disabled. Figure 9.12 shows how the instance-level resource plan could dynamically be set to the TECHNICAL plan within the POWER_USERS resource consumer group.

**FIGURE 9.12** Setting the instance's resource plan dynamically

```
SQL> alter system set resource_manager_plan = technical;

System altered.
```

If you specify a non-existent resource plan in the init.ora, Oracle will return an ORA-07452 "Specified Resource Manager Plan Does Not Exist in the Data Dictionary Error at Instance Startup" error message.

Oracle also gives you the ability to dynamically change the active RCG for an individual connected user. Figure 9.13 demonstrates how the POWER_USERS RCG could be activated in Betty's session by using the SWITCH_CONSUMER_GROUP_FOR_USER procedure in the DBMS_RESOURCE_MANAGER package.

**FIGURE 9.13** Changing the active resource consumer group for a connected user

```
SQL> EXECUTE dbms_resource_manager.switch_consumer_group_for_user ( user => 'BETTY', consumer_group => 'POWER_U
SERS');

PL/SQL procedure successfully completed.
```

However, in some applications, the application itself connects to the database with the same database username for all users (even though each application user has a unique login name). In these cases, the above technique cannot be used since all connected users would then have the same RCG activated. In this situation, you can use the SWITCH_CONSUMER_GROUP_FOR_SESS procedure in the DBMS_RESOURCE package to change the active RCG for an individual user's session—even if that user is connected to the database with the same username as another connected user. This procedure accepts the SID and SERIAL# of the session you wish to change as input parameters. Both SID and SERIAL# are identified by querying V$SESSION. Figure 9.14

demonstrates how this procedure could be used to change the RCG for just Betty's session when all application users connect to the database using the database username APPS.

**FIGURE 9.14** Changing the active resource consumer group for a specified session

```
SQL> SELECT sid, serial#, username, osuser
  2  FROM v$session
  3  WHERE osuser = 'betty';

       SID    SERIAL# USERNAME   OSUSER
---------- ---------- ---------- ----------
        13         14 APPS       betty

1 row selected.

SQL> EXECUTE dbms_resource_manager.switch_consumer_group_for_sess ( session_id => 13, session_serial => 14, con
sumer_group => 'POWER_USERS');

PL/SQL procedure successfully completed.
```

# Monitoring Resource Manager

Once resource consumer groups, resource plans, and plan directives have been created, you can use several views to monitor Resource Manager–related topics, such as which consumer groups exist, which plan is active, and which plans have been assigned to each user. These views are of two types: V$ dynamic performance views, and DBA data dictionary views.

## Resource Manager *V$* Views

The three dynamic performance views that contain information related to Resource Manager are:

- V$SESSION
- V$RSRC_CONSUMER_GROUP
- V$RSRC_PLAN

The two other V$ views related to Resource Manager are V$RSRC_PLAN_CPU_MTH and V$RSRC_CONSUMER_GROUP_CPU_MTH. These two views contain only one column, NAME, which displays the available resource-allocation methods for both resource consumer groups and resource plans, respectively. By default, the method used is ROUND–ROBIN.

### V$SESSION

The RESOURCE_CONSUMER_GROUP column in V$SESSION displays the current RCG for each session. The following query on V$SESSION shows the contents of this column:

```
SQL> SELECT username, resource_consumer_group
  2  FROM v$session
  3  WHERE username IS NOT NULL;


USERNAME    RESOURCE_CONSUMER_GROUP
----------  -----------------------
DBSNMP      DEFAULT_CONSUMER_GROUP
SYSTEM      SYS_GROUP
APPS        POWER_USERS
BETTY       POWER_USERS
```

### V$RSRC_CONSUMER_GROUP

The V$RSRC_CONSUMER_GROUP dynamic performance view contains detail about the resource allocations that have been made to the active resource consumer groups. Table 9.3 describes the contents of this view.

**TABLE 9.3**   Contents of the V$RSRC_CONSUMER_GROUP View

| Column | Description |
|---|---|
| NAME | The name of the resource consumer group |
| ACTIVE_SESSIONS | The number of sessions that are currently assigned to this resource consumer group |
| EXECUTION_WAITERS | The number of sessions assigned to this resource consumer group that are waiting to be allotted resources before they can execute |
| REQUESTS | The total number of database requests that have been executed by users in this resource consumer group |
| CPU_WAIT_TIME | The total time that users in this resource consumer group have had to wait for access to the CPU (in 100th of a second) |

**TABLE 9.3** Contents of the V$RSRC_CONSUMER_GROUP View *(continued)*

| Column | Description |
|--------|-------------|
| CPU_WAITS | The total number of times that users in the resource consumer group have waited for access to the CPU |
| CONSUMED_CPU_TIME | The total amount of CPU time that users in this resource consumer group have consumed (in 100th of a second) |
| YIELDS | The number of times users in this resource consumer group have had to yield the CPU to users in other resource consumer groups with greater priority |
| SESSIONS_QUEUED | The number of user sessions assigned to this resource consumer group that are waiting to become active |

Ideally, if your users have been assigned to resource consumer groups effectively, users with high priority in the database should be experiencing few CPU waits (EXECUTION_WAITERS and CPU_WAIT_TIME) and not have many unserviced sessions (SESSIONS_QUEUED). If this is not the case, you may want to re-examine the resource allocations you have created to try and minimize these events.

### V$RSRC_PLAN

The V$RSRC_PLAN dynamic performance view displays the names of all the currently active resource plans. There is only one column in this view, NAME, which contains the name of the resource plan that is active at the instance-level. The following query shows how V$RSRC_PLAN could be used to determine the active resource plan:

```
SQL> SELECT *
  2  FROM v$rsrc_plan;

NAME
--------------------------------
TECHNICAL
```

## Resource Manager DBA Views

There are five data dictionary views that contain information related to Resource Manager:

- DBA_RSRC_PLANS
- DBA_RSRC_PLAN_DIRECTIVES
- DBA_RSRC_CONSUMER_GROUPS
- DBA_RSRC_CONSUMER_GROUPS_PRIVS
- DBA_USERS

### DBA_RSRC_CONSUMER_GROUPS

The DBA_RSRC_CONSUMER_GROUPS view contains information on each resource consumer group in the database. These are the same parameters that are specified at the creation of the resource consumer group. Table 9.4 lists the contents of this view.

**TABLE 9.4**  Contents of the DBA_RSRC_CONSUMER_GROUPS View

| Column | Description |
| --- | --- |
| CONSUMER_GROUP | The name of the resource consumer group. |
| CPU_METHOD | The CPU allocation method used to assign CPU resources to this consumer group. |
| COMMENTS | The comments (if any) specified for the resource consumer group at its creation. |
| STATUS | The status of the resource consumer group. New, uncommitted RCGs have a status of PENDING. Committed RCGs have a status of ACTIVE. |
| MANDATORY | Indicates whether or not the resource consumer group is mandatory. Mandatory RCGs cannot be deleted or modified. |

The following query on DBA_RSRC_CONSUMER_GROUPS shows the summary information for the POWER_USERS resource consumer group created earlier:

```
SQL> SELECT consumer_group, cpu_method,
  2           status, mandatory
  3  FROM dba_rsrc_consumer_groups
  4  WHERE consumer_group = 'POWER_USERS';


CONSUMER_GROUP    CPU_METHOD   STATUS       MAN
--------------    ----------   ----------   ---
POWER_USERS       ROUND-ROBIN  ACTIVE       NO
```

### DBA_RSRC_CONSUMER_GROUP_PRIVS

The DBA_RSRC_CONSUMER_GROUP_PRIVS view shows which users or roles in the database have been granted to each resource consumer group. Table 9.5 lists the columns found in this view.

**TABLE 9.5**  Contents of the DBA_RSRC_CONSUMER_GROUP_PRIVS View

| Column | Description |
|--------|-------------|
| GRANTEE | The username or role that has been granted a resource consumer group |
| GRANTED_GROUP | The name of the resource consumer group the user or role has been granted |
| GRANT_OPTION | Indicates whether the user has the ability to pass the privilege, assigned via the resource consumer group, on to other users |
| INITIAL_GROUP | Indicates whether the resource consumer group is the user's default RCG |

The following query shows the resource consumer group privileges for the two users, Apps and Betty, which were referenced in prior examples:

```
SQL> SELECT *
  2  FROM dba_rsrc_consumer_group_privs;
```

```
GRANTEE        GRANTED_GROUP              GRA INI
-----------    ------------------------   --- ---
APPS           POWER_USERS                NO  NO
BETTY          POWER_USERS                NO  YES
PUBLIC         DEFAULT_CONSUMER_GROUP     YES YES
PUBLIC         LOW_GROUP                  NO  NO
SYSTEM         SYS_GROUP                  NO  YES
```

## DBA_RSRC_PLANS

The DBA_RSRC_PLANS view shows all the resource plans that have been created in the database. Table 9.6 shows the contents of this view.

**TABLE 9.6**  Contents of the DBA_RSRC_PLANS View

| Column | Description |
|---|---|
| PLAN | The name of the plan. |
| NUM_PLAN_DIRECTIVES | The number of directives within the plan. |
| CPU_METHOD | The method used to allocate CPU resources to the plan (emphasis method). |
| MAX_ACTIVE_SESS_TARGET_MTH | Not currently defined, reserved for future use. |
| PARALLEL_DEGREE_LIMIT_MTH | The method used to allocate parallel resources to the plan (absolute method). |
| COMMENTS | The comments defined at plan creation (if any). |
| STATUS | The status of the resource plan. New uncommitted plans have a status of PENDING. Committed plans have a status of ACTIVE. |
| MANDATORY | Indicates whether or not the resource plan is mandatory. Mandatory plans cannot be modified or deleted. |

The following query shows the output from DBA_RSRC_PLANS for the TECHNICAL and FUNCTIONAL resource plans created in a previous example. It also shows an uncommitted resource plan called AR_CLERK:

```
SQL> SELECT plan, status, mandatory
  2  FROM dba_rsrc_plans;


PLAN            STATUS        MAN
-------------   ----------    ---
SYSTEM_PLAN     ACTIVE        NO
FUNCTIONAL      ACTIVE        NO
TECHNICAL       ACTIVE        NO
AR_CLERK        PENDING       NO
```

## DBA_RSRC_PLAN_DIRECTIVES

DBA_RSRC_PLAN_DIRCECTIVES displays the specific resource allocations that were assigned to each resource plan. Table 9.7 shows descriptions of some of the columns found in this view.

**TABLE 9.7** Contents of the DBA_RSRC_PLAN_DIRECTIVES View

| Column | Description |
| --- | --- |
| PLAN | The name of the plan to which this directive has been assigned. |
| CPU_P1 | The emphasis percentage assigned to CPU allocation at each level. There are seven other columns (CPU_P2 through CPU_P8) that are also used to report the plan's CPU allocation at those levels. |
| COMMENTS | The comments defined at plan creation (if any). |
| STATUS | The status of the resource plan. New, uncommitted plans have a status of PENDING. Committed plans have a status of ACTIVE. |
| MANDATORY | Indicates whether or not the resource plan is mandatory. Mandatory plans cannot be modified or deleted. |

The following query shows the output from DBA_RSRC_PLAN_
DIRECTIVES for the plan directives created in previous examples:

```
QL> SELECT plan, cpu_p1, cpu_p2, cpu_p3,
  2          cpu_p4, status, mandatory
  3  FROM dba_rsrc_plan_directives;
```

| PLAN | CPU_P1 | CPU_P2 | CPU_P3 | CPU_P4 | STATUS | MAN |
|------|--------|--------|--------|--------|--------|-----|
| TECHNICAL | 100 | 0 | 0 | 0 | ACTIVE | NO |
| FUNCTIONAL | 80 | 0 | 0 | 0 | ACTIVE | NO |
| TECHNICAL | 0 | 50 | 0 | 0 | ACTIVE | NO |
| FUNCTIONAL | 0 | 80 | 0 | 0 | ACTIVE | NO |
| TECHNICAL | 0 | 0 | 50 | 0 | ACTIVE | NO |
| FUNCTIONAL | 0 | 0 | 80 | 0 | ACTIVE | NO |
| TECHNICAL | 0 | 0 | 0 | 25 | ACTIVE | NO |
| FUNCTIONAL | 0 | 0 | 0 | 20 | ACTIVE | NO |

## DBA_USERS

The DBA_USERS view has a single column, INITIAL_RSRC_CONSUMER_GROUP,
which indicates the resource consumer group that has been assigned to a user
as their default. The following query shows the initial resource consumer
group assigned to Betty in a previous example:

```
SQL> SELECT username, initial_rsrc_consumer_group
  2  FROM dba_users
  3  WHERE username = 'BETTY';
```

| USERNAME | INITIAL_RSRC_CONSUMER_GROUP |
|----------|-----------------------------|
| BETTY | POWER_USERS |

# Summary

**O**racle Resource Manager is used to allocate CPU and parallel query resources to users. The resource plan directives are where the actual CPU and degree-of-parallelism allocations are defined using the DBMS_RESOURCE_MANAGER PL/SQL package. Once directives are defined, they are assigned to resource plans, which are assigned to resource consumer groups, which are in turn assigned to database users or roles. The resource plan for the instance can be defined using the RESOURCE_MANAGER_PLAN parameter in the init.ora or by issuing the ALTER SYSTEM SET RESOURCE_MANAGER_PLAN command. Several data dictionary and dynamic performance views are available to monitor and manage the resource consumer groups, resource plans, and resource plan directives.

# Key Terms

**B**efore you take the exam, make sure you're familiar with the following terms:

resource consumer group

resource plan directives

resource plan

pending area

emphasis method

absolute method

# Review Questions

**1.** Which Oracle versions contain the Resource Manager feature?

   **A.** Oracle8i

   **B.** Oracle8i Lite

   **C.** Personal Oracle8i

   **D.** Oracle8i Enterprise Edition

**2.** A group of database users who have similar resource needs can be assigned to a:

   **A.** Resource plan

   **B.** Resource consumer group

   **C.** Resource plan directive

   **D.** Consumer resource group

**3.** Which of the following is made up of a collection of resource plan directives?

   **A.** Resource consumer group

   **B.** DBMS_RESOURCE_MANAGER

   **C.** Resource plan

   **D.** Consumer plan group

**4.** Which of the following database resources can be assigned to a resource plan using plan directives? (Choose all that apply.)

   **A.** Memory

   **B.** CPU

   **C.** Disk I/O

   **D.** Degree of parallelism

5. At how many levels can CPU allocation be defined?

   **A.** Only two

   **B.** Four or less

   **C.** Up to eight

   **D.** The number is unlimited.

6. Which of the following Oracle-supplied PL/SQL packages is used to grant a user the ability to create and administer resource management objects and privileges?

   **A.** DBMS_RESOURCE_MANAGER

   **B.** GRANT_RESOURCE_MANAGER_PRIVS

   **C.** DBMS_RESOURCE_MANAGER_PRIVS

   **D.** DBMS_RSRC_MANAGER_PRIVS

7. The pending area is used to store new Resource Manager consumer groups, plans, or directives until they are:

   **A.** Committed to the database

   **B.** Recorded in the archive logs

   **C.** Assigned to a database user or role

   **D.** Dropped from the database

8. The process of examining the contents of the pending area and determining that the resource consumer groups, resource plans, and resource plan directives found there are defined correctly is called:

   **A.** Certification

   **B.** Validation

   **C.** Examination

   **D.** Stabilization

**9.** Which of the following PL/SQL packages is used to create a new resource consumer group?

**A.** DBMS_RESOURCE_MANAGER

**B.** DBMS_CREATE_CONSUMER_GROUP

**C.** DBMS_RESOURCE_GROUP

**D.** DBMS_RSRC_CONSUMER_GROUP

**10.** Which of the following default resource groups has the highest database priority?

**A.** OTHER_GROUPS

**B.** SYS_GROUP

**C.** LOW_GROUP

**D.** DEFAULT_CONSUMER_GROUP

**11.** Which of the following resource consumer groups is active when a user is not a member of the currently active resource plan?

**A.** LOW_GROUP

**B.** DEFAULT_GROUP

**C.** DEFAULT_CONSUMER_GROUP

**D.** OTHER_GROUPS

**12.** The SET_INITIAL_CONSUMER_GROUP procedure in the DBMS_ RESOURCE_MANAGER PL/SQL package is used to:

**A.** Set the default resource plan for the instance

**B.** Set the resource plan that will be active when a user logs in

**C.** Create the four default resource consumer groups

**D.** Alter a connected user's current resource plan

13. Which `init.ora` parameter is used to define the default resource plan at the instance level?

    **A.** INSTANCE_RESOURCE_PLAN

    **B.** RESOURCE_PLAN

    **C.** RESOURCE_MANAGER_PLAN

    **D.** RSRC_MANAGER_PLAN

14. Which of the following procedures in the DBMS_RESOURCE_MANAGER package can change the active resource group for a connected user? (Choose all that apply.)

    **A.** SWITCH_CONSUMER_GROUP_FOR_USER

    **B.** SWITCH_CONSUMER_GROUP_FOR_SESS

    **C.** SWITCH_USER_CONSUMER_GROUP

    **D.** SWITCH_CURRENT_CONSUMER_GROUP

15. How many of a database's resource plans can be active at the instance-level at the same time?

    **A.** All of them

    **B.** None of them

    **C.** One of them

    **D.** Up to four

16. The default resource plan created at database creation is called:

    **A.** DEFAULT_PLAN

    **B.** SYSTEM_DEFAULT

    **C.** SYSTEM_PLAN

    **D.** PLAN_DEFAULT

17. Which of the following views shows information about which users have been assigned to each resource consumer group?

    **A.** DBA_RSRC_CONSUMER_GROUP

    **B.** DBA_RSRC_CONSUMER_GROUP_PRIVS

    **C.** DBA_RSRC_CONSUMER_GROUPS_GRANTED

    **D.** DBA_RSRC_CONSUMER_GROUPS

18. Which of the following views shows the resource plan that is currently active in the instance?

    **A.** V$RSRC_ACTIVE_PLAN

    **B.** V$RSRC_CURRENT_PLAN

    **C.** V$RSRC_PLAN

    **D.** V$RSRC_PLAN_ACTIVE

19. Which of the following views shows the CPU allocation directives that have been assigned to particular resource plan?

    **A.** DBA_RSRC_PLAN_DIRECTIVES

    **B.** DBA_RSRC_DIRECTIVES

    **C.** DBA_RSRC_DIRECTIVE_CPU

    **D.** DBA_RSRC_CPU

20. When creating a resource consumer group, resource plan, or resource plan directive, which of the following is true? (Choose all that apply.)

    **A.** Each parameter must be preceded by a =>.

    **B.** Each parameter must be enclosed in quotes.

    **C.** The command must be typed all on one line.

    **D.** All of the above are correct.

# Answers to Review Questions

1. D. Only Oracle8i Enterprise Edition contains the Resource Manager feature.

2. B. Users who share the same needs for access to database resources can be grouped together and assigned the same resource consumer group.

3. C. Resource plans are made up of one or more resource plan directives. The directives describe how database resources related to CPU and degree of parallelism should be allocated among users.

4. B, D. Currently, only CPU and the parallel query degree of parallelism can be defined using resource plan directives.

5. C. Varying degrees of CPU allocation can be defined at up to eight levels. Each succeeding level receives CPU access whenever excess CPU time is left over from the previous level.

6. C. The ADMINISTER_RESOURCE_MANAGER procedure in the DBMS_RESOURCE_MANAGER_PRIVS package can be used to assign a user the privileges needed to create and administer Resource Manager.

7. A. New resource consumer groups, resource plans, and resource plan directives are held in the pending area until they are validated and written to the database.

8. B. The procedure VALIDATE_PENDING_AREA in the DBMS_RESOURCE_MANAGER PL/SQL package must be used to validate new Resource Manager objects before they are written to the database.

9. A. The CREATE_CONSUMER_GROUP procedure of the DBMS_RESOURCE_MANAGER package is used to create new resource consumer groups.

10. B. The SYS and SYSTEM database users are members of the SYS_GROUP resource consumer group.

11. D. The OTHER_GROUPS resource consumer group is used to assign resource privileges to a user who is not a member of the resource plan that is currently active at the instance level.

12. B. When a user initiates a new connection to the database, the resource consumer group specified as their initial RCG will be active.

13. C. The default resource plan for an instance is determined at instance startup according to the RESOURCE_MANAGER_PLAN parameter in the init.ora.

14. A, B. SWITCH_CONSUMER_GROUP_FOR_USER changes the current resource consumer group for a connected user by username. SWITCH_ CONSUMER_GROUP_FOR_SESS changes the current resource consumer group for a connected user by SID and SERIAL#.

15. C. Only one of the database's resource plans can be defined at the instance level at a time.

16. C. Every database includes at least one resource plan, called SYSTEM_ PLAN. This plan is created when the database is created.

17. B. The DBA_RSRC_CONSUMER_GROUP_PRIVS view also contains information about whether this is the user's initial resource consumer group.

18. C. The V$RSRC_PLAN view will show which of the available resource plans is active at the instance-level.

19. A. The DBA_RSRC_PLAN_DIRECTIVES view will show how much CPU has been allocated to each resource plan at each of the eight allocation levels.

20. A, C. Not all parameters used when creating a resource consumer group, resource plan, or resource plan directive are in quotes. For example, the parameters for CPU emphasis and degree of parallelism are not enclosed in quotes.

# Chapter

# 10

# Oracle Expert

## ORACLE8i PERFORMANCE TUNING EXAM OBJECTIVES COVERED IN THIS CHAPTER:

✓ Describe the features of Oracle Expert.

Exam objectives are subject to change at any time without prior notice and at Oracle's sole discretion. Please visit Oracle's Training and Certification Web site (http://education .oracle.com/certification/index.html) for the most current exam objectives listing.

**A**s you have seen from the previous nine chapters, there is a great deal of information that must be taken into account when executing a thorough performance tuning exercise on an Oracle database. Remembering every statistic and its associated tuning recommendation is a daunting task. It can also be difficult to apply these tuning techniques consistently over time when other demands are placed on your busy schedule.

*Oracle Expert* is designed to assist busy DBAs with the important task of performance tuning. Oracle Expert is a GUI-based performance tuning tool that is a component of the Oracle Enterprise Manager Performance Pack. The Oracle Expert tool allows you to specify which aspects of the Oracle Tuning Methodology you wish to tune. It then monitors those areas for a user-specified period of time before making tuning recommendations based on the collected data. In this way, Oracle Expert provides you with consistent, relevant tuning information for your Oracle databases.

**NOTE** While Oracle Expert is an extra-cost option included with the Oracle Enterprise Manager Performance Pack, a free demonstration copy of the software can be downloaded from http://technet.oracle.com/software/products/oem/ software_index.htm.

Does the advent of software like Oracle Expert mean that all the things you've learned so far can be forgotten and replaced by this GUI tool? Not at all. In fact, Oracle Expert requires a good understanding of the previous topics in order to be able to analyze and interpret which of the tuning recommendations suggested by Oracle Expert are appropriate for you.

# Starting Oracle Expert

**O**racle Expert can be launched either from the OEM Console or by clicking the Oracle Expert icon. When you start the Oracle Expert GUI tool, you are presented with the login screen shown in Figure 10.1.

**FIGURE 10.1** Oracle Expert's Login screen

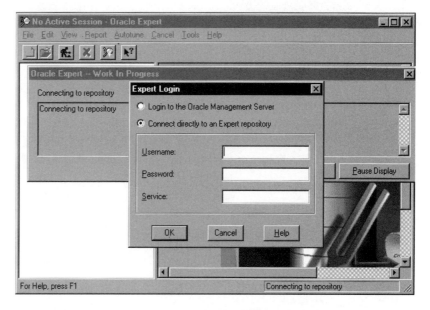

In addition to the usual Username, Password, and Service prompts common on many Oracle GUI tools, this login screen also includes the following connection options:

- Login to the Oracle Management Server
- Connect Directly to an Expert Repository

## Using a Management Server

As mentioned in Chapter 2: Sources of Tuning Information, the Oracle Management Server (OMS) acts as the central repository for the OEM configuration. By connecting via the OMS, you can also run Oracle Expert from an X Windows, Windows, or browser-based client. The OMS can be located on either a Windows NT or UNIX server. Both types of OMS can be used to access databases running on Windows NT or UNIX.

Initial connections to an Oracle Management Server are made using the SYSMAN username and the password oem_temp. The OMS will force you to change this password after the first login to the new management server. Once connected, the Oracle Management Server will build the OMS repository in the schema and database specified for this purpose.

## Using an Expert Repository

If you connect without the OMS, Oracle Expert establishes a direct connection with the database it will be monitoring. In order to use Oracle Expert in this type of configuration, the Oracle Expert *repository* information that is normally kept in the OMS is located in the target database instead. If the schema you used to connect to the target database does not already contain an Oracle Expert repository, you will be prompted by Repository Manager to build one. The schema you use to connect to the database must have the following database privileges in order for the repository to be built successfully:

- CREATE SESSION
- ALTER SESSION
- CREATE CLUSTER
- CREATE DATABASE LINK
- CREATE SEQUENCE
- CREATE SYNONYM
- CREATE TABLE
- CREATE VIEW
- CREATE PROCEDURE
- CREATE TRIGGER
- CREATE TYPE
- SELECT ANY TABLE

When connecting without the OMS, you should create a database user account just for the purpose of housing the Oracle Expert repository. This user should also have their own default tablespace dedicated solely to the storage of the repository objects.

This repository is nothing more than a collection of tables that Oracle Expert uses to hold things like gathered database statistics and tuning rules. Figure 10.2 shows what this Repository Manager screen looks like.

**FIGURE 10.2** Oracle Expert's Repository Manager screen

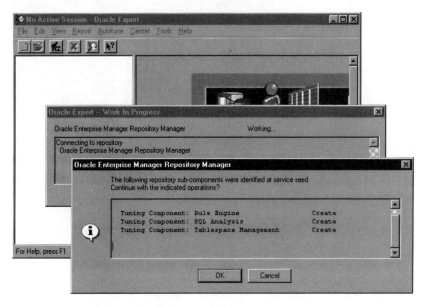

Once the Oracle Expert repository is built, you will see the Tuning Session Wizard Welcome screen shown in Figure 10.3.

**FIGURE 10.3** Tuning Session Wizard Welcome screen

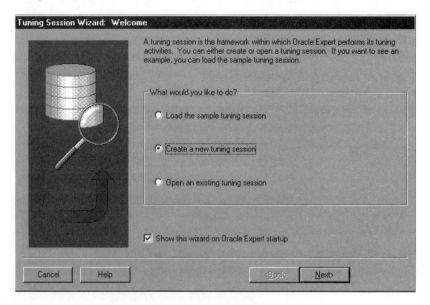

The welcome screen offers the ability to create a new tuning session using all new statistics and parameters, or to open an existing tuning session that uses previously defined statistics and parameters. After selecting which type of tuning session you would like to use, you can begin your Oracle Expert tuning session by following the Oracle Expert tuning process. This tuning process is dictated by the options available to you within the GUI tool. This process involves:

- Specifying the tuning scope

- Collecting tuning statistics

- Viewing the tuning statistics and editing the tuning rules as needed

- Analyzing the tuning statistics according to the tuning rules

- Reviewing Oracle Expert's tuning recommendations and generating script files

- Implementing Oracle Expert's recommendations where appropriate

Each of these steps in the Oracle Expert tuning process has an associated tab within the Oracle Expert GUI interface. Performing a tuning session using Oracle Expert essentially consists of selecting and examining the entries on each of these tabs, while working your way from the leftmost tab to the rightmost tab. The contents and parameters for each tab—Scope, Collect, View/Edit, Recommendations, and Scripts—are discussed in the following sections.

# Oracle Expert Scope

**Y**ou begin your tuning session on the leftmost tab, Scope. Figure 10.4 shows the contents of the Scope tab.

**FIGURE 10.4**  Oracle Expert's Scope tab

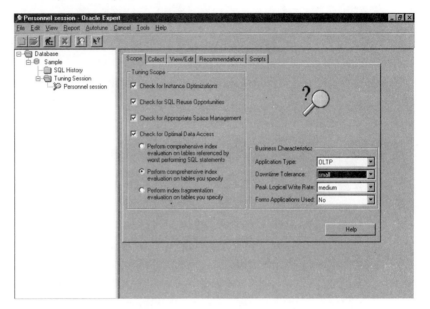

The contents of this tab are broken into two broad categories: Tuning Scope and Business Characteristics.

## Specifying the Tuning Scope

The Tuning Scope section of the Scope tab allows you to pinpoint which broad aspects of performance you wish to monitor and analyze during the tuning session. This section is composed of four subcategories:

- Check for Instance Optimizations
- Check for SQL Reuse Opportunities
- Check for Appropriate Space Management
- Check for Optimal Data Access

## Instance Level Optimizations

By selecting this option, you are instructing Oracle Expert to examine and recommend tuning strategies that will maximize the performance of the instance. This examination encompasses all aspects of the instance including the SGA and Oracle background processes as well as `init.ora` parameters related to I/O, sorting, and O/S-specific options.

## SQL Reuse Opportunities

Choosing this option tells Oracle Expert to examine how well your application is reusing the SQL code issued by application users. As discussed in Chapter 4: Tuning the Shared Pool, a high degree of SQL reuse improves the hit ratios for the Shared Pool.

## Appropriate Space Management

If you select this option, Oracle Expert will examine the manner in which segments are using the space allocated to them in the tablespaces, and whether the placement of the database datafiles is optimal.

## Optimal Data Access

By choosing this option, you are instructing Oracle Expert to examine whether your application is making appropriate use of indexes and full table scans, as well as which indexes are candidates for rebuilding because they are not using space efficiently. This option also recommends the use of Bitmapped, Reverse Key, and Index Organized Tables where appropriate.

Oracle Expert uses the Cost-based Optimizer when determining optimal data access paths.

To better specify where you would like to focus your tuning effort, Oracle Expert allows you to break down this area even further. It offers the following data access subcategories:

- Perform comprehensive index evaluation on tables referenced by worst performing SQL statements

- Perform comprehensive index evaluation on tables you specify

- Perform index fragmentation evaluation on tables you specify

### Worst Performing SQL

Selecting this option instructs Oracle Expert to capture statistics on the most poorly performing SQL statements executed during the statistics gathering period. Poor performance in this case is measured in terms of the number of physical reads performed by a statement. Once the poorly performing statements are identified, Oracle Expert ranks them from the worst of the worst to the best of the worst.

### Specified Tables

By choosing this option, you tell Oracle Expert to capture statistics on the suitability of the indexes for the specific tables you will identify on the Collect tab. Oracle Expert recommends whether new indexes should be built, old indexes should be dropped, or existing indexes should be rebuilt.

### Index Fragmentation

Selecting this option directs Oracle Expert to examine the tables you will specify on the Collect tab and identify which indexes would perform better if they were rebuilt.

## Specifying Business Characteristics

The Business Characteristics section of the Scope tab allows you to give Oracle Expert a broad idea of your application requirements. Since this type of information is not available from the database itself, you will have to supply it before you begin. This section is also composed of four subcategories:

- Application Type

- Downtime Tolerance

- Peak Logical Write Rate

- Forms Applications Used

### Application Type

This option offers three choices: OLTP, Multipurpose, and Data Warehousing. As their names imply, the OLTP option is for transactional systems, Data Warehousing is for DSS systems, and Multipurpose is intended for use with hybrid systems. By selecting the appropriate application type for your system, Oracle Expert applies the correct rules for your tuning effort.

## Downtime Tolerance

This option offers four choices: Large, Medium, Small, and None. This parameter is used to specify how much downtime is acceptable for your system. Table 10.1 shows how Oracle Expert defines each of these options.

**TABLE 10.1** Oracle Expert Definitions for Downtime Tolerance

| Option | Description |
|--------|-------------|
| None | No unscheduled downtime is allowed. |
| Small | A small amount of unscheduled downtime is allowed. |
| Medium | A moderate amount of unscheduled downtime is allowed. |
| Large | A large amount of unscheduled downtime is allowed. |

Changing these values makes Oracle Expert weigh factors like checkpoint intervals and instance recovery times at varying levels of importance.

## Peak Logical Write Rate

This option offers four choices: Low, Medium, Large, and Huge. This parameter is used to tell Oracle Expert the amount of logical I/O (i.e., writes to memory) that is performed during the busiest times in the database. Table 10.2 shows how Oracle Expert defines the values associated with each of these options.

**TABLE 10.2** Oracle Expert Definitions for Peak Logical Write Rate

| Value | Description |
|-------|-------------|
| Low | Five DML transactions per second or lower |
| Medium | Between five and 50 DML transactions per second |
| Large | Between 50 and 500 DML operations per second |
| Huge | More than 500 DML operations per second |

### Forms Applications

This option is used to tell Oracle Expert whether your application uses Oracle's Developer/2000 or Developer 6i Forms as its user interface. When this option is set to Yes, certain `init.ora` parameters that impact the performance of Developer/2000-based applications will be examined.

# Collecting Tuning Statistics

O racle Expert's Collect tab allows you to specify which performance statistics should be gathered for both the database and the instance. Figure 10.5 shows the contents of the Collect tab.

**FIGURE 10.5**  Oracle Expert's Collect tab

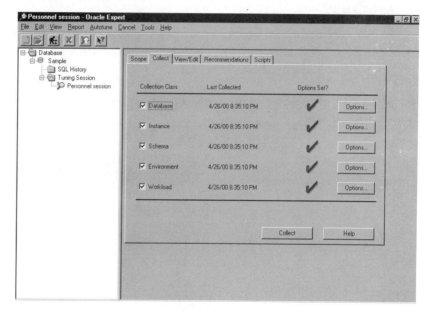

The Collect tab allows you to gather statistics from the following areas:

- Database
- Instance
- Schema
- Environment
- Workload

Each of these areas is included or excluded from the tuning session by either checking or clearing the check box under the Collection Class column. The statistics gathered for the checked areas can be specified in even greater detail by using the Options button. If green check marks appear under the Options Set? column, then the options associated with this area of data gathering are ready for data collection. If a red X appears under the Options Set? column, then the options have not yet been set and will need to be examined before data collection can occur.

Not all collection classes and options will be active at the same time. Oracle Expert automatically enables collection classes based on the options you choose on the Scope tab.

## Database

If you select this option, Oracle Expert gathers statistics about the physical characteristics of the database itself. Figure 10.6 shows the options for the database collection class.

**FIGURE 10.6** Oracle Expert's options for database collection class

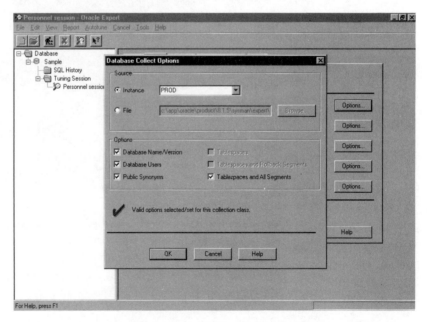

Statistics for the selected Database Collection Class options are gathered primarily from V$ dynamic performance views and DBA static data dictionary views. Make sure the instance has been active for a sufficient period of time for meaningful statistics to exist before collecting the database information.

## Instance

Choosing this option tells Oracle Expert to gather statistics about the characteristics of the instance. Figure 10.7 shows the options for the instance collection class.

**FIGURE 10.7**    Oracle Expert's options for instance collection class

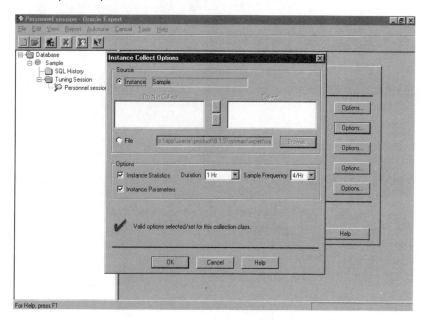

Selecting the Instance Statistics option on this screen causes Oracle Expert to gather instance statistics according to the frequency that has been specified in the Sample Frequency box and for the length of time specified in the Duration box. The default duration is fifteen minutes (1/4 hr). The default frequency is twelve samples per hour (i.e., every five minutes).

Oracle recommends taking at least 10 samples, of any duration, before asking Oracle Expert to generate tuning recommendations.

## Schema

By selecting this option, you instruct Oracle Expert to examine specified schemas for performance-related problems. Figure 10.8 shows the options for the schema collection class.

**FIGURE 10.8** Oracle Expert's options for schema collection class

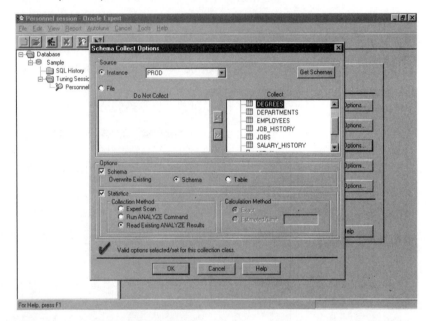

Clicking the Get Schemas button causes all database schemas (except SYS and SYSTEM) to be listed under the Do Not Collect window at the middle of the screen. You can designate which schemas Oracle Expert should monitor during processing by selecting the schemas under the Do Not Collect window and sending them to the Collect window using the right-pointing arrow head that separates the two windows.

Once you have designated which schemas to collect performance statistics for, you must also designate whether Oracle Expert should overwrite any existing collected data for this schema and/or tables that were gathered in a prior tuning session. To activate this setting, select either the Schema or Table option in the Overwrite Existing section of the window. This feature is useful if you have fixed a previously identified performance problem with a particular schema or table and don't want the old statistics to interfere with any subsequent analysis.

Using the Statistics option, you can specify how the statistics for the analysis should be gathered. The choices for this option are:

- Expert Scan

- Run ANALYZE Command

- Read Existing ANALYZE Records

Selecting Expert Scan causes Oracle Expert to gather cardinality statistics during the collection of the instance and database statistics.

Selecting Run ANALYZE Command causes Oracle Expert to issue the ANALYZE TABLE or ANALYZE INDEX command for each table or index in the schema that has been selected for monitoring. When statistics are gathered using either of these two methods, you can instruct Oracle to perform the analysis using either the Exact option, which is the Oracle Expert equivalent of ANALYZE...COMPUTE, or the Estimated/Limit option, which is the Oracle Expert equivalent of ANALYZE...ESTIMATE.

The Read Existing ANALYZE Records option tells Oracle Expert to not gather any new statistics, but instead to use the ones already in the data dictionary from a previous ANALYZE command.

## Environment

By selecting this option, you tell Oracle Expert to include factors specific to your environment in the tuning analysis. Figure 10.9 shows the options for the environment collection class.

**FIGURE 10.9**  Oracle Expert's options for environment collection class

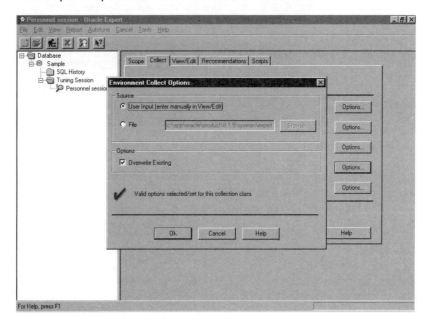

Examples of environment data that are relevant to this collection class include the following:

- Amount of physical memory in the server

- CPU utilization

- Operating block and page size data

Since this type of data exists outside both the database and the instance, Oracle Expert is not able to collect the data directly. You must either enter the data manually on the View/Edit tab or import the data from a previous Oracle Expert session.

Statistics and data can be exported and imported between Oracle Expert tuning sessions using the File ➢ Export and File ➢ Import choices on the Oracle Expert menu. Oracle Expert export files have a .XDL extension.

## Workload

Choosing this option instructs Oracle Expert to consider specific tuning goals related to workload when formulating tuning recommendations. Figure 10.10 shows the options for the schema collection class.

**FIGURE 10.10** Oracle Expert's options for workload collection class

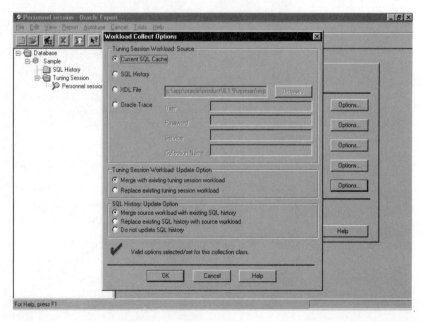

This window offers fours ways for Workload data to be determined: Current SQL Cache, SQL History, XDL File, or Oracle Trace.

**Current SQL Cache**    If you select this option, Oracle Expert examines the SQL in the Shared Pool to determine what statements are most frequently issued and therefore which portions of the application comprise the majority of the workload. The SQL cache data that is gathered during this tuning session can be added to previously gathered SQL cache statistics, used to replace previously gathered SQL cache statistics, or just used on its own without affecting previously gathered SQL cache statistics. This functionality is specified in the SQL History: Update Option section at the bottom on this window.

**SQL History**    Choosing this option instructs Oracle Expert to use only SQL cache statistics gathered during previous tuning sessions and to disregard the current SQL cache completely.

**XDL File**    This option makes Oracle Expert use workload statistics from an Oracle Expert export file. This can be a very useful feature because it allows you to compare tuning recommendations made under a consistent workload model.

**Oracle Trace**    With this option, you can instruct Oracle Expert to use the output from the Oracle Trace GUI tool as input for workload data. This is generally the most complete source of workload data for a tuning session.

New workload data can be either merged into existing workload data already stored in the Oracle Expert repository or used to overwrite data already stored in the Oracle Expert repository.

# Viewing Statistics and Editing Rules

**O**nce you have described the scope and collection methods for your tuning session you can move to the View/Edit tab on the Oracle Expert console. Figure 10.11 shows the View/Edit tab.

**FIGURE 10.11** Oracle Expert's View/Edit tab

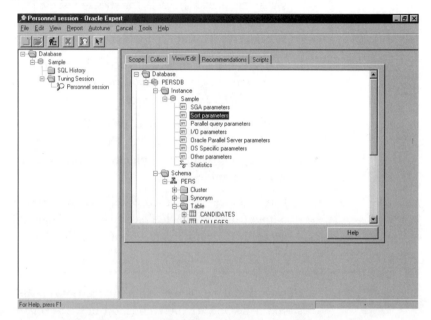

This tab is used to review all the options you have specified for your tuning session. In addition, you can modify, delete, or update the values shown to perform "what-if" analysis on your system. Examples of this type of analysis might include:

- Testing the effect of doubling the physical memory in your server

- Measuring the impact of adding additional CPUs to your server

- Determining the performance implications of doubling the number of application users

Values are changed in this window by expanding the appropriate section of the database, environment, or workload folders and then clicking the value you wish to examine. The resulting Edit window is composed of two tabs, Attributes and Rules.

## Attributes

Figure 10.12 shows the Attribute Edit screen for the instance value I/O parameter.

**FIGURE   10.12**    Attribute Edit screen for instance I/O parameters

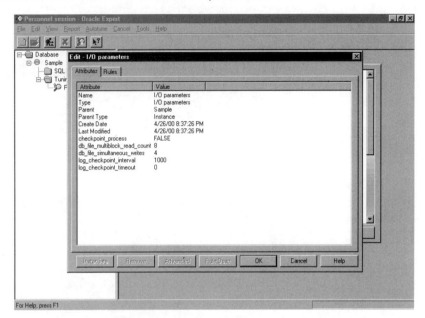

Clicking the desired attribute, entering a new value for that attribute, and then clicking the OK button can change attribute values on this screen. However, if an attribute is read-only, you will not be allowed to change its value.

If you have already gathered statistics using Oracle Expert, changing attribute values may result in inaccurate tuning recommendations. Attributes should be changed before statistics are gathered on the Recommendations tab.

## Rules

The second tab in the attribute Edit window is the Rules tab. Figure 10.13 shows an example of the contents of this tab for tablespace-specific rules.

**FIGURE 10.13** Rule screen for tablespace parameters

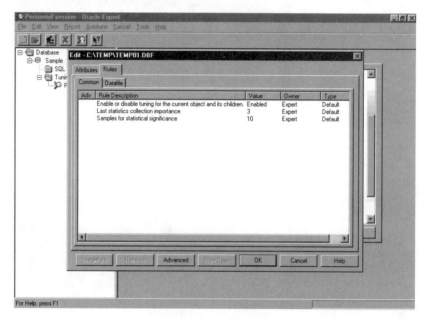

This tab displays some of the rules that Oracle Expert will apply to the gathered statistics in order to make its tuning recommendations. These rules represent a distillation of the combined knowledge of several of Oracle Corporation's performance tuning experts.

**NOTE** These rules are different from those associated with the Rule-based Optimizer discussed in Chapter 3: SQL Statement Tuning and Application Design. In addition, not all rules that Oracle Expert uses in its performance tuning recommendations are viewable.

You can see a description of each rule by selecting a rule and then clicking the Rule Desc button at the bottom of the window. The rule description for the I/O parameter `Last statistics collection importance` is shown in Figure 10.14.

**FIGURE 10.14** Sample Oracle Expert rule description

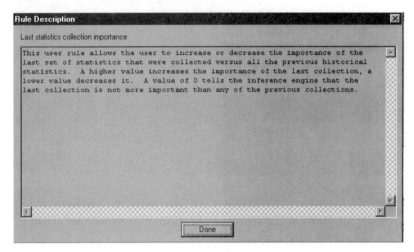

There are three types of rules in the Oracle Expert tool:

- Default rules
- Modified rules
- Advanced rules

**Default Rules**   The Oracle Expert *default rules* are those that are used without modification. Only some of the default rules are viewable, but you can change the default values associated with any viewable default rule.

**Modified Rules**   The Oracle Expert *modified rules* are those that you have changed from their defaults or have modified in some way.

**Advanced Rules**   The Rules tab only displays the basic rules for an object by default. You can view the *advanced rules* by clicking the Advanced button at the bottom of the window. Advanced rules are denoted by an X next to the rule under the Adv column of the window. Figure 10.15 shows the advanced rules for the `DBWR_IO_SLAVES` object of the `I/O parameters` instance parameter.

**FIGURE  10.15**   Sample Oracle Expert advanced rules listing

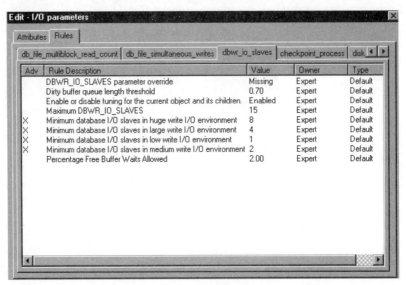

| Adv | Rule Description | Value | Owner | Type |
|---|---|---|---|---|
| | DBWR_IO_SLAVES parameter override | Missing | Expert | Default |
| | Dirty buffer queue length threshold | 0.70 | Expert | Default |
| | Enable or disable tuning for the current object and its children. | Enabled | Expert | Default |
| | Maximum DBWR_IO_SLAVES | 15 | Expert | Default |
| X | Minimum database I/O slaves in huge write I/O environment | 8 | Expert | Default |
| X | Minimum database I/O slaves in large write I/O environment | 4 | Expert | Default |
| X | Minimum database I/O slaves in low write I/O environment | 1 | Expert | Default |
| X | Minimum database I/O slaves in medium write I/O environment | 2 | Expert | Default |
| | Percentage Free Buffer Waits Allowed | 2.00 | Expert | Default |

Care should be taken when editing the advanced rules. Be sure you completely understand their purpose and impact before relying on Oracle Expert recommendations, which are made using modified advanced rules.

# Reviewing Recommendations and Generating Scripts

**A**fter leaving the View/Edit tab on the Oracle Expert GUI interface, the tab to the right is the Recommendations tab. This tab is not only used for viewing Oracle Expert's tuning recommendations; it is also used to actually generate those recommendations using all the parameters you have previously established on the Scope, Collect, and View/Edit tabs. Figure 10.16 shows the layout of the Recommendations tab.

**FIGURE 10.16** Oracle Expert's Recommendations tab

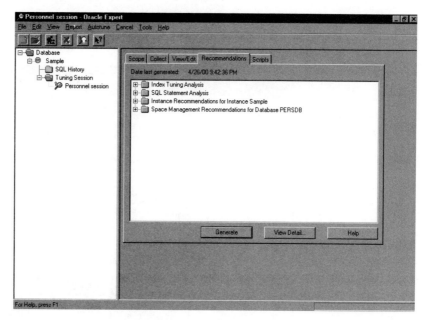

 Before any recommendations can be viewed, you must click the Generate button at the bottom of the Recommendations tab.

The time it takes Oracle Expert to generate your tuning recommendations is directly related to how many areas, which areas, and in what manner you chose to analyze the database on the Scope, Collect, and View/Edit tabs. The generation time can vary from several minutes to several hours.

Once the recommendation generation is complete, the results will be displayed as shown in Figure 10.16. The results are broken into up to four areas depending on which options you selected on prior tabs:

- Index Tuning Analysis

- SQL Statement Analysis

- Instance Recommendations for Instance Sample

- Space Management Recommendations for Database

As shown in Figure 10.17, each of these areas can be further expanded to display the specific recommendations for each area.

**FIGURE 10.17** Sample expanded Oracle Expert recommendations

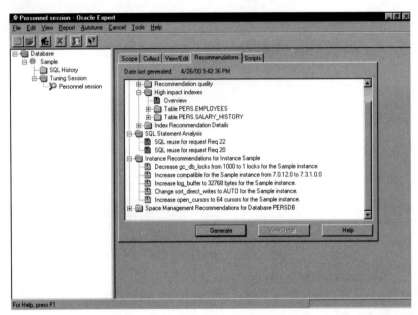

Once an area is expanded, you can then click any individual tuning recommendation and use the View Detail button at the bottom of the Recommendations tab to see a full explanation of the rationale behind Oracle Expert's tuning recommendation. A sample tuning detail for recommended changes to the Redo Log Buffer is shown in Figure 10.18.

**FIGURE 10.18** Sample tuning recommendation detail

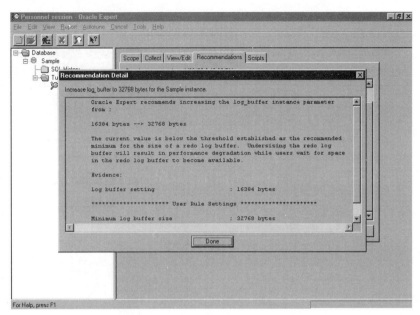

In the next tab, Scripts, Oracle Expert will generate SQL scripts and sample init.ora files that can be used to implement all the tuning recommendations listed on the Recommendations tab. Before generating these files, you can choose to either accept or decline any of the tuning recommendations shown on the Recommendations tab. By default, all recommendations are accepted. To decline a tuning recommendation, simply right-click while selecting the recommendation you wish to change, and select Decline from the pop-up menu. Figure 10.19 shows the red circle with a line through it that Oracle Expert uses to denote a declined tuning recommendation.

**FIGURE 10.19** Sample declined tuning recommendation

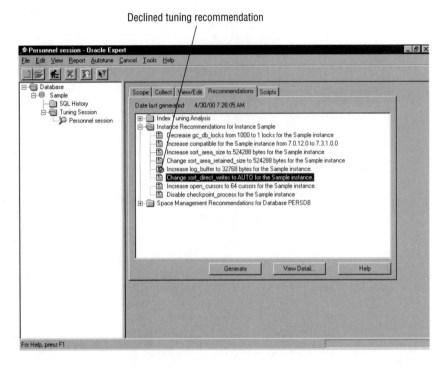

A detailed, written report of Oracle Expert's tuning recommendations is also available. This report is a full text document complete with a table of contents, title page, and complete explanations of each tuning recommendation. This report is generated in ASCII text format by selecting Report ➢ Recommendation Summary from the Oracle Expert menu. Figure 10.20 shows a portion of the output from this report.

**FIGURE 10.20** Sample output of full text recommendation summary

```
2.3.3.1  EMPLOYEES_SORTED_IDX_003

   Due to its calculated high relative importance, this change


                        Analysis Summary Report
                        Index Tuning Analysis                  Page 6


   recommendation is considered a high impact adjustment.  High impact
   refers to the relative performance enhancement that may be achieved by
   implementing the suggested change.

   Index:       EMPLOYEES_SORTED_IDX_003
   Index type:  BITMAPPED
   Status:      New


     Recommended columns
     -------------------

     SEX
         1 reference by an equality operator.


2.3.3.2  EMPLOYEES_SORTED_IDX_001

   Due to its calculated high relative importance, this change
   recommendation is considered a high impact adjustment.  High impact
```

# Implementing Recommendations

The final tab on the Oracle Expert main window is the Scripts tab. Reaching this tab represents the end of the current tuning session. Figure 10.21 shows the Scripts tab window.

**FIGURE 10.21** Oracle Expert's Scripts tab

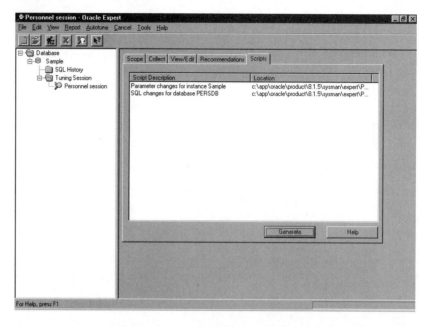

This tab is used to generate the SQL scripts and sample init.ora files that are needed to implement the tuning changes that Oracle Expert has identified. You can specify the locations for your implementation scripts and files by editing the Location value shown in this window. The default location for these files is $ORACLE_HOME/sysman/expert on UNIX systems and %ORACLE_HOME%\sysman\expert on Windows NT systems. The scripts are created in these locations by clicking the Generate button. Figure 10.22 shows a sample of a script generated to implement changes in init.ora parameters.

**FIGURE 10.22** Sample generated script for init.ora changes

```
# Oracle Expert 2.0.4                                    4/26/00 9:52:56 PM
#                         Recommended Instance Parameters
#
#
# Tuning Session: Personnel session
# Database Name:  PERSDB
# Instance Name:  Sample
#---------------------------------------------------------------------------
compatible = 7.3.1.0.0                      #previous value:
gc_db_locks = 1                             #previous value: 1000
log_buffer = 32768                          #previous value: 16384
open_cursors = 64                           #previous value: 50
sort_direct_writes = AUTO                   #previous value: FALSE
```

These changes are implemented by simply copying the recommended changes into the appropriate init.ora file and then restarting the instance.

Figure 10.23 shows a sample SQL script for making physical changes to the database.

**FIGURE 10.23** Sample generated script for SQL changes

```
|-- Oracle Expert 2.0.4                                  4/26/00 9:53:18 PM
--                          Recommended SQL changes
--
--
-- Tuning Session: Personnel session
-- Database Name:  PERSDB
-- Analysis Date:  4/26/00 9:42:36 PM
--------------------------------------------------------------------------------


--------------------------------------------------------------------------------
--  How to Use This Implementation File
--------------------------------------------------------------------------------


/*
For recommendations made on a SQL object; for example, an index, a
tablespace or a database user, Oracle Expert attempts to generate complete,
valid SQL.  However, there may be situations where this is not possible.
In these cases, the generated SQL includes the string '<tbs>' in places
where you must provide appropriate information.  Note the Analysis Report
may include suggestions for what should be specified.

After correct information has been entered, the statements in this file can
be executed.
*/


--------------------------------------------------------------------------------
--  CREATE Tablespace Recommendations
--------------------------------------------------------------------------------


CREATE TABLESPACE RBS
    DATAFILE
        '<tbs>rbs01.dbf' SIZE <tbs>K
        DEFAULT STORAGE (
            MINEXTENTS 20
            MAXEXTENTS 4096)
```

Before using this script, you will have to examine it for places where Oracle Expert has inserted < > symbols. These symbols are used to indicate that a site-specific variable like a device name, datafile name, or tablespace name needs to be specified in place of the < > in order to implement the required tuning recommendation. Once the script has been reviewed and edited accordingly, the script can be executed from SQL*Plus so that the recommended tuning actions take effect.

# Summary

**O**racle Expert is a GUI tool designed to simplify the complex process of tuning an Oracle database. Using a collection of tuning rules created by the performance tuning experts at Oracle Corporation, Oracle Expert examines and analyzes the behavior of the database and instance before generating tuning recommendations that are based on your specific environment.

In order to perform an Oracle Expert Tuning session, you must complete the appropriate sections of the Scope, Collect, and View/Edit tabs before generating the tuning recommendations and implementation scripts on the Recommendations and Scripts tabs. The final recommendations are created in the form of written reports and in ready-to-use sample `init.ora` and SQL scripts.

## Key Terms

Before you take the exam, make sure you're familiar with the following terms:

Oracle Expert

repository

default rules

modified rules

advanced rules

# Review Questions

**1.** Which of the following methods of connecting to Oracle Expert will cause a repository to be built in the target database if a repository does not already exist?

   **A.** Connecting using an Oracle Management Server

   **B.** Connecting as SYSDBA

   **C.** Connecting directly to an Expert repository

   **D.** Connecting via a non-Net8 network

**2.** An Oracle Expert repository is:

   **A.** A collection of SQL scripts used to store Oracle Expert tuning information

   **B.** The second tab on the main Oracle Expert screen

   **C.** The final ASCII text document that is produced at the end of a tuning session

   **D.** A collection of tables used to store Oracle Expert tuning information

**3.** Which system privilege does the owner of the Oracle Expert repository *not* need?

   **A.** SELECT ANY TABLE

   **B.** CREATE USER

   **C.** CREATE SESSION

   **D.** CREATE TABLE

**4.** In general, which tab on the Oracle Expert main window represents the first step in a tuning session?

   **A.** Scripts

   **B.** Recommendations

   **C.** Scope

   **D.** View/Edit

5. Which tab on the Oracle Expert main window allows you to see and modify the statistics that will be gathered and the rules that will be applied during the Recommendation stage?

   A. Scope

   B. View/Edit

   C. Scripts

   D. Collect

6. Selecting the SQL Reuse Opportunities option in the Scope tab will cause Oracle Expert to analyze:

   A. Which SQL statements are not using indexes properly

   B. Whether the application code benefits from the caching behavior of the Shared Pool

   C. The worst performing SQL statements

   D. Whether statements are using optimal access paths

7. In Oracle Expert, which of the following is *not* a valid Application Type in the Business Characteristics section of the Scope tab?

   A. Hybrid

   B. OLTP

   C. Data Warehousing

   D. Multipurpose

8. If your application was required to be available 24 hours a day, 7 days a week, which option in Oracle Expert would you choose for Downtime Tolerance?

   A. Low

   B. Small

   C. None

   D. Zero

**9.** If your system experiences between 50 and 100 DML operations per second, what value would you specify for `Peak Logical Write Rate` in Oracle Expert?

    **A.** Low

    **B.** Medium

    **C.** Large

    **D.** Huge

**10.** The default sample duration in Oracle Expert is:

    **A.** Five minutes

    **B.** 15 minutes

    **C.** 30 minutes

    **D.** One hour

**11.** How many samples does Oracle recommend be taken before relying on the tuning recommendations from Oracle Expert?

    **A.** 1

    **B.** 10

    **C.** 100

    **D.** 1000

**12.** Which of the following options in the Schema section of the Collect tab will cause Oracle Expert to generate cardinality statistics for selected tables?

    **A.** Expert Scan

    **B.** Run ANALYZE Command

    **C.** Read Existing ANALYZE Records

    **D.** None of the above

**13.** Which of the following is an example of an environment statistic that must be manually entered in Oracle Expert because its value is not stored in the database?

   **A.** Oracle block size

   **B.** Total size of database datafiles

   **C.** Location of background trace files

   **D.** The total physical memory in your server

**14.** Workload information can be imported into Oracle Expert from what type of export file?

   **A.** .XLS

   **B.** .XLT

   **C.** .XLD

   **D.** .XOE

**15.** No recommendations will appear on the Recommendations tab in Oracle Expert until you click which button?

   **A.** Generate

   **B.** Analyze

   **C.** Recommend

   **D.** OK

**16.** The View Detail button on the Recommendations tab of the Oracle Expert main Window is used to:

   **A.** See how long the tuning session lasted

   **B.** See which `init.ora` parameters Oracle Expert recommends changing

   **C.** See which users were logged in during the tuning session

   **D.** See a detailed explanation of the tuning recommendation

**17.** To create a complete written recommendation report, you need to choose which option on Oracle Expert's Report menu?

    **A.** Text Summary

    **B.** Summary Report

    **C.** Recommendation Summary

    **D.** Export

**18.** What two types of files does Oracle Expert create when you click the Generate button on the Scripts tab?

    **A.** `init.ora` sample file incorporating suggested changes

    **B.** User trace files of each session that was connected during the tuning session

    **C.** SQL script that can be used to implement new indexes, tablespaces, etc.

    **D.** Complete written report of tuning recommendations in ASCII text format

**19.** By default, to which location are the output files from Oracle Expert written on a UNIX system?

    **A.** `$ORACLE_HOME`

    **B.** Location specified by `USER_DUMP_DEST`

    **C.** The user's working directory

    **D.** `$ORACLE_HOME/sysman/expert`

**20.** When generating a SQL script on the Scripts tab, which characters does Oracle Expert use to denote that site-specific information must be supplied in the script?

    **A.** { }

    **B.** ( )

    **C.** /* */

    **D.** < >

# Answers to Review Questions

1. C. Connecting directly to an Oracle Expert repository requires that the schema you are using have an Oracle Expert repository in the target database.

2. D. The Oracle Expert repository is composed of several tables, indexes, sequences, and PL/SQL packages.

3. B. The owner of the Oracle Expert repository needs only the following privileges: ALTER SESSION, CREATE CLUSTER, CREATE DATABASE LINK, CREATE SEQUENCE, CREATE SESSION, CREATE SYNONYM, CREATE TABLE, CREATE VIEW, CREATE PROCEDURE, CREATE TRIGGER, CREATE TYPE, and SELECT ANY TABLE.

4. C. The Scope tab allows you to specify the broad characteristics of your system.

5. B. The View/Edit tab contains a summary of all the tuning selections you have made on the Scope and Collect tabs.

6. B. High reuse of cached SQL code improves the Library Cache hit ratio in the Shared Pool. This is a major determinant of application performance.

7. A. The Multipurpose option is used for hybrid systems.

8. C. Specifying a value of None for the Downtime Tolerance option will cause Oracle Expert to use the most stringent rules related to archiving, checkpoint activity, and maximum recovery times.

9. C. Oracle Expert considers 50 to 500 DML operations per second to be a large Peak Logical Write Rate.

10. B. By default, Oracle Expert gathers performance statistics every 1/4 hour.

11. B. Oracle recommends that at least 10 samples be gathered using Oracle Expert before generating tuning recommendations.

**12.** A. Run ANALYZE Command gathers statistics regarding number of rows, row length, etc., but not cardinality data. Read Existing ANALYZE Records causes no new data to be gathered. Instead, Oracle Expert uses the current table statistics if they exist in the data dictionary.

**13.** D. Supplying these non-database environment statistics help Oracle Expert know what resources are available to it when it makes its tuning recommendations.

**14.** C. Exported Oracle Expert data is stored in files that use the .XLD extension.

**15.** A. Clicking the Generate button on the Recommendations tab will cause Oracle Expert to start gathering and analyzing the database according to the options you selected on the Scope, Collect, and View/Edit tabs.

**16.** D. The View Detail button shows a complete explanation of the rationale for the associated tuning recommendation.

**17.** C. The Recommendation Summary option generates a complete written report in ASCII text format. The report includes a title page, table of contents, and page numbers.

**18.** A, C. The init.ora changes can be copied to the existing init.ora to implement the suggested changes. The SQL script must be executed from SQL*Plus.

**19.** D. Entering a new path on the Scripts tab on the main Oracle Expert window can also specify alternative locations for these files.

**20.** D. Anything enclosed in < > in the generated SQL script must be replaced with site-specific information before the script can be executed. This site-specific information includes device names, directory paths, and tablespace names.

# Introduction to Network Administration

## ORACLE8i NETWORK ADMINISTRATION EXAM OBJECTIVES COVERED IN THIS CHAPTER:

- ✓ Define the issues the DBA should consider when implementing an Oracle Network.

- ✓ Define the responsibilities of the Database Administrator in terms of network management.

- ✓ Define the various Network Configurations.

- ✓ Describe the base functionality of Net8.

- ✓ Describe the optional configuration features of Net8.

- ✓ Describe the features of the Advanced Security Option.

- ✓ Describe what the Net8 Assistant does.

- ✓ Describe the Oracle Gateway Products.

- ✓ Describe some of the tools the DBA can use to troubleshoot the network environment.

Exam objectives are subject to change at any time without prior notice and at Oracle's sole discretion. Please visit Oracle's Training and Certification Web site (http://education.oracle.com/certification) for the most current exam objectives listing.

etworks have evolved from simple terminal-based systems to complex multi-tier systems. Modern networks can be comprised of many computers on multiple operating systems using a wide variety of protocols and communicating across wide geographic areas. One need look no further than the explosion of the Internet to see how networking has matured and what a profound impact networks are having on the way we work and communicate with one another.

While networks have become increasingly complex, they also have become easier to use and manage. All of us can take advantage of the Internet without knowing or caring about the components that make this communication possible. The complexity of the network is completely hidden from us.

The experienced Oracle Database Administrator has seen this maturation process in the Oracle Network architecture as well. From the first version of SQL*Net to the latest releases of Net8, Oracle has evolved its network strategy and infrastructure to meet the demands of the rapidly changing landscape of network communications.

This chapter highlights the areas that database administrators need to consider when implementing an Oracle Network strategy. It also looks at the responsibilities the database administrator has when managing an Oracle Network. The chapter explores the most common types of network configurations and introduces the features of Net8—the connectivity management software that is the backbone of the Oracle Network architecture.

# Network Design Considerations

There are many factors involved in making network design decisions. The Oracle Network architecture is flexible and configurable, and has the scalability to accommodate small or large networks. There are a variety of network configurations to choose from. The sections that follow summarize the areas the DBA needs to consider when designing the Oracle Network infrastructure.

## Network Complexity Issues

The complexity of the network plays an important role in many of your network design decisions. Consider the following questions in terms of network complexity:

- How many clients will the network need to support?

- What type of work will the clients be doing?

- What are the locations of the clients? In complex networks, clients may be geographically dispersed over a wide area.

- What types of clients are going to be supported? Will these be PC-based clients or terminal-based clients? Will these be thin clients that do little processing or fat clients that will do the majority of the application processing?

- What is the projected growth of the network?

- Where will the processing take place? Will there be any middle-tier servers involved, such as an application server or transaction server?

- What types of network protocols will be used to communicate between the clients and servers?

- Will Oracle Servers have to communicate with other Oracle Servers in the enterprise?

- Will the network involve multiple operating systems?

- Are there any special networking requirements of applications that will be used? This is especially important to consider when dealing with third-party applications.

# Network Security Issues

Network security has become even more critical as companies expose their systems to larger and larger numbers of users through internets and intranets. Consider the following questions in terms of network security:

- Does the organization have any special requirements for secure network connections? What kinds of information will be sent across the Oracle Network?

- Can we ensure secure connections across a network without risk of information tampering? This may involve sending the data in a format that makes it tamper proof and also ensures that the data cannot be captured and read by other parties besides the client and the intended Oracle Server.

- Is there a need to centralize the authorizations an individual has to each of the Oracle Servers? In large organizations with many Oracle services, this can be a management and administration issue.

# Interfacing Existing Systems with New Systems

The following issues should be considered when existing computer systems must communicate with Oracle Server networks:

- Does the application that needs to perform the communication require a seamless, real-time interface?

- Does the existing system use a non-Oracle database such as DB2 or Sybase?

- Will information be transferred from the existing system to the Oracle Server on a periodic basis? If so, what is the frequency and what are the transport mechanisms to use? Will the Oracle Server need to send information back to the existing system?

- Do applications need to gather data from multiple sources, including Oracle and non-Oracle databases simultaneously?

- What are the applications involved that require this interface?

- Will these network requirements necessitate design changes to existing existing systems?

# Network Responsibilities for the DBA

The database administrator has many design issues to consider and plays an important role when implementing a network of Oracle Servers in the enterprise. Here are some of the key responsibilities of the DBA in the Oracle network implementation process:

- Understand the network configuration options available and know which options should be used based on the requirements of the organization.

- Understand the underlying network architecture of the organization in order to make informed design decisions.

- Work closely with the network engineers to ensure consistent and reliable connections to the Oracle Servers.

- Understand the tools available for configuring and managing the network.

- Troubleshoot connection problems on the client, middle-tier, and server.

- Ensure secure connections and use the available network configurations, when necessary, to attain higher degrees of security for sensitive data transmissions.

- Stay abreast of trends in the industry and changes to the Oracle architecture that may have an impact on network design decisions.

# Network Configurations

There are three basic types of network configurations to select from when designing an Oracle infrastructure. The simplest type is the single-tier architecture. This has been around for years and is characterized by the use of terminals for serial connections to the Oracle Server. The other types of network configurations are the two-tier or client/server architecture and most recently introduced n-tier architecture. Let's take a look at each of these configuration alternatives.

## Single-Tier Architecture

*Single-tier architecture* was the standard for many years before the birth of the PC. Applications utilizing single-tier architecture are sometimes referred to as "green screen applications" because most of the terminals using them, such as the IBM 3270 terminal, had green screens. Single-tier architecture is commonly associated with mainframe-type applications.

This architecture is still in use today for many mission critical applications, such as Order Processing and Fulfillment and Inventory Control, because it is the simplest architecture to configure and administer. Since the terminals are directly connected to the host computer, the complexities of network protocols and multiple operating systems don't exist. Users interact with the database using terminals. These terminals were non-graphical character-based devices. Figure 11.1 shows an example of the single-tier architecture. In a single-tier architecture, client terminals are directly connected to larger server systems such as mainframes. All of the intelligence exists on the mainframe, and all processing takes place there. Simple serial connections also exist on the mainframe. Although no complex network architecture is necessary, single-tier architecture is somewhat limiting in terms of scalability and flexibility. All of the processing must take place on the server, and the server can become the bottleneck to increasing performance.

**FIGURE 11.1**  Single-tier architecture

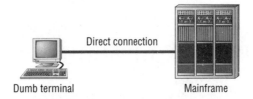

Dumb terminal                Mainframe

## Two-Tier Architecture

*Two-tier architecture* gained popularity with the introduction of the PC and is commonly referred to as client/server computing. In a two-tier environment, clients connect to servers over a network using a network protocol. The protocol is the agreed-upon method for the client to communicate with the server. TCP/IP is a very popular network protocol and has become the de facto standard of network computing. Both the client and the server must be able to understand the protocol. Figure 11.2 shows an example of two-tier architecture.

**FIGURE  11.2**    Two-tier architecture

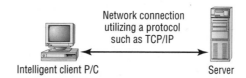

Network connection utilizing a protocol such as TCP/IP

Intelligent client P/C                           Server

This architecture had definite benefits over single-tier architecture. Client/server computing introduced the graphical user interface. The graphical user interface was easier to understand and learn and offered more flexibility than the traditional character-based interfaces of the single-tier architecture. Two-tier architecture also allowed the client computer to share the application processing load. To a certain degree, this reduced the processing requirements of the server.

The two-tier architecture does have some faults. At one time, it was thought that client/server computing would be the panacea of all networking architectures. Unfortunately, the problem of scalability persists. Notice the term "client/server computing" contains a slash "/". The slash represents the invisible component of the two-tier architecture and the one that is often overlooked: the network!

When prototyping projects, many developers fail to consider the network component and soon find out that what worked well in a small environment may not scale effectively to larger more complex systems. There was also a great deal of redundancy in this model, because application software is required on every desktop.  Many companies end up with bloated PCs and large servers that still do not provide adequate performance. What is needed is a more scalable model for network communications. That is what n-tier architecture provides.

## N-Tier Architecture

*N-tier architecture* is the next logical step after two-tier architecture. Instead of dividing application processing work among a client and a server, you divide the work up among three or more machines. The n-tier architecture introduces the "middleware" component, which can be used for a variety of tasks. Some of those tasks include:

- Moving data between machines that work with different network protocols.

- Serving as firewalls that can control client access to the servers.

- Offloading processing of the business logic from the clients and servers to the middle tier.

- Executing transactions and monitor activity between clients and servers to balance the load among multiple servers.

- Acting as a gateway to bridge existing systems to new systems.

The Internet provides the ultimate n-tier architecture with the browser as a consistent presentation layer. This common interface means less training of staff and also increases the potential reuse of client-side application components. N-tier architecture makes it possible to take advantage of technologies such as the network computer. These devices can make for economical, low-maintenance alternatives to the personal computer. Much of the application processing can be done by application servers. This means the client computing requirements are greatly reduced. The processing of transactions can also be offloaded to transaction servers. This reduces the burden on the database servers.

The n-tier model is a very scalable architecture that divides the tasks of presentation, business logic and routing, and database processing among many machines, which means it accommodates large applications. The reduction of processing load on the database servers means that the servers can do more work with the same amount of resources. The transaction servers can balance the flow of network transactions intelligently, and application servers can reduce the processing and memory requirements of the client (see Figure 11.3).

**FIGURE 11.3** N-tier architecture

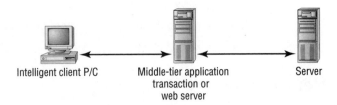

Intelligent client P/C          Middle-tier application          Server
                                transaction or
                                web server

# Overview of Net8 Features

**N**et8 is the glue that bonds the Oracle Network together. Net8 serves all implementations of Oracle and is responsible for handling client-to-server and server-to-server communications. Net8 can be configured on both the client and the server. It manages the flow of information in the Oracle Network infrastructure. Net8 is used to establish the initial connection to the Oracle Server and then acts as the messenger, passing requests from the client back to the server or between two Oracle Servers. Net8 handles all negotiations between the client and server during the client connection. In Chapter 12, we discuss the architectural design of Net8.

Net8 supports the use of middleware products such as Oracle Application Server and Oracle Connection Manager. These middleware products allow for n-tier architectures to be used in the enterprise, which increases the flexibility and performance of application designs. Read the following sections to learn more about some of the features of Net8.

## Multi-Protocol Support

Net8 supports a wide range of industry standard protocols including TCP/IP, LU6.2, IPX, Named Pipes, and DECnet. This allows for connectivity to a wide range of computers and a wide range of operating environments. The multi-protocol support is handled transparently by Net8. In Chapter 16, you will learn about Connection Manager, which allows systems communicating with protocols that are different than the Oracle Server to communicate with the server.

## Multiple Operating Systems

Net8 can operate on many different operating system platforms, from Windows NT to all variants of UNIX to large mainframe-based operating systems. This range allows users to bridge existing systems to other UNIX or PC-based systems, which increases the data access flexibility of the organization, without making wholesale changes to the existing systems.

## Java Connectivity

With the introduction of Oracle8i, Net8 now allows connectivity to Oracle Servers from applications using Java components such as Enterprise Java-Beans and Common Object Request Broker Architecture (CORBA), which is a standard for defining object interaction across a network. Oracle Net8 supports standard Internet connectivity solutions such the Internet Inter-Orb Protocol (IIOP) and the General Inter-Orb Protocol (GIOP). These features are discussed in Chapter 20.

# Open API

The Net8 architecture has an open *Applications Program Interface*, or API. The product, Net8 Open, allows third-party software vendors to construct interfaces to Net8 for both Oracle database and non-database connectivity using a programming language such as C. You can take advantage of functionality such as creating a program that utilizes the Net8 infrastructure to connect and interact with your program.

# Optional Configuration Features

Net8 supports several optional configuration features that enhance its scalability and flexibility. As the number of supported clients in an enterprise grows, the complexity of managing the available services increases. The strain on existing resources increases as the number of connections to continue to grow. The Oracle Names Server and Oracle Connection Manager options address these network issues.

## Oracle Names Server

The *Oracle Names Server* option is used to centralize all of the Oracle services within the enterprise. This centralized approach makes the management and administration of the services in an Oracle Enterprise easier.

The Name Server acts as a central lookup facility for clients attempting to contact an Oracle Server in the enterprise. The client interaction with the Name Server could be compared to making an operator-assisted phone call. The advantage of this approach is that clients only need to know the location of the Name Server, not the locations of all of the Oracle services in the enterprise. If new Oracle Servers are introduced into the enterprise, the DBA can add new listings to the Names Server. These new listings are immediately available to any client that can connect to the Names Server. The Names Server can accommodate both dedicated and multithreaded connection requests. The Names Server is completely configurable using the graphical Net8 Assistant tool. Chapter 15 discusses the configuration and operational details of the Names Server.

## Oracle Connection Manager

*Oracle Connection Manager* is a middleware solution that provides three additional scalability features:

**Connection Concentration**   Connection Manager can group together many client connections and send them as a single multiplexed network connection to the Oracle Server. This reduces the total number of network connections the server has to manage.

**Client Access Control**    Connection Manager can be configured with rules that allow it to function as a "mini firewall." The rules-based configuration can be set up to accept or reject client connection requests. Connections can be restricted by point of origin, destination server, or Oracle Server.

**Multi-Protocol Interchange**    This feature allows clients and servers that use different network protocols to communicate. Connection manager acts a translator, doing two-way protocol conversion.

Oracle Connection Manager is controlled by a set of background processes that manage the communications between clients and servers. This option is not configured using the graphical Net8 Assistant tool. We will discuss Connection Manager in more detail in Chapter 17.

# Advanced Security Option

The threat of data tampering is becoming an issue of increasing concern to many organizations as network systems continue to grow in number and complexity and as users gain increasing access to systems. Sensitive business transactions are being conducted with greater frequency and, in many cases, are not protected from unauthorized tampering or message interception.

The *Advanced Security Option*, which was known in earlier releases as the Advanced Networking Option, provides the tools necessary to ensure secure transmissions of sensitive information and provides mechanisms to confidently identify and authenticate users in the Oracle Enterprise.

The Advanced Security Option, when configured on the client and the Oracle Server, supports secured data transactions by encrypting and optionally checksumming the transmission of information that is sent in a transaction. Oracle supports encryption and checksumming by taking advantage of industry standard algorithms, such as RSA RC4 encryption, DES encryption, and MD5 checksumming. These security features ensure that data transmitted from the client has not been altered during transmission to the Oracle Server.

The Advanced Security Option also gives the database administrator the ability to authenticate users connecting to the Oracle Servers. There are a number of authentication features for ensuring that users are really who they claim to be. These are offered in the form of token cards, which use a physical card and a user identifying PIN number to gain access to the system and the biometrics option, which uses fingerprint technology to authenticate user connection requests.

Another feature of the Advanced Security Option is the ability to have a single sign-on mechanism for clients. Single sign-on is accomplished with a centralized security server that allows the user to connect to any of the Oracle services in the enterprise using a single user ID and password. Oracle leverages the industry standard features of Kerberos to enable these capabilities. This greatly simplifies the privilege matrix that administrators must manage when dealing with large numbers of users and systems. The Advanced Security Option is covered in detail in Chapter 18.

# Oracle Gateway Products

The *Oracle Procedural Gateway* and the *Oracle Transparent Gateway* products allow Oracle to communicate with non-Oracle data sources in a seamless configuration. Oracle gateways integrate existing systems with the Oracle environment allowing you to leverage your investment in those systems. The gateways allow for two-way communication and replication from Oracle data sources to non-Oracle data sources.

**Procedural Gateway**  The Oracle Procedural Gateway allows contact with non-Oracle data sources through a PL/SQL procedure interface. Users call PL/SQL stored procedures, which initiate conversations with non-Oracle data sources. All the user needs to know is the name of the procedure. The user does not need to know the whereabouts of the external data source. This is all controlled via the procedure. The gateway offers full transaction support features such as two-phase commit and rollback. The procedural gateways can interact with transaction monitoring or message queueing software, which can route transactions to the appropriate data source.

**Transparent Gateway**  The transparent gateway product seamlessly extends the reach of Oracle to non-Oracle data stores. The transparent gateways allow you to treat non-Oracle data sources as if they were part of the Oracle environment. The user is not aware of the fact that the data being accessed is coming from a non-Oracle source. This can significantly reduce the time and investment necessary to transition from existing systems to the Oracle environment. Transparent gateways fully support SQL and the Oracle transaction control features and currently support access to more than 30 non-Oracle data sources.

# The Net8 Assistant

The *Net8 Assistant* is a graphical user interface tool that allows database administrators to configure the most critical components of the Net8 infrastructure. Using Net8 Assistant, the DBA can configure both the client and server components of Net8. The Net8 Assistant is a Java-based tool that has a common look and feel across different operating systems.

The Net8 Assistant allows you to configure all of the various names resolution options including localnaming, hostnaming, and the Oracle Names Server. It also lets you configure the server-side files that support the Oracle listener. Figure 11.4 shows an example of the opening screen of the Net8 Assistant. The Net8 Assistant is covered in detail throughout this book. You will see how to use this tool to configure all of the important components of Net8.

**FIGURE 11.4**    Net8 Assistant opening screen

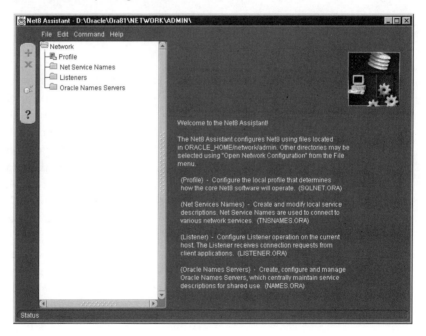

# Troubleshooting Utilities

If Oracle Network problems do arise, you can use a variety of methods for resolving the problem. The database administrator can look at log files that are generated by clients, middle-tier, and server processes. These log files may hold information that can help resolve the problem. The DBA can also configure tracing, which provides a more detailed analysis of the network connection process.

Oracle also comes with connection testing tools, such as `tnsping`, that provide you with a way to check client connectivity. Oracle also provides a tool that allows you to format the output of trace files. This tool can provide valuable information about the flow of network traffic for a session. Chapter 19 contains details about the methods to use when troubleshooting connection problems. It discusses many of the common Oracle Network errors, as well as the causes and remedies of these errors.

# Summary

This chapter covered the issues that a database administrator needs to consider when implementing an Oracle Network. You should be able to list the responsibilities of the database administrator with respect to network administration. Can you define the basic network configuration choices and summarize strengths and weaknesses of these options?

You should understand what Net8 is and the functionality it provides. You should know the basic concept of the Oracle Names Server and Oracle Connection Manager options of Net8. You should be able to define the basic concepts of the Advanced Security Option and know when to consider it for use in the enterprise.

You should be able to define the uses of the Procedural and Transparent Gateways and know the situations in which these options are useful. You should also be able to describe some of the tools available for troubleshooting connection problems in the Oracle Enterprise.

# Key Terms

**B**efore you take the exam, make sure you're familiar with the following terms:

Advanced Security Option

Applications Program Interface

Net8 Assistant

n-tier architecture

Oracle Connection Manager

Oracle Names Server

Oracle Procedural Gateway

Oracle Transparent Gateway

single-tier architecture

two-tier architecture

# Review Questions

1. The following are all examples of networking architectures *except*:

   **A.** Client/Server

   **B.** N-tier

   **C.** Single-tier

   **D.** Two-tier

   **E.** All of the above

2. You manage one non-Oracle database and several Oracle databases. An application needs to access the non-Oracle databases as if it were part of the Oracle databases. What tool will solve this business problem?

   **A.** Oracle Names Server

   **B.** Oracle Connection Manager

   **C.** Oracle Transparent Gateways

   **D.** Net8

   **E.** None of the above

3. Which of the following is *true* about Net8?

   **A.** It is not an option included in the Oracle Enterprise installation.

   **B.** It only works on TCP/IP platforms.

   **C.** It has an open API.

   **D.** It is never installed directly on a client workstation.

4. A DBA wants to centrally administer all of the Oracle Network services in a large organization with many network services. Which tool would best provide this functionality at minimal cost?

   **A.** Advanced Security

   **B.** Localnaming

   **C.** Hostnaming

   **D.** Oracle Names Server

**5.** TCP/IP, DECNET, and LU6.2 are all examples of:

   **A.** Computer programming languages

   **B.** Net8 connection tools

   **C.** Networking protocols

   **D.** Network programming languages

**6.** Which feature of Net8 best describes this statement: Net8 supports TCP/IP and SPX/IPX.

   **A.** GUI Tools integration

   **B.** Robust tracing and diagnostic tools

   **C.** Zero configuration on the client

   **D.** Network transport protocol support

**7.** A solution that Oracle8i employs with Net8, which allows connectivity of Java Components such as Enterprise JavaBeans is:

   **A.** LU6.2

   **B.** IPA

   **C.** GIOP

   **D.** Oracle Names Server

**8.** Which of the following are *true* of Oracle Names Servers? (Choose two.)

   **A.** It does not support dedicated connections.

   **B.** It supports only Multithreaded Server.

   **C.** It is a centralized naming solution.

   **D.** It can be configured using the Net8 Assistant.

**9.** Which of the following are *true* of the Net8 Assistant? Choose all that apply.

   **A.** It allows for configuration of localnaming.

   **B.** It allows for configuration of Connection Manager.

   **C.** It allows for configuration of hostnaming.

   **D.** It allows for configuration of the listener.

10. Complete the following statement: The Net8 Assistant was one of the first Oracle Tools...

    **A.** Written in Java

    **B.** Written in PL/SQL

    **C.** Written in C

    **D.** Written in C++

11. IIOP is an example of:

    **A.** Tools to use for Net8

    **B.** Oracle Network Integration utilities

    **C.** Internet Network Protocol

    **D.** Portions of the Net8 Stack

12. Finish this sentence: Connection Manager provides... (Choose all that apply.)

    **A.** Multiplexing

    **B.** Cross protocol connectivity

    **C.** Network access control

    **D.** All of the above

13. A Company has a need for certain end users to send secure transmissions to the database. This could be accomplished with what Oracle8i solution?

    **A.** Advanced Networking Option

    **B.** Advanced Security Option

    **C.** Enterprise Security Option

    **D.** Enterprise Networking Option

14. Other benefits of the solution in question #13 are: (Choose all that apply.)

    **A.** Zero client setup and administration

    **B.** Hot standby databases

    **C.** Hot Failure capabilities

    **D.** Authentication Services

    **E.** None of the above

**15.** One of the benefits of Net8 is an open API. API stands for:

   **A.** Applications Production Interface

   **B.** Advanced Program Interaction

   **C.** Advanced Program Interface

   **D.** Applications Program Interface

**16.** A client workstation connects to a transaction server, which passes on requests to the Oracle database. This is a description of:

   **A.** Single-tier architecture

   **B.** Client/server architecture

   **C.** N-tier architecture

   **D.** None of the above

**17.** Which Oracle Net8 networking product can best be described as middleware?

   **A.** Oracle Names Server

   **B.** Oracle Connection Manager

   **C.** Oracle Advanced Networking

   **D.** Oracle Multithreaded Server

**18.** Which of the following are characteristics of complex networks?

   **A.** Multiple protocols

   **B.** Desperate geographic locations

   **C.** Multiple operating systems

   **D.** Multiple hardware platforms

   **E.** All of the above

**19.** An Oracle Names Server could most closely be compared to:

   **A.** A party line

   **B.** An interpreter

   **C.** An operator assisted phone call

   **D.** A phone call made directly to the caller

**20.** One of the requirements of using encryption is:

**A.** Client and server must be running the same operating system.

**B.** Client and server must be using the same network protocol.

**C.** Client and server must be configured with the Advanced Networking Option.

**D.** Client and server must be configured with the Advanced Security option.

**E.** None of the above

# Answers to Review Questions

1. E. Networking can be as simple as a dumb terminal connected directly to a server via a serial connection to an n-Tier architecture that may involve clients, middleware, the Internet, and database servers. All of these are examples of network connectivity configurations.

2. C. The Oracle Names Server alone would not solve this application problem. Net8 would be part of the solution, but another Oracle Network component is necessary. Connection Manager would also not be able to accommodate this requirement on its own. The Oracle gateways are products that allow cross-platform connectivity to non-Oracle databases.

3. C. Net8 is included in the Oracle Enterprise installation and works with a variety of protocols. It has a client and a server component. The only statement that is true about Net8 is that it has an open Applications Program Interface (API), which means that third-party software can write to these specifications to interact directly with Net8.

4. D. Although hostnaming and localnaming can be done in a somewhat centralized manner, these solutions would not be the best alternative. The Advanced Security option could provide this functionality, but is an additional cost item. The best solution to the problem is the Oracle Names Server to facilitate centralized naming.

5. C. TCP/IP, DECnet, and LU6.2 are all examples of network protocols.

6. D. Net8 allows for support of multiple protocols. TCP/IP and SPX/IPX are two examples of the protocols that Net8 supports.

7. C. The General Inter-Orb Protocol is a protocol that supports connectivity of Java components.

8. C, D. Oracle Names Server is a centralized network naming solution that can be configured using Net8 Assistant. It does not have anything to do with the kind of connection (dedicated or multithreaded) that is ultimately made to the Oracle Server.

**9.** A, C, D. The Net8 Assistant allows for configuration of most of the network infrastructure files that are utilized by Oracle. Users can configure client, server, and Name Server files through Net8 Assistant. You would not use it to configure Connection Manager.

**10.** A. The Net8 Assistant was one of the first Oracle tools to be transferred to the JAVA environment.

**11.** C. IIOP is an example of an Internet network protocol.

**12.** D. Connection Manager is a middleware solution that provides for multiplexing of connections, cross protocol connectivity, and network access control. All of the answers describe Connection Manager.

**13.** B. Oracle8i networking has an optional product that allows for robust network security configurations within the enterprise. The Advanced Security Option provides many features of network security.

**14.** D. The Advanced Security Option provides authentication services that allow administrators to be confident about the identity of the clients connecting to the Oracle environment.

**15.** D. API stands for Applications Program Interface. This is implemented by using the NET8 Open feature of Net8. Programmers can write software that can connect to Oracle and non-Oracle sources utilizing Net8.

**16.** C. When you introduce middle tiers into the processing of a transaction, this is known as n-tier architecture.

**17.** B. The Connection Manager option is a middle-tier option that provides multi-protocol interchange, connection concentration, and client access control.

**18.** E. All of these are characteristics of complex networks.

**19.** C. An Oracle Names Server is similar to an operator-assisted phone call. The client contacts the Names Server to provide information on where a specific Oracle service can be located.

**20.** D. In order to take advantage of encryption, both the client and the server have to be configured with the Advanced Security Option.

# Chapter

# 12

# Oracle8i Net8 Architecture

---

## ORACLE8i NETWORK ADMINISTRATION EXAM OBJECTIVES COVERED IN THIS CHAPTER:

- ✓ List the steps in establishing network connections to an Oracle database.
- ✓ Describe the various components involved in establishing a network connection.
- ✓ Define a network service name.
- ✓ Describe the various client names resolution solutions.
- ✓ Describe how servers can respond to connection requests.
- ✓ Describe situations where a connection fails.
- ✓ List the ways in which clients can terminate connections.
- ✓ Define the structure of the Oracle communications stack.
- ✓ Describe Net8 connectivity through the Internet.

Exam objectives are subject to change at any time without prior notice and at Oracle's sole discretion. Please visit Oracle's Training and Certification Web site (http://education .oracle.com/certification/index.html) for the most current exam objectives listing.

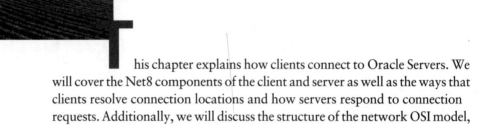

his chapter explains how clients connect to Oracle Servers. We will cover the Net8 components of the client and server as well as the ways that clients resolve connection locations and how servers respond to connection requests. Additionally, we will discuss the structure of the network OSI model, the Net8 stack configuration, and connectivity options through the Internet.

# Establishing Connections to Oracle Servers

It is important to understand what occurs when a client requests a connection to an Oracle Server. This information can assist you if problems arise with network connections.

The following is a common set of steps used to establish a connection to an Oracle Server:

1. The client enters connection information.

2. The client attempts to resolve the location of the Oracle Server.

3. If the location is resolved, the client contacts the Oracle Server.

4. The server receives the connection request and determines if it is valid.

5. If the server accepts the request, it sends a response back to the client, and the connection is established.

6. If the request fails, an error message is sent back to the client about why the connection was failed.

Let's take a closer look at each of these steps.

## Entering Connection Information

To establish a connection to an Oracle Server, the client needs to supply three pieces of information: an Oracle user ID and password and the location of the Oracle Server. Some programs, like SQL*Plus, call the location information a connect string. The proper name for this is a *net service name.* A net service name is the identification of some location of an Oracle Server. You could compare the net service name to a synonym in an Oracle database. It allows you to hide the complexity of the connection information by using a simple identifier.

For example, if a user called Matt with a password of **casey** wants to connect to an Oracle database called **payroll** using SQL*Plus, he would enter:

```
sqlplus matt/casey@payroll
```

The example below shows the graphical version of SQL*Plus with the same connection information. When entering connection information at the command line like in the example above, the @ sign separates the user ID and password combination from the net service name. In the graphical version of SQL*Plus, no @ sign is used when entering the connect string.

# Attempting to Resolve the Location of the Oracle Server

Once the connection information is entered, the next step is to resolve the location of the Oracle Server. The net service name itself does not contain specific location information. Every valid net service name refers to some *connect descriptor*. A connect descriptor contains information the client needs to contact the appropriate Oracle Server. The connect descriptor contains:

- The network path that the client will follow to get to the server.

- A *service name,* which is a logical identification of an Oracle database. Earlier releases of Oracle referred to this as the Oracle System Identifier, or Oracle SID.

Connect descriptor information can be kept in four different locations. Each of the locations is associated with a different option that can be used to resolve a net service name. These options include:

**The Localnaming Option**   Connect descriptors can be kept in a local file on the client. The file is called the *tnsnames.ora* file. The term localnaming comes from the fact that the `tnsnames.ora` file is normally located locally on the client machine and contains all of the necessary name information to connect to an Oracle Server. The client looks in various locations to find this file. Once it is found, it performs a lookup to see if the file contains a reference to the net service name. If it does, the client will contact the Oracle Server utilizing connect descriptor information located in the file.

**The Oracle Names Server Option**   You can configure an Oracle Names Server, which contains connect descriptor information. The client contacts the Names Server and supplies the server with the net service name. The server responds with connect descriptor information that the client needs to complete the connection.

**The Hostnaming Option**   There are some special requirements to use the *hostnaming* option. This option can only be used in a TCP/IP network environment. It also requires that you maintain net service name information in some existing external naming service environment such as Domain Names Server (DNS) or the client-side `HOSTS` file.

**The External Naming Service Option**   The *external naming service option* is third-party software that contains connect descriptor information. The client would access this information from some network location. Examples of third party software would be Novell's Network Directory Service (NDS) and Network Information Service (NIS).

You can use any combination of these options to resolve a net service name. If multiple options are used, you can specify the order in which to check each option by setting a parameter in the `sqlnet.ora` file on the client. The `sqlnet.ora` file contains optional configuration parameters and can exist on both the client and the server.

The parameter in the `sqlnet.ora` file that specifies the order of the options is `NAMES.DIRECTORY_PATH`. The following listing contains an example of the `NAMES.DIRECTORY_PATH` setting. The order in which the names resolutions options appear in the parameter is the order in which they are checked. In the code listed below, the Names Server option is checked first, followed by the localnaming option and finally the hostnaming option.

```
# C:\V8I\NETWORK\ADMIN\SQLNET.ORA Configuration
# File:C:\v8i\NETWORK\ADMIN\sqlnet.ora
# Generated by Oracle Net8 Assistant

NAMES.DIRECTORY_PATH= (ONAMES, TNSNAMES, HOSTNAME)
```

If this parameter is not present, Oracle will try to resolve the net service name first by using the localnaming method. The client will search for a `tnsnames.ora` file. If unsuccessful, the client looks for an Oracle Names Server. If neither search is successful, the client will try resolving the service using the hostnaming method. Table 12.1 shows a listing of the possible settings for the `NAMES.DIRECTORY_PATH` parameter.

**TABLE 12.1**   `NAMES.DIRECTORY_PATH` Settings

| Title Setting | Title Definition |
| --- | --- |
| CDS | Cell Directory Server |
| HOSTNAME | Hostnaming Option |
| NDS | Netware Directory Service |
| NIS | Network Information Service |
| ONAMES | Oracle Names Server |
| TNSNAMES | Local Naming Option |

## Using the LocalNaming Option

The localnaming option uses the `tnsnames.ora` file. This file contains connect descriptors that resolve the locations of net service names. The `tnsnames.ora` file is similar to an index in a book. Just as you look up subjects in an index to find their location in a book, the client scans the `tnsnames.ora` file for a matching network service name. If it finds one, the entry provides the client with connect descriptor information for the network service name. A `tnsnames.ora` file looks like this:

```
# C:\V8I\NETWORK\ADMIN\TNSNAMES.ORA Configuration
# File:C:\v8i\NETWORK\ADMIN\tnsnames.ora
# Generated by Oracle Net8 Assistant

PAYROLL =
  (DESCRIPTION =
    (ADDRESS_LIST =
      (ADDRESS = (PROTOCOL = TCP)(HOST = MAD01ORA)(PORT =
1521))
    )
    (CONNECT_DATA =
      (SERVICE_NAME = v8i)
    )
  )
```

The default location for the `tnsnames.ora` file and the `sqlnet.ora` file is `$ORACLE_HOME/network/admin` on UNIX systems and `%ORACLE_HOME%\network\admin` on Windows NT systems.

If you move these files to a different location, set the environmental variable `TNS_ADMIN` to the directory path where these files were moved. In Unix systems, `TNS_ADMIN` can be exported to the user's shell environment or be set in the user's profile. In Windows NT, this setting is placed in the registry.

The Windows NT registry key that stores the `TNS_ADMIN` may vary depending on your particular setup. Generally, it can be found somewhere under the `Hkey_local_machine/software/oracle` registry key. It may be at a lower level depending on your configuration. The `regedit` or `regedt32` utilities are used to add this registry information. Figure 12.1 shows an example of the `TNS_ADMIN` setting in the Windows NT registry.

**FIGURE 12.1**    Windows NT Registry display

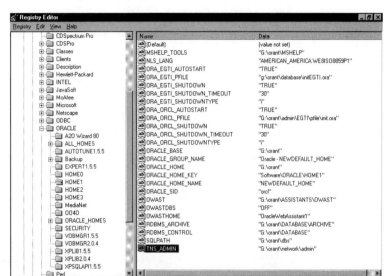

Setting TNS_ADMIN in a Windows NT environment involves modifying the Windows NT registry. Extreme care should be taken when making modifications to the registry. Windows NT may not function properly if the registry is damaged.

There is a default search hierarchy for the `tnsnames.ora` file and `sqlnet.ora` files. Net8 first looks for these files in the current working directory of the application. If it cannot locate the files there, it looks in the TNS_ADMIN location. If this variable is not set, it will look in the platform specific default location. Figure 12.2 shows how the localnaming option functions. The localnaming connection steps are as follows:

**1.** The client looks up service information in the `tnsnames.ora` file.

**2.** The client contacts the Oracle Server.

**3.** The server spawns a dedicated process, redirects the connection to a prespawned process, or redirects the connection to a dispatched process.

**4.** The server passes the connection information back to the client.

**5.** The client is now in direct contact with the server process or dispatcher.

**FIGURE 12.2** Localnaming option

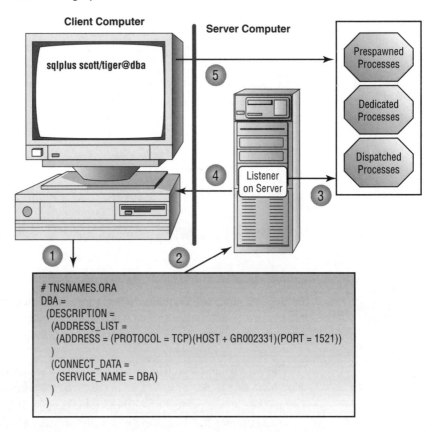

The details of the connect descriptor syntax for the tnsnames.ora file are described in Chapter 14: Configuring Oracle8i Net8 for the Client.

## Using the Oracle Names Server Option

Using the Oracle Names Server option is similar to making an operator-assisted phone call. When you call the operator to find a phone number, you supply the operator with the name and the city of the person you wish to call. The operator looks up the information and gives you the number to dial. The Names Server does the same thing, only you are supplying a net service name instead of a person's name and city.

A client contacts an Oracle Names Server and passes it a net service name. The Names Server then looks up the net service name information. If the information is found, the Names Server sends connect descriptor information back to the client. The client can then contact the appropriate Oracle Server.

The Names Server is only used for a brief period while the connection description is being looked up. Once it sends the information back to the client, the Names Server is free to process other client requests. Figure 12.3 depicts the interaction of the client and the Oracle Names Server. The Names Server connection steps are as follows:

**1.** The client contacts the Names Server.

**2.** The Names Server returns the connect descriptor.

**3.** The client contacts the Oracle Server.

**4.** The server spawns a dedicated process, redirects the connection to a prespawned process, or redirects the connection to a dispatched process.

**5.** The server passes connection information back to the client.

**6.** The client is now in direct contact with the server process or dispatcher.

**FIGURE 12.3** Names Server option

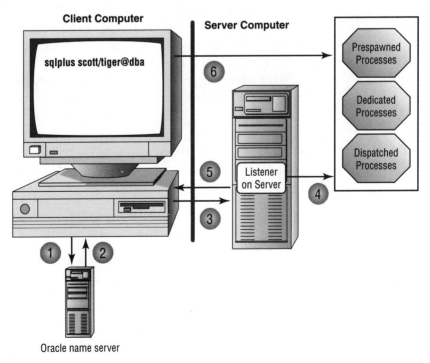

The Names Server can be configured to keep connection descriptor information in operating system files or in a database. The Names Server will respond in the same manner in either configuration. We will discuss how to configure the Names Server in Chapter 15. Once a Names Server has been created, the client should be configured with information about the location of the Names Server. Through a process called discovery, a client will build a list of Names Servers that it can use to resolve service names. Chapter 15 details how to initiate the discovery process on the client. There are three types of Names Servers a client will search for during the discovery process: Preferred Names Servers, Well-Known Names Servers, and Local Names Server.

### Preferred Names Servers

A client can keep a list of Names Servers. These are called Preferred Names Servers. The list of Preferred Names Servers is kept in the `sqlnet.ora` file and is defined by the `NAMES.PREFERRED_SERVERS` parameter. Typically, a preferred Names Server should be a Names Server that the client is able to contact most quickly and contains the net service names most frequently accessed. In Chapter 15, we will discuss details on configuring preferred Names Servers on the client.

### Well-Known Names Servers

A client can contact a well-known Names Server to resolve net service names. A well-known Names Server has a name that is hard coded into the Net8 software. The names of these well-known Names Servers depend on the type of network protocol that is being used to communicate with the Oracle Server. Table 12.2 contains a list of the names of the well-known Names Servers by protocol. These well-known Names Servers must be defined in your external naming environment, such as DNS, or in the HOSTS file on the client.

**TABLE 12.2** Well-Known Names Servers

| TCP/IP Protocol | Named Pipes | SPX Protocol |
| --- | --- | --- |
| Oranamesvrv0 | ORANAMESRVR0 | Oranamesrvr |
| Oranamesvrv1 | ORANAMESRVR1 | |
| Oranamesvrv2 | ORANAMESRVR2 | |
| Oranamesvrv3 | ORANAMESRVR3 | |
| Oranamesvrv4 | ORANAMESRVR4 | |

### Local Names Server

A local Names Server runs on the same machine as the client. This type of configuration only works with the TCP/IP protocol, and the Names Server must be listening for connection requests on port 1575.

## Using the Hostnaming Option

The hostnaming option, unlike the other options discussed, does not require any configuration on the client. In simple Oracle networks with few servers to manage, this may be an option to consider.

When a client uses the hostnaming option, the client supplies the net service name that is actually the hostname of the Oracle Server the client wants to connect to. This hostname must be defined in either the Domain Name Server (DNS) or the client HOSTS file. These external environments pass the network address of the Oracle Server back to the client. The client builds the remainder of the connect descriptor with some default values. Figure 12.4 shows how the hostnaming option works. The hostnaming connection steps are as follows:

1. The client contacts the DNS server or uses the local HOSTS file.

2. The client contacts the Oracle Server.

3. The server spawns a dedicated process, redirects the connection to a prespawned process, or redirects the connection to a dispatched process.

4. The server passes connection information back to the client.

5. The client is now in direct contact with the server process or dispatcher.

**FIGURE 12.4** Hostnaming option

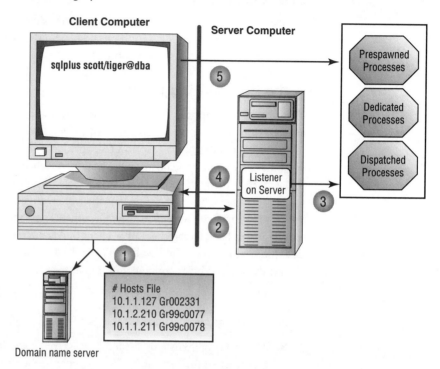

Domain name server

There are some parameters on the server that need to be used to enable host-naming. We will discuss how to configure hostnaming on the Oracle Server in Chapter 14.

The hostnaming option can only be used with the TCP/IP protocol.

## Using the External Naming Option

The external naming option uses third-party software to establish connections to an Oracle Server. The external naming option contains connect descriptor information that resolves the Oracle net service name. It works similarly to the Oracle Names Server option, but uses third-party packages that can control a variety of network services, not just connect descriptor information. As mentioned previously, Novell's Network Directory services

(NDS) is an example of an external naming service. Figure 12.5 shows how the external naming service for NDS option functions. The external naming connection steps are as follows:

1. The client contacts the external naming server.

2. The Names Server returns the connect descriptor.

3. The client contacts the Oracle Server.

4. The server spawns a dedicated process, redirects the connection to a prespawned process, or redirects the connection to a dispatched process.

5. The server passes connection information back to the client.

6. The client is now in direct contact with the server process or dispatcher.

**FIGURE 12.5** External naming option

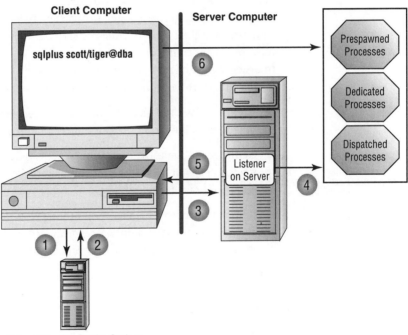

For further reading on how to configure external naming, refer to *The Oracle Net8 Administrator's Guide* (part number A67440-01).

## Establishing Contact with the Oracle Server

Once the client has resolved the network service name and has connect descriptor information, it will contact the Oracle Server on the network.

The Oracle Server has a special process running on it called the *listener*. You can think of the listener as a big ear that is listening for connection requests from clients. When a client contacts the listener, it provides the listener with the service name part of the connect descriptor.

The service names that the listener can listen for are configured in the listener.ora file. This is the configuration file for the listener.

A listener is configured to listen for particular service names. If the listener is configured to listen for the requested service, it has to determine how it will connect the client to the Oracle Server.

In order for the client to communicate with the Oracle Server, the listener has to do one of three things on behalf of the client:

- Create a new process that will be dedicated to serving the needs of this one client connection. This is called a *dedicated server connection*.

- Redirect the client to an existing process that will be dedicated to serving the needs of this one client connection. This is called a *prespawned dedicated server connection*.

- Redirect the client to an existing process that may be shared with many clients. This is called a *multithreaded connection*. The process to which the listener redirects the client is called a *dispatcher*.

Let's take a closer look at these three options.

### Dedicated Connections

Dedicated connections are the most common kind of connections established in an Oracle environment. The listener creates a process that will service all of the client's requests. This is known as spawning a process.

After the listener has spawned the process, it has to relinquish control of the client connection to the process that was just spawned. This is known as bequeathing the process. In fact, another name for a dedicated connection is a *bequeath session*. Once the listener has relinquished control of the connection to the server process, all client communications to the database flow through the server process. The listener goes back to serving other connection requests. Figure 12.6 illustrates the following steps of connecting to an Oracle Server using a dedicated connection:

1. The client contacts the Oracle Server after resolving the service name.

2. The server spawns a dedicated process and bequeaths control of the connection process.

3. The Server Process manages the client server requests.

**FIGURE  12.6**    Dedicated connection

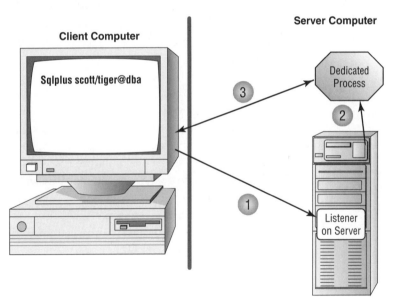

You can think of the dedicated server as the personal waiter to client processes. The dedicated server process carries out any request the client sends to the server, such as retrieving rows from a table or running a stored procedure.

There is also something known as the Bequeath protocol adapter. The bequeath protocol adapter allows clients to establish communications to the database server without using the listener. The bequeath protocol adapter is installed by default and used when a client application is running on the same machine as the Oracle Server. When a client connects to an Oracle database using this adapter, it is referred to as a *local connection* because both the client and server process reside on the same physical machine and the listener is not involved in making the connection. In order for this to work, the environmental variable *ORACLE_ SID* needs to be set to the name of the instance you wish to connect to.

## Prespawned Connections

Prespawned connections are a form of dedicated connection. They allow for faster connection times to the Oracle Server because a client does not have to wait for the listener to spawn a new process. By default, if prespawned processes exist on the Oracle Server, these will be utilized before a listener will spawn a new process.

You configure the listener to start a pool of prespawned processes when the listener starts. The configuration parameters for prespawned server processes will be discussed in Chapter 13: Configuring Oracle8i Net8 on the Server.

Instead of the listener spawning a new process when a client issues a connection request, it sends a message back to the client, telling the client to redirect communication to the address of one of the prespawned servers. Once this happens, the listener and client do not have to communicate with each other any more. All network conversations to the Oracle Server from this client will flow through the prespawned dedicated server. Figure 12.7 illustrates the steps of connecting to an Oracle Server using a dedicated prespawned connection. The prespawned connection steps are as follows:

1. The listener spawns server processes when it is started.

2. The client contacts the Oracle Server after resolving the service name.

3. The server redirects client connection to the prespawned server process.

4. The server process manages client server requests.

**FIGURE 12.7** Prespawned connection

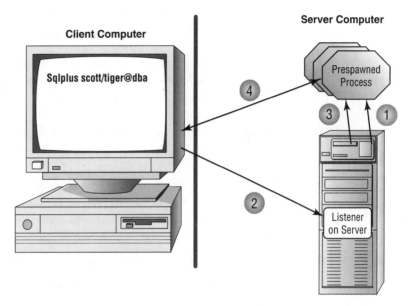

You can maintain a pool of prespawned processes. After the listener redirects the client to a prespawned process, it may spawn a new idle server process to replace the one just assigned. You can specify the maximum number of prespawned processes that are allowed by the maximum number of prespawned processes allowed in the `listener.ora` file. As long as this number has not been reached, the listener can spawn new processes. Once this number is reached, no more prespawned processes will be created, and subsequent clients will connect with dedicated connections until some of the prespawned processes become available through disconnections.

## Multithreaded Connections

Multithreaded connections are used if the Oracle Server is configured with the Multithreaded Server option (MTS). This is the default connection method for clients unless the client requests a dedicated connection or no multithreaded connections are currently available.

Multithreaded Server connections involve processes called dispatchers. Dispatchers are shared processes that are spawned when an Oracle instance is started. Parameters in the `init.ora` file must be set for dispatchers to start when the instance starts. We will see how to configure the Multithreaded Server in Chapter 16.

The process of connecting to a dispatcher is very similar to the process of connecting to a prespawned dedicated server process. Instead of the listener spawning a new process when a client issues a connection request, it sends a message back to the client, telling the client to redirect communication to the address of one of the dispatcher processes. Once this happens, the listener and client do not have to communicate with each other any more. All network conversations to the Oracle Server from this client will flow through the dispatcher process.

The last step is that the dispatcher will notify the listener to update information about the connection. This is done so the listener is aware of the number of connections the dispatcher is managing. It is important for the listener to know this information so as not to exceed the maximum number of connections the dispatcher is configured to handle. Figure 12.8 illustrates the steps of connecting to an Oracle Server using a multithreaded connection. The multithreaded connection steps are as follows:

1. Dispatcher processes are spawned when the instance is started.

2. The client contacts the Oracle Server after resolving the service name.

3. The server redirects client connection to the dispatcher that is least busy.

4. The dispatcher process manages client server requests.

5. The dispatcher registers the connection information with the listener.

**FIGURE 12.8** Multithreaded connection

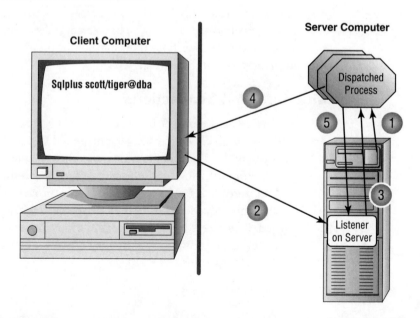

Dispatchers are responsible for processing the requests of many connections. You can think of dispatchers like hostesses in a diner. When you go to a diner, a hostess takes your order and brings you your food, but is also responsible for other patrons in the diner as well. This is true of dispatchers. Each dispatcher can be responsible for many client connections.

# Connection Request Failures

A connection request may fail for many reasons. You will learn how to diagnose and troubleshoot a variety of connection problems later in this book. Here are a few of the most common reasons for connection failures:

## The Service Name Supplied Is Invalid

If the user supplies a service name the listener is not listening for, the listener will return an error. This means the service name associated with connect descriptor information supplied by the client is invalid. The following code shows the results of connecting with an invalid server name:

```
D:\>sqlplus system/manager@dba


SQL*Plus: Release 8.1.5.0.0 - Production on Sun Feb 6
14:12:34 2000
(c) Copyright 1999 Oracle Corporation.  All rights
reserved.


ERROR:
ORA-12514: TNS:listener could not resolve SERVICE_NAME
given in connect descriptor


Enter user-name:
```

## Rejection Due to Invalid Net Service Name

If the net service name cannot be resolved, you will receive an error. This means the client could not find the net service name using the names resolution options available to it. This code shows that the user will receive an ORA-12154 error because of this rejection.

```
D:\>sqlplus system/manager@dba1

SQL*Plus: Release 8.1.5.0.0 - Production on Sun Feb 6
14:39:45 2000
(c) Copyright 1999 Oracle Corporation.
All rights reserved.

ERROR:
ORA-12154: TNS:could not resolve service name

Enter user-name:
```

## The Oracle Instance is Not Running

If the Oracle instance that the user wants to connect to is not available, the connection will be rejected. Following is an example of this occurrence:

```
D:\>sqlplus system/manager@dba

SQL*Plus: Release 8.1.5.0.0 - Production on Sun Feb 6
 14:25:38 2000
(c) Copyright 1999 Oracle Corporation.
All rights reserved.

ERROR:
ORA-01034: ORACLE not available

Enter user-name:
```

## The User Supplied an Invalid User ID or Password

If the user supplies an invalid user ID or password, the connection will be rejected. In this situation, the server process on the Oracle Server is created. The server process validates the user ID and password against the known users and passwords on the Oracle database. If no match is found, the connection fails. When a user supplies an invalid password or user ID, it looks something like this:

```
D:\>sqlplus system/manage@dba

SQL*Plus: Release 8.1.5.0.0 - Production on Sun Feb 6
14:48:27 2000
```

```
(c) Copyright 1999 Oracle Corporation.
All rights reserved.

ERROR:
ORA-01017: invalid username/password; logon denied

Enter user-name:
```

### The Listener Process is Not Running

If the listener process is not available, the connection will fail. The following code shows the resulting error from this situation:

```
D:\>sqlplus system/manager@dba

SQL*Plus: Release 8.1.5.0.0 - Production on Sun Feb 6
14:51:16 2000
(c) Copyright 1999 Oracle Corporation.
All rights reserved.

ERROR:
ORA-12541: TNS:no listener

Enter user-name:
```

# Terminating Sessions

Once a connection has been established with the Oracle Server, all session information is passed between the client and either a dedicated or multithreaded server process. The connection can remain open indefinitely. There are no time-out mechanisms that are built in to the Net8 architecture.

You can configure an option called Profiles. Profiles allow you to specify a time-out period for connections that remain inactive for a certain length of time, as well as other resource monitoring parameters. Profiles are an option of the Oracle database and configured within the Oracle database itself, not within the Net8 architecture. Some operating systems also allow you to specify time limits on inactive network sessions. Once a certain amount of inactive time has passed, the operating system will force the session to be terminated. Consult your operating system documentation to find out if time limits can be enforced by the operating system. Consult the Oracle Server documentation to learn more about profiles.

At some point, a connection will be terminated. The termination can happen as a result of the client exiting the application, a DBA terminating a server process for various reasons (such as to backup the system), or an abnormal condition. Let's examine what occurs when sessions terminate under normal and abnormal conditions.

## Normal Terminations of Sessions

Connections are terminated when a client disconnects from the server. If the client is connected to a dedicated server and terminates the connection normally, the associated dedicated process will also terminate.

If the client disconnects normally from a dedicated prespawned process, this prespawned process may remain available but be in an idle state. You can specify the number of prespawned idle processes to maintain by setting an initialization parameter in the `listener.ora` file called *POOL_SIZE* (you will see how to configure prespawned processes in Chapter 13). If the number of idle prespawned connections exceeds the `pool_size`, the prespawned process may wait for a number of minutes before terminating. The time that the process will wait before terminating is set by the `listener.ora` parameter *timeout*.

If the client disconnects normally from a dispatched process, the dispatched process will remain available to serve other connections.

On some systems, clients can disconnect by issuing a break request generated by entering Ctrl+C or Ctrl+Break. These interrupts can cause termination of the session. The break requests are handled as in-band breaks or out-of-band breaks. In-band breaks are break requests that are sent as part of the regular data transmission from the client. In the case of out-of-band breaks, the break request is given priority and sent ahead of any other requests that my be waiting in the clients network transmission queue. These are called urgent messages because they are given priority. Out-of-band breaks will cause a faster disconnection because they are given priority over other transmission data. Net8 can handle either of these types of requests.

Whether in-band breaks or out-of-band breaks are used depends on how your operating system sends the network signal. Many implementations of UNIX support out-of-band breaks.

## Abnormal Terminations of Sessions

Connections may also terminate as the result of some abnormal condition. Examples of abnormal termination are a client powering down a P/C without first disconnecting from the session or a failure in the underlying network connection, such as the TCP/IP daemon failing or a router failure.

In situations like these, the server-side process may remain running for a period of time. The time that the process remains running is operating system dependent. The process may take only a few minutes, or it could remain running indefinitely. The PMON process is responsible for cleaning up terminated server processes, but PMON cannot detect certain situations where the client process has terminated. If this type of situation happens often enough, the server could have many of these "orphan" processes that may actually start to impact server resources. You can also run into problems with operating system process limits.

### Dead Connection Detection

There is a feature called *dead connection detection* that can be configured on the Oracle Server. When dead connection detection is enabled, a packet is sent periodically to the client from the Oracle Server to check the health of the connection. If the server session does not receive a valid response from the client, the session will be terminated on the server. When dedicated server processes are used, these processes will be killed.

Dead connection detection is enabled by setting the SQLNET.EXPIRE_TIME parameter in the sqlnet.ora file on the server. This parameter is set to a number of minutes. After this number of minutes have elapsed since the last contact with a client, the Oracle Server sends a packet to the client to see if the client is still alive. If the client does not respond, the Oracle background process PMON kills the associated server process and rolls back any work in progress for the session.

# The Net8 Stack Architecture

The Net8 software is comprised of a series of programs that form a type of stack architecture. Each of these programs is responsible for handling various aspects of network communications and comprises a layer of the stack. This section discusses the architecture of the Net8 stack and defines the responsibilities of each portion of the stack. An understanding of the structure and responsibilities of the Net8 stack is important to successful completion of the OCP exam.

## The OSI Model

The *Open Systems Interconnection* (OSI) model is a widely accepted model that defines how data communications are carried out across a network. There are seven layers in the OSI model, with each layer responsible for some aspect of network communication. The upper layers of the model handle responsibilities such as communicating with the application and presenting data. The lower layers are responsible for transporting data across the network. The upper layers pass information, such as the destination of the data and how the data should be handled, to the lower layers. The lower layers communicate status information back to the upper layers. Table 12.3 shows the layers of the OSI model and the responsibilities of each of the layers in executing communications across a network. This layered approach allows for a separation of responsibilities. It also allows for the separation of the logical aspects of network communications, such as presentation and data management, from the physical aspects of communications, such as the physical transmission of bits across a network.

**TABLE 12.3** The Layers of the OSI Model

| OSI Model Layer | Responsibilities |
| --- | --- |
| Application Layer | Interacts with the user. Accepts commands and returns data. |
| Presentation Layer | Responsible for settling data differences between client and server. Also responsible for data format. |
| Session Layer | Manages network traffic flow. Determines whether data is being sent or received. |

**TABLE  12.3**   The Layers of the OSI Model  *(continued)*

| OSI Model Layer | Responsibilities |
| --- | --- |
| Transport Layer | Handles interaction of the network processes on the source and destination. Error correction and detection occurs here. |
| Network Layer | Responsible for delivery of data between nodes. |
| Data Link Layer | Responsible for connection reliability and retransmission functionality. |
| Physical Layer | Transmits electrical signals across the network. |

# The Oracle Communications Stack

The OSI model is the foundation of the Oracle communications stack architecture. Each of the layers of the Oracle communications stack has characteristics and responsiblities that are patterned after the OSI model.

Net8 is an integral component of the Oracle communications stack architecture. It is based on the Transparent Network Substrate (TNS). TNS allows Net8 to be a very flexible architecture, interfacing with a wide variety of network protocols. The TNS interface shields both the client and server from the complexities of network communications.

Oracle uses Net8 on the client and server to facilitate communications. The communications stack functions as a conduit to share and manage data between the client and server. The layers of Oracle communications stack are:

- Application or Server
- Oracle Call Interface (OCI) or Oracle Program Interface (OPI)
- Two Task Common (TTC)
- Transparent Network Substrate (TNS)
- Oracle Protocol Adapters (OPA)
- Network Specific Protocols
- Network Program Interface (NPI for server-to-server communications only)

Figure 12.9 depicts the relationship of each of the layers of the stack on both the client and the server. The client process makes network calls that traverse down the Net8 client layers to the network protocol. The server receives the network request, processes it, and returns the results to the client.

**FIGURE 12.9** Net8 stack architecture

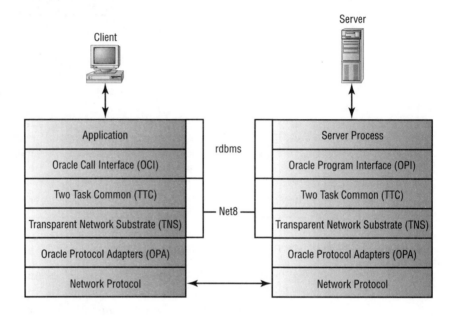

## The Application Layer

The application layer of the Oracle communications stack provides the same functionality as the application layer of the OSI model. This layer is responsible for interaction with the user, providing the interface components and screen and data control elements. Interfaces such as a forms or menus are examples of the application layer. This layer communicates with the Oracle Call Interface (OCI) layer.

## The Oracle Call Interface (OCI) Layer

The *Oracle Call Interface (OCI)* is responsible for all of the SQL processing that occurs between a client and the Oracle Server. The OCI layer exists on the client only. There is an analogous server component called the Oracle Program Interface (OPI) on the server. The OCI layer is responsible for opening and closing cursors, binding variables in the server's shared memory space, and fetching rows. Because the OCI is an open architecture, third-party products can write applications that interface directly with this layer of the communications stack. The OCI layer passes information directly to the Two-Task Common (TTC) layer.

## The Two-Task Common (TTC) Layer

The *Two-Task Common (TTC)* layer is responsible for negotiating any datatype or character set differences between the client and the server. The Two-Task Common layer acts as a translator, converting values from one character set to another. The TTC will determine if any datatype differences are present when the connection is established. The TTC layer passes information to the Transparent Network Substrate (TNS) layer.

## The Transparent Network Substrate (TNS) Layer

The Transparent Network Substrate (TNS) is the level of the communications stack where the Net8 software interfaces with the other layers of the stack. This layer provides the interface to the underlying protocols. The TNS layer provides the level of abstraction necessary to make Net8 a flexible and adaptable architecture. It compensates for differences in connectivity issues between machines and underlying protocols. It also handles interrupt messages and passes information directly to the Oracle Protocol Adapters (OPA). The TNS layer is made up of several sublayers:

### Network Interface Sublayer (NI)

The network interface sublayer provides a common interface on which the clients and servers can process functions. This layer of the stack is also responsible for handling any break requests.

### Network Routing Sublayer (NR)

This is where Net8 keeps its network roadmap of how to get from the source or client to the destination or server.

### Network Naming Sublayer (NN)

This layer takes network alias information and changes it into Net8 destination address information.

### Network Authentication Sublayer (NA)

This layer is responsible for any negotiations necessary for authenticating connections.

### Network Session Sublayer (NS)

The network session layer handles the bulk of activity in an Oracle network connection. This layer is responsible for such things as negotiating the initial connection request from the client. It is also responsible for managing the Net8 buffer contents and passing the buffer information between the client and the server. It also handles special features of connection management such as buffer pooling and multiplexing if these options are used.

### The Oracle Protocol Adapters (OPA) Layer

The *Oracle Protocol Adapters (OPA)* interface directly with the underlying network transport protocol. They map the TNS functions to the analogous functions in the underlying protocol. There are different adapters for each protocol supported.

### The Network Protocol Layer

This is the actual transport layer that carries the information from the client to the server. Some of the protocols supported by Net8 include TCP/IP, IPX, DECnet, and SPX/IPX. These protocols are not supplied with the Oracle software and must be in place to facilitate network communications.

### The Network Program Interface (NPI)

The *Network Program Interface (NPI)* is found only on the Oracle Server. It is analogous to the OCI on the client. This layer is responsible for server-to-server communications and is used in distributed environments where databases communicate with each other across database links.

## Changes to Net8 for Internet Communications

Oracle has made modifications to the Net8 communications stack to accommodate Java and Internet connections. Net8 now supports the General Inter-Orb Protocol (GIOP). This is a new presentation level of the stack that supports client connections with the Java option. The Internet Inter-Orb protocol (IIOP) is a flavor of GIOP running under the TCP/IP protocol. It also supports the Secured Sockets Layer (SSL) for making secured network connections across the Internet.

These changes reduce the amount of Net8 layers that have to be present on both the client and the server. The only portion of Net8 that is required is TNS. This streamlined communications stack allows for more efficient connectivity of Oracle Servers through Web-based interfaces and across the Internet. Figure 12.10 shows how the modifications streamline the Oracle Communications stack.

**FIGURE 12.10** IIOP stack communications

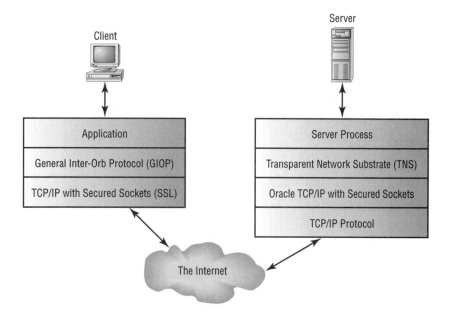

# Summary

To be successful on the OCP exam, you need to understand the network connection process. The client uses a net service name to target a specific Oracle service to connect to. These net service names are resolved to connect descriptors using localnaming, hostnaming, the Oracle Names Server, or an external naming service. Once the client resolves the service name, it uses the connect descriptor to connect to the listener running on the Oracle Server. The listener will then connect the client to the appropriate service using dedicated, prespawned, or multithreaded connections.

Connections can sometimes fail. The user may enter an invalid user ID or password or enter an incorrect net service name. The listener may not be available, or the Oracle Server may be unavailable. These are some of the problems you may encounter working with Net8 connections.

Clients can terminate a connection with a normal exit request, or the connection can be terminated abnormally. If an abnormal termination occurs, the background process PMON is responsible for cleaning up the terminated server process.

The Net8 architecture is based upon the Open Systems Interconnection, or OSI, model of network computing. This model divides the responsibility of conducting network transactions among various layers. Oracle Net8 is a layered architecture. On the client, these layers are Application, Oracle Call Interface, Two-Task Common, Transparent Network Substrate, Oracle Protocol Adapters, and the underlying network protocol. The server has an identical network layer structure, with the addition of the Network Program Interface for server-to-server communications.

# Key Terms

**B**efore you take the exam, make sure you're familiar with the following terms:

bequeath session

connect descriptor

dead connection detection

dedicated server connection

dispatcher

external naming service option

hostnaming

listener

local connection

multithreaded connection

Oracle Call Interface (OCI)

net service name

Open Systems Interconnection (OSI)

Network Program Interface (NPI)

ORACLE_SID

pool_size

prespawned process

Oracle Protocol Adapters (OPA)

Two-Task Common (TTC)

timeout

TNS_ADMIN

# Review Questions

**1.** What is another name for a connection location?

   **A.** Oracle name

   **B.** Database

   **C.** ORACLE_SID

   **D.** Network service name

   **E.** None of the above

**2.** The DBA wants to put the client side files in a non-default location. The environmental variable that will be set to accomplish this is:

   **A.** TNS_NAMES

   **B.** TNS_LOCATION

   **C.** TNS_ADMIN

   **D.** SERVICE_LOCATION

**3.** What are the two main components of a connect descriptor?

   **A.** The path to the requested Oracle Server

   **B.** The location of the tnsnames.ora file

   **C.** A network service name

   **D.** A service name

**4.** The DBA would like to avoid problems with abnormal termination of client processes, which causes problems with system resources. What could be configured to aid the DBA?

   **A.** Expiration time Setting

   **B.** Dead connection detection on the client

   **C.** Dead connection detection on the server

   **D.** None of the above

**5.** What is the standard that the Net8 communications stack is based on?

**A.** OCI

**B.** NPI

**C.** OSI

**D.** API

**6.** "Responsible for moving bits across the wire" describes:

**A.** Application layer

**B.** Physical layer

**C.** Data Link layer

**D.** Network layer

**7.** The file that contains optional client and server parameters is:

**A.** Sqlnet.trc

**B.** Tnsnames.ora

**C.** Sqlnet.ora

**D.** Sdns.ora

**E.** None of the above

**8.** Oracle now supports Internet connectivity using what Internet connection protocol?

**A.** IHOP

**B.** GHOP

**C.** NPI

**D.** IIOP

**9.** What are two possible ways in which a user's session may be terminated?

**A.** User termination

**B.** Automatic termination

**C.** Abnormal termination

**D.** Default termination

**10.** A DBA configures Novell Netware Directory Services for resolving service names. This is an example of:

    **A.** Localnaming

    **B.** External naming

    **C.** Hostnaming

    **D.** Oracle Names Server

**11.** Another name for a dedicated non-prespawned session is:

    **A.** Local session

    **B.** Global session

    **C.** Bequeath session

    **D.** Dispatcher session

**12.** "Displays the graphical use interface" best describes:

    **A.** The Net8 layer

    **B.** The application layer

    **C.** The Oracle call interface layer

    **D.** The two-task common layer

    **E.** None of the above

**13.** Which of the following is true about the OCI layer?

    **A.** It displays the graphical interface.

    **B.** Its datatype conversions are handled.

    **C.** It interfaces directly with the protocol adapters.

    **D.** It interfaces directly with the TTC layer.

    **E.** None of the above

**14.** "Responsible for datatype conversions" best describes:

    **A.** OCI

    **B.** Application layer

    **C.** OPA

    **D.** TNS

    **E.** TTC

**15.** All of the following are false regarding the OCI layer except:

    **A.** It handles break requests.

    **B.** It interfaces directly with the user.

    **C.** It performs character set translations.

    **D.** It parses SQL statements.

**16.** Which of the following is a protocol supported by Net8?

    **A.** LU6.2

    **B.** APX

    **C.** OSA

    **D.** TTC

    **E.** IPC

**17.** "Handles server-to-server communications" best describes:

    **A.** TTC

    **B.** OPA

    **C.** OSI

    **D.** NPI

**18.** Which of the following is true of the OPA?

    **A.** It interfaces directly with the database.

    **B.** It consists of several sublayers.

    **C.** It interfaces directly with TCP/IP.

    **D.** Provides for server call definitions.

**19.** All of the following exist in the client Net8 stack except:

    **A.** NPI

    **B.** TTC

    **C.** OPA

    **D.** OPI

**20.** A client workstation is running the US7ASCII character set. The database is running with the WE8ISO8859PI character set. Which layer of the Net8 stack will compensate for this difference?

**A.** Application

**B.** NPI

**C.** TTC

**D.** OPA

**E.** None of the above

# Answers to Review Questions

1.  D. Connect strings resolve to some location on the network that will provide some service to the end user. The service does not necessarily have to be the same as an ORACLE_SID or an Oracle database. In Oracle8i, a database may be known by multiple service names, so the connection strings are now referred to as network service names.

2.  C. It is common to move the network files from the default location to some other location. Sometimes, DBAs will try to create a pseudo centralized naming structure by placing this information on shared or mounted devices. As long as the client knows the location of the files, service names can be resolved. The TNS_ADMIN environmental variable is set to the non-default directory location of the network files. All of the other choices are invalid variables.

3.  A, C. A connect descriptor contains the path that the client will follow to the Oracle Server and the service name. The net service name is the name used to identify an associated connect descriptor. The location of the tnsnames.ora file is not identified in the connect descriptor.

4.  C. Dead connection detection is configured on the server. This prevents abnormally terminated processes from piling up on the server.

5.  C. The Net8 communications stack is based on the Open Systems Interconnection (OSI) model. NPI and OCI are parts of the Net8 stack and API stands for Applications Program Interface.

6.  B. The physical layer is responsible for sending the actual data bits across the network. The other layers are all above this base layer.

7.  C. Optional parameters can be set up on the client and/or the database server. These optional parameters are kept in the sqlnet.ora file. Tnsnames.ora contains names resolution information, and sdns.ora contains names server information.

8.  D. The Internet Inter-Orb protocol (IIOP) is used to facilitate connections across the Internet.

**9.** A, C. Users can elect to terminate their own sessions. Exiting SQL*Plus is one example of user termination. A connection can also be disconnected by an expiration time. This is the case when a client abnormally disconnects from an application and the server process remains active on the server. If dead connection detect is enabled, these rouge server processes will be detected and killed. There are no default or automatic disconnect options available.

**10.** B. This would be an example of the external naming option. External naming is when third-party software is used to resolve service names.

**11.** C. Local and global sessions are incorrect. There are no such session types. A dispatcher session is not a form of dedicated session. Bequeath sessions are sessions where the listener passes control (hence the name bequeath) to a process that the listener spawns.

**12.** B. This is a question dealing with the Net8 architecture. Net8 is divided into a series of layers, with each layer responsible for some aspect of network activity. The layer that is closest to the user is the layer that is responsible for displaying the application. So, the application layer is correct. The call interface layer and two-task common layers are valid, but incorrect.

**13.** C. The OCI layer is below the application layer and above the two-task common (TTC) layer. The call interface handles such things as cursor management and SQL execution. This information is passed on to the two-task common layer.

**14.** E. Datatype conversions are handled by the Two-Task Common (TTC) layer. These conversions can happen when the client and server are running different character sets. The TTC layer compensates for these character set differences.

**15.** D. The OCI is not responsible for break management. This is handled by the TNS (Transparent Network Substrate) layer. Character set translations are managed by the TTC (Two-Task Common) layer. The OCI layer does not directly interface with the user. The application layer serves that purpose. The OCI layer manages and processes SQL statements.

16. A. Some of the protocols supported by Net8 include: TCP/IP, DECnet, SPX/IPX, and LU6.2. Answers B to E are not valid protocols.

17. D. When two servers need to communicate with one another, for example, across a database link, another layer of the Net8 stack manages this communication. The Network Program Interface (NPI) functions in much the same way as the OCI layer does. This layer accomodates the construction of server-to-server SQL calls.

18. C. The Oracle Protocol Adapters (OPA) allow interaction with industry standard protocols, such as TCP/IP and IPX. The adapters provide and interface for Net8 to these protocols. This layer does not have any direct database interaction nor does it contain sublayers. The NPI is responsible for server calls. The phrase "Interfaces directly with TCP/IP" best describes the OPA.

19. D. Become familiar with the abbreviations of the Net8 layers. The only choice that is not valid is OPI because it is not a valid layer of the Net8 stack.

20. C. The Two-Task Common layer (TTC) is responsible for compensating for differences in the client-to-server or server-to-server character sets. An example would be two servers, one 7-bit ASCII and one 8-bit ASCII, involved in a distributed transactional environment. The Two-Task Common layer would provide the necessary conversion between the two disparate character sets.

# Chapter

# 13

# Configuring Oracle8i Net8 on the Server

**ORACLE8i NETWORK ADMINISTRATION EXAM OBJECTIVES OFFERED IN THIS CHAPTER:**

✓ Define the Net8 Listener.

✓ List the responsibilities of the listener.

✓ Compare and contrast dedicated, prespawned, and dispatched connections.

✓ Configure the listener using the Net8 Assistant.

✓ Describe and interpret the contents of the `listener.ora` file.

✓ Explain the `lsnrctl` command line utility.

✓ Stop and start the listener.

✓ Display the list of services and the status of the listener.

✓ List and define the `lsnrctl SET` commands.

✓ Define and configure Autoregistration.

Exam objectives are subject to change at any time without prior notice and at Oracle's sole discretion. Please visit Oracle's Training and Certification Web site (`http://education .oracle.com/certification/index.html`) for the most current exam objectives listing.

he DBA must configure the Oracle Server to allow for client connections. This chapter will focus on configuring the basic elements of the Oracle Server. We'll discuss ways to manage and configure the main Oracle Server network component and the listener process, as well as how to use the Net8 Assistant and the lsnrctl command line utility. We'll also discuss the Autoregistration feature, which was introduced in Oracle8i to allow instances to automatically register with listeners on an Oracle Server.

# The Oracle Listener

The Oracle *listener* is the main server-side Oracle networking component that allows connectivity to an Oracle database. As stated in Chapter 12, you can think of the listener as a big ear that listens for connection requests. A client connection can be initiated from the same machine the listener resides on, or may come from some remote location.

The listener listens for connection requests to Oracle services. The Oracle service is part of the connection descriptor information supplied by the process requesting a connection. The service name resolves to an Oracle database. The listener can listen for any number of databases configured on the server.

The listener file is configured using a centralized file called *listener.ora*. There is one listener.ora file configured per machine. Later in the chapter, we will discuss the content and structure of the listener.ora file.

There can be multiple listeners configured on a single server. You may configure multiple listeners to balance connection requests and minimize the burden of connections on a single listener. The listener.ora file contains all of the configuration information for every listener configured on the server.

The listener is able to listen for requests being transported on a variety of protocols, such as TCP/IP, DECnet, and SPX/IPX.

Every listener is a named process that is running on the server. The default name of the Oracle listener is LISTENER. If you configure multiple listeners, each one would have a unique name.

## How Do Listeners Respond to Connection Requests?

In Chapter 12, we discussed the way that the listener responds to connection requests. The listener can spawn a new process and pass control of the client session to this new process. This is called a dedicated connection (see Figure 12.6 in Chapter 12). Another name for this connection is the bequeath connection. Figure 13.1 shows the connection process for the dedicated connection steps listed here:

1. The client contacts the Oracle Server after resolving the service name.

2. The server spawns a dedicated process and bequeaths control of the connection to the process.

3. The server process manages the client requests.

**FIGURE 13.1** Dedicated connection process

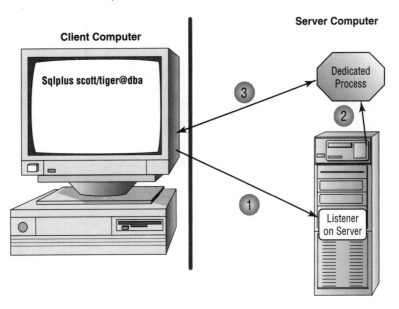

The listener can redirect the user to a process that already exists (see Figure 12.7 in Chapter 12). This is called a prespawned dedicated session (see Figure 13.2). Clients will be connected to prespawned sessions before the listener will start to spawn new processes. These prespawned processes take up system resources, but allow for faster connect times. The following are the prespawed connection steps:

1. When started, the listener spawns a number of server processes.

2. After resolving the net service name, the client contacts the Oracle Server.

3. The listener redirects the client to one of the prespawned processes.

4. The prespawned server process now manages the client connection.

**FIGURE 13.2** Prespawned connection process

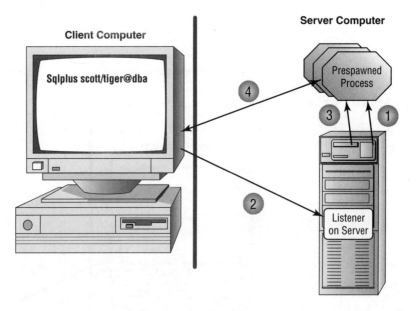

In a multithreaded connection, the listener can redirect the user to a process called a dispatcher (see Figure 12.8 in Chapter 12). If Multithreaded Server is configured, this is the default connection type. The following steps are illustrated in Figure 13.3:

1. Dispatcher processes are spawned when instance is started.

2. The client contacts the Oracle Server after resolving the service name.

3. The server redirects the client connection to the least busy dispatcher.

4. The dispatcher process manages the client server requests.

5. The dispatcher registers connection information with the listener.

**FIGURE 13.3** Multithreaded connection process

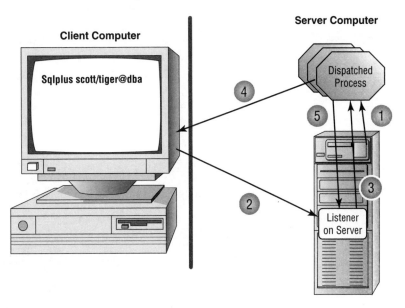

# Starting and Using the Net8 Assistant

**N**et8 Assistant is a tool used to create and manage most client- and server-side configuration files. The Net8 Assistant has evolved from the Oracle7 tool, Network Manager, to the latest Oracle8i 8.1.5 version, which is written in Java. The first Java release of the Net8 tool was in Oracle8 and was at times a bit challenging to work with. The Oracle8i release has been retooled to allow for a consistent look and feel across platforms and is a more stable product.

We strongly recommend using the Net8 Assistant for creating and managing all of your network files. These files need to be in a specific format, and the Net8 Assistant ensures the files are created in that format. Failure to put the files in the correct format can result in problems with your network connections. Something as subtle as an extra space or tab can cause problems with network connections. So if you were used to "cutting and pasting" old entries to create new entries in these files, it is better now to use Net8 Assistant to create new entries.

If you are using a Windows NT environment, you can start the Net8 Assistant by running: Start ➤ Programs ➤ *Your Oracle8i Programs choice* ➤ Network Administration ➤ Net8 Assistant.

In a UNIX environment, it can be started by running `./netasst` from your `$ORACLE_HOME/bin` directory.

Figure 13.4 shows the Net8 Assistant opening page.

**FIGURE 13.4** Net8 Assistant opening page

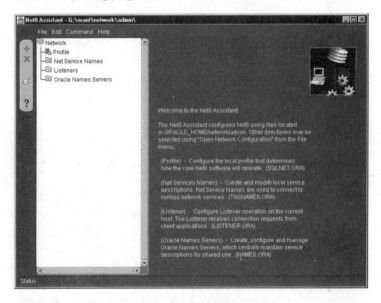

# Configuring the Listener Using the Net8 Assistant

You will want to use the Net8 Assistant to configure the listener. As stated earlier, the Net8 Assistant provides an easy-to-use graphical interface for configuring most of the network files you will be using. Using Net8 Assistant will ensure that the files are created in a consistent format, which will reduce connection problems.

When you first start the Net8 Assistant, the opening screen displays a list of icons down the right-hand side of the screen under the Network folder. The choices under the Network folder relate to different network configuration files. Table 13.1 shows the different network file choices and what each configures.

**TABLE 13.1**  Files Configured by the Net8 Assistant Icons

| Icon | File Configured |
| --- | --- |
| Profile | sqlnet.ora |
| Net Service Names | tnsnames.ora |
| Listeners | listener.ora |
| Oracle Names Servers | names.ora |

## Creating the Listener

The first step in configuring the listener with Net8 Assistant is to create the listener definition. The Net8 Assistant has a wizard interface for creating most of the basic network elements, such as the listener.ora and tnsnames.ora files.

Follow these steps to create the listener:

1. Click the Listener icon

2. Click the Plus sign icon or select Create from the Edit menu.

**3.** The Choose Listener Name dialog box appears. If this is the first listener being created, the Net8 Assistant defaults to LISTENER as the name. Click OK if this is correct or enter a new name.

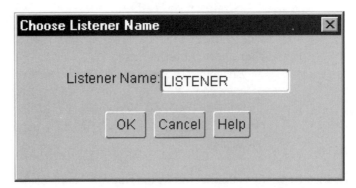

**4.** After you have chosen a name for the listener, you are presented with the screen shown in Figure 13.5. To configure the listening locations, click the Listening Locations drop-down list box and make your selection. Then click the Add Address button at the bottom of the screen.

**FIGURE 13.5** Listening Locations screen

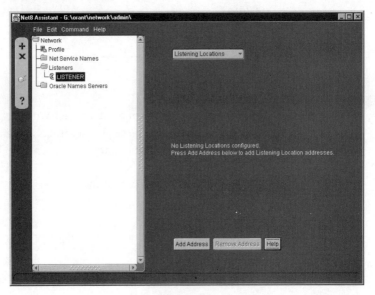

**5.** A new screen appears on the right side of Net8 Assistant. Depending on your protocol, the prompts will be somewhat different. By default, the TCP/IP protocol information is displayed. If you are using the TCP/IP protocol, Host and *Port* information is filled in for you. The Host is the name of the machine where the listener is running, and the Port is the listening location for TCP/IP connections. The default value for the Port is 1521. (The Port default was 1526 for older versions of SQL*Net. This Port default may change in a future release.) The Net8 Clients choice should be selected in the Protocol Stack Support field (see Figure 13.6).

**FIGURE 13.6** Add listening locations information

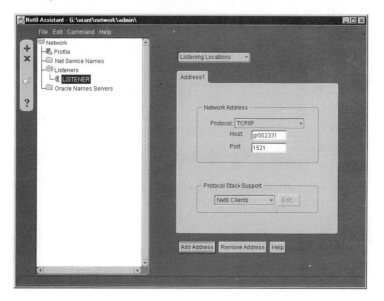

**6.** Save your information by selecting File ➤ Save Network Configuration. After saving your information, look in the directory where it was saved.

You always know where the files are stored by looking at the top banner of the Net8 Assistant screen.

The Net8 Assistant actually creates three files in this process: listener.ora, tnsnames.ora, and sqlnet.ora. The tnsnames.ora and sqlnet.ora do not contain any information. The sqlnet.ora file may contain a few entries at this point, but these can be ignored for right now. The listener.ora file will contain information as shown in the code listed below. We will discuss the structure and content of the listener.ora file later on in the chapter.

```
# C:\V8I\NETWORK\ADMIN\LISTENER.ORA Configuration
# File:C:\v8i\NETWORK\ADMIN\listener.ora
# Generated by Oracle Net8 Assistant

LISTENER =
  (DESCRIPTION =
    (ADDRESS = (PROTOCOL = TCP)(HOST = gr99c0073)(PORT =
1521))
    (PROTOCOL_STACK =
      (PRESENTATION = TTC)
      (SESSION = NS)
    )
  )
```

## Adding Additional Protocols to a Listener

A listener can listen for multiple protocols. For example, if clients can connect to the Oracle Server using TCP/IP and SPX/IPX, a single listener could accommodate both kinds of connections.

To configure a listener with another protocol, choose the Listening Locations value from the drop-down list box at the top right of the screen and click the Add Address button at the bottom of the screen. A new Address2 tab will appear. Fill in the details for the new protocol type. Table 13.2 shows the other protocols and the prompts for each.

**TABLE 13.2** Protocol Prompt Summary from Net8 Assistant

| Protocol | Parameter | Definition |
|----------|-----------|------------|
| IPC | KEY | Normally set to Listener Name. |

**TABLE 13.2**  Protocol Prompt Summary from Net8 Assistant

| Protocol | Parameter | Definition |
|---|---|---|
| Named Pipes | SERVER | Name of server. |
| | PIPE | Name of pipe to connect to server. Can be the same as SERVER. |
| SPX/IPX | SERVICE | Name of Oracle Service. |
| TCP/IP | PORT | Listening Location. Default is 1521. |
| | HOST | Hostname of machine where listener resides. |

The following code is an example of a `listener.ora` file configured to listen for TCP/IP connections and SPX/IPX connections used in a Novell environment:

```
# C:\V8I\NETWORK\ADMIN\LISTENER.ORA Configuration
# File:C:\v8i\NETWORK\ADMIN\listener.ora
# Generated by Oracle Net8 Assistant

LISTENER =
  (DESCRIPTION_LIST =
    (DESCRIPTION =
      (ADDRESS = (PROTOCOL = TCP)(HOST = gr99c0073)
      (PORT = 1521))
      (PROTOCOL_STACK =
        (PRESENTATION = TTC)
        (SESSION = NS)
      )
    )
    (DESCRIPTION =
      (ADDRESS = (PROTOCOL = SPX)(SERVICE = DBA))
      (PROTOCOL_STACK =
        (PRESENTATION = TTC)
        (SESSION = NS)
      )
    )
  )
```

## Adding Service Name Information to the Listener

After the listener has been created with the name, protocol, and listening location information, you define the network services that the listener is responsible for connecting users to. There is no limit to the number of network service names that a listener can listen for.

The steps to add the service name information are as follows:

1. Select the listener to configure by clicking the Listeners icon and highlighting the name of the listener you wish to configure.

2. After selecting the listener, choose Database Services from the dropdown list box at the top right of the screen.

3. Click the Add Database button at the bottom of the screen.

4. Enter values in the prompts for Global Database Name, Oracle Home Directory, and SID. The SID and the global database name are the same if you are using a flat naming convention. See Figure 13.7. We will discuss flat and hierarchical naming conventions in the next chapter.

5. If you want to configure prespawned dedicated server processes, click the Use Prespawned Dedicated Servers option.

**FIGURE 13.7** Add Services screen

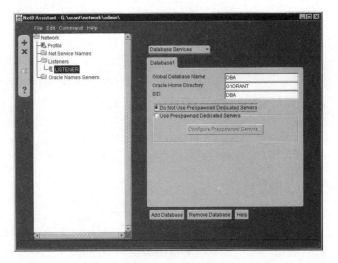

**6.** Prespawned dedicated servers can be configured for variety of protocols. Choose the protocol to configure. TCP/IP is chosen by default.
Select the number of prespawned processes you would like the listener
to maintain. This is called the pool size.

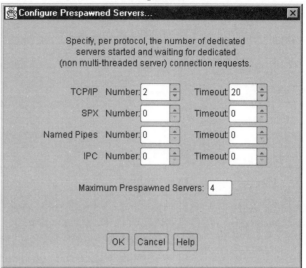

**7.** Choose the timeout value. This value specifies how long a dedicated
prespawned process will remain active after a user has disconnected
from it. A value of zero means the process will remain active indefinitely. This only applies to prespawned processes after they have had
an active connection and the connection has terminated.

**8.** Finally, choose the maximum number of prespawned processes the listener can maintain. This number must be at least the total number of your
`pool_size`.

**9.** Click File ➢ Save to save your configuration. The following code shows
the result of the changes that have been made to the `listener.ora` file:

Comments have been added to the `listener.ora` file below for clarification.

```
# C:\V8I\NETWORK\ADMIN\LISTENER.ORA Configuration
# File:C:\v8i\NETWORK\ADMIN\listener.ora
# Generated by Oracle Net8 Assistant
```

```
LISTENER =
  (DESCRIPTION =
    (ADDRESS = (PROTOCOL = TCP)(HOST = gr99c0073)
    (PORT = 1521))
    (PROTOCOL_STACK =
      (PRESENTATION = TTC)
      (SESSION = NS)
    )
  )

SID_LIST_LISTENER =
  (SID_LIST =
    (SID_DESC =
      (GLOBAL_DBNAME = DBA)
      (ORACLE_HOME = c:\orant)
      (SID_NAME = DBA)
      (PRESPAWN_MAX = 4) - Maximum  prespawned processes
      (PRESPAWN_LIST =
        (PRESPAWN_DESC =
          (PROTOCOL = TCP) -> Use TCP/IP for
                                    prespawned processes
          (POOL_SIZE = 2) -> Keep 2 TCP/IP
                                    prespawned processes
  (TIMEOUT = 2) -> 2 minute timeout for
                      terminated prespawns
        )
      )
    )
  )
```

Table 13.3 describes each of the `listener.ora` parameters for the Listening Location section of the `listener.ora` file.

**TABLE 13.3** Description of `listener.ora` Parameters for the Listening Location Section of the File

| Parameter | Description |
| --- | --- |
| LISTENER | Indicates the starting point of a listener definition. This is actually the name of the listener being defined. The default name is LISTENER. |
| DESCRIPTION | Describes each of the listening locations. |
| ADDRESS | Starts an Address definition. |
| PROTOCOL | Designates the protocol for this listening location. |
| HOST | Name of the machine the listener resides on. |
| PORT | Address the listener is listening on. |
| PROTOCOL STACK | Defines the client type that will use this listener. This defines the interface type and determines what session layers will be used, for example TNS or IIOP for internet connections. |
| PRESENTATION | Defines the presentation. For typical network clients, this will be set to TTC (Two Task common). For internet sessions, this will be set to IIOP. |
| SESSION | Describes this as a Network Session (NS). This would be a typical client/server connection. |

## Adding Additional Listeners

To add more listeners, follow the steps outlined above. Listeners must have unique names and listen on separate ports, so give the listener a new name and assign it to a different Port, for example 1522. You also must assign service names to the listener. The following code shows an example of two configured listeners, one called LISTENER and one called LISTENER1, both listening for TCP/IP connections. Notice that each listener has a separate section for listening locations and service names and that the name of the listener is appended to the `sid_list` definition so we know which service names belong each listener definition.

```
# C:\V8I\NETWORK\ADMIN\LISTENER.ORA Configuration
# File:C:\v8i\NETWORK\ADMIN\listener.ora
# Generated by Oracle Net8 Assistant

LISTENER1 =
  (DESCRIPTION =
    (ADDRESS = (PROTOCOL = TCP)(HOST = gr99c0073)
    (PORT = 1522))
    (PROTOCOL_STACK =
      (PRESENTATION = TTC)
      (SESSION = NS)
    )
  )

LISTENER =
  (DESCRIPTION =
    (ADDRESS = (PROTOCOL = TCP)(HOST = gr99c0073)
    (PORT = 1521))
    (PROTOCOL_STACK =
      (PRESENTATION = TTC)
      (SESSION = NS)
    )
  )

SID_LIST_LISTENER1 =
  (SID_LIST =
    (SID_DESC =
      (GLOBAL_DBNAME = PROD)
      (ORACLE_HOME = C:\V8I)
      (SID_NAME = PROD)
    )
  )
```

```
SID_LIST_LISTENER =
  (SID_LIST =
    (SID_DESC =
      (GLOBAL_DBNAME = DBA)
      (ORACLE_HOME = c:\orant)
      (SID_NAME = DBA)
    )
  )
```

## Optional *listener.ora* Parameters

You can set optional parameters that add functionality to the listener. Additional parameters are added by choosing the General Parameters drop-down list box at the top right of the screen. Table 13.4 describes the additional parameters and where they can be found in the Net8 Assistant.

The optional parameters also have the listener name appended to them so you can tell which listener definition they belong to. For example, if the parameter STARTUP_WAIT_TIME is set for the default listener, the parameter created is START_WAIT_TIME_LISTENER.

**TABLE 13.4**    Optional `listener.ora` Parameter Definitions

| Net8 Assistant Prompt | listener.ora Parameter | Description |
| --- | --- | --- |
| Startup Wait Time | STARTUP_WAIT_TIME | How long a listener will wait to respond to a STATUS command in the `lsnrctl` command line utility. |
| Connect Timeout | CONNECT_TIMEOUT | Defines how long a listener will wait for a valid response for a client once a session is initiated. The default is 10 seconds. |

**TABLE 13.4** Optional `listener.ora` Parameter Definitions *(continued)*

| Net8 Assistant Prompt | `listener.ora` Parameter | Description |
|---|---|---|
| Save configuration on shutdown | SAVE_CONFIG_ON_STOP | Specifies whether modifications made during a `lsnrctl` session should be saved when exiting. |
| Register Services with Oracle names | USE_PLUG_AND_PLAY | This specifies whether a listener will register information with a well known Names Server. Only valid when using the Version 2 Dynamic Discovery option. |
| SNMP contact information | None | Message to send when using SNMP. |
| Log File | LOG_FILE–Will not be in `listener.ora` file if default setting is used. By default, listener logging is enabled with the log created in the default location. | Specifies where a listener will write log information. This is ON by default and defaults to %ORACLE_HOME%\network\log\listener.log. |
| Trace Level | TRACE_LEVEL–Not present if tracing is disabled. Default is OFF. | If tracing listener connections, this sets the level of detail. Valid values: Off, User, Support, Admin. |
| Trace File | TRACE_FILE | Location of listener trace information. Defaults to %ORACLE_HOME\network\trace\listener.trc. |

**TABLE 13.4** Optional `listener.ora` Parameter Definitions *(continued)*

| Net8 Assistant Prompt | listener.ora Parameter | Description |
|---|---|---|
| Require a Password for listener operations | PASSWORDS | Password required to perform administrative tasks in the lsnrctl command line utility. |

# Managing the Listener Using *lsnrctl*

Once you have created and saved the listener definition, you need to start the listener. The listener must be started before clients can connect to it and request database connections. The listener cannot be started or stopped from the Net8 Assistant.

The listener is started using the command line tool *lsnrctl*. Other Oracle network components, such as Oracle Names Server and Connection Manager, have command line tools that are used to stop and start the associated processes.

On Windows NT, the listener runs as a service. Services are programs that run in the background on Windows NT. You can start the listener from the Windows NT Services panel. Choose Start ➤ Settings ➤ Control Panel ➤ Services. Then select the name of the listener service from the list of services. If your %ORACLE_HOME% directory was ORANT and the name of your listener was Listener, you would look for a name such as Orant-TNSListener. Highlight the listener name and choose Start.

The lsnrctl utility is located in the %ORACLE_HOME%\bin directory on Windows NT and in $ORACLE_HOME/bin on UNIX systems. Windows NT users familiar with earlier releases of Oracle will notice that utility names no longer have version extensions. For example in Oracle8, the tool was called lsnrctl80. All of the tools now have a consistent name across platforms, so the version extensions have been dropped to comply with this.

Type **lsnrctl** at the command line. The code below shows what a login screen looks like:

```
Microsoft(R) Windows NT(TM)
(C) Copyright 1985-1996 Microsoft Corp.
```

```
C:\>lsnrctl

LSNRCTL for 32-bit Windows: Version 8.1.5.0.0
 - Production on 08-FEB-00 07:52:14

(c) Copyright 1998 Oracle Corporation.  All rights
    reserved.

Welcome to LSNRCTL, type "help" for information.

LSNRCTL>
```

## Starting the Listener

The listener has commands to perform various functions. Type **help** at the LSNRCTL> prompt to get a list of the commands. To start the default listener named LISTENER, type **start** at the prompt. If you want to start a different listener, you would have to type in the listener name after **start**. For example, *start listener1* would start the LISTENER1 listener. The following code shows the results of starting the listener:

```
LSNRCTL> start
Starting tnslsnr: please wait...

Service Oraclev8iTNSListener start pending.
Service Oraclev8iTNSListener started.
TNSLSNR for 32-bit Windows: Version 8.1.5.0.0
        - Production
System parameter file is C:\v8i\network\admin
                              \listener.ora
Log messages written to C:\v8i\network\log
                              \listener.log

Listening on:
(DESCRIPTION=(ADDRESS=(PROTOCOL=TCP)(HOST=gr99c0073)
            (PORT=1521))(PROTOCOL_
STACK=(PRESENTATION=TTC)(SESSION=NS)))
```

```
Connecting to (DESCRIPTION=(ADDRESS=(PROTOCOL=TCP)
                (HOST=gr99c0073)(PORT=1521))(P
ROTOCOL_STACK=(PRESENTATION=TTC)(SESSION=NS)))
STATUS of the LISTENER
------------------------
Alias        LISTENER
Version      TNSLSNR for 32-bit Windows:
             Version 8.1.5.0.0 - production
Start Date   08-FEB-00 09:40:43
Uptime       0 days 0 hr. 0 min. 2 sec
Trace Level              off
Security                 OFF
SNMP                     OFF
Listener Parameter File  C:\v8i\network\admin
                            \listener.ora
Listener Log File        C:\v8i\network\log\listener.log
Services Summary...
   DBA          has 1 service handler(s)
   PROD         has 1 service handler(s)
The command completed successfully
```

This listing shows a summary of information presented, such as the services the listener is listening for, the log locations, and whether tracing is enabled for the listener.

## Reloading the Listener

If the listener is running and modifications are made to the listener.ora file either manually or with Net8 Assistant, the listener has to be reloaded to refresh the listener with the most current information. The RELOAD command will reread the listener.ora file for the new definitions. It is not necessary to stop and start the listener. The following code shows an example of the RELOAD command. Stopping and restarting the listener can also accomplish a reload, but using the RELOAD command is better because the listener is not actually stopped. Reloading the listener has no effect on clients connected to the Oracle Server.

```
LSNRCTL> reload
```

```
Connecting to
(DESCRIPTION=(ADDRESS=(PROTOCOL=TCP)(HOST=gr99c0073)
                (PORT=1521))(
PROTOCOL_STACK=(PRESENTATION=TTC)(SESSION=NS)))
The command completed successfully
LSNRCTL>
```

## Showing the Status of the Listener

You can display the status of the listener by using the STATUS command. The STATUS command shows if the listener is active, the locations of the logs and trace files, how long the listener has been running, and the services for the listener. This is a quick way to verify that the listener is up and running with no problems. The code below shows the result of the lsnrctl STATUS command.

```
C:\>lsnrctl status

LSNRCTL for 32-bit Windows: Version 8.1.5.0.0
                - Production on 08-FEB-00 13:48:26


(c) Copyright 1998 Oracle Corporation.
    All rights reserved.

Connecting to
(DESCRIPTION=(ADDRESS=(PROTOCOL=TCP)(HOST=gr99c0073)
                (PORT=1521))
(PROTOCOL_STACK=(PRESENTATION=TTC)(SESSION=NS)))
STATUS of the LISTENER
------------------------
Alias                   LISTENER
Version                 TNSLSNR for 32-bit Windows:
                        Version 8.1.5.0.0 - Production
Start Date              08-FEB-00 13:48:20
Uptime                  0 days 0 hr. 0 min. 7 sec
Trace Level             off
Security                OFF
SNMP                    OFF
```

```
Listener Parameter File    C:\v8i\network\admin
                              \listener.ora
Listener Log File          C:\v8i\network\log\listener.log
Services Summary...
   DBA           has 1 service handler(s)
   PROD          has 1 service handler(s)
The command completed successfully
```

## Listing the Services for the Listener

The lsnrctl SERVICES command displays information about the services, such as whether or not the services have any dedicated prespawned server processes or dispatched processes associated with them, and how many connections have been accepted and rejected per service. Use this method to check if a listener is listening for a particular service. The following code shows an example of running the SERVICES command.

```
Lsnrctl> services

LSNRCTL for 32-bit Windows: Version 8.1.5.0.0
          - Production on 08-FEB-00 14:15:16

(c) Copyright 1998 Oracle Corporation.  All rights
                                        reserved.

Connecting to
(DESCRIPTION=(ADDRESS=(PROTOCOL=TCP)(HOST=gr99c0073)
          (PORT=1521))
(PROTOCOL_STACK=(PRESENTATION=TTC)(SESSION=NS)))
Services Summary...
   DBA           has 1 service handler(s)
     DEDICATED SERVER established:0 refused:0
       LOCAL SERVER
   PROD          has 1 service handler(s)
     DEDICATED SERVER established:0 refused:0
       LOCAL SERVER
The command completed successfully
```

## Other Commands in *lsnrctl*

There are other commands that can be run in lsnrctl. Table 13.5 shows a summary of the other commands. Type the command at the lsnrctl prompt to execute it.

**TABLE 13.5** Summary of the lsnrctl Commands

| Command | Definition |
|---|---|
| CHANGE_PASSWORD | Allows a user to change the password needed to stop the listener. |
| DBSNMP_STOP | Stops the Oracle Intelligent Agent. |
| DBSNMP_START | Starts the Oracle Intelligent Agent. |
| DBSNMP_STATUS | Shows the status of the Oracle Intelligent Agent. |
| DEBUG LISTENER | Attempts to contact the listener. If successful, returns "Not an error." |
| EXIT | Exits the lsnrctl utility. |
| QUIT | Same as EXIT. |
| RELOAD | Rereads listener.ora file without stopping the listener. Used to refresh the listener if changes are made to the file. |
| SAVE_CONFIG | Makes a copy of the listener.ora file called listener.bak when changes are made to the listener.ora file from lsnrctl. |
| SERVICES LISTENER | Lists a summary of services and details information on the number of connections established and the number of connections refused for each protocol service handler. |
| START LISTENER | Starts the named listener. |
| STATUS LISTENER | Shows the status of the named listener. |

**TABLE  13.5**   Summary of the `lsnrctl` Commands *(continued)*

| Command | Definition |
|---|---|
| STOP LISTENER | Stops the named listener. |
| TEST LISTENER | Same as DEBUG LISTENER. |
| TRACE | Turns on tracing for the listener. |
| VERSION | Displays the version of the Net8 software and protocol adapters. |

## SET Commands in *lsnrctl*

The `lsnrctl` utility also has commands called SET commands. These commands are issued by typing *set <commandname>* at the LSNRCTL> prompt. The SET commands are used to make modifications to the `listener.ora` file, such as setting up logging and tracing. Most of these parameters can be set using the Net8 Assistant. To display the current setting of a parameter, use the SHOW command. SHOW is used to display the current settings of the parameters set using the SET command. Table 13.6 shows a summary of the `lsnrctl` SET Commands. If you just type in **set** or **show**, you will see a listing of all of the commands.

**TABLE  13.6**   Summary of the `lsnrctl` SET Commands

| SET Command | Description |
|---|---|
| CURRENT_ LISTENER | Sets the listener to make modifications to or show the name of the current listener. |
| CONNECT_ TIMEOUT | Defines how long a listener will wait for a valid response for a client once a session is initiated. The default is 10 seconds. |
| DISPLAYMODE | Sets display for lsnrctl utility to RAW, COMPACT, NORMAL, or VERBOSE. |
| LOG_STATUS | Shows whether logging is on or off for the listener. |

**TABLE 13.6** Summary of the lsnrctl SET Commands *(continued)*

| SET Command | Description |
| --- | --- |
| LOG_FILE | Shows the name of listener log file. |
| LOG_DIRECTORY | Shows the log directory location. |
| RAWMODE | Shows more detail on STATUS and SERVICES when set to ON. Values: ON or OFF. |
| STARTUP_ WAITTIME | Sets the length of time a listener will wait to respond to a STATUS command in the lsnrctl command line utility. |
| SAVE_CONFIG_ ON_STOP | Saves changes to the listener.ora file when exiting lsnrctl. |
| TRC_LEVEL | Sets the trace level to OFF, USER, ADMIN, SUPPORT. |
| TRC_FILE | Sets the name of the listener trace file. |
| TRC_DIRECTORY | Sets the name of the listener trace directory. |
| USE_ PLUGANDPLAY | Enables listener to register services with well-known Names Servers. |

## Stopping the Listener

In order to stop the listener, you must issue the *lsnrctl stop* command. This command will stop the default listener. To stop a nondefault listener, include the name of the listener. For example, to stop the LISTENER1, type **lsnrctl stop listener1**. If you are in the lsnrctl> facility, you will stop whatever listener is the current listener defined by the current_listener setting. Use the SHOW command to see what it is set to. The default value is LISTENER.

Stopping the listener does not affect clients connected to the database. It only means that no new connections can use this listener until the listener is restarted. The following code shows what the STOP command looks like:

```
LSNRCTL> stop
Connecting to (DESCRIPTION=(ADDRESS=(PROTOCOL=TCP)
            (HOST=gr99c0073)(PORT=1521))
(PROTOCOL_STACK=(PRESENTATION=TTC)(SESSION=NS)))
The command completed successfully
LSNRCTL>
```

# New Feature: Automatic Registration of Services

**O**racle8i has a new feature that allows an Oracle Server to automatically pass service information to a listener. The instance will register with the listener defined on the local machine. *Automatic instance registration* allows you to take advantage of other new Oracle8i Net8 features such as load balancing and automatic failover. These will be discussed in Chapter 14.

When automatic registration is used, you will not see the service listed in the `listener.ora` file. Run the `lsnrctl SERVICES` command and you should see the service listed. If the listener is started after the Oracle instance, there may be a time lag before the instance actually registers information with the listener.

In order for an instance to automatically register with a listener, the listener must be configured as a default listener, or you must specify the `init.ora` parameter LOCAL_LISTENER. The LOCAL_LISTENER parameter defines the location of the listener that you want the Oracle Server to register with. A default listener definition is show below:

```
Listener Name = LISTENER
Port = 1521
Protocol = TCP/IP
```

Here is an example of the LOCAL_LISTENER parameter used to register the Oracle Server with a non-default listener:

```
local_listener="(ADDRESS_LIST = (Address =
(Protocol = TCP) (Host=weishan) (Port=1522)))"
```

In the example above, the Oracle Server will register with the listener listening on Port 1522 using the TCP/IP protocol. This is a non-default Port location, so you must use the LOCAL_LISTENER parameter in order for the registration to take place.

Two other new `init.ora` parameters need to be configured to allow an instance to register information with the listener. There are two new parameters used to allow automatic registration, `instance_name` and `service_names`.

The `instance_name` parameter is set to the name of the Oracle instance you would like to register with the listener. The `service_name` parameter is a combination of the instance name and the domain name. The domain name is set to the value of the DB_DOMAIN initialization parameter. For example, if your

DB_DOMAIN is set to GR.COM and your Oracle instance was DBA, the parameters would be set as follows:

```
Instance_name = DBA
Service_names = DBA.GR.COM
```

If you are not using domain names, the instance_name and service_names parameters should be set to the same values.

# Summary

**Y**ou can connect to an Oracle Server using dedicated, prespawned, or dispatched processes. With a dedicated connection, each Oracle session is served by its own server process, which is created when the client connects to the Oracle Server. With prespawned processes, a pool of Oracle Server processes are started when the listener is started. When a client requests a connection, they are redirected to one of the existing prespawned process. In a Multithreaded Server environment, client connections are served by dispatcher processes. A dispatcher process can service requests from many clients.

The listener process serves as a big ear, listening for client connection requests. When a client needs to get connected to an Oracle Server, it contacts the listener, and the listener will connect the client in one of the three methods mentioned above. The listener then continues to listen for other client connection requests.

You configure the listener by using the Net8 Assistant. The Net8 Assistant provides a graphical interface for creating most of the Net8 files you will use for Oracle. When you create the listener, you must decide on a name for the listener, the listening location of the listener, and what services the listener will be listening for. This is all configured using the Net8 Assistant. This process creates the listener.ora file, which is the configuration file for the listener. The file contains information about the listener's listening locations, the services the listener is listening for, and optional listener parameters. There is one listener.ora file per server. If multiple listeners are configured, each one will have a separate entry in the listener.ora file.

You stop and start the listener using the lsnrctl command line utility. This utility also provides commands to check the status of the listener and make modifications to the listener.ora file. The lsnrctl SET and SHOW commands allow you to see the current settings for the listener and make modifications to listener settings.

Oracle 8i provides a new feature called Autoregistration. This feature allows an Oracle instance to automatically register itself with a listener. The listener must be configured with the TCP/IP protocol and listening on Port 1521. It also must have the default name of LISTENER. You have to set the parameters `instance_name` and `service_name` in the `init.ora` file for the Oracle instance to enable Autoregistration.

# Key Terms

**B**efore you take the exam, make sure you're familiar with the following terms:

listener

`listener.ora`

Port

`lsnrctl`

`lsnrctl stop`

Automatic Instance Registration

# Review Questions

1. Which file must be present on the Oracle Server to start the Oracle listener?

   A. `listener.ora`

   B. `lsnrctl.ora`

   C. `sqlnet.ora`

   D. `tnsnames.ora`

2. What are the possible ways in which the listener may connect a user to an Oracle instance? (Choose three.)

   A. Prespawned connection

   B. Master/slave connection

   C. Bequeath connection

   D. Multithreaded connection

   E. Multipass connection

3. The default name of the Oracle listener is:

   A. `lsnrctl`

   B. Listen

   C. `sqlnet`

   D. `tnslistener`

   E. None of the above

**4.** What is the maximum number of databases a listener processes can listen for?

**A.** 1 database

**B.** 2 databases

**C.** 10 databases

**D.** 25 databases

**E.** None of the above

**5.** What is the maximum number of `listener.ora` files that should exist on a server?

**A.** one

**B.** two

**C.** four

**D.** eight

**E.** None of the above

**6.** Choose the correct order of steps for the user connection process:

**A.** A listener receives a request.

**B.** A client issues a connect request.

**C.** Start the listener.

**D.** The listener spawns a new process to handle the client request.

**E.** The listener continues listening for connections.

**F.** The session is bequeathed to the spawned process.

**7.** The types of redirect sessions are: (Choose two.)

**A.** Local session

**B.** Dispatcher session

**C.** Prespawned session

**D.** Bequeath session

**E.** IPC session

**8.** Which of the following are *not* default `listener.ora` settings? (Choose two.)

**A.** `Listener name = LISTENER`

**B.** `Port = 1521`

**C.** `Protocol = IPX`

**D.** `Protocol = TCP/IP`

**E.** `Listener name = lsnrctl`

**9.** The command line interface to administer the listener is:

**A.** `LISTENER`

**B.** `lismgr`

**C.** `TCPCTL`

**D.** `lsnrctl`

**E.** None of the above

**10.** Which Net8 Assistant icon should you choose to manage listeners?

**A.** Services

**B.** Listener Names

**C.** Profile

**D.** Listeners

**E.** None of the above

**11.** Which parameter sets the number of seconds a server process waits to get a valid client request?

   **A.** `connect_waittime_`*`listener_name`*

   **B.** `connect_wait_`*`listener_name`*

   **C.** `timeout_`*`listener_name`*

   **D.** `connect_timeout_`*`listener_name`*

**12.** Which of the following is *true* about listener logging?

   **A.** It is on by default.

   **B.** It is off unless we configure the `LOGGING_`*`listener_name`* parameter.

   **C.** It gathers more information than tracing.

   **D.** It cannot be enabled from the Net8 Assistant.

**13.** The maximum number of listeners that can be configured for a server are:

   **A.** One

   **B.** Two

   **C.** Four

   **D.** Eight

   **E.** None of the above

**14.** There is a listener called listenerA. The correct command to start the listener is:

   **A.** `lsnrctl startup listenerA`

   **B.** `lsnrctl start`

   **C.** `listener start`

   **D.** `listener startup`

   **E.** `lsnrctl start listenerA`

**15.** There is a listener called listener. The correct method to start the listener would be:

**A.** `lsnrctl startup listener`

**B.** `lsnrctl start`

**C.** `listener start`

**D.** `listener start listener`

**16.** Modifications have been made to the `listener.ora` file from Net8 Assistant. When will these modifications take effect?

**A.** Immediately

**B.** After exiting the Net8 Assistant

**C.** Upon saving the `listener.ora` file

**D.** After executing `lsnrctl refresh`

**E.** None of the above

**17.** There is a listener called listener1. How would the listener be chosen to make modifications using the `lsnrctl` facility?

**A.** By setting `current_listener listener1`

**B.** By accepting `current_listener listener1`

**C.** By reloading `listener listener1`

**D.** By refreshing `listener listener1`

**18.** Modifications have been made using the `lsnrctl` facility. What must be set to ON in order to make the changes permanent?

**A.** `save_configuration`

**B.** `save_listener.ora`

**C.** `save_config_on_stop`

**D.** `configuration_save`

**19.** The administrator or DBA wants to make a backup of the listener file after making changes using `lsnrctl`. Which command must you implement to make this backup from the `lsnrctl` facility?

**A.** `create_backup`

**B.** `save_config_on_stop`

**C.** `save_config`

**D.** `save_backup`

**20.** The administrator wants to display the setting for one of the listener parameters using the `lsnrctl` facility. What command will accomplish this?

**A.** `DISPLAY`

**B.** `SHOW`

**C.** `PRINT`

**D.** `ECHO`

**E.** None of the above

# Answers to Review Questions

**1.** A. The listener is the process that manages incoming connection requests. The `listener.ora` file is used to configure the listener. The `sqlnet.ora` file is an optional client- and server-side file. The `tnsnames.ora` file is used for doing localnaming resolution. There is no such file as `lsnrctl.ora`.

**2.** A, C, D. The listener can handle a connection request in one of three ways: it can spawn a process and bequeath (pass) control to that process, it can assign the connection to a prespawned process, or it can assign the process to a dispatcher when using Multithreaded Server.

**3.** E. When creating a listener with the Net8 Assistant, the Assistant recommends LISTENER as the default name. When starting and stopping the listener via the command line tool, the tool assumes the name of the listener is LISTENER if no listener name is supplied.

**4.** E. There is no physical limit to the number of services a listener can listen for. So, the answer is again E, none of the above.

**5.** A. Although a listener can listen for an unlimited number of services, only one `listener.ora` file is used. If multiple listeners are configured, there will still be only one listener.

**6.** C, B, A, D, F, E. The correct sequence to process connections is:

1. The listener must be available before any network connections can use it.

2. The client will issue a request to connect to a net service.

3. The listener receives the request.

4. The listener spawns a new dedicated server process.

5. The session is passed on to the new dedicated server.

6. The listener continues to listen for new connection requests.

**7.** C, B.  Answers A and E are incorrect because these are invalid session types. A bequeath session is created when the listener spawns a new process. Prespawned sessions and dispatcher sessions are redirected to existing processes.

**8.** C, E.  A default listener has a name of LISTENER and listens on Port 1521 for TCP/IP connections.

**9.** D.  LISTENER is the default name of the Oracle listener. There is no such utility as lismgr. TCPCTL was actually an old utility used to start and stop the SQL*NET version 1 listener. The lsnrctl command is used to manage the listener.

**10.** D.  Become familiar with the Net8 Assistant interface. Listeners is the correct choice. Profile is used for sqlnet.ora administration. The other choices are not valid menu options.

**11.** D.  When a user makes a connection request, the listener passes control to some server process or dispatcher. Once the user is attached to this process, all negotiations and interaction with the database pass through this process. If the user supplies an invalid user ID or password, the process waits for a period of time for a valid response. If the user does not contact the Server Process with a valid response in the allotted time, the Server Process terminates, and the user must contact the listener so the listener can again spawn a process or redirect the client to an existing prespawned process or dispatcher. This period of time that the process waits is specified by the connect_timeout_*listener_name* parameter. This parameter is specified in seconds.

**12.** A.  By default, listener logging is enabled. A trace will generate significantly more information than a log. Both logging and tracing can be enabled using the Net8 Assistant.

**13.** E.  There is no maximum number of listeners that can be configured per server.

**14.** E. Oracle expects the listener to be called LISTENER by default. The name of the facility to start the listener is lsnrctl. Using lsnrctl start will start the default listener. To start a listener with another name, enter **lsnrctl start *listener_name*.**

**15.** B. As stated earlier, the default listener name is LISTENER. Since this is the default, simply enter lsnrctl start. The name LISTENER is assumed to be the listener to start in this case.

**16.** E. Anytime modifications are made to the listener file using the Net8 Assistant, either manually or using lsnrctl, the listener must be reloaded for the modifications to take effect. Get to a command line and enter **lsnrctl reload**. Stopping and starting the listener will also have the same effect. Since lsnrctl reload is not one of the choices, none of the above is the correct answer.

**17.** A. If you want to administer any listener besides the default listener when using lsnrctl, you must target the listener. SET commands are used to change lsnrctl session settings. So, setting current_ listener listener1 would be the correct method.

**18.** C. Changes made to the listener.ora file in the lsnrctl facility can be made permanent. To make changes permanent, set the save_ config_on_stop option to ON.

**19.** C. The DBA can make a backup of the existing listener.ora file after making modifications to it using lsnrctl. The backup will be named listener.bak. This is done with the save_config option.

**20.** B. Any of the listener options and their current settings can be displayed with the SHOW command. All other choices are invalid options.

# Configuring Oracle8i Net8 for the Client

## ORACLE8i NETWORK ADMINISTRATION EXAM OBJECTIVES OFFERED IN THIS CHAPTER:

- ✓ Define the various client-side names resolution options.
- ✓ Describe the two net service naming models.
- ✓ Define the prerequisites of hostnaming.
- ✓ Configure the hostnaming option.
- ✓ Configure Localnaming on the client using Net8 Assistant.
- ✓ Describe the various `tnsnames.ora` parameters.
- ✓ Define and configure load balancing.
- ✓ Define and configure failover.
- ✓ Troubleshooting client connections.

Exam objectives are subject to change at any time without prior notice and at Oracle's sole discretion. Please visit Oracle's Training and Certification Web site (http://education.oracle.com/certification/index.html) for the most current exam objectives listing.

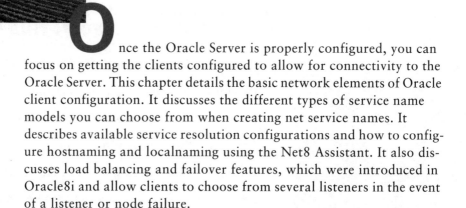

**O**nce the Oracle Server is properly configured, you can focus on getting the clients configured to allow for connectivity to the Oracle Server. This chapter details the basic network elements of Oracle client configuration. It discusses the different types of service name models you can choose from when creating net service names. It describes available service resolution configurations and how to configure hostnaming and localnaming using the Net8 Assistant. It also discusses load balancing and failover features, which were introduced in Oracle8i and allow clients to choose from several listeners in the event of a listener or node failure.

# Client-Side Names Resolution Options

**W**hen a client needs to connect to an Oracle Server, the client must supply three pieces of information: their user ID, password, and net service name. The net service name provides the necessary information, in the form of a connect descriptor, to locate an Oracle service in a network. As we stated in Chapter 12, a connect descriptor describes the path to the Oracle Server and its service name. The service name is an alias for an Oracle database.

You can use a number of different methods to resolve connect descriptor information. This information is kept in different locations depending on the names resolution method that you choose.

The four net service names resolution methods are: hostnaming, localnaming, external naming, and the Oracle Names Server. Normally, you will choose one of these methods, but you can use any combination.

Hostnaming is advantageous when you want to reduce the amount of configuration work necessary. There are prerequisites to using this option that we will talk about later in the chapter. This option is typically used in small networks with few Oracle Servers to maintain.

Localnaming involves configuring the `tnsnames.ora` file. This file contains the connect descriptor information to resolve the net service names. Localnaming is the most popular names resolution method used. You will see how to configure hostnaming and localnaming later in the chapter.

An Oracle Names Server is advantageous in complex networks with many Oracle Servers. The Names Server allows the DBA to configure and manage net service names and connect descriptor information in a central location. We will look at configuring the Names Server in the next chapter.

External naming allows the DBA to use third-party software, such as NDS and NIS, to manage connect descriptor information. It is important to understand that external naming is available, but knowledge of how to configure the various third-party products is not necessary for success on the OCP exam.

# Decide on a Network Service Naming Model

When setting up net service names, you must first decide what kind of naming model you want to use. You can use a flat naming model or a hierarchical-naming model.

In a *flat naming model* (Figure 14.1), every Oracle service name and net service name is unique and all services reside in a single *domain*.

**FIGURE 14.1**  Flat naming model

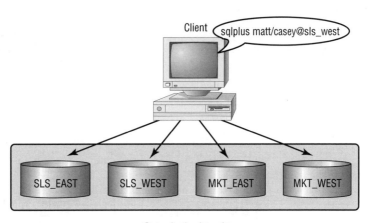

One single domain

A domain is nothing more than a collection of related Oracle services. You can think of a domain as structurally (not functionally) similar to a role in a database. You associate privileges with a role in a database and assign users to the role. This role becomes an aggregate point for privileges. If users need more privileges, you assign the privileges to the role. This level of abstraction makes administering the privileges easier.

Just as a role serves as a way to aggregate privileges, domains serve to aggregate groupings of Oracle services. The domain groups may be defined along logical boundaries, such as grouping similar applications services together, or physical boundaries, such as grouping by geographic locations. Domains can also be grouped together in Net8 and referred to as Administrative Regions. Collections of clients and servers running the same protocol are referred to as a community. Administrative regions and communities are used in the definition of Oracle Names Servers. Configuring the Oracle Names Server is discussed in more detail in Chapter 15.

*Hierarchical naming models* (Figure 14.2) allows multiple domains to maintain an orderly structure to your Oracle services by grouping like services together under each domain. Multiple domains can ease administration of network services and enhance the flexibility of your service naming. You also gain the advantage of being able to specify the same service names in different domains. This isn't possible in a flat naming model with one domain.

**FIGURE 14.2** Hierarchical naming model

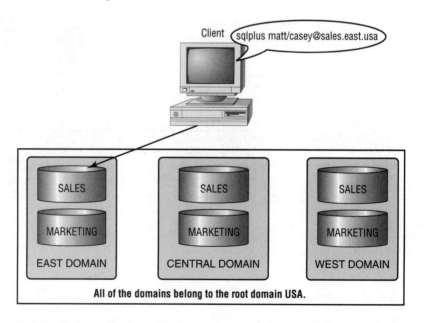

The domains are specified by extensions to the base Oracle net service name. A user can supply the domain information or the domain information can be appended automatically. The parameter NAMES.DEFAULT_DOMAIN in the sqlnet.ora file on the client contains the default domain to append. If a client supplies an unqualified net service name and the NAMES.DEFAULT_ DOMAIN parameter exists, it would be appended to the base net service name. An unqualified service name is a net service name with no extension.

For example, if the net service name of DBA is specified, and the NAMES.DEFAULT_DOMAIN parameter is set to GR.COM, the net service name to resolve is DBA.GR.COM. The following steps show an example of using the NAMES.DEFAULT_DOMAIN parameter:

1. A client enters the following command: **Sqlplus matt/casey@DBA**

2. The DBA has configured the sqlnet.ora file on the client machine with the parameter NAMES.DEFAULT_DOMAIN = GR.COM. This is appended to the net service name of the DBA that was supplied by the client.

3. The client performs a lookup on a net service name of DBA.GR.COM because of the appended default domain.

Oracle has a "Master" domain called WORLD. In earlier releases, the NAMES.DEFAULT_DOMAIN parameter in the sqlnet.ora file was initialized to this value. This caused problems with connections that did not utilize domain names because the WORLD extension was appended to unqualified service names. If you have problems when resolving service names, check the value of this parameter in the sqlnet.ora file. If it is set, remove the parameter and try the connection again. Oracle no longer places this default value in the sqlnet.ora file.

# The Hostnaming Method

In small networks with few Oracle Servers to manage, you can take advantage of hostnaming. Hostnaming saves you from having to do configuration work on the clients, although it does have limitations. There are four prerequisites to using hostnaming:

- You must use TCP/IP as your network protocol.

- You must have a listener defined on the server listening on port 1521.

- You must have an external naming service, such as DNS, or have a HOSTS file available to the client.

- The listener must be set up with the GLOBAL_DBNAME parameter equal to the name of the machine.

The Connection Manager option does not support the hostnaming method.

## Configuring the Hostnaming Method

By default, Oracle will only attempt to use the hostnaming method from the client after attempting connections using localnaming and the Oracle Names Server. If you want to override this default search path for resolving names, set the NAMES.DIRECTORY_PATH parameter in the sqlnet.ora file on the client to search for hostnaming only. You can configure this parameter using the Net8 Assistant (see Figure 14.3). To configure the parameter using Net8 Assistant, choose Profile from the main screen and select Naming from the drop-down list at the top of the screen. This brings up a list of naming methods that are available. The Selected Methods list displays the naming methods being used and the order in which the methods are used to resolve service names. The Available Methods list displays the methods that have not been included in the selected methods. To change the list of available methods, use your mouse to highlight a method name and click the arrow key (>) to include it in the list of selected methods. You can remove a name by selecting it in the list of selected methods and clicking the other arrow key (<). You can also use the Demote and Promote buttons to change the order of the list. Select a name from the Selected Methods list and click the Demote button to move the name down the list or the Promote button to move the name to up the list.

**FIGURE 14.3**    Net8 Assistant `sqlnet.ora` Profile screen

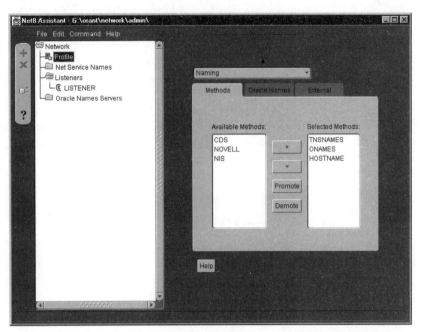

The hostnaming method does not require any client-side configuration. As long as the client has the TCP/IP protocol adapter installed and can connect to the server, the client can use the hostnaming method. You can check TCP/IP connectivity from the client using the TCP/IP utility ping. *Ping* attempts to contact the server by sending a small request packet. The server will respond in kind with an acknowledgment. The following code shows an example of how Ping works and how fast the round trip takes from client to server and back:

```
C:\>ping mil02ora

Pinging mil02ora [10.1.5.210] with 32 bytes of data:

Reply from 10.1.5.210: bytes=32 time<10ms TTL=128
Reply from 10.1.5.210: bytes=32 time<10ms TTL=128
Reply from 10.1.5.210: bytes=32 time<10ms TTL=128
Reply from 10.1.5.210: bytes=32 time<10ms TTL=128
```

The server must be configured with a listener running the TCP/IP protocol. The listener must be listening on the default port of 1521. You also must configure the listener with the GLOBAL_DBNAME parameter (Chapter 13 explains how to configure the listener). The code listed below shows what the listener.ora file looks like configured with the parameter. In this example, the hostname is GR99c0073. This is the name of the physical machine the listener process is running on.

```
# C:\V8I\NETWORK\ADMIN\LISTENER.ORA Configuration
# File:C:\v8i\NETWORK\ADMIN\listener.ora
# Generated by Oracle Net8 Assistant

LISTENER =
  (DESCRIPTION =
    (ADDRESS = (PROTOCOL = TCP)(HOST = gr99c0073)
    (PORT = 1521))
    (PROTOCOL_STACK =
      (PRESENTATION = TTC)
      (SESSION = NS)
    )
  )

SID_LIST_LISTENER =
  (SID_LIST =
    (SID_DESC =
      (GLOBAL_DBNAME = GR99c0073) - machine listener is on
      (ORACLE_HOME = c:\v8i)
      (SID_NAME = DBA)
    )
  )
```

Figure 14.4 shows the Net8 Assistant screen, which is where the global database name is to be set when configuring a listener.

**FIGURE 14.4**    Net8 Assistant `listener.ora` setup for hostnaming

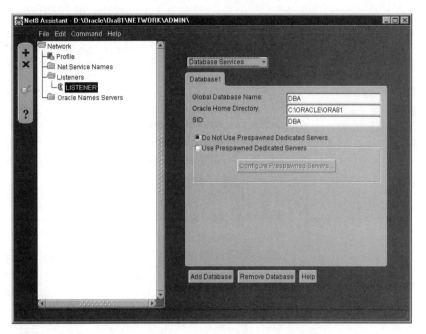

## Connection Process when Using Hostnaming

When using hostnaming, the client supplies a user ID and password along with the name of the machine the user wants to connect to. For example, if the user Matt with password of *casey* wants to connect to a database residing on machine GR99c0073, the user would enter **Sqlplus matt/casey@gr99c0073.**

The hostname would be resolved through either a HOSTS file or from an external naming environment, such as DNS. The following code contains an example of a HOSTS file from a Windows NT environment. The default location for the HOSTS file on UNIX is in the /etc directory. On Windows NT, the default location is c:\winnt\system32\drivers\etc. Once the hostname is resolved, the connection is made to the machine.

```
Copyright (c) 1993-1995 Microsoft Corp.
#
# This is a sample HOSTS file used by Microsoft
# TCP/IP for Windows NT.
#
# This file contains the mappings of IP addresses
# to host names. Each
# entry should be kept on an individual line.
```

```
# The IP address should
# be placed in the first column followed
# by the corresponding host name.
# The IP address and the host name should be separated
# by at least one
# space.
#
# Additionally, comments (such as these) may be
# inserted on individual
# lines or following the machine name denoted
# by a '#' symbol.
#
# For example:
#
#   102.54.94.97      rhino.acme.com    # source server
#    38.25.63.10      x.acme.com        # x client host

127.0.0.1          localhost
10.2.0.91          gr99c0073 # Oracle Database Server
```

The listener receives the request and looks for a matching GLOBAL_ DBNAME. If it is found, the connection is established as a dedicated, prespawned, or multithreaded connection, depending on the configuration of the Oracle Server. Figure 14.5 illustrates the following hostnaming connection process.

1. The client contacts the DNS server or local HOSTS file.

2. The client contacts the Oracle Server.

3. The server spawns a dedicated process, redirects connection to a prespawned process, or redirects connection to a dispatched process.

4. The server passes connection information back to the client.

5. The client is now in direct contact with the server process or dispatcher.

**FIGURE 14.5** Hostnaming connection summary

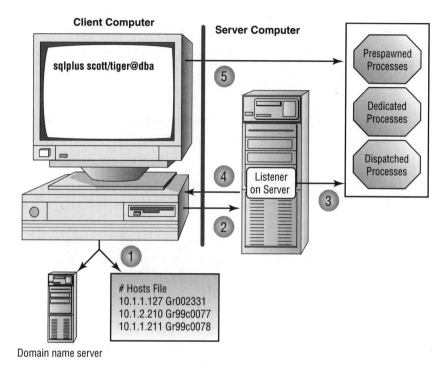

## Configuring Multiple Services on the Same Host Using Hostnaming

If you have multiple Oracle Servers on the same machine, it is possible to continue using the hostnaming method. You must have separate hostname address entries in your HOSTS file or in your external naming service for each of the separate Oracle services. For example, if we had two Oracle services, one called DBA and one called PROD, on a machine with an IP address of 10.2.0.91, you could configure your HOSTS name with following entry:

```
10.2.0.91       DBA  # Alias for MACH1 server for DBA   DBA
10.2.0.91       PROD # Alias for MACH1 server for PROD
PROD
```

Notice that each of these names resolve to the same IP address. You also need to configure your listener with two entries, one for DBA and one for PROD, both with the GLOBAL_DBNAME parameter set to DBA and PROD respectively (if you were using the hierarchical naming model with domain names, include the domain name on the GLOBAL_DBNAME parameter).

## The Localnaming Method

The localnaming method is probably the most widely used and well-known method of resolving net service names. Most users know this method as the tnsnames.ora method because it uses the tnsnames.ora file.

The localnaming method requires configuration of the tnsnames.ora file, which can be in any location, as long as the client can get to it. The default location for the tnsnames.ora file and the sqlnet.ora file is %ORACLE_HOME%\network\admin on Windows NT, and $ORACLE_HOME/ network /admin on UNIX systems. If you want to change the location of this file, set the environmental variable TNS_ADMIN. In UNIX-based systems, TNS_ADMIN can be exported to the user's shell environment or be set in the user's profile. In Windows NT, this setting is placed in the registry. The Windows NT registry key that stores the TNS_ADMIN may vary depending on your particular setup. Generally, it can be found somewhere under the Hkey_local_machine/software/oracle registry key. It may be at a lower level depending on your configuration

Most installations probably keep the files in these default locations on the client and server. Some users create shared disks and place the tnsnames.ora and sqlnet.ora files in this shared location to take a centralized approach to managing these files. If server-to-server communication is necessary, these files need to be on the server. The default location on the server is the same as the default location on the client.

### Configuring the Localnaming Method Using Net8 Assistant

The localnaming method is configured using the Net8 Assistant. Open the Net8 assistant and click the Net Service Names icon. Click the plus sign or choose Create from the Edit menu (see Figure 14.6).

**FIGURE 14.6**   Net8 Assistant title screen with Net Service Names option chosen

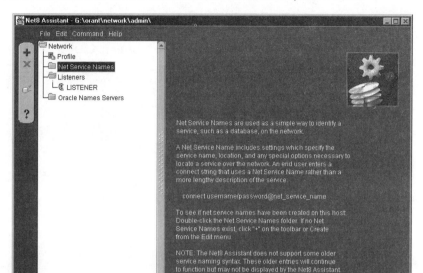

The Net8 Assistant will present you with the Net Service wizard. The wizard will guide you through the process of creating the net service names definition.

### Choose a Net Service Name

Choosing a net service name is the first step. This is the name the user enters when referring to the location they want to connect to. The name you supply should not include the domain portion if you are using the hierarchical naming mode. Click the Next button to continue.

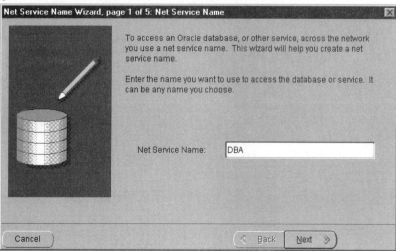

## Choose a Network Protocol

The next step is to enter the type of protocol to use when the client connects to the server for this net service name. By default, TCP/IP is chosen. The list of protocols will vary depending on your platform. Click the Next button to continue.

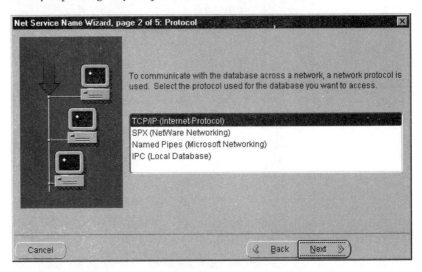

## Choose the Host Name and the Port

This step will vary depending on the protocol chosen in the previous step. Assuming TCP/IP was chosen, you are prompted for the Host Name and the Port Number. The Host Name is the name of the machine where the listener process is running. The Port Number is the listening location for the listener. The default port is 1521.

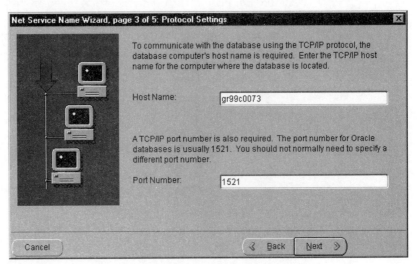

Table 14.1 shows a summary of the prompts you will see for the other protocols.

**TABLE 14.1** Prompts in Net8 Assistant for Other Protocols

| Protocol | Prompt | Definition |
|---|---|---|
| SPX/IPX | SPX Service Name | SPX service name for the database. This is the protocol used in Novell networks. |
| IPC | Key Value | Identifies the server. Oracle recommends using the listener name. IPC stands for Inter-Process Communication and is used for client connections that originate from the same machine as the Oracle Server. |
| Named Pipes | Server Name | Name of server where database resides. |
| Named Pipes | Pipe Name | Name of pipe to use; defaults to orapipe. |

### Choose the Service Name

The next step is to define the service name. For Oracle8i Net8, the service name does not have to be the same as the ORACLE_SID, as it was in the past. A database can have multiple service names defined for it. In Oracle8i Net8, the service name is normally the same as the global database name. This is the service name that is supplied to the listener, so the listener has to be listening for this service.

### Test the Net Service Name Connection

The last step is to test the net service name. This test will verify that all of the connection information entered is correct. Press the Test button to test the network connection.

The test connection will try to connect to the database with a username of Scott and a password of *tiger* by default. If your connection fails, check to see if you have a Scott/tiger user. You can change which login to test with by clicking the Change Login button in the Test Connection screen. You can also create the user Scott by running a script called scott located in the $ORACLE_HOME/rdbms /admin directory on UNIX or %ORACLE_HOME%\rdbms\admin on Windows NT.

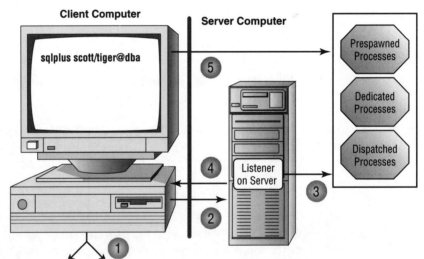

If everything is correct, you should see a result similar to Figure 14.7.

**FIGURE 14.7** Net8 Assistant tnsnames.ora wizard test result screen

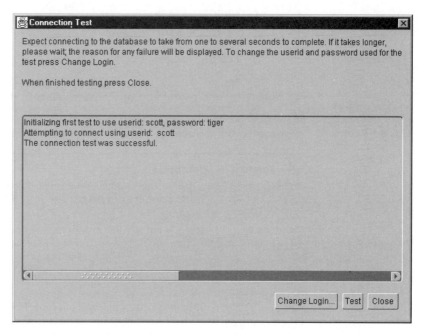

The last step is to save your changes by choosing Save Network Configuration from the File menu. This saves and creates the tnsnames.ora file.

## Contents and Structure of the *tnsnames.ora* file

The process above creates the tnsnames.ora file. The following code shows an example of the tnsnames.ora file:

```
# D:\ORACLE\ORA81\NETWORK\ADMIN\TNSNAMES.ORA
# Configuration
# File:D:\Oracle\Ora81\NETWORK\ADMIN\tnsnames.ora
# Generated by Oracle Net8 Assistant

DBA =
  (DESCRIPTION =
    (ADDRESS_LIST =
      (ADDRESS = (PROTOCOL = TCP)(HOST = gr99c0073)
      (PORT = 1521))
```

```
      )
      (CONNECT_DATA =
        (SERVICE_NAME = DBA)
      )
    )
```

Table 14.2 has a summary of the parameters in the tnsnames.ora file.

**TABLE 14.2** tnsnames.ora Parameters

| Parameter | Description |
|---|---|
| Description | Starts connect descriptor section of file. |
| Address_ list | Starts a list of all connect descriptor address information. |
| Address | Specifies connect descriptor for net service name. |
| Protocol | Specifies protocol used such as TCP/IP. |
| Host | Specifies name of the machine where listener is running. An IP address can also be specified in TCP/IP. |
| Port | Specifies listening location of listener specific to TCP/IP protocol. |
| Connect_ data | Starts the services section for this net service name. |
| Service_ name | Replaces the SID parameter from older releases of Oracle. Defines what service to connect to. Can be the same as the ORACLE_SID or set to the global database name. Databases can now be referred to by more than a single service name. |

# Configuring Load Balancing and Failover

Two new features of Oracle8i Net8 are load balancing and failover. Load balancing is the ability to distribute connections evenly. There are two types of load balancing: client load balancing and connection load balancing. Failover is the ability to connect to a second listener or database if one listener or database connection attempt fails.

## Configuring Client Load Balancing

*Client load balancing* occurs when a client randomly chooses among a list of listeners to contact a net service name. This achieves an even distribution of connections across a set of listeners for a given service. Client load balancing is accomplished with the `tnsnames.ora` parameter (`LOAD_BALANCE=ON`). When this parameter is set (and there are multiple listening locations defined for a net service name), you can take advantage of load balancing. The following code listing shows an example of a `tnsnames.ora` file with client load balancing configured:

```
# D:\ORACLE\ORA81\NETWORK\ADMIN\TNSNAMES.ORA
# Configuration
# File:D:\Oracle\Ora81\NETWORK\ADMIN
# \tnsnames.ora
# Generated by Oracle Net8 Assistant

DBA =
  (DESCRIPTION =
    (ADDRESS_LIST =
      (LOAD_BALANCE = ON)
      (FAILOVER = ON)
      (ADDRESS = (PROTOCOL = TCP)
      (HOST = weishan)(PORT = 1521))
      (ADDRESS = (PROTOCOL = TCP)
      (HOST = weishan)(PORT = 1522))
    )
    (CONNECT_DATA =
      (SERVICE_NAME = DBA)
    )
  )
```

The following steps show you how to use the Net8 Assistant to configure client load balancing:

1. From the Net8 Assistant screen, click Net Service Names and choose a net service name to modify.

2. Add a second address as a listening location. Make sure that the listeners are listing on different ports if TCP/IP is used.

3. Then click the Advanced button in the Address Configuration section. This screen allows you to configure the client load balancing.

4. Uncheck the box next to the Use Options Compatible with Net8 8.0 Clients option.

5. Select the radio button next to the Try Each Address, Randomly, Until One Succeeds option. Click OK and save your modifications.

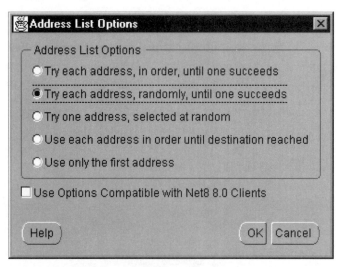

## Configuring Connection Load Balancing

*Connection load balancing* is the other kind of load balancing. Connection load balancing evenly distributes a set of connections across a set of dispatchers in a multithreaded server environment. You can also configure connection load balancing to distribute the load evenly among a set of instances. The listener will determine which dispatcher or instance is the least loaded and connect the user to that instance.

Connection load balancing can only be used if an instance has been automatically registered with a set of listeners. Also, this feature can only be used with the Multitheaded Server option.

See Chapter 13 for more information on server-side configuration to enable autoregistration for an instance.

## Configuring Connection Failover

*Connection failover* can occur at two levels: listener failover or instance failover.

*Listener failover* occurs when two listeners are listening for the same service. The tnsnames.ora file on the client is configured with both listening addresses. If the client attempts to contact the first listener, and the listener is not available, the client will failover and attempt to connect using the second listener. The following code is an example of a tnsnames.ora file configured for listener failover:

```
# C:\V8I\NETWORK\ADMIN\TNSNAMES.ORA Configuration
File:C:\v8i\NETWORK\ADMIN\tnsnames.ora
# Generated by Oracle Net8 Assistant

DBA =
  (DESCRIPTION =
    (ADDRESS_LIST =
      (SOURCE_ROUTE = OFF)
      (LOAD_BALANCE = OFF)
      (FAILOVER = ON)
      (ADDRESS = (PROTOCOL = TCP)(HOST = gr99c0073)(PORT =
1521))
      (ADDRESS = (PROTOCOL = TCP)(HOST = gr99c0073)(PORT =
1522))
    )
    (CONNECT_DATA =
      (SERVICE_NAME = DBA)
    )
  )
```

*Instance failover* is a tnsnames.ora file configured with one or more listener definition, each listening for the same service on different machines. If a client contacts the first listener and the instance is down, the client attempts to contact the second listener on the other machine. The following code is an example of a tnsnames.ora file configured with instance failover:

```
# C:\V8I\NETWORK\ADMIN\TNSNAMES.ORA Configuration
# File:C:\v8i\NETWORK\ADMIN\tnsnames.ora
# Generated by Oracle Net8 Assistant

DBA =
  (DESCRIPTION =
```

```
    (ADDRESS_LIST =
      (SOURCE_ROUTE = OFF)
      (LOAD_BALANCE = OFF)
      (FAILOVER = ON)
      (ADDRESS = (PROTOCOL = TCP)(HOST = gr99c0073)(PORT =
1521))
      (ADDRESS = (PROTOCOL = TCP)(HOST = mil02ora)(PORT =
1521))
      )
    (CONNECT_DATA =
      (SERVICE_NAME = DBA)
      )
    )
```

The advantages of using failover are that you can configure clients to be resilient in situations where database servers or listener processes are unavailable. This is especially valuable when using standby databases. No modifications to the network files are necessary for the user to reconnect to a standby instance if the primary instance fails.

You can use the Net8 Assistant to configure connection failover. From the Net8 Assistant screen, click Net Service Name and choose a net service name to modify.

Next, add a second address as a listening location. Click the Advanced button in the Address Configuration section. This screen allows you to configure the client load balancing. Uncheck the Use Options Compatible with Net8 8.0 Clients box. Select the Try Each Address in Order, Until One Succeeds option or the radio button. Then click OK.

# Summary

There are four names resolution methods available for clients: hostnaming, localnaming, an Oracle Names Server, and External Naming. Hostnaming, which can only be used if you are using the TCP/IP protocol, is mainly used for very simple Oracle Networks. Localnaming is the most popular of the names resolution methods and uses the `tnsnames.ora` file to resolve net service names. This file is typically located on each client. The client looks up the net service name in the `tnsnames.ora` file and uses the resulting connect descriptor information to connect to the Oracle Server. An Oracle Names Server is used when organizations want to centralize all of the service names. The Names Server is described in detail in Chapter 15. External Naming uses a HOSTS file located on the client, or an external naming service such as DNS to resolve the service names. The hostnaming, localnaming, and Oracle Names Server methods are configured using the Net8 Assistant.

You can also use Net8 Assistant to configure load balancing and failover. Load balancing is when a client will randomly choose from a list of listeners when connecting to an Oracle Server, provided there are multiple listeners to choose from. The service definition in the `tnsnames.ora` file contains multiple listener entries for a service name definition. You cannot configure load balancing when hostnaming is used. Load balancing provides for even distribution of connections across listeners. This is beneficial on systems that may experience heavy connection loads.

Failover is the ability of the client to choose a secondary listener to connect to when the primary listener connection fails. This can be useful if a database fails and you want clients to be able to connect to an alternate location without having to make modifications to the service definitions on the client.

# Key Terms

**B**efore you take the exam, make sure you're familiar with the following terms:

connection failover

connection load balancing

domain

flat naming model

hierarchical-naming models

instance failover

listener failover

# Review Questions

1. The ways in which a client may resolve a net service name are: (Choose three.)

    **A.** Localnaming

    **B.** Hostnaming

    **C.** Globalnaming

    **D.** Oracle Names Server

2. When configuring a client, what file must be present to accomplish localnaming?

    **A.** `lsnrctl.ora`

    **B.** `names.ora`

    **C.** `tnsnames.ora`

    **D.** `sdns.ora`

    **E.** None of the above

3. Which of the following is a prerequisite to hostnaming?

    **A.** You must use `tnsnames.ora` on the client.

    **B.** You must be using TCP/IP.

    **C.** You must have an Oracle Names Server present.

    **D.** You must have a `sqlnet.ora` file present on the client.

    **E.** None of the above

4. Which of the following statements about `tnsnames.ora` is *false*?

    **A.** Used to resolve an Oracle service name

    **B.** Can exist on the client

    **C.** Used for localnaming

    **D.** Used for globalnaming

5. Which entry in the `sqlnet.ora` file would change the default service resolution search path?

   A. `Names.directory_path=(TNSNAMES,ONAMES,HOSTNAME)`

   B. `Names.search_path=(TSNAMES,HOSTNAME,ONAMES)`

   C. `Names.directory_path=(HOSTNAME,ONAMES,TNSNAMES)`

   D. `Names.search_path=(HOSTNAME,TNSNAMES,ONAMES)`

6. Which option in the Net8 Assistant is used to configure `tnsnames.ora`?

   A. Profile

   B. Listeners

   C. tnsnames

   D. Net service names

   E. Network names

7. The user Bob with the password *apple* needs to connect to the DBA service. Which one of the following connect statements would work?

   A. `sqlplus apple/bob@DBA`

   B. `sqlplus bob/apple@DBA`

   C. `sqlplus DBA@bob/apple`

   D. `sqlplus bob\apple@DBA`

   E. `sqlplus bob/apple#DBA`

8. Which phrase best completes the sentence: A net service name is...

   A. The name of the `ORACLE_SID`

   B. The database name

   C. Another name for a database location on my network

   D. The same as my `DB_NAME` `init.ora` setting

   E. None of the above

9. Which section of the `tnsnames.ora` file contains the parameter `SERVICE_NAME`?

   **A.** Address

   **B.** Connect_Data

   **C.** Host

   **D.** Description

10. Which parameters have replaced `ORACLE_SID` in the `tnsnames.ora` file in version 8i (choose 2):

    **A.** SERVICE_NAME

    **B.** DATABASE_NAME

    **C.** CONNECT_STRING

    **D.** INSTANCE_NAME

    **E.** ORACLE_INSTANCE

11. Which of the following is a prerequisite for connection load balancing:

    **A.** A dedicated server

    **B.** Multithreaded Server

    **C.** IPX protocol adapter

    **D.** AUTOMATIC_IPC=ON

12. For which of the following is the `INSTANCE_NAME` parameter required in the `tnsnames.ora` file?

    **A.** Bequeath connections

    **B.** Parallel server

    **C.** Dedicated server

    **D.** Local connections

**13.** Which parameter gets appended to the service name if present in the `sqlnet.ora` file?

    **A.** `Names.default_path`

    **B.** `Names.default_domain`

    **C.** `Names.service_name`

    **D.** `Names.connection_name`

**14.** In which situation would an administrator choose to use hostnaming?

    **A.** The administrator has a complex network with many instances to manage.

    **B.** The administrator is interested in minimal client-side configuration.

    **C.** The administrator does not want to use the Net8 Assistant.

    **D.** The administrator want to use a `tnsnames.ora` file to contain the configuration settings.

    **E.** None of the above

**15.** "Allows users to randomly choose between listeners" describes:

    **A.** Connection load balancing

    **B.** Client load balancing

    **C.** Instance failover

**16.** When configuring `tnsnames.ora` using the Net8 Assistant, what protocol is the default selection?

    **A.** TCP/IP

    **B.** IPX

    **C.** Named Pipes

    **D.** IPC

**17.** Which phrase best completes this sentence: The network protocol...

**A.** Is installed by default by the Oracle installer

**B.** Is another name for the Oracle protocol adapters

**C.** Is not necessary for doing client/server connections

**D.** Needs to be present for client/server connections

**18.** One utility that you can use to test the TCP/IP network protocol is:

**A.** `trcasst`

**B.** `lsnrctl`

**C.** `namesctl`

**D.** Ping

**E.** None of the above

**19.** Which of the following are *true* with respect to the hierarchical naming model?

**A.** Each database within a domain must have a unique network service name.

**B.** Each database can have the same network service name provided they are in different domains.

**C.** Each database must be named uniquely in all domains.

**D.** All of the above

**20.** Which section of the `tnsnames.ora` file is correct?

**A.** `(ADDRESS =(PROTOCOL = TCP)(HOST = MILO2ORA)(PORT = 1521))`

**B.** `(ADDRESS= (HOST=MILO2ORA) (PORT=1521)(PROTOCOL=TCP))`

**C.** `(ADDRESS=(PROTOCOL=TCP, HOST=MILO2ORA,PORT=1521))`

**D.** `(ADDRESS=(PROTOCOL=TCP) (HOST=MILO2ORA,PORT=1521))`

# Answers to Review Questions

1. A, B, D. Oracle uses service names in networks in much the same way it uses synonyms in the database. Service names provide location transparency and hide the complexity of connect string information. We have three ways to configure Net8 to accomplish this: hostnaming, localnaming, and Oracle Names Server. We can set a global name for the database connect string, but we would do that in the context of one of these three names resolution solutions.

2. C. Localnaming is more often referred to as TNSNAMES naming, since we use the `tnsnames.ora` file to resolve a service name. There is no such file as `lsnrctl.ora`, and `sdns.ora` is a file that is created by certain actions involved with the Oracle Names Server.

3. B. Hostnaming is typically used in small installations with few Oracle databases. This is an attractive option when the DBA wants to minimize client-side configuration. One of the prerequisites of hostnaming is that you must use TCP/IP.

4. D. A `tnsnames.ora` file is configured when we want to use localnaming and typically exists on the client workstation. It is also used to resolve a service name. Answer D, globalnaming, is not a names resolution technique.

5. C. The DBA has the capability of modifying the default search path for resolving a name. The default search path is (`TNSNAMES, ONAMES, HOSTNAME`) in Oracle8i. This is set using the `sqlnet.ora parameter names.directory_path`. Answer C changes the `NAMES.DIRECTORY_PATH` setting from its default search path to a different search path.

6. E. Network names configures the `tnsnames.ora` file. Profile is used to configure `sqlnet.ora`. The other choices are not valid choices. A good knowledge of the Net8 Assistant interface will definitely help you succeed on the OCP exam.

7. B. When we specify a connection to the database via SQL*Plus, the syntax is `sqlplus userid/password@service_name`. All of the other choices would result in a failed connection attempt.

8. C. Net service names resolve to locations somewhere in the enterprise. It may not necessarily be the same as the `ORACLE_SID` or the database name. This means the correct answer is C.

9. B. The `SERVICE_NAME` parameter is new in Oracle8i and is part of the `Connect_Data` portion of the `tnsnames.ora` file.

10. A, D. The `SERVICE_NAME` and `INSTANCE_NAME` parameters have replaced the `ORACLE_SID`. A single database can now be associated with multiple service names. The `INSTANCE_NAME` parameter in the `tnsnames.ora` file is set to the INSTANCE_NAME parameter found in the `init.ora` file. The `SERVICE_NAME` is normally configured as the global database name. This is a combination of the instance name and the domain name.

11. B. Connection load balancing can only be used when you are configured with multithreaded server.

12. B. INSTANCE_NAME is only required in the parallel server environment when more than one instance can be associated with a single database.

13. B. An enterprise may have many domains, each with its own services. In a hierarchical naming model, service names may be the same across domains. To differentiate between service names, the `names.default_domain` parameter is appended to a service that does not contain a domain name. For example, if a user specifies DBA and `names.default_domain=GR.COM`, the resultant service name to be searched for is `DBA.GR.COM`.

14. B. Hostnaming is used in situations where there are few overall databases to administer and you want to minimize client-side configuration. Complex networks would probably be candidates for the Names Server. The Net8 Assistant can be used to configure any of the name resolution possibilities and `tnsnames.ora` files are used for localnaming. The correct answer is B.

**15.** B. Client load balancing allows clients to randomly choose between listener processes to connect to for an instance. This allows for an even distribution of connection requests across listeners.

**16.** A. TCP/IP is probably the most widely used network protocol today. The Net8 Assistant chooses this by default.

**17.** D. All network data is transported from a client to a database server by an underlying network protocol. This protocol needs to be in place for Net8 to function correctly. Protocols are independent of the Oracle software and are not the same as the Oracle protocol adapters. The adapters are what allow Net8 to talk to the underlying protocol. The answer is D.

**18.** D. Protocols come with tools that allow you to test network connectivity. One such utility for TCP/IP is Ping. The user supplies either an IP address or a hostname to the Ping utility. It then searches the network for this address. If it is found, it will display information on data that is sent and received and how quickly it found this address. The other choices are Oracle-supplied utilities.

**19.** A, B. Each service name within a domain must be unique, but names can be repeated if they reside in different domains.

**20.** A. Review the syntax and formatting of the network files. All of the other syntax is incorrect.

# Centralizing Services with Oracle Names Server

---

## ORACLE8i NETWORK ADMINISTRATION EXAM OBJECTIVES OFFERED IN THIS CHAPTER:

✓ Describe how an Oracle Names Server functions.

✓ List the advantages of using an Oracle Names Server.

✓ Configure an Oracle Names Server using Net8 Assistant.

✓ Describe the checkpoint file implementation of the Oracle Names Server.

✓ Configure a region database for a Names Server.

✓ Define a well-known Names Server.

✓ Start up and shut down a Names Server using Net8 Assistant.

✓ Register services with a Names Server using Net8 Assistant.

✓ Use the namesctl command line facility to administer the Names Server.

✓ Startup and shutdown the Names Server using namesctl.

✓ Get status information about the Names Server with namesctl.

✓ Gain familiarity with the namesctl commands.

✓ Register a service manually using namesctl.

✓ Define dynamic discovery.

✓ Perform dynamic discovery of Names Servers from a client.

✓ Define preferred Names Servers for a client using Net8 Assistant.

✓ Register a listener with a Names Server.

Exam objectives are subject to change at any time without prior notice and at Oracle's sole discretion. Please visit Oracle's Training and Certification Web site (http://education .oracle.com/certification) for the most current exam objectives listing.

As the number and complexity of Oracle Servers grows in an organization, it can become increasingly difficult to effectively manage the Oracle network services with the hostnaming or localnaming conventions. This chapter describes the Oracle Names Server and the benefits of utilizing Names Servers as a means to resolve services.

You will learn how to configure the Names Server using the Net8 Assistant and administer the Names Server from both the Net8 Assistant and the namesctl command line interface. You will discover how to configure clients to take advantage of Names Server service resolution and the concepts of dynamic discovery, preferred Names Servers, and well-known Names Servers. This chapter also discusses how an Oracle listener process can register service definitions with Names Servers.

# The Oracle Names Server

A Names Server acts like a telephone operator. When you call the operator to find a person's phone number, the operator asks you for the name and city of the person whom you want to contact. If the number is listed, the operator will give you the person's phone number and you can then place your call.

The Names Server works in much the same way. When you want to contact an Oracle Server, you place a "call" to the Names Server supplying it with the net service name. If the net service name is "listed," the Names Server will respond with connect descriptor information and service name information. You can then place your "call" to the appropriate location on the network.

## Advantages of a Names Server

Oracle Names Servers allow you to define a central location for managing connect descriptor and service name information. If you are currently using other Names resolution methods such as localnaming, you will appreciate having one central location to manage this information.

With information stored in one or more Names Servers, you minimize the chance of having errors in connection information. In large organizations, it can be a difficult task to determine what the current copy of the `tnsnames.ora` file should be and where the most current copy is located. With the localnaming method, deploying changes to the service information located on clients scattered across the organization is inefficient and not very flexible. It can also introduce errors.

With only one or a few Names Servers to manage, administering connect descriptor and service name information becomes much easier. This makes the administrative staff more effective at keeping the information accurate and up-to-date. If you take advantage of a centralized database configuration, all of the Names Servers will share a central image of service name and connect descriptors. This makes for truly centralized naming.

## How Names Servers Resolve Service Names

The following is a summary of the steps taken when a client issues a request to connect to an Oracle Server using Oracle Names.

A client issues a request for a connection to some net service name. For example, if user Matt with a password of *casey* wants to use SQL*Plus to connect to a net service of *payroll*, he would issue the following command:

```
sqlplus matt/casey@payroll
```

The client has to be aware that Names Servers exist and should be used. The client is made aware of Names Servers in two ways. The client can discover Names Servers, or the client can be configured with a list of Names Servers. Later on in the chapter you will learn about discovering Names Servers and configuring the list of Names Servers on the client.

By default, a client will make an attempt to use Names Servers as a means to resolve a net service name. As described in Chapter 12, the default search hierarchy is to first attempt to resolve the net service name by using localnaming, then to use the Oracle Names Server, and finally to use hostnaming. You can modify the search hierarchy for the client by setting the `names.directory_path` variable. You will see how this is done using the Net8 Assistant later in the chapter.

If a Names Server exists, the client contacts the Names Server. The Names Server listens for client's request. The client supplies the Names Server with the net service name information. If the Names Server has information about the net service name requested, the Names Server returns the connection descriptor and service name information to the client. The client then contacts the listener using the connect descriptor information that the Names Server supplied.

The Names Server is only used to supply the information to the client. If a Names Server fails and clients are already connected to their destinations, those clients are unaffected. If a client contacts a Names Server that is not active, the client will receive an error indicating that the net service name was not found.

# Configuring a Names Server with Net8 Assistant

Names Servers are configured using the Net8 Assistant. Most management of Names Servers is done from the Net8 Assistant, which includes defining the Names Server, starting and stopping the Names Server, and registering services with the Names Server. There is a command line interface tool that can be used to administer Names Servers. Later in the chapter, you will see how to use this tool and what functions can be performed.

Names Servers are implemented using two methods. You can choose to create Names Servers that store the connection descriptor and service name information in *checkpoint files,* or you can configure them to store the connect descriptor and service name information in a database. If multiple Names Servers are configured and you select the checkpoint naming convention, they are synchronized by replicating the information from one Names Server to the next. This is known as *cache replication.* You will see how to configure cache replication later in this chapter. For small installations, this can be a feasible solution.

A database is probably a better solution for managing service names because it eliminates the need for cache replication, and it provides more secure storage since databases are likely backed up by the DBA on a regular basis.

# Configuring a Names Server Using Checkpoint Files

The first method is using checkpoint files with cache replication. This type is suitable for smaller Oracle installations with centralized service naming.

## Creating a Names Server Using Net8 Assistant

Follow these steps to create a Names Server using Net8 Assistant:

1. Start the Net8 assistant and choose the Oracle Names Server icon. If this is the first Names Server being created, you will get a message box asking you to search for existing Names Servers or create a new Names Server. Click OK if this is the first Names Server being defined.

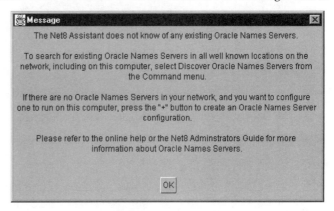

2. Click the plus sign or choose Create from the Edit menu. This starts the Names Wizard. The wizard guides you step by step through the creation process.

3. The first two screens contain introductory information. The first screen informs you that the wizard will lead you step by step through

the Names Server creation process. Click Next and move on to the second screen.

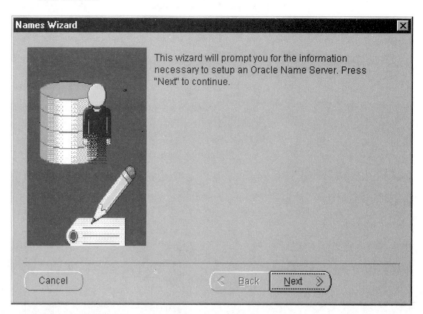

4. The second screen suggests creating the necessary user and table definitions in a database if you are going to configure a database to store the service names. Click Next and move on to the next screen.

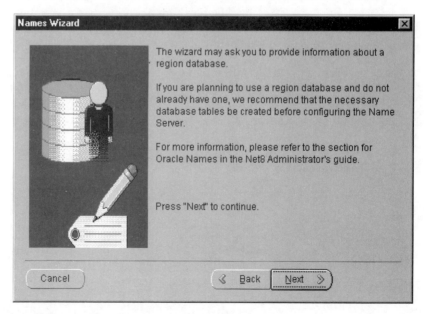

## Choosing a Name and Protocol for the Names Server

Follow these steps to choose a name and protocol for the Names Server:

1. The Names Server has to be given a name. There is no default value. If you are using a hierarchical naming model for your organization, append the domain name to the base name for the Names Server. Click Next and move on to the next screen.

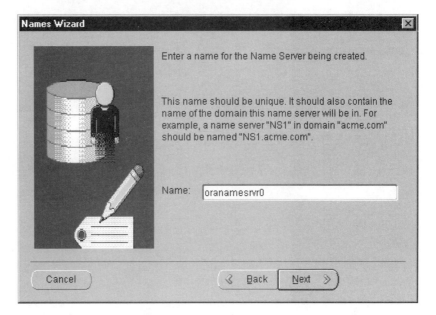

2. The Names Server listens for client requests using a specific protocol. Choose the protocol you want to use. The default is TCP/IP. If you use TCP/IP, supply the host and port designation. The host is the name of the machine where the Names Server resides, and the port location

designates the listening location of the Names Server. The default port location for the Names Server is 1575.

Depending on your protocol, you will see different prompts. Table 15.1 shows the prompts you see depending on the protocol you choose.

**TABLE 15.1** Names Server Protocols and Prompts in Net8 Assistant

| Protocol chosen | Prompt |
| --- | --- |
| TCP/IP | Host and Port |
| SPX | SPX Service |
| IPC | IPC Key |
| NMP | Machine Name and Pipe Name |

After filling in the information, click Next to move on. The next screen is an information screen that gives details on Names Server configurations. Click Next to move on.

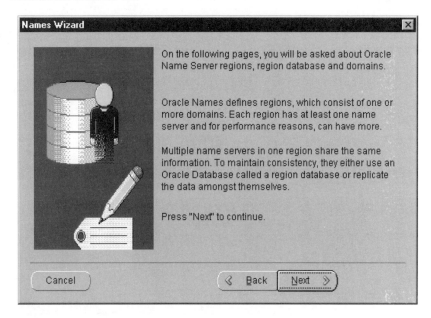

## Choosing a Configuration: Checkpoint Files or a Region Database

Choose whether you want to store connect descriptor information in checkpoint files or a region database. The default is to use a region database. In Chapter 14, the term region was defined as a collection of domains. Oracle recommends that a region database be configured, especially if more than one Names Server will exist. You will learn how to configure a region database later in the chapter. Follow these steps to configure a Names Server using checkpoint files:

1. Since you are configuring the Names Server with the checkpoint files option, choose the Don't Use a Region Database option and click Next.

For a discussion of regions and the different naming models, see Chapter 14.

**2.** If this is the first Names Server in the region, click Next on this screen.

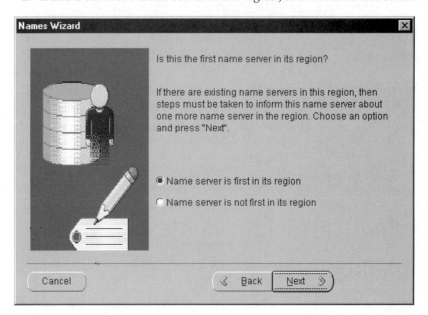

If this is not the first Names Server defined, choose the Names Server Is Not First in Its Region option and click the Next button.

3. You have the option of discovering other Names Servers or entering information about their locations. This is done to make new Names Servers aware of previously defined Names Servers and so that synchronization of service information can be done between all of the Names Servers in the region by performing cache replication.

If you choose to discover Names Servers, Oracle searches for them. Well-known Names Servers are those that have specific, hard-coded names in the Net8 environment. Chapter 12 contains the list of default names for well-known Names Servers.

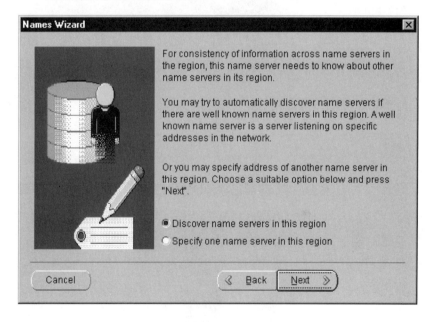

For consistency of information across name servers in the region, this name server needs to know about other name servers in its region.

You may try to automatically discover name servers if there are well known name servers in this region. A well known name server is a server listening on specific addresses in the network.

Or you may specify address of another name server in this region. Choose a suitable option below and press "Next".

○ Discover name servers in this region
○ Specify one name server in this region

4. If you choose to enter Names Server information, or if the discovery process does not find any well-known Names Servers, you must supply information about their location on this screen. This information varies depending on the protocol (see Table 15.1). If you are using TCP/IP, which is the default, enter the Host and Port location of the other listener in the region. When you press the Next button, the Wizard attempts to contact the Names Server to verify its existence. If it cannot contact the Names Server,

you will receive an error. Enter the correct information and attempt the connection again.

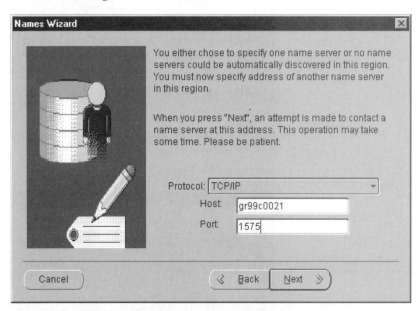

**5.** If this Names Server resides in the root region, select Yes and click Next.

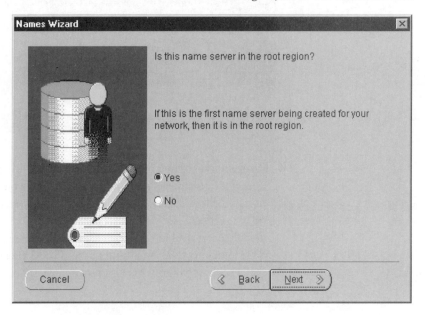

If this Names Server is in a different region, select No and click Next.

**6.** Enter the name of the domain where this Names Server resides. Click Next.

See Chapter 14 for a discussion of domains and regions.

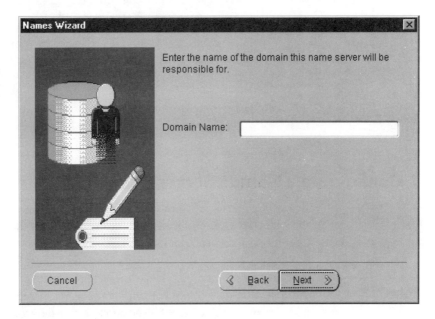

## Completing Definition of Name Server

Once you click Finish, you will get a message box informing you of the creation of your Names Server.

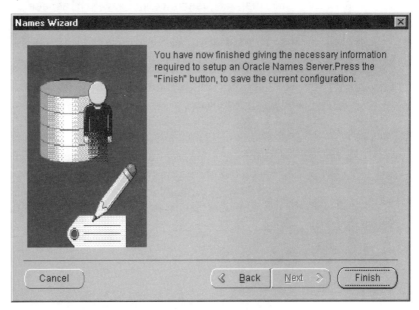

The definition of the Names Server is complete.

```
┌─────────────────────────────────────┐
│ 🖳 Names Server Created          [×] │
├─────────────────────────────────────┤
│     A Names Server, oranamesrvr0, has│
│    been created with default settings. Use│
│     the Configure Server section to modify│
│         the default configuration.   │
│                                      │
│                                      │
│              ┌──────┐                │
│              │  OK  │                │
│              └──────┘                │
└─────────────────────────────────────┘
```

# Configuring a Names Server Using a Region Database

Before you can use a region database to store information, you have to create the necessary user and table definitions on the database that will store the definition of the service information.

Connect to the database that will serve as the Names Server repository, and create a new user. You need to run a script called namesini.sql. This script creates the tables that store connect descriptor and service name information. This script is located in the $ORACLE_HOME/network/admin directory on UNIX systems and %ORACLE_HOME%\network\admin\names on Windows NT systems. See the listing below for an example:

```
sql> CREATE user names identified by password rachel01
tablespace users temporary tablespace temp;
sql> CONNECT names/rachel01
sql> @$oracle_home/network/addmin/namesini.sql;
```

The Names Server needs to connect to the database server that stores connect descriptor information. Enter the login information defining the user and server where the service name information is stored. The Names Server connects to the database when it is started and retrieves connect descriptor and service name information.

Use the Net8 Assistant to define the login information. To enter service name and connect descriptor information manually, choose Oracle Names Servers and select the names server to modify. Then choose Manage Data from the drop down list box at the top of the screen. Select the Add radio button to add an individual entry. After completing the entry, click the Execute button (see Figure 15.1).

**FIGURE 15.1** Names Server database definition

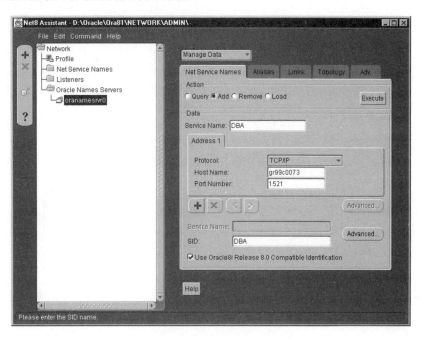

## Creating the *names.ora* File

After completing the definition, save your work by choosing File ➢ Save Network Configuration. This creates a new file called names.ora. The names.ora file is the main configuration file for the Oracle Names Server. This file contains information about the name and listening location for the Names Server. The location of this file is ORACLE_HOME\network\admin. Here is a sample names.ora file:

```
# C:\V8I\NETWORK\ADMIN\NAMES.ORA Configuration
# File:C:\v8i\NETWORK\ADMIN\names.ora
# Generated by Oracle Net8 Assistant

NAMES.SERVER_NAME = NS1

NAMES.ADDRESSES =
  (ADDRESS = (PROTOCOL = TCP)(HOST = gr99c0073)(PORT =
1575))
```

## Starting and Stopping the Names Server Using Net8 Assistant

After completing the definition of the Names Server, start the Names Server. The Names Server can be started from either the Net8 Assistant or the command line interface, lsnrctl. We will discuss the command line interface later in this chapter.

To start the Names Server using the Net8 Assistant, choose Manage Server from the drop-down list box at the top right of the screen. A screen that allows you to start and stop the Names Server is displayed. Click the Apply button at the bottom of the screen. A message appears that the Names Server has been started. In UNIX, a new background process is created, and in Windows NT, a new service is created and started.

Names Servers can be stopped by choosing the Shut Down radio button and clicking Apply at the bottom of the screen.

## Registering Service Names Using Net8 Assistant

The Names Server is now started, but is not listening for any Oracle services. The next step is to define Oracle services and connect descriptor information for the Names Server. Choose Manage Data from the drop-down list box located in the upper right-hand part of the screen (see Figure 15.2).

**FIGURE 15.2**    Manage data information from Net8 Assistant.

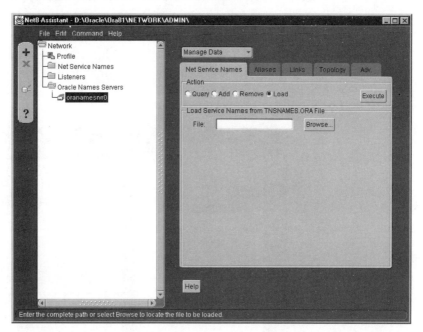

## Loading Existing Service Data from a *tnsnames.ora* File

You can load connect descriptor and service name information from an existing tnsnames.ora file. This saves you a good deal of time, especially if you have a number of service names to enter.

Choose the Load radio button and enter the path for the tnsnames.ora file you want to load. You can also choose Browse and Search for the tnsnames.ora file in your directory structure.

Once the file prompt has been filled in with the tnsnames.ora file, press Execute. Net8 Assistant responds with the number of service definitions loaded from the file. This loads the data from the tnsnames.ora files into the Names Server. The Names Server is now capable of responding to requests for services that were loaded from the tnsnames.ora file.

### Adding Net Service Definitions Manually

If you don't have an existing `tnsnames.ora` file, or you need to enter the net service definitions manually, choose the Add radio button from the Manage Data screen. Fill in the details of the net service's name service, connect descriptor, and service name information (see Figure 15.3).

**FIGURE 15.3** Add new service definitions manually.

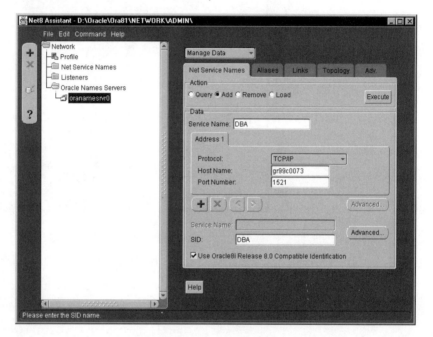

Once you have completed the prompts, click the Execute button to save connect descriptor information.

## Checkpoint Files that Store Service Information

Connect descriptor information is kept in several operating system files. There are three checkpoint files, besides the `names.ora` file, that are used with this method. By default, files are located in the `$ORACLE_HOME/network/names` directory on UNIX and the `%ORACLE_HOME\network\names` directory on NT and hold different information.

Table 15.2 gives a summary of the files and the contents of each file.

**TABLE 15.2**   Checkpoint Files Used to Store Names Server Configuration Information

| File Name | Definition of contents |
|---|---|
| Ckpcch.ora | Cache checkpoint file that stores client cache information |
| Ckpcfg.ora | Configuration checkpoint file that stores Names Server configuration information |
| Ckpreg.ora | Region checkpoint file that stores net services information like tnsnames.ora |

The following code shows examples of these files. The Names Server is responsible for managing these files; they should not be modified by hand.

```
# ckpreg.ora THIS FILE IS AUTOMATICALLY GENERATED BY
# THE NAMES SERVER AS
# ITS NORMAL OPERATION.  IF YOU EDIT THIS FILE, YOUR
# CHANGES WILL BE
# OVERWRITTEN BY THE NAME SERVER WITHOUT WARNING.
#
# Generation date:              11-FEB-00 09:23:19
# Server version banner:        Oracle Names for 32-bit
# Windows: Version 8.1.5.0.0 - Production
#
. = (DATA_LIST=(FLAGS=0x11)
    (DATA=(TYPE=ns.smd.)(NAME=NS1.) )
    )

DBA. = (DATA_LIST=(FLAGS=0x1)(TTL=86400)
    (DATA=(TYPE=a.smd.)(DESCRIPTION = (ADDRESS_LIST =
    (SOURCE_ROUTE = OFF) (LOAD_BALANCE = OFF)
 (FAILOVER = ON) (ADDRESS = (PROTOCOL = TCP)
(HOST = gr99c0073)(PORT = 1522))
 (ADDRESS = (PROTOCOL = TCP)(HOST = gr99c0073)
(PORT = 1521))) (CONNECT_DATA =
(SERVICE_NAME = DBA))) )
```

```
      )
# ckpcfg.ora THIS CONFIGURATION PARAMETER CHECKPOINT
# FILE IS # GENERATED BY THE NAME SERVER AS PART OF ITS
STARTUP
 PROCESS.  IF YOU EDIT THIS  FILE, YOUR CHANGES WILL BE
OVERWRITTEN
 WITHOUT WARNING THE
# NEXT TIME THE  SERVER STARTS OR RESTARTS.
#
# Generation date:              11-FEB-00 09:23:19
# Server version banner:        Oracle Names for 32-bit
Windows: Version 8.1.5.0.0 - Production
# Region's ROS data store:
#
NAMES.SERVER_NAME = NS1
names.domains = (DOMAIN_LIST=(DOMAIN=(NAME=)
(MIN_TTL=86400)))
NAMES.ADDRESSES = (ADDRESS = (PROTOCOL = TCP)
(HOST = gr99c0073)(PORT = 1575))
```

## Discovering Other Names Servers in a Region

If other Names Servers exist in the same region as the one being defined, discovery needs to occur. The discovery process is necessary so the new Names Server is aware of other Names Servers to contact for cache replication. Discovery is also a process that is performed on the client. This is discussed later in this chapter.

During the discovery process, Oracle searches for any Names Server defined as:

- Well-known Names Server. See Chapter 12 for a discussion of well-known Names Servers.

- Preferred Names Servers. We will discuss configuration of preferred Names Servers later on in this chapter.

- Local Names Server. This is a Names Server on the local machine that is configured using TCP/IP listening on the default port of 1575.

To discover Names Servers from Net8 Assistant, choose Discover Oracle Names Servers from the Command menu at the top of the screen. Depending on the size of your network and the number of Names Servers defined in the region, this process could take a while to execute.

The discovery process creates the `sdns.ora` file. This file contains a list of all of the Names Servers discovered. This is used during cache replication so Names Servers are aware of other Names Servers in the region. Here is a listing of the `sdns.ora` file contents:

```
\ = (ADDRESS=(PROTOCOL=IPC)(KEY=ONAMES))
NS1 = (ADDRESS = (PROTOCOL = TCP)(HOST = gr99c0073)(PORT =
1575))
```

Later in the chapter you will see how to discover Name Servers using the `namesctl` command line utility.

## Cache Replication between Names Servers in a Region

Cache replication is used for the checkpoint file model. Replication is a way to synchronize all of the Names Servers in a given region with each other. If you use a database to store service information, no replication is necessary.

Replication of Names Servers information can be done in two ways: autoregistration or replication. With auto registration, a listener automatically registers information with a Names Server. When the listener starts, it registers all of its service name information with any well-known Names Servers defined. This is called the plug-and-play option.

If you have multiple regions with multiple Names Servers, information is replicated among the Names Servers on a periodic basis. The period of time that this replicated information remains fresh is called the time-to-live (TTL). By default, this time is set to 24 hours. This means that if replicated information on a Names Server is more than 24 hours old, it needs to be refreshed when a request for a connection is made to one of the replicated connect descriptors. The Names Server contacts the original Names Server that provided it with connect descriptor information and refreshes its own copy.

The time to live is configurable in Net8 (see Figure 15.4). Choose Configure Server from the drop-down list box at the top part of the screen. Choose the Domains tab and enter the domain where the Names Server resides and the time to live information in days, hours, minutes and seconds. This means that Names Servers in this domain will refresh with other Names Servers using this time-to-live interval.

**FIGURE 15.4** Domains definitions screen

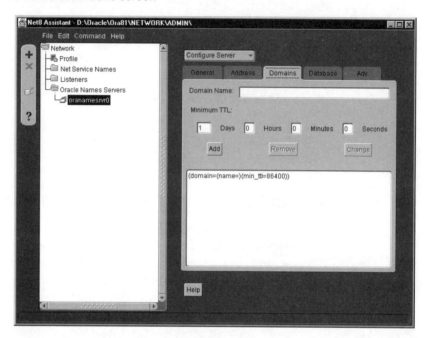

# The *namesctl* utility

The Names Server command line utility namesctl is used to administer the Names Server. It is similar to the lsnrctl facility for the listener. The utility has commands for starting, stopping, and receiving status information about the Names Server.

Other commands can be executed such as registering new services with a Names Server.

## Starting and Stopping Names Servers

To start the utility, type namesctl from a command line prompt. The output below shows how the utility is initialized. If a Names Server is found by the utility, it displays information about the current Names Server.

```
Microsoft(R) Windows NT(TM)
(C) Copyright 1985-1996 Microsoft Corp.

C:\>namesctl

Oracle Names Control for 32-bit Windows: Version
8.1.5.0.0 - Productionon 11-FEB-00 10:54:27

(c) Copyright 1997 Oracle Corporation.
  All rights reserved.

Currently managing name server "NS1"
Version banner is "Oracle Names for 32-bit Windows:
 Version 8.1.5.0.0 - Production"

Welcome to NAMESCTL, type "help" for information.

NAMESCTL>
```

To start a Names Server, you would type **start** from the following prompt:

```
NAMESCTL> start
Starting "names.exe"...Service Oraclev8iNamesNS1 start
pending.
Service Oraclev8iNamesNS1 started.
server successfully started

Currently managing name server "NS1"
Version banner is "Oracle Names for 32-bit Windows:
 Version 8.1.5.0.0 - Production"

Server name:                              NS1
Server has been running for:              1.53 seconds
Request processing enabled:               yes
Request forwarding enabled:               yes
```

```
Requests received:                              0
Requests forwarded:                             0
Foreign data items cached:                      0
Region data next checked for reload in:         not set
Region data reload check failures:              0
Cache next checkpointed in:                     not set
Cache checkpoint interval:                      not set
Cache checkpoint file name:
        C:\v8i\network\names\ckpcch.ora
Statistic counters next reset in:               not set
Statistic counter reset interval:               not set
Statistic counters next logged in:              not set
Statistic counter logging interval:             not set
Trace level:                                    0
Trace file name:
        C:\v8i\network\trace\names9e.trc
Log file name:
        C:\v8i\network\log\names.log
System parameter file name:
        C:\v8i\network\admin\names.ora
Command-line parameter file name:               " "
Administrative region name:                     " "
Administrative region description:              " "
ApplTable Index:                                0
Contact                                         " "
Operational Status                              0
Save Config on Stop                             no
NAMESCTL>
```

## Register Service Names from *namesctl*

You can use the namesctl utility to register service information. For example, suppose you have a database on host gr99c0073 with an instance name of DBA and a TCP/IP listener listening for connections for this service. To register this service, use the Register command manually with the Names Server, as shown below:

```
NAMESCTL> register dba -t oracle_database -d
(DESCRIPTION=(ADDRESS=(PROTOCOL=TCP)(HOST=gr99c0073)
```

```
(PORT=1521)))(CONNECT_DATA=(SERVICE_NAME=DBA)))
Total response time:    0.08 seconds
Response status:        normal, successful completion
```

The response, `successful completion`, indicates that you have success-fully registered the service. If you do not get a valid response, make sure you typed the command in exactly as shown above. The `namesctl` utility is very sensitive about proper spacing. Do not put spaces between any of the paren-theses. You can register Oracle services, other Names Servers, or listeners using the `register` command.

To remove a registration, you would use the `unregister` command. The form of this command is identical to the `register` command.

```
NAMESCTL> unregister dba -t oracle_database -d
(DESCRIPTION=(ADDRESS=(PROTOCOL=TCP)(HOST=gr99c0073)
(PORT=1521)))(CONNECT_DATA=(SERVICE_NAME=DBA)))
Total response time:    0.08 seconds
Response status:        normal, successful completion
```

## Other Commands in *namesctl*

There are over 30 commands available from the `namesctl` utility. Table 15.3 summarizes some of the common commands. For a complete listing of the com-mands, refer to the *Oracle Net8 Administrator's Guide* (Part #A67440-01).

**TABLE 15.3**    Commonly Used namesctl Commands

| Command | Description |
| --- | --- |
| Exit | Exits namesctl utility. |
| Help | Lists available commands. |
| Ping | Contacts the current or referenced Names Server. |
| Query | Allows a user to query network services associated with a Names Server. |

**TABLE 15.3** Commonly Used namesctl Commands *(continued)*

| Command | Description |
| --- | --- |
| Register | Allows users to register new services with a Names Server. |
| Reload | Refreshes Names Server information. |
| Reorder_ns | Used to discover other Names Server from a client or an existing Name Server. This command creates the sdns.ora file. |
| Save_config | Saves any modifications to the names.ora file and creates a backup file containing the original settings. |
| Startup | Starts the current Names Server. |
| Start_client_ cache | Starts the client-side cache option. |
| Shutdown | Stops the current Names Server. |
| Status | Shows the status of the current Names Server. |
| Unregister | Removes a service definition from the Names Server. |

## Set and Show Commands in *namesctl*

There are other commands used in the namesctl utility. These commands are also available from the Net8 Assistant. The commands are used in conjunction with the SET keyword. Table 15.4 shows a summary of the commands. These commands are used to change various parameters in the names.ora file such as turning on logging and tracing for the Names Server. To check the current value of any parameter, use the SHOW command.

**TABLE 15.4**   SET Commands for the namesctl Utility

| SET parameter | Description |
| --- | --- |
| Cache_checkpoint_ interval | Sets frequency of how often replicated names service data is saved to the Names Server cache. |
| Default_domain | Sets the current default domain |
| Forwarding available | Allows a Names Server to act as the routing mechanism for route connection requests between Names Servers. This only works for Names Servers in the root region. |
| Log_stats_interval | Sets how often statistics are written to the log file. |
| Log_file_name | Sets the name of the names log file. |
| Namesctl_trace_level | Sets the level of tracing. Values are OFF, USER, ADMIN, and SUPPORT. |
| Password | Sets the Names password for stopping Names Server. |
| Requests_enabled | Enables and Disables the Names Server from accepting client requests. |
| Reset_stats_interval | Changes how often Names Server statistics are cleared. |
| Save_config_interval | Sets the save interval in seconds for changes made to the names file during a session. |
| Save_config_on_stop | Will save modifications to the names.ora file when exiting the namesctl utility. |
| Server | Sets the name of the Names Server to manage. |

**TABLE 15.4** SET Commands for the `namesctl` Utility *(continued)*

| SET parameter | Description |
| --- | --- |
| Trace_level | Sets the Names Server trace level to OFF, USER, ADMIN or SUPPORT. |
| Trace_file_name | Sets the name of the trace file. |
| Log_file_name | Sets the name of the log file. |

# Configure Clients to Use Names Servers

After configuring and starting the Names Server, you will configure the clients to use the Names Server. Names Servers are defined for clients in two ways. You can specify preferred Names Servers for a client or you can discover Names Servers the client can use.

## Defining Preferred Names Servers on the Client

You can supply a client with a list of Name Servers to use. These are called preferred Names Servers. Create the list of preferred Names Servers by using the Net8 Assistant. A preferred Names Server is the Names Server that contains the most common service names for the client and is most likely to be closest in proximity to the client site.

To use Net8 Assistant to configure preferred Names Servers, choose Profile from the main Net8 Assistant Screen. Choose the Preferred Oracle Names Server option from the drop-down list box on the right-hand side of the screen. Choose New if this is the first preferred Names Server being defined.

Enter the information about the location of the Names Server (see Figure 15.5). This will vary with the type of protocol used by the Names Server. If you are configuring TCP/IP, which is the default, enter the hostname for the Names Server and the port where the Names Server is listening. After this is complete, save your work by selecting Save Network Configuration from the File menu.

**FIGURE 15.5**    Define preferred Names Servers for the client.

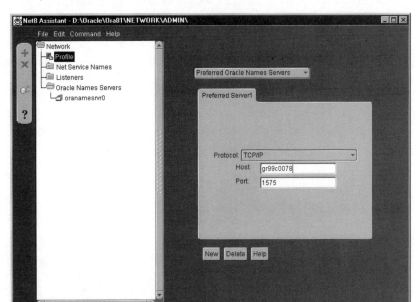

This creates an entry in the sqlnet.ora file. The following listing shows the sqlnet.ora file with a preferred Names Server defined. The Names.preferred_servers parameter contains the list of preferred Names Servers for the client.

```
# C:\V8I\NETWORK\ADMIN\SQLNET.ORA Configuration
# File:C:\v8i\NETWORK\ADMIN\sqlnet.ora
# Generated by Oracle Net8 Assistant

NAMES.PREFERRED_SERVERS =
  (ADDRESS_LIST =
    (ADDRESS = (PROTOCOL = TCP)(HOST = gr99c0073)
(PORT = 1575))
  )
```

## Discover Names Servers from the Client

You can also perform discovery of Names Servers from the Client. The discovery process is done using the `namesctl` utility. You attempt to discover Names Servers from the client that are defined as preferred Names Servers, well-known Names Servers or local Names Servers. (See Chapter 12 for a discussion of these types of Names Servers.)

Once a client discovers a Names Server, it looks for other Names Servers that belong to the same region as the client. The client creates a list of all the Names Servers contacted and how long it took to contact each Names Server. The list is saved in the `sdns.ora` file. The `reorder_ns` command is used from the `namesctl` utility to discover Names Servers. For example:

```
NAMESCTL> reorder_ns
```

## Define the Names Resolution Search Hierarchy

By default, localnaming is checked first, followed by Oracle Names Servers, and finally hostnaming. But you can select a different search hierarchy to resolve service names. Set the `names.directory_path` parameter in the `sqlnet.ora` file from the Net8 Assistant to modify the search hierarchy.

To change the setting for the client, choose the Profile icon. Select Naming from the drop-down list box on the right-hand side of the screen. You will see two columns, Available Methods and Selected Methods. The Selected Methods column shows you the current names resolution search hierarchy. The Available Methods column shows a list of all supported names resolution methods. You can change the order of the naming methods by using the Demote and Promote buttons. You can also move methods from one side to another by clicking the method followed by the appropriate arrow key (see Figure 15.6). Chapter 12 has a listing of the `sqlnet.ora` file with the `names.directory_path` parameter configured.

**FIGURE  15.6**    Profile screen naming methods

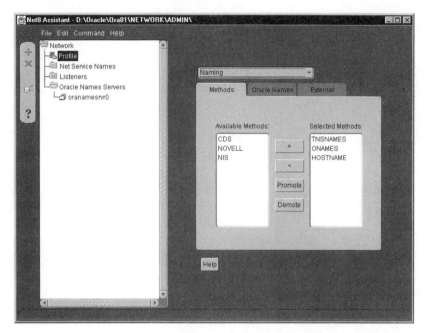

## Client-Side Cache Option

Clients can be configured with a mechanism that saves connect descriptor information from recent contacts made to Oracle Servers. The *client-side cache* option allows the client to contact an Oracle server directly without having to contact a Names Server by using information stored in the client cache. The client cache runs as a background process on UNIX or a service on Windows NT.

The first time a client makes contact with a Names Server to resolve a net service name while the client cache is active, it saves connect descriptor and service information in the cache for a period of time. The time-to-live, by default, is 24 hours. If the client makes subsequent contacts to the same Oracle Server, the client first checks its own cache to see if it can resolve the service. If the client had made contact to this Oracle Server in the last 24 hours, it uses the cached information. Otherwise, it will contact the Names Server and get the latest connect descriptor information from the Names Server. This is beneficial if the Names Server is unavailable. The client can use the cached information to resolve the service name.

To start the client cache, you can run the `start_client_cache` option from the `namesctl` utility. For example:

```
Namesctl> start_client_cache
```

## Other Client-Side Parameters for Oracle Names

There are some optional parameters that you can configure on the client when using the Oracle Names Server. These options are set using the Net8 Assistant. Choose the Profile icon and select Naming from the drop-down list box on the right side of the screen. Table 15.5 is a summary of the prompts and the definitions of the prompts. These parameters are placed in the `sqlnet.ora` file on the client.

**TABLE 15.5**  Optional Client `sqlnet.ora` Parameters for Names Servers

| Prompt | Parameter | Definition |
|---|---|---|
| Default_domain | Names.default_domain | Specifies the domain name to append to an unqualified net service name (for example, GR.COM). |
| Maximum wait each attempt | Names.initial_retry_timeout | Specifies how many seconds a client waits to receive a valid response from a Names Server. Specify 1-600 seconds. |
| Attempts per names server | Names.request_retries | Specifies how many times a client will attempt to contact a Names Server before failure. Specify 1–5. |
| Maximum open connections | Names.max_open_connections | Specifies how many connections a single client can have open to a Names Server. Specify 3–64. |
| Initial preallocated requests | Names.message_pool_start_size | Specifies how many messages to preallocate in the clients message pool. Specify 3–256. |

# Auto-Registration of Services with a Names Server

Listeners can register automatically with Oracle Names Servers. When the listener is started, it contacts the Names Servers that it knows. These can be well-known Names Servers or Names Servers listed in the `sdns.ora` file. The listener passes connect descriptor and service information to the Names Server. This provides a more dynamic approach to keeping Names Servers aware of the latest service information.

To use the autoregistration feature, the listener has to be configured and made aware of the Names Servers available in the region. The listener attempts to contact preferred Names Servers listed in a server-side `sqlnet.ora` file, discovered Names Servers listed in a server-side `sdns.ora` file, and well-known Names Servers defined in the external naming service with hard coded names.

## Configure Autoregistration Using Net8 Assistant

You can use the Net8 Assistant to configure a listener to auto-register with Names Servers. Start Net8 Assistant and choose the listener you want to configure. Select General Parameters from the drop-down list box at the top right of the screen (See Figure 15.7). Choose Register Services with Oracle Names and save your changes.

**FIGURE 15.7** Configure autoregistration

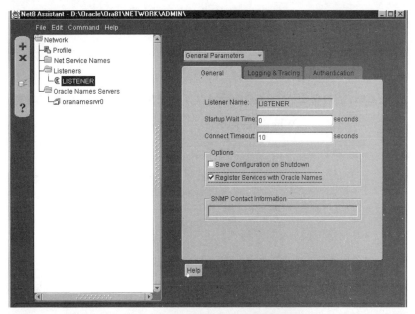

This makes an entry in the listener.ora file. The parameter use_plug_and_play is added to the listener.ora file. Below is an example of the listener.ora file:

```
# C:\V8I\NETWORK\ADMIN\LISTENER.ORA Configuration
# File:C:\v8i\NETWORK\ADMIN\listener.ora
# Generated by Oracle Net8 Assistant

USE_PLUG_AND_PLAY_LISTENER = ON ‡ Auto registration

LISTENER =
  (DESCRIPTION =
    (ADDRESS = (PROTOCOL = TCP)(HOST = gr99c0073)
    (PORT = 1521))
    (PROTOCOL_STACK =
      (PRESENTATION = TTC)
      (SESSION = NS)
    )
  )

SID_LIST_LISTENER =
  (SID_LIST =
    (SID_DESC =
      (GLOBAL_DBNAME = GR99c0073)
      (ORACLE_HOME = c:\v8i)
      (SID_NAME = DBA)
    )
  )
```

## Verifying Listener Autoregistration to Names Servers

When the listener is started, it attempts to contact the Names Servers that it knows about. You can verify that a listener has registered with Names Server at the time it starts. If the registration is done correctly, you will see the word *registered* after the service names. Here is an example of what you would see if you start the listener with autoregistration enabled.

```
D:\ORACLE\ORA81\NETWORK\ADMIN>lsnrctl start

LSNRCTL for 32-bit Windows: Version 8.1.5.0.0 -
Production on 12-FEB-00 17:46:12
(c) Copyright 1998 Oracle Corporation.
All rights reserved.
Starting tnslsnr: please wait...
Service OracleOraHome81TNSListener start pending.
Service OracleOraHome81TNSListener started.
TNSLSNR for 32-bit Windows: Version 8.1.5.0.0 - Production
System parameter file is D:\Oracle\Ora81\network\
admin\listener.ora
Log messages written to D:\Oracle\Ora81\network\log\
listener.log
Listening on:
(DESCRIPTION=(ADDRESS=(PROTOCOL=TCP)(HOST=gr99c0073)
(PORT=1521))(PRO
TOCOL_STACK=(PRESENTATION=TTC)(SESSION=NS)))
Listening on:
(DESCRIPTION=(ADDRESS=(PROTOCOL=IPC)(KEY=DBA))
(PROTOCOL_STACK=(PRESENTATION=TTC)(SESSION=NS)))

Connecting to
(DESCRIPTION=(ADDRESS=(PROTOCOL=TCP)(HOST=gr99c0073)
(PORT=1521))(PRO
TOCOL_STACK=(PRESENTATION=TTC)(SESSION=NS)))
STATUS of the LISTENER
-----------------------
Alias                   LISTENER
Version                 TNSLSNR for 32-bit Windows:
Version 8.1.5.0.0 - Production
Start Date              12-FEB-00 17:46:22
Uptime                  0 days 0 hr. 0 min. 3 sec
Trace Level             off
Security                OFF
SNMP                    OFF
```

```
Listener Parameter File   D:\Oracle\Ora81\network\
admin\listener.ora
Listener Log File         D:\Oracle\Ora81\network\log\
listener.log
Services Summary...
  DBA  (registered)       has 1 service handler(s)
The command completed successfully
```

# Summary

**T**o do well on the OCP exam, you need to understand what an Oracle Names Server is and the advantages of using it. The Names Server centralizes the resolution of service names in the Oracle enterprise to make for easier and more accurate management of the service names. You use the Net8 Assistant to configure the Oracle Names Server. Net8 Assistant allows you to choose between a checkpoint file or database to store the Names Server information. If you store the information in a database, you must run some scripts to configure the database to accept the Names Server data.

You can use the Net8 Assistant to start and stop the Names Server, as well as register service name information with the Names Server. The names.ora file is the main configuration file that stores information about the location of the Names Server.

There is a command line utility, namesctl, that you can use to administer the Names Server. The utility lets you start and stop the Names Server, see the status of the Names Server, and change settings of the Names Server. You can also register new service names using this utility.

Name Servers and clients can dynamically discover other Names Servers in a region. This can be done with the reorder_ns command of the namesctl utility or from the Net8 Assistant. The discovery process is necessary so the new Names Server is aware of other Names Servers to contact for cache replication. The client needs to be able to contact the Names Servers to resolve service names. The discovery process creates the sdns.ora file that contains information about the discovered Name Servers. You can also designate a list of preferred Name Servers in the sqlnet.ora file.

You can change the default search hierarchy for Names resolution on the client by setting the names.directory_path setting in the sqlnet.ora file. You can also configure a client cache that will enable clients to retain connect descriptor information gathered from recent contacts with Names Servers. This can save extra trips to a Names Server.

Autoregistration allows a listener to automatically register service names with a well-known Names Server. The use_plug_and_play parameter in the listener.ora file enables this option. When the listener starts, it contacts the Names Server and passes all of the services for which it is listener on to the Names Server.

## Key Terms

Before you take the exam, make sure you're familiar with the following terms:

Cache replication

Checkpoint option

Client cache option

Database option

reorder_ns

sdns.ora

# Review Questions

1. The following are benefits of using an Oracle Names Server *except*:

   **A.** Simplifies administration

   **B.** Eliminates duplication of naming information across the enterprise

   **C.** Eliminates the need for listeners

   **D.** Increases efficiency by storing service names in centralized locations

2. Choose the phrase that best completes this sentence: A Names Server...

   **A.** Must use an Oracle Database to store service names

   **B.** Must reside on the same server as an Oracle Database

   **C.** May use an Oracle Database to store service names

   **D.** Must not be used with Multithreaded Server

   **E.** None of the above

3. Which of the following is *not* a step in resolving a service name using Oracle Names Server?

   **A.** The Names Server sends a request to the destination database.

   **B.** The Names Server receives a request from a client.

   **C.** The client receives information from the Names Server regarding the resolved sevice name.

   **D.** The Names Server sends resolved service name information back to the client.

   **E.** All of these are steps in resolving a service name.

**4.** The two kinds of domain naming models that are used when establishing your enterprise are:

   **A.** Flat naming model

   **B.** Multidimensional naming model

   **C.** Hierarchical naming model

   **D.** Enterprise naming model

**5.** Which of the following is a characteristic of the flat naming model?

   **A.** Used to reduce configuration work on the client

   **B.** All names are common within a single domain

   **C.** All names are distinct within a single domain

   **D.** Must be used when the database is setup in multi-threaded server mode

**6.** DBA.GR.COM is an example of:

   **A.** A Checkpoint naming model

   **B.** A Multidimensional naming model

   **C.** A Hierarchical naming model

   **D.** A Enterprise naming model

**7.** In order to keep all service names in one central location, the DBA would most likely configure:

   **A.** Cache replication

   **B.** A region database

   **C.** Region concentration

   **D.** Region pooling

   **E.** None of the above

8. Which best characterizes the Oracle Names Server?

   **A.** Host naming

   **B.** Global naming

   **C.** Centralized naming

   **D.** Enterprise naming

   **E.** None of the above

9. Multiple Names Servers are kept synchonized by which methods? (Choose two.)

   **A.** Cache replication

   **B.** Cache cohesion

   **C.** Cache fusion

   **D.** By defining a region database

10. The icon used to configure an Oracle Names Server using the Net8 Assistant is:

    **A.** Services

    **B.** Listeners

    **C.** Tnsnames servers

    **D.** Oracle Names Server

    **E.** None of the above

11. Server names that are hard coded into the Names Server environment are called:

    **A.** Enterprise Names Servers

    **B.** Universal Names Servers

    **C.** Well-known Names Servers

    **D.** Default Names Servers

**12.** The file that is created when the Names Server is configured is:

**A.** `sdns.ora`

**B.** `onames.ora`

**C.** `names.ora`

**D.** `namesctl.ora`

**E.** None of the above

**13.** The location of the file created in question #12 is:

**A.** `$ORACLE_HOME/net81/admin`

**B.** `$ORACLE_HOME/network/names`

**C.** `$ORACLE_HOME/network/admin`

**D.** `$ORACLE_HOME/network/onames`

**14.** The drop-down list box choice from the Net8 Assistant to start the Names Server is:

**A.** Start Server

**B.** Manage Server

**C.** Configure Server

**D.** Manage Data

**15.** Which of the following syntax from the file created in question #12 is correct?

**A.** `NAMES.ADDRESSES=(ADDRESS= (PROTOCOL=TCP) (HOST=GR.COM) (PORT=1575))`

**B.** `NAMES.ADDR=(ADDRESS=(PROTOCOL=TCP) (HOST=GR.COM)(PORT=1575))`

**C.** `ONAMES.ADDRESSES=(ADDRESS=(PROTOCOL=TCP) (HOST=GR.COM)(PORT=1575))`

**D.** `NAMES.ADDRESSES=(ADDRESS=(PROTOCOL=TCP, HOST=GR.COM,PORT=1575))`

**16.** If the DBA stops the Names Server, what will happen to open database connections that utilized the Names Server to establish a connection?

**A.** Connections will be disconnected immediately.

**B.** An error message will be generated next time they access the database.

**C.** They will be enabled to execute queries.

**D.** Connections will be disconnected but receive no error messages.

**E.** None of the above

**17.** The DBA wants to configure client workstations to use Names Server net service name resolution before checking any other names resolution options. Which line would correctly satisfy this request:

**A.** NAMES.SEARCH_PATH=(ONAMES,HOSTNAME, TNSNAMES)

**B.** NAMES.SEARCH_HEIRARCHY=(ONAMES, TNSNAMES.HOSTNAME)

**C.** NAMES.DIRECTORY_PATH=(ONAMES, HOSTNAME,TNSNAMES)

**D.** NAMES.SEARCH_ARGS=(ONAMES,HOSTNAMES,TNSNAMES)

**18.** Which file on the database server would the line from question #17 be added to?

**A.** sqlnet.trc

**B.** sqlnet.ora

**C.** tnsnames.ora

**D.** names.ora

**E.** None of the above

**19.** The DBA wants to start the Oracle Names Server from the command line. Which line would accomplish this?

**A.** `nmctl start`

**B.** `onames start`

**C.** `namesctl start`

**D.** `start names`

**E.** None of the above

**20.** Which command creates a file that will contain Names Server and address information?

**A.** `discover_names`

**B.** `find_ns`

**C.** `reorder_ns`

**D.** `create_names`

**E.** None of the above

# Answers to Review Questions

1. C. Oracle Names Servers allow for the centralized configuration and management of network services across an enterprise. Because network service information is centralized, administration is simplified which greatly reduces duplication of service name information. All of these options are true, but using a Names Server does not eliminate the need for listeners. Listeners will still be listening on Oracle Servers for client requests.

2. C. Names Servers can reside on any supported server in the enterprise. No database has to be present on the server to utilize a Names Server. Multithreaded connections can utilize a Names Server for names resolution. A Names Server may use a database to store service names information.

3. A. It almost sounds as if all of these are true statements. Names Servers do receive requests from clients, and clients do receive connection information back from a Names Server. But the Names Server never contacts the destination server directly. It is only used to pass connection information back to the client.

4. A, C. Naming conventions can be established as either flat (the most common) or hierarchical. Hierarchical naming has the advantage of allowing duplicate service names access the enterprise. The domain name is appended onto the service name to make the network service unique. Both of these are naming models that encompass the enterprise.

5. C. For both hierarchical and checkpoint naming models, no network service names can be the same within a given domain.

6. C. When the network service name is used in conjunction with a domain name, you get a name such as DBA.GR.COM. This would be used in the hierarchical model.

**7.** B. For truly centralized naming, a database is probably the best option when configuring Names Servers. Multiple Names Servers can share a region database. The database stores all information related to network services. This also reduces network traffic between Names Server because no cache replication is necessary.

**8.** C. We stay with the theme of having a single place to resolve service name information. Hence, the correct answer would be C, Centralized naming. Hostnaming requires the `tnsnames.ora` file, and global-naming is not a type of names resolution offering. However, global names can be used to resolve services.

**9.** A, D. If Names Servers are sharing a region database, then all Names Servers will be sharing the same information from the database. If no region database is configured, Names Servers can be kept synchronized by enabling cache replication. Replication will force Names Servers to update each other periodically with the latest service names information.

**10.** D. The Oracle Names Servers icon in the Net8 Assistant is used to configure the Oracle Names Server.

**11.** C. Some service names are "hard wired" into the Names Server environment. These are well-known names. They are well known because they are defined with common names within the network's external naming environment. The dynamic discovery option uses these names, if they exist within the enterprise, when building a list of possible Names Servers. This saves the clients from having to be told explicitly about preferred Names Servers.

**12.** C. Like most of the network's components, a Names Server needs a configuration file. And it is named appropriately—`names.ora`.

**13.** C. The `names.ora` file is located·on the Names Server in the default location of: `$ORACLE_HOME/network/admin`. On Windows NT, the path would be `%ORACLE_HOME\network\admin`.

**14.** B. There are several ways to start and stop the Names Servers. The command line utility `namesctl` can be used. On NT, the names service can be started from the NT services window. And from the Net8 Assistant, the drop-down choice of Manage Server can be chosen to start and stop Names Servers.

15. A. The `names.addresses` choice is added to the `names.ora` file after completing the configuration of the Names Server in Net8 Assistant. It looks very similar to an entry in the `listener.ora` file. The protocol, host, and port all need to be specified. Each choice is enclosed in parentheses, and the entire entry after the equals sign is also enclosed in parentheses. The correct name of the entry is `names.addresses`.

16. C. The Names Server is not a middleware component. Once a Names Server has looked up service information for a client, it is out of the processing loop. It operates similarly to a listener in that regard. Nothing happens to *existing* connections if the Names Server goes down. New connections that rely upon the Names Server for service resolution will have problems getting connected, but existing connections are unaffected. They will be able to execute queries or any other database commands.

17. C. By default, a Names Server will be searched if localnaming via `tnsnames.ora` fails to satisfy a user request. If the DBA wants to alter the search path, then the `names.directory_path sqlnet.ora` parameter on the client workstation would be set to an alternate search path.

18. B. As stated in the answer to #17, the `names.directory_path` parameter is added to the `sqlnet.ora` file on the client workstation to alter the default names resolution search path.

19. C. The command line choice to start the Names Server is `namesctl start`. This is similar to other `start` commands such as `lsnrctl start` and `cmctl start`. Remember that `ctl` is the last part of the names for all of these commands. (NOTE: In older releases of Oracle, the names of these commands on Windows NT were appended with the release number extension, such as `namesctl80`. This is no longer the case in Version 8i.)

20. E. If a client needs to discover what Names Servers are in a region, a command needs to be run on the client that collects this information and stores it in a common location on the client. The `reorder_ns` command can be run from the `namesctl` command line utility. This creates a file called `sdns.ora` (`.sdns.ora` on Unix) that contains information about Names Servers that the client can contact for resolving service names. None of these answers correctly states the filename.

# Configuring the Multithreaded Server Option

## ORACLE8i NETWORK ADMINISTRATION EXAM OBJECTIVES COVERED IN THIS CHAPTER:

✓ Describe the features of MTS.

✓ Describe the situations when it is advantageous to use MTS.

✓ Define the architecture of MTS.

✓ Outline the steps of an MTS connection.

✓ Configure MTS on the Oracle Instance.

✓ Administer MTS using the V$ views.

✓ Configure the Large Pool for MTS.

✓ Configure connection pooling in MTS.

✓ Configure a client to request dedicated connections in an MTS environment.

✓ Tune the MTS environment.

Exam objectives are subject to change at any time without prior notice and at Oracle's sole discretion. Please visit Oracle's Training and Certification Web site (http://education .oracle.com/certification) for the most current exam objectives listing.

**A**s the number of users connecting to Oracle services in the enterprise grows, the system requirements of the servers increase—particularly the memory and process requirements. This chapter discusses the *Oracle Multithreaded Server option* and its benefits. You will learn the steps of the connection process as well as the configuration of the Multithreaded Server option. A discussion of how user requests are processed in a Multithreaded Server configuration is provided. You will also learn how to manage the Multithreaded Server environment by utilizing various Oracle data dictionary views. You will see how to configure clients to request dedicated connections when connecting to an Oracle database configured with Multithreaded Server. You will learn how to configure connection pooling when you are using a Multithreaded Server. You will also learn where to find information to assist you in tuning the Multithreaded Server.

# Multithreaded Server Configuration

**M**ultithreaded Server (MTS) is an optional configuration of the Oracle Server that allows support for a larger number of concurrent connections without increasing physical resource requirements. This is accomplished by sharing resources among groups of users.

# Dedicated Server versus Multithreaded Server

If you have ever gone to a very upscale restaurant, you may have had your own personal waiter. The waiter is there to greet you and escort you to your seat. The waiter will take your order for food and drinks and even help in the preparation of your order. No matter how many other patrons enter the restaurant, your waiter is responsible for serving only your requests. Therefore, your service is very consistent—if the person is a good waiter.

A dedicated server environment works in much the same way. Every client connection has an associated dedicated server process on the machine where the Oracle Server exists. No matter how many other connections are made to the server, you always have the same dedicated server responsible for processing only your requests. You utilize the services of that server process until you disconnect from the Oracle Server.

Most restaurants tend to be more like Multithreaded Servers. When you walk in, you are assigned a waiter or waitress. They may have many other tables they are responsible for serving. This is good for the restaurant, because they can serve more customers without increasing the staff. It may be fine for you as well, if the restaurant is not too busy and the waiter or waitress is not responsible for too many tables. Also, if most of the orders are small, the staff can keep up with the requests and service will be as good as if you had your own personal waiter.

In the diner, the waitress takes your order and places it on a turnstile. If the diner has multiple cooks, the order is picked up from the turnstile and prepared by one of the available cooks. When the cook completes the preparation of the dinner, it is placed in a location where the waitress can pick it up and bring it back to your table.

This is how a Multithreaded Server environment works. In a multithreaded environment, clients share processes on the Oracle Server. These shared processes are called *dispatchers*. Dispatchers are like the waiter or waitress in the diner. A dispatcher can be responsible for taking the orders of many clients.

When you request something from the server, it is the dispatcher's responsibility to take your request and place it in a location called a *request queue*. The request queue functions like the turnstile in the diner analogy. There is one request queue where all of the dispatcher processes place their client requests. The request queue is a structure contained in the SGA.

*Shared server processes*, like cooks in a diner, are responsible for fulfilling the client requests. The shared server process executes the request and places the result into an area of the SGA called a *response queue*. Every dispatcher has its own response queue. The dispatcher picks up the completed request from the response queue and returns the results back to the client. Figure 16.1 depicts the processing steps for a Multithreaded Server request shown here:

1. The client passes a request to the dispatcher serving it.

2. The dispatcher places the request on a request queue in the SGA.

3. One of the shared server processes executes the request.

4. The shared server places the completed request on the dispatchers' response queue of the SGA.

5. The dispatcher picks up the completed request from the response queue.

6. The completed request is passed back to the client.

**FIGURE 16.1** Request processing in Multithreaded Server

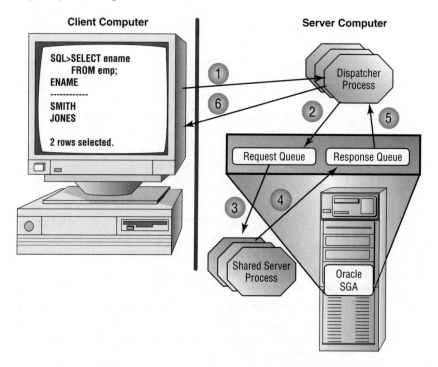

## Advantages of Multithreaded Server

A Multithreaded Server is used in situations where server resources, such as memory and active processes, become constrained. People tend to throw more hardware at problems like these. It will likely remedy the problem, but may be an unnecessary expense.

If your system is experiencing these problems, multithreaded allows you to support the same or greater number of connections without additional hardware requirements. Multithreaded Server tends to decrease the overall memory and process requirements on the server.

An average dedicated connection takes roughly 2 to 4 megabytes of memory. A multithreaded connection takes about 2 megabytes of memory. As you can see, there will be some overall memory reduction. Also, because clients are sharing processes, the total number of processes is reduced. These translate into resource savings on the server.

Multithreaded Server is also required to take advantage of certain network options, such as connection concentration when using Connection Manager. Connection Manager is discussed in Chapter 17: Configuring Connection Manager.

## Applications Suited to Multithreaded Server

Multithreaded Server is suitable for "high think" applications. High think applications are comprised of small transactions with natural pauses in the transaction patterns. These types of applications are good candidates for multithreaded connections. An example of a high think application would be an order entry system. Order entry systems tend to have small transactions with natural pauses in the work pattern of entering the information.

## Drawbacks of Multithreaded Server

Applications that generate a significant amount of network traffic or result in large result sets are not good candidates for multithreaded connections. Think of the diner analogy from the previous discussion. Your service is fine until two parties of twelve people show up. All of a sudden the waitress is overwhelmed with work from these two other tables and your service begins to suffer. The same thing would happen in a multithreaded environment. If requests for large quantities of information start going to the dispatchers, the dispatchers can become overwhelmed by these large requests, and you may see performance suffer for the other clients connected to the dispatcher. This, in turn will increase your response times. Dedicated processes better serve these types of applications.

There are some functions that are not allowed when you are using a multithreaded connection. You cannot start up, shut down or perform certain kinds of recovery of an Oracle Server when connected via a multithreaded connection.

## Scalability versus Performance

Multithreaded Server is a scalability enhancement option, not a performance enhancement option. If you are looking for an increase of performance, Multithreaded Server is not what you should be configuring. Only use Multithreaded Server if you are experiencing the system constraint problems discussed earlier. You will always have equal or better performance in a dedicated server environment.

## Oracle Server Changes in a Multithreaded Environment

When Multithreaded Server is configured, Oracle adds two new types of structures to the System Global Area (SGA): request queues and response queues. These structures do not exist in a dedicated server environment. There is one request queue for MTS and a response queue for each dispatcher process. The request queue is a location in the SGA where the dispatcher places client requests. These requests are then executed by a shared server process. The shared server process then places the competed request in the dispatchers' response queue.

You have to configure the number of dispatcher and shared server processes that you want to start with when the instance starts. You also have to configure the maximum number of each of these structures. Later, you will see how to determine the starting number of dispatchers and shared server processes.

In a dedicated environment, each dedicated server has a memory segment called a Program Global Area (PGA). The PGA is an area of memory where information about each client session is maintained. This information includes bind variables, cursor information, and the client's sort area. In a multithreaded environment, this information is moved from the PGA to an area of the SGA called the User Global Area, or UGA. You can configure a special area of the SGA called the *Large Pool* to accommodate the bulk of the UGA. In older releases of Oracle, the entire UGA was stored in the Shared Pool. As of Oracle8, the majority of the UGA can be stored in the Large Pool. You will see how to configure the Large Pool later. Figure 16.2 shows how the SGA and PGA structures differ between a dedicated and multithreaded environment.

**FIGURE 16.2** SGA dedicated vs Multithreaded Server

Dedicated Server SGA

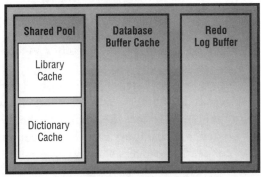

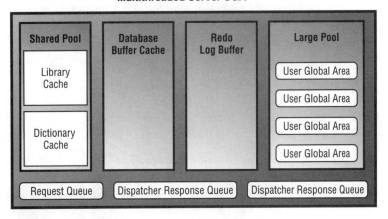

# The Role of the Listener in a Multithreaded Environment

The listener plays an important role in the multithreaded environment. The listener is responsible for supplying the client with the address of the dispatcher to connect to when a user requests connections to a Multithreaded Server. When the dispatcher receives the redirected connection request, it notifies the listener, so the listener is aware of the number of connections the dispatcher is managing. This information allows the listener to take advantage of dispatcher load balancing. Dispatcher Load balancing is something new in Oracle8i.

Load balancing allows the listener to make intelligent decisions about which dispatcher to redirect client connections to, so no one dispatcher becomes overburdened. When the listener receives a connection request, it looks at the current connection load for each dispatcher and redirects the client connection request to the least loaded dispatcher. By doing so, the listener ensures that connections are evenly distributed across dispatchers. When a client connection terminates, the listener is updated to reflect the change in the number of connections the dispatcher is handling. Figure 16.3 depicts the steps of the multithreaded connection process shown here:

1. The dispatcher processes are spawned when an instance is started.

2. The client contacts the Oracle Server after resolving the service name.

3. The server redirects the client connection to the least busy dispatcher.

4. The dispatcher process manages the client server request.

5. The dispatcher registers connection information with the listener.

**FIGURE  16.3**   Multithreaded Server connection process

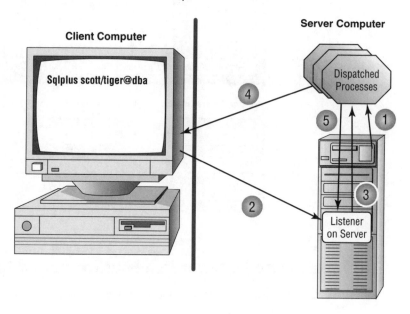

# Configuring the Multithreaded Server Option

**M**ultithreaded Server requires additional parameters in the init.ora file. These parameters identify the number and type of dispatchers, the number of shared servers, and the name of the database that you want to associate with the Multithreaded Server.

## *MTS_DISPATCHERS* Parameter

This parameter configures the number of dispatchers to start when the instance is started. Specify the number of dispatchers and the type of protocol that the dispatchers can respond to. You can add additional dispatchers dynamically using the ALTER SYSTEM command. This allows you to increase the number of dispatchers without bringing the instance down.

This command has a number of optional attributes. The two main attributes are the number of dispatchers and the protocol the dispatcher will listen for. For example, say you wanted to configure three TCP/IP dispatchers and two IPC dispatchers. You would set the parameter as follows:

```
mts_dispatchers = "(PRO=TCP)(DIS=3)(PRO=IPC)(DIS=2)"
```

All of the attributes for this parameter can be abbreviated. Table 16.1 shows the other attributes you can set with the MTS_DISPATCHERS parameter. Of the three attributes, ADDRESS, DESCRIPTION, or PROTOCOL, only one needs to be specified for a MTS_DISPATCHERS definition.

**TABLE 16.1** Summary of MTS_DISPATCHER attributes

| Attribute | Abbreviations | Description |
|-----------|---------------|-------------|
| Address | ADD or ADDR | Old Net8 syntax for the network address of where the dispatchers listen |
| Description | DES or DESC | The network description of the endpoint where the dispatcher is listening, including the protocol being listened for |

**TABLE 16.1** Summary of MTS_DISPATCHER attributes *(continued)*

| Attribute | Abbreviations | Description |
|---|---|---|
| Dispatchers | DIS or DISP | The number of dispatchers to start when the instance is started |
| Listener | LIS or LIST | The address of the listener that the dispatchers register with |
| Protocol | Pro or Prot | The network protocol for the dispatcher to listen for |
| Service | SER or SERV | The name of the Oracle Service |
| Sessions | SES or SESS | The maximum number of network sessions allowable for this dispatcher |

## Determining the Number of Dispatchers to Start

The number of dispatchers you start will vary depending on your particular configuration. Your operating system may place a limit on the number of connections that one dispatcher can handle. Consult your Operating system documentation to get this information.

Use the following formula as a guide when deciding how many dispatchers to initially configure:

```
Number of Dispatchers = CEIL  (maximum number of
concurrent sessions / connections per dispatcher)
```

For example, if you have 200 concurrent TCP/IP connections, and you want each dispatcher to manage 20 concurrent connections, you would need 10 dispatchers. You would set your MTS_DISPATCHERS parameter as follows:

```
mts_dispatchers = "(PRO=TCP)(DIS=10)"
```

You can determine the number of concurrent connections by querying the V$SESSION view. This view shows you the number of clients currently connected to the Oracle Server. Here is an example of the query:

```
SQL> select sid,serial#,username,server,program
from v$session
  2* where sid > 6
```

| SID | SERIAL# | USERNAME | SERVER | PROGRAM |
|-----|---------|----------|--------|---------|
| 7 | 13 | SCOTT | DEDICATED | SQLPLUS.EXE |
| 8 | 12 | SCOTT | DEDICATED | SQLPLUS.EXE |
| 9 | 4 | SYSTEM | DEDICATED | SQLPLUS.EXE |

In this example, you see three users connected to the server. In the SQL statement, you can ignore the first six sessions. These entries refer to the background processes such as PMON and SMON. Take a sampling of this view over a typical work period to get an idea of the average number of concurrent connections for your system. Use this number as a guide when establishing the starting number of dispatchers.

## Allocating Additional Dispatchers

You can start additional dispatchers dynamically using the ALTER SYSTEM command. You can start any number of dispatchers up to the MTS_MAX_SERVERS setting. Here is an example of adding three TCP/IP dispatchers to a system configured with two TCP/IP dispatchers:

```
ALTER SYSTEM SET mts_dispatchers="(PRO=TCP)(DIS=5)";
```

Notice that you set the number to the total number of dispatchers you want, not the number of dispatchers you want to add.

## *MTS_MAX_DISPATCHERS* Parameter

Set this parameter to the maximum number of dispatchers you anticipate needing for the Oracle Server. This number cannot be set dynamically. The maximum number of processes a dispatcher could run concurrently is operating system dependent. Use the following formula to set this parameter:

```
mts_max_dispatchers = (maximum number of dispatchers/
connections per dispatcher)
```

Here is an example of the parameter:

```
mts_max_dispatchers = 5
```

### *MTS_SERVERS* Parameter

This parameter specifies the number of shared servers to start when the Oracle instance is started. This parameter can be altered dynamically with the ALTER SYSTEM command.

The number of servers necessary will vary depending on the type of activities your users are performing. Generally, for the types of high think applications that will be using multithreaded connections, 15 to 20 connections per shared server should be adequate. If your users are going to require larger result sets or are doing more intensive processing, then you will want to reduce this ratio.

Here is an example of the parameter:

```
mts_servers = 3
```

## Allocating Additional Shared Servers

You can start additional shared servers dynamically using the ALTER SYSTEM command. You can start any number of dispatchers up to the MTS_MAX_ DISPATCHERS setting. Here is an example of adding three additional shared servers to a system initially configured with two shared servers:

```
ALTER SYSTEM SET mts_servers = 5;
```

Notice that you set the number to the total number of shared servers you want, not the number of shared servers you want to add.

### *MTS_MAX_SERVERS* Parameter

Set this parameter to the maximum number of shared servers you anticipate needing for the Oracle Server. This number cannot be set dynamically. Generally, you should set this parameter to accommodate your heaviest work times.

Here is an example of the parameter:

```
mts_max_servers = 5
```

# Starting the Instance and Managing Multithreaded Server

**A**fter you have completed the configuration work in the init.ora file, you will need to restart your database. Once you have restarted your database, you should query the V$ views to see if the instance has started the shared servers and the dispatcher processes. Later in this chapter, we will discuss the various data dictionary views used to manage Multithreaded Server.

> ### Troubleshooting Startup Problems after Configuring Multithreaded Server
>
> If you have problems starting the instance, chances are that you have a problem with one of the Net8 files. If you receive an error that states the MTS_DISPATCHERS parameter is incorrect, make a backup of all of your Net8 files, such as tnsnames.ora and listener.ora, and recreate these files using the Net8 Assistant. Most problems we have experienced with the Multithreaded Server can be traced back to modifications made to these files without using Net8 Assistant. Even cutting and pasting service information to create new service definitions can cause problems. After you have recreated your files, try to restart your instance.

## Registering Dispatcher Information with the Listener

When Multithreaded Server is started, it will register dispatcher information with the listener. You can query the listener to see this registered information. The listener will keep track of the current connection load across all of the dispatchers. This information is necessary so that the listener can take advantage of dispatcher load balancing.

## Displaying Information about Multithreaded Connections Using lsnrctl

You can user the lsnrctl command line utility to see information about the dispatcher processes. Use the *lsnrctl services* query to view information about dispatchers. The example below shows a listener listening for two TCP/IP dispatchers. Notice that the listing displays how many connections each dispatcher is managing, the listening location of the dispatcher, and the process ID of the dispatcher. This example has three active connections, two on the first dispatcher and one on the second dispatcher:

```
D:\>lsnrctl services

LSNRCTL for 32-bit Windows: Version 8.1.5.0.0 -
Production on 13-FEB-00 18:41:02
(c) Copyright 1998 Oracle Corporation.
All rights reserved.

Connecting to (DESCRIPTION=(ADDRESS=(PROTOCOL=TCP)
(HOST=gr99c0073)
```

```
(PORT=1521))(PROTOCOL_STACK=(PRESENTATION=TTC)
(SESSION=NS)))
Services Summary...
  DBA              has 4 service handler(s)
 DEDICATED SERVER established:0 refused:0
     LOCAL SERVER
   DISPATCHER established:2 refused:0 current:2 max:254
   state:ready
     D000 <machine: gr99c0073, pid: 151>
     (ADDRESS=(PROTOCOL=tcp)(HOST=gr99c0073)(PORT=1191))
   DISPATCHER established:1 refused:0 current:1 max:254
   state:ready
     D001 <machine: gr99c0073, pid: 167>
     (ADDRESS=(PROTOCOL=tcp)(HOST=gr99c0073)(PORT=1192))
```

# Data Dictionary Views for Multithreaded Server

The data dictionary provides views you can query to gather information about the multithreaded environment. These views provide information about the number of dispatchers and shared servers configured, the activity among the shared servers and dispatchers, the activity in the request and response queue, as well as the clients that are connected with multithreaded connections. We have included the column definitions for each of these views. You will see later in this chapter how you can use these views when you are tuning the Multithreaded Server. For a complete listing of all of the column definitions for the V$ views, consult the *Oracle 8i Reference, Release 8.1.5* (Part #A67790-01).

### V$DISPATCHER Dictionary View

The V$DISPATCHER view contains information about the dispatchers. You can collect information about the dispatchers' activity, the number of connections the dispatchers are currently handling, and the total number of connections each dispatcher has handled since instance startup. Here is a sample output from the V$DISPATCHER view:

```
SQL> select name,status,messages,idle,busy,bytes,breaks
from
   2  v$dispatcher


NAME STATUS  MESSAGES    IDLE BUSY BYTES BREAKS
---- ------  ---------- ------- ---- ------ ------
D000 WAIT           168 389645  108 12435      0
D001 WAIT            94 389668   48  6940      0
```

### *V$DISPATCHER_RATE* Dictionary View

The V$DISPATCHER_RATE view shows statistics for the dispatchers, such as the average number of bytes processed, the maximum number of inbound and outbound connections, and the average rate of bytes processed per client connection. This information can be useful when taking load measurements for the dispatchers. Below is a sample of the output from this view:

```
SQL>select name,avg_event_rate,avg_msg_rate,
    avg_svr_byte_rate from v$dispatcher_rate
```

| NAME | AVG_EVENT_RATE | AVG_MSG_RATE | AVG_SVR_BYTE_RATE |
| ---- | -------------- | ------------ | ----------------- |
| D000 | 12 | 0 | 0 |
| D001 | 14 | 0 | 1 |

### *V$QUEUE* Dictionary View

The V$QUEUE dictionary view contains information about the request and response queues. The information deals with how long requests are waiting in the queues. This information is valuable when you are trying to determine if more shared servers are needed. The following example shows the COMMON request queue and two response queues:

```
SQL> select * from v$queue;
```

| PADDR | TYPE | QUEUED | WAIT | TOTALQ |
| -------- | ---------- | --------- | --------- | --------- |
| 00 | COMMON | 0 | 0 | 152 |
| 03C6C244 | DISPATCHER | 0 | 0 | 91 |
| 03C6C534 | DISPATCHER | 0 | 0 | 71 |

### *V$CIRCUIT* Dictionary View

V$CIRCUIT displays information about multithreaded client connections, such as the volume of information that has passed between the client and the dispatcher and the current status of the client connection. The SADDR column displays the session address for the connected session. This can be joined to the V$SESSION view to display information about the user to whom this connection belongs. See the listing below:

```
SQL> select circuit,dispatcher,server,waiter WTR,
    2 status,queue,bytes from v$circuit;
```

```
CIRCUIT  DISPATCH SERVER   WTR STATUS QUEUE  BYTES SADDR
-------- -------- -------- --- ------ ------ ----- ------
03E2A624 03C6C244 00        00  NORMAL NONE   47330 03C7AB68
03E2A724 03C6C534 03C6BC64 00  NORMAL SERVER 43572 03C79BE8
```

### V$SHARED_SERVER Dictionary View

This view contains information about the shared server processes. It displays information about the number of requests and the amount of information processed by the shared servers. It also indicates the status of the shared server (i.e. whether it is active or idle).

```
SQL> select name,status,messages,bytes,idle,busy,
        requests from v$shared_server;
```

| NAME | STATUS | MESSAGES | BYTES | IDLE | BUSY | REQUESTS |
| ---- | ------ | -------- | ----- | ----- | ---- | -------- |
| S000 | EXEC | 372 | 86939 | 98472 | 300 | 175 |
| S001 | EXEC | 26 | 9851 | 98703 | 38 | 13 |

### V$SESSION Dictionary View

This view contains information about the client session. The SERVER column indicates whether this client is using a dedicated session or a dispatcher. The listing below shows an example of the V$SESSION view displaying the server information. This listing ignores any rows that do not have a username to avoid listing information about the background processes. Notice that user Scott has a server value of SHARED. This means Scott is connected to a dispatcher. The SYSTEM user is connected using a local connection because the status is NONE. If a user connected using a dedicated connection, the status would be DEDICATED.

```
SQL> select username,program,server from v$session
        where username is not null;
```

| USERNAME | PROGRAM | SERVER |
| --------------- | --------------- | --------- |
| SYSTEM | SQLPLUS.EXE | NONE |
| SCOTT | SQLPLUS.EXE | SHARED |

### *V$MTS* Dictionary View

This view contains information about the configuration of the dispatchers and shared servers. This includes the maximum number of connections for each dispatcher, the number of shared servers that have been started and stopped, and the highest number of shared servers that have been active at the same time. This view gives you an indication of whether more shared server processes should be started. The sample below shows output from this view:

```
SQL> select MAX_CONNECTIONS MAX_CONN, SERVERS_STARTED
SRV_STARTED, SERVERS_TERMINATED SRV_TERM,
SERVERS_HIGHWATER SRV_HW
FROM V$MTS;


MAX_CONN SRV_STARTED SRV_TERM SRV_HW
-------- ----------- -------- ------
      60           0        0      2
```

# Requesting a Dedicated Connection in a Multithreaded Environment

**Y**ou can have multithreaded and dedicated servers connecting to a single Oracle Server. This is advantageous in situations where you have a mix of activity on the Oracle Server. Some users may be well suited to multithreaded connections while other types of users may be better suited to use dedicated connections.

By default, if Multithreaded Server is configured, a client is connected to a dispatcher unless the client explicitly requests a dedicated connection. As part of the connection descriptor, the client has to send information requesting a dedicated connection. Configure this option using the Net8 Assistant. Clients may request this type of connection if the names resolution method is localnaming or a Name Server is used. This option cannot be used with hostnaming.

## Configuring Dedicated Connections When Hostnaming is Used

If you are using hostnaming, Open the Net8 Assistant and click the Net Service Names icon. Select the service name that you want to modify. Click the **Advanced** icon in the Service Identification section, and the Advanced Service Options screen will appear. Choose the Use a Dedicated Server box. Click OK and save your configuration. This places an entry in your tnsnames.ora file. The following listing shows the tnsnames.ora file with the (SERVER=DEDICATED) parameter added to the DBA net service name. The SERVER parameter can also be abbreviated to SRVR.

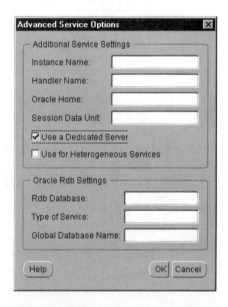

```
# D:\ORACLE\ORA81\NETWORK\ADMIN\TNSNAMES.ORA Configuration
# File:D:\Oracle\Ora81\NETWORK\ADMIN\tnsnames.ora
# Generated by Oracle Net8 Assistant

DBA =
  (DESCRIPTION =
    (ADDRESS_LIST =
      (ADDRESS = (PROTOCOL = TCP)(HOST = weishan)
    (PORT = 1521))
    )
    (CONNECT_DATA =
      (SERVICE_NAME = DBA)
```

```
        (SRVR = DEDICATED) " Request a dedicated connection
    for DBA
        )
    )
```

## Configuring Dedicated Connections
## When a Name Server is Used

If you are using the Oracle Names Server method, Open the Net8 Assistant and choose the Names Server you want to modify. Choose Manage Data from the drop down list box at the top right-hand side of the screen. Click the Add radio button to add a new net service definition. Enter the net service name and protocol information. Click the Advanced button at the lower right side of the screen. You will see the same screen as the one below. Click OK and save your modifications.

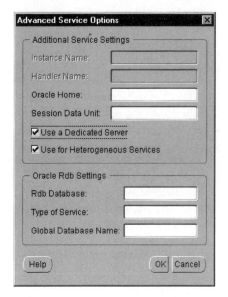

# Connection Pooling

**C**onnection pooling is another scalability feature of Net8. This option allows client connections to share a finite number of network connections. This is conceptually similar to a party line telephone call. Party lines allow for multiple parties to share the same phone line.

Connection pooling takes the concept of shared dispatcher processes one step further. Now, you not only maximize the use of the processes on the server, you also maximize the use of the physical network connections. Connection pooling can only be used with Multithreaded Server.

Connection pooling works like this: You define a dispatcher to be able to handle a certain number of concurrent connections. This is done using the CONNECTIONS option in the MTS_DISPATCHERS parameter. You also have to configure a value that specifies how many total connections a dispatcher can handle at one time. This is done using the SESSIONS option of the MTS_DISPATCHERS parameter. The difference between SESSIONS and CONNECTIONS is called the pool size and is the number of connections that can be waiting for a free line to connect to the dispatcher.

You also need to set the POOL option of the MTS_DISPATCHERS parameter. This option specifies how pooling will be done. You can have pooling for incoming requests, outgoing requests, or for both incoming and outgoing connections.

---

### Connection Pooling Example

Say you want to configure a dispatcher to be able to handle 10 concurrent connections, but no more than 15 maximum connections. This means the dispatcher could have 15 clients connected, but only 10 could be doing any work. The difference of five represents clients that are connected but are idle or waiting for an idle connection. You would have 10 physical network connections servicing 15 clients.

You also have to specify how long a client is willing to wait for an idle connection. This is specified with the TICKS parameter. The TICKS parameter is specified in 10-second increments, so a value of four means the client will wait up to 40 seconds for an idle connection. The following line would be placed in the init.ora file:

```
mts_dispatchers="(PRO=TCP)(CON=10)(DIS=2)(POO=ON)(TIC=4)
(SESS=15)"
```

If you have 10 clients actively working, and a new client wants to establish a connection, this client will wait for one of the 10 working clients to become idle. When this happens, the dispatcher disconnects the old client from the network connection and connects new the client to the now available network connection. If the disconnected client needs to process another request, this client has to wait for an idle client. In this way, we are able to connect more clients with fewer physical connections.

Connection pooling is advantageous with Internet or intranet applications where you may have a large number of clients connecting to a database. To conserve resources, you don't want each of these clients to have a physical connection.

The downside of connection pooling is that clients may have to wait for idle connections. If you cannot afford to have clients wait, or your system is already experiencing unwanted delays, then connection pooling will not be a viable alternative.

## Configure Connection Pooling

Configure connection pooling by setting MTS_DISPATCHERS parameters. New options are added to the MTS_DISPATCHERS parameter. Table 16.2 summarizes the optional attributes of the MTS_DISPATCHERS parameter you use to configure connection pooling.

**TABLE 16.2** Optional Attributes of the MTS_DISPATCHERS parameter

| Attribute | Description |
| --- | --- |
| Connection (CON) | Specifies the maximum number of connections that the dispatcher can handle. |
| Sessions (SES) | Specifies the maximum number of concurrent connections that the dispatcher can handle. The difference between the number of SESSIONS and the number of CONNECTIONS is the pool size. This is the number of connections that are waiting for network connections. |
| Ticks (TIC) | This is the length of time a client is willing to wait for an idle connection. The ticks are specified in 10 second increments. So, if TIC is set to three, a client will wait up to 30 seconds to get an idle connection. The default is 10 increments, or 100 seconds. |

**TABLE 16.2** Optional Attributes of the MTS_DISPATCHERS parameter *(continued)*

| Attribute | Description |
| --- | --- |
| Poo (Poo) | Specifies whether connection pooling is enabled. The value can be set to ON, YES, TRUE, BOTH, IN, or OUT. This specifies whether connection pooling is enabled and in what direction connection pooling will work—in both directions, for incoming messages only, or for outgoing messages only. |

# Tuning the Multithreaded Server Option

**B**efore tuning the Multithreaded Server, you should examine the performance of the dispatchers and the shared server processes. You want to make sure that you have enough dispatchers so clients are not waiting for dispatchers to respond to their requests. You want to have enough shared server processes so requests are not waiting to be processed. You also want to configure the Large Pool SGA memory area. The *Large Pool* is used to store the User Global Area (UGA). The UGA takes the place of the Program Global Area (PGA) that is used for dedicated servers.

The Large Pool is designed to allow the database to request large amounts of memory from a separate area of the SGA. Before the database had a Large Pool design, memory allocations for Multithreaded Server came from the Shared Pool. This caused Multithreaded Server to compete with other processes updating information in the Shared Pool. The Large Pool alleviates the memory burden on the Shared Pool and enhances performance of the Shared Pool.

## Configure the Large Pool

Configure the Large Pool by setting the parameter `large_pool_size` in the `init.ora` file. The `large_pool_size` parameter can be set to a minimum of 300K and a maximum of 2GB. If you do not configure a Large Pool, Oracle will place the UGA into the Shared Pool. You should configure a Large Pool when using Multithreaded Server so you don't affect the performance of the Shared Pool. Here is an example of setting the `large_pool_size` parameter in the `init.ora` file:

```
Large_pool_size = 50M
```

You can see how much space is being used by the Large Pool by querying the `v$sgastat` view. The *free memory* row shows the amount available in the Large Pool and the *session heap* row show the amount of space used in the Large Pool. Here is a listing that shows an example of the query:

```
SQL> select * from v$sgastat where pool = 'Large Pool';

POOL          NAME                                    BYTES
-----------   --------------------------   ---------
large pool    free memory                            251640
large pool    session heap                            48360
```

## Sizing the Large Pool

The Large Pool should be large enough to hold information for all of your multithreaded connections. Generally, each connection will need between one and three megabytes of memory, but this depends on that client's type of activity. Clients that do a great deal of sorting or open many cursors will use more memory.

You can gauge how much memory multithreaded connections are using by querying the `v$sesstat` view. This view contains information about memory utilization per user. The query below shows how to measure the maximum amount of memory for all multithreaded sessions since the instance was started. You can use this as a guide to determine how much memory you should allocate for the Large Pool. This example shows that the maximum amount of memory used for all multithreaded sessions is around 240k:

```
select sum(value) "Max MTS Memory Allocated"
from v$sesstat ss, v$statname st
where name = 'session uga memory max'and ss.statistic# =
st.statistic#;

Max MTS Memory Allocated
------------------------
                  244416
```

## Determine Whether You Have Enough Dispatchers

The dispatcher processes can be monitored by querying the v$dispatcher view. This view contains information about how busy the dispatcher processes are. Query this view to determine whether it will be advantageous to start more dispatchers.

The sample query below runs against the v$dispatcher view to show what percentage of the time dispatchers are busy:

```
Select network "Protocol"
(SUM(busy) / (SUM(busy) + sum(idle)))*100
"Dispatcher % busy Rate"
From v$dispatcher
Group by Network;


Protocol          Dispatcher % Busy Rate
-----------       --------------------------

tcp               10.134
```

This TCP/IP dispatcher is only busy a little more than 10 percent of the time. If dispatchers are busy more than 50 percent of the time, you should consider starting more dispatchers. This can be done dynamically with the ALTER SYSTEM command. Add one or two more dispatchers and monitor the busy rates of the dispatchers to see if they fall below 50 percent.

## Determine How Long Users Are Waiting for Dispatchers

To measure how long users are waiting for the dispatchers to execute their request, look at the combined v$queue and v$dispatcher views. See the listing below for an example:

```
SELECT decode(sum(totalq),0,'No Responses',
              Sum(wait)/sum(totalq)) "Average Wait time"
FROM v$queue q, v$dispatcher d
WHERE q.type = 'DISPATCHER'
AND q.paddr = d.paddr;


Average Wait Time
------------------
   .0413
```

The average wait time for dispatchers is a little more than four hundredths of a second. Monitor this measure over time. If the number is consistently increasing, you should consider adding more dispatchers.

## Determine Whether You Have Enough Shared Servers

You can monitor shared servers by using the `v$shared_server` and `v$queue` dictionary views. The shared servers are responsible for executing client requests and placing the requests in the appropriate dispatcher response queue.

The measurement you are most interested in is how long client requests are waiting in the request queue. The longer the request remains in the queue, the longer the client will wait for a response. The following statement will tell you how long requests are waiting in the queue:

```
Select decode(totalq,0,'No Requests'),
Wait/totalq || ' hundredths of seconds'
"Average Wait time per request"
from v$queue
where type = 'COMMON'


Average Wait time per request
-----------------------------
.023132 hundredths of a second
```

The average wait time in the request queue is a little more than two hundredths of a second. Monitor this measure over time. If the number is consistently increasing, you should consider adding more shared servers.

# Summary

**T**he Multithreaded Server is a configuration of the Oracle Server that allows you to support a greater number of connections without the need for additional resources. In this configuration, user connections share processes called dispatchers. Dispatchers replace the dedicated server processes in a dedicated server environment. The Oracle Server is also configured with shared server processes that can process the requests of many clients.

The Oracle Server is configured with a single request queue where dispatchers place the client requests for the shared servers to take and process. Each dispatcher has its own response queue. The shared server processes place completed requests in the appropriate dispatchers' response queue. The dispatcher sends the completed request back to the client. These request and response queues are structures added to the SGA.

There are a number of parameters that are added to the init.ora file to configure Multithreaded Server. These parameters are MTS_DISPATCHERS, MTS_SERVERS, MTS_MAX_DISPATCHERS, and MTS_MAX_SERVERS. Dispatchers and shared servers can be added dynamically after the Oracle Server has been started. You can add more shared servers and dispatchers up to the maximum value specified.

There are several new V$ views that are used to monitor Multithreaded Server. These include V$QUEUE, V$DISPATCHER, V$SHARED_SERVER, V$MTS, V$CIRCUIT, and V$DISPATCHER_RATE. The information contained in these views pertains to dispatchers, shared server processes, and the clients that are connected to the dispatcher processes.

You can also take advantage of connection pooling to increase the number of simultaneous connections that Multithreaded Server can support. Connection pooling is similar to a party line. Client processes can share connections. A client may have to wait for a connection to become idle before taking over the connection to process a request. Dispatchers have a maximum queue size that determines how many clients may be waiting for an idle connection to become available. Connection pooling is configured with additional arguments of the MTS_DISPATCHERS parameter.

You can use the V$ views to tune the Multithreaded Server. It is most important to measure how long clients are waiting for dispatchers to process their requests and how long it is taking before a shared server processes the client requests. These factors may lead to increasing the number of shared server and dispatcher processes. You also want to monitor the usage of the Large Pool.

# Key Terms

connection pooling

dispatcher

Large Pool

MTS_DISPATCHERS

MTS_MAX_DISPATCHERS

MTS_MAX_SERVERS

MTS_SERVERS

Oracle Multithreaded Server Option

request queue

response queue

shared server

User Global Area (UGA)

# Review Questions

1. All of the following are reasons to configure the server using Multi-threaded Server *except*:

   A. Reduction of overall memory utilization.

   B. The system is predominantly used for decision support with large result sets returned.

   C. The system is predominantly used for small transactions with many users.

   D. Reduction of the number of idle connections on the server.

2. The following are *false* about Multithreaded Server *except*:

   A. Dedicated connections cannot be made when Multithreaded Server is configured.

   B. Bequeath connections are not possible when Multithreaded Server is configured.

   C. The database can be started when connected via Multi-threaded Server.

   D. The database cannot be stopped when connected via Multi-threaded Server.

3. The administrator wants to allow a user to connect via a dedicated connection into a database configured in Multithreaded Server mode. Which of the following lines would accomplish this:

   A. (SERVER=DEDICATED)

   B. (CONNECT=DEDICATED)

   C. (INSTANCE=DEDICATED)

   D. (MULTITRHEADED=FALSE)

   E. None of the above

**4.** In what file would the change in question #3 be made?

    **A.** listener.ora

    **B.** mts.ora

    **C.** init.ora

    **D.** tnsnames.ora

    **E.** sqlnet.ora

**5.** One of the components of Multithreaded Server is:

    **A.** Shared user processes

    **B.** Checkpoint processes

    **C.** Dispatcher processes

    **D.** Dedicated server processes

**6.** The DBA wants to put the database in Multithreaded Server mode. In what file will modifications be made?

    **A.** tnsnames.ora

    **B.** cman.ora

    **C.** names.ora

    **D.** init.ora

**7.** What choice in the Net8 Assistant allows for the configuration of Multithreaded Server?

    **A.** Services

    **B.** Listeners

    **C.** MTS

    **D.** Profile

    **E.** None of the above

8. The DBA wants two TCP/IP dispatchers and one IPC dispatcher to start when the instance is started. Which line will accomplish this?

   **A.** `dispatchers=(protocol=tcp)(dispatchers=2)`
   `(protocol=IPC)(dispatchers=1)mts_`
   `dispatchers=(protocol=tcp)(dispatchers=2)`
   `(protocol=IPC)(dispatchers=1)`

   **B.** `mts_dispatchers="(protocol=tcp)(dispatchers=2)`
   `(protocol=IPC)(dispatchers=1)"`

   **C.** `dispatchers_start=(protocol=tcp)(dispatchers=2)`
   `(protocol=IPC)(dispatchers=1)`

9. The following parameters cannot be modified without bringing the instance down *except*:

   **A.** `MTS_DISPATCHERS`

   **B.** `MTS_MAX_DISPATCHERS`

   **C.** `LOCAL_LISTENER`

   **D.** `MTS_MAX_SERVICES`

   **E.** None of the above

10. The first step after a dispatcher has received a request from the user is:

   **A.** The dispatcher passes the request to a shared server.

   **B.** The dispatcher places the request in a request queue in the PGA.

   **C.** The dispatcher places the request in a request queue in the SGA.

   **D.** The dispatcher processes the request.

11. The following statements are *true* about dispatchers *except*:

   **A.** Dispatchers can be shared by many connections.

   **B.** More dispatchers can be added dynamically with the ALTER SYSTEM command.

   **C.** A dispatcher can listen for multiple protocols.

   **D.** Each dispatcher has its own response queue.

**12.** When configured in Multithreaded Server mode, which of the following is contained in the PGA?

**A.** Cursor state

**B.** Sort information

**C.** User session data

**D.** Stack space

**E.** None of the above

**13.** Which of the following is *false* about shared servers?

**A.** Shared servers can process requests from many users.

**B.** Shared servers receive their requests directly from dispatchers.

**C.** Shared servers place completed requests on a dispatcher response queue.

**D.** The MTS_SERVERS parameter configures the number of shared servers to start at instance startup.

**14.** Which of the following is *not* a step in the processing of a multi-threaded request?

**A.** Shared servers pass information back to the client process.

**B.** Dispatchers place information in a request queue.

**C.** Users pass requests to a dispatcher.

**D.** The dispatcher picks up completed requests from its response queue.

**E.** None of the above

**15.** When configuring Multithreaded Server, which initialization parameter would likely need to be increased?

   **A.** DB_BLOCK_SIZE

   **B.** DB_BLOCK_BUFFERS

   **C.** SHARED_POOL_SIZE

   **D.** MTS_BUFFER_SIZE

   **E.** None of the above

**16.** Which of the following is *false* about request queues?

   **A.** They reside in the SGA.

   **B.** They are shared by all of the dispatchers.

   **C.** Each dispatcher has its own request queue.

   **D.** The shared server processes remove requests from the request queue.

**17.** The DBA is interested in gathering information about users connected via multithreaded connections. The view that would contain this information is:

   **A.** v$mts_users

   **B.** v$queue

   **C.** v$sess_stats

   **D.** v$circuit

   **E.** None of the above

**18.** Which of the following is *not* a characteristic of connection pooling?

   **A.** It can only be used for multithreaded connections.

   **B.** Users share a finite number of simultaneous physical connections.

   **C.** The wait time to get a connection is non-configurable.

   **D.** It is a method to increase the possible number of connections to the database.

**19.** What is the purpose of (TIC=4) in the following syntax: `mts_dispatchers = "(PRO=TCP)(CON=10)(POO=ON)(TIC=4)(SESS=30)(DIS=2)"`

 **A.** The user will be allowed only 4 simultaneous connections.

 **B.** These dispatchers only supports 4 simultaneous connections.

 **C.** A user will wait 40 seconds to get a connection if all multithreaded connections for these dispatchers are busy.

 **D.** A user will wait 4 seconds to get a connection if all multithreaded connections for these dispatchers are busy.

**20.** What command can be executed to give details about the number of sessions connected via Multithreaded Server?

 **A.** `mtslsnr check`

 **B.** `lsnrctl mts`

 **C.** `lsnrctl status`

 **D.** `lsnrctl services`

 **E.** None of the above

# Answers to Review Questions

1. B.   Mulithreaded server is a scalability option of Oracle. It provides a way to increase the number of supported user processes while reducing the overall memory usage. This configuration is well suited to high-volume, small transaction-oriented systems with many users connected. Because users share processes, there is also an overall reduction of the number of idle processes. It is not well suited for large data retrieval type applications like decision support.

2. D.   Users can still request dedicated connections in a Multithreaded Server configuration. Bequeath and dedicated connections are one and the same. The database cannot be stopped or started when a user is connected over a multithreaded connection.

3. A.   A user must explicitly request a dedicated connection when a server is configured in Multithreaded Server mode. Otherwise, the user will get a multithreaded connection. The correct parameter is (SERVER=DEDICATED).

4. D.   The change is made in the `tnsnames.ora` file on the client workstation.

5. C.   In Multithreaded Server, users connect to a pool of shared resources called dispatchers. A client connects to the listener and the listener redirects the request to a dispatcher. While shared servers also exist, it is the dispatchers that handle all of the user requests for the session. Many users can share dispatchers.

6. D.   Since the database has to be configured in Multithreaded Server mode, changes have to be made to the database initialization file. That file is the `init.ora` file. The other choices are also configuration files, but none of them are used to configure Multithreaded Server.

**7.** E.   This is one of the tricky questions again! Many options and files can be configured by the Net8 Assistant, including `tnsnames.ora` and `sqlnet.ora`. But, since Multithreaded Server is a characteristic of the database server and not of the network, Net8 Assistant is not used to configure it. So the answer is none of the above.

**8.** B.   Back to syntax again! The `mts_dispatchers` `init.ora` parameter is used to configure dispatchers. So, the correct answer is option B. All of the other choices are invalid parameters.

**9.** A.   Once the maximum dispatchers and servers are set up, the only way to modify these settings is by changing the `init.ora` file and restarting Oracle. The `LOCAL_LISTENER` parameter can only be set when the instance is shutdown. The only parameter of these that can be configured dynamically with the `ALTER SYSTEM` command is the `MTS_DISPATCHERS`. Dispatchers can be dynamically added with this parameter.

**10.** C.   Once a dispatcher receives a request from the user process, it places the request on the request queue. Remember that in a Multi-threaded Server environment, a request can be handled by a shared server process. This is made possible by placing the request and user information in the SGA.

**11.** C.   Many users can connect to dispatchers and dispatchers can be added dynamically. Also, each dispatcher does have its own response queue. The only one that is false is option C. Dispatchers can listen for only one protocol. Multiple dispatchers can be configured so that each is responsible for different protocols.

**12.** D.   A small PGA is maintained even though most of the user specific information is moved to the SGA (specifically called the UGA in the Shared Pool or the Large Pool). The only information left in the reduced PGA is stack space.

**13.** B.   Shared servers can process requests from many users. The completed requests are placed into the dispatchers' response queue. The servers are configured with the `MTS_SERVERS` parameter. Shared servers do not receive requests directly from dispatchers. The requests are taken from the request queue.

**14.** A.  This is similar to #13. Study the steps of what happens during a request via Multithreaded Server. Dispatchers receive requests from users and place the requests on request queues. Only dispatchers interact with client processes. Shared servers merely execute the requests and place the results back on the dispatchers' response queue.

**15.** C.  Multithreaded Server requires a shift of memory away from individual session processes to the SGA. More information has to be kept in the SGA (in the UGA) within the Shared Pool. A Large Pool can also be configured and would probably be responsible for the majority of the SGA space allocation. But, since that was not a choice, option C is the correct answer. The block size and block buffers settings do not affect Multithreaded Server.

**16.** C.  Request queues reside in the SGA, and there is one request queue per instance. This is where shared server processes pick up requests that are made by users. Dispatchers have their own response queues but *share* a single request queue.

**17.** D.  There are several V$ views that can be used to manage the Multithreaded Server. V$queue gives information regarding the request and response queues. V$mts_users and v$sess_stats are not valid views. V$circuit will give information about the users who are connected via multithreaded connections. V$circuit will provide the necessary information.

**18.** C.  Connection pooling is a feature of Multithreaded Server that allows users to share connections. If a user needs a connection and none are available, they will wait for an idle connection. If one is found, the current user surrenders the line and the new user takes over the connection. This is a means to support an even greater number of users with a finite number of connections. The wait time is configurable.

**19.** C.  How long a user waits for a valid connection during connection pooling is set by the TIC option of the mts_dispatchers parameter. The TICs are in 10-second increments, so TIC=4 would mean that a user would wait 40 seconds for a connection to become available.

**20.** C.  Dispatchers register with listeners so that when a listener redirects a connection to a dispatcher, the listener knows how many active connections the dispatcher is serving. The `lsnrctl status` command summarizes the number of connections established, connections currently active, and other valuable information regarding Multithreaded Server. The `lsnrctl services` command only gives a summary of dispatchers, not any details about connections.

# Connection Manager Configuration

## ORACLE8i NETWORK ADMINISTRATION EXAM OBJECTIVES COVERED IN THIS CHAPTER:

- ✓ Describe the features of Connection Manager.
- ✓ Define connection concentration.
- ✓ Define multi-protocol interchange.
- ✓ Define connection access control.
- ✓ Describe the components of Connection Manager.
- ✓ Describe the CMGW process responsibilities.
- ✓ Describe the CMADM process responsibilities.
- ✓ Define the parts of the cman.ora file.
- ✓ Configure connection concentration.
- ✓ Configure multi-protocol interchange.
- ✓ Configure connection access control.
- ✓ Configure a client to utilize Connection Manager.
- ✓ Use Connection Manager with an Oracle Names Server.

Exam objectives are subject to change at any time without prior notice and at Oracle's sole discretion. Please visit Oracle's Training and Certification Web site (http://education .oracle.com/certification) for the most current exam objectives listing.

**O**racle Connection Manager is an optional feature of the Oracle Net8 architecture that functions in a manner similar to routers. In this chapter, you will explore the architecture of Connection Manager and how to properly configure the three main features of Connection Manager: *connection concentration, connection access control,* and *multi-protocol interchange.* You will learn the contents of the `cman.ora` configuration file and how to stop and start Connection Manager using the `cmctl` command line interface. You will also learn how to configure the client to make connections through the Connection Manager facility. This chapter also features a discussion on CMGW and CMADMIN, the two main Connection Manager background processes.

# Connection Manager Features

**C**onnection Manager (abbreviated CMAN) is a middle-tier product that offers three primary functions: connection concentration, multi-protocol interchange, and connection access control. Connection Manager is configured as a stand-alone product. It can reside on its own machine or it can be configured on the same machine as an Oracle Server. Clients establish connections to the Connection Manager middle tier. Connection Manager then routes all client requests to the appropriate Oracle Server.

Unlike the listener or the Oracle Names Server, Connection Manager is a persistent middle-tier product. This means that as long as the client is connected to the server, all requests to the Oracle Server from the client will pass through Connection Manager, and Connection Manager will return all requested information from the server back to the client. If the Connection Manager process fails, the client connection will be lost. Let's review the primary features of Connection Manager.

# Connection Concentration

Connection concentration is a feature that involves multiple clients connecting to a Connection Manager middle-tier. Connection Manager takes these separate incoming connections and establishes a single, multiplexed, outgoing connection to the Oracle Server utilizing a single protocol.

The net result is that the number of physical connections to the Oracle Server is reduced, which allows for increased scalability of your network. You can support a greater number of clients without increasing the number of physical connections to the Oracle Server, which conserves server resources such as memory and active process counts. Figure 17.1 shows an example of how connection concentration functions. Connection concentration requires that the Oracle Server be configured in Multithreaded Server mode. See Chapter 16 for instructions on configuring the Multithreaded Server.

**FIGURE 17.1** CMAN connection concentration

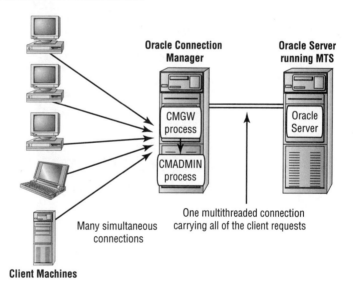

## Multi-Protocol Interchange

Connection Manager also allows clients and servers to converse with one another even if they are using disparate protocols. This feature is a replacement for the multi-protocol interchange features of SQL*Net V2.

The Connection Manager middle tier handles all of the necessary protocol conversion activities to transfer messages from the client to the server (see Figure 17.2). This means that a client running the DECnet protocol could carry on a conversation through Connection Manager to an Oracle Server configured only with TCP/IP.

**FIGURE 17.2** CMAN multi-protocol interchange

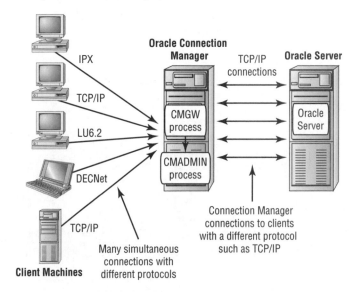

## Connection Access Control

Connection Manager can act as a "mini firewall" to your Oracle Servers. The connection access control feature is a rule-based authorization mechanism that enables you to configure Connection Manager to allow or restrict access to Oracle Servers based on a set of criteria. That criterion is the source address of the client, the destination address of the host where the Oracle Server resides, and the destination Oracle Server service. This feature is only available for TCP/IP-based installations (see Figure 17.3).

**FIGURE 17.3** CMAN access control

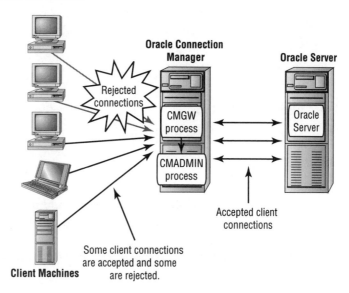

# Connection Manager Processes

**C**onnection Manager is comprised of two background processes that are responsible for different aspects of the networking process. In Windows NT, these processes are implemented as services; in a UNIX environment, they run as background processes. Both of these processes are started when Connection Manager is started.

## CMGW process

The *Connection Manager Gateway (CMGW)* process is the main background process of Connection Manager. Connection Manager Gateway routes client connection requests to the appropriate destination. Once a connection is established, the gateway process acts as the middleman between the client and server by passing client requests to the server and relaying server responses back to the client. The gateway is responsible for managing connection concentration, client access control, and multi-protocol interchange.

Connection Manager Gateway registers with the Connection Manager Administrator process for connection concentration. By default, Connection Manager Gateway is configured to listen for requests using the TCP/IP protocol on port 1630. Connection Manager Gateway responds to both SQL*Net V2 and Net8 requests.

## CMADMIN Process

The *Connection Manager Administrator (CMADMIN)* process is the administrative process of Connection Manager. This process is responsible for maintaining address information and processing the registration information for the Connection Manager Gateway. It identifies listeners that are serving Oracle Servers, locates and monitors listeners that are registered with Oracle Names Servers, and periodically updates the Oracle Names Server cache with current service information. The CMADMIN process defaults to the TCP/IP protocol and listens on port 1650.

# The *cman.ora* file

The *cman.ora* file is the configuration file used by Connection Manager. The file is divided into three sections, the cman section, the cman_profile section, and the cman_rules section.

The Oracle Server comes with a sample file definition, which should be located in the %ORACLE_HOME\network\admin\samples directory on NT or $ORACLE_HOME/network/admin/samples directory on UNIX. You can use this file as a guide when creating the cman.ora file. This file is not created or maintained by using the Net8 Assistant, but is instead configured manually.

## cman Section

The cman section is the top section of the file, which contains the listening locations for Connection Manager. If you are using a TCP/IP network, the default port address is 1630 for the CMGW process and 1650 for the CMADMIN process. The following code listing shows an example of the cman section of the file:

```
# Connection Manager config file
# cman.ora - The file is used by cman and cman_admin.
#
#
#CMAN = (ADDRESS_LIST=<tnsaddr1><tnsaddr2>...<tnsaddrn>)
```

```
#
# These are cman's listening addresses (one or more)
# for the purpose of
# relaying TNS sessions.
#
     CMAN = (ADDRESS=(PROTOCOL=tcp)(HOST=gr99c0073)
    (PORT=1630))
#
#       port 1630 is the default listening location for
#       connection
#       manager

#CMAN_ADMIN = tnsaddr
#
#
     CMAN_ADMIN = (ADDRESS=(PROTOCOL=tcp)(HOST=)
    (PORT=1650))
#
```

## cman_profile Section

The *cman_profile* section is the second section of the cman.ora file and contains optional configuration parameters, such as logging and tracing parameters. The file is located by default in the %ORACLE_HOME\network\admin directory on Windows NT and $ORACLE_HOME/network/admin on UNIX. The example below shows the cman_profile section. Table 17.1 shows a summary and description of each parameter.

```
CMAN_PROFILE = (PARAMETER_LIST=
                       (maximum_relays=100)
                       (log_level=1)
                       (tracing=yes)
                       (trace_directory='c:\oraclass\trace')
                       (relay_statistics=<valuen>)
                       (show_tns_info=yes)
                       (use_async_call=yes)
                       (authentication_level=0)
```

```
                                    (maximum_connect_data=1024)
                                    (answer_timeout=30)
                                    (max_freelist_buffers=10240)
                        )
```

**TABLE 17.1**   cman_profile Parameters

| Parameter | Description |
| --- | --- |
| MAXIMUM_RELAYS | Maximum number of concurrent connections that Connection Manager supports. The default is 128, and the maximum is 2048. |
| LOG_LEVEL | Specifies whether Connection Manager will perform logging. Values are 0–4. Higher numbers produce more output. |
| TRACING | Specifies if Connection Manager will perform tracing. values YES and NO. |
| TRACE_DIRECTORY | Directory where trace file is placed. |
| RELAY_STATISTICS | If set to YES, this captures information about network traffic, such as number of bytes and packets sent and received. Defaults to NO. |
| SHOW_TNS_INFO | If set to YES, allows tns information to be recorded in the log. You will see connection requests per Oracle service passing through Connection Manager. |
| USE_ASYNC_CALL | If set to YES, tells cman to use asynchronous network session calls. Defaults to YES. |
| AUTHENTICATION_ LEVEL | If set to 1, will require authentication of a client through SNS. Default is 0, and no authentication is required. |
| MAXIMUM_CONNECT_ DATA | Sets the maximum value of the connect string. The default is 1024, and the maximum is 4096. |

**TABLE 17.1**   cman_profile Parameters *(continued)*

| Parameter | Description |
|---|---|
| ANSWER_TIMEOUT | The number of seconds that Connection Manager will wait to receive a handshake signal from the requested Oracle Server. The default = 0, which means the Connection Manager will wait indefinitely. |
| MAX_FREELIST_ BUFFERS | The maximum number of freelist buffers to keep after a network session has closed. The default is 2048, and the maximum is 10240. |

## cman_rules Section

The *cman_rules* section contains information about the types of connection requests that should be accepted or rejected. This section defines the client access control, which allows cman to act like a firewall, preventing unauthorized connections to the Oracle Server through Connection Manager. This feature is only available on TCP/IP protocols.

The cman_rules stipulate what clients are allowed to connect to what hosts and services. The rules take the following format:

(RULE=(SRC=<source_host>)(DST=<dest_ host>)(SRV=<service>)(ACT=accept|reject))

Table 17.2 shows a list of the definitions for the attributes of the cman_ rule parameter.

**TABLE 17.2**   cman_rules Attributes

| Attribute | Definition |
|---|---|
| SRC | The source of the client. This is the hostname or the IP address. |
| DST | The destination of the client. This is the hostname or IP address. |
| SRV | The requested service name. |
| ACT | The action, which accepts (ACC) or rejects (REJ) the connection. |

If you want to allow a client with hostname of `client1` to connect to a service name called `prod` located on `MACH1`, the rule would be:

```
(RULE=(SRC=client1)(DST=mach1)(SRV=prod)(ACT=acc))
```

You can also use wildcards. The wildcard character is a lowercase *x*. For example, if you wanted to allow any client to connect to the `prod` service on `mach1`, you would enter:

```
(RULE=(SRC=x)(DST=mach1)(SRV=prod)(ACT=acc))
```

The wildcard character can be used in any of the attributes. You can use IP addresses instead of hostnames. If you use the IP address format `d.d.d.d`, any of the portions of the IP address can contain a wildcard. For example, if you wanted to allow client1 to access any service that was located in the 10.10 subnet of your network, you would enter:

```
(RULE=(SRC=client1)(DST=10.10.x.x)(SRV=x)(ACT=acc))
```

When a client contacts Connection Manager, Connection Manager will attempt to find a rule match for the source client, destination server, and the destination service. The first rule match found is applied and is either accepted or rejected depending on the setting of the `action` attribute.

If you define Connection Manager rules, Connection Manager follows the principle, "That which is not expressly permitted is prohibited." So, if rules are defined, only those rules that allow connections will be permitted to pass. If a client connects to Connection Manager and there is no rule expressly permitting the client to establish a connection, the connection attempt will be rejected. The following is a complete example of the `cman.ora` file:

```
# Connection Manager config file cman.ora
#
# ======================================================
# cman's listening addresses
# ======================================================

cman = (ADDRESS_LIST=
            (ADDRESS=(PROTOCOL=tcp)(HOST=)(PORT=1630))
        )
```

```
cman_admin = (ADDRESS=(PROTOCOL=tcp)(HOST=)(PORT=1650))


# ======================================================
# cman_profile optional paramters
# ======================================================


cman_profile = (parameter_list=
                    (MAXIMUM_RELAYS=1024)
                    (LOG_LEVEL=1)
                    (TRACING=no)
                    (RELAY_STATISTICS=yes)
                    (SHOW_TNS_INFO=yes)
                    (USE_ASYNC_CALL=yes)
                    (AUTHENTICATION_LEVEL=0)
                )
# ======================================================
# cman_rules section
# ======================================================

cman_rules=
 (rule_list=

(rule=(src=gr99c0073)(dst=mad01ora)(srv=dba)(act=reject))
    (rule=(src=10.10.25.40)(dst=10.10.172.200)(srv=prod)
    (act=accept))

(rule=(src=gr002210)(dst=mil01ora)(srv=v8i)(act=accept))
 )
```

# Managing Connection Manager

**C**onnection Manager is started and stopped from the command line utility, CMCTL. You can start, stop, and get status information using this utility.

To start Connection Manager, login to the computer configured with Connection Manager. At a command line prompt, enter **CMCTL START** to start the Connection Manager processes. When you start Connection Manager, the

Connection Manager Gateway and Connection Manager Administrator processes are started. The following is an example of starting Connection Manager:

```
D:\>cmctl start

CMCTL for 32-bit Windows: Version 8.1.5.0.0 - Production
on 18-FEB-00 09:09:28

(c) Copyright 1998 Oracle Corporation.  All rights
reserved.

Service OracleOraHome81CMAdmin start pending.
Service OracleOraHome81CMAdmin started.
ADMIN Status:
(STATUS=(VERSION=8.1.5.0.0)(STARTED=18-FEB-00 09:09:29)
(STATE=RUNNING))
Service OracleOraHome81CMan start pending.
Service OracleOraHome81CMan started.
CMAN Status:
(STATUS=(VERSION=8.1.5.0.0)(STARTED=18-FEB-00 09:09:36)
(STATE=running))
```

To stop Connection Manager, enter **CMCTL STOP** from the command line. If active client connections are using Connection Manager, you will be given a warning that there are active connections using Connection Manager. If Connection Manager is stopped, the client's network connection is broken. If they attempt to communicate with the database after the connection is broken, they receive an error message. Connection Manager must be started again, and all clients that were disconnected will need to reconnect to the server.

The example below shows how to stop Connection Manager and the warning you would receive if there are active connections:

```
CMCTL> stop
 The Connection Manager has active connections. Do you
still want to stop it (y/
n)? y
```

Clients receive the following error:

```
SQL> select ename from scott.emp;
select ename from scott.emp
*
ERROR at line 1:
```

```
ORA-03113: end-of-file on communication channel
```

You can check if Connection Manager is active by entering the **CMCTL STATUS** command:

```
C:\>cmctl status

CMCTL for 32-bit Windows: Version 8.1.5.0.0 - Production
on 18-FEB-00 10:20:35

(c) Copyright 1998 Oracle Corporation.  All rights
reserved.

CMAN Status:
(STATUS=(VERSION=8.1.5.0.0)(STARTED=18-FEB-00 10:19:26)
(STATE=running))
ADMIN Status:
(STATUS=(VERSION=8.1.5.0.0)(STARTED=18-FEB-00 10:19:16)
(STATE=RUNNING))
```

The CMCTL STATUS command lists ACTIVE_RELAYS, which is the number of active connections Connection Manager is servicing. TOTAL_RELAYS is the total number of connections handled by Connection Manager. MOST_RELAYS is the maximum number of concurrent connections established. TOTAL_REFUSED is the number of connections refused. OUT_OF_RELAY is the number of connections refused because the maximum number of connections has been reached. All of these totals are cumulative since Connection Manager was last started.

```
CMAN Status:
(STATISTICS=(TOTAL_RELAYS=1)(ACTIVE_RELAYS=1)(MOST_
RELAYS=1)(OUT_OF_RELAY=0)(TOTAL_REFUSED=0))
```

Table 17.3 has a summary of all of the commands you can use with the CMCTL utility.

**TABLE 17.3** CMCTL Commands

| Command | Description |
| --- | --- |
| EXIT | Exits CMCTL utility |
| START | Starts Connection Manager |
| STOP | Stops Connection Manager |
| STOP NOW | Stops without prompting user |
| STATUS | Displays if Connection Manager is running |
| STATS | Displays statistics such as total connections, active connections, and total connections refused |

# Configuring Connection Concentration

To enable connection concentration, you need to configure the client-side network files. Use the Net8 Assistant to configure connection concentration. The server must be configured with the Multithreaded Server option to use connection concentration.

## Connection Concentration with Localnaming

If localnaming is used, select the Net Service Names icon from the main Net8 Assistant screen to add or modify net service name definitions. See Chapter 14 for instructions on adding a net service name for the localnaming method.

The first address configured is the address of the Connection Manager host. Enter the name of the Connection Manager host in the Host Name field and the listening location for Connection Manager in the Port Number field. You must then add a second address, which is the address of the Oracle Server destination. Click the plus sign in the Address Configuration section. An Address 2 tab appears. Enter the Hostname of the Oracle Server and the Port Number of the listener. Figure 17.4 shows an example of Net8 Assistant with these configurations.

**FIGURE 17.4** Net8 Assistant with multiple addresses configured for connection concentration

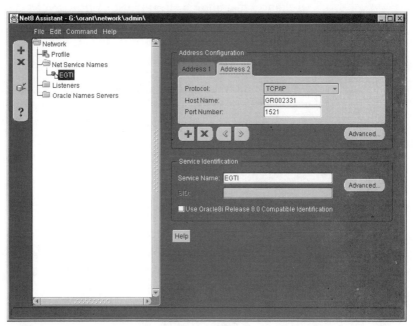

You have to ensure that clients first contact Connection Manager and that Connection Manager then forwards the connection request to the appropriate Oracle Server. This means the addresses must be used in the order in which they appear in the `tnsnames.ora` file.

To ensure clients use the addresses in order, click the Advanced icon in the Address Configuration section. The Address List Options screen appears. Click the radio button next to Use Each Address in Order Until Destination Is Reached. This ensures the client will not attempt to randomly select from the address list.

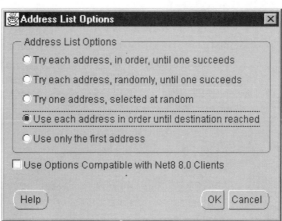

Save your changes. The following example shows the `tnsnames.ora` file changes that allow a client to use Connection Manager. The `tnsnames.ora` file contains a new address for Connection Manager and the `SOURCE_ROUTE` parameter. This tells the client to use the addresses listed in order and not to randomly choose an address.

```
# D:\ORACLE\ORA81\NETWORK\ADMIN\TNSNAMES.ORA Configuration
File:D:\Oracle\Ora81\NETWORK\ADMIN\tnsnames.ora
# Generated by Oracle Net8 Assistant

DBA =
  (DESCRIPTION =
    (SOURCE_ROUTE = ON) " Use addresses in order
    (ADDRESS_LIST =
      (ADDRESS = (PROTOCOL = TCP)(HOST = weishan)
      (PORT = 1630))
      (ADDRESS = (PROTOCOL = TCP)(HOST = weishan)
      (PORT = 1521))
    )
    (CONNECT_DATA =
      (SERVICE_NAME = DBA)
      (SRVR = DEDICATED)
    )
  )
```

## Using Connection Concentration with Names Server

If Oracle Names Server is used, the CMADMIN process automatically updates the Names Server with address information. Names Servers can also send requests to Connection Manager to inform Connection Manager of their presence. The `sqlnet.ora` parameter USE_CMAN=TRUE must be initialized on the client and on the Names Server to indicate use of Connection Manager, if possible. If Connection Manager is not available, the client attempts to connect directly to the listener. If Names Servers are used, this parameter must be set in both the client `sqlnet.ora` and the Names Server `sqlnet.ora` files.

To set the USE_CMAN parameter using Net8, select the Profile icon and select General from the drop-down list box. Then choose the routing tab. Select the Prefer Connection Manager Routing option and save your change. This adds the parameter to the `sqlnet.ora` file. If multiple Connection Manager connections are involved in routing a client to an Oracle Server, then you cannot use an Oracle Names Server to resolve the net service name.

## Enabling Connection Pooling with Connection Concentration

To use connection concentration in conjunction with connection pooling, you need to specify an additional attribute on the MTS_DISPATCHERS parameter in the init.ora file. The attribute MUL is used to allow connection pooling with connection concentration. Here is an example of setting the attribute:

```
MTS_DISPATCHERS = "(PRO=TCP)(DIS=2)(MUL=ON)"
```

The MUL attribute can be set to ON, TRUE, or BOTH to enable connection pooling with multiplexing for incoming and outgoing requests. If it is set to IN, then multiplexing is only used for incoming requests. If it is set to OUT, then it is used only for outgoing requests. If it is set to OFF, NO, or FALSE, connection multiplexing is disabled. The default is OFF.

# Configure Multi-Protocol Interchange

**M**ulti-protocol interchange allows clients and servers using different protocols to communicate with each other through Connection Manager. Connection Manager serves as the interpreter, handling any protocol conversion issues. The client is first configured to connect to Connection Manager using one protocol and then to the Oracle Server using a different protocol.

Configuring the client for multi-protocol interchange is identical to configuring the client for connection concentration. The only difference is that the protocol for the first address definition is different from the protocol for the second address definition.

For example, if you have a client that needs to connect to Connection Manager using TCP/IP and then to the Oracle Server using IPC, you would configure the first address for TCP/IP and the second address for IPC. The following code listing shows an example of how the tnsnames.ora file would look:

```
# D:\ORACLE\ORA81\NETWORK\ADMIN\TNSNAMES.ORA Configuration
# File:D:\Oracle\Ora81\NETWORK\ADMIN\tnsnames.ora
# Generated by Oracle Net8 Assistant

DBA =
  (DESCRIPTION =
    (SOURCE_ROUTE = ON)
```

```
      (ADDRESS_LIST =
        (ADDRESS = (PROTOCOL = TCP)(HOST = gr99c0073)
        (PORT = 1630))
        (ADDRESS = (PROTOCOL = IPC)(Key = DBA))
      )
      (CONNECT_DATA =
        (SERVICE_NAME = DBA)
        (SRVR = DEDICATED)
      )
    )
```

# Summary

Connection Manager provides you with three main features: connection concentration, multi-protocol interchange, and client access control. Connection concentration is a feature that allows the Connection Manager middle tier to funnel many incoming connections into one outgoing connection to the Oracle Server. This reduces the total number of network connections on the Oracle Server. In order to use this feature, your Oracle Server must be configured as a Multithreaded Server. Multi-protocol interchange allows Connection Manager to function as a middleware interpreter between clients and servers that utilize different protocols. The client access control feature allows Connection Manager to function as a firewall, allowing or rejecting client connections based on client location, destination location, and the Oracle Server Name.

Connection Manager is comprised of two processes, CMADMIN and CMADMIN. The CMADMIN process manages the flow of traffic between clients and servers, and the CMADMIN process supports CMGW. Connection Manager normally runs on a separate machine functioning as a middle tier product.

The cman.ora file is the main configuration file for Connection Manager. The file is comprised of three sections: cman, cman_profile, and cman_rules. The cman section contains information about the listening location of Connection Manager. The cman_profile section contains optional parameters for Connection Manager, such as the number of connections to support, as well as logging and tracing parameters. The cman_rules section describes the rules for allowing or rejecting client connections if you are using the client access control features of Connection Manager.

Clients must be configured to connect to the Connection Manager machine, which can be done with the Net8 Assistant. If the client is using localnaming, the `tnsnames.ora` file entry for a net service name using Connection Manager will have two addresses: one for Connection Manager and one for the Oracle Server. The `SOURCE_ROUTE` parameter tells Oracle to use the addresses in order.

Connection Manager is managed by the `CMCTL` command line utility, which is used to stop and start Connection Manager as well as accessing statistical information. If you stop Connection Manager when there are active connections, the client will receive an error the next time the database is accessed.

If you are using an Oracle Names Server, you can configure connection concentration to work with connection pooling in a Multithreaded Server environment.

## Key Terms

Before you take the exam, make sure you're familiar with the following terms:

`cman.ora`

`cman_profile`

`cman_rules`

`cmctl`

connection access control

connection concentration

Connection Manager Administrator (CMADMIN)

Connection Manager Gateway (CMGW)

multi-protocol interchange

# Review Questions

1. The main functions Oracle Connection Manager provides are: (Choose three.)

   **A.** Connection concentration

   **B.** Multi-protocol interchange

   **C.** Network access control

   **D.** Connection Pooling

2. The command line function to start Connection Manager is:

   **A.** CMAN

   **B.** CMANCTL

   **C.** CMCTL

   **D.** STARTCM

3. The processes that are started by CMAN are: (Choose two.)

   **A.** CMAN

   **B.** CMGW

   **C.** CMCTL

   **D.** CMADMIN

4. What is the default port that the Connection Manager Gateway process listens for on TCP/IP connections?

   **A.** 1521

   **B.** 1610

   **C.** 1526

   **D.** 1630

**5.** What client-side file contains information that would be used by the client to establish a connection to an Oracle Server via Connection Manager?

    **A.** `tnsnames.ora`

    **B.** `listener.ora`

    **C.** `cman.ora`

    **D.** `ckpreg.ora`

**6.** What parameter needs to be present in the client file to take advantage of Connection Manager?

    **A.** CONNECT_DATA

    **B.** SOURCE_ROUTE

    **C.** CMAN_CONNECT

    **D.** CMAN_PATH

    **E.** None of the above

**7.** The DBA has a client using IPX and needs to have the client connect to the database server using TCP/IP. The DBA could take advantage of which Connection Manager feature?

    **A.** Connection concentration

    **B.** Connection pooling

    **C.** Multi-protocol interchange

    **D.** Connection filtering

    **E.** None of the above

**8.** Which of the following is *true* about Connection Manager?

    **A.** It must be started on the same server as the database.

    **B.** It cannot be started on the same server as the database.

    **C.** Connection Manager passes clients requests to the database server.

    **D.** Connection Manager will not allow bequeathed connection requests.

9. Which file is used to configure Connection Manager?

   **A.** cmctl.ora

   **B.** cman.ora

   **C.** connect.ora

   **D.** cman.ctl

   **E.** None of the above

10. The cman.ora file is divided into three sections. The section that records information about Connection Manager's listening location is called:

    **A.** cman_listener

    **B.** cman

    **C.** cman_profile

    **D.** cman_rules

    **E.** None of the above

11. If a default Connection Manager configuration is used, which of the following lines would you find in the section of the file from question #10?

    **A.** (ADDRESS= (PROTOCOL=TCP)(HOST=GR01)(PORT=1630))

    **B.** (ADDRESS=(PROTOCOL=TCP)(HOST=GR01)(PORT=1521))

    **C.** (ADDRESS=(PROTOCOL=TCP)(HOST=GR01)(PORT=1526))

    **D.** (ADDRESS=(PROTOCOL=TCP)(HOST=GR01)(PORT=1522))

12. In the following syntax:
    MTS_DISPATCHERS="(PRO=TCP)(DIS=3)(MUL=ON)"
    what does (MUL=ON) allow for?

    **A.** Connection pooling with Connection Manager

    **B.** Connection concentration with Connection Manager

    **C.** Connection filtering with Connection Manager

    **D.** Multi-protocol interchange with Connection Manager

    **E.** None of the above

**13.** The DBA wants to disallow access to the database server from workstation WS1 to the DBA database on machine MACH1 through Connection Manager. Which line below will accomplish this?

**A.** `cman_rules = (RULES_LIST = (RULE= (SRC = WS1)`
`(DST=MACH1)(SRV=DBA)(ACT=TRUE)))`

**B.** `cman_rules = (RULES_LIST = (RULE= (SRC = WS1)`
`(DST=MACH1)(SRV=DBA)(ACT=REJECT)))`

**C.** `cman_rules (RULES_LIST = (RULE= (SRC = WS1)`
`(DST=MACH1)(SRV=DBA)(REJ=TRUE)))`

**D.** `cman_rules (RULES_LIST = (RULE= (SRC = WS1)`
`(DST=MACH1)(SRV=DBA)(ACT=FALSE)))`

**14.** When defining Connection Manager rules, which of these statements is *true*:

**A.** That which is not expressly prohibited is accepted.

**B.** That which is not expressly accepted is prohibited.

**C.** Rules defined in Connection Manager must have matching rules in the `init.ora` file.

**D.** Rules defined in Connection Manager must also be defined in the `listener.ora` file.

**15.** The maximum number of concurrent connections allowed by Connection Manager is:

**A.** 256

**B.** 512

**C.** 1024

**D.** 2048

**E.** None of the above

**16.** Which Connection Manager parameter is used to alter the maximum number of concurrent connections?

**A.** MAX_CONNECTIONS

**B.** MAX_CONNECTS

**C.** MAXIMUM_RELAYS

**D.** MAXIMUM_CONNECTIONS

**E.** None of the above

**17.** The DBA needs to start Connection Manager. Which Net8 Assistant menu option will be chosen to accomplish this?

**A.** Profile

**B.** CMAN

**C.** Oracle Names Server

**D.** Connection Manager

**E.** None of the above

**18.** The DBA wants to start Connection Manager from the command line. What command line option will be chosen?

**A.** CMCTL START

**B.** CMAN START

**C.** CMAN_ORA STARTUP

**D.** CMAN STARTUP

**E.** None of the above

**19.** The DBA stops Connection Manager while users are connected to the database. What happens to the sessions that connected to the database using Connection Manager?

    **A.** An immediate error message is received.

    **B.** The session is unaffected, and clients can continue working.

    **C.** An error message is received the next time they try to access the database.

    **D.** Clients will not be able to access the database, but will not receive an error message.

    **E.** None of the above

**20.** Which of the following is *true* about connection concentration?

    **A.** It cannot be used with Multithreaded Server.

    **B.** It must be used with Multithreaded Server.

    **C.** The (POO=ON) parameter needs to be specified in the `cman.ora` file to enable this feature.

    **D.** This feature supports connection pooling.

    **E.** None of the above is true.

# Answers to Review Questions

1. A, B, C. Connection Manager provides Oracle with greater connection scalability, the ability to connect disparate protocols through a central location, and the ability to secure network access. Connection pooling is a function of the Multithreaded Server.

2. B. The command line function to start Connection Manager is CMCTL. The names of most Oracle command line tools end in *ctl* such as lsnrctl and namesctl.

3. B, D. Two processes start when Connection Manager is started. The main process, CMGW, is responsible for handling user requests for connections to Oracle databases, along with other functions. The CMADMIN process is responsible for all of the administrative functions for Connection Manager. CMAN is another name for Connection Manager and CMCTL is the command line utility to start and stop Connection Manager.

4. D. Port 1521 is the default port designation for a listener on TCP/IP. Port 1526 is another port that is typically configured for listeners. Port 1630 is the common port designations for TCP/IP when using Connection Manager.

5. A. In order for a client to use Connection Manager, it has to know the host and port information for Connection Manager. This information is kept in the tnsnames.ora file.

6. B. SOURCE_ROUTE tells the client to use the two addresses in order. The first is the Connection Manager address and the second is the service address that is to be connected to. CONNECT_DATA is the part of the file where SOURCE_ROUTE is specified.

7. C. This is an example of multi-protocol interchange. Connection concentration allows for multiple users to share a common network connection with the database; connection filtering is the access control capability of Connection Manager; and connection pooling is a feature of Multithreaded Server.

**8.** C. Connection Manager *could* be located on the same server as the database and *could* be started from that location. Connection Manager does allow dedicated (bequeath) connections to database destinations. The correct answer is C, it passes the client requests on to the database server.

**9.** B. Answers A, C, and D are non-existent files. So, the answer is `cman.ora`, which is Connection Manager's configuration file.

**10.** B. The Connection Manager file specifies information about Connection Manager's listener location, any optional parameters, and any connection rules that govern access control. The `cman` section has information about the listening location for Connection Manager.

**11.** A. All are syntactically correct, but only one is listening on one of the default ports for Connection Manager, which is 1630. The other ports, while they could be used, are typically ports used by the Oracle Listener.

**12.** B. To use connection concentration, the database must be configured in Multithreaded Server mode. In order to allow connection concentration with MTS, the parameter (`MUL=ON`) must be set.

**13.** B. Look carefully at the syntax. All of the syntax is identical except for the last parameter. The possible setting for the `ACT` (short for action) setting are `ACC` (short for accept) and `REJ` (short for reject). This is used for configuring access control.

**14.** B. If Connection Manager rules are not defined, then all connections are allowed. If rules are defined, then any connection attempt not covered by the rules is rejected. Therefore option B is the correct answer. In other words, once you start defining rules, any client connection not explicitly allowed by a defined rule is rejected.

**15.** D. Connection Manager can handle up to 2048 concurrent connections.

**16.** C. This is one of the parameters that can be set in the `cman.ora` file. The `MAXIMUM_RELAYS` parameter is configurable up to 1024 with 8 being the default. Answer C is correct. All other choices are non-existent parameters.

**17.** E. This is one of those trick questions that seem simple on the surface. Connection Manager cannot be started from within the Net8 Assistant. Read the questions carefully!

**18.** A. Connection Manager *is* started from the command line. The CMCTL command is used to start Connection Manager.

**19.** C. Unlike the listener, Connection Manager remains in the middle of all database conversations. It acts as a gateway, passing requests from the client on to the database server. If Connection Manager goes down, the user will notice this the next time a database request is made.

**20.** B. This is another one of those subtly difficult questions that requires careful reading. Connection concentration requires the Multithreaded Server option to be used, so option A is incorrect. The (POO=ON) parameter does need to be configured, but it is located in the init.ora file, not the cman file. The answer is B, connection concentration can only be used when the server is configured with the Multithreaded Server option.

# Advanced Security Option

**ORACLE8i NETWORK ADMINISTRATION EXAM OBJECTIVES COVERED IN THIS CHAPTER:**

- ✓ Define security concerns in the enterprise.
- ✓ Define the features of the Advanced Security option.
- ✓ Understand the features of data security.
- ✓ Examine how data encryption functions.
- ✓ Examine how checksumming functions.
- ✓ Define the authentication features of the Advanced Security option.
- ✓ Understand the token card and Biometric options.
- ✓ Define KERBEROS and RADIUS support features.

Exam objectives are subject to change at any time without prior notice and at Oracle's sole discretion. Please visit Oracle's Training and Certification Web site (`http://education .oracle.com/certification/index.html`) for the most current exam objectives listing.

Ensuring a secure database is a primary concern of database administrators. As organizations grow and databases are distributed throughout an organization, the need for tighter security becomes an important issue. This chapter introduces the Oracle Advanced Security option and its features. You will learn about the benefits this option provides to organizations that require a high level of data and user security. This chapter also explains how the Advanced Security option integrates into an Oracle Enterprise, and how it can be utilized to ensure a high level of data integrity and privacy and prevent unauthorized personnel from accessing Oracle resources. Finally, you will learn about what third-party products the Oracle Security Server supports.

Oracle offers the Oracle Advanced Security option to accommodate the needs of organizations that require a higher degree of connectivity security and data security than what the base Oracle installation provides. The option offers a level of functionality that allows for secure and validated connections to an Oracle Enterprise. It also provides for high-level data security of network transactions through encryption and checksumming.

Intimate knowledge of the Advanced Security option is not necessary for success on the Oracle8i Network Administration certification exam. However, it is important to understand the types of security concerns within an organization, the benefits and features that the Advanced Security option offers, and some of the significant parameters used in conjunction with this option.

The Oracle Advanced Security option is an add-on product to the base Oracle Net8 Server and Net8 client software.

# Security Concerns in the Enterprise

The size and complexity of distributed, mission-critical applications continue to grow. The amount of sensitive information being transmitted across a network by these applications, such as credit card numbers and bank account numbers, is increasing. The rise of the Internet has been a boon for organizations interested in large-scale deployment of mission critical of applications carrying sensitive information. Yet because the Internet provides an open platform that anyone with a Web browser can access, this openness and flexibility can come at the price of increased security risks. These risks include the following:

- Unauthorized data modifications during the transmission process

- Unauthorized viewing of information during data transmissions

- Individuals masquerading as real users accessing sensitive information

- Individuals gaining unauthorized access to the database because of breakdowns in security

These types of security breaches fall into four main categories: data integrity, data privacy, client authentication, and client authorization.

## Data Integrity

Data integrity can be jeopardized if network intruders gain access to the network and intercept information passed between the client and the Oracle Server. The information could be modified and transmitted to the Oracle Server without detection. Figure 18.1 illustrates a data integrity security violation.

**FIGURE 18.1** Data integrity security violation

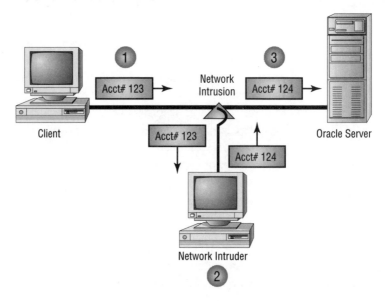

In this example, the information is being captured by an intruder. The intruder captures and modifies account information and sends the modified information on to the server. Both the client and server are unaware that this modification has taken place.

## Data Privacy

A network intruder could gain access to and intercept sensitive information, thus violating data privacy. This sensitive information, such as bank account numbers, usernames, and passwords, could then be used for malicious activities. Figure 18.2 illustrates a data privacy security violation.

**FIGURE 18.2** Data privacy security violation

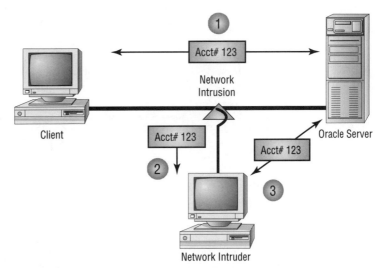

In this example, an intruder captures a bank account number and PIN number for the account. With this information, the potential exists for the intruder to gain electronic access to the user's account, compromising the data privacy.

## Client Authentication

An intruder could impersonate a user who is authorized to the system. This can occur if an intruder gains access to a network transmission and captures information such as login and password data. Thus client authentication—ensuring that clients are truly whom they claim to be—is imperative. Figure 18.3 illustrates a client authorization security violation.

**FIGURE 18.3** Client authorization security violation

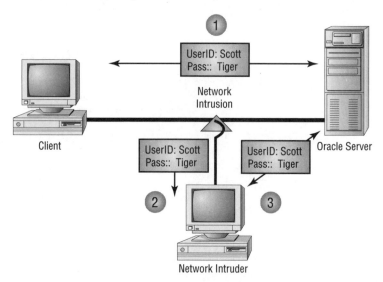

In this example, an intruder captures a user ID and password. With this information, the intruder could then masquerade as the real user, connect to the system and do significant harm to the information that the real user has access to.

### Client Authorization

You must ensure that a client has only the necessary authorizations to carry out business processes. While Oracle does have internal privilege mechanisms, the Advanced Security option enhances the standard security and authorization model.

# Data Security Features

Oracle's Advanced Security option provides a framework that guarantees secure transmissions of sensitive information and provides mechanisms to confidently identify and authenticate users in the Oracle Enterprise. Oracle provides two mechanisms that protect data transmissions from being compromised: encryption and checksumming. Encryption ensures privacy of data by electronically scrambling the data. This prevents a would-be intruder from capturing and reading the transmitted data. Checksumming ensures data integrity by attaching a computed checksum value with each packet sent across a network. This same computation is performed by the server upon receipt of the packet to make sure that none of the information in the packet has been modified. This prevents a would-be intruder from capturing and modifying the information being sent across the network.

## Encryption: Protection of Data Privacy

The Advanced Security option allows for the *encryption* of data transmissions across a network. Oracle supports two encryption methods:

- The RSA RC4 method by Data Security Inc.
- The DES Data Encryption Standard method

Encrypted data utilizes an electronic "key" to ensure that data is protected. The recipient can decrypt the data if they have the proper decryption key. Special hardware is required for this option.

When data is *encrypted*, the information is scrambled during transmission using an encryption key. Encryption keys can be from 40 bits to 128 bits in length depending on the type of encryption method employed. The larger the encryption key, the more difficult it is for a would-be intruder to decipher the encrypted data.

Both client and server must be configured with the Advanced Security option to take advantage of encryption. Oracle supports the RC4 Encryption method from RSA Data Security and the Data Encryption Standard (DES) method of encryption. The RC4 method of encryption supports key lengths of 40, 56, and 128 bits. The DES encryption method uses a 56-bit method of encryption for domestic databases and, because of government restrictions, a 40-bit key length for non-domestic databases that are exported outside of the United States.

## Checksumming: Protection of Data Quality

*Checksumming* protects client-transmitted data from modification prior to reaching the intended Oracle Server as well as from being duplicated and repeatedly sent across a network. When checksumming is used, each packet is labeled and sequenced. Also, a message digest is attached to each packet sent across the network. The message digest contains a calculated hash number. When the server receives the packet, it performs an identical hash calculation and compares its value to the hash number in the message digest to ensure that the data has not been modified. If the values do not match, the server rejects the transmission.

Oracle supports the Message Digest 5 (MD5) checksumming algorithm. As explained above, if any of the data has been modified during transmission, the checksum value created by the algorithm will change, thus allowing the server to detect the fact that the data was modified.

## Negotiations for Encryption and Checksumming Enforcement

The client and server can negotiate as to whether encryption and checksumming are enforced. This is done by specifying the appropriate parameters in the `sqlnet.ora` file on both the client and the server. These parameters are listed below:

*SQLNET.CRYPTO_CHECKSUM_CLIENT*   This parameter specifies if client-side checksumming is enforced.

*SQLNET.CRYPTO_CHECKSUM_SERVER*   This specifies if server-side checksumming is enforced.

*SQLNET.ENCRYPTION_CLIENT*   This specifies if client-side encryption is enforced.

*SQLNET.ENCRYPTION_SERVER*   This specifies if server-side encryption is enforced.

There are four possible values for these parameters: ACCEPTED, REJECTED, REQUESTED, and REQUIRED.

**ACCEPTED**   Encryption or checksumming is active if the other side of the connection specifies "REQUESTED" or "REQUIRED." The same or compatible algorithm must be available on the other side of the network transmission or the security measure will be inactive. ACCEPTED is the default if no values are specified on the client or the server for encryption or checksumming. The service will be turned on if the other side of the connection wants it.

**REJECTED**   If a parameter is set to REJECTED, the service cannot be active. Connection failure occurs if "REQUIRED" is specified on the other side of the request. The service will not be activated even if the other side wants it.

**REQUESTED**   The service will be active if the other side specifies "ACCEPTED," "REQUESTED," or "REQUIRED" and there is a compatible algorithm available on the other side; it will be inactive otherwise. The service will be turned on if the other side of the connection allows it.

**REQUIRED** If a parameter is set to REQUIRED, the service must be active. The connection fails if the other side of the network transmission specifies "REJECTED" or if there is no compatible algorithm on the other side. The service must be turned on or the connection will not be made.

The Advanced Security server defaults to ACCEPTED for all of these parameters if they are not specified. The encryption and checksumming parameters can be set independently, allowing you to use encryption, checksumming, or both.

Table 18.1 shows the negotiation matrix for each combination of parameters.

**TABLE 18.1** Client/Server Security Negotiation Matrix

| Client Parameter | Accepted | Rejected | Requested | Required |
|---|---|---|---|---|
| Server Accepted | Off | Off | On | On |
| Server Rejected | Off | Off | Off | Connect Failure |
| Server Requested | On | Off | On | On |
| Server Required | On | Connect Failure | On | On |

## Client- and Server-Side Settings

You have the option of specifying which methods of encryption or checksumming to use. It is possible that the client and the server may support more than one type of encryption algorithm. It is the server that decides what type of algorithm to use based on what is made available in the `sqlnet.ora` file. The server chooses the first algorithm in its list that is also in the list supplied by the client. If either side does not have a list, then all of the algorithms supplied from the other side are made available.

The parameters described next control what type of encryption algorithm is used by the connection and if checksumming will be used. These parameters are also specified in the `sqlnet.ora` file.

*SQLNET.CRYPTO_CHECKSUM_TYPES_CLIENT*　Specifies if checksumming will be used on the client. The only valid value is MD5.

*SQLNET.CRYPTO_CHECKSUM_TYPES_SERVER*　Specifies if checksumming will be used on the server. The only valid value is MD5.

*SQLNET.ENCRYPTION_TYPES_CLIENT*　Specifies the type of encryption to use on the client. Valid values are RC4_40, RC4_56, RC4_128, DES, and DES40.

*SQLNET.ENCRYPTION_TYPES_SERVER*　Specifies the type of encryption to use on the server. Valid values are RC4_40, RC4_56, RC4_128, DES, and DES40.

# Authentication Methods

**A**n organization must have confidence in the fact that clients connecting to an Oracle Server are actually whom they claim to be. Therefore, the Oracle Advanced Security option supports a variety of authentication methods including *Secured Sockets Layer (SSL)*, *RADIUS*, *KERBEROS*, and CyberSAFE. These services allow organizations to take advantage of robust, industry-standard authentication mechanisms. Generally, these methods are maintained in a separate authentication server that is responsible for allowing or denying access to Oracle services based on some formal identification method such as the use of credentials, shared secrets, token cards (such as the SecurID Smartcards), or fingerprints through the use of the Biometric option. All of these methods can provide the organization with a high degree of confidence that the clients connecting to the Oracle environment are genuine and not intruders.

Figure 18.4 shows an example of how an authentication server would process a connection request. The following steps occur when a client connects using an authentication server:

1. A client desires to connect to some Oracle Server. Before this can be done, the client must make a request to an authentication server using some type of identifying characteristic, such as a password or PIN number.

2. If the authentication server verifies this client as valid, information is passed back to the client. This information allows access to the desired Oracle Server for a specified period of time.

3. The client passes this information to the Oracle Server.

**4.** The Oracle Server contacts the authentication server to verify that this is a valid and authenticated connection request.

**5.** The authentication server will either accept or reject the information from the server as being authentic. If the information is valid, then the client is allowed access to the server. If it is rejected, the client is denied access to the server.

**FIGURE 18.4** Authentication security example

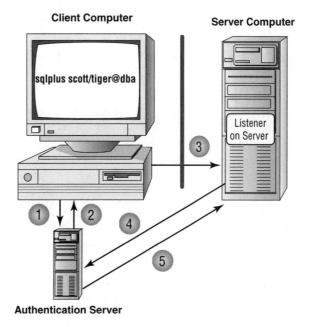

# Token Cards

*Token cards*, such as Smartcards, are similar to credit cards, but are intelligent and have a built-in processor and memory. A reader device is necessary to use these types of cards. Some token cards have a small panel that displays a randomly generated alphanumeric key that changes every sixty seconds. These keys are synchronized with the information on the authentication server and are only valid for as long as they are displayed on the card.

Because of multi-factored security, token cards can be an effective measure at deterring security breaches. When attempting to connect to an Oracle Server, the client must use a PIN (personal identification number) along with this unique key. Thus, these types of cards rely on two levels of authentication: a PIN number the client knows and a physical card that has the uniquely generated key.

Other types of token cards use a challenge-response method of authentication. With these cards, a user enters a response via a keypad to a challenge offered by the server at the time a connection request is made.

## Biometric Option

The *Biometric option* offers authentication of a client through the identification of a fingerprint. Oracle supports the Indentix Touchsafe II Biometric device, which is used to read and store fingerprint information in an authentication server database. A user places one of their fingers on a fingerprint reader, and the fingerprint is scanned and compared to other scanned fingerprints known to the authentication server. If a match is found, the client is authenticated and allowed to access the Oracle service.

## KERBEROS and CyberSAFE Support

The Oracle Advanced Security option supports single sign-on capabilities and centralized password storage though the use of the *KERBEROS* and *Cyber-SAFE* network security adapters. KERBEROS was developed by MIT for providing secure, authenticated connections across a network. It is a trusted third-party authentication system that relies on shared secrets called private keys. Only the client and server know these secrets. CyberSAFE is an authentication adapter that KERBEROS supports. The CyberSAFE TrustBroker™ security server establishes trusted relationships and secure connections on as needed basis between clients and Oracle Servers by leveraging the features of both public key and private key authentication via KERBEROS.

## RADIUS Support

*RADIUS*, or Remote Authentication Dial-In Service, is an emerging industry standard for enforcing authentication of clients accessing an Oracle Server remotely. The RADIUS protocol supports a number of different authentication methods, such as token cards, and makes these services more transparent by providing a gateway and common protocol to the appropriate authentication server. With the use of RADIUS, authentication methods can be changed without any modifications to the Oracle client or Server.

The RADIUS adapter must be installed and configured to be utilized.

When clients connect to an Oracle environment using a RADIUS server, the client contacts the appropriate Oracle Server and the server contacts the RADIUS server. The RADIUS server, in turn, contacts the authentication server that is configured for the authentication method being utilized. For example, if Smartcards are being used, the authentication server may be configured with Secure Dynamics ACE/Server software. The authentication server validates the client information and passes information back to the RADIUS server. Then the RADIUS server notifies the Oracle Server as to whether or not the client has been validated and can connect to the Oracle Server.

The RADIUS server, authentication server, and the Oracle Server can be on the same physical machine or on different physical machines.

## Secured Sockets Support

The Advanced Security option also supports network connections using the Secured Sockets Layer (SSL). The Secured Sockets Layer is an industry-standard protocol developed by Netscape Communications to provide security in a networked environment. SSL interfaces with the Oracle protocol adapters and supports authentication and encryption between clients and servers as well as between servers.

The security features of SSL can be used individually or in concert with any of the other various authentication methods supported by the Advanced Security option. SSL is also very flexible and can be configured to require authentication on a client, a server, or both client and server.

## Distributed Computing Environment (DCE)

Oracle supports the ability of single sign-on by utilizing the *Distributed Computing Environment (DCE)* set of integrated network services. DCE, developed by the Open Software Foundation (OSF), is situated between the application and the operating system and allows users to create distributed applications that work across a variety of operating platforms and environments. The security components of DCE provides the following capabilities:

- Authentication of clients and single sign-on capabilities

- Protection of data from tampering

- Protection of data privacy

# Authentication Configuration Parameters

**Y**ou configure the authentication methods by setting parameters in the sqlnet.ora file on the client and server machines and in the init.ora file on the Oracle Server. The following is a summary of the significant parameters for authentication:

**SQLNET.AUTHENTICATION_SERVICES**   This parameter specifies the type of authentication method that will be used. The client side and server side sqlnet.ora files should contain this parameter. For example, if you were to configure KERBEROS as the authentication mechanism, the parameter would be

```
SQLNET.AUTHENTICATION_SERVICES = (Kerberos5)
```

**REMOTE_OS_AUTHENT**   This parameter allows certain types of remote clients to connect to Oracle Servers without supplying a user ID or password. This is called *operating system authentication*. This parameter is located in the init.ora file on the Oracle Server. It should be set to FALSE when you are using the Advanced Security option authentication methods. If this parameter is set to TRUE and you are using operating system authentication (such as the use of OPS$ accounts), it could allow a client to connect without proper authorization. This is because the operating system serves as the authenticating mechanism and not the Advanced Security option authentication method chosen. This can occur with non-secure protocols such as TCP/IP. Here is an example for the proper setting of this parameter in the init.ora file:

```
REMOTE_OS_AUTHENT = FALSE
```

**OS_AUTHENT_PREFIX**   The OS_AUTHENT_PREFIX parameter in the init.ora file on the Oracle Server should also be set to NULL. The default for this parameter is OPS$. The advantages to setting this parameter to NULL are that. NULL allows for longer usernames and you do not have to maintain a separate username for externally authenticated users. An externally authenticated user is a user that is defined in the operating system and also defined in Oracle. This type of user does not have to supply a password when connecting to Oracle because they are being authenticated by the operating system. In other words, if they have adequate security clearance to connect to the machine where the Oracle Server exists, they also have rights to connect to the Oracle Server. Here is an example of setting this parameter:

```
OS_AUTHENT_PREFIX = ""
```

For more detailed instructions on configuring the Advanced Security option, see the *Oracle Advanced Security Administrator's Guide, Release 8.1.5* (Part# A67766-01).

# Summary

This chapter emphasized the importance of providing a secure setting for conducting business activities across a network in an Oracle environment. The Oracle Advanced Security option provides an organization with a higher degree of security than is possible with the Oracle Server alone. It offers sophisticated security measures that ensure not only the security and integrity of the transactions across the network, but it also provides the business with confidence in the identity of the clients who are gaining access to and using this information. You should understand the types of security breaches that this option protects an organization from, such as data privacy and data integrity breaches and access to the enterprise from unauthorized sources.

The Advanced Security option ensures accurate and secure transaction processing in an Oracle network by providing encryption and checksumming of transactional information. These options are configured on the client and the server and allow transactions to be conducted in a secure environment. Oracle supports industry-standard methods of encryption and checksumming.

The Advanced Security option also provides a wide variety of authentication mechanisms including the token cards, the Biometric option, KERBEROS and CyberSAFE, and SSL. This array of choices is enhanced by the support of RADIUS and DCE.

# Key Terms

**B**efore you take the exam, make sure you're familiar with the following terms:

Biometric option

checksumming

Distributed Computing Environment (DCE)

encryption

KERBEROS

OS_AUTHENT_PREFIX

RADIUS

REMOTE_OS_AUTHENT

Secured Sockets Layer (SSL)

SQLNET.AUTHENTICATION_SERVICES

SQLNET.CRYPTO_CHECKSUM_CLIENT

SQLNET.CRYPTO_CHECKSUM_SERVER

SQLNET.ENCRYPTION_CLIENT

SQLNET.ENCRYPTION_SERVER

token cards

# Review Questions

1. Which of the following is an example of a security risk?

   **A.** A user typing in an invalid user ID

   **B.** A user attempting to capture a data transmission

   **C.** A user entering an invalid service name

   **D.** None of the above

2. You want to ensure that the database server receives data being transmitted from a client workstation without modification. This is an example of:

   **A.** Data privacy

   **B.** Data authentication

   **C.** Data integrity

   **D.** Data correctness

3. A company would like to give users the ability to log in to a set of database services with only one user ID and password. This is an example of:

   **A.** Data authentication

   **B.** Single sign-on

   **C.** Enterprise security

   **D.** Database authorization

   **E.** None of the above

4. The two encryption methods supported by the Security server are:

   **A.** DEA

   **B.** DES

   **C.** RSA1

   **D.** RSA

   **E.** RSA4

5. Which of the following best describes what occurs on a client when checksumming is employed?

   **A.** Packets are labeled and sequenced before transmission to the server.

   **B.** Packets are encoded before transmission to the server.

   **C.** Packets are encrypted before transmission to the server.

   **D.** None of the above is correct.

6. What would result when a client requires checksumming but the server rejects checksumming?

   **A.** The client connection will fail.

   **B.** The client connection will succeed with checksumming employed.

   **C.** The client connection will succeed without checksumming employed.

   **D.** None of the above is correct.

7. Which of the following are possible server-side settings for encryption? (Choose two.)

   **A.** ALLOWED

   **B.** REQUESTED

   **C.** MANDATORY

   **D.** REQUIRED

   **E.** OPTIONAL

8. In what file would the encryption parameters reside?

   **A.** `listener.ora`

   **B.** `init.ora`

   **C.** `sqlnet.ora`

   **D.** `names.ora`

   **E.** None of the above

**9.** What is the encryption parameter you would set on the server?

   **A.** `SQLNET.ENCRYPTION_SERVER`

   **B.** `INIT.ENCRYPTION_SERVER`

   **C.** `LISTENER.ENCRYPTION_CHECKSUM_SERVER`

   **D.** `SQLNET.CRYPTO_CHECKSUM_SERVER`

**10.** Which of the following methods are available for user authentication using the security server?

   **A.** Passkeys

   **B.** Credit cards

   **C.** Token cards

   **D.** Voice recognition

   **E.** None of the above

**11.** When using an authentication server, which of the following are true? (Choose all that apply.)

   **A.** Client contacts the authentication server.

   **B.** Authentication server passes information back to the client.

   **C.** Client passes authentication information to the database server.

   **D.** The server either accepts or rejects the client credentials.

   **E.** All of the above are true.

**12.** A user places their finger on a fingerprint reader in order to gain access into the database. This is an example of:

   **A.** The Fingerprint option

   **B.** The Biologic option

   **C.** The Biometric option

   **D.** The Token Card option

13. You want to use KERBEROS as your authentication mechanism. Which of the following will work?

    **A.** SQLNET.REMOTE_OS_AUTHENT=(KERBEROS)

    **B.** SQLNET.OS_AUTHENT_PREFIX=(KERBEROS)

    **C.** REMOTE_LOGIN_PASSWORDFILE=(KERBEROS)

    **D.** SQLNET.AUTHENTICATION_SERVICES=(KERBEROS)

    **E.** None of the above

14. In which file would the SQLNET.AUTHENTICATION_SERVICES parameter be placed?

    **A.** init.ora

    **B.** sqlnet.ora

    **C.** tnsames.ora

    **D.** listener.ora

    **E.** None of the above

15. The DBA simply wants to use the user ID and password to authenticate users connecting to the server. Which of the following will satisfy this need?

    **A.** REMOTE_OS_AUTHENT=OFF

    **B.** SQLNET.AUTHENTICATION_SERVICES=TRUE

    **C.** SQLNET.AUTHENTICATION_SERVICES=NONE

    **D.** SQLNET.AUTHENTICATION_SERVICES=PASS

    **E.** None of the above

16. SSL stands for:

    **A.** Sqlnet Security List

    **B.** Sqlnet Services Layer

    **C.** Single Sign-on Layer

    **D.** Secured Sockets Layer

**17.** Which of the following are security factors of token cards? (Choose two.)

   **A.** A checksum value

   **B.** Something the person knows

   **C.** Something the person posesses

   **D.** A challenging question the user must answer

**18.** RADIUS stands for:

   **A.** Remote Authentication Device Input User Service

   **B.** Real Active Device Input User System

   **C.** Remote Authentication Dial-in User Service

   **D.** Ready Access Device Input User System

   **E.** None of the above

**19.** What integration platform supports the ability of single sign-on?

   **A.** OSF

   **B.** SSL

   **C.** DCE

   **D.** OPA

**20.** Which of the following parameters should be set to NULL in the `init.ora` file when using the Advanced Security option?

   **A.** SQLNET.ENCRYPTION_CLIENT

   **B.** OS_AUTHENT_PREFIX

   **C.** REMOTE_OS_AUTHENT

   **D.** SQLNET.ENCRYPTION_SERVER

# Answers to Review Questions

1. B. If a user tries to capture a data transmission, this is a data privacy security violation. An invalid user ID or service name is not considered a breach of security.

2. C. If data is transmitted from the client to a server and is modified in the process, the data integrity has been compromised.

3. B. Single sign-on is a feature of the Advanced Security option that allows a DBA to define a set of credentials to a centralized authentication server such as CyberSAFE, which is a KERBEROS-based server.

4. B, D. RSA and DES are two types of supported encryption methods.

5. A. Packets are labeled and sequenced before transmission to the server. This prevents unauthorized interceptions and modifications of the data.

6. A. The client connection to the server will fail because the client requires checksumming to be available.

7. B, D. REQUESTED and REQUIRED are two settings for encryption. The other two settings are ACCEPTED and REJECTED, which are used when clients and server are negotiating whether to turn on checksumming and/or encryption.

8. C. These settings are found in the `sqlnet.ora` file.

9. A. The `SQLNET.ENCRYPTION_SERVER` parameter specifies how a server will react to a client requesting encryption.

10. C. SecurID Token cards can be used as a security solution. These cards display a number that changes every sixty seconds. The client must supply a PIN number and the number currently displayed on the card to gain access to the Oracle Server.

11. E. These are all steps in the connection process when using an authentication server.

12. C. The Biometric option supports fingerprint scanning as a means to verify a client and allow access to the Oracle Server.

13. D. The `SQLNET.AUTHENTICATION_SERVICES` parameter specifies which authentication adapter is used.

14. B. The `sqlnet.ora` file stores information about which authentication adapters are being used.

15. C. You can disable the authentication services by setting the `SQLNET.AUTHENTICATION_SERVICES` parameter to NONE in the `sqlnet.ora` file.

16. D. SSL stands for Secured Sockets Layer. SSL is a standard protocol for providing secure network connections.

17. B, C. For a user to gain access to the Oracle Server when using token cards, the person must know a PIN number and possess the SecurID card, which has a dynamically changing number.

18. C. Remote Authentication Dial-in User Service is a security option that enables remote access and authentication of clients.

19. C. The Distributed Computing Environment, or DCE, supports single sign-on capabilities.

20. B. The `OS_AUTHENT_PREFIX` parameter should be set to NULL when using the Advanced Security option.

# Chapter

# 19

# Troubleshooting Oracle8i Net8

## ORACLE8i NETWORK ADMINISTRATION EXAM OBJECTIVES COVERED IN THIS CHAPTER:

- ✓ Define the types of problems you may encounter.
- ✓ Define the server-side troubleshooting techniques.
- ✓ Define the middle-tier troubleshooting techniques.
- ✓ Define the client-side troubleshooting techniques.
- ✓ Define logging and tracing.
- ✓ Configure client-side logging using Net8 Assistant.
- ✓ Configure server-side tracing using Net8 Assistant.
- ✓ Configure Oracle Names logging.
- ✓ Configure Connection Manager logging.
- ✓ Learn how to use Oracle Trace Assistant.

Exam objectives are subject to change at any time without prior notice and at Oracle's sole discretion. Please visit Oracle's Training and Certification Web site (http://education .oracle.com/certification/index.html) for the most current exam objectives listing.

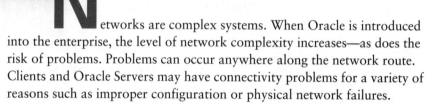

**N**etworks are complex systems. When Oracle is introduced into the enterprise, the level of network complexity increases—as does the risk of problems. Problems can occur anywhere along the network route. Clients and Oracle Servers may have connectivity problems for a variety of reasons such as improper configuration or physical network failures.

Ensuring reliable connections is vitally important to the organization. Thus the Oracle Database Administrator needs to have an understanding of the types of failures that can occur in an Oracle Network. The Database Administrator also needs to understand the tools available to diagnose problems and to solve them.

This chapter focuses on the types of problems that can arise in an Oracle Network and on the tools the Database Administrator can use to troubleshoot these problems. You will learn a systematic approach to solving connection errors as well as how to configure logging and tracing. Finally, the chapter reviews how trace files can be formatted to yield further information.

# Diagnosing and Correcting Connection Problems

**N**etwork errors occur for a number of reasons:

- The client, middle tier, or Oracle Server may not be configured properly.

- The client may not be able to resolve the net service name.

- The underlying network protocol may not be active on the server; for example, the TCP/IP process on the server may not be running.

- The user may enter an incorrect net service name, user ID, or password.

These types of errors can be diagnosed and corrected easily.

When a client has a connection problem that is up to you to fix, it is helpful to first gather information about the situation. Make sure you record the following information:

- The Oracle error received.

- The location of the client. Is the client connecting from a remote location, or is the client connected directly to the server?

- The name of the Oracle Server to which the client is attempting to connect.

- Check if other clients are having connection problems. If other clients are experiencing problems, are these clients in the same general location?

- Ask the user what is failing: Is it the application being used or the connection?

We will now look at the particular network areas to check and the methods used to further diagnose connection problems. We will also look at the Oracle error codes that will help to identify and correct the problems.

## Server-Side Checks

First things first: Start with the server. Make sure the machine is running, that the Oracle Server is available, and that the listener is active. Here is a summary of checks to perform on the server:

**Check the server machine.**   Make sure the server machine is active and available for connections. On some systems, it is possible to start a system in a restricted mode that only allows supervisors or administrators to log in to the computer. Make sure that the computer is open and available to all users.

**Check the database.**   Make sure the database is running. Connect to the Oracle Server and log in to the database using a tool like SQL*Plus. You should first attempt to do a local connection, which does not use the Oracle Listener.

To connect to the Oracle Server using a local connection, set your ORACLE_SID environmental variable to the name of the Oracle Instance you want to connect to. Then, attempt to connect to SQL*Plus. The following example is a connection sequence on Windows NT that fails because the database is not running. For example, if the database you are attempting to connect to were named

PROD, the following code example could be used in a Windows NT environment for your test:

```
C:\>set ORACLE_SID=PROD
C:\>sqlplus system/manager

SQL*Plus: Release 8.1.5.0.0 - Production on Sat Feb 19
20:07:51 2000

(c) Copyright 1999 Oracle Corporation.  All rights
reserved.

ERROR:
ORA-01034: ORACLE not available
```

An ORA-01034 error means the Oracle Instance is not running. You need to start up the Oracle Instance.

On Windows NT, you will receive an ORA-12500 error from SQL*Plus or an ORA-12560 error from Server Manager when the Oracle Service for the instance is not running. Start the service and attempt to connect to the Oracle Server.

**Verify that the database is open to all users.**   A database can be opened in restricted mode. This means only users with restricted mode access can use the system. This is not a networking problem but will lead to clients being unable to connect to the Oracle Server.

```
C:\sqlplus scott/tiger@Database Administrator

SQL*Plus: Release 8.1.5.0.0 - Production on Sat Feb 19
20:32:17 2000

(c) Copyright 1999 Oracle Corporation.  All rights
reserved.

ERROR:
ORA-01035: ORACLE only available to users with
RESTRICTED SESSION privilege
```

**Check the listener.** Make sure the listener is running on the Oracle Server. Make sure you check the services for all of the listeners on the Oracle Server. You can use the lsnrctl status command. The following command shows the status of the default listener named LISTENER:

```
C:\>lsnrctl status

LSNRCTL for 32-bit Windows: Version 8.1.5.0.0 -
Production on 19-FEB-00 20:19:44

(c) Copyright 1998 Oracle Corporation.  All rights
reserved.

Connecting to
(DESCRIPTION=(ADDRESS=(PROTOCOL=TCP)(HOST=weishan)(PORT
=1521))(PROTOCOL_STACK=(PRESENTATION=TTC)(SESSION=NS)))
STATUS of the LISTENER
-----------------------
Alias                     LISTENER
Version                   TNSLSNR for 32-bit Windows:
Version 8.1.5.0.0 - Production
Start Date                19-FEB-00 20:19:36
Uptime                    0 days 0 hr. 0 min. 8 sec
Trace Level               off
Security                  OFF
SNMP                      OFF
Listener Parameter File
D:\Oracle\Ora81\network\admin\listener.ora
Listener Log File
D:\Oracle\Ora81\network\log\listener.log
Services Summary...
   PROD             has 1 service handler(s)
The command completed successfully
```

Also check the services for which the listener is listening. You must see the service to which the client is attempting to connect. If the service is not listed, the client may be entering the wrong service, or the listener may not be configured to listen for this service.

**Check the *GLOBAL_DBNAME* parameter.** If the client is using the hostnaming method, make sure the GLOBAL_DBNAME parameter is set to the name of the host machine. You can find this parameter in the service definition of the listener.ora file. Verify the setting by reviewing the listener.ora configuration.

Chapter 13: Configuring Oracle8i Net8 on the Server shows an example of the GLOBAL_DBNAME setting.

**Check the listener protocols.** Check the protocols the listener is configured for. This is displayed by the lsnrctl services command. Make sure the protocol of the service matches the protocol the client is using when requesting a connection. If the client is requesting to connect with a protocol the listener is not listening for, the user will receive an ORA-12541 "No Listener" error. You will see how to check the client protocol later on in this chapter.

**Check the server protocols.** Make sure the underlying network protocol on the server is active. For systems that run TCP/IP, you can attempt to use the ping command to ping the server. This will verify that the TCP/IP daemon process is active on the server. There are other ways to check this, such as verifying the services on Windows NT or with the ps command on UNIX. An example of the ping command can be found later in the chapter.

**Check the server protocol adapters.** Make sure the appropriate protocol adapters have been installed on the server. On most platforms, you can invoke the Oracle Universal Installer program and check the list of installed protocols. On UNIX platforms, you can use the adapter utility to make sure the appropriate adapters have been linked to Oracle. An example of how to run this utility is provided below. This utility is located in the $ORACLE_HOME/bin directory.

```
[root@localhost] ./adapters oracle

Net protocol adapters linked with oracle are:

   BEQ
   IPC
   TCP/IP
   RAW

Net Naming Adapters linked with oracle are:

   Oracle TNS Naming Adapter
   Oracle Naming Adapter
Advanced Networking Option/Network Security products
 linked with oracle are:

   Oracle Security server Authentication Adapter
```

If the required protocol adapter is not listed, you have to install the adapter. This can be done by using the Oracle Installer: installing the Net8 Server software and choosing the appropriate adapters during the installation process.

**Check the user privileges.**   Make sure the user attempting to establish the connection has been granted the create session privilege to the database. This privilege is needed for a user to connect to the Oracle Server. If the client does not have this privilege, you must grant it to the user. To do so, follow this example:

```
D:\ORACLE\ADMIN\DATABASE ADMINISTRATOR\pfile>sqlplus
matt/casey@Database Administrator

SQL*Plus: Release 8.1.5.0.0 - Production on Sat Feb
19 20:52:13 2000

(c) Copyright 1999 Oracle Corporation.  All rights
reserved.

ERROR:
ORA-01045: user MATT lacks CREATE SESSION privilege;
logon denied
```

**Check for connection timeouts.** If the client is receiving an ORA-12535 or an ORA-12547 error, the client is timing out before a valid connection is established. This can occur if you have a slow network connection. You can attempt to solve this problem by increasing the time that the listener will wait for a valid response from the client; simply set the CONNECT_TIMEOUT parameter to a higher number. This is the number of seconds the listener waits for a valid response from the client when establishing a connection.

For more information on configuring the CONNECT_TIMEOUT parameter, see Chapter 13.

## Middle-Tier Checks

If you are using a middle-tier product, such as Connection Manager, make sure the product is functional. Specifically for Connection Manager, you want to ensure that it is active and that the connection rules have been configured correctly.

**Check Connection Manager.** Make sure that Connection Manager is running. You can verify this by logging on to the Connection Manager machine and entering **cmctl status**. This displays information about active Connection Manager processes. The following listing shows an example of the status command. If Connection Manager is not running, start it with the **cmctl start** command.

```
Microsoft(R) Windows NT(TM)
(C) Copyright 1985-1996 Microsoft Corp.

C:\>cmctl status

CMCTL for 32-bit Windows: Version 8.1.5.0.0 - Production
on 20-FEB-00 13:30:12

(c) Copyright 1998 Oracle Corporation.  All rights
reserved.
```

```
CMAN Status:
(STATUS=(VERSION=8.1.5.0.0)(STARTED=20-FEB-00 13:12:53)
(STATE=running))ADMIN Status:
(STATUS=(VERSION=8.1.5.0.0)(STARTED=20-FEB-00 13:12:50)
(STATE=RUNNING))
```

**Check *CMAN_RULES*.**   Make sure that you have defined the rules for the client. Remember, if you are using rules, you must define all of the rules. Connection Manager is governed by the principle "That which is not expressly permitted is rejected." If you do not have the rules properly configured, the client will receive an error similar to the following:

```
C:\>sqlplus system/manager@Database Administrator

SQL*Plus: Release 8.1.5.0.0 - Production on Sun Feb 20
13:13:06 2000

(c) Copyright 1999 Oracle Corporation.  All rights
 reserved.

ERROR:
ORA-12564: TNS:connection refused
```

## Names Server Checks

If you are using a Names Server, make sure it is active and is listening for the correct net service names. Then perform the following checks.

**Check the Names Server status.**   You can check if the Oracle Names Server is running by using the namesctl status command, as shown here:

```
C:\>namesctl status

Oracle Names Control for 32-bit Windows: Version 8.1.5.0.0
- Production on 20-FEB-00 13:20:55

(c) Copyright 1997 Oracle Corporation.  All rights
reserved.

Currently managing name server "oranamesrvr0"
Version banner is "Oracle Names for 32-bit Windows:
```

```
Version 8.1.5.0.0 - Production"

Version banner is "Oracle Names for 32-bit Windows:
 Version 8.1.5.0.0 - Production"

Server name:                                oranamesrvr0
Server has been running for:                24.17 seconds
Request processing enabled:                 yes
Request forwarding enabled:                 yes
Requests received:                          4
Requests forwarded:                         0
Foreign data items cached:                  0
Region data next checked for reload in:     not set
Region data reload check failures:          0
Cache next checkpointed in:                 not set
Cache checkpoint interval:                  not set
Cache checkpoint file name:
c:\ora81\network\adminckpcch.ora
Statistic counters next reset in:           not set
Statistic counter reset interval:           not set
Statistic counters next logged in:          not set
Statistic counter logging interval:         not set
Trace level:                                0
Trace file name: c:\ora81\network\trace\namesd7.trc
Log file name:
c:\ora81\network\log\names.log
System parameter file name:
c:\ora8\network\admin\names.ora
Command-line parameter file name:           " "
Administrative region name:                 " "
Administrative region description:          " "
ApplTable Index:                            0
Contact                                     " "
Operational Status                          0
Save Config on Stop                         no
```

**Verify the Names Server services.**   Make sure the Names Server is listening for the correct net service names. You can verify this with the Net8 Assistant:

1. Connect to the Net8 Assistant and select the Names Server from the Oracle Names Server icon (see Figure 19.1).

2. Select Manage Data from the drop-down menu at the top of the screen.

3. Select the Query radio button and enter the service name you want to query in the Service Name field.

4. Click the Execute button.

You should see a summary of connect descriptor information for this net service name displayed. The box has a scroll bar so you can move back and forth to see the entire connect descriptor.

**FIGURE  19.1**    Net8 Assistant Names Server query services screen

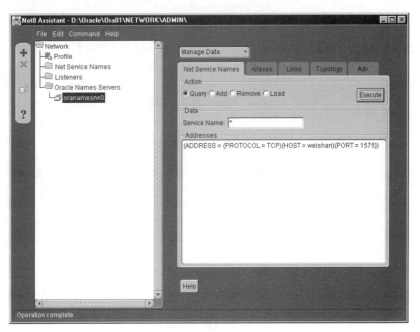

## Client-Side Checks

The client must be able to contact both the computer where the Oracle Server is located and the listener listening for connections to the Oracle Server. The client must also be able to resolve the net service name. Let's take a look at the checks to perform on the client to verify connectivity to the Oracle Server.

**Can the client contact the server?**   Make sure the client can see the host computer. If you are using the TCP/IP protocol, you can attempt to ping the host computer. Simply type **ping** and the name of the host. If the host is not found, try using the IP address of the host computer instead of the host-name. If this works, the problem may be that your hosts file is not correct or your domain Names Server does not recognize the host computer name. For example, you could ping a computer with the host name of gr99c0073 as follows:

```
C:\>ping gr99c0073

Pinging gr99c0073 [127.1.10.1] with 32 bytes of data:

Reply from 127.1.10.1: bytes=32 time<10ms TTL=128
Reply from 127.1.10.1: bytes=32 time<10ms TTL=128
Reply from 127.1.10.1: bytes=32 time<10ms TTL=128
Reply from 127.1.10.1: bytes=32 time<10ms TTL=128
```

**Can the client see the listener?**   Next, check to see if the client can contact the listener. You can use a utility called tnsping to verify this. tnsping is an Oracle utility that attempts to contact an Oracle server. It works similarly to ping in that you can enter a net service name and the number of times to contact the listener. This utility verifies that the client can contact the listener. However, it does not verify that the client can actually connect to the Oracle Server. You can also specify a number of attempts. In the example below, three attempts are made to contact the PROD database.

```
C:\>tnsping PROD  3

TNS Ping Utility for 32-bit Windows: Version 8.1.5.0.0
- Production on 19-FEB-00
 21:18:25

(c) Copyright 1997 Oracle Corporation.  All rights
```

```
reserved.

Attempting to contact
(ADDRESS=(PROTOCOL=TCP)(HOST=gr0073)(PORT=1521))
OK (270 msec)
OK (40 msec)
OK (30 msec)
```

The `tnsping` utility shows how long the round trip took to contact the listener. This information can also assist you in uncovering the connection problem, as the accompanying sidebar reveals.

---

### The Mysterious Timeout Problem

I have used `tnsping` to help troubleshoot some very interesting connection problems. One such problem involved a client experiencing intermittent connection timeouts. Sometimes the client could connect, but other times the client received a timeout error. The client also reported that it always took an inordinate amount of time to log in to the Oracle Server.

This problematic client machine happened to be sitting adjacent to another client machine that had no connection or timeout problems whatsoever. I ran some connection tests with `tnsping` and discovered that the client having problems took on average 3000 milliseconds to connect to the listener while the other client took only 30 milliseconds. Both clients were using the same network routes to connect to the server.

After further investigation, it was discovered that the machines were using different implementations of TCP/IP. This was causing the intermittent timeout problems. With the help of the `tnsping` utility, I was able to narrow down the problem to a difference in the client machine configurations.

---

**Can the client locate the Names Server?**   If you are using an Oracle Names Server, you need to configure the client with either preferred Names Servers or discovered Names Servers. As we discussed in Chapter 15, preferred Names Servers are Names Servers listed in the `sqlnet.ora` file. Discovered Names Servers would be listed in the `sdns.ora` file and are discovered by running the `reorder_ns` command from the `namesctl` utility. Preferred Names Servers are configured with the NAMES.PREFERRED_ SERVERS parameter in the `sqlnet.ora` file. In order to discover Names Servers, you need to run the `reorder_ns` command from the `namesctl` utility. This will create the `sdns.ora` file.

See Chapter 15: Centralizing Services with Oracle Names Server for more information on configuring the client when using a Names Server.

**Verify localnaming configuration files.**   If the client is using the localnaming method for net service name resolution, check the entries in the `tnsnames.ora` file. Make sure the entries are syntactically correct and that there is an entry for the net service name. Also make sure the protocol is correct.

**Check network file locations.**   One of the most common problems I have encountered is clients moving network files and not setting the TNS_ ADMIN environmental variable to the new file location. Oracle expects the `tnsnames.ora` and `sqlnet.ora` files to be in the default location. If it cannot locate the files and you have not set TNS_ADMIN, you receive an ORA-12154 error. Below is an example of this error. You also receive this error if the supplied net service name is invalid.

```
D:\ORACLE\ORA81\NETWORK\ADMIN>sqlplus system/
manager@Database Administrator

SQL*Plus: Release 8.1.5.0.0 - Production on Sat
Feb 19 21:40:12 2000

(c) Copyright 1999 Oracle Corporation.  All rights
 reserved.

ERROR:
ORA-12154: TNS:could not resolve service name
```

If you decide to move network files, be sure to set the TNS_ADMIN environmental variable to the location of the files. Oracle first searches the default location for the files and then searches the TNS_ ADMIN location for the files.

See Chapter 12: Oracle8i Net8 Architecture for information on how to set the TNS_ADMIN environmental variable.

**Check *NAMES.DIRECTORY_PATH* parameter.**   Make sure that the client has the proper names resolution setting. The NAMES.DIRECTORY_PATH parameter in the sqlnet.ora file controls the order in which the client resolves net service names. If the parameter is not set, the default is local-naming, Oracle Names Server, and then hostnaming. (See Chapter 12 for the allowable settings.)

If this parameter is set incorrectly, the client may never check the appropriate names resolution type. For example, if you are using localnaming and the parameter is set to ONAMES, the tnsnames.ora file will never be used to resolve the net service name. You will receive an ORA-12154 "Cannot Resolve Service Name" error.

**Check *NAMES.DEFAULT_DOMAIN* parameter.**   NAMES.DEFAULT_DOMAIN is another common error. It was more common in older releases of Oracle because the parameter defaulted to WORLD. Check the client sqlnet.ora file to see if the parameter is set. If the parameter has a value and you are using unqualified net service names, the parameter value is appended to the end of the net service name.

For example, if a user entered **Sqlplus matt/casey@PROD**, and the NAMES.DEFAULT_DOMAIN was set to WORLD, then Oracle would append WORLD to the net service name; Oracle will pass the command as sqlplus matt/casey@PROD.WORLD. You will receive an ORA-12154 "Cannot Resolve Service Name" error if the service name should only be Database Administrator. You use this parameter only if you are using a hierarchical naming convention.

**Check the client protocol adapters.**   Verify that the appropriate protocol adapters have been installed on the client. You can invoke the Universal Installer and check the client setup. Look for the listing of client protocol adapters installed.

## Other Network Areas to Check

In addition to the server-side, middle-tier, Names Server, and client-side checks, other network areas should be looked at when troubleshooting Net8. These areas include the following:

- Check any other machines, such as routers, hubs, or gateways, that may lie between the client and the server.

- Check the network route the client is taking to get to the Oracle Server. If you are using the TCP/IP protocol, you can use a tool such as `traceroute`, which will show you the route the client is taking to the server destination.

- If you are connecting through a firewall, make sure the client has privileges to connect through the firewall. I have seen problems with network connections if the firewall is not configured properly. Check with your network administrator on any issues with connections through a firewall.

Network sniffers or network analyzers can also be used to track down sporadic network connection problems. These tools allow you to monitor network traffic, and some allow you to inspect the network packets as they are passed back and forth from client to server.

# Net8 Logging and Tracing

If a network problem persists, you can use logging and tracing to help resolve it. Oracle generates information into log files and trace files that can assist you in tracking down network connection problems. You can use logging to find out general information about the success or failure of certain components of the Oracle Network. Tracing can be used to get in-depth information about specific network connections.

By default, Oracle produces logs for clients, the listener, and the Oracle Names Server. Client logging and Names Server logging cannot be disabled.

*Logging* records significant events, such as starting and stopping the listener, along with certain kinds of network errors. Errors are generated in the log in the form of an error stack. (Later in the chapter, you will see an example of the error stack produced from a client log.) The listener log records information such as the version number, connection attempts, and the protocols it is listening for. Logging can be enabled at the client, middle tier, and server.

*Tracing*, which you can also enable at the client, middle-tier, or server location, records all events that occur on a network, even when an error does not happen. The trace file provides a great deal of information that logs do not, such as the number of network round trips made during network connection or the number of packets sent and received during a network connection. Tracing enables you to collect a thorough listing of the actual sequence of the statements as a network connection is being processed. This gives you a much more detailed picture of what is occurring with connections the listener is processing.

**WARNING** Tracing uses much more space than logging and can also have an impact on system performance. Enable tracing only if other methods of troubleshooting fail to resolve the problem.

Use the Net8 Assistant to enable most logging and tracing parameters. Many of the logging and tracing parameters are found in the `sqlnet.ora` file. Let's take a look at how to enable logging and tracing for the various components in an Oracle Network.

## Server Logging

By default, the listener is configured to enable the generation of a log file. The log file records information about listener startup and shutdown, successful and unsuccessful connection attempts, and certain types of network errors. By default, the listener log location is `$ORACLE_HOME/network/log` on UNIX and `%ORACLE_HOME%\network\log` on Windows NT. The default name of the file is `listener.log`.

The format of the information in the `listener.log` file is a fixed-length, delimited format with each field separated by an asterisk. If you want to do further analysis of the information in the log, the data in the log can be loaded into an Oracle table using a tool like SQL*Loader. Notice in the sample listing below that the file contains information about connection attempts, the name of the program executing the request, and the name of the client attempting to connect. The last field will contain a zero if a request was successfully completed.

```
TNSLSNR for 32-bit Windows: Version 8.1.5.0.0 -
Production on 20-FEB-00 12:22:32

(c) Copyright 1998 Oracle Corporation.  All rights
reserved.

System parameter file is D:\Oracle\Ora81\network\admin
```

```
\listener.ora
Log messages written to D:\Oracle\Ora81\network\log
\listener.log

Listening on: (DESCRIPTION=(ADDRESS=(PROTOCOL=TCP)
(HOST=weishan)(PORT=1521))(PROTOCOL_STACK=
(PRESENTATION=TTC)(SESSION=NS)))
TIMESTAMP * CONNECT DATA [* PROTOCOL INFO] *
EVENT [* SID] * RETURN CODE
20-FEB-00 12:22:34 * service_register * PROD  * 0
20-FEB-00 12:22:35 * (CONNECT_DATA=(CID=(PROGRAM=)(HOST=)
(USER=Administrator))(COMMAND=status)(ARGUMENTS=64)
(SERVICE=LISTENER)(VERSION=135286784)) * status * 0
20-FEB-00 12:22:53 * service_register * PROD  * 0
20-FEB-00 12:23:42 * (CONNECT_DATA=(SERVICE_NAME=PROD
)(CID=(PROGRAM=D:\Oracle\Ora81
\bin\SQLPLUS.EXE)(HOST=WEISHAN)(USER=Administrator))) *
(ADDRESS=(PROTOCOL=tcp)(HOST=127.0.0.1)(PORT=1039))
 * establish * PROD  * 0
20-FEB-00 12:52:54 * PROD  *
(ADDRESS=(PROTOCOL=tcp)(HOST=127.0.0.1)(PORT=1039))
 * service_update * PROD  * 0
20-FEB-00 13:00:36 * ping * 0
```

## Disabling Server Logging

You can disable listener logging from the Net8 Assistant. Choose the listener from the Listeners icon. Then select General Parameters from the drop-down list box. Select the Logging & Tracing tab and select the Logging Disabled radio button (see Figure 19.2).

**FIGURE  19.2**    Net8 Assistant listener general parameters logging and tracing screen

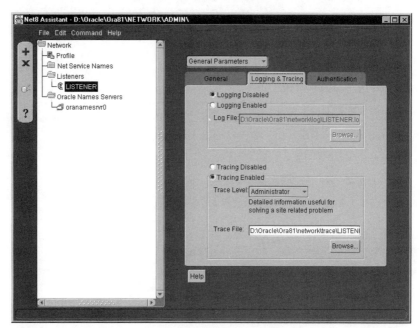

## Server Tracing

As mentioned earlier, tracing gathers information about the flow of traffic across a network connection. Data is transmitted back and forth in the form of packets. A packet contains sender information, receiver information, and data. Even a single network request may generate a large amount of packets.

In the trace file, each line of the file starts with the name of the procedure executed, in one of the Net8 layers followed by a set of hexadecimal numbers. The hexadecimal numbers are the actual data transmitted. If you are not encrypting the data, sometimes you will see the actual data after the hexadecimal numbers.

Each of the Net8 procedures is responsible for a different action. Each packet has a different code type depending on the action being taken. All of the packet types start with *NSP*. Table 19.1 summarizes the common packet types.

**TABLE 19.1**   Net8 Packet Types

| Packet Keyword | Packet Type |
| --- | --- |
| NSPTAC | Accept |
| NSPTRF | Refuse |
| NSPTRS | Resend |
| NSPDA | Data |
| NSPCNL | Control |
| NSPTMK | Marker |

If you are doing server-to-server communications and have a sqlnet.ora file on the server, you can enter information in the Server Information section of the Net8 Assistant tracing screen (see Figure 19.5). This provides tracing information for server-to server-communications.

## Enabling Server Tracing

You can enable server tracing from the same Net8 Assistant screen as shown earlier in Figure 19.2. Simply choose the Tracing Enabled radio button. The default file name and location is ORACLE_HOME/network/trace/listener.trc in UNIX and ORACLE_HOME\network\trace\listener.trc on Windows NT. You can set the trace level to USER, ADMIN, or SUPPORT. The USER level will detect specific user errors. The ADMIN level contains all of the user-level information along with installation-specific errors. SUPPORT is the highest level and can be used to produce information that may be beneficial to Oracle Support personnel. The following listing shows an example of a listener trace file:

```
nsglldprm: Resolved "CONNECT_TIMEOUT_LISTENER" to: 10
nsglldprm: Resolved "STARTUP_WAIT_TIME_LISTENER" to: 0
nsglma: entry
```

```
nsglma: Reporting the following error stack:
TNS-01152: All addresses specified for the
listener name, LISTENER, failed
nsmal: 339 bytes at 0xb03e70
nsdo: cid=0, opcode=67, *bl=339, *what=10,
uflgs=0x0, cflgs=0x3
nsdo: rank=64, nsctxrnk=0
nsdo: nsctx: state=2, flg=0x4204, mvd=0
nsdo: gtn=152, gtc=152, ptn=10, ptc=2023
nscon: sending NSPTRF packet
nspsend: plen=12, type=4
nspsend: 12 bytes to transport
```

You can tell what section of the Net8 stack the trace file is in by looking at the first two characters of the program names in the trace file. In the example above, nscon refers to the Network Session (NS) sublayer of the transparent network substrate. A message is being sent back to the client in the form of an NSPTRF packet. This is a *refusal packet*, which means that the requested action is being denied.

You see the Oracle error number embedded in the error message. In the example, a TNS-01152 error was generated. This error means the listener failed to start for some reason. This could be a problem with another process listening on the same location or a syntax problem in the listener.ora file. The most recent errors are located at the bottom of the file. These are the error messages you are most interested in. The next example shows a section of the listener.ora file with the logging and tracing parameters enabled:

```
# D:\ORACLE\ORA81\NETWORK\ADMIN\LISTENER.ORA Configuration
# File:D:\Oracle\Ora81\NETWORK\ADMIN\listener.ora
# Generated by Oracle Net8 Assistant

TRACE_LEVEL_LISTENER = ADMIN
TRACE_FILE_LISTENER = LISTENER.trc
TRACE_DIRECTORY_LISTENER = D:\Oracle\Ora8\network\trace
LOG_DIRECTORY_LISTENER = D:\Oracle\Ora8\network\log
LOG_FILE_LISTENER = LISTENER.log
```

Remember that trace files can grow very large, so you want to use tracing sparingly and only if other means of problem resolution do not help.

## Names Server Logging

The Oracle Names log file contains diagnostic startup and shutdown information about the Names Server. You can also gather statistical information such as the number of Names Server lookup requests received, the number of failed lookup attempts, and the number of messages sent and received.

By default, Oracle generates a log files for the Names Server. The default location of the Names Server log is $ORACLE_HOME/network/log on UNIX and %ORACLE_HOME%\network\log on Windows NT. The parameters to specify the directory and name of the names log file are NAMES.DIRECTORY_LOG and NAMES.FILE. The default filename is names.log. You can set these parameters using the Net8 Assistant. To do so, follow these steps:

1. Select the Names Server to manage from the main Net8 Assistant screen.

2. Choose Configure Server from the drop-down list and choose the Advanced (Adv.) tab (see Figure 19.3).

3. Enter the Log Directory and the Log File name.

4. Save your changes by selecting the Save Configuration option from the File menu.

**FIGURE 19.3** Net8 Assistant Configure Names Server Advanced tab

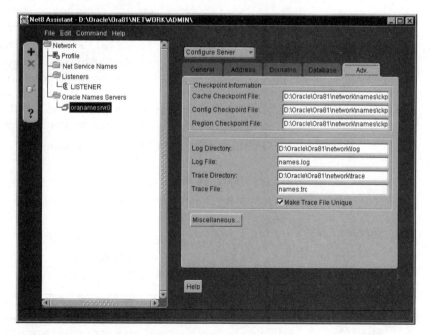

Following is an example of the entry from the names.ora file:

```
NAMES.LOG_FILE = d:\oracle\ora81\network\log\names1.log
```

You can also modify this information using the namesctl command-line utility. The following example shows how to use the tool to set the log filename and directory:

```
NAMESCTL> set log_file_name d:\oracle\ora81\network\
log\names1.log
Log file name is now d:\oracle\ora81\network\log\
names1.log
NAMESCTL> show log_file_name
Log file name is currently d:\oracle\ora81\network\log
\names1.log
```

## Gathering Names Server Statistics

You can enable the statistics gathering facility by setting the LOG_STATS_ INTERVAL parameter. This parameter enables the Names Server to capture statistics that are useful when trying to determine the amount of requests the Name Server is processing. The parameter specifies the number of seconds to wait before recording the current Names Server statistics. Here is an example of setting the parameter using the namesctl utility:

```
NAMESCTL> set log_stats_interval 100
Statistic counter logging interval is now 1 minute 40
seconds.
```

The following listing summarizes the information captured in the name.log file. The statistics portion is included to show you what information is captured when statistics gathering is enabled. Notice the warning that a database is not being used. This is because this example is configured to read from checkpoint files. Also notice the information about the startup time and stop time of the Names Server.

```
System parameter file is
D:\Oracle\Ora81\network\admin\names.ora
Log messages written to
D:\Oracle\Ora81\network\log\names.log


NNO-00268: warning: configuration database is not used,
using checkpoint data instead
NNO-00260: loading configuration data from checkpoint file
"D:\Oracle\Ora81\network\names\ckpcfg.ora"
```

```
NNO-00315: server is listening on address
(ADDRESS=(PROTOCOL=TCP)(HOST=oranamesrvr0)(PORT=1575))
NNO-00060: loading server topology from checkpoint file
"D:\Oracle\Ora81\network\names\ckpreg.ora"
NNO-00065: loading cached data from checkpoint file
"D:\Oracle\Ora81\network\names\ckpcch.ora"
26-FEB-00 19:55:15: NNO-00303: server "oranamesrvr0"
started with process ID 205
26-FEB-00 20:18:02: NNO-00326: server statistic counter
dump follows
Query requests received:                        4
Messages received:                              4
Corrupted messages received:                    0
Requests refused, processing disabled:          0
Messages sent:                                  4
Responses sent:                                 4
Alias loops detected:                           0
Cache lookup requests:                          40
Names created on lookup:                        22
Cache lookup failures:                          4
Cache lookup exact matches:                     14
Cache checkpoints:                              0
Cache checkpoint failures:                      0
Timeouts, name TTL expired:                     0
Forwarding failures:                            0
Timeouts, server not responding:                0
Not forwarded, no servers found:                0
Reforwarded requests expired:                   0
Authoritative answers when authority:           0
Non-authoritative NACKs received:               0
Objects received with no TTL:                   0
Responses received:                             0
Unmatched responses received:                   0
Requests received:                              4
Requests forwarded:                             0
Foreign data items cached:                      0
26-FEB-00 20:38:24: NNO-00301: server will shut down in 0
seconds
26-FEB-00 20:38:24: NNO-00302: server stopped
```

# Names Server Tracing

In addition to Names Server logging, you can also enable tracing to gather detailed information about the connection requests the Names Server processes. You can set the trace parameters from the same Net8 Assistant screen where you set the log parameters (shown earlier in Figure 19.3).

The Names Server trace parameters are NAMES.TRACE_FILE and NAMES.TRACE_UNIQUE. If NAMES.TRACE_UNIQUE is set, then a unique trace file is created for each trace session by appending a process ID number to the end of the trace file name. You can also set these parameters using the namesctl utility with the set trace_file_name and set trace_level options. The trace levels can be set to OFF, USER, ADMIN, or SUPPORT. The SUPPORT level provides the most detailed information. Following is a small sample of the output from the Names trace file:

```
nscon: sending NSPTAC packet
nspsend: entry
nspsend: plen=94, type=2
nspsend: 94 bytes to transport
nspsend: packet dump
nspsend:00 5E 00 00 02 00 00 00  |.^......|
nspsend:01 36 00 00 08 00 10 00  |.6......|
nspsend:01 00 00 3E 00 20 00 00  |...>. ..|
nspsend:00 00 00 00 00 00 00 00  |........|
nspsend:28 41 44 44 52 45 53 53  |(ADDRESS|
nspsend:20 3D 20 28 50 52 4F 54  | = (PROT|
nspsend:4F 43 4F 4C 20 3D 20 54  |OCOL = T|
nspsend:43 50 29 28 48 4F 53 54  |CP)(HOST|
nspsend:20 3D 20 6F 72 61 6E 61  | = orana|
nspsend:6D 65 73 72 76 72 30 29  |mesrvr0)|
nspsend:28 50 4F 52 54 20 3D 20  |(PORT = |
nspsend:31 35 37 35 29 29 00 00  |1575))..|
nspsend: normal exit
nscon: doing connect handshake...
nscon: nsctxinf[0]=0x0, [1]=0x0
nsconbrok: asking transport to enable NTOBROKEN
nscon: normal exit
nsdo: nsctxrnk=0
nsdo: normal exit
```

## Connection Manager Logging

You can configure logging for Connection Manager by manually setting the LOG_LEVEL parameter in the cman.ora file. The log level can be set from zero to four. Following is a summary of the log levels and what each log level represents:

- Level 0: No logging
- Level 1: Basic reporting
- Level 2: RULE_LIST Matchup report
- Level 3: Relay blocking report
- Level 4: Relay I/O counts report

Both of the Connection Manager processes create log files. The log files are called CMAN_PID.LOG for the Connection Manager Gateway Process and CMADM_PID.LOG for the Connection Manager Administrator Process. The PID portion of the filename is the number for the associated process that was started for the Connection Manager Gateway Process and the Connection Manager Administrator Process. These logs are found in $ORACLE_HOME/network/log for UNIX systems and %ORACLE_HOME%\network\admin for Windows NT. You can specify a different location by setting the LOG_DIRECTORY parameter in the CMAN_PROFILE section of the cman.ora file. The following listings show examples of the CMAN log and the CMADM log.

```
*** CMAN LOG ***
 (TIMESTAMP=22-FEB-00
21:18:42)(EVENT=10)(VERSION=8.1.5.0.0)
(TIMESTAMP=22-FEB-00 21:18:42)(EVENT=36)(rule_list=
(rule=(src=weishan)(dst=x)(srv=x)(act=rej)))
(TIMESTAMP=22-FEB-00 21:18:42)(EVENT=32)(PARAMETER_LIST=
(MAXIMUM_RELAYS=1024)(RELAY_STATISTICS=yes)
(AUTHENTICATION_LEVEL=0)(LOG_LEVEL=1)(SHOW_TNS_INFO=yes)
(ANSWER_TIMEOUT=0)(MAXIMUM_CONNECT_DATA=1024)
(USE_ASYNC_CALL=yes)(TRACING=no)(TRACE_DIRECTORY=default)
(MAX_FREELIST_BUFFERS=0))
(TIMESTAMP=22-FEB-00 21:18:43)(EVENT=34)(ADDRESS_LIST=
(ADDRESS=(PROTOCOL=tcp)(HOST=)(PORT=1630)(QUEUESIZE=32)))
(TIMESTAMP=22-FEB-00 21:18:44)(EVENT=38)(COMMAND=2)
```

```
(TIMESTAMP=22-FEB-00
21:25:10)(EVENT=20)(RLYNO=0)(REASON=17)
ADDRESS=(PROTOCOL=tcp)(HOST=127.0.0.1)(PORT=1106))

**** CMADM LOG ***
(TIMESTAMP=22-FEB-00 21:18:35)
(EVENT=Sent Admin Status to UI)
(TIMESTAMP=22-FEB-00 21:18:43)(EVENT=CMan Registration)
```

There are many different event codes that are reported in the Connection Manager CMAN log file. In the example above, the last line of the file contains a REASON code of 17. This event code means a connection request has been rejected because the client failed the cman_rules.

The *Oracle Net8 Administrator's Guide, Release 8.1.5* (Part #A67440-01) contains a complete list of the Connection Manager log reason codes.

## Connection Manager Tracing

Tracing can also be configured to monitor the flow of packets through Connection Manager. Trace files can be formatted using the Trace Assistant tool, which is discussed later in the chapter.

You turn on tracing for Connection Manager by using the TRACING parameter and the TRACE_DIRECTORY parameter. These parameters are specified in the CMAN_PROFILE section of the cman.ora file.

By default, Connection Manager tracing is turned off. If tracing is turned on, the default directory is $ORACLE_HOME/network/trace for UNIX and %ORACLE_HOME%\network\trace for Windows NT. The trace file output of Connection Manager is similar to the trace file output from the listener trace. For an example of what trace files look like, see the earlier section on Names Server tracing.

## Client Logging

By default, clients are configured with logging enabled. The log information is written to the $ORACLE_HOME/network/log directory on UNIX and the %ORACLE_HOME%\network\log directory on Windows NT. The default name is sqlnet.log. The log file will record error messages in the form of an error stack. This error stack, which will only be updated when connection errors occur, contains details about network connection errors that the clients receive. This is especially helpful if the client does not recall the error that was generated.

The following listing shows an example of a client stack error from the sqlnet.log. The ORA-12564 error was a result of failing the Connection Manager rules.

```
************************************************************
*************
Fatal NI connect error 12564, connecting to:
 (DESCRIPTION=(SOURCE_ROUTE=ON)(ADDRESS_LIST=
(ADDRESS=(PROTOCOL=TCP)(HOST=weishan)(PORT=1630))
(ADDRESS=(PROTOCOL=TCP)(HOST=weishan)(PORT=1521)))
(CONNECT_DATA=(SERVICE_NAME=DATABASE
ADMINISTRATOR)(CID=(PROGRAM=D:\Oracle\Ora81\bin
\SQLPLUS.EXE)(HOST=WEISHAN)(USER=Administrator))))

 VERSION INFORMATION:
    TNS for 32-bit Windows: Version 8.1.5.0.0 - Production
    Windows NT TCP/IP NT Protocol Adapter for 32-bit
Windows: Version 8.1.5.0.0 - Production
  Time: 24-FEB-00 20:21:40
  Tracing not turned on.
  Tns error struct:
    nr err code: 0
    ns main err code: 12564
    TNS-12564: TNS:connection refused
    ns secondary err code: 0
    nt main err code: 0
    nt secondary err code: 0
    nt OS err code: 0
```

Figure 19.4 shows a Net8 Assistant screen with client logging configured. Log Directory specifies the location where the client log information will be placed. Log File specifies the name of the file that is created. By default, the file will be created with an extension of .log, so there is no need to place an extension on the file name.

**FIGURE 19.4**    Net8 Assistant client logging screen

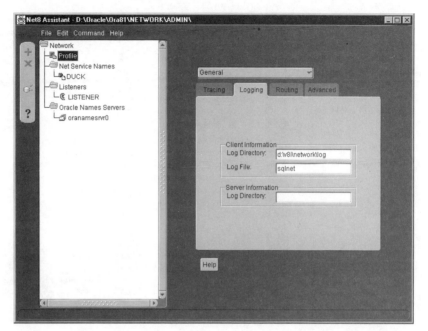

## Client Tracing

Tracing is enabled for clients by setting the following parameters in the
`sqlnet.ora` file: `TRACE_LEVEL_CLIENT`, `TRACE_DIRECTORY_CLIENT`,
`TRACE_FILE_CLIENT`, and `TRACE_UNIQUE_CLIENT`. The trace levels are
OFF, USER, ADMIN, and SUPPORT. You can also use the numbers 0,
4, 6, and 16 to represent the different trace levels. These parameters can
be enabled from the Net8 Assistant by selecting Profile and choosing
General from the drop-down list box on the right side of the screen.
Choose the Tracing tab and enter information in the Client Information
section (see Figure 19.5).

**FIGURE 19.5** Net8 Assistant client tracing screen

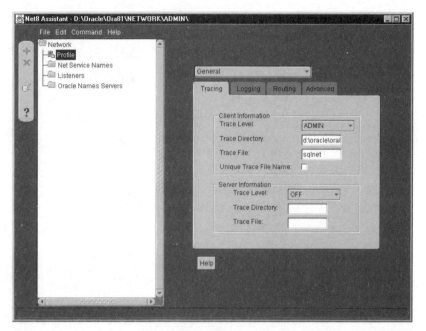

The three trace levels offer varying degrees of detail. The USER trace level will show client errors. The ADMIN level shows all of the user-level information plus any installation type errors. SUPPORT is the highest level of tracing. This level details the actual flow of packets sent and received. This information can then be analyzed using the Trace Assistant to yield information on packet flow and volume.

Also, there are two optional parameters you can add to the sqlnet.ora file that will allow you to add tracing to the tnsping command-line tool. These parameters are TNSPING.TRACE_LEVEL and TNSPING.TRACE_ DIRECTORY, and they allow you capture trace information from the tnsping command to a file. The trace levels are the same as for client tracing, which can be helpful when testing connections from a client. For more information, see the discussion on tnsping in the "Client-Side Checks" section earlier in the chapter.

When using the trace files, you are most interested in finding error conditions. On some platforms, the error condition will be identified with the word **error** or **data**. The following example shows a client trace file generated from tnsping tracing. In this example, the error is found on the **nserror** line. The ns=12541 specifies that the error occurred in the network Session layer of the Net8 transparent network substrate and was an ORA-12541, which is an error that occurs when the client cannot contact the specified listener.

```
nttcnp: creating a socket.
nttcnp: exit
nttcni: entry
nttcni: trying to connect to socket 92.
ntt2err: entry
ntt2err: soc 92 error - operation=1, ntresnt[0]=511,
 ntresnt[1]=61, ntresnt[2]=0
ntt2err: exit
nttcni: exit
nttcon: exit
nserror: entry
nserror: nsres: id=0, op=65, ns=12541, ns2=12560;
 nt[0]=511, nt[1]=61, nt[2]=0
nsopen: unable to open transport
nsbfr: entry
nsbfr: normal exit
nsmfr: entry
nsmfr: 1676 bytes at 0x1c47178
nsmfr: normal exit
nsmfr: entry
nsmfr: 412 bytes at 0xaa4520
nsmfr: normal exit
```

When you enter the name of the trace file in the Net8 Assistant, do not include
an extension or your file will end up with two extensions. For example, if you
enter `sqlnet.trc` in the Trace File box, your file will be called `sqlnet.trc.trc`!
This is not an error, but it may make for some confusion.

## The Oracle Trace Assistant Utility

You can produce more meaningful output from any trace files created by
formatting the information using Oracle's Trace Assistant. The Trace
Assistant is a command-line tool that allows you to see network connection
information, such as the number of packets that were sent and received. If
you set your trace level to SUPPORT, you can even review the contents of
the packets and the order in which the packets that were sent and received.

The Trace Assistant can be run to produce either a detailed report or a summarized report of information. Trace Assistant produces information that will give you insights into the performance of your applications that are using the network, because it analyzes information at the two-task common layer of the Net8 stack. This can be important when you are attempting to gauge the performance of your network; it helps to identify any potential network trouble spots.

Trace Assistant comes with command-line options. The following example shows the Help screen you see if you type **trcasst** at the command line. Notice that the default for the Trace Assistant includes most of the meaningful options you would want, such as displaying statistical information and error information.

```
D:>trcasst
Usage: trcasst [options] <filename>
                [options]  default values are: -odt -e -s
                <filename> is always the last argument
   Options can be zero or more of the following:
   -o   Enables display of SQL*Net and TTC information
        After the -o the following options can be used:
         c or d for summary or detailed SQL*Net
information respectively
         u or t for summary or detailed TTC I
         Information respectively
         q displays SQL commands (used together with u)

   -p   Enables application performance measurement
   -s   Enables display of statistical information
   -e   Enables display of error information
        After the -e, zero or one error decoding
        level may follow:
         0 or nothing, translates NS error numbers
         1 displays NS error translation plus all
           other errors
         2 displays error number without translation
```

Here is an example of the statistics you can produce with the Trace Assistant:

```
D:\ORACLE\ORA81\NETWORK\TRACE>trcasst -s names.trc


Trace Assistant Utility for 32-bit Windows: Version
8.1.5.0.0 - Production on 2-FEB-00 15:09:23
```

```
Trace File Statistics:
-----------------------------------------------------------
-

SQL*Net:
    Total Calls:           81 sent,           81 received,  0
upi
    Total Bytes:        28514 sent,         6781 received
    Average Bytes:        352 sent,           83 received
    Maximum Bytes:        867 sent,          426 received

    GRAND TOTAL PACKETS  sent: 81             received:    81
```

# Summary

**U**pon completion of this chapter, you should be familiar with the kinds of problems you can encounter in establishing a network connection. There are three areas on which to concentrate your effort: the server, the middle tier (if you are using one), and the client. Before you do any troubleshooting, make sure to record information about who is experiencing the problem and the error message the client received.

Next, make sure the server, the Oracle database, the listener, and the underlying network protocol are all available. Then perform the following steps:

1. Attempt to log in to the database using a local connection.

2. Ensure that the client has connect privileges to the Oracle Server.

3. If you are using a middle tier such as Connection Manager, make sure that it is also functioning.

4. For Connection Manager, make sure that the CMAN_RULES are defined correctly.

5. Check what type of names resolution the client is using. If a Names Server is used, make sure the client can see the Names Server.

6. Make sure the client has the appropriate files, such as `tnsnames.ora`, for localnaming.

7. Check the location of these files. If the files were moved from the default locations, make sure that `TNS_ADMIN` is set correctly.

8. Check entries such as `NAMES.DEFAULT_DOMAIN` and `NAMES.DIRECTORY_PATH` in the `sqlnet.ora` file. You can use the `tnsping` and `adapters` utilities to verify connectivity to the Oracle Listener and the `ping` utility to make sure the client can contact the appropriate server.

You can configure logging and tracing using the Net8 Assistant where appropriate for the client, server, and Oracle Names Server. Logging records significant events, such as starting and stopping the listener, along with certain kinds of network errors. Errors are generated in the log in the form of an error stack. Tracing records all events that occur even when an error does not happen. The trace file provides a great deal of information that logs do not. Tracing uses much more space than logging and can also have an impact on system performance. Enable tracing only if other methods of troubleshooting fail to resolve the problem. You can use the Oracle Trace Assistant to format the output of trace files.

## Key Terms

Before you take the exam, make sure you're familiar with the following terms:

tnsping

tracing

logging

trcasst

# Review Questions

1. Which of the following files will the Database Administrator *not* find on a client workstation?

   **A.** Sqlnet.ora

   **B.** Sqlnet.log

   **C.** Listener.log

   **D.** Client.trc

2. A user is having difficulty getting connected to the database named PROD. Which of the following could be done from the user's workstation to troubleshoot the connection problem?

   **A.** Check the listener.log.

   **B.** Run cmctl status.

   **C.** Ping PROD.

   **D.** tnsping PROD.

   **E.** None of the above are correct.

3. Look at the output below:

   (ADDRESS=(PROTOCOL=TCP)(HOST=GR00210)(PORT=1521))

   OK (200 msec)

   OK (120 msec)

   OK (40 msec)

   Which of the following would produce the above results?

   **A.** Listener services 3

   **B.** Lsnrctl status 3

   **C.** tnsping PROD 3

   **D.** Ping PROD 3

   **E.** None of the above

4. The Database Administrator wants to turn on logging on the client workstation. What Net8 Assistant menu choice would be chosen to accomplish this?

   **A.** Listeners

   **B.** Net service names

   **C.** Profile

   **D.** Oracle Names Server

5. Which line does Net8 assistant add to the client file if the Database Administrator turned on logging on the client workstation?

   **A.** LOG_CLIENT = TRUE

   **B.** LOG_CLIENT_PROFILE = TRUE

   **C.** LOG_FILE_CLIENT = sqlnet.log

   **D.** LOG_FILE = sqlnet.log

   **E.** None of the above

6. In what client-side file would the answer from question #5 be present?

   **A.** Tnsnames.ora

   **B.** Logging.ora

   **C.** Sqllog.ora

   **D.** Sqlnet.ora

   **E.** None of the above

7. In order to designate a location for the log from question #4, what line would be added to the client file?

   **A.** LOG_LOCATION = c:\log

   **B.** LOG_DIRECTORY=c:\log

   **C.** LOG_FILE_LOC=c:\log

   **D.** LOG_DIRECTORY_CLIENT=c:\log

8. The Database Administrator is interested in configuring tracing on a client. Which of the following would be done first?

   A. `Trcasst -e sqlnet.trc.`

   B. Start Connection Manager.

   C. `TRACE_LEVEL_CLIENT = USER.`

   D. Start the Oracle Names Server.

9. Where would the Database Administrator do the work for question #8?

   A. `Sqlnet.ora` on the database server

   B. `Sqlnet.ora` on the client workstation

   C. `Tnsnames.ora` on the client workstation

   D. Run from the command line on the client

   E. None of the above

10. Which of the following is true about Net8 tracing?

    A. The instance must be shut down to enable tracing.

    B. The listener must be stopped to enable tracing.

    C. Tracing can use a large amount of disk space.

    D. Tracing is enabled by default.

    E. None of the above is true.

11. The Database Administrator is interested in gathering information about network packet traffic from a particular client workstation. Which of the following lines will satisfy this?

    A. `TRACE_LEVEL_CLIENT=USER`

    B. `TRACE_LEVEL_CLIENT=SUPPORT`

    C. `TRACE_ADMIN_CLIENT=ADMIN`

    D. `TRACE_LEVEL_ADMIN=SUPPORT`

    E. None of the above

**12.** In which file would the Database Administrator place the line from question #11?

**A.** tnsnames.ora

**B.** trace.ora

**C.** sqllog.ora

**D.** sqlnet.ora

**E.** None of the above

**13.** Net8 tracing can gather information about the sublayers of the Net8 network communications stack. When analyzing the trace file, the Database Administrator sees the following lines:

nigini: entry

nigini: Count in NI global area now 2:

nigini: exit

What portion of the Net8 communications stack does this trace information refer to?

**A.** TTC

**B.** TNS

**C.** OPA

**D.** NPI

**E.** NII

**14.** In order to produce the output from the last question, the Database Administrator would use:

**A.** nettrace

**B.** lsnrctl

**C.** tcpctl

**D.** netasst

**E.** trcasst

**15.** The Database Administrator is interested in analyzing information about network packet traffic from a particular client workstation. Which of the following lines will satisfy this?

**A.** `Nettrace -s sqlnet.trc`

**B.** `Lsnrctl -s sqlnet.trc`

**C.** `Tcpctl -s sqlnet.trc`

**D.** `Trcasst -s sqlnet.trc`

**E.** None of the above

**16.** The trace level that will produce the largest amount of information is:

**A.** ADMIN

**B.** USER

**C.** ALL

**D.** SUPPORT

**E.** None of the above

**17.** Which choice from the drop-down list of choices in Net8 Assistant would be used to configure client-side tracing?

**A.** Client parameters

**B.** Client settings

**C.** General

**D.** Trace settings

**E.** None of the above

**18.** The Database Administrator wants to ensure that each trace file created on the client has a unique name. How would this be done?

**A.** `TRACE_NAMES_UNIQUE = ON`

**B.** `TRACE_UNIQUE = TRUE`

**C.** `TRACE_CLIENT_UNIQUE=ON`

**D.** `TRACE_UNIQUE_CLIENT=ON`

**19.** The Database Administrator enters sqlnet.trc in the trace file prompt for client tracing in the Net8 Assistant tool. What would be the name of the trace file generated by the client workstation?

**A.** `sqlnet.trc`

**B.** `sqlnet.trc.log`

**C.** `sqlnet.log`

**D.** `sqlnet.trc.trc`

**20.** A user gets the ORA-12154 "TNS: Could Not Resolve Service Name".error when attempting to login. Which of the following is the most likely cause of this kind of error?

**A.** The user input an invalid user ID.

**B.** The user input an invalid password.

**C.** The listener is down.

**D.** The user entered an invalid service name.

**E.** All of the above are correct.

# Answers to Review Questions

1. C. The `sqlnet.ora` is an optional file that can reside on the client or server. If logging or tracing are enabled on the client, then log files such as `sqlnet.log` and/or trace files such as `client.trc` may be found. The only file that would not be found would be the `listener.log`.

2. D. The `listener.log` would not be found on the client. `Cmctl` is the Connection Manager utility. Pinging would be something that may help, but it only works if an IP address or a DNS name is supplied. The service name cannot be pinged. `tnsping` is the best choice, for it tests to see if the client can see this network service. It also gives indications that the listener is running and how quickly the name is getting resolved.

3. C. This is a continuation of question #2. The `tnsping` utility will create the response listed. An optional parameter can be added to `tnsping` that specifies the number of attempts to make to the network service.

4. C. Logging information on the client is kept in the `sqlnet.ora` file. The Listeners icon is chosen to update server-side information about the listener, and the Net Service Names choice is selected to update information in the `tnsnames.ora` file. The `sqlnet.ora` file is where client-side logging information is kept.

5. C. The `log_file_client` choice would be set in order to enable logging of connections from a client. All of the other choices are invalid parameters.

6. D. All client-side logging and tracing parameters are kept in the `sqlnet.ora` file. `tnsnames.ora` will only store net service names resolution information. The other choices are invalid parameters.

7. D. Choices A, B, and C refer to non-existent parameters. `LOG_DIRECTORY_CLIENT` is the correct choice to set up a non-default logging directory on the client.

**8.** C. In order to enable tracing on the client, a parameter must be set up in the `sqlnet.ora` file. The parameter `TRACE_LEVEL_CLIENT` has four possible settings: OFF, USER, ADMIN, and SUPPORT. This parameter can be set manually or by using the Net8 Configuration Assistant tool. Once set up, tracing of user connections will take place on the user's workstation.

**9.** B. As stated above, the trace parameter needs to be configured in the `sqlnet.ora` file on the client workstation in order to enable tracing.

**10.** C. Client-side tracing can be enabled without having to stop the database or the listener. By default, tracing is not enabled. This is due to the fact that tracing can generate a significant amount of information and create large files.

**11.** B. There are various levels of tracing, each producing progressively more detail about network connections. The highest level of tracing will actually capture information about packet-level traffic sent and received from the client workstation. To enable this capability, set `TRACE_LEVEL_CLIENT=SUPPORT`. This is the highest level of tracing available.

**12.** D. To enable tracing on the client, the trace parameters must be set in the `sqlnet.ora` file. This file contains optional configuration information for clients and servers.

**13.** B. The Net8 stack contains a set of layers that have different network communications responsibilities. The Net8 layers that have a set of sublayers associated with them are the Transparent Network Substrate (TNS) and the Oracle Protocol Adapters (OPA). This eliminates answers A, D, and E. TNS contains the NI, NR, NN, NS, and NA sublayers, and OPA contains the NS and NT sublayers. The trace file uses these two-letter codes as part of its trace output. This output describes the TNS layer because of the NI two-letter code as the leading portion of the name.

**14.** E. The output produced from question #13 would be produced using the `trcasst` command line tool. This tool reads a trace file and produces formatted output.

**15.** D. The `trcasst` with the –S option will give summary information about the packets that were sent and received from a client to the Oracle Server.

**16.** D. The highest level of tracing available is the SUPPORT level. This is the level that would be used to trace packet traffic information.

**17.** C. Client-side tracing can be configured using the Net8 Configuration Assistant. The trace parameters are stored in the `sqlnet.ora` file on the client. The icon used to modify the `sqlnet.ora` file is Profile, which contains a drop-down list box of areas to choose from to configure the `sqlnet.ora` file. The General drop-down choice allows for client-side tracing information to be input.

**18.** D. Trace files can be generated with a common name and overwritten every time or with a unique name to preserve the contents. To preserve each trace file as a unique file, set `TRACE_UNIQUE_CLIENT=ON` in the `sqlnet.ora` file.

**19.** D. This is a little tricky. When entering the name of the trace file, a `.trc` extension is implied on the filename. If the user enters sqlnet.trc, the resulting filename will be `sqlnet.trc.trc`. The `.trc` gets appended to the name entered. Be careful when setting this to ensure that the expected filename is produced.

**20.** D. This can be caused by a number of circumstances. When the client tries to look up a service name and it cannot be found, this is the error that will be produced. Answers A and B are incorrect because in order to have an invalid user ID or password, contact must have been made to the server. If the listener is down, the user would get a different error message. The most likely cause is an invalid network service name being entered by the user. -

# Appendix A

# Oracle8i Performance Tuning Practice Exam

1. In what order would the Oracle Tuning Methodology suggest you perform the following tuning steps?

   A. Tune the application, tune I/O, tune memory allocation, tune contention

   B. Tune memory allocation, tune I/O, tune the application, tune contention

   C. Tune the application, tune contention, tune memory allocation, tune I/O

   D. Tune the application, tune memory allocation, tune I/O, tune contention

2. Which of the following is the best example of a throughput benchmark?

   A. The time it takes for an end-of-month report to return values

   B. The time it takes for the instance to startup

   C. The number of customer reservations that can be input into a reservation system in one minute

   D. Any of the above are good examples of throughput.

3. Which of the following components of the Oracle architecture is not part of the System Global Area?

   A. Shared Pool

   B. Redo log

   C. Database Buffer Cache

   D. Redo Log Buffer

4. Setting specific tuning goals helps in the database tuning process because:

   A. It allows you to understand how your changes are affecting the system.

   B. It allows you to focus your tuning on specific aspects of the system.

   C. It gives you a tentative endpoint when the tuning effort can end.

   D. All of the above are true.

5. Which data dictionary view will show you information on an index-organized table and its associated overflow segment?

   **A.** DBA_TABLES

   **B.** DBA_INDEXES

   **C.** DBA_SEGMENTS

   **D.** DBA_IOT_TABLES

6. The Alert log file contains information about which of the following database events?

   **A.** Instance startup and shutdown

   **B.** Segments that could not acquire additional space in a tablespace

   **C.** Redo log switches

   **D.** Any of the above information might be found in an alert log.

7. Background processes generate trace files. Which trace file would you look at if you were having I/O problems writing to datafiles on a UNIX system?

   **A.** pmon_3456.trc

   **B.** smon_3456.trc

   **C.** dbw0_3456.trc

   **D.** lgwr_3456.trc

8. Which two data dictionary views would you use to match a connected user to their trace file?

   **A.** V$SESSION and V$TRACE

   **B.** V$SESSION and V$PROCESS

   **C.** V$SESSION and DBA_USERS

   **D.** V$SESSION and V$SESSTAT

9. DBA users can activate tracing in another user's session using which procedure in the DBMS_SYSTEM PL/SQL package?

   A. SET_TRACE

   B. SET_SQL_TRACE_ON

   C. SET_SQL_TRACE_IN_SESSION

   D. SET_SQL_TRACE_ON_IN_SESSION

10. The init.ora parameter that can be used to limit the maximum size of a user trace file is called:

    A. USER_MAX_DUMP

    B. MAX_USER_DUMP_SIZE

    C. MAX_DUMP_FILE_SIZE

    D. MAX_DUMP_USER_FILE

11. Which TKPROF parameter will eliminate the recursive SQL from the formatted trace file?

    A. RECURSE=NO

    B. SYS=NO

    C. SYSTEM=NO

    D. SYS=FALSE

12. By default, which of the following tables stores explain plan information following an EXPLAIN PLAN FOR command?

    A. EXPLAIN_TABLE

    B. EXPLAINED

    C. PLAN_TABLE

    D. PLANNING_TABLE

13. When reading the output from an explained SQL statement, the first table that was accessed will be:

    **A.** The table at the top of the plan

    **B.** The table at the bottom of the plan

    **C.** The table with the most indenting

    **D.** The table with the longest name

14. Which method of gathering database statistics would sample 30 percent of the rows in the EMPLOYEE table?

    **A.** ANALYZE TABLE employee ESTIMATE STATISTICS

    **B.** ANALYZE TABLE employee ESTIMATE STATISTICS SAMPLE 30 PERCENT

    **C.** ANALYZE TABLE employee ESTIMATE STATISTICS SAMPLE 30 ROWS

    **D.** ANALYZE TABLE employee COMPUTE STATISTICS SAMPLE 30

15. Which of the following Oracle-supplied PL/SQL packages can back up the old statistics before new statistics are gathered?

    **A.** DBMS_STATS

    **B.** DBMS_UTILITY

    **C.** DBMS_SYSTEM

    **D.** None of the above

16. Which dynamic performance view is used to monitor the usage of the Shared Pool reserved area?

    **A.** V$LIBRARYCACHE

    **B.** V$SHARED_POOL_RESERVED_SIZE

    **C.** V$SHARED_POOL_RESERVED

    **D.** Any of the above can be used.

17. Step 7 in the Oracle Tuning Methodology: Tuning Memory Allocation deals with tuning which of the following SGA structures?

    **A.** The Shared Pool

    **B.** The Database Buffer Cache

    **C.** The Redo Log Buffer

    **D.** All of the above are included in Step 7.

18. For two issued SQL statements to be considered a Library Cache miss, they must:

    **A.** Match each other exactly

    **B.** Make use of bind variables

    **C.** Differ in some way

    **D.** None of the above

19. The parsed version of a cached statement that is stored in the Shared Pool is called:

    **A.** Execution Plan

    **B.** P-Code

    **C.** Data Dictionary Statistics

    **D.** SQL Text

20. In order to determine the hit ratio for the Data Dictionary Cache using REPORT.TXT you must:

    **A.** Sum the GET_REQS and GET_MISS columns.

    **B.** Divide the sum of the GET_MISS by the sum of the GET_REQS and subtract it from 1.

    **C.** Both A and B are correct.

    **D.** Neither A or B is correct.

**21.** The Database Buffer Cache hit ratio is calculated using which of the following statistics?

**A.** db block gets

**B.** physical reads

**C.** consistent gets

**D.** All of the above

**22.** Which of the following dynamic performance views contain information useful for determining which tables might benefit from being altered to CACHE tables?

**A.** V$BH

**B.** V$CACHE

**C.** Both of the above

**D.** Neither of the above

**23.** Which of the following Oracle background processes writes the buffers from the Database Buffer Cache to disk?

**A.** LGWR

**B.** PMON

**C.** User Server Process

**D.** DBW0

**24.** Using the following output from a REPORT.TXT file:

```
SQL> set numwidth 12;
SQL> Rem The total is the total value of the statistic between the time
SQL> Rem bstat was run and the time estat was run.  Note that the estat
SQL> Rem script logs on as "internal" so the per_logon statistics will
SQL> Rem always be based on at least one logon.
SQL> select n1.name "Statistic",
  2         n1.change "Total",
  3         round(n1.change/trans.change,2)  "Per Transaction",
  4         round(n1.change/logs.change,2)   "Per Logon",
  5         round(n1.change/(to_number(to_char(end_time,    'J'))*60*60*24 -
  6                     to_number(to_char(start_time, 'J'))*60*60*24 +
  7                     to_number(to_char(end_time,    'SSSSS')) -
  8                     to_number(to_char(start_time, 'SSSSS')))
  9              , 2) "Per Second"
 10    from stats$stats n1, stats$stats trans, stats$stats logs, stats$dates
 11    where trans.name='user commits'
 12     and  logs.name='logons cumulative'
 13     and  n1.change != 0
 14    order by n1.name;
```

| Statistic | Total | Per Transaction | Per Logon | Per Second |
|-----------|-------|-----------------|-----------|------------|
| consistent gets | 3509007 | 13563.39 | 156826.69 | 929.69 |
| db block changes | 526837 | 2847.77 | 32927.31 | 195.2 |
| db block gets | 890921 | 3192.01 | 36907.56 | 218.79 |
| physical reads | 1244343 | 8349.42 | 96540.19 | 572.3 |
| physical writes | 45001 | 243.25 | 2812.56 | 16.67 |

What is the approximate Database Buffer Cache hit ratio?

**A.** 72 percent

**B.** 28 percent

**C.** 1 percent

**D.** 99 percent

**25.** High or increasing values for the statistics free buffer inspected and free buffer waits might indicate that which SGA structure is too small?

**A.** Shared Pool

**B.** Database Buffer Cache

**C.** Both of the above

**D.** Neither of the above

**26.** The Redo Log Buffer retry ratio is calculated using which two statistics from V$SYSSTAT? (Choose two.)

**A.** `redo buffer entries`

**B.** `redo entries`

**C.** `redo buffer allocation retries`

**D.** `redo buffer allocation errors`

**27.** When examining the output from a REPORT.TXT file, what should the difference between the values for `log checkpoint started` and `log checkpoint completed` be?

**A.** 50 or more

**B.** 20 or less

**C.** 1 or 0

**D.** More than 100

**28.** A value of `WAITED FOR SHORT TIME` in the V$SESSION_WAIT dynamic performance view means that the session:

**A.** Is waiting at the very moment

**B.** Waited an undetermined period of time

**C.** Waited for 2 minutes

**D.** Waited for less than 1/100th of a second

**29.** The value for TIME_WAITED in V$SYSTEM_EVENT is expressed in:

**A.** Minutes

**B.** Seconds

**C.** 10th of a second

**D.** 100th of a second

30. Seeing the message `Checkpoint not complete` in the Alert log might indicate that:

    A. The Redo Log Buffer is too small

    B. The Database Buffer Cache is too small

    C. The redo log files are too small

    D. The archive destination is full

31. Suppose that you use the `V$FILESTAT` dynamic performance view to monitor datafile I/O. If you notice that a majority of the read and write activity is against the datafiles that make up the SYSTEM tablespace, what might you conclude?

    A. The Database Buffer Cache is too small.

    B. The Shared Pool is too small.

    C. There may be non-data dictionary segments stored in the SYSTEM tablespace.

    D. The redo logs are switching too quickly for ARC0 to keep up.

32. Increasing the value of the `init.ora` parameter `DB_FILE_MULTIBLOCK_READ_COUNT` helps the performance of:

    A. LGWR

    B. Full table scans

    C. B-Tree indexes

    D. WHERE clauses

33. High or steadily increasing values for the statistics `buffer busy wait`, `db file parallel write`, or `write complete waits` in `V$SYSTEM_EVENT` may all indicate that:

    A. ARC0 is not writing quickly enough.

    B. LGWR is not writing quickly enough.

    C. User Server Processes are not finding the data blocks they need in memory.

    D. DBW0 is not writing quickly enough.

**34.** Larger block sizes are preferred to smaller block sizes in DSS systems for all the following reasons *except*:

**A.** They are less likely to lead to block contention.

**B.** They store more rows in less blocks.

**C.** They require fewer I/O to retrieve table data.

**D.** They favor the sequential I/O found on most DSS systems.

**35.** Increasing the size of the redo log members improves the performance of the ARC0 background process because:

**A.** The redo logs are less likely to become corrupt.

**B.** The redo logs will switch less frequently, allowing ARC0 more time to archive each redo log.

**C.** The redo logs can then be placed on several devices.

**D.** The redo logs will not fill up the archive destination as fast.

**36.** Which of the following steps in the Oracle Tuning Methodology occur before Tuning Contention? (Choose all that apply.)

**A.** Tuning Memory Allocations

**B.** Tune I/O and Physical Structure

**C.** Tune the Underlying Platform

**D.** Tune the Access Paths

**37.** Which of the following columns in V$LATCH can be used to determine if a miss occurred when a Willing-to-Wait latch was accessed?

**A.** MISSES

**B.** WILLING_TO_WAIT_MISSES

**C.** WTW_MISSES

**D.** IMMEDIATE_MISSES

**38.** Free List contention might occur whenever:

   **A.** Several users are performing updates on the same table

   **B.** Many users are performing deletes on the same table

   **C.** Many users are performing inserts on the same table

   **D.** Many users are performing DDL on the same table

**39.** Which of the following lock modes is the most restrictive?

   **A.** Share Table (S)

   **B.** Share Row Exclusive (SRX)

   **C.** Exclusive Table (X)

   **D.** Table Row Share (RS)

**40.** When lock contention is occurring, which of the following views is used to find a user's SID and SERIAL# so that their session can be killed?

   **A.** V$SYSTEM

   **B.** V$SESSION

   **C.** V$LOCK

   **D.** V$LOCKED_OBJECT

**41.** Which of the following portions of Resource Manager is used to group together users with similar resource requirements?

   **A.** Resource consumer role

   **B.** Resource consumer profile

   **C.** Resource consumer group

   **D.** Resource consumer privilege

**42.** Which of the following PL/SQL procedures in the DBMS_RESOURCE_ MANAGER package is used to create a new resource group?

**A.** CREATE_RESOURCE_GROUP

**B.** CREATE_GROUP

**C.** CREATE_RESOURCE

**D.** CREATE_GROUP_RESOURCE

**43.** Every resource plan directive must include which resource consumer group in order to avoid validation errors?

**A.** OTHER

**B.** OTHER_GROUPS

**C.** DEFAULT_GROUPS

**D.** SYS_GROUP

**44.** Which of the following resources are affected by Resource Manager settings? (Choose two.)

**A.** Disk I/O

**B.** CPU

**C.** Memory usage

**D.** Parallel query execution

**45.** Which of the following init.ora parameters is used to set the resource plan at the instance level?

**A.** RESOURCE_MANAGER_PLAN

**B.** RESOURCE_PLAN_DEFAULT

**C.** RESOURCE_PLAN

**D.** DEFAULT_RESOURCE_PLAN

46. Which of the following is the first area configured by the DBA when performing a tuning session with Oracle Expert?

    **A.** Collect tuning statistics

    **B.** Review tuning recommendations

    **C.** Specify tuning scope

    **D.** Implement Oracle Expert recommendations

47. Selecting the SQL Reuse option on the Scope tab of Oracle Expert will cause Oracle Expert to monitor the instance for:

    **A.** How well space is utilized in the database

    **B.** How well the application reuses existing cached statements

    **C.** Whether the instance uses indexes appropriately

    **D.** How many times a single user issues the same SQL statement

48. Which optimizer mode does Oracle Expert use when accessing the instance for optimal data access?

    **A.** Rule-based optimizer

    **B.** Cost-based optimizer

    **C.** Index-based optimizer

    **D.** All-rows optimizer

49. In Oracle Expert, the term Peak Logical Write Rate refers to:

    **A.** The amount of logical I/O performed during busy database periods

    **B.** The amount of physical I/O performed during busy database periods

    **C.** The amount of logical I/O performed during slow database periods

    **D.** The amount of logical I/O performed to access index data

50. Which of the following types of schema analysis cause Oracle Expert to gather cardinality data?

    **A.** Expert Scan

    **B.** Run ANALYZE command

    **C.** Read existing ANALYZE records

    **D.** Use Cost-based optimizer

# Answers to Practice Exam

1. D. Application tuning has the biggest performance impact. Oracle Server tuning of the instance's memory, I/O, and resource contention are secondary. See Chapter 1 for more information.

2. C. Throughput refers to the amount of work that a system can do in a specified period of time. See Chapter 1 for more information.

3. B. Redo logs are part of the Oracle database, not the instance. See Chapter 1 for more information.

4. D. Establishing specific tuning goals helps you know why you're tuning and what areas to start with. Goals also help you know when you've reached the end of a given tuning iteration. See Chapter 1 for more information.

5. A. Overflow segment information is shown in both DBA_SEGMENTS and DBA_TABLES. However, only DBA_TABLES shows the index-organized table name and the matching overflow segment. See Chapter 2 for more information.

6. D. The alert log contains numerous kinds of messages including database creation, instance startup and shutdown, redo log switches, creation and modification of tablespaces, and block corruption errors. See Chapter 2 for more information.

7. C. Since Database Writer (DBW0) is the process that writes to datafiles, its trace file may contain useful information about any possible I/O errors. See Chapter 2 for more information.

8. B. The V$PROCESS and V$SESSION data dictionary views can be joined on their PADDR and ADDR columns, respectively. Once joined, the SPID column of the V$PROCESS table will contain the same number found in the corresponding user's trace file. See Chapter 2 for more information.

9. C. The DBMS_SYSTEM.SET_SQL_TRACE_IN_SESSION procedure can be used to activate tracing in the session of another user. See Chapter 2 for more information.

10. C. The `MAX_DUMP_FILE_SIZE` parameter limits the maximum size that a user's trace file can grow to. The maximum size can be specified in terms of the number of OS blocks or bytes that can be written to the user dump destination. See Chapter 2 for more information.

11. B. The `SYS=NO` option of the `TKPROF` utility omits the recursive SQL that was issued in support of the statement from the formatted file. See Chapter 3 for more information.

12. C. The `PLAN_TABLE` table stores the results of an explained SQL statement. Querying this table will display the execution plan of the statement. See Chapter 3 for more information.

13. C. Explain plan output is read from the innermost operation out. If two tables are accessed at the same level, the top table is accessed first. See Chapter 3 for more information.

14. B. The `ANALYZE` command used with the `SAMPLE … PERCENT` clause will generate statistics for a sample size equal to the percentage specified. If the specified percentage is greater than 50 percent, then all the rows are sampled. See Chapter 3 for more information.

15. A. The `DBMS_STATS` package can back up old statistics before new statistics are gathered using the `EXPORT_TABLE_STATS` procedure. See Chapter 3 for more information.

16. C. You can determine if your Shared Pool reserved area is properly sized by using the `REQUEST_MISSES` and `REQUEST_FAILURES` columns in `V$SHARED_POOL_RESERVED`. See Chapter 4 for more information.

17. D. Tuning all the SGA's memory structures, including the UGA and Large Pool, are included in the category Tuning Memory Allocation. See Chapter 4 for more information.

18. C. Cache misses occur when two SQL or PL/SQL statements do not hash to the same value. This causes the statement to be parsed even if an essentially identical statement is already in the Library Cache. If the two statements differ in any way, they will not hash to the same value and will cause a cache miss. See Chapter 4 for more information.

**19.** B. The Oracle Server caches P-Code (Parsed Code) for each SQL or PL/SQL statement that is cached in memory. See Chapter 4 for more information.

**20.** C. You must sum the GET_REQS and GET_MISS columns found in the Data Dictionary Cache section of REPORT.TXT. Using these totals, you can then use the following formula to calculate the hit ratio: (1- sum(GET_REQS)/sum(GETS)). See Chapter 4 for more information.

**21.** D. The Database Buffer Cache hit ratio is the ratio of physical reads to the total numbers of buffers read (db block gets and consistent gets). See Chapter 5 for more information.

**22.** C. The Oracle Parallel Server views V$BH and V$CACHE are also useful for determining which tables to cache because they show which segments the buffers in memory belong to. See Chapter 5 for more information.

**23.** D. The Database Writer (DBW0) background processes writes the buffers from the Database Buffer Cache to the datafiles on disk. See Chapter 5 for more information.

**24.** A. The Database Buffer Cache hit ratio is calculated by dividing the physical reads by the total buffer reads (db block gets and consistent gets) and subtracting the result from 1. See Chapter 5 for more information.

**25.** B. High or steadily increasing values for these statistics indicate that user Server Processes are spending too much time locating and accessing free buffers in the Database Buffer Cache. Increasing the size of the Database Buffer Cache minimizes this problem by making more buffers available. See Chapter 5 for more information.

**26.** B, C. The ratio of redo buffer allocation retries to redo entries tells you how often user Server Processes that want to place entries in the Redo Log Buffer are experiencing a wait for access to that resource. See Chapter 6 for more information.

27. C. Since we would like every checkpoint that starts to also complete successfully, the difference between these two values should ideally be 0. The value of 1 is acceptable, too, since this probably indicates that a checkpoint started, but did not complete during the time the REPORT.TXT file was being generated. See Chapter 6 for more information.

28. D. Waits for resources that are less than $1/100^{th}$ of a second are only recorded as WAITED FOR SHORT TIME in V$SESSION_WAIT. Any other measurable waits longer than $1/100^{th}$ of a second are indicated by the statistic WAITED KNOWN TIME. See Chapter 6 for more information.

29. D. As with most timings that are displayed in the V$ dynamic performance views, the timings in V$SYSTEM_EVENT are expressed in $100^{th}$ of a second. See Chapter 6 for more information.

30. C. One of the events that cause a checkpoint to occur is a Redo log switch. If these logs are too small and switching too quickly as they fill with redo information from the Redo Log Buffer, the frequent switching may cause two checkpoints to occur close together causing this error. Making the redo logs bigger will minimize this problem. See Chapter 6 for more information.

31. C. If application tables and indexes are stored in the SYSTEM tablespace the I/O activity on its datafiles will be higher than it would be if these segments where properly placed in their own tablespaces. See Chapter 7 for more information.

32. B. Increasing the value for DB_FILE_MULTIBLOCK_READ_COUNT improves the performance of full table scans by reducing the total number of I/O required to read all of the table's blocks. See Chapter 7 for more information.

33. D. All of these statistics indicate that Database Writer may not be writing database buffers from the Database Buffer Cache to the datafiles fast enough to satisfy user requests. See Chapter 7 for more information.

34. A. Larger block sizes actually increase the likelihood that block contention will occur since many more rows are stored per block than are stored with smaller block sizes. See Chapter 7 for more information.

**35.** B. The larger the redo log members are, the longer it will take LGWR to fill the logs with entries from the Redo Log Buffer. This reduces the frequency of redo log switches and lessens the likelihood that ARC0 will still be archiving a redo log when it is time for LGWR to write to it again. See Chapter 7 for more information.

**36.** A, B, D. Nearly every area of database tuning is addressed prior to examining latch and Free List contention as well as locking issues. See Chapter 8 for more information.

**37.** A. The MISSES column in V$LATCH reports the number of Willing-to-Wait latch misses that have occurred since instance startup. The IMMEDIATE_MISSES column indicates how many Immediate latch misses have occurred. See Chapter 8 for more information.

**38.** C. When many users are attempting to find and use free blocks to hold newly inserted data into a table, Free List contention can occur. See Chapter 8 for more information.

**39.** C. Exclusive table locks prevent all DML against the locked table until the lock is released. See Chapter 8 for more information.

**40.** B. The V$SESSION view contains the SID and SERIAL# values needed to issue the ALTER SYSTEM KILL SESSION command. See Chapter 8 for more information.

**41.** C. Using resource plans and directives, resource consumer groups are used to assign resources to users who have similar resource requirements. See Chapter 9 for more information.

**42.** A. The CREATE_RESOURCE_GROUP procedure creates a new resource consumer group based on the CONSUMER_GROUP and COMMENT parameters that are passed into the procedure. See Chapter 9 for more information.

**43.** B. OTHER_GROUPS must be defined for each resource directive so that users who are not part of that resource group have default access to resources when that plan is active at the instance level. See Chapter 9 for more information.

44. B, D. Currently only CPU and degree of parallelism for parallel query can be controlled using Resource Manager. See Chapter 9 for more information.

45. A. In addition to the `init.ora` parameter RESOURCE_MANAGER_PLAN, the instance resource plan can also be set dynamically using the ALTER SYSTEM SET RESOURCE_MANAGER_PLAN command. See Chapter 9 for more information.

46. C. Before beginning an Oracle Expert tuning session, the scope of the tuning session must be defined in terms of instance optimizations, SQL reuse, space management, and optimal data access. See Chapter 10 for more information.

47. B. This option monitors the effectiveness of the Shared Pool by measuring how often application users are reusing cached statements. See Chapter 10 for more information.

48. B. Oracle Expert uses the Cost-based optimizer when determining whether the instance uses indexes effectively to achieve optimal access paths. See Chapter 10 for more information.

49. A. Oracle Expert defines Peak Logical Write Rate activity as "low" if it is less than 5 DML transactions per second, "medium" if it is between 5 and 50 DML transactions per second, "large" if it is between 50 and 500 transactions per second, and "huge" when it is greater than 500 transactions per second. See Chapter 10 for more information.

50. A. Checking the Expert Scan option on the Oracle Expert Collect tab will cause Oracle Expert to determine how many distinct values are in each indexed column. See Chapter 10 for more information.

# Appendix

# B

# Oracle8i Network Administration Practice Exam

1. Oracle8i Net8 provides all of the following *except*:

   **A.** Support for multiple operating systems

   **B.** Support for multiple protocols

   **C.** An open Applications Program Interface

   **D.** A robust configuration tool

   **E.** All of the above

2. Two options that enhance the flexibility of Oracle8i Net8 are:

   **A.** Advanced Network option

   **B.** Advanced Security option

   **C.** Connection Manager

   **D.** Bequeath option

3. The Oracle8i Net8 Assistant provides for configuration of all of these files except:

   **A.** `tnsnames.ora`

   **B.** `listener.ora`

   **C.** `cman.ora`

   **D.** `names.ora`

4. Oracle8i Net8 Logging can be configured: (Choose all that apply.)

   **A.** For the listener on the server

   **B.** On the client workstation

   **C.** For Connection Manager on a middle tier

   **D.** For the Multithreaded Server option

**5.** A terminal connected directly to a server via a serial connection is an example of:

    **A.** N-tier architecture

    **B.** Two-tier architecture

    **C.** Single-tier architecture

    **D.** None of the above

**6.** A client connects to an Oracle Server using the following command: `sqlplus system/manager@DBA`. Which of the following are true? (Choose all that apply.)

    **A.** The client must use a Names Server to connect to DBA.

    **B.** DBA is the network service name.

    **C.** If `names.directory_path=(TNSNAMES)` is set in the client `sqlnet.ora` file and no entry for DBA is found in the `tnsnames.ora` file, this command will fail.

    **D.** This connection will succeed using hostnaming if there is a hostname of DBA in the client `HOSTS` file, and if a listener is listening on port 1521 using the TCP/IP protocol with `GLOBAL_DBNAME=DBA` in the `listener.ora` file.

**7.** A listener can respond to a service request in which of the following ways? (Choose all that apply.)

    **A.** Spawn a bequeath session

    **B.** Redirect to a dispatcher

    **C.** Spawn a shared server process

    **D.** Return an error to the client if no service is found

    **E.** All of the above

8. A user issues a Ctrl-C, and the message is handled along with the other data traffic. This is an example of:

   A. Out-of-band breaks

   B. In-band breaks

   C. Priority requests

   D. Priority signals

9. The TNS layer of the Net8 stack is responsible for:

   A. Interrupt handling

   B. Datatype conversions

   C. Communicating directly with the underlying network protocols

   D. Validating SQL syntax

   E. None of the above

10. The OCI layer of the Net8 stack is responsible for:

    A. Interrupt handling

    B. Datatype conversions

    C. Communicating directly with the underlying protocols

    D. Validating SQL syntax

    E. None of the above

11. A connection to an Oracle service may be unsuccessful if:

    A. A valid network service name is entered by the client, but the listener is unavailable

    B. The listener is available, but the client entered an invalid network service name

    C. An invalid password was entered by the client

    D. All of the above

12. A client enters **sqlplus system/manager@DBA** and receives the ORA-12154 "TNS Could Not Resolve Service Name" error. Which of the following is a possible cause of this problem?

    **A.** The user entered an invalid user ID.

    **B.** The user entered an invalid password.

    **C.** Names.default_domain=WORLD is located in the client sqlnet.ora file.

    **D.** The listener is down.

    **E.** None of the above

13. A client wants to use the default search path for resolving service names. The default search path is:

    **A.** (TNSNAMES, ONAMES, HOSTNAME)

    **B.** (ONAMES, TNSNAMES, HOSTNAME)

    **C.** (HOSTNAME, TNSNAMES, ONAMES)

    **D.** There is no default search path for resolving service names.

14. A client wants to take advantage of Oracle8i Net8 failover capabilities. Which of the following parameters will accomplish this?

    **A.** LOAD_BALANCE=ON

    **B.** NET8_FAILOVER=ON

    **C.** FAILOVER=ON

    **D.** None of the above

15. In what file would the parameter FAILOVER be placed?

    **A.** sqlnet.ora

    **B.** tnsnames.ora

    **C.** sdns.ora

    **D.** listener.ora

    **E.** None of the above

**16.** Which of the following is *true* about the `listener.ora` file?

  **A.** The file contains information about listening locations.

  **B.** The file can contain information for more than one listener.

  **C.** Only one `listener.ora` file should be configured on the server.

  **D.** All of the above

**17.** Changes have been made and saved to the `listener.ora` file. What is the next command the DBA should issue that will make the changes available with minimal disruption?

  **A.** `lsnrctl services`

  **B.** `lsnrctl stop/lsnrctl start`

  **C.** `lsnrctl status`

  **D.** `lsnrctl reload`

**18.** The DBA issues the command `lsnrctl` stop. Which of the following are *true*? (Choose all that apply.)

  **A.** Clients can no longer access services using this listener.

  **B.** If another listener is configured on the server and is listening for this service, clients could access services if `FAILOVER=ON` is configured.

  **C.** Existing client connections are not disrupted.

  **D.** The `tnsping` command would fail for all services on this server if there were only one listener on the server.

**19.** To configure the listener using the Net8 Assistant, which icon is chosen?

  **A.** Services

  **B.** Listeners

  **C.** Networks

  **D.** Profile

**20.** Which parameter controls the destination of the listener trace file?

   **A.** `trace_location_listenername`

   **B.** `trace_directory_location_listenername`

   **C.** `trace_directory_listenername`

   **D.** The trace file can only be written to the Oracle default trace directory.

**21.** In what locations would well-known Name Servers be listed? (Choose two.)

   **A.** In an external naming environment, such as DNS

   **B.** In a HOSTS file

   **C.** In the `tnsnames.ora` file

   **D.** In the `sqlnet.ora` file on the server

**22.** The main advantage of a Names Server over other service resolution techniques is:

   **A.** Location transparency

   **B.** No client-side configuration necessary

   **C.** Centralized net service names

   **D.** Can use Net8 Assistant to configure the Names Server

**23.** Which of the following commands would enable a client to capture and retain information about services that have been recently accessed?

   **A.** `Namesctl enable_client_cache`

   **B.** `Namesctl start_client_cache`

   **C.** `Namesctl client_cache_start`

   **D.** `Namesctl start_cache`

**24.** When a client discovers Names Servers, what file is created on the client?

    **A.** names.ora

    **B.** servers.ora

    **C.** sdns.ora

    **D.** sqlnet.ora

    **E.** None of the above

**25.** Which command is used to start a Names Server?

    **A.** namesctl start

    **B.** namesctl startup

    **C.** namesctl status

    **D.** namesctl reload

**26.** Complete the sentence: Each dispatcher has its own...

    **A.** Response queue

    **B.** Shared server

    **C.** Request queue

    **D.** UGA

**27.** What optional area of the SGA can the DBA configure when running in Multithreaded Server mode?

    **A.** Shared Pool

    **B.** Large Pool

    **C.** Database Buffer Cache

    **D.** UGA

**28.** Complete the sentence: Shared servers...

   **A.** Can handle requests from many users

   **B.** Are responsible for placing information into request queues

   **C.** Cannot be allocated dynamically

   **D.** Belong to only one dispatcher

**29.** Complete this sentence: When connecting to a Multithreaded Server, clients...

   **A.** Receive a dedicated connection unless a multithreaded connection is requested

   **B.** Are not connected to the database if no dispatchers are available

   **C.** Can request a bequeath connection

   **D.** Can only be connected to dispatchers

**30.** The DBA is interested in gathering information about how long requests are waiting before being processed by shared servers. The V$ view that can assist the DBA is:

   **A.** v$dispatcher

   **B.** v$circuit

   **C.** v$queue

   **D.** v$shared_servers

**31.** For which of the following is the CMADMIN process responsible?

   **A.** Process user requests coming into connection manager

   **B.** Passing client requests on to the server

   **C.** Updating Oracle Names Servers

   **D.** Passing initial client connection requests on to servers

**32.** The three parts of the `cman.ora` file are:

**A.** CMAN_FILTER

**B.** CMAN

**C.** CMAN_PROFILE

**D.** CMAN_RULES

**33.** Connection concentration can only be used with:

**A.** Dispatched processes

**B.** Bequeath processes

**C.** Prespawned processes

**D.** All of the above

**34.** Which of the following best describes this line:

`(RULE = (SRC = GR0021) (DST =MAD01ORA)(SRV=DBA)(ACT=ACC))`

**A.** Connection Manager will accept requests for the MAD01ORA database.

**B.** Connection Manager will reject service requests coming from GR0021.

**C.** Connection Manager will accept all requests from GR0022 for service DBA.

**D.** Connection Manager will only allow GR0021 to access the DBA database on MAD01ORA.

**35.** What client-side parameter must be set to ensure proper connections to Connection Manager?

**A.** ORACLE_SID

**B.** SOURCE_ROUTE

**C.** TNS_ADMIN

**D.** NAMES.DIRECTORY_PATH

**36.** We want to allow a user access to all Oracle services in an enterprise with one login ID. This could be accomplished with:

**A.** Encryption

**B.** Checksumming

**C.** Authentication server running DCE

**D.** All of the above

**37.** The default value for SQLNET.ENCRYPTION_CLIENT is:

**A.** Rejected

**B.** Accepted

**C.** Requested

**D.** Required

**38.** "Turn on the Security service or do not allow the connection" describes which of the following settings for checksumming and encryption?

**A.** Rejected

**B.** Accepted

**C.** Requested

**D.** Required

**39.** Which sqlnet.ora parameter sets the value of the authentication method to use when using Security server?

**A.** sqlnet.authentication_adapters

**B.** sqlnet.authentication_devices

**C.** sqlnet.authentication_services

**D.** None of the above

**40.** DCE stands for:

  **A.** Distributed Computing Environment

  **B.** Dynamic Computing Enterprise

  **C.** Distributed Computing Enterprise

  **D.** Development Computer Environment

**41.** TNS_ADMIN is set to C:\ORA8I\NETWORK. What does this mean?

  **A.** A client will find the listener.ora file in this directory.

  **B.** A client will search this directory before any other directories to resolve a service name.

  **C.** The client will search the current working directory and then C:\ORA8I\NETWORK for service names.

  **D.** This is the last location the client will look to resolve a service name.

**42.** A client types in the following: **TNSPING DBA 4**. What does the 4 mean?

  **A.** Wait 4 seconds before returning a result.

  **B.** Make 4 attempts to contact the DBA database.

  **C.** Wait 40 seconds before timing out.

  **D.** Wait 4 seconds before timing out.

**43.** A client receives the ORA-03113 "End of Communication Channel" error. What is one possible cause of this problem?

  **A.** The Connection Manager background processes died.

  **B.** The client did not supply a valid password.

  **C.** The DBA has stopped the listener.

  **D.** The Names Server is down.

  **E.** All of the above

**44.** The `trcasst` utility can be used to:

**A.** Run diagnostics on network connections

**B.** Check the availability of a network service

**C.** Format trace files

**D.** Ping a listener

**45.** By default, the location of the `listener.log` file is:

**A.** `ORACLE_HOME\rdbms\log`

**B.** `ORACLE_HOME\network\admin`

**C.** `ORACLE_HOME\network\trace`

**D.** `ORACLE_HOME\network\log`

**46.** A DBA wants to ensure that all client connections that abnormally terminate are cleaned up. What can be set to accommodate this request?

**A.** `SQLNET.EXPIRE_TIME`

**B.** `CONNECT_TIMEOUT`

**C.** `SQLNET.ABORT_TIMEOUT`

**D.** `CONNECTION_ABORT`

**47.** Connection Manager would be used in:

**A.** Single-tier architecture

**B.** Client-server architecture

**C.** Multithreaded architecture

**D.** N-tier architecture

**48.** Which option is utilized in a way similar to making an operator-assisted phone call?

**A.** Oracle Connection Manager

**B.** Oracle Transparent Gateway

**C.** Oracle Name Server

**D.** Oracle Multithreaded Server

**E.** None of the above

**49.** Which of these are restrictions of the hostnaming option? (Choose all that apply.)

**A.** Cannot use a bequeath connection

**B.** Cannot be used with Multithreaded Server

**C.** Cannot be used with Connection Manager

**D.** Does not support IPX

**50.** A collection of related Oracle services is called a:

**A.** Region

**B.** Collection

**C.** Domain

**D.** Schema

# Answers to Practice Exam

1. E. Oracle8i Net8 provides all of the functions described above. See Chapter 11 for more information.

2. B, C. The Advanced Security option and Connection Manager are two of the options provided to enhance the flexibility of Net8. See Chapter 11 for more information.

3. C. The Net8 Assistant provides for configuration of many of the Net8 files. However, `cman.ora` is not one of these files. This is the configuration file for Connection Manager. See Chapter 17 for more information.

4. A, B, C. Logging is provided for all of these areas except for the Multithreaded Server. See Chapter 19 for more information.

5. C. Single-tier architecture is characterized by the use of dumb terminals connecting to a centralized server. This is a popular configuration with mainframe architecture. See Chapter 11 for more information.

6. B, C, D. In this example, all are true except that a Names Server must be used. See Chapter 12 for more information.

7. A, B, D. The listener may do any of the above except spawn a shared server process. Listeners do not spawn these processes. These are part of the Multithreaded Server option. See Chapter 16 for more information.

8. B. In-band breaks are break requests handled along with the other data of a network transmission. See Chapter 12 for more information.

9. A. One of the responsibilities of the Transparent Network Substrate, or TNS, is that it handles interrupts. See Chapter 12 for more information.

10. D. The Oracle Call Interface, or OCI, is responsible for validating the SQL syntax issued by a client. See Chapter 12 for more information.

11. D. Any of these may cause an unsuccessful connection. See Chapter 12 for more information.

**12.** C. If an invalid user ID or password is entered, this is not the error message that you would see. If you are using a flat naming model and the `names.default_domain` value is appended to the end of the net service name, the net service name will not be found. In this example, DBA becomes DBA.WORLD and could cause this error to occur. See Chapter 12 for more information.

**13.** A. The default search hierarchy is to check `tnsnames`, then for a Names Server, and then for a hostname resolution to a net service name. See Chapter 12 for more information.

**14.** C. The `FAILOVER` parmeter is used when a client wants to be able to failover to another listener when the first listener attempted is not available. This parameter is specified in the `tnsnames.ora` file and can also be used with the Oracle Names Server. See Chapter 14 for more information.

**15.** B. This parameter is specified in the `tnsnames.ora` file if the client is using the localnaming option. See Chapter 14 for more information.

**16.** D. All of these statements are true about the `listener.ora` file. See Chapter 13 for more information.

**17.** D. The `lsnrctl` utility is used to administer the listener. You can update an active listener with the `lsnrctl` reload option. See Chapter 13 for more information.

**18.** A, B, C, D. All of these are true when the listener is stopped. See Chapters 13 and 19 for more information.

**19.** B. The Listeners icon is used to configure the listener. See Chapter 13 for more information.

**20.** C. The `trace_directory_listenername` parameter is used to specify the location of listener trace files. See Chapter 19 for more information.

**21.** A, B. Well-known Names Servers are those that are defined with hard code names that are common to the Net8 environment. You would find well-known Names Servers defined in an external naming environment or in a `HOSTS` file. See Chapter 12 for more information.

**22.** C. A Names Server allows you to have a centralized way of managing the net service names in an your organization. See Chapter 15 for more information.

**23.** B. A client may cache information about recently accessed Oracle services if the client cache is active. This prevents extra trips to a Names Server to resolve a recently accessed net service name. See Chapter 15 for more information.

**24.** C. The `sdns.ora` file contains information about discovered Names Servers. See Chapter 15 for more information.

**25.** A. The `namesctl start` command is used to start a Name Server. You can also start a Name Server from the Net8 Assistant. See Chapter 15 for more information.

**26.** A. Each dispatcher process has its own response queue. See Chapter 16 for more information.

**27.** B. The Large Pool is used to take the place of Program Global Areas (PGA) that are used in a dedicated server environment. See Chapter 16 for more information.

**28.** A. Shared servers can handle requests from many users. All of the rest of the statements are false. See Chapter 16 for more information.

**29.** C. Clients can explicitly request a bequeath connection in a Multithreaded Server environment. Another name for a bequeath connection is a dedicated connection. See Chapter 16 for more information.

**30.** C. The `v$queue` view will supply this information to the DBA. See Chapter 16 for more information.

**31.** C. One of the responsibilities of the Connection Manager Administrator process or CMADMIN is to update Oracle Name Servers. See Chapter 17 for more information.

**32.** B, C, D. The `cman.ora` file contains information about the Connection Manager listening location in the CMAN section, optional configuration parameters in the CMAN_PROFILE section, and client access control information in the CMAN_RULES section. See Chapter 17 for more information.

**33.** A. Connection concentration can only be used with dispatched processes in a Multithreaded Server environment. See Chapter 17 for more information.

**34.** D. The best description of this is that client GR0021 will be allowed to access the DBA database on MAD01ORA. This is an example of client access control. See Chapter 17 for more information.

**35.** B. The SOURCE_ROUTE parameter specifies that the addresses listed under a net service name must be used in the order specified. This ensures the client will first connect to Connection Manager, and then Connection Manager will connect the client to the requested net service location. See Chapter 17 for more information.

**36.** C. An authentication server running DCE would meet this requirement. See Chapter 18 for more information.

**37.** B. If no values are specified on the client for encryption, then the value defaults to ACCEPTED. See Chapter 18 for more information.

**38.** D. When using encryption or checksumming, this is the behavior of the REJECTED setting. See Chapter 18 for more information.

**39.** C. The sqlnet.authentication_services parameter specifies the authentication method to use. See Chapter 18 for more information.

**40.** A. DCE stand for Distributed Computing Environment and provides for features such as authentication and single sign-on. See Chapter 18 for more information.

**41.** C. This parameter specifies the location of the Net8 network files the client will search after searching the current working directory. See Chapter 12 for more information.

**42.** B. The client will make four attempts to contact the net service name supplied. See Chapter 19 for more information.

**43.** A. The only one of these problems that would cause an interruption in service and cause this error would be the Connection Manager process dying. See Chapter 17 for more information.

**44.** C. This utility is used to format the network trace files into a more readable format. See Chapter 19 for more information.

**45.** D. The default location is ORACLE_HOME\network\log on NT or $ORACLE_HOME/network/log on UNIX. See Chapter 19 for more information.

**46.** A. The SQLNET.EXPIRE_TIME parameter sets the number of minutes that a server will wait between receiving valid client contact. If the server has not heard from the client in that time period, a packet is sent from the server to the client. If no response or an invalid response is received, the server process will be terminated. See Chapter 12 for more information.

**47.** D. The Connection manager would be used in N-tier architecture. See Chapter 11 for more information.

**48.** C. The Oracle Name Server is used in a way similar to making an operator-assisted phone call. See Chapters 12 and 15 for more information.

**49.** C, D. The hostnaming option cannot be used with Connection Manager and can only be used in a TCP/IP environment. See Chapter 14 for more information.

**50.** C. A Domain is a collection of related Oracle services. See Chapter 14 for more information.

# Glossary

# A

**Absolute Method**   A method of assigning resources to consumer groups by designating a specific value allowed for each resource. Parallel query degree-of-parallelism resources are assigned in this manner.

**Advanced Rules**   Detailed rules that Oracle Expert uses when performing a performance analysis. Some advanced rules cannot be modified.

**Advanced Security Option**   Allows secured transactions across the network in an Oracle Net8 environment. Also used for client authentication.

**Alert Log**   Text file generated by the Oracle instance that contains information about instance-level activity against the database.

**Applications Program Interface**   Allows third parties to interact with Net8 through languages such as C.

**Archive Log File**   The archived contents of an online redo log file.

**Archiver (ARC0)**   The Oracle background process responsible for copying the contents of the redo log files to archive logs in the archive destination.

**Archiving**   The process of copying the contents of the redo logs to a secondary location prior to being reused by LGWR.

**Asynchronous**   A method of performing disk I/O that does not require the assistance of an OS layer. These are usually referred to as "raw" devices.

**Automatic Instance Registration**   The feature that allows Oracle Servers to automatically register service information with listeners.

**Autotrace**   The utility for generating Explain Plan and resource usage information for SQL statements from with SQL*Plus.

# B

**BACKGROUND_DUMP_DEST**   The `init.ora` parameter that specifies the directory where trace files generated by the Oracle background processes should be created.

**Bequeath Session**   Another name for a dedicated connection.

**Bind Variable**   Containers that hold passed-in values in SQL statements so that the actual values themselves are not included in the statement. Use of bind variables increases the Shared Pool hit ratio.

**Biometric Option**   This option provides a method of authentication by use of fingerprints.

**Bitmap**   The binary mapping of the contents of an indexed column. Used when Bitmap indexes are created on table columns.

**B-Tree**   The balanced tree index structure used by several Oracle index types.

# C

**Cache Hit**   The act of finding an object you need in memory and therefore not having to read it from disk (in the case of the Database Buffer Cache) or parse it (in the case of the Shared Pool).

**Cache Miss**   The act of not finding an object you need in memory and therefore having to read it from disk (in the case of the Database Buffer Cache) or parse it (in the case of the Shared Pool).

**Cache Replication**   The technique that keeps multiple Names Servers synchronized by replicating the information from one Names Server to the next.

**Cache Table**   A table whose buffers are placed at the most recently used end of the LRU List even when accessed via a full table scan.

**Chained Row**   A row of table data that is too large to fit into a single database block.

**Checkpoint Option**   The option that stores Names Server information in operating system files.

**Checkpoint Process (CKPT)**   The Oracle background process that updates the control file and datafile headers at a database checkpoint event.

**Checksumming**   This method provides data security by calculating and storing information in each packet sent in a network transaction. The information is then recalculated and compared to the original to ensure no modifications have been made to the data.

**Client Cache Option**   The option that allows the client to maintain a copy of the connect descriptor.

**Cluster**   A physical storage method that allows the data from one or more tables to be stored in the same physical blocks and clustered around a common value (the cluster key).

**cman.ora**   The Connection Manager configuration file.

**cman_profile**   The section of the cman.ora file that contains optional configuration parameters.

**cman_rules**   The section of the cman.ora file that contains client access control constraints.

**cmctl**   The command line utility used to start up and shut down Connection Manager.

**Common Object Request Broker Architecture (CORBA)**   An architectural specification that defines methods for interaction of objects in a networked environment.

**Connect Descriptor**   Information the client needs to contact the appropriate Oracle Server such as hostname and listening port location.

**Connection Access Control**   Connection Manager feature that allows clients to be accepted or rejected based on client, destination, or Oracle Server information. This is controlled by entering rules in the CMAN_RULES section of the cman.ora file. These rules indicate if clients are allowed to establish connections to servers or services in the Oracle Enterprise.

**Connection Concentration**   Connection Manager feature that allows multiple incoming connections to be managed as a single outgoing connection to an Oracle Server.

**Connection Failover**   A configuration that allows a client to use a secondary listener if the primary listener connection fails.

**Connection Load Balancing**   The ability to distribute connections evenly across multiple listeners.

**Connection Manager Administrator**   This is one of the two processes that make up Oracle Connection Manager. This process is responsible for maintaining address information and processing the registration information for the Connection Manager Gateway.

**Connection Manager Gateway (CMGW)**   The other process that makes up the Connection Manager server. This process is responsible for routing client connection requests to the appropriate destination.

**Connection Pooling**   This option allows client connections to share a finite number of network connections to a multithreaded Oracle Server.

**Control File**   The physical database files that store information about the database's name, physical structure, and recovery timestamps.

**Cost-based Optimizer**   The Oracle optimizer mode that examines all possible execution plans for a given SQL statement and then chooses the one with the lowest execution cost.

# D

**Data Concurrency**   The process of allowing as many users as possible to access segment data by using the least restrictive locks.

**Data Consistency**   The process of always presenting an application user with data that is consistent within their session.

**Data Dictionary Cache**   The section of the Shared Pool that caches data dictionary information.

**Data Dictionary View**   The DBA views that show static database, user, and segment information.

**Data Lock**   A lock that is taken out on segments when DML is being performed on those segments.

**Database Checkpoint**   The moment in time when the contents of the Database Buffer Cache and the Redo Log Buffer are written to disk and the database control file and datafile headers are updated to record occurrence of the event.

**Database Event**   A specific action that occurs at the database level. Specific events can be monitored and managed by the OEM Intelligent Agent.

**Database Option**   The option that stores Names Server information in an Oracle database.

**Database Writer (DBW0)**   The Oracle background process that writes database buffers from the SGA to the Datafiles.

**Datafile**   The physical database files that store the application's tables and indexes.

**Dead Connection Detection**   A function of Net8 that will detect when a client process has disconnected, so the server process can be terminated.

**Deadlock**   The special locking problem where two or more users are each waiting for the other to release a lock before their processing can proceed.

**Decision Support Systems**   A system that is characterized by long, query-based access of large tables in order to gain insights into trends or patterns in the data.

**Dedicated Server Connection**   A server process that processes the requests of a single session.

**Default Pool**   The Database Buffer Cache buffer pool used to cache any segments that have not been designated for storage in the Keep or Recycle Pools.

**Default Rules**   Oracle Expert tuning rules that are used just as delivered, without modification.

**Dictionary Lock**   A lock that is taken out on segments when DDL commands are being performed on those segments.

**Dirty List**   The list of buffers in the Database Buffer Cache whose contents do not match the copy of the block on disk.

**Dispatcher**   A dispatcher is an Oracle Server process that is responsible for processing the requests of many clients.

**Dispatcher**   A server process that processes the request of many sessions. Used in a multithreaded server environment.

**Distributed Computing Environment (DCE)**   A set of middleware network services that allows users to create distributed applications that work across a variety of operating platforms and environments.

**Domain**   A collection of related Oracle services.

**Dynamic Performance View**   The V$ views which show statistical information collected from the time the instance was started until the present.

# E

**Emphasis Method**   A method of assigning resources to consumer groups by specifying a value between 0 and 100 percent for the resource. CPU resources are assigned in this manner.

**Encryption**   A method of altering data in a transaction across a network to ensure only a receiver of information with the proper decryption key can read the data.

**Enqueue**   The process Oracle uses to keep track of the type and sequence of locking requests issued by application users.

**Enterprise JavaBeans (EJB)**   Java-based transactional applications in a distributed environment.

**Execute**   The stage in SQL statement processing where the action specified in the statement is actually performed.

**Extent**   A contiguous set of database blocks that belong to a particular segment.

**Extent Map**   An entry in the header block of the initial extent of a segment that tells the segment where the rest of the segment's extents are located and their sizes.

**External Naming Service Option**   A way of resolving service names through an outside source such as Novell Network Directory Services (NDS).

# F

**Fetch**   The stage in SQL statement processing when the rows selected by the statement are returned to the user.

**Fixit Job**   A job that runs when a specific triggering event associated with that Fixit Job occurs in the database.

**Flat Naming Model**   Every Oracle service name and net service name is unique and all services reside in a single domain.

**Free List**   The list of database blocks belonging to a particular segment that are available for inserts.

**Free List Contention**   Excessive requests for access to a table's Free List that result in waits for users performing insert activity.

# G

**General Inter-Orb Protocol (GIOP)**   A Presenttion-layer protocol used in Java to provide for messaging.

**Graphical User Interface (GUI)**  Software that utilizes graphics instead of command-line syntax as a user interface.

# H

**Hash Cluster**  A physical storage method that allows Oracle to find row values using a hashing algorithm instead of using a conventional B-Tree index.

**Hierarchical Naming Models**  A naming model that allows multiple domains to maintain an orderly structure to your Oracle services by grouping like services together under each domain.

**High Water Mark**  The block ID of the highest block number used to store data for a table. All blocks up to the high water mark block are read during a full table scan.

**Hints**  Keywords which, when embedded within SQL statements, cause the Oracle optimizer to behave in the specified manner.

**Hostnaming**  Using a `tnsnames.ora` file to resolve net service names.

# I

**Immediate**  A latch type that immediately retries obtaining a previously busy latch without waiting.

`init.ora`  The physical file that contains the database and instance configuration parameters.

**Instance Failover**  One or more listeners, each listening for the same service on different machines. If a client contacts the first listener and the instance is down, the client attempts to contact the second listener on the other machine.

**Intelligent Agent**  The process that runs on each node that the Oracle Enterprise Manager GUI tool is managing. The agent reports events for all databases on that node to the OEM console.

**Internet Inter-Orb Protocol (IIOP)**  An implementation of GIOP over TCP/ IP.

# K

**Keep Pool**  The Database Buffer Cache buffer pool used to cache frequently used segments.

**KERBEROS**  This is an industry-standard method of providing for authentication in a networked environment.

# L

**Large Pool**  A portion of the SGA that is set aside for buffering the activities of I/O intensive operations like Recovery Manager and I/O Slaves as well as multi-threaded server information.

**Latch**  A mechanism used to protect access to Oracle's shared memory structures.

**Least Recently Used (LRU)**  The type of algorithm used by the Oracle Server to determine which objects should be moved out of the SGA in order to make room for new objects.

**Library Cache**  The section of the Shared Pool that caches SQL statements, PL/SQL blocks, triggers and sequences.

**Listener**  A process that listens for and services connection requests on an Oracle Server.

**Listener Failover**  One or more listeners, each listening for the same service on the same machine. If a client fails in its attempt to contact the first listener, the client attempts to contact the second listener.

`listener.ora`  The configuration file for the listener.

**Local Connection**  A connection made to an Oracle Server without using the listener.

**Locally Managed Tablespace**  A tablespace whose space allocation and management is handled by an extent map in the header of the tablespace's datafile instead of by the data dictionary.

**Lock Contention**  Excessive waits caused by locks that are too restrictive or are held too long.

**Log Writer (LGWR)**  The Oracle background process responsible for emptying the contents of the Redo Log Buffer to the online redo log.

**Logging**  This process records significant information, such as errors, about a network connection.

`lsnrctl`  A command-line utility used to administer the listener.

# M

**Materialized View**  A view that physically stores the summary results of a query against the view's base tables.

`MAX_DUMP_FILE_SIZE`  The `init.ora` parameter that specifies the maximum size that a user trace file can grow to.

**Migrated Row**   A row of table data that originally fit into a single database block, but which was moved to a new block with more free space when the row was updated.

**Modified Rules**   Oracle Expert rules that you have modified from their default settings in some way.

**MTS_DISPATCHERS**   A parameter that specifies the number and type of dispatchers to start when the Oracle Server is started.

**MTS_MAX_DISPATCHERS**   The maximum number of dispatchers to allow.

**MTS_MAX_SERVERS**   The maximum number of shared server processes allowed.

**MTS_SERVERS**   The number of shared servers to start when the Oracle Server starts.

**Multi-protocol Interchange**   Connection Manager feature that allows clients and servers to communicate across different network protocols.

**Multithreaded Connection**   A connection made to an Oracle Server utilizing a dispatched process.

# N

**Net Service Name**   A net service name is the identification of some location of an Oracle Server.

**Net8 Assistant**   The graphical tool used to configure many of the Net8 configuration files.

**Network Program Interface (NPI)**   The layer of Net8 stack responsible for server-to-server communications.

**N-tier Architecture**   Connection architecture characterized by a client, middle-tier server, and database server. Processing can be split among the multiple tiers.

# O

**Online Transaction Processing**   A system that is characterized by short DML transactions that emphasize response time.

**Open Systems Interconnection (OSI)**   A model of network architecture that uses a layered approach to networking.

**Optimal Flexible Architecture**   The naming convention for devices and directories that are home to Oracle-related products and files.

**Oracle Call Interface (OCI)**   Responsible for all of the SQL processing that occurs between a client and the Oracle Server. Exists on the client only.

**Oracle Connection Manager**   Middle-tier product that offers connection concentration, multi-protocol support, and client access filtering.

**Oracle Enterprise Manager**   The set of tools that enable DBAs to manage and monitor Oracle databases in a GUI environment.

**Oracle Expert**   The component of the Oracle Enterprise manager Oracle Performance Pack used to gather and analyze performance statistics in order to make tuning recommendations according to a stored rule base.

**Oracle Multithreaded Server Option**   The Server option that allows clients to share server processes on the Oracle Server.

**Oracle Names Server**   The product that serves as a repository for connection information to the Oracle services. This offers a centralized approach to service name management.

**Oracle Procedural Gateway**   The Oracle Procedural Gateway allows contact with non-Oracle data sources through a PL/SQL procedure interface.

**Oracle Protocol Adapters (OPA)**   The layer of the Net8 stack that maps the TNS functions to the analogous functions in the underlying protocol.

**Oracle Transparent Gateway**   The transparent gateway product that seamlessly extends the reach of Oracle to non-Oracle data stores.

**ORACLE_SID**   The identifier of an Oracle Server.

**OS_AUTHENT_PREFIX**   This is an init.ora setting that is used when employing operating system authentication is used. It should be set to NULL when using the Advanced Security option.

# P

**Parse**   The stage in SQL statement processing where the statement is checked for syntactic correctness, security, and object resolution.

**Parse Lock**   The lock type taken out on an object at parse time.

**Password File**   The physical file used by Oracle to authenticate database users who are connecting with SYSDBA or SYSOPER privileges.

**Pending Area**   The location where resource consumer groups, resource plans, and resource plan directives are temporarily stored until they are committed to the database.

**Performance Manager**   The OEM GUI tool that allows you to graphically monitor the performance of a selected database.

**Plan Equivalence**   The determining factor of whether a stored outline will be used to execute a particular query. If the plans are equivalent, the stored outline will be used.

**pool_size**   A `listener.ora` parameter that specifies the number of prespawned servers to maintain.

**Port**   A listening location for connection requests.

**Prespawned Servers**   Dedicated server processes started when the listener starts.

**Process Global Area**   The memory space used to support the activities of each user's Server Process.

**Process Monitor (PMON)**   The Oracle background process responsible for cleaning up failed user connections.

# R

**RADIUS**   Remote Authentication Dial-In Service provides for a common gateway and protocol into various methods of authentication.

**RAID**   A hardware solution designed to minimize downtime by striping data across several devices. A failure by any one device will not interrupt processing since the remaining devices can reconstruct the data from the missing device.

**Recycle Pool**   The Database Buffer Cache buffer pool used to cache infrequently used segments.

**Redo Log**   The physical database files that store transaction recovery information.

**Redo Log Buffer**   The portion of the SGA that stores information needed to recover user transactions.

**REMOTE_OS_AUTHENT**   This `init.ora` parameter allows a client to connect in a non-secured manner when using operating system authentication. This parameter should be set to FALSE when using the Advanced Security option.

**reorder_ns**   A command in the `namesctl` utility that will discover Names Servers in the enterprise.

**Repository**   The collection of tables that store the Oracle Expert rule base, tuning preferences, and gathered statistics.

**Request Queue**   The location in the SGA where the dispatcher places a client request to be executed by a shared server.

**Resource Consumer Group**   A group of users who have similar needs for database resources.

**Resource Plan**   A collection of resource plan directives that are used to implement resource management.

**Resource Plan Directive**   Specifies the CPU and degree-of-parallelism resources allocated to a particular resource plan.

**Response Queue**   The location in the SGA where shared servers place completed client requests. Each dispatcher has its own response queue.

**Response Time**   The amount of time it takes to perform a specific operation on a system.

**Reverse Key**   A B-Tree index type that reverses the contents of the indexed column before creating the index.

**Rule-based Optimizer**   The Oracle optimizer mode that uses a set of pre-defined rules when determining the best execution plan for a given SQL statement.

# S

**sdns.ora** A file that contains information about discovered Names Servers. This file is created by the reorder_ns command.

**Secured Sockets Layer (SSL)** This industry-standard protocol developed by Netscape Communications provides security in a networked environment.

**Shared Pool** The portion of the SGA that caches SQL statements issued against the instance.

**Shared Pool Reserved Area** Portion of the Shared Pool that can be set aside specifically for use by large PL/SQL packages and triggers.

**Shared Server** The Oracle processes responsible for executing a client request in a multithreaded server environment.

**Single-tier Architecture** Connection architecture characterized by a simple terminal connection to a server that does all of the processing.

**SQLNET.AUTHENTICATION_SERVICES** This is an sqlnet.ora parameter that determines the type of authentication method to use.

**SQLNET.CRYPTO_CHECKSUM_CLIENT** This is a client-side checksum parameter in the sqlnet.ora file.

**SQLNET.CRYPTO_CHECKSUM_SERVER** This is a server-side checksum parameter in the sqlnet.ora file.

**SQLNET.ENCRYPTION_CLIENT** This is a client-side encryption parameter in the sqlnet.ora file.

**SQLNET.ENCRYPTION_SERVER** This is a server-side encryption parameter in the sqlnet.ora file.

**Stored Outlines** The predetermined, stored execution plan for a given SQL statement that is used each time that statement is issued.

**Striping** The process of causing a datafile to span multiple physical devices in order to improve I/O.

**Synchronous** A method of performing disk I/O that does require the services of an OS layer. These are usually referred to as file systems or "cooked" devices.

**System Global Area (SGA)** Oracle's shared memory structure used to cache SQL statements, data buffers, and transaction recovery information.

**System Monitor** The Oracle background process responsible for performing instance recovery, managing sort segments, and coalescing of free space in tablespaces.

# T

**Tablespace Manager** The OEM GUI tool for creating, managing, monitoring, and dropping tablespaces.

**Throughput** The amount of work performed by a system in a given period of time.

**TKPROF** The Oracle command line utility for formatting user trace files so that the resulting file can be examined for tuning information.

**TNS_ADMIN** An environmental variable that specifies the location of the Net8 network configuration files.

**tnsping** This utility checks if a client can contact an Oracle Listener process using a net service name.

**Token Cards** These credit card–like cards, when used with a card-reading device, control access to an Oracle server.

**TopSessions** The OEM GUI tool for identifying and monitoring the user and background processes that are interacting with the instance.

**Trace File** A text file that contains information about all the actions performed by a user or background process during the time that tracing was active.

**Trace Manager** The OEM GUI tool for collecting data from Oracle-based applications by using Oracle Trace application program interface calls.

**Tracing** This method records extensive information about a network connection.

**Transparent Network Substrate (TNS)** The layer of the Net8 stack that compensates for differences in connectivity issues between machines, and differences in underlying protocols.

**trcasst**   The Oracle Trace Assistant is a utility that formats trace files generated by enabling tracing of network connections.

**Two-Task Common (TTC)**   Responsible for negotiating any datatype or character set differences between the client and the server.

**Two-tier Architecture**   The connection architecture characterized by a client database server. Processing can be split among the client and server.

# U

**User Global Area**   The section of the Shared Pool that caches shared user information when using the Multithreaded Server mode.

**USER_DUMP_DEST**   The init.ora parameter that specifies the directory where trace files generated by the Oracle Server processes should be created.

**UTLBSTAT.SQL**   The Oracle-supplied script that is run at the beginning of the tuning period to be examined.

**UTLESTAT.SQL**   The Oracle-supplied script that is run at the end of the tuning period that to be examined. The script also generates the output file REPORT.TXT.

# W

**Willing-to-Wait**   A latch type that waits before trying to obtain a previously busy latch again.

# Index

**Note to Reader:** In this index, **boldfaced** page numbers refer to primary discussions of the topic; *italics* page numbers refer to figures.

## E

## F

## J

## K